DISCARDED

Short
Stories
for Students

National Advisory Board

Short Stories

for Students

**Presenting Analysis, Context, and Criticism on
Commonly Studied Short Stories**

Volume 8

Ira Mark Milne, Editor

GALE GROUP

™

Detroit
New York
San Francisco
London
Boston
Woodbridge, CT

Short Stories for Students

Staff

Editorial: Ira Mark Milne, *Editor.* Tim Akers, Dave Galens, Polly Vedder, Kathleen Wilson, *Contributing Editors.* James P. Draper, *Managing Editor.*

Research: Victoria B. Cariappa, *Research Team Manager.* Cheryl Warnock, *Research Specialist.* Patricia T. Ballard, Corrine A. Boland, Wendy Festerling, Tamara Nott, Tracie A. Richardson, *Research Associates.* Timothy Lehnerer, Patricia Love, *Research Assistants.*

Permissions: Maria Franklin, *Permissions Manager.* Kimberly Smilay, *Permissions Specialist.* Kelly Quin, *Permissions Associate.* Sandra K. Gore, Erin Bealmear, *Permissions Assistants.*

Production: Mary Beth Trimper, *Production Director.* Evi Seoud, *Assistant Production Manager.* Cindy Range, *Production Assistant.*

Imaging and Multimedia Content Team: Randy Bassett, *Image Database Supervisor.* Robert Duncan, Michael Logusz, *Imaging Specialists.* Pamela A. Reed, *Imaging Coordinator.*

Product Design Team: Cynthia Baldwin, *Product Design Manager.* Pamela A. E. Galbreath, *Senior Art Director.* Gary Leach, *Graphic Artist.*

Copyright Notice

Table of Contents

Why Study Literature At All?

Short Stories for Students is designed to provide readers with information and discussion about a wide range of important contemporary and historical works of short fiction, and it does that job very well. However, I want to use this guest foreword to address a question that it does *not* take up. It is a fundamental question that is often ignored in high school and college English classes as well as research texts, and one that causes frustration among students at all levels, namely—why study literature at all? Isn't it enough to read a story, enjoy it, and go about one's business? My answer (to be expected from a literary professional, I suppose) is no. It is not enough. It is a start; but it is not enough. Here's why.

First, literature is the only part of the educational curriculum that deals directly with the actual world of lived experience. The philosopher Edmund Husserl used the apt German term *die Lebenswelt*, "the living world," to denote this realm. All the other content areas of the modern American educational system avoid the subjective, present reality of everyday life. Science (both the natural and the social varieties) objectifies, the fine arts create and/or perform, history reconstructs. Only literary study persists in posing those questions we all asked before our schooling taught us to give up on them. Only literature gives credibility to personal perceptions, feelings, dreams, and the "stream of consciousness" that is our inner voice. Literature wonders about infinity, wonders why God permits evil, wonders what will happen to us after we die. Literature admits that we get our hearts broken, that people sometimes cheat and get away with it, that the world is a strange and probably incomprehensible place. Literature, in other words, takes on all the big and small issues of what it means to be human. So my first answer is that of the humanist—we should read literature and study it and take it seriously because it enriches us as human beings. We develop our moral imagination, our capacity to sympathize with other people, and our ability to understand our existence through the experience of fiction.

My second answer is more practical. By studying literature we can learn how to explore and analyze texts. Fiction may be about *die Lebenswelt*, but it is a construct of words put together in a certain order by an artist using the medium of language. By examining and studying those constructions, we can learn about language as a medium. We can become more sophisticated about word associations and connotations, about the manipulation of symbols, and about style and atmosphere. We can grasp how ambiguous language is and how important context and texture is to meaning. In our first encounter with a work of literature, of course, we are not supposed to catch all of these things. We are spellbound, just as the writer wanted us to be. It is as serious students of the writer's art that we begin to see how the tricks are done.

Seeing the tricks, which is another way of saying "developing analytical and close reading skills," is important above and beyond its intrinsic literary educational value. These skills transfer to other fields and enhance critical thinking of any kind. Understanding how language is used to construct texts is powerful knowledge. It makes engineers better problem solvers, lawyers better advocates and courtroom practitioners, politicians better rhetoricians, marketing and advertising agents better sellers, and citizens more aware consumers as well as better participants in democracy. This last point is especially important, because rhetorical skill works both ways—when we learn how language is manipulated in the making of texts the result is that we become less susceptible when language is used to manipulate us.

My third reason is related to the second. When we begin to see literature as created artifacts of language, we become more sensitive to good writing in general. We get a stronger sense of the importance of individual words, even the sounds of words and word combinations. We begin to understand Mark Twain's delicious proverb—"The difference between the right word and the almost right word is the difference between lightning and a lightning bug." Getting beyond the "enjoyment only" stage of literature gets us closer to becoming makers of word art ourselves. I am not saying that studying fiction will turn every student into a Faulkner or a Shakespeare. But it will make us more adaptable and effective writers, even if our art form ends up being the office memo or the corporate annual report.

Studying short stories, then, can help students become better readers, better writers, and even better human beings. But I want to close with a warning. If your study and exploration of the craft, history, context, symbolism, or anything else about a story starts to rob it of the magic you felt when you first read it, it is time to stop. Take a break, study another subject, shoot some hoops, or go for a run. Love of reading is too important to be ruined by school. The early twentieth century writer Willa Cather, in her novel *My Antonia*, has her narrator Jack Burden tell a story that he and Antonia heard from two old Russian immigrants when they were teenagers. These immigrants, Pavel and Peter, told about an incident from their youth back in Russia that the narrator could recall in vivid detail thirty years later. It was a harrowing story of a wedding party starting home in sleds and being chased by starving wolves. Hundreds of wolves attacked the group's sleds one by one as they sped across the snow trying to reach their village. In a horrible revelation, the old Russians revealed that the groom eventually threw his own bride to the wolves to save himself. There was even a hint that one of the old immigrants might have been the groom mentioned in the story. Cather has her narrator conclude with his feelings about the story. "We did not tell Pavel's secret to anyone, but guarded it jealously—as if the wolves of the Ukraine had gathered that night long ago, and the wedding party had been sacrificed, just to give us a painful and peculiar pleasure." That feeling, that painful and peculiar pleasure, is the most important thing about literature. Study and research should enhance that feeling and never be allowed to overwhelm it.

Thomas E. Barden
Professor of English and
Director of Graduate English Studies
The University of Toledo

Introduction

Purpose of the Book

The purpose of *Short Stories for Students* (*SSfS*) is to provide readers with a guide to understanding, enjoying, and studying short stories by giving them easy access to information about the work. Part of Gale's "For Students" Literature line, *SSfS* is specifically designed to meet the curricular needs of high school and undergraduate college students and their teachers, as well as the interests of general readers and researchers considering specific short fiction. While each volume contains entries on classic stories frequently studied in classrooms, there are also entries containing hard-to-find information on contemporary stories, including works by multicultural, international, and women writers.

The information covered in each entry includes an introduction to the story and the story's author; a plot summary, to help readers unravel and understand the events in the work; descriptions of important characters, including explanation of a given character's role in the narrative as well as discussion about that character's relationship to other characters in the story; analysis of important themes in the story; and an explanation of important literary techniques and movements as they are demonstrated in the work.

In addition to this material, which helps the readers analyze the story itself, students are also provided with important information on the literary and historical background informing each work.

This includes a historical context essay, a box comparing the time or place the story was written to modern Western culture, a critical overview essay, and excerpts from critical essays on the story or author. A unique feature of *SSfS* is a specially commissioned overview essay on each story by an academic expert, targeted toward the student reader.

To further aid the student in studying and enjoying each story, information on media adaptations is provided, as well as reading suggestions for works of fiction and nonfiction on similar themes and topics. Classroom aids include ideas for research papers and lists of critical sources that provide additional material on the work.

Selection Criteria

The titles for each volume of *SSfS* were selected by surveying numerous sources on teaching literature and analyzing course curricula for various school districts. Some of the sources surveyed include: literature anthologies, *Reading Lists for College-Bound Students: The Books Most Recommended by America's Top Colleges; Teaching the Short Story: A Guide to Using Stories from Around the World,* by the National Council of Teachers of English (NTCE); and "A Study of High School Literature Anthologies," conducted by Arthur Applebee at the Center for the Learning and Teaching of Literature and sponsored by the National Endowment for the Arts and the Office of Educational Research and Improvement.

Input was also solicited from our expert advisory board, as well as educators from various areas. From these discussions, it was determined that each volume should have a mix of "classic" stories (those works commonly taught in literature classes) and contemporary stories for which information is often hard to find. Because of the interest in expanding the canon of literature, an emphasis was also placed on including works by international, multicultural, and women authors. Our advisory board members—current high-school teachers—helped pare down the list for each volume. Works not selected for the present volume were noted as possibilities for future volumes. As always, the editor welcomes suggestions for titles to be included in future volumes.

How Each Entry Is Organized

Each entry, or chapter, in *SSfS* focuses on one story. Each entry heading lists the title of the story, the author's name, and the date of the story's publication. The following elements are contained in each entry:

- **Introduction:** a brief overview of the story which provides information about its first appearance, its literary standing, any controversies surrounding the work, and major conflicts or themes within the work.

- **Author Biography:** this section includes basic facts about the author's life, and focuses on events and times in the author's life that may have inspired the story in question.

- **Plot Summary:** a description of the events in the story, with interpretation of how these events help articulate the story's themes.

- **Characters:** an alphabetical listing of the characters who appear in the story. Each character name is followed by a brief to an extensive description of the character's role in the story, as well as discussion of the character's actions, relationships, and possible motivation.

  Characters are listed alphabetically by last name. If a character is unnamed—for instance, the narrator in "The Eatonville Anthology"—the character is listed as "The Narrator" and alphabetized as "Narrator." If a character's first name is the only one given, the name will appear alphabetically by that name.

- **Themes:** a thorough overview of how the topics, themes, and issues are addressed within the story. Each theme discussed appears in a separate subhead, and is easily accessed through the boldface entries in the Subject/Theme Index.

- **Style:** this section addresses important style elements of the story, such as setting, point of view, and narration; important literary devices used, such as imagery, foreshadowing, symbolism; and, if applicable, genres to which the work might have belonged, such as Gothicism or Romanticism. Literary terms are explained within the entry, but can also be found in the Glossary of Literary Terms.

- **Historical and Cultural Context:** This section outlines the social, political, and cultural climate *in which the author lived and the work was created.* This section may include descriptions of related historical events, pertinent aspects of daily life in the culture, and the artistic and literary sensibilities of the time in which the work was written. If the story is historical in nature, information regarding the time in which the story is set is also included. Long sections are broken down with helpful subheads.

- **Critical Overview:** this section provides background on the critical reputation of the author and the story, including bannings or any other public controversies surrounding the work. For older works, this section may include a history of how story was first received and how perceptions of it may have changed over the years; for more recent works, direct quotes from early reviews may also be included.

- **Sources:** an alphabetical list of critical material quoted in the entry, with bibliographical information.

- **For Further Study:** an alphabetical list of other critical sources which may prove useful for the student. Includes full bibliographical information and a brief annotation.

- **Criticism:** an essay commissioned by *SSfS* which specifically deals with the story and is written specifically for the student audience, as well as excerpts from previously published criticism on the work.

In addition, each entry contains the following highlighted sections, if applicable, set separate from the main text:

- **Media Adaptations:** where applicable, a list of film and television adaptations of the story, including source information. The list also includes stage adaptations, audio recordings, musical adaptations, etc.

- **Compare and Contrast Box:** an ''at-a-glance'' comparison of the cultural and historical differences between the author's time and culture and late twentieth-century Western culture. This box includes pertinent parallels between the major scientific, political, and cultural movements of the time or place the story was written, the time or place the story was set (if a historical work), and modern Western culture. Works written after the mid-1970s may not have this box.

- **What Do I Read Next?:** a list of works that might complement the featured story or serve as a contrast to it. This includes works by the same author and others, works of fiction and nonfiction, and works from various genres, cultures, and eras.

- **Study Questions:** a list of potential study questions or research topics dealing with the story. This section includes questions related to other disciplines the student may be studying, such as American history, world history, science, math, government, business, geography, economics, psychology, etc.

Other Features

SSfS includes ''Why Study Literature At All?,'' a guest foreword by Thomas E. Barden, Professor of English and Director of Graduate English Studies at the University of Toledo. This essay provides a number of very fundamental reasons for studying literature and, therefore, reasons why a book such as *SSfS,* designed to facilitate the study of literature, is useful.

A Cumulative Author/Title Index lists the authors and titles covered in each volume of the *SSfS* series.

A Cumulative Nationality/Ethnicity Index breaks down the authors and titles covered in each volume of the *SSfS* series by nationality and ethnicity.

A Subject/Theme Index, specific to each volume, provides easy reference for users who may be studying a particular subject or theme rather than a single work. Significant subjects from events to broad themes are included, and the entries pointing to the specific theme discussions in each entry are indicated in **boldface.**

Entries may include illustrations, including an author portrait, stills from film adaptations (when available), maps, and/or photos of key historical events.

Citing **Short Stories for Students**

When writing papers, students who quote directly from any volume of *SSfS* may use the following general forms to document their source. These examples are based on MLA style; teachers may request that students adhere to a different style, thus, the following examples may be adapted as needed.

When citing text from *SSfS* that is not attributed to a particular author (for example, the Themes, Style, Historical Context sections, etc.) the following format may be used:

> ''The Celebrated Jumping Frog of Calaveras County.'' *Short Stories for Students.* Ed. Kathleen Wilson. Vol. 1. Detroit: Gale, 1997. 19-20.

When quoting the specially commissioned essay from *SSfS* (usually the first essay under the Criticism subhead), the following format may be used:

> Korb, Rena. Essay on ''Children of the Sea.'' *Short Stories for Students.* Ed. Kathleen Wilson. Vol. 1. Detroit: Gale, 1997. 42.

When quoting a journal essay that is reprinted in a volume of *Short Stories for Students,* the following form may be used:

> Schmidt, Paul. ''The Deadpan on Simon Wheeler.'' *The Southwest Review* XLI, No. 3 (Summer, 1956), 270-77; excerpted and reprinted in *Short Stories for Students,* Vol. 1, ed. Kathleen Wilson (Detroit: Gale, 1997), pp. 29-31.

When quoting material from a book that is reprinted in a volume of *SSfS,* the following form may be used:

> Bell-Villada, Gene H. ''The Master of Short Forms,'' in *Garcia Marquez: The Man and His Work* (University of North Carolina Press, 1990); excerpted and reprinted in *Short Stories for Students,* Vol. 1, ed. Kathleen Wilson (Detroit: Gale, 1997), pp. 90-1.

We Welcome Your Suggestions

The editor of *Short Stories for Students* welcomes your comments and ideas. Readers who wish to suggest short stories to appear in future volumes, or who have other suggestions, are cordially invited to contact the editor. You may write to the editor at:

Editor, *Short Stories for Students*
The Gale Group
27500 Drake Rd.
Farmington Hills, MI 48331-3535

Literary Chronology

1821: Gustave Flaubert is born in France on December 12.

1843: Henry James is born in New York, New York, on April 15.

1861: The U.S. Civil War begins when Confederate forces capture Fort Sumter in South Carolina.

1862: Edith Wharton is born in New York, New York, on January 24.

1865: The U.S. Civil War ends; Abraham Lincoln is assassinated.

1877: "A Simple Heart" by Gustave Flaubert is published in his *Three Tales.*

1880: Gustave Flaubert dies on May 5.

1882: James Joyce is born in Dublin, Ireland, on February 2.

1885: Isak Dinesen is born in Rungsted, Denmark, on April 17.

1885: D. H. Lawrence is born in Eastwood, Nottinghamshire, England, on September 11.

1891: Zora Neale Hurston is born in Eatonville, Florida, on January 7.

1897: William Faulkner is born in New Albany, Mississippi on September 25.

1899: Vladimir Nabokov is born in St. Petersburg, Russia, on April 23.

1899: Ernest Hemingway is born in Oak Park, Illinois, on July 21.

1902: John Steinbeck is born in Salinas, California, on February 27.

1903: "The Beast in the Jungle" by Henry James is published in his short story collection, *The Better Sort.*

1911: "The Odour of Chrysanthemums" by D. H. Lawrence is published in the *English Review.*

1912: The *U.S.S. Titanic* sinks on her maiden voyage.

1914: With the assassination of Archduke Ferdinand of Austria, long-festering tensions in Europe erupt into what becomes known as the Great War.

1914: "The Dead" by James Joyce is published in his short story collection *Dubliners.*

1916: Henry James dies in London, England, on February 28.

1916: "The Easter Rising," in which Irish nationalists take control of the Dublin post office and declare a provisional government apart from British rule, takes place on April 24.

1917: Russian Revolution takes place. Czar Nicholas II abdicates the throne and a provisional government is established.

1918: World War I, the most deadly war in history, ends with the signing of the Treaty of Versailles.

1920: The 18th Amendment, outlawing the sale, manufacture, and transportation of alcohol—known as Prohibition—goes into effect. This law led to the creation of ''speakeasies''—illegal bars—and an increase in organized crime. The law is repealed in 1933.

1920: The efforts of the Women's Suffrage movement, directed by women such as Susan B. Anthony and Elizabeth Cady Stanton, finally succeeds. The 19th Amendment, which granted the right to vote to women, is adopted.

1921: Edith Wharton wins the Pulitzer Prize for fiction for her novel *The Age of Innocence.*

1925: ''Spunk'' by Zora Neale Hurston is published in *Opportunity: A Journal of Negro Life.*

1925: ''A Guide to Berlin'' by Vladimir Nabokov is published.

1927: ''Hills Like White Elephants'' by Ernest Hemingway is published in the magazine *transition.*

1928: Gabriel Garcia Marquez is born in Aracataca, Columbia, on March 6.

1929: The stock market crash in October signals the beginning of a worldwide economic depression.

1929: *The Sound and the Fury* by William Faulkner is published.

1930: D. H. Lawrence dies of tuberculosis in Vence, France, on March 2.

1930: John Barth is born in Cambridge, Maryland, on May 27.

1930: ''A Rose for Emily'' by William Faulkner is published in *Forum.*

1931: ''Pomegranate Seed'' by Edith Wharton is published in *Ladies' Home Journal.*

1937: ''The Chrysanthemums'' by John Steinbeck is published in *Harper's* magazine.

1937: Edith Wharton dies in St. Brice-sous-Foret, France, on August 11.

1938: Raymond Carver is born in Clatskanie, Oregon, on May 25.

1939: World War II begins when Nazi Germany, led by Adolf Hitler, invades Poland; England and France declare war in response.

1940: John Steinbeck is awarded the Pulitzer Prize for Fiction for *The Grapes of Wrath.*

1941: James Joyce dies in Zurich, Switzerland, on January 13.

1941: John Edgar Wideman is born in Washington, D.C., on June 14.

1945: World War II ends in August with the atomic bombing of Hiroshima and Nagasaki, Japan.

1947: Octavia Butler is born in Pasadena, California, on June 22.

1949: William Faulkner wins Nobel Prize for literature.

1950: Senator Joseph McCarthy of Wisconsin sets off the ''Red Scare'' that leads to government hearings and blacklisting of suspected communists.

1952: Rohinton Mistry is born in Bombay, India.

1953: Ernest Hemingway is awarded the Nobel Prize for Literature.

1954: United States Supreme Court, in *Brown vs. Board of Education of Topeka,* rules unanimously that public school segregation is unconstitutional under the 14th amendment.

1958: ''The Ring'' by Isak Dinesen is published her short story collection *Anecdotes of Destiny.*

1960: Zora Neale Hurston dies in Fort Pierce, Florida, on January 28.

1961: Ernest Hemingway commits suicide in Ketchum, Idaho, on July 2.

1962: John Steinbeck is awarded the Nobel Prize for Literature.

1962: William Faulkner dies in Byhalia, Mississippi, on July 6.

1962: Isak Dinesen dies in Rungsted, Denmark, on September 7.

1963: President John F. Kennedy is assassinated in Dallas, Texas, on November 22.

1967: ''Lost in the Funhouse'' by John Barth is published in the *Atlantic Monthly.*

1968: ''A Very Old Man with Enormous Wings'' by Gabriel Garcia Marquez is published.

1968: John Steinbeck dies of heart disease in New York, New York, on December 20.

1972: President Richard Nixon resigns following the Watergate scandal.

1973: John Barth is awarded the National Book Award for his novel *Chimera.*

1975: Saigon, the South Vietnamese capital, falls to the North Vietnamese army, bringing an end to the Vietnam War.

1977: Vladimir Nabokov dies in Monteux, Switzerland, on July 2.

1981: "Cathedral" by Raymond Carver is published in *Atlantic Monthly.*

1982: Gabriel Garcia Marquez wins the Nobel Prize for Literature.

1984: John Edgar Wideman wins the PEN/Faulkner award for fiction for *Sent for You Yesterday.*

1984: "Bloodchild" by Octavia Butler is published in *Isaac Asimov's Science Fiction Magazine.*

1985: Octavia Butler is awarded both the Hugo and Nebula Awards for best novellette for "Bloodchild."

1987: "Swimming Lessons" by Rohinton Mistry is published in his short story collection *Tales from Firozsha Baag.*

1988: Raymond Carver dies of lung cancer in Port Angeles, Washington, on August 2.

1989: The Berlin Wall, a symbol of the 28 years of division between East and West Germany, is torn down.

1989: "Fever" by John Edgar Wideman is published in his short story collection *Fever.*

1990: Soviet leader Mikhail Gorbachev's policy of *glasnost* results in the fracturing of the Iron Curtain. By December the Soviet flag is lowered from the Kremlin.

Acknowledgments

The editors wish to thank the copyright holders of the excerpted criticism included in this volume and the permissions managers of many book and magazine publishing companies for assisting us in securing reproduction rights. We are also grateful to the staffs of the Detroit Public Library, the Library of Congress, the University of Detroit Mercy Library, Wayne State University Purdy/Kresge Library Complex, and the University of Michigan Libraries for making their resources available to us. Following is a list of the copyright holders who have granted us permission to reproduce material in this volume of *SSFS*. **Every effort has been made to trace copyright, but if omissions have been made, please let us know.**

COPYRIGHTED EXCERPTS IN *SSFS*, VOLUME 8, WERE REPRODUCED FROM THE FOLLOWING PERIODICALS:

Ball State University Forum, v. XXIII, Winter, 1982. © 1982 Ball State University. Reproduced by permission.—*English Language Notes,* v. 20, May-June, 1983. © copyrighted 1983, Regents of the University of Colorado. Reproduced by permission.—*Essays in Literature,* v. XV, Fall, 1988. Copyright 1988 by Western Illinois University. Reproduced by permission.—*The George Eliot Fellowship Review,* 1991. Reproduced by permission.—*George Eliot - George Henry Lewes Studies,* v. 18-19, September, 1991; v. 24-25, 1993. Both reproduced by permission.—*Journal of the Southwest,* v. 30, Autumn, 1988. Copyright © 1988 by the Arizona Board of Regents. All rights reserved. Reproduced by permission.—*Linguistics in Literature,* v. 2, 1977. Reproduced by permission.—*MELUS: Society for the Study of the Multi-Ethnic Literature of the United States,* v. 5, Winter, 1978. Copyright, *MELUS, The Society for the Study of Multi-Ethnic Literature of the United States,* 1978. Reproduced by permission.—*Modern Fiction Studies,* v. 22, Summer, 1976. Copyright © 1976 by Purdue Research Foundation, West Lafayette, IN 47907. All rights reserved. Reproduced by permission of The Johns Hopkins University.—*The New York Times Book Review,* March 1, 1959. Copyright © 1959 by The New York Times Company. Reproduced by permission.—*South Atlantic Bulletin,* v. 38, 1973. Copyright © 1973 by South Atlantic Modern Language Association. Reproduced by permission.—*The Southern Literary Journal,* v. XXI, Spring, 1989; v. XXII, Fall 1989. Copyright 1989 by the Department of English, University of North Carolina at Chapel Hill. Both reproduced by permission.—*Studies in American Fiction,* v. 15, 1987. Copyright © 1987 Northeastern University. Reproduced by permission.—*Studies in Short Fiction,* v. VI, Winter, 1969; v. VII, Spring, 1970; v. 10, Winter, 1973; v. 18, Summer, 1981; v. 19, Winter, 1982; v. 20, SpringSummer, 1983; v. 20, Fall, 1983; v. 22, Summer, 1985; v. 25, 1988; v. 29, Spring, 1992; v. 30, 1993. Copyright 1969, 1970, 1973, 1981, 1982, 1983, 1985, 1988, 1992, 1993 by

Newberry College. All reproduced by permission.—*Studies in the Humanities,* v. 3, 1972. Reproduced by permission.—*The University of Mississippi Studies in English,* v. 1, 1980. Copyright © 1980 The University of Mississippi. Reproduced by permission.

COPYRIGHTED EXCERPTS IN *SSFS,* VOLUME 8, WERE REPRODUCED FROM THE FOLLOWING BOOKS:

Daly, Brenda O. From "'How Do We [Not] Become These People Who Victimize Us?': Anxious Authorship in the Early Fiction of Joyce Carol Oates" in *Anxious Power: Reading, Writing, and Ambivalence in Narrative by Women.* Edited by Carol J. Singley and Susan Elizabeth Sweeney. State University of New York Press, 1993. Copyright © 1993 by the State University of New York. All rights reserved. Reproduced by permission of the State University of New York Press.—George, Albert J. From *Short Fiction in France 1800-1850.* Syracuse University Press, 1964. Copyright © 1964 by Syracuse University Press. All rights reserved. Reproduced by permission.—Gilbert, Elliot L. From *The Good Kipling: Studies in the Short Story.* Ohio University Press, 1970. Copyright © 1970 by Elliot L. Gilbert. Reproduced by permission of the Literary Estate of Elliot L. Gilbert.—Hamblen, Abigail Ann. From *The New England Art of Mary E. Wilkins Freeman.* The Green Knight Press, 1966. © 1966. Reproduced by permission of the author.—Hanson, Clare, and Andrew Gurr. From *Katherine Mansfield.* St. Martin's Press, 1981. Copyright © Clare Hanson and Andrew Gurr 1981. All rights reserved. Reproduced by permission of Macmillan Press Ltd. In North America with permission of St. Martin's Press, Incorporated.—Lodge, David. From "'Mrs. Bathurst': Indeterminacy in Motion" in *Kipling Considered.* Edited by Phillip Mallett. Macmillan Press, Ltd., 1989. © Phillip Mallett 1989. All rights reserved. Reproduced by permission of Macmillan Press Ltd.—Martin, Jay. From *Harvests of Change: American Literature 1865-1914.* Prentice-Hall, 1967. Copyright © 1967 by Prentice-Hall, Inc. All rights reserved. Reproduced by permission of the author.—Morris, Gregory L. From *A World of Order and Light: The Fiction of John Gardner.* University of Georgia Press, 1984. Copyright 1984 by University of Georgia Press, Athens. All rights reserved. Reproduced by permission.—Rait, A. W. From *Prosper Merimee.* Eyre & Spottiswoode, 1970. © 1970 A. W. Rait. Reproduced by permission of the author.—Richman, Sidney. From *Bernard Malamud and the Critics.* Edited by Leslie A. Field and Joyce W. Field. New York University Press, 1979. Copyright © 1979 by New York University. Reproduced by permission.—Ryan, Maureen. From "Stopping Places: Bobbie Ann Mason's Short Stories" in *Women Writers of the Contemporary South.* Edited by Peggy Whitman Prenshaw. University Press of Mississippi, 1984. Copyright © 1984 by The Southern Quarterly. All rights reserved. Reproduced by permission.—Seyersted, Per. From *Leslie Marmon Silko.* Boise State University, 1980. Copyright 1980 by the Boise State University Western Writers Series. All rights reserved. Reproduced by permission of the publisher and the author.—Ward, Bruce K. From *Dostoyevsky's Critique of the West: The Quest for the Early Paradise.* Wilfrid Laurier University Press, 1986. Copyright © 1986 by Wilfrid Laurier University Press. Reproduced by permission.—Winther, Per. From *The Art of John Gardner: Introduction and Exploration.* State University of New York Press, 1992. (c) 1992 State University of New York. All rights reserved. Reproduced by permission of the State University of New York Press.

PHOTOGRAPHS AND ILLUSTRATIONS APPEARING IN *SSFS,* VOLUME 8, WERE RECEIVED FROM THE FOLLOWING SOURCES:

A farm plow, April 1981, photograph. CORBIS/Gunter Marx. Reproduced by permission. Aerial view of a forest in South Africa, photograph by Marco Polo. Phototake. Reproduced by permission.—Aiken, Conrad, photograph. The Library of Congress.—Alden, Priscilla, in the garden, sewing, illustration. Rare Books.—Blood transfusion, 1882, drawing by Dr. Roussel. The Library of Congress.—Blue spruce tree, covered with snow, photograph by James Lee Sikkema. Reproduced by permission.—Bridges over water in Prague, Czech Republic, photograph by Ryan Wrocklage. Mira Bossowska. Reproduced by permissions.—Dostoevski, Fyodor Mikhailovich, photograph. The Library of Congress.—Eliot, George (veil on back of hair), drawing. The Library of Congress.—English ambulance driver (standing next to truck), c. 1918, Italy, photograph. UPI/Corbis-Bettmann. Reproduced by permission.—Engraving by Fritz Eichenberg. From Tales of Edgar Allan Poe, by Edgar Allan Poe. Random House, 1944. Copyright, 1944, by Random House, Inc. Reproduced by permission.—Formal garden design, photograph by Frederik Lewis. Archive Photos, Inc. Reproduced by permission.—Freeman, Mary E. Wilkins, photograph. The Library of Congress.—Freud, Sigmund (sitting, holding cigar), photograph. The Library of Congress.—From a jacket of Hoboes: Wandering in America, 1870-1940, by Richard Wormser. Walker and Company, 1994. Jacket photograph courtesy of The Library of Congress. Reproduced by permission.—Gardner, John (smoking pipe), photograph by Lutfi Ozkok. Reproduced by permission.—Hemingway, Ernest, photograph. Archive Photos, Inc. Reproduced by permission.—High rise buildings downtown (and water tower), Detroit, Michigan, photograph by Robert J. Huffman. Field Mark Publications. Reproduced by permission.—Illustration from The Legend of Sleepy Hollow. By Washington Irving. Corbis-Bettmann. Reproduced by permission.—Irving, Washington (dark coat and tie, cleft chin), painting. The Library of Congress.—Malamud, Bernard, photograph. The Library of Congress.—Man and woman of Laguna Pueblo, New Mexico, photograph by Ben Wittick. National Archives and Records Administration.—Mansfield,

Katherine, photograph. Corbis-Bettmann. Reproduced by permission.—Map of Italy, line drawing by Bill Bourne. Bourne Graphics. The Gale Group.—Mason, Bobbie Ann, photograph by Jerry Bauer. © Jerry Bauer. Reproduced by permission.—Merimee, Prosper, portrait. The Library of Congress.—Oates, Joyce Carol (seated at table, leafing through book), 1991, photograph. AP/Wide World Photos. Reproduced by permission.—Porter, Katherine Ann (facing front, arms up in front, wearing a fuzzy dark V-necked top), 1940, photograph by George Platt Lynes. NYWTS/The Library of Congress.—Silko, Leslie Marmon (wearing black shirt, parrot pin), photograph by Robyn McDaniels. © Robyn McDaniels. Reproduced by permission.—Villa, Francisco "Pancho," Zapata, Emiliano (sitting together, surrounded by large group), Mexico City, Mexico, ca. 1916, photograph by Agustin Cassola. Archive Photos. Reproduced by permission.—Warren, Robert Penn, photograph. The Library of Congress.

Contributors

ANDREWS HENNINGFELD, Diane. Associate professor of English at Adrian College in Michigan; has written extensively for a variety of educational and academic publishers. Entries: "Redemption" and "Residents and Transients."

BARDEN, Thomas E. Professor of American Studies and Director of Graduate Studies at the University of Toledo. Commissioned Essay for Entry: "Residents and Transients."

BERTONNEAU, Thomas. Has been a Temporary Assistant Professor of English and the Humanities at Central Michigan University, and Senior Policy Analyst at the Mackinac Center for Public Policy. Entries: "Mateo Falcone" and "Silent Snow, Secret Snow."

BILY, Cynthia. Instructor of English at Adrian College in Michigan. Contributor to reference publications including *Feminist Writers, Gay and Lesbian Biography,* and *Chronology of Women Worldwide.* Entries: "The Grand Inquisitor" and "The Legend of Sleepy Hollow."

BRENT, Liz. Ph.D. in American Culture, specializing in cinema studies, from the University of Michigan. Teacher of courses in American cinema, freelance writer and editor. Entries: "The Lifted Veil" and "The Masque of the Red Death." Commissioned Essay for Entry: "Residents and Transients."

GOLUBOFF, Benjamin. Has taught English at Lake Forest College in Lake Forest, Illinois. Entry: "The Magic Barrel."

MADSEN HARDY, Sarah. Ph.D. in English literature from the University of Michigan, freelance writer, and editor. Entry: "Flowering Judas."

MERCY, Andrew. Has been a freelance writer and a doctoral candidate at the University of California-Berkeley. Entry: "Mrs. Bathurst."

PAUL, Angelina. Doctoral candidate in English literature at the University of Hyderabad and a Fulbright Visiting Researcher in South Asia Regional Studies at the University of Pennsylvania; has published literary criticism in *American Literature Today* and the *Indian Journal of American Studies.* Entry: "The Man to Send Rain Clouds."

PIEDMONT-MARTON, Elisabeth. Teaches American literature and directs the writing center at Southwestern University in Texas; writes frequently about the modern short story. Entries: "Blackberry Winter" and "How I Contemplated the World. . . ."

RICH, Jennifer. Instructor of literature, composition, and gender issues at Marymount Manhattan College. Entry: "The Garden Party."

WILLIAMS, Deborah M. Instructor in the Writing Program at Rutgers University. Entry: "A New England Nun."

ZAM, Michael. Associate professor at Fordham College and New York University, as well as a writer for the *Harvard Gay and Lesbian Review* and *Details* magazine. Entry: ''In Another Country.''

Blackberry Winter

Robert Penn Warren

1946

The novelette *Blackberry Winter* was originally published separately in 1946 and subsequently collected in Robert Penn Warren's first and only volume of short stories, *The Circus in the Attic*, initially published in 1947. *Blackberry Winter* is widely believed to be Penn's finest work of short fiction. It has been included in many anthologies and has garnered the interest of critics and readers. Since its first publication, critics have noted Warren's deft evocation of the textures and rhythms of rural Tennessee and his ear for dialogue. One of the reasons for the story's popularity is the universal appeal of the narrator, whose boyhood innocence is as convincing as his adult ambivalence and restlessness.

Author Biography

A Southerner by birth and by nature, Robert Penn Warren was born in 1905 in Guthrie, Kentucky and died of cancer at his Vermont vacation home in September, 1989. His legacy includes major contributions to fiction, poetry, drama, and criticism. In a tribute to Warren in the *Kenyon Review*, a journal he helped establish, editor David Lynn commemorated ''the end of a miraculous career of an American laureate.'' Other than, perhaps, [Ralph Waldo] Emerson,'' Lynn continues, ''no other American has ever stood among the first rank in so many genres.''

Not only did Warren write literature (he published nearly three dozen books), but he changed the way literature was taught and studied. His books (written with Cleanth Brooks), *Understanding Poetry* and *Understanding Fiction,* "influenced, in Lynn's words, "a generation (and more) of students and teachers," and his essays on other writers "remain models of level-headed judgment, insight, and passion, and are bedrock for other critics."

After completing his early education in Guthrie, the young Warren was sent across the state line to Clarksville High School in Tennessee. A tall red-headed boy with aspirations for a career as a military officer, he suffered an eye injury that forced him to resign his appointment to the United States Naval Academy after graduating from high school at sixteen. Instead, he entered Vanderbilt University in Nashville, Tennessee. At Vanderbilt he soon fell in with an extraordinarily bright and ambitious group of students and faculty who cultivated his talent and honed his critical skills. Soon he was committed to a career in literary studies. He graduated with highest honors from Vanderbilt and began graduate study at the University of California at Berkeley. After receiving his master's degree he was awarded a prestigious Rhodes Scholarship and studied at Oxford University in England until eye trouble brought him back to the States in 1929.

Newly married and armed with an advanced degree from Oxford, Warren then embarked on the teaching career that would support and complement his writing until his retirement in the mid-1970s. After holding posts at Vanderbilt, Louisiana State University and the University of Minnesota, in 1949 Warren accepted a position at Yale University in New Haven, Connecticut, and settled in a New York City apartment. A year later he divorced his wife and married fellow writer Eleanor Clark, who soon gave birth to Warren's first child, Rosanna and three years later to a son, Gabriel. Fatherhood and marriage to Eleanor helped spark a creative rebirth for Warren as he entered into the second half of his life and career.

Despite all his travels, however, Warren never lost touch with his Kentucky roots. He participated in the literary and social movements known as the Agrarians and the Fugitives, who aimed to preserve and nurture the cultural heritage of the south, and with Cleanth Books at Louisiana State University he founded the distinguished literary journal, the *Southern Review.* "Blackberry Winter," the finest

piece in the only collection of short fiction Warren ever published, was written in 1946 while Warren was living in the north. Its detailed and evocative rendering of a boy's life on a farm in the first decades of the century is testimony not only to Warren's skill as a writer, but also to his attachment to the memories of summers on his grandfather's farm in the hills of southern Kentucky.

Plot Summary

This novelette is a recollection of one memorable day in the childhood of Seth, the narrator, then nine years old. It is told as a first-person narrative, more than thirty-five years later. The title refers to the weather phenomenon of a period of cool temperatures in June. The story takes place in middle Tennessee.

On this unseasonably cold day Seth's mother forbids him to go outside barefoot, but he disobeys her, wanting to "rub [his] feet over the wet shivery grass and make the perfect mark of [his] foot in the smooth, creamy, red mud." But before he can get out the door, Seth notices something unusual: "Out of the window on the north side of the fireplace I could see the man . . . still far off, come along by the path of the woods." The boy watches the man follow a path where the family's fence meet the woods. From a distance he can tell that the man is a stranger and that he is approaching the house. After Seth's mother calls off the dogs the man is near enough for closer inspection, and the boy sees that he is carrying a paper parcel in one hand and a switch-blade knife in the other. According to the narrator's assessment of the stranger, "Everything was wrong about what he wore." His worn khaki pants and dark wool coat and hat, his tie stuffed in a pocket and his city shoes mark him as both strange and menacing. Despite premonitions of danger, however, the boy is fascinated and drawn to the man who has come looking for a handout or work.

Seth watches the man work, disdainfully picking up the dead chicks and pitching them into a basket, "with a nasty, snapping motion." Then the boy watches while the tramp washed his dirty but uncalloused hands before eating. Finally the man makes the boy feel so uncomfortable that he leaves, suddenly remembering that "the creek was in flood over the bridge, and that people were down there watching it."

When he arrives at the bridge the first person he sees is his father, "sitting on his mare over the heads of the other men who were standing around admiring the flood." Seth's father scoops him "up to the pommel of his McClellan saddle" so he can see better. Seth and the men watch as the swollen creek carries debris along its course, and they are fascinated by the sight of a dead cow. Uncomprehending, Seth listens as the men discuss whose cow it likely was and whether a man could get hungry enough to eat a drowned cow.

Although his father takes him to the gate of their farm, Seth does not go home immediately. Instead he decides to stop off at a sharecropper family's cabin, where his playmate Jebb lives with his parents Dellie and Old Jebb. He expects to be welcomed by the usual cheer at the cabin, but instead encounters Dellie sick in bed and Old Jebb forecasting that the cold weather is a sign of the end of the world as we've known it, evidence that the earth is tired of "sinful folks." The most disturbing incident in the cabin, however, is that Dellie suddenly reaches out from her sick bed and slaps her son across the face. Although Seth tells Old Jebb about the man at the house with a knife, the news barely penetrates the gloom of the cabin and the preoccupation of the family.

The story reaches a climax when the stranger comes head to head with the father. Seth's father tells the tramp that he won't be hiring him for another day's work and pays him a half dollar for a half day's work (the going rate). Then the man curses the farm, mocks Seth's father, and spits on the ground just "six inches from the toe of [the] father's right boot." Seth's father stares the man down and he retreats. Seth, however, still cannot resist the man's horrible appeal and follows him "the way a kid would, about seven or eight feet behind." Seth asks where he came from and the man rebuffs him, but the young boy keeps following. Finally, the tramp threatens: "Stop following me. You don't stop following me and I cut yore throat, you little son-of-a-bitch."

The story ends with the older Seth explaining that both his parents are now dead, Jebb is in the penitentiary, Dellie's dead, but Old Jebb is still alive and well over a hundred years of age. The narrator also confesses that although the tramp had threat-

Robert Penn Warren

ened to kill him for following him, that he "did follow him, all the years."

Characters

Dellie

Dellie is the wife of the sharecropper Old Jebb and mother of Seth's sometime playmate Jebb. She works as a cook for Seth's family. They are an African-American family who live in a cabin on the narrator's family's farm. On the day the story takes place, Dellie is sick in bed with an unspecified "female" illness. Young Seth is shocked by her ravaged appearance and stunned when she lashes out and slaps her son so hard that he cries.

Father

The father's first or last name never appears in the story, but he plays a prominent role both in the events of the day and in the elder Seth's recollections. From the information provided, however, he seems to be a leader in the community, an affectionate father, and a fearless protector of his family. He embodies the virtues of his rural southern roots: chivalry, loyalty, resourcefulness, and restraint. In the boy's eyes, he is everything the tramp is not, and despite the boy's attraction to the malevolent stranger, it's clear that he loves and respects his father. The elder narrator remembers that his father "was a tall, limber man and carried himself well. I was always proud to see him sit a horse, he was so quiet and straight, and when I stepped through the gap of the hedge that morning, the first thing that happened was, I remember, the warm feeling I always had when I saw him up there on a horse, just sitting." He dies just a few years after the events of the story.

Jebb

Sometimes called Little Jebb, the son of Dellie and Old Jebb, Jebb is about two years older than Seth. He lives with his sharecropper parents in a cabin provided by Seth's father. On the day the story takes place, his mother viciously slaps him for making too much noise playing with Seth. In the epilogue to the story Seth explains that Jebb "grew up to be a mean and fiery Negro. [He] killed another Negro in a fight and got sent to the penitentiary."

Mother

Seth's mother, whose name is Sallie, is tough and brave. She is the one who puts limits on the young boy and tries to keep him from going outside in the cold air barefoot. The older Seth remembers his mother for her other, non-maternal qualities. When his mother confronts the strange man with the knife in his pocket, the narrator acknowledges, many women would have been afraid, "But my mother wasn't afraid. She wasn't a big woman, but she was clear and brisk about everything she did and looked everybody and everything right in the eye from her own blue eyes in her tanned face." It is later revealed that she died within three years of Seth's father's death, "right in the middle of life."

Old Jebb

Old Jebb is Jebb's father and the live-in partner of Dellie. The narrator remembers that he was an old man, "up in his seventies," back then, "but he was strong as a bull." Young Seth is drawn to him because he had "the kindest and wisest face in the world, the blunt, sad, wise face of an old animal peering tolerantly out on the goings-on of the merely human before him."

Seth

Seth is the narrator and the main character in the actions of the story. The first and only time his name is used in the story is when his father calls out to him from the crowd looking at the flooding creek.

The nine-year-old Seth is completely at home in his world and lives a child's innocent existence, free from the constraints of time and unthreatened by death and evil. As events unfold, however, he experiences and witnesses events that begin to change the way he sees himself and his world. The older Seth understands much better what happens that day, but the fact that he needs to go back and tell the story indicates that he still has unresolved feelings and unanswered questions. The biggest mystery about the Seth is what happens to him in the thirty-five years between the events and the telling of the story.

The Tramp

The tramp—or simply, the man, or the man with a knife—is the malevolent stranger with the inappropriate city clothes who walks up the path from the woods to the back door of Seth's family's farmhouse. Seth notices at first glance that "Everything was wrong about what he wore," and his menacing appearance proves to be an accurate predictor of his behavior. First, he's a surly and poor worker. Next, he swears and spits at Seth's father, and finally he snarls at and threatens Seth himself. Nevertheless, his exotic and singular rebelliousness is a powerful attraction for the young Seth, and apparently has remained so throughout his life, according to the narrator's cryptic comments in the epilogue.

Themes

Fathers and Sons

Throughout his career, Warren was interested in exploring and writing about the relationship between fathers (and grandfathers) and sons, and in *Blackberry Winter* the theme takes center stage. In an interview, Warren agrees with his critics who say that the search for the father is a recurrent theme in his work: "I've been told, and I think it's true, that the 'true' father and the 'false' father are in practically every story I've written." Though Warren goes on to say (rather disingenuously) that he has "no idea" what that means, but readers of *Blackberry Winter* can hardly fail to notice that the young boy is drawn to two strong and contrasting figures in the father and the tramp.

Surely the tramp embodies the opposite of his father: the tramp is cowardly, weak and squeamish, and perhaps worst of all, ungentlemanly. His choice of the switchblade as a weapon demonstrates his untrustworthiness and cowardice, but the blade itself naturally appeals to the boy. When the tramp is repulsed by the dead chicks, the boy "who did not mind hog-killing or frog-gigging," suddenly sees them anew and feels "hollow in the stomach." But it's the tramp's swearing and spitting at the boy's father that makes him at once repulsive and irresistible. The boy follows him because he's the only one he's ever seen who has not deferred to his father, and because like all boys he will eventually have to do the same in order to become a man, and he wants to know how.

Seth's father, on the other hand, is a model of strength, affection, and manly southern virtues. At the creek his father displays both civic leadership among the other men and paternal affection by lifting his son up to his horse and placing a hand on his thigh to steady him. When the father finally encounters the tramp on his property, he knows exactly what to do and exercises restraint when the man accosts him. Nevertheless, the portrayal of the father is undercut somewhat by the older Seth's epilogue when the narrator reveals that the tramp is the man whose image walked before him "all these years."

Innocence

Warren's depiction of the farm in *Blackberry Winter* is most likely drawn from his own boyhood experiences on his grandfather's farm in Cerulean, Kentucky. In the narrator's memory, it is a place of unspoiled innocence—until that cold day in June when the stranger walked up to the house from the path by the woods.

Seth's boyhood world on the morning of that day is June is a kind of garden of Eden, a "first paradise," in the language of critic Winston Weathers. The narrator describes how the boy's understanding of time differs from the adult view: ". . . and when you are nine years old, what you remember seems forever; for you remember everything and everything is important and stands big and full and fills up Time and is so solid that you can walk around and around it like a tree and look at it."

Of course, innocence is a state of being only understood from the perspective of its opposite—experience. In Judeo-Christian terms, the opposite of innocence is sin, and the consequences of the fall include being expelled from the garden of Eden. The older narrator of *Blackberry Winter* is recalling the day when his paradise was lost, when death (the

Topics for Further Study

- What were the lives of tobacco farmers like early in the century? What is likely to happen to the families whose crops are washed away in the flood?

- There are many interpretations of what the narrator means when he says he did follow the tramp "all the years." What do you think he means? Write a brief narrative describing what happens to Seth during those thirty-five years.

- The story provides no motivation for the tramp's behavior. What do you think he wants when he walks up to the farmhouse? Does Seth's mother's fearlessness make him change his plans?

- The whole town seems to be represented at the bridge over the flooding creek. Describe the social and economic structure of the area where Seth's family lives.

baby chicks, the dead cow in the creek), the destructive force of nature (the flood), and evil (the snarling, malevolent tramp) entered his world and changed him forever. In the words of critic Charles Bohner, "In the span of a single morning, the child has experienced his own blackberry winter. He has been thrust suddenly and violently from the warmth of his childish innocence to the chill knowledge of the 'jags and injustices' of an adult world."

Style

Narration

The story is told by a first-person narrator who is recalling events that happened to him sometime in the past. Not until the epilogue does he reveal that thirty-five years separate the events of that June day from the narration. This distance sets up a contrast between the nine-year-old Seth's point of view and the forty-four-year-old narrator's. This structure not only invites comparison between the boy's perception of events and the man's, it also asks readers to consider how the mechanism of memory works. In other words, is it the events of that June day that are important, or the recollection of those events over the intervening time period?

Because the adult narrator is capable of understanding and interpreting the events of the day better than the child is, the narrative structure of the story anticipates an explanation. Readers expect that by the end, the elder Seth will provide the missing pieces and a narrative overlay to connect the fragments and explain the significance of the events of the day. Warren never gives his narrator a chance to offer a full resolution, however. Though it is clear throughout the narrator's story that he understands events much better now than he did then, he still cannot account for the bigger mysteries. "The man is looking backward on the boy he once was," Bohner explains, "recalling objectively his childhood bewilderment. The events of the day had puzzled the child, but the man, remembering the experience, is not puzzled. Rather he now sees the experience as a paradigm of a problem he has carried into adulthood. He has come to terms with the problem—it is one mark of his maturity—but it is a problem that is never finally resolved."

Setting

The southern rural setting of *Blackberry Winter* is significant in several ways. Warren considered himself a Southerner and a southern writer his entire career, despite the years he spent living in Minnesota, New York, and abroad. He, like Flannery O'Connor wrote years later, believed that the south would produce a richer literature because the experience of the Civil War and its repercussions meant that the region had "already had its fall," had already acquired a deeper and more tragic vision of the human condition. For Warren the rural life in Kentucky and Tennessee (where the story is set) conjures images of an agrarian way life in the south that he believed was being threatened by the intrusion of homogenous northern industrialism (see below).

On a more personal level, though, the farm in *Blackberry Winter* evokes his grandfather's place in Cerulean, Kentucky, where Warren spent summers as a boy. Living in Minneapolis in 1946, where snow in May was not uncommon, Warren was apparently nostalgic for the warmer spring of his youth and found himself with a string of memories that became the story that many consider his best piece of short fiction.

Historical Context

The New Criticism

Warren's legacy to literary studies goes far beyond the novels, stories, poems and plays he created. He was one of the founders of a school of criticism called the New Criticism, which dominated the field of English studies for more than a generation. He accomplished this through his role as teacher to countless undergraduate and graduate students who would go on to be teachers and professors, through his influence as founder and editor of two highly influential literary journals (*Southern Review* and *Kenyon Review*), and perhaps most important, through the defining textbooks he wrote with fellow Louisiana State University professor and critic Cleanth Brooks.

The theory and methods of the New Criticism will seem to today's students both obvious and outdated. Simply put, they argued that poems (and other genres, but poems especially) could be read and interpreted on the merits of their own internal and formal qualities. The methods grew out of the practices of a loose group of students and professors (called the Fugitives) at Vanderbilt University who met regularly to talk about poetry and to read and discuss each other's work. Though one of the youngest members of the group when he first began attending, Warren was quickly recognized as one of its brightest lights, contributing as both a poet and as an adept reader of other members' work. The critical methods that members of the group employed, careful word by word scrutiny of the text as separate from its author, became part of the classroom practices of the professors and professors to be. When Warren took up a teaching post at Louisiana State University in 1934 he collaborated with his colleague Cleanth Brooks to write the textbook that formalized these methods, *Understanding Poetry*, which was published in 1938 and still in use in some college classrooms forty years later.

Today, most critics find New Criticism limited in its ability to account for the cultural context of a work of literature, and believe that its insistence on discounting the personal life of the author erases important differences in gender, ethnicity, and other features of authorial identity. Nonetheless, many—if not most—professors and critics in literary studies today were taught by professors who were trained in these methods. Though the New Criticism is no longer an end in itself, its methods for close

Compare & Contrast

- **1940s:** Workers during the Great Depression are faced with unemployment rates as high as 25% and relief comes through socialistic government programs. The United States also increases defense spending as the nation enters World War II.

   1990s: Unemployment stands around 6%, but corporate downsizing has many workers concerned about their future. The government must reduce a multi-billion dollar deficit, yet the stock market continues its strong performance.

- **1940s:** Blacks are excluded from the suburban housing boom of the era. The Federal Housing Authority practices "redlining": on city maps it draws red lines around predominantly black inner-city areas and refuses to insure loans for houses in those areas. This practice contributes to the demise of the inner city.

1990s: Though many upper- and middle-class blacks live and work in the suburbs, poor blacks are often confined to substandard housing in decaying urban areas, or ghettos.

- **1940s:** Race relations are tense as blacks grow frustrated with segregation and discrimination. In southern states, poll taxes and literacy tests are used to prevent blacks from voting. Tempers explode during race riots in Detroit and Harlem in the summer of 1943.

   1990s: Though civil rights legislation enacted during the 1960s has improved the conditions of minorities, particularly African Americans, the nation was polarized along racial lines in the debates over the Rodney King and O. J. Simpson trials.

---

reading of a text are often the first step in any teacher's or critic's approach to a work of literature.

The New South and the Old South

The cultural context of the literary circle at Vanderbilt is important. Vanderbilt was at the time the site of vigorous intellectual activity, and a great deal of the discussion, quite naturally, had to do with the state of the American South. Members of the Fugitive group who met to discuss literature and culture were interested in preserving the cultural uniqueness of the southeast, but were also "intent of repudiating the magnolia-and-julip tradition of southern letters," as Bohner puts it. The Fugitives' positions were complex and contradictory, but in general, they were concerned that the northern industrial culture would eclipse what was left of the southern way of life. In particular they "were distressed by what they considered to be the results of a culture based on the machine: the accelerating tempo of life, the chaotic individualism, the blatant materialism, the debasement of human effort and human dignity," as Bohner defines it. By 1930, four

of the regular attendees of Fugitive meetings, Warren, John Crowe Ransom, Allen Tate, and Donald Davidson joined eight other southern writers to publish a collection of essays called *I'll Take my Stand*.

Critical Overview

Blackberry Winter first appeared in November of 1946 at a time when Warren's novel *All the King's Men* was on the *New York Times* best-seller list. Because of the success of the novel, Warren's agent was able to get him an unusually large amount of money for the publication of his novelette. When Warren collected his short fiction into the volume called *The Circus in the Attic and Other Stories* in 1948, he received what was for him an exceptionally large advance against royalties.

Early reviews praised the title story and *Blackberry Winter* (the second story in the book), but the critical consensus then and now is that the short

Two hoboes walking on railroad tracks, pictured on the cover of "Hoboes: Wandering in America, 1870–1940," by Richard Wormser.

story is not Warren's finest genre. Within a year of the book's publication, Warren told a colleague, "I know that the collection is, at the best, uneven, but if I was ever to publish them I reckoned I might as well go ahead and hope for the best." In his recent critical biography of Warren, Joseph Blotner sums up the reaction of critics: "It was indeed uneven, achieving distinction only in the first two and the last story. His range of characters and inventive imagination would be praised along with the atmosphere and continuity of the stories, but there would also be numerous cavils and rather general agreement that in prose fiction he was a novelist rather than a short-story writer. It was to be his first and last collection of stories."

Blackberry Winter, however, has been frequently anthologized and has received considerable critical attention. Commentators in the first decades after the story's publication tended to focus on Warren's use of poetic imagery and universal themes, using critical methods from the New Criticism that Warren himself had helped to define. Writing in the *New York Times* Granville Hicks noted that Warren had "developed a colloquial style that is just about as

good as anything one can find in contemporary literature," and that he has "also acquired greater and greater subtlety in his explorations of personality."

Another reviewer in *U. S. Quarterly Booklist* praises Warren's ability to capture "the characteristic rhythms and homely idioms of Southern rural speech," as well as the stories' "strong sense of the uses and beauties of tangible things." A reviewer in *Time*, however, concluded that although "each story has a rural or small-town setting and is marked by a notebook quality of careful, detailed observation . . . there is not one story that rises from notebook level to finished fiction."

H. N. Smith, writing in *The Saturday Review of Literature* concludes that "Despite the occasional triumphs of the earlier pieces, none of them is an entirely satisfactory thing-in-itself. They suggest, in fact, that Mr. Warren is a novelist rather than a short-story writer." As it turns out, recent critical attention has focused less on Warren's novels and more on the long narrative poems that occupied the late phase of his career. Joseph Blotner's 1997 critical biography of Warren devotes little space to Warren's short fiction, but does single out *Blackberry Winter* as the best and most enduring of the collection.

Criticism

Elisabeth Piedmont-Marton

Elisabeth Piedmont-Marton teaches American literature and directs the writing center at Southwestern University in Texas. She writes frequently about the modern short story. In this essay she discusses how the tramp's appearance rearranges Seth's conception of himself and the protected world he lives in.

Critics of Warren's finest story, "Blackberry Winter," have focused on his presentation of universal themes and his deft use of imagery and atmosphere. While it certainly is true that the story invokes age-old and timeless human narratives, like the expulsion from the garden of Eden and the rebellion against the father, it can also be understood in its own particular historical and cultural context. Because the events that happen to young Seth that day in June, and which continue to haunt him thirty-five years later, is about how human beings create and

What Do I Read Next?

- *All the King's Men* (1946) is Warren's famous novel about an ambitious political leader. It is funny, exciting, and every bit as relevant to politics today as it was the day it was published.

- "A Good Man is Hard to Find," by Flannery O'Connor is also a short story in which the ordinary events in the life of a family are disrupted by the arrival of a menacing stranger.

- *Ellen Foster* (1989) is the coming-of-age story of a young girl struggling to grow up amidst poverty and sorrow in rural North Carolina.

carve out identity from their surroundings, it seems especially important to attend to where these events transpire in time and space, to the here and now-ness of the story. "Blackberry Winter," for all its symbolic resonance, is very much the story of a thoughtful young (white) boy's experiences in and around his parents' farm in middle Tennessee at the beginning of the second decade of the twentieth century.

The first indication that this day will be significant, and possibly transformative, appears in the story's opening paragraphs when the child assesses how this moment seems unique, different from each that has come before. Seth's understanding of time and the passing of the seasons is childlike: if it is June, you can go barefoot. It never crosses his mind, he says, "that they would try to stop you from going barefoot in June, no matter if there had been a gully-washer and a cold spell." For Seth, time and nature are familiar and knowable things, not the troubling abstractions they become for adults. At that age, "you remember everything and everything is important and stands big and full and fills up Time and is so solid that you can walk around and around it like a tree and look at it." His connection to nature is similarly seamless: "When you are a boy and stand in the stillness of woods, which can be so still that your heart almost stops beating and makes you want to stand there in the green twilight until you feel your very breathing slow through its pores like the leaves." Poets and theologians would define Seth's state of mind at the beginning of the story as "innocence." He has no understanding of his self as separate or different from the world

around him. Psychologists would call Seth's identity "undifferentiated."

During the course of the day, Seth begins the wrenching process of differentiation, of exploring the boundaries where self ends and other begins, of understanding that his particular reality cannot be mistaken for universal truth, and of recognizing that he only knows who he is by defining others as "not him." What makes Warren's story so poignant and effective is that Seth's self-knowledge comes incrementally and tangibly. The landscape which he traverses is not some vague, mythical place, not are the other characters he interacts with merely empty symbols themselves. Instead, Seth's experiences that day have everything to do with rural Tennessee, with the south, with who his father is, with the arrestingly cool weather of blackberry winter. The arrival of the stranger sets in motion a series of events that cause Seth to redefine himself and his place in the world, and, as he will come to understand more deeply in the thirty-five years before he narrates the story, he will lose forever the innocent certainty of being perfectly at home in the world.

That morning, when Seth first sees the man out the window, he is struck by the incongruity, the strangeness, of the sight. In fact, the hallmark of the man is his strangeness: he does not know anything about dogs, his clothes are all wrong, and he carries a mysterious package. To Seth, the man is more than strange, however, his entrance into the world defies explanation and challenges the laws of Seth's universe. Even Seth's mother cannot account for his presence. She says that she does not "recognize him," and when Seth asks her where he could be

> " It is as if Seth realizes for the first time that his friend and his family are black, that he his white, and that in the time and place where they live, that signifies an unerasable and fundamental difference."

coming from, all she can say is "I don't know." Shutting his eyes and hoping the figure of the man will disappear, Seth thinks, "There was no place for him to have come from, and there was no reason for him to come where he was coming, toward the house." But he is there, and his presence does not just challenge Seth's world view, it forever changes it. Now Seth must include new phenomena in his comprehension of what is possible, and furthermore, he will no longer enjoy the feeling of certainty with which he began the day. Even thirty-five years later, the narrator still cannot make sense of the encounter with the stranger. The man's voice, he remembers "seemed to have a wealth of meaning, but a meaning which I could not fathom." In retrospect, he can still only hazard a guess that "it probably was not pure contempt."

The tramp's intrusion into Seth's world changes everything. The strange man's emergence from the woods, "like a man who has come a long way and has a long way to go," is trespassing in several senses of the word. He is a trespasser in the legal sense in that he walks across the family's property (and surely the property of others as well) without permission or regard for their rights. But trespass also means to sin or transgress. The tramp's entrance into Seth's world is literally a transgression, a crossing of boundaries (the fence), and figuratively (stepping over the line between the possible and the impossible). His sin does not take the form of any specific act, however. Rather, he is sin embodied and his very presence forces Seth to acknowledge the existence of sin and evil in the world. That knowledge, in turn, alters the way he perceives himself and everything else in his now fallen world.

The familiar sights of his world suddenly look strange to Seth. When he arrives at the bridge, for example, a ritual repeated every spring flood, the faces of the men look "foreign" and "not friendly." When he comes up along side his father "within touching distance of his heel," Seth is unable to "read" his father's "impassive" face. The spectacle of the dead cow also takes on new dimensions for Seth, who understands for the first time that the cow is not just "dead as a chunk." It represents a devastating loss to Milt Alley and his "pore white trash family." Seth's concern and empathy for Mr. Alley and his "thin-faced" children is genuine, but part of his interest in their circumstances is triggered by his dawning awareness that the brutal forces of the rural economy make the Alleys poor and his family comfortable. He seems to recognize that his relative wealth depends on their poverty, that the idyllic comfort of his family's farm is built on the hard work of others. After Seth listens, only half understanding, to the men and boys discuss what hunger will do to a man, he gets another glimpse of life outside of the garden of innocence. And once he has that knowledge in his possession, he cannot return to his former state of consciousness. This inability to return to innocence is symbolized by Seth's choice not to go home after his father drops him off at the gate to the farmhouse.

Shivering, both from the cold and from uncertainty, Seth goes instead to Dellie and Jebb's cabin where he hopes to be able to play with Little Jebb, the boy close to his own age. Expecting warmth and reassurance in the family's humble cabin, Seth finds instead disarray, sickness, and violence. The first thing that Seth notices is "that the drainage water had washed a lot of trash and filth out from under Dellie's house." Like the appearance of the tramp coming across the yard, and revelations of poverty at the bridge, the trash in Dellie's yard is jarring because it defies the laws of the universe as Seth has understood them up to this point. Although the cabin looks "just as bad as the yards of the other cabins." To Seth's eye's "it was worse . . . because it was a surprise." The interior of the cabin is no less familiar. Dellie herself is sick, and looks so strange that Seth "scarcely recognized" her face. When she calls Jebb over to her bedside and then slaps him so hard that he cries silently, the last of Seth's illusions are shattered. He is forced to acknowledge the psychological consequences of poverty and to accept his role in the social and economic mechanisms that keep Jebb and his family in a dirt-floored cabin. It is as if Seth realizes for the first time that his friend and his family are black, that he his white, and that in the time and place where they live, that signifies an unerasable and fundamental difference.

Everything changes after the tramp arrives on Seth's family's property. He does not do anything menacing or sinful, or destroy or change anything, but when he walks in to Seth's garden from the outside world, he represents the intrusion of the outside world into the fading agrarian ideal of the south. He represents the city, industrialism, materialism and the ruthless cult of success. The stranger's presence destroys their shared illusions about race, class and identity in the south. Now, Seth sees, black and white are not just unequals, they are adversaries. In short, the tramp represents everything that threatens the middle Tennessee rural way of life and once Seth sees the world through the tramp's eyes, he is destined to follow him "all the years" because he knows he cannot stay where he is.

Source: Elisabeth Piedmont-Marton, for *Short Stories for Students*, The Gale Group, 2000.

Bryan Dietrich

In the following essay, Dietrich interprets "Blackberry Winter" in terms of its religious context, casting the tramp as an antichrist who negates Christian belief in the face of the disillusionment of life.

For four and half decades readers, professors, and critics seem to have stumbled, at least the first time through, over the last line of Robert Penn Warren's short story, "Blackberry Winter." If we know the basic story line, the adult narrator's final, backward-looking observation, "But I did follow him, all the years," is plain enough on the surface. It simply refers to the tramp of the story and to an experience the narrator is remembering in the context of 35 interim years. But as readers, we know there is a deeper level, and it is the deeper level that throws us. Seth, the narrator, has not literally spent the years since he was nine years old following that one tramp. But if we believe a metaphor is at work here and that that metaphor succeeds, then we must be seeing evidence, clues, or keys to its interpretation, in the larger body of the story.

Floyd C. Watkins argues that such a key to adequate understanding of the last line (and ultimately, I suppose, the whole tale) is lacking. Watkins acknowledges that the "concluding sentence is as dramatic as the threat of the tramp," but also suggests,

> **One can easily read a Pied Piper legend into this work, or see a Lucifer figure in the person of the tramp; but if we take the incidentals of the story as symbolic and religious references rather than simple metaphors, the tramp becomes an antichrist figure."**

the older narrator did *not* specify how he followed him. There are many possibilities: following him into the urban world; growing old; adopting a life of rootlessness and violence; or simply growing up into knowledge.

In other words, Watkins continues,

> The tramp moves into the experiences of the world, but the story does not provide one glimpse of his understanding or of the events of the narrator's later life. . . . the author lets the last sentence of the story, mysterious as it is, fall flat on its face into a puddle of meaning.

If we believe Watkins, then, Warren has neglected to provide a solid context in which to see the ending, and it is only natural that the reader should trip over the last line.

Most other critics, however, seem to disagree. Thomas W. Ford, in a charming essay that compares "Blackberry Winter" to Emily Dickinson's poem, "These are the days when Birds come back," sees

> the recognition of hunger and starvation as a possible human condition . . . the trash washed up by the flood that spoiled Dellie's always clean yard; the awful and uncharacteristic slap administered by Dellie to her small son during the misery of her menopause; and, most important of all, the conversation with Old Jebb . . . [as] the metaphorical center of the story.

I think Ford would agree with Warren himself, who wrote of his story, and of the meaning of the last line in particular,

> the tramp had said to the boy: "You don't stop following me and I cut yore throat, you little son-of-a-bitch."

Had the boy then stopped or not? Yes, of course, literally, in the muddy lane. But at another level—no. In so far as later he had grown up, had really learned something of the meaning of life, he had been bound to follow the tramp all his life, in the imaginative recognition, with all the responsibility which such a recognition entails, of this lost, mean, defeated, cowardly, worthless, bitter being as somehow a man. (Warren, "Recollection")

And for Warren himself, then, the ending is one of hope, an ending that indicates no matter what or how much we realize about the inadequacies of men, no matter how awful those realizations may be (especially for a nine-year-old), we tend to find that we can overcome self-pity when we accept a kind of basic humanity in even the most inhumane of men.

If such a hopeful outlook is the interpretation we are to arrive at, Ford's assertion of the central metaphor will do nicely. All the images of human frailty that he notes—images that illustrate the basic, underlying contradictions of human nature—provide sufficient context with which to read the last eight words as positive. Ford goes on to say,

So a nineteenth-century Amherst spinster in a poem about a New England Indian summer and a twentieth-century southern agrarian in a short story about a Tennessee blackberry winter stretch out long arms across space and time, clasp hands, and become metaphorical twins in creative response to and recognition of the uncertainty of the human condition.

But the above interpretation is not the only interpretation. Ford himself suggests that there is a strong "rite of passage" element at work in Warren's story, and this particular rite can be seen in a more negative context, despite Warren's own assertion: "no tramp ever leaned down at me and said for me to stop following him or he would cut my throat. But if one had, I hope that I might have been able to follow him anyway, in the way the boy in the story does" (Warren, "Recollection").

Kenneth Tucker sees the underlying contextual metaphor as related to the German legend of the Pied Piper. Such a parallel is a fairly simple one to make if we break the action of both the story and the legend down into general terms:

In both stories appear the coming of a catastrophe, the hiring of a stranger to undo the harm, the employer's reneging on the wage, the stranger's impulse to seek vengeance, and children or a child irresistibly following the departing stranger.

Tucker, however, takes the analogy even further, deftly describing the tramp's accouterments, not necessarily as "pied," but certainly as "motley." He then elaborates, defining the Tramp/piper

character as a symbol of evil, specifically as "an embodiment of the Trickster archetype" and later explains, "The Trickster's basic significance resides in his delight in disorder."

Tucker argues that Seth understands the basic "evil" inherent in the tramp, but

like the Pied Piper, the tramp gains a victory over the employer who has not paid the promised wage. As the Piper leads the children from the town, the tramp lures Seth psychologically from the orderly but restrictive world of his parents.

This particular interpretation makes fairly clear how Tucker sees that "the provocative [last] line also implies that in trailing after the tramp, Seth has followed and faced villainy in himself."

In his essay, "'Blackberry Winter' and the Use of Archetypes," Winston Weathers anticipates Tucker's argument, but suggests an even more sinister view of the tramp. For Weathers, "Warren's handling of the 'Mysterious Stranger' is traditional" yet he believes Warren creates a "Mephistophelian form of the archetype." Weathers, continuing, writes, "Of the Mephistophelian possibilities—the harlequinesque rogue or the black punchinello—Warren leans somewhat toward the latter." In other words, for Weathers, the tramp is more than a simple Trickster or Pied Piper who leads Seth into (presumably) redeemable villainy; the tramp is cut from a decidedly darker pattern of Luciferan cloth. Thus, Seth's admission to having followed the tramp all his days becomes less an admission of guilt, and more an admission of damnation.

Few if any of these interpretations take the middle way into consideration. Yes, the metaphoric context is there; yes, the last line is justified by that metaphor; yes, the ending is hopeful; but yes, also, the tramp figure is a harbinger of "evil." These statements are not mutually exclusive if the tramp is seen as a dual figure himself. We will return to the dual nature of the tramp later, but first we must look at the metaphoric context: In what light should we see the tramp? Much of that light, the light that shines from behind the words of the text, can be viewed as religious, at least as pseudo-religious.

Prime examples of such a "religious" reading can be found early in the story, in the awed descriptions of time and the woods that rattle through Seth's head. There is little doubt that the depth of caring, the breathlessness, and the nod to universal significance that appear in these internal descriptions approach a kind of mystic revelation. These are short textual examples, but both descriptions hold positions of prominence in the overall thrust of the story. These descriptions, in fact, set the tone for the entire piece. Other scenes follow in the same religious context, some specifically Christian, some, like the awed responses to nature, not. Moreover, the religion, the belief that these undertones allude to, can also be seen as a fading belief.

The religious context, the atmosphere of faith that is set up early in the story, is gradually undermined. Belief becomes disillusionment. We see this undermining in several places throughout "Blackberry Winter," most notably in Jebb's speeches, in Seth's brief historical summary at the end, and in a handful of specific Christian (or New Testament) allusions. In both of Jebb's extended speeches, his disillusionment is clear. In the first, he describes the blackberry winter as a sign of the end. Here, by "end," he means the apocalypse in the Judeo-Christian tradition. If we are to take him literally, he and Seth and all the characters have been left behind by God, left to walk the Earth as it becomes a living hell. Jebb, 35 years later, again echoes this kind of disillusionment when he says that God answered his prayers, gave him strength, and left him. This strength has allowed him to live too long in a world that has lost its significance, in a world God himself has forsaken.

Other images of fading belief, of the undermining of faith, appear in the scenes outlined by Ford earlier, but what about Seth's adult description of what has happened to his family? His father, a man who believed in the way of farming, died on his own blade. Seth's mother, a woman who believed in loving her husband, died of a broken heart. Those very beliefs, the faith in what they were that *made* them what they were—farmer or mother, man of the land or wife—killed them.

The final images of disillusionment can be found in what appear to be direct allusions to the New Testament. The time frame and setting of "Blackberry Winter" are, after all, rooted in "down-home" Christian tradition. If we are to see the metaphoric context of this story as a descent into disillusionment, it only makes sense that the basic faith of the given place and time, Christianity, is also challenged, at least symbolically. When the county people come to see the results of the flood, the narrator informs us, "Everybody always knew what it would be like when he got down to the bridge, but people always came. It was like church or a funeral". Here we have people gathering in a

church-like atmosphere to witness something for reasons they do not really understand. We have a boy, small of stature, who comes to this "religious" gathering and who sees his father mounted on a horse. His father, seeing Seth on the ground, commands him up onto the horse where the boy can see better.

We see a similar set of events and actions in the Gospel of Luke, 19:1–6, when Jesus enters Jericho. The people have gathered to see Jesus, to witness the coming of something they do not fully understand. Zacchaeus, a rich man, but a man small of stature, climbs a sycamore tree to see better. Jesus, passing by, commands Zacchaeus to come down. Of course the parallels are not exact; Seth mounts his father's horse to see better, he does not climb a tree. But all of the same elements are here, as well as tantalizing similarities: Seth's smallness of stature, his climbing up to see better, the people gathered and unsure about *what* they have gathered to witness. Even more important, arguably, are the differences. Seth's father commands him up onto the horse. Jesus commands Zacchaeus to "come down." There is at one and the same time a kind of familiarity with the scene and a kind of reversal. After all, what the masses witness in "Blackberry Winter" is not a coming (or even a second coming) of Christ; rather, they witness the coming of a cow. This cow—if we see it as a symbol, as reminiscent of roughly parallel pagan symbols—is yet another indication that faith has fallen degenerate. Not only is it potentially pagan, and thus the antithesis to Christ, it is also quite dead. Another, possibly even more oblique, parallel to the New Testament is the relationship between Christ's parable of the vineyard, in which a laborer contests unequal pay (Matthew 20:1–16) and the hostility that arises between Seth's father and the tramp over what the tramp sees as a "breach of contract."

What about the tramp himself? Seth mentions, when he first sees the vagabond on the road, "Nobody ever went back there except people who wanted to gig frogs in the swamp or to fish in the river . . ." This simple statement is far more intriguing when we view it in light of what Christ says to Simon and Andrew by the Sea of Galilee in Mark 1:17: "Come ye after me, and I will make you to become fishers of men." Is the tramp then, himself, a kind of "fisher of men"? He "reels in" Seth quite handily; in fact he does so by reversing what Christ says in Matthew 8: 22. While Christ asks his disciples to "Follow me," the tramp eventually says to Seth, "Stop following me," the exact opposite.

One can easily read a Pied Piper legend into this work, or see a Lucifer figure in the person of the tramp; but if we take the incidentals of the story as symbolic and religious references rather than simple metaphors, the tramp becomes an antichrist figure. The tone of near-cathedral-like reverence toward time and nature early in the story; the church-like atmosphere of the gathering on the river bank; the increasing tempo of disillusionment with any belief, but specifically with belief in Christian ideas; the loose parallels to Christ and Christian mythos throughout; and, specifically, the command of the tramp, a command that echoes an exact negation of Christ's words—all these elements lead to the conclusion that the last eight words are an admission that Seth did not (necessarily) follow the path of hope, villainy, *or* damnation alone. Rather, he followed all the paths by following the path of an antichrist.

This is not to say that Seth fell under the spell of that antichrist—merely that he followed in the footsteps of disillusionment. Disillusionment holds within it all paths, the temptation toward despair, for example (as Jebb would solidly testify). But it also presupposes the possibility of enlightenment, the possibility of recognizing the face of the deceiver and changing course. And who better than a deceiver, an antichrist, to bring us the message of a dual- or even multi-faced coin? To a society whose preeminent belief system is Judeo-Christian, whose system is now faltering, an antichrist comes, and he flips that coin. He shakes things up, because if one does not question one's beliefs, one prays to a sedentary God.

Whether the deceiver arrives in the form of Pied Piper, Lucifer, tramp, antichrist or Christ himself, the revealed deception is always a seed of hope. And Seth, the narrator of "Blackberry Winter," intimates the possibility of such hope by the very knowledge that he *did* follow that deceiver, that tramp, all the years.

Source: Bryan Dietrich, "Christ or Antichrist: Understanding Eight Words in 'Blackberry Winter,'" in *Studies in Short Fiction*, Vol. 29, No. 2, Spring, 1992, pp. 215–20.

Floyd C. Watkins

In the following essay, Watkins suggests that the puzzling ending to "Blackberry Winter" (that the boy followed the tramp) is incomplete and lacks clues from the story necessary for an adequate understanding of how the boy did follow the tramp.

Robert Penn Warren wrote his short stories in the late 1930s and the first half of the 1940s. He did not publish any poems from his *Selected Poems* (1943) until *Brother to Dragons* (1953) and then the poems collected into the Pulitzer Prize winning *Promises* (1957). Brevity and compactness (and perhaps the intensity of writing short fiction) interfered with Warren's composition of poetry. On the other hand, he has said that the emotional turbulence of the last stages of his marriage to Cinina Brescia also ran counter to the mood which produces poetry.

Preciseness of imagery, distinctness of characterization, and revelation of meaning give Warren's "Blackberry Winter" many traits of his poems. The story begins with childhood in the country recalled by a forty-four-year-old man. The progression is toward increasing conflict on a day on the farm and an abrupt shift in time at the end of the story when the narrator takes a hard look at the meaning of his following a tramp after that day. An interpretation by Warren written twelve years after the story was published serves as the author's criticism of his own story. This afterword on "Blackberry Winter" increases the complexity and puzzlements, the variety of possible meanings, and perhaps the questions.

The remembered day in Tennessee is cold and uncomfortable, and mother and son argue about whether the boy may go outdoors barefooted. Putting on his shoes, he lifts his head and sees a man out the window. "What was strange was that there should be a man there at all," but what is even stranger is the kind of man he is — a complete foreigner to the farm. He prepares to defend himself against the farm dogs with "the kind of mean knife just made for devilment and nothing else"; "everything was wrong about what he wore"; when the boy's mother speaks to him, he "stopped and looked her over" — suggesting hostility and perhaps even an appraisal of her sexually. He wants work, but told to bury some drowned young turkeys, he says, "What are them things — poults?" Working in a flower bed, he feels "a kind of impersonal and distant marveling that he should be on the verge of grubbing in a flower bed." The series of images which reveal how this tramp is from a different world end in a scene of conflict between the tramp and the boy's father. Learning that the tramp has a "mean knife," the father fires him. In contempt, the man spits close to the father's foot, and the son notices the contrast between the father's "strong cowhide boots" and the tramp's "bright blob" of spit and his "pointed-toe, broken, black shoes. . . ."

The stranger brings to the farm the disorder of a mechanized, violent, urban world. Disorder also comes from nature. It is blackberry winter, a day of cold rain, storms, and floods. A dead cow floats down the flooding creek, and hunger in the lives of the poor is revealed. A big gangly boy asks, "Reckin anybody ever et drownt cow?" The storm mangles the flowers around Dellie's cabin, and trash washes from under the house of her and Jebb — admirable blacks who live on the farm.

These destructive forces enter the nine-year-old's stable world from a foreign culture and the storms of nature. It is for him a time of definition. His childhood until that time had not been "a movement, a flowing, a wind," but a world in which living things and people stood "solid in Time like the tree that you can walk around." Before, the wind had not shaken the tree but only the leaves "a little . . . on the tree which is alive and solid." Decades later the boy remembered the stable environment: the strength of his mother, the courage of his father, and the suffering of poor countrymen like Milt Alley, who silently watched the cow and the crops being washed away.

The entire story is a description of this cold day, except for five final short paragraphs. They are told when the boy is forty-four years old, thirty-five years later. The ending summarizes a variety of disasters since that time: the natural, the accidental, and the violent and the evil. The father died of lockjaw after a cut; the mother, of a broken heart; Little Jebb grew up to be "mean and ficey" and killed a man. But the most extraordinary future awaited the boy. At the end of his long recollection, he comes back to the tramp and tells how he followed him as he left the farm. The man showed his teeth and said: "'Stop following me. You don't stop following me and I cut yore throat, you little son-of-a-bitch.' That was what he said, for me not to follow him. But I did follow him, all the years." The concluding sentence is as dramatic as the threat of the tramp, but the older narrator did *not* specify how he followed him. There are many possibilities: following him into the urban world; growing old; adopting a life of rootlessness and violence; or simply growing up into knowledge.

In the last five paragraphs the characters also seem to have followed the tramp — the good people lived on into a sadder world; they died of accident and lockjaw, of grief, the Negroes Jebb and Dellie lived on for many years; their son, Little Jebb, went out into the violent world. All, then, apparently

> "Warren now believed that if the narrator 'had really learned something of the meaning of life, he had been bound to follow the tramp all his life, in the imaginative recognition . . . of this lost, mean, defeated, cowardly, worthless bitter being as somehow a man.'"

moved into a greater knowledge of complexities and depravities. The way the boy followed the tramp is not at all enacted in the story. Warren indicates only that he lived at least forty-four years, arrived at some state of knowledge, and indulged in a long reverie about that ancient day. The man ponders the meanings rather than the actions of the later time. The story ends without the causes being embodied in the world's body and the events of the boy's life. The actions and decisions of several characters were not like those of the tramp. The narrator's life was like the tramp's, or perhaps not. Not everyone must follow the tramp into the same kind of knowledge.

Warren's "Recollection" of his writing the story begins with the admission that the writing was "complicated" and that "I shall never know the truth, even in the limited, provisional way the knowing of truth is possible in such matters." In unfavorable terms he remembered the tramp who came into the story and left it: "city bum turned country tramp, suspicious, resentful, contemptuous of hick dumbness, bringing his own brand of violence, . . . a creature altogether lost and pitiful, a dim image of what, in one perspective, our human condition is." In contrast, he remembers the "mother's self-sufficency," and there is never an indication that she too followed a route like the tramp's. Warren remembered later that he "wanted the story to give some notion that out of change and loss a human recognition may be redeemed, more precious for being no longer innocent." At the ending, I believe, there is a decline from embodied incident to general statement. Either when Warren wrote the ending of the story or when he wrote his interpretation of it, he considered only one way of following the tramp. Warren now believed that if the narrator "had really learned something of the meaning of life, he had been bound to follow the tramp all his life, in the imaginative recognition . . . of this lost, mean, defeated, cowardly, worthless bitter being as somehow a man." The boy followed the tramp at least in his meditations. If following is mere recognition, the last sentence is "an impersonal generalization about experience" — as Warren calls it in his own recollection. But that is not the best method of enactment in fiction. That ending makes a heavy demand on a reader who is told of the murderous life of Little Jebb and of other terrible matters. In his recollection, Warren says that no tramp ever threatened him as the one in the story did the boy, "but if one had, I *hope* that I might have been able to follow him anyway, in the way the boy in the story does" [italics mine].

But what way is that? The story has not specified, and the recollection has given almost no additional clue. The tramp moves into the experiences of the world, but the story does not provide one glimpse of his understanding or of the events of the narrator's later life. Certainly this ending has not ruined one of Warren's best short stories and one of the most accomplished American short stories. But neither has it entirely fulfilled the fiction. By switching altogether to the narrator's meditation and by making a *statement* of a view of life, the author lets the last sentence of the story, mysterious as it is, fall flat on its face into a puddle of meaning. At the end of Warren's explanation, one can only wonder if he has left his interpretation incomplete, if the recollection is wrong, or if the story itself has a misleading last sentence.

Source: Floyd C. Watkins, "Following the Tramp in Warren's 'Blackberry Winter,'" in *Studies in Short Fiction*, Vol. 22, No. 3, Summer, 1985, pp. 343.

James E. Rocks

In the following essay, Rocks argues that the tramp in "Blackberry Winter" represents the idea of the original corruption of the will in Adam.

Robert Penn Warren wrote "Blackberry Winter" shortly after he completed *All the King's Men* and "A Poem of Pure Imagination: an Experiment in Reading," the long essay on *The Ancient Mariner*; these three works, written during 1945 and 1946, are notable examples of their respective genres and reveal Warren's varied literary talents. That "Blackberry Winter" was written soon after the novel and essay suggests that it might be read critically in the light of the two earlier works. It is unlikely that they influenced the short story in any definite way, but the essay on Coleridge and *All the King's Men* do foreshadow some of the themes, symbols and techniques of the story and indicate that Warren was thinking about similar problems as he wrote each work. *All the King's Men* and "Blackberry Winter" share the same mood of impending disorder and express a similar view of the idea of change, a major theme in Warren's work.

In "Writer at Work: How a Story was Born and How, Bit by Bit, It Grew," Warren describes the origin of "Blackberry Winter" in World War II, when he felt civilization might never again be the same. A line in Melville's poem "The Conflict of Convictions" carried for him the frightening reminder that wars threaten to uncover the "slimed foundations" of the world, an image that is reminiscent in tone of the decay, corruption and death in the novel and the story. His tale grew, he says, from the association of various experiences in his own life and was an attempt to treat the "adult's grim orientation" toward the fact of time and the fall of man into moral awareness. As Warren writes, "I wanted the story to give some notion that out of change and loss a human recognition may be redeemed, more precious for being no longer innocent." This condition of growth into maturity, with its concomitant gains and losses, is shared by Jack Burden in *All the King's Men* and Seth in "Blackberry Winter."

Warren's essay on "Blackberry Winter" gives us some clues in reading both the story and *All the King's Men*, but it is like Poe's "The Philosophy of Composition" or Allen Tate's "Narcissus as Narcissus" in that it leaves most of the important pieces of the puzzle for the reader to assemble. Warren expects the reader, like the writer in the act of composing, to be a creative and discerning individual. The quest for knowledge that fictional characters undergo is interpreted by a sympathetic and imaginative reader, who must discover in the work the symbols, myths and archetypes that the writer has used to dramatize the universal human condition. As a New Critic, Warren affirms the significance of a symbolic reading of literature and states that a "poem is the light by which the reader may view and review all the areas of experience with which he is acquainted." A story, like a poem, uses symbol and has rich texture. Warren stresses the varied and suggestive meaning of any symbol, particularly one ''rooted in our universal natural experience.'' The sun, moon, stars and wind that he identifies in Coleridge are examples of such fundamental symbols, which like the archetypes of rebirth and the journey in Coleridge are to be found in Warren's own work, including, of course, ''Blackberry Winter'' and *All the King's Men.*

Warren's discussion of Coleridge's sacramental conception of the universe, violated by the Mariner's crime against the sanctity of nature, is relevant to a reading of ''Blackberry Winter.'' The short story examines how the prideful individual can isolate himself from what Warren calls the sense of the ''One Life'' in which a creation participates. In ''Blackberry Winter'' the older Seth arrives at a similar knowledge as he looks back at his day's journey: like the Mariner, he learns about the beauty and terror of the universe and the natural process of change that both renews and destroys. Seth, like all men, must reenact the fall of the first father, Adam, whose third son we are told in Genesis was named Seth. Although the story, in its series of episodes and recurring symbols, seems to emphasize decay and death (the ''slimed foundations''), it asserts finally the triumph of human perception over the natural forces that age and destroy. Seth, whose fall is fortunate, has moved, like Jack Burden and Ann Stanton in *All the King's Men,* ''into history and the awful responsibility of Time.'' The adult Seth, like Jack and Anne, has learned the meanings of sin and guilt, isolation and community.

The tramp, or the Mysterious Stranger, represents, as Warren finds them in Coleridge's poem, the ideas of sin and guilt and the isolation that attends them. Warren maintains that Coleridge was interested in the mystery of original sin—not hereditary sin, however, but sin that is original with the sinner and is a manifestation of his own will. In the Mariner, Warren says, we witness the corruption of the will, which is the beginning of the moral history of man. The Mariner's killing of the albatross reenacts the fall and is a condition of the will and results from no single human motive. Although a comparison between the Mariner and Willie Stark certainly cannot be carried too far, one may see in Stark an example of the corruption of the will that Warren finds in the Mariner. Like the Mariner, Willie makes his own convenience the measure of an act and therefore isolates himself from the ''One Life.'' One might argue, then, that Willie Stark and the tramp in ''Blackberry Winter'' represent in Warren's fiction the corruption of the will and the

> **''** Man's knowledge makes him aware that he is a fallen creature, Warren is saying, but that he has gained more than he has lost. . . .**''**

isolation of sin he finds in Coleridge. Both men are agents in the narrators' initiations and can be viewed as primarily beneficial in their influence on them. Stark may be corrupt in the means of his politics but he is often motivated by altruistic ends; goodness, as Jack Burden learns, can be accomplished by the morally bad agent. Like Stark, the tramp is also a human being, however sinful and violent he may appear. In ''Blackberry Winter,'' as Warren states in ''Writer at Work,'' Seth remembers ''this lost, mean, defeated, cowardly, worthless, bitter being as somehow a man'' who had come ''out of the darkening grown-up world of time.'' The Ancient Mariner, Willie Stark and the tramp are alike in that they serve to elicit the emotions of pity and terror from the reader and suggest the knowledge that man must apprehend if he is to avoid a similar fate. Each of these men enters a ''darkening grown-up world of time''; so, also, do their observers, the wedding guest, Jack Burden and Seth. An awareness of time is a central concern of Warren's characters, and in his story he depicts the truth that Jack Burden and Seth must suffer to learn; life is motion toward knowledge.

The title ''Blackberry Winter'' foreshadows the principal knowledge that Seth will gain: what man thinks has been permanent and will always remain permanent is subject to unexpected and devastating change. As a boy Seth believes that what he has done before will remain possible forever—that in June, for example, one need never wear shoes:

> . . . when you are nine years old, what you remember seems forever; for you remember everything and everything is important and stands big and full and fills up Time and is so solid that you can walk around and around it like a tree and look at it. You are aware that time passes, that there is a movement in time, but that is not what Time is. Time is not a movement, a flowing, a wind then, but is, rather, a kind of climate in which things are, and when a thing happens it begins

to live and keeps on living and stands solid in Time like a tree that you can walk around. And if there is a movement, the movement is not Time itself, any more than a breeze is climate, and all the breeze does is to shake a little the leaves on the tree which is alive and solid. When you are nine, you know that there are things that you don't know, but you know that when you know something you know it. You know how a thing has been and you know that you can go barefoot in June.

At the time the story opens, however, an unseasonable cold spell, blackberry winter, and a gully washer have just interrupted the anticipated plan of boyhood activity. From the beginning of the story, we are aware that the apparent security of the boy's world will be upset by a series of episodes revealing the mystery of change. The four scenes of the story—the first at his house, the second at the bridge, the third at the Negro cabin and the fourth at his house—are structured to suggest the idea of cycle or return, a going forth and a coming back. This pattern, like the notion that the gain of knowledge is worth the loss of innocence, argues for an interpretation of the story that stresses rebirth and renewal—if not the regeneration of life, at least the enlightenment of the mind. In the epilogue that concludes the story, the older Seth looks back from the year 1945—when Warren felt that the "slimed foundations" of the world might be exposed—and considers the profound ironies of change: that the father who seemed invincible to him as a boy has died early, a victim of the machine, not of nature; and that the mother who seemed strong has died of a broken heart; and that Old Jebb, who most wanted the release of death to end his fatigue and who had prophesied the end of the world, lives on like an aging Samson. Most important of all, Seth realizes the value of his memory, which has kept alive the image of the tramp for thirty-five years.

This tramp and not the cold spell first disturbs the harmony of Seth's world, his "One Life." Seeing the tramp emerge from the woods, he is struck by "the strangeness of the sight" and he tries to "walk around" in his mind the idea of such unpredictable behavior. The tramp is completely out of place; his appearance and his manner suggest the origin of the city, a complex world unknown to the country boy. In the figure of the tramp Warren creates the archetype of the outsider, a character who threatens the security of a closed world; a vagabond or maverick, he is the type of the failure of the American dream of success. The tramp's nondescript eyes and "perfectly unmemorable face" are like a confusing mask to the boy, making him all the more inquisitive of the reality underneath. The

boy's "steady and self-reliant" mother, in whom he can feel confidence, offers the tramp the work of burying the dead chicks and cleaning up the trash in the flower beds. This description of the littered setting, suggesting the destruction and death of the animate world, foreshadows the vivid descriptions in succeeding scenes of the trash that runs in the creek and of the trash under Dellie's cabin. The boy begins to see the capacity of nature to ravage what it creates (chickens) and what man creates (flower beds). Seth will grow to realize that man does not control his environment and that he cannot be certain either of his expectations or of the satisfaction of his desires.

Seth does not perceive the full devastation of nature until he arrives at the strange sight of the bridge over the swollen creek, which is described as "boiling," "frothing," "hissing," "steaming" and "tumbling"—words that suggest natural cataclysm and foreshadow the Biblical tone of Old Jebb's later description of the next great and annihilating flood. On the bank the boy's tall, proud father sits on his horse, above the heads of the other men, who are mostly poor white tenant farmers and in Seth's mind of a lower social class. In this episode Seth begins to learn about poverty, a condition largely unknown to him. The dead cow that floats past reminds the onlookers of their probable hunger in the future. The cow, which suggests the idea of maternity, foreshadows Dellie's condition of menopause, Old Jebb's remark that mother earth might stop producing and his own mother's death some years later. Each of these images gives unity to the story and affirms the idea of death to man and nature, a death out of which there will seem to be no renewal.

When the young spectator at the bridge asks whether anyone has ever eaten a drowned cow, the response is stunned silence; but the question becomes ironic in the light of Old Jebb's statement later that if the earth stops producing man will eat up everything. Jebb's wisdom is anticipated in an old Civil War veteran's response to the boy: "you live long enough and you'll find a man will eat anything when the time comes." This man speaks, it might be said, rather like a character out of Southwestern humor; his words demonstrate knowledge of the comic and the tragic. He is, like Old Jebb, the sage and seer, to whom time and experience have brought wisdom.

The third episode of the story, at the Negro cabin, falls into two parts—in the first, Seth talks with the family cook Dellie and, in the second, with her common-law husband Old Jebb. Both of them have always been proud of their clean, orderly house and yard; but, much to Seth's surprise, the yard has also become littered by the storm. Contrary to what he had come to expect, the yard is full of the trash and filth that had always remained hidden under the house. Seth learns that appearances or order, cleanliness and health can be deceptive, that dirt, ugliness and decay lie beneath the surface of things. This new awareness is reaffirmed when he sees Dellie, normally healthy and active, lying sick under her quilt, which, like the house hiding the litter, covers the reality of the decay underneath. Dellie is suffering menopause, what Old Jebb later calls "the change of life and Time." This change signals the end of her ability to reproduce and thus the approach of a kind of death. When Seth says he is sorry to hear that she is ill, he realizes that the word is an empty one. Language fails to express the emotions of loss or sorrow, and, like the men watching the creek, Seth stands a mute and powerless witness to this example of natural change and human suffering.

The culmination of the boy's journey is reached in his dialogue with Jebb, who unlike the tramp has a wise, sad, kind face and represents the security of love and fatherly wisdom. A prophet figure, Jebb speaks like Noah, who foretells a flood but who has not heard God's word of a possible salvation for man; he is also like the preacher of Ecclesiastes, but his message is that the sun will never rise again, that the earth will not abide forever. Old Jebb will not tell Seth why Dellie is ill, and his response, "Time come and you find out everything," reveals the Negro's understanding that all things change and that time is needed for man to be aware of the nature of change and of his part in it. Time, Jebb knows, is maturity.

Seth argues with Jebb that because it is June the cold spell will pass. Jebb contradicts the boy's belief that what has been will always be when he says that the cold may have come to stay:

> Cause this-here old yearth is tahrd. Hit is tahrd and ain't gonna perduce. Lawd let hit come rain one time forty days and forty nights, 'cause he was tahrd of sinful folks. Maybe this-here old yearth say to the Lawd, Lawd, I done plum tahrd, Lawd, lemme rest.

Like Dellie, mother earth will lose her fecundity and man will be faced with extinction. The irony of Old Jebb's speech is that man feels no awe for the earth's seemingly infinite bounty or no concern to preserve it; the Lord rested on the seventh day and so does man, but the earth can never rest. As Seth

leaves, the cold penetrating his spirit as well as his bare feet, Jebb tells him to hurry home before "you ketch yore death." Young Seth will also have to endure the process of change and decay; like all men, he has caught his death. Back at his home, in the concluding episode that brings the action full circle, Seth follows the tramp up the drive toward the pike and into the memory of the future.

In the epilogue, the adult Seth provides a perspective on his youthful experiences and reveals that he is not unlike the Ancient Mariner in his need to articulate the meaning of what happened to him on that day. The story provides for him and for the reader an epiphany that gains value in the narrator's dual vantage point of youth, which feels, and age, which interprets. The fullest insight belongs to the reader, however, for it is he who perceives the entire significance of Seth's experience. The epiphany we participate in is a discovery of the self in relation to one's environment and to other individuals, not unlike Robinson Crusoe's discovery of the footprint, a mark that signalled a change in his life. (Seth thinks early in the story about this moment of self-awareness in Defoe's work.) The image of a footprint is particularly meaningful in the light of its importance as a symbol of man's relation to nature, which is both his sustainer and his destroyer. Seth's bare feet grip the earth but they are unprotected from the cold and dirt; they let him know nature as she is. As the foot is an important symbol in the story, so is the hand, which can grasp hold of reality. Each of the adult characters has strong hands, which presumably can control and shape destiny—or at least that seems so to young Seth. But the painful truth is that these people cannot alter their lives, that they will become victims of their mortality. Their condition is almost like that of the character in *All The King's Men* who has what Jack Burden calls the Great Twitch, which determines that man is a victim of uncontrollable forces. The characters in "Blackberry Winter" have the freedom to choose and to act but no certainty that their choices and acts won't be overwhelmed by nature.

"Blackberry Winter," like *The Ancient Mariner* and *All the King's Men,* creates in literary form, as Warren writes in "Knowledge and the Image of Man," "a vision of experience . . . fulfilled and redeemed in knowledge, the ugly with the beautiful, the slayer with the slain, what was known as shape now known as time, what was known in time now known as shape, a new knowledge." This definition of the ordering of experience into a literary image comments on the theme of his own fiction, particularly ''Blackberry Winter.'' Man has a right, states Warren, to define himself and to achieve his own identity, or an image of himself. He says that this notion of personality is part of the heritage of Christianity, in which every soul is valuable to God and in which the story of every soul is the story of its choice of salvation or damnation. In the quest for knowledge, Warren declares, man discovers his separateness and the pain of self-criticism and of isolation; but he also learns that his condition is shared by all men alike:

> In the pain of isolation he may achieve the courage and clarity of mind to envisage the tragic pathos of life, and once he realizes that the tragic experience is universal and a corollary of man's place in nature, he may return to a communion with man and nature.

Man's knowledge makes him aware that he is a fallen creature, Warren is saying, but that he has gained more than he has lost:

> Man can return to his lost unity, and if that return is fitful and precarious, if the foliage and flower of the innocent garden are now somewhat browned by a late season, all is the more precious for the fact, for what is now achieved has been achieved by a growth of moral awareness.

These two passages provide a perfect gloss of Warren's story and novel written a decade earlier.

The essay on *The Ancient Mariner* and *All the King's Men* share with ''Blackberry Winter'' similar themes of sin, isolation, change and growth, similar characters who lose their innocence because of others who embody evil and guilt or because of forces over which they have no apparent control and similar techniques of rich texture, narrative point-of-view and the treatment of time. Reading ''A Poem of Pure Imagination,'' *All the King's Men* and ''Blackberry Winter'' together enhances the reader's appreciation of each of the works.

Source: James E. Rocks, ''Warren's 'Blackberry Winter': A Reading,'' in *The University of Mississippi Studies in English*, Vol. 1, 1980, pp. 97–105.

Robert Penn Warren

In the following essay, Warren informs the reader that he wanted the story to tell about the effect of time in bringing harsh change and loss to human relationships but also to show that one can still recognize human qualities in the struggle.

I once wrote a story called ''Blackberry Winter.'' It has the form of a recollection, many years after the events narrated, by a fictional first person. On a June morning, a young boy on a farm in Tennessee is being prevented by his mother from going barefoot because a gullywasher the night before makes the morning unseasonably cold. As they argue, they see a tramp, a citified tramp, coming up the lane, and wonder how he ever got back there in the river woods. The mother gives the tramp some work. The boy goes off to explore the damage and excitement of the storm, and then to play with the son of Dellie, the cook, who is sick in one of the tenant cabins. In a moment of annoyance Dellie, ordinarily a loving mother, savagely cuffs her son. The boy, disturbed, goes to hunt Old Jebb (Dellie's common-law husband) who says this isn't merely blackberry winter—that the earth maybe is tired the way Dellie is, and won't produce any more. The boy goes back to the house and sees his father firing the tramp. The tramp is about to resent the firing, but the father overawes him, and the tramp goes off, the boy following until the tramp turns and snarls at him. Then there is a little summary of what had happened to the boy's family and Dellie's family in later years. Then:

> That is what has happened since the morning when the tramp leaned his face down at me and showed his teeth and said: ''Stop following me. You don't stop following me and I cut yore throat, you little son-of-a-bitch.'' That was what he said, for me not to follow him. But I did follow him, all the years.

I remember with peculiar distinctness the writing of the story, especially the tension between a sense of being trapped in a compulsive process, and the flashes of self-consciousness and self-criticism. I suppose that most attempts at writing have some such tension, but here the distinction between the two poles of the process was peculiarly marked, between the ease and the difficulty, the elation and, I am tempted to say, the pain.

The vividness with which I remember this may come from the time and situation in which the story was written. It was the winter of 1945–46, just after the war, and even if one had had no hand in the blood-letting, there was the sense that one's personal world would never be the same. I was then reading Melville's poetry, and remember being profoundly impressed by ''The Conflict of Convictions,'' a poem about the American Civil War. Whatever the rights and wrongs, the war, Melville said, would show the ''slimed foundations'' of the world. There was the sense in 1945 that we had seen the slimed foundations, and now as I write this, the image that comes to mind is the homely one from my story—the trash washed out from under Dellie's cabin to foul her pridefully clean yard. So Melville, it seems, belongs in the package.

For less remote background, I had just finished two long pieces of work, a novel called *All the King's Men* and a study of Coleridge's *The Ancient Mariner*. Both of these things were impersonal, that is, about as impersonal as the work of a man's hand may be. At the same time I was living in a cramped apartment over a garage in a big, modern, blizzardbit Northern city. So the circumstances of my life and the work that had held me for so long were far from the rural world of my childhood. As for my state of mind, I suppose I was living in some anxiety about my forthcoming pieces of work, and in the unspoken, even denied conviction that, with my fortieth birthday lately passed, I was approaching some watershed of experience.

Out of this situation the story began, but by a kind of accident. Some years earlier I had written a story about a Tennessee sharecropper, a bad story that had never been published; now I thought I saw a way to improve it. So with that story I began to turn my feelings back into an earlier time. I can't say whether I began writing "Blackberry Winter" before I rewrote the other story. It doesn't really matter much. What mattered was that I was going back. I was fleeing, if you wish. Hunting old bearings and bench-marks, if you wish. Trying to make a fresh start, if you wish. Whatever people do in their doubleness of living in a present and a past.

I recollect the particular thread that led me back into the past: the feeling you have when, after vacation begins, you are allowed to go barefoot. Not that I ever particularly liked to go barefoot. But the privilege was important, an escape from the tyranny of winter, school, and, even, family. It was like what the anthropologists call rite of passage. But it had another significance; it carried you over into a dream of nature, the woods, not the house, was now your natural habitat, the stream not the street. Looking out into the snow-banked alley of that iron latitude, I had a vague nostalgic feeling and wondered if spring would ever come. It finally came—and then on May 5 there was again snow, and the heavy-headed blooms of lilac were beautiful with their hoods of snow and beards of ice.

With the recollection of going barefoot came another, which had been recurrent over the years: the childhood feeling of betrayal when early sum-

> "I should give a false impression if I imply that this story is autobiographical. It is not."

mer gets turned upside down and all its promises are revoked by the cold spell, the gully-washer. So by putting those two recollections together, I got the story started. I had no idea where it was going, if anywhere. Sitting at the typewriter was merely a way of indulging nostalgia. But something has to happen in a story, if there is to be more than a dreary lyric poem posing as a story to promote the cause of universal boredom and deliquescent prose. Something had to happen, and the simplest thing ever to have happen is to say: *"Enter, mysterious stranger."* And so he did.

The tramp who thus walked into the story to cut short the argument between mother and son had been waiting a long time in the wings of my imagination—an image based, no doubt, on a dozen unremembered episodes from childhood, the city bum turned country tramp, suspicious, resentful, contemptuous of hick dumbness, bringing his own brand of violence into a world where he half-expected to find another kind, enough unlike his own to make him look over his shoulder down the empty lane as dusk came on, a creature altogether lost and pitiful, a dim image of what, in one perspective, our human condition is. But then, at that moment, I was thinking merely of the impingement of his loose-footedness and lostness on a stable and love-defined world of childhood.

Before the tramp actually appeared, however, I had known he was coming, and without planning I began to write the fourth paragraph of the story, about the difference between what time is when we grow up and what it was when we stood on what, in my fancy phrase in the story, I called the glistening auroral beach of the world—a phrase which belonged to a boy who had never seen a beach but whose dreams were of the sea. Now the tramp came up, not merely out of the woods, but out of the darkening grown-up world of time.

The boy, seeing the tramp, tries to think of him coming up through the woods. He sees the image of the tramp blundering along, not like a boy who might stand in absolute quiet, almost taking root and growing moss on himself, trying to feel himself into that deep vegetative life. This passage, too, was written on impulse, but as soon as it began I knew its import; I was following my nose, trusting, for better or worse, my powers of association in relation to an emerging pattern of contrasts. It was natural, therefore, after a little about the tramp's out-of-waterness, to set over against him the brisk self-sufficiency of the mother at the time of the incident, and then over against that portrait a thought of the time later when she would be dead and only a memory—though back then in the changeless world of childhood, as the narrator says, it had never crossed the boy's mind that "she would ever be dead."

In the instant I wrote that clause I knew, not how the story would end, for I was still writing by guess and by God, but on what perspective of feeling it would end. I knew that it would end with a kind of detached summary of the work of time, some hint of the adult's grim orientation toward that fact. From now on, the items that came on the natural wash of recollection came not only with their, to me, nostalgic quality, but also with the freighting of the grimmer possibilities of change—the flood, which to the boy is only an exciting spectacle but which will mean hunger to some, the boy's unconscious contempt for poor white trash like Milt Alley (the squatter who lived up the hill), the recollection of hunger by the old man who had ridden with Nathan Bedford Forrest, Dellie suffering her "woman mizry." But before I had got to Dellie, I already had Old Jebb firmly in mind with some faint sense of the irony of having his name remind one—or at least, me—of the dashing Confederate cavalryman killed at Yellow Tavern.

Perhaps what I did with Dellie had, in fact, stemmed from the name I gave Old Jebb. Even if the boy would see no irony in that echo of J. E. B. Stuart's fame, he would get a shock when Dellie slapped her beloved son, and would sense that that blow was, in some deep way, a blow at him. I knew this, for I knew the inside of that prideful cabin, and the shock of early realization that beneath mutual kindliness and regard a dark, tragic, unresolved thing lurked. And with that scene with Dellie I felt I was forecasting the role of the tramp in the story. The story, to put it another way, was now shifting emphasis from the lyricism of nostalgia to a concern with the jags and injustices of human relationships. What had earlier come in unconsciously, reportorially, in regard to Milt Alley, now got a conscious formulation.

I have said the end was by now envisaged as a kind of summary of the work of time on the human relationships. But it could not be a mere summary: I wanted some feeling for the boy's family and Jebb's family to shine through the flat surface. Now it struck me that I might build the summary with Jebb as a kind of pilot for the feeling I wanted to get; that is, by accepting, in implication at least something of Jebb's feeling about his own life, we might become aware of our human communion. I wanted the story to give some notion that out of change and loss a human recognition may be redeemed, more precious for being no longer innocent. So I wrote the summary.

When I had finished the next to the last paragraph I still did not know what to do with my tramp. He had already snarled at the boy, and gone, but I sensed in the pattern of things that his meaning would have to coalesce now with the meaning I hoped to convey in the summary about the characters. Then, for better or worse, there it was. In his last anger and frustration, the tramp had said to the boy: "You don't stop following me, and I cut yore throat, you little son-of-a-bitch."

Had the boy stopped or not? Yes, of course, literally, in the muddy lane. But at another level—no. In so far as later he had grown up, had really learned something of the meaning of life, he had followed the tramp all his years, in the imaginative recognition, with all the responsibility which such a recognition entails, of this lost, mean, defeated, cowardly, worthless, bitter being as somehow a man.

So what had started out as an escape into the simplicities of childhood from the complications of the present, had turned, as it always must if we accept the logic of our lives, into an attempt, however bumbling, to bring something meaningfully out of that simple past into the complication of the present. And now, much later, I see that this story, and the novel then lately finished, and my reading of Coleridge's poem all bore on the same end.

I should give a false impression if I imply that this story is autobiographical. It is not. I never knew these particular people. And no tramp ever leaned down at me and said for me to stop following him or he would cut my throat. But if one had, I hope that I would have been able to follow him anyway, in the way the boy in the story does.

Source: Robert Penn Warren, ''Writer at Work: How a Story Was Born, and How, Bit by Bit, It Grew,'' in *New York Times Book Review*, Vol. CVIII, No. 36,926, March 1, 1959, pp. 4–5, 36.

Weathers, Winston. ''*Blackberry Winter* and the Use of its Archetypes,'' in *Studies in Short Fiction*, Vol. 1, pp. 45–51.

Sources

Blotner, Joseph. *Robert Penn Warren: A Biography*, New York: Random House, 1997.

Bohner, Charles. *Robert Penn Warren*, Twayne United States Author Series, Boston: G. K. Hall, 1981.

Hicks, Granville. Review of *Circus in the Attic*, in the *New York Times*, January 25, 1948, p.5.

Lynn, David H. [In Memoriam], in *Kenyon Review*, N.s., Vol. 11, No. 4, Fall, 1989.

Review of *Circus in the Attic*, in *Time*, January 26, 1948.

Review of *Circus in the Attic*, in *U.S. Quarterly Booklist*, June, 1948.

Smith, H. N. Review, in *Saturday Review of Literature*, January 1, 1948.

Watkins, Floyd C. and John T. Heirs, eds. *Robert Penn Warren Talking: Interviews 1950–1978*, New York: Random House, 1980.

Further Reading

Conkin, Paul. *The Southern Agrarians*, Knoxville: University of Tennessee Press, 1988.

> With the benefit of historical perspective and newer critical methods, Conkin offers a fresh perspective on the literary and scholarly contributions of the group of writers who called themselves The Agrarians. Contains a careful explanation of Warren's sometimes strained relationship with the group.

Runyon, Paul Randolph. *The Taciturn Text: The Fiction of Robert Penn Warren*, Columbus: Ohio State University Press, 1990.

> In this comprehensive study of Warren's fiction, Runyon organizes his analysis historically. Chapter Four is a careful reading of the volume of stories of which ''Blackberry Winter'' is a part, and contains useful discussion of common themes and stylistic features.

Flowering Judas

Katherine Anne Porter

1930

Katherine Anne Porter allegedly wrote "Flowering Judas" in a single evening in December of 1929. After writing the story, she then rushed out after midnight that same night to mail it to the literary magazine *Hound and Horn*. Regardless of this anecdote's accuracy, it is indisputable that "Flowering Judas" represented an artistic breakthrough for Porter. The next year—1930—she named her debut collection of short stories after this richly symbolic tale of an alienated young American woman set in Mexico City just after the Mexican Revolution. *Flowering Judas and Other Stories* garnered enthusiastic critical praise. Reviewers were consistently impressed with Porter's original narrative style, her complex and tightly controlled symbolism, and her beautifully intricate language. "Flowering Judas" remains a staple of anthologies and is considered one of the best works of a master of the short story form. Its complex symbolism has intrigued several generations of readers and scholars.

The character of Laura, the story's protagonist, is set against that of Braggioni, a corrupt revolutionary leader who is courting her. The story takes place during an evening they spend together, as Braggioni's singing and conversation mirrors Laura's growing disenchantment with the revolutionary ideal that brought her to Mexico. Laura, a former Catholic, rejects the hypocrisy of the socialist revolutionaries who have come to power and she rejects the advances of Braggioni and several other ardent suitors, which leads to a crisis of faith and a sense of acute

isolation. The theme of lost faith is amplified through the story's Christian imagery, central to which is the complex figure of the flowering Judas, named for Christ's betrayer.

Author Biography

Porter was born Callie Russell Porter on May 15, 1890, in a two-room log cabin in the Texas frontier community of Indian Creek. Porter's mother died when she was two and her father brought his five children to live with his mother, Catherine Anne. Later, Porter took her grandmother's name. When the grandmother died in 1901 the family suffered from emotional and financial instability. Porter and her sister helped support the family by giving singing and acting lessons, and she aspired to be an actress.

After the family resettled in San Antonio, Porter attended a private Methodist school for two years, which comprised her only formal education. The Porters were Methodists, though Porter later claimed that she had been raised Catholic. She converted to Catholicism upon her marriage, at age sixteen, to a Catholic man.

Porter was a free spirit who defied convention. At age 25 she left her husband and set out to pursue an acting career. She worked at a movie studio in Chicago and as a traveling singer-dancer in Louisiana. Her life's course took an important turn in 1918 when she became seriously ill with influenza and nearly died. She reevaluated her goals and emerged with a new aspiration to be a writer. She found work as a reporter in Denver and then moved to New York City where she met a group of young Mexican artists and revolutionaries. In 1920 she went to Mexico City to witness the aftermath of the Mexican Revolution and to gather material for her fiction. The first short story she published in 1922, "Maria Conception," was set in Mexico and inspired by events she observed during this visit.

In 1930 Porter published *Flowering Judas and Other Stories*, the work that established her critical reputation. The following year she won a Guggenheim Fellowship, which allowed her to return to Mexico and then to travel extensively in Europe. She continued to write, working on short stories, a biography, and a novel, but published only sporadically, often distracted by love affairs, politics, and illness. She returned to the United States and continued to live a nomadic life, traveling from one teaching position to another. Her next several books of short stories, *Pale Horse, Pale Rider* and *The Leaning Tower* solidified her reputation as a masterful stylist. With her 1962 novel, *Ship of Fools*, she became a best-selling author. In 1966 she received a Pulitzer Prize and a National Book Award for her *Collected Stories*.

Porter was a beautiful, charismatic woman with a tendency toward self-dramatization. Though she lived an exceptionally independent life for a woman of her generation, she was at times paralyzed by a chaotic personal life. She had numerous lovers and married four times, twice to men far younger than she. Despite her success as a writer, she remained insecure about her lack of education and poor Texas upbringing. Some facts of her biography remain uncertain because Porter was evasive about many aspects of her life and misleading about others. She died in 1980 at age ninety.

Plot Summary

A young American woman, Laura has come to Mexico City in the aftermath of the Mexican Revolution in order to work for the revolutionary cause, in support of a socialist regime. She is a schoolteacher and also acts as a go-between for the local revolutionary leader, Braggioni, and his adherents. Braggioni has a personal interest in the lovely but cold young woman and he pays her nightly visits, hoping to seduce her. As the story opens, Braggioni is in Laura's room, singing to her. It is the end of the day and Laura is tired, but she receives Braggioni's attention politely, not wishing to offend the powerful man.

There is little action in the story. The events are mostly internal, as Braggioni's terrible singing and bantering conversation triggers Laura's thoughts and emotions. Laura knows that Braggioni would like to seduce her and that she "must resist tenaciously without appearing to resist." She finds him grossly sensual and corrupt, but Braggioni is a local hero, embodying all of the hypocrisy that threatens the ideals of the socialist revolution. Laura longs to flee from him and from the disillusioning cynicism of the revolutionaries, but she sees no other option than to continue her commitment.

As they sit together, Braggioni flaunts his elegant clothing, telling Laura that she is more like him

Katherine Anne Porter

than she realizes and warning her that she will be as disappointed in life as he is. Laura wonders about her devotion to the cause, thinking about her duties teaching English to Indian children, attending union meetings, and delivering messages and supplies to political prisoners. Despite her disgust with Braggioni's blatant hypocrisy, Laura has her own lapses as good socialist. The revolutionaries are politically opposed to the Catholic Church, but Laura sometimes goes to church and prays, though she is no longer faithful. She also has a secret love of luxury, favoring handmade lace, which also runs counter to socialist ideology.

Braggioni continues to sing to Laura and flirt with her. Laura has had several suitors in Mexico in addition to Braggioni. She has skillfully rebuffed the pass of a former soldier in the army of another revolutionary faction. She draws a parallel between this "rude folk-hero" and the children she teaches, who express a surprising and unrequited affection for her.

The other suitor is a young union activist who serenades her according to the Mexican tradition. Laura's maid advised her to toss him a flower from the Judas tree outside her window in order to stop his singing. She does this, not realizing that this is actually a signal of encouragement. The young man

continues to follow and watch her. She ignores him, but does not regret her mistake. She maintains an attitude of stoicism and negativity in all of her interactions.

Braggioni goes on to tell her about the confrontation planned for the next day in the nearby town of Morelia, where a Catholic festival for the Blessed Virgin will coincide with a celebration of labor activism by the Socialists. He predicts violence and asks her to clean and oil his weapons, which she does obediently. She returns his guns to him and, with uncharacteristic boldness, tells him to "go kill someone in Morelia, and you will be happier." She then reveals that a prisoner, one of Braggioni's adherents, whom she had visited earlier that night, had committed suicide by taking sleeping pills she had brought to him the day before. Braggioni pretends indifference, but he leaves abruptly and reconciles with his wife.

After Braggioni leaves, Laura undresses and goes to bed, plagued by oppressive feelings of guilt and alienation. When she finally falls asleep she has a disturbing dream. The prisoner who committed suicide is beckoning her from the house. She says she will follow him only if she can hold his hand, but when he refuses her, calling her a murderer, she follows him anyway. He offers her flowers from the Judas tree to eat, and when she consumes them greedily he again calls her a murderer and cannibal. She awakens to the sound of her own voice crying "No!" and is afraid to fall asleep again.

Characters

Braggioni

Braggioni is the most powerful revolutionary leader in town, as well as Laura's suitor. She also works for him carrying messages to members of the movement who are in prison or in hiding. He comes to her house every night to sit and talk with her and to sing songs he has composed as part of a campaign to seduce her. Braggioni is vain and self-obsessed; Laura is repulsed by him, but she accepts his attention because his is a powerful man. Fat and disgusting, he represents the corruption and cynicism of the revolutionary movement. Some critics note that he embodies all of the Seven Deadly Sins. He personifies the hypocrisy of the movement—he is a "good revolutionist" because "he has the malice, the cleverness, the wickedness, the sharpness of wit, the hardness of heart, stipulated for loving the world profitably."

Mrs. Braggioni

Braggioni's wife is, in her husband's view, an "instinctively virtuous woman." She remains faithful to him and to his cause while he indulges his appetites and philandering impulses. During the month preceding the evening when the story takes place, Braggioni has been living separately from his wife and courting Laura. His wife has spent much of this time weeping. After he visits Laura, Braggioni returns home to his wife who greets him by weeping and begging his forgiveness. She washes his feet in an act of obeisance that echoes Mary's washing of Jesus's feet, in an ironic reflection of Braggioni's role as savior of his people. In contrast to Laura, Braggioni's wife has completely given herself over to love and martyrs herself before the powerful man.

Eugenio

Eugenio is one of Braggioni's followers, an activist in the revolution who has been imprisoned for political reasons. On the night that the story takes place Laura has just returned from visiting him in prison, where she finds him near death from an overdose of sleeping pills. When Laura tells Braggioni about the suicide Braggioni calls him a fool, but his mood changes and he leaves her. That night, Eugenio comes to Laura in a symbolic dream that serves as the ambiguous resolution of the plot. Eugenio beckons her toward death and offers her flowers from the Judas tree to eat, saying, "This is my body and my blood," a reference to the Eucharist, thus identifying him as a Christ figure. He then calls her a murderer and a cannibal, to which Laura responds, "No!"

Laura

Laura is the protagonist of the story. She is a young American woman living in Mexico and working for the socialist revolution. She is a schoolteacher and also performs tasks, such as running messages, for Braggioni as part of her revolutionary commitment. She is very idealistic but yet cold; thus she is disgusted by Braggioni's sensuality and corruption. "She cannot help feeling that she has been betrayed irreparably by the disunion between her way of living and her feeling of what life should be." However, she continues to be loyal to the revolution despite her misgivings. She is a lapsed Catholic but she occasionally enters a church and says a Hail Mary, even though this is against the

Media Adaptations

- "Flowering Judas" is included on an audiotape read by Sioban McKenna, *The Collected Stories of Katherine Anne Porter*, recorded in 1990 by Publishing Group West.

beliefs of the revolutionary movement. She feels both betrayed by and guilty of betraying her Mexican comrades.

Laura is graceful, womanly, and virginal. She conducts herself with reserve and dresses in nun-like clothes. When she finds herself the unwilling recipient of the romantic interest of several young revolutionaries she rebuffs them, while she skillfully keeps Braggioni at arm's length while appearing to indulge him. Braggioni comments that he does not understand her commitment to the revolutionary ideal since she does not love a man who is involved. Laura is an isolated and sexually repressed figure, refusing to admit to a need for love. However, the figure of Eugenio—who is both ominous and seductive—suggests that she longs for merging and communion even as she denies it.

Lupe

Lupe is Laura's maid. She advises Laura to throw her suitor a flower from the Judas tree outside her window so that he will stop serenading her and tells her not to trust him or any man. But she does not tell her that the flower is encouragement for him to return night after night. Lupe's familiarity with the culture and its social conventions underscore Laura's alienation.

The Serenading Youth

A young man who is an organizer of the Typographer's Union. He courts Laura by singing serenades outside of her window, following the elaborate romantic rituals of his culture. She unintentionally encourages him by tossing him a flower, so he pursues her further. She is "pleasantly disturbed'' when she notices him watching her, a phrase signaling her sexual repression and ambivalence.

The Young Captain

A young captain—a hero of the Mexican Revolution—makes a pass at Laura, attempting to embrace her as she dismounts her horse at the end of a ride. She avoids his embrace by covertly spurring her horse. Described as ''gentle'' and a ''rude folk hero,'' he represents a model of the kind of man through whom she might express her love of revolution sensually. Instead, she rejects him.

Themes

Faith and Betrayal

In ''Flowering Judas'' there is no faith that is not betrayed. The story is structured through a series of contrasts and parallels between religious faith, faith in revolutionary ideals, and romantic-sexual fidelity, all of which are misguided or transgressed. For example, Laura is a Roman Catholic and has been raised in the Catholic tradition. Yet the revolution rejects religion, in particular the Catholic Church. Unable to divorce herself from either her religious beliefs or her political ideals, she ends up feeling as if she has violated both.

Braggioni is a hero who fought for the redistribution of wealth to the masses, only to indulge his every whim for luxury and power when he became part of the new ruling elite. He furthermore expresses his supposed love of humanity through womanizing, betraying his wife's fanatical devotion. Even Eugenio, a martyr of the revolution whom Laura betrays by enabling his suicide, kills himself out of boredom rather than for any principle.

Ideals and Reality

The contrast between ideals and reality is closely tied to the contrast of faith and betrayal in ''Flowering Judas.'' Laura has high ideals, but the reality of her situation is very disappointing to her. Her loss of faith is presented as an inevitable part of life. Extremely disillusioned, she feels she has no other choice than to continue with her mission.

The reprehensible Braggioni becomes for Laura ''a symbol of her many disillusions.'' Despite his corruption, he is a successful leader, representing the pragmatism and self-interest that permeate the political system. Though Laura is herself no longer

idealistic about the cause she works for, neither can she adopt the blithe attitude of her cohorts that corruption and betrayal are merely part of reality. Instead, Laura continues her denial, refusing to regret her choices but also declining to truly participate in life. She can no longer say yes to her ideals, but she continues to say no to reality, leaving her radically alienated from those around her.

Alienation

Laura is a young American woman living in a foreign country and participating in a political struggle that has nothing to do with her own interests or history. The revolutionary ideal that she works for is invested in the unity and cultural pride of Mexican workers and peasants, a population with whom she has little in common. She confronts belief systems and behaviors that are objectionable to her and hard for her to understand. She speaks the language poorly and misreads cultural cues, as when she throws the flower to her suitor. These factors, in addition to her own philosophical crisis in faith, characterize Laura as an alienated individual. She does not belong anywhere or believe in anything. Her condition is more extreme than mere loneliness. Everyone appears as a stranger to her and she is ''not at home in the world,'' so she has little chance of overcoming her acute isolation.

Love

One way of understanding Laura's alienation is to attribute it to her inability to love. She is disciplined in her commitment to the cause but she lacks the love for the Mexican people that underlies the revolutionary ideals she professes. She is cold in response to the peasant children's affection and to her various suitors' fervent advances. Related to this shortcoming are Laura's sexual repression and her loss of faith in Catholicism.

She lacks the capacity not only for socialist love of humanity, but divine Christian love and erotic love as well. Braggioni doubts her commitment to the revolution given that she does not love any man who is a fighter in it, which he sees as the only way a woman can participate in revolution. Braggioni, in contrast, is a ''professional lover of humanity.'' He 'loves' the Mexican people, especially women, indiscriminately and selfishly. Braggioni is cruel, but not cold in the sense that Laura is. He abuses the faith of his followers and of his wife, but sees their faith in him as good in itself. In this way, he encourages participation in what he sees as the reality of love and its inevitable counter-

Topics for Further Study

- At one point in the story Braggioni tells Laura, "We are more alike than you realize in some things." Are these two contrasting characters at all alike? Find some descriptions of Braggioni and Laura from the text to support your ideas about the characters.

- Porter concludes "Flowering Judas" with a strange and complicated dream. How does the dream connect to themes, images, and issues raised earlier in the story? To what extent does it offer a resolution?

- Research the role that Judas Iscariot plays in the New Testament. How does his background and

relationship to Jesus reflect on the themes of faith and betrayal in the story?

- Research the role of Catholicism in Mexican culture and the role of the Catholic Church in the Mexican Revolution. How does this historical context enrich your reading of the story?

- Braggioni finds Laura's political commitment confusing in light of the fact that she is not attached to any man in the revolution. Research the role of women in the Mexican Revolution. How is Laura typical or exceptional in her political activities?

---

part, betrayal, while Laura ignores her appetites and suffers from the despair of self-denial, isolation, and faithlessness.

Style

Symbolism

Symbolism is the most important stylistic feature of "Flowering Judas." The most important thing to understand about Porter's use of symbolism is that it is multi-faceted and ambiguous. Indeed, symbols that Porter employs often refer to one idea and also its opposite. The story's central symbol, the flower from the Judas tree, is a example. The flower first appears when Laura tosses it out the window, which misleads her suitor. She uses the flower, an encouraging sign, in order to say "No" to her suitor—the "holy talismanic word" from which Laura draws her strength. The exotic flower is a sensuous image, and the fact that she uses it to reject the man suggests Laura's sexual ambivalence and repression. When the flower appears later in Laura's nightmare it is again a sensual image—she eats it greedily—but this time it doubles as a symbol of

the Eucharist, wherein the body and blood she consumes belong not to Christ but to Eugenio. The flower is thus simultaneously a sign of purification and corruption.

The flower's name refers to Judas Iscariot, Christ's betrayer. The tree is named for Judas because, according to mythology, it is the tree from which he hanged himself out of repentance for his deed. The flower is a symbol of the betrayal of Christ, reflecting Laura's alienation from the Catholicism of her girlhood and also from the revolutionary cause. She is, in this way, like Judas.

Yet she also sees those around her—most exaggeratedly, Braggioni—as betrayers and hypocrites themselves, which is one source of her loss of faith. Braggioni and Eugenio represent contrasting Christ figures, with Braggioni serving as a grotesque perversion of Christ's self-sacrifice and "love of humanity" while Eugenio represents Christ's martyrdom. Braggioni's self-aggrandizement and Eugenio's self-negation are connected through this figure.

The central matrix of Christian symbolism is only one example of how Porter's use of symbolism gives the story meaning. On a simpler level, Braggioni's opulent, garish clothes represent his hypocrisy and sensuality. They serve as a contrast to Laura's severe high-necked dress, but the hand-made lace collar that is her secret luxury suggests an underlying similarity to Braggioni's self-indulgence. Thus, again, things that seem like opposites are revealed as similar. The "monstrous" confusion between opposites that Laura refers to as she drifts off into her nightmare characterizes Porter's use of symbolism throughout. Laura longs for clear distinctions and purity, but the very language which Porter uses to tell her story reveals this as impossible.

Setting

Porter sets "Flowering Judas" in Mexico City in the aftermath of the Mexican Revolution. The dramatic foreign setting and the loaded historical moment are evoked in an oblique way, described only in relation to the ideas and feelings they trigger in Laura as she sits in the upper room of her house listening to Braggioni's singing and conversation. Eudora Welty's description of Porter's style suggests that one may understand "Flowering Judas" as actually being set inside of Laura's distressed mind. "Most good stories are about the interior of our lives, but Katherine Anne Porter's take place there," Welty writes in *The Eye of the Story*. "They show surface only at her choosing. Her use of the physical world is enough to meet her needs and no more."

For example, Porter offers exquisitely detailed physical descriptions of the exterior world only as they reflect Laura's inner conflicts, such as the "battered doll-shape of some male saint whose white, lace-trimmed drawers hang around his ankles below the dignity of his velvet robe" that she observes as she furtively visits a Mexican church. But the larger social and physical environs are, for the most part, characterized in abstract or subjective terms. For example, Porter's description of Laura's duty as a messenger for Braggioni highlights Laura's state of isolation: "She knocks at unfamiliar doors not knowing whether a friend or a stranger shall answer, and even if a known face emerges from the sour gloom of that unknown interior, still it is the face of a stranger."

Point of View

"Flowering Judas" is narrated in the third person by an omniscient narrator. That is, the narrator is not an actor in the story, but has access to the thoughts, motivations, and feelings of characters. While a third-person narrator's omniscience signifies a position of knowledge, often making this a straightforward mode of storytelling, the fact that the narrator in "Flowering Judas" is so tied to Laura's conflicted perspective makes the narration obscure and disorienting. Indeed, as Welty suggests, the narration is so tied to Laura's inner experiences that the story creates the effect of taking place within her consciousness. And the fact that she feels so alienated from what is going on around her creates a further barrier between Laura's thoughts and the reality of the outside world.

Historical Context

The Mexican Revolution

Porter based the story on events she experienced and observed in Mexico during 1920 and 1921, in the aftermath of the Mexican Revolution. In 1910 the revolution started as a struggle against political and economic repression; in Mexico at that time, a dictator controlled the government under a one-party system and an elite class of landowners controlled the country's resources. After the dictator was overthrown, a series of factions formed and struggled for power over the next decade. A socialist agenda of land reform (the redistribution of land to the common people), workers' rights, and the separation of the educational system from the control of the Catholic Church were among the main objectives of the revolutionary position as laid out in the Constitution of 1917.

However, the revolutionaries who assumed political power failed to live up to these ideals. There was an ongoing struggle for leadership between agrarian revolutionaries who strongly supported the interests of the workers, led by Pancho Villa and Emiliano Zapata, and bourgeois revolutionaries who subordinated these interests to those of developing a capitalist economy. The latter faction eventually prevailed. It included Alvaro Obregon, a former general in the Mexican Revolution who became president in 1920 and served until 1924. The Obregon presidency was marked by compromise and has been referred to as "the rule of the millionaire socialists." Though he gave lip service to socialist ideals in order to appeal to the radicalized population of Mexican peasants, Obregon's accomplish-

Compare
&
Contrast

- **1920s:** In 1920 Mexico's *Partido Nacional Revolucionario* (PNR), the National Revolutionary Party, is founded out of a coalition of military, labor, and peasant leaders. The party takes a conservative approach to the reforms demanded by socialist revolutionaries, seeking economic and political stability above social justice. According to the government that is established, the president of Mexico can only serve one term but chooses his successor, creating a one-party democracy.

  1990s: The PNR, renamed PRI (*Partido Revolucionario Institucional*, the Revolutionary Institutional Party) has ruled Mexico for seventy years, holding the presidency and both legislative houses. In 1997 the PRI lost the lower legislative house for the first time in what has been called the ''freest election in Mexican history.'' The PRI still holds the upper house and the presidency.

- **1920s:** The capitalist PNR slowly and ineffectively implements the socialist policy of land reform—the redistribution of land from large private estates to the peasant farmers. Between 1920 and 1930 over four thousand villages receive more than eight million hectares of land, but less than a quarter of that is arable, and peasants are not given the supplies, machinery, and credit necessary for success. Grain production falls precipitously and land reform is deemed a failure.

  1990s: The economy of Mexico is dominated increasingly by the private sector. There are fewer than 200 state-owned enterprises. Income distribution is unequal, with 20% of the population owning 55% of the wealth.

- **1920s:** Mexico remains an overwhelmingly Catholic country, but the institution of the Catholic Church, which had been closely affiliated with the former dictatorship, wanes in power. Conservative Catholic clerics organize service strikes, boycotts, and guerrilla attacks in protest of the PNR's secular cultural policies.

  1990s: 97% of Mexicans are Catholic. The institution of the Catholic Church remains politically conservative, but, since the Second Vatican Council in 1962, a branch of Catholicism inspired by a school of thought called Liberation Theology has become associated with grassroots activism and social change.

- **1920s:** The federal government seizes control of Mexico's schools from the Catholic Church. The new secular schools have a mission to educate Mexico's native Indian peoples, whose assimilation is considered important for the creation of a stable capitalist Mexico. A well-funded program to bring literacy to remote pueblos and to distribute free copies of cheaply-printed literary classics is launched.

  1990s: Mexico has a literacy rate of 87%. The school system is public, funded by the federal government. Fifteen percent of school-age children don't attend school. In rural areas education is particularly poor, with secondary schools virtually nonexistent.

---

ments were centrist, pragmatic, and, in the eyes of many, marred by corruption.

The story takes place in the early days of the Obregon presidency when the revolution was over but Mexico was still undergoing a complex political and cultural upheaval. The country was devastated and divided from the years of war. The human costs of the revolution were enormous. War casualties were so great that the Mexican population had declined by a million people since 1910. The revolution had also shaken Mexico's rigid class system to its base. In the aftermath of the war, many generals of peasant origins who had gained status during the revolution vied for positions in a governmental structure that maintained many features of the earlier dictatorship. Thus the heroes of the socialist revolution assumed roles of the power elite. In the words of Benjamin Keen and Mark Wasserman's *A History of Latin America*," Obregon summed up the problem when he said that the days of revolutionary banditry had ended because he had brought all the bandits with him to the capital to keep them out of trouble." The ethos of Mexican leaders, who were worn down from years of war and political instability, became marked by a certain amount of irony or cynicism about the revolutionary cause. The character of Braggioni is a hyperbolic representation of this attitude.

Porter spent much time in Mexico during her life. Her first visit to Mexico was in 1920. At first, she went to Mexico for education and adventure and was drawn into revolutionary circles by her artistic friends. By her second visit in 1922 she was completely disillusioned by the country and its government. Porter claimed that the story was inspired by an acquaintance of hers, a young American Catholic woman named Mary Doherty who was a zealous supporter of the revolution, but scholars have shown that some of the events portrayed are also inspired by her own experiences.

Modernism

"Flowering Judas" reflects not only the political context of 1920 Mexico, but also the aesthetic and cultural ethos among Porter's artistic peers—most notably, the literary movement of modernism. Modernist writers focused on the aesthetic qualities of language and pushed images to their limits, often resulting in an inconclusive meaning. This style reflected—and often mourned—a loss of faith in those sources of meaning that had organized art and civilization previously, including belief systems such as religion and scientific rationality. Modernist experiments with plot and imagery also reflected the confusing and disorienting aspects of modern life, in which traditional communities and ways of life were uprooted. Porter's statement that Laura "is not at home in the world" reflects this modernist sentiment.

The flower from the Judas tree that Laura throws to her suitor and recurs in her dream of Eugenio provides the story with its title and ties it to Porter's aesthetic influences. The Judas tree is named for Judas Iscariot, Christ's betrayer in the New Testament. According to myth, Judas hung himself from this tree in repentance for his betrayal of Christ. Many scholars have pointed out that the figure of the flowering Judas is an allusion to a poem by T. S. Eliot, one of the great masters of modernism. In his poem "Gerontion" the following lines appear. "In the juvenescence of the year / Came Christ the tiger // In depraved May, dogwood and chestnut, flowering judas, / To be eaten, to be divided, to be drunk / Among hispers." Eliot's poem relates to the story's themes of betrayal and loss of faith. Its images of eating and drinking also correspond to the dream at the end of "Flowering Judas".

Critical Overview

When Porter hurried out after midnight to mail the just-finished manuscript of "Flowering Judas" to the editors of the magazine *Hound and Horn* in 1929, Porter was an obscure writer, hoping that she was on the verge of a breakthrough. Because she had not yet established her reputation when Harcourt Brace accepted a collection including "Flowering Judas" and five other stories for publication the following year, they agreed to print the book only as a limited edition. *Flowering Judas and Other Stories* did not sell widely for this reason, but the collection received uniformly favorable reviews and, on its strength, Porter was awarded a Guggenheim Fellowship in 1931.

Reviewers gave elaborate praise to Porter's stories, in particular her controlled and original use of language. In *Bookmark*, E. R. Richardson maintained of the stories: "All are exquisitely done, with feeling for dramatic values, with clarity, with delicate delineation of characters, and in language transcendently beautiful." Allen Tate of the *Nation* commented that "her style is beyond doubt the most economical and at the same time the richest in American fiction," and that "every sentence, whether of description, narrative, or dialogue, create[s] not only an inevitable and beautiful local effect, but contribute[s] directly to the final tone and climax of the story."

Louise Bogan, writing for the *New Republic,*, singled out the title story of the collection for praise. "The firm and delicate writing in Miss Porter's "Flowering Judas," a story startling in its com-

Francisco "Pancho" Villa, wearing military uniform and seated in gilded chair next to Emiliano Zapata.

plexity, were it not based on recognizable fact, would be to no purpose. As it is, its excellence rises directly from the probity of the conception. It is as impossible to question the characters . . . as it is to find a flaw or lapse in the style that runs clear and subtle, from the story's casual beginning to the specter of life and death at the end.''

The *New York Times Book Review* also comments on the "scrupulous distinction of phrase" in the story, though it finds its dream conclusion confused. When an enlarged edition, with two additional stories, appeared four years later, Porter had arrived on the literary scene. She was at the height of her powers and had come to be widely considered one of the finest short story stylists of her time.

The startling complexity of "Flowering Judas" attracted much critical commentary. Much of the early scholarship unraveled the meanings of the story's symbolism. The figure of the flowering Judas was resonant with modernist themes of alienation and lost faith and thus appealed to modern critics. Furthermore, Porter's dense prose lent itself well to New Criticism, the dominant school of literary scholarship in the mid-twentieth century. New Criticism is a language-based approach to

literary criticism, where symbols are decoded through close reading. Ray B. West, in a chapter of his 1949 *The Art of Modern Fiction*, offered an extensive New Critical explication of the symbolism in "Flowering Judas," that served as a point of departure for many later critics. West focused on religious symbolism, arguing that Braggioni is capable of redemption, while Laura, who is unable to love, is not.

In the 1960s the first book-length critical studies of Porter appeared, notably those by Ray B. West, Brother William Nance, and George Hendrick. Though this kind of academic study signaled Porter's status as a historically significant literary figure, Porter objected to the interpretations offered by all three scholars. Scholarship focused on autobiographical elements of her work—which Porter particularly resented—and her use of symbolism. Later scholars reevaluated Porter's fiction according to more accurate biographical information as it became available and, in keeping with the academic trends, with more attention to her feminism, her politics, and the historical context of her work. She remains of interest to scholars of modernism and of Southern regional writing and is considered one of the finest American short story writers of the twentieth century.

Criticism

Sarah Madsen Hardy

Madsen Hardy has a doctorate in English literature and is a freelance writer and editor. In the following essay, she discusses Laura's alienation through an exploration of the concepts of home and 'homelessness' in "Flowering Judas."

Laura, the troubled young protagonist of "Flowering Judas," is disillusioned with Mexican politics, but her unhappiness goes much further than this. She walks through life feeling anxious and detached, always afraid, though she knows not of what. "She is not at home in the world," Porter writes, summing up Laura's state of mind. This overarching sense of 'homelessness' may be seen as the crux of Laura's problem. *Home* refers to a physical and geographical place and it also refers to a set of feelings—security, belonging, connectedness, even love. Laura has none of these. The entire story takes place inside Laura's house—her nominal Mexican home—where Braggioni's overbearing presence makes Laura feel pressured and ill at ease. It is easy to see why she does not feel at home there. It is also understandable why, as a foreigner, a *gringita*, Laura does not feel at home in Mexico, and why, as a supporter of socialist revolution, she does not feel at home in her native capitalist America. However, not only does Laura not feel at home in any particular place, but she also does not feel at home "in the world" at large. Such alienation—that is, such separation and disharmony between the self and the outside world—is a feeling that many writers of Porter's generation sought to express in their fiction.

Laura is 22 years old when the story takes place, sometime during Alvaro Obregon's 1920–24 term as president of Mexico. Born approximately at the turn of the century, Laura may therefore be seen as a representative of what is known as the "lost generation." The "lost generation" refers broadly to Americans who were born around 1900. Not unlike "generation X," the "lost generation" found it difficult to put faith in the ideals and beliefs that had given meaning and structure to the lives of their parents. They rejected given values, but remained "lost" because they did not find new ones to replace the old. More narrowly, the "lost generation" refers to a circle of writers who defined the spirit of the age in their fiction, many of whom chose to express their alienation from their native culture by living abroad in self-imposed exile. In *Exile's Return*, his canonical portrait of "lost gen-

eration" writers, essayist Malcolm Cowley describes the process that defined the generation as primarily geographical. He writes that the generation was lost "first of all, because it was uprooted, schooled away and almost wrenched away from its attachment to any region or tradition." According to Cowley, the "lost generation" saw themselves as "homeless citizens of the world." Indeed, being lost suggests being out of place, not belonging anywhere or with anyone.

Central to Laura's feeling of homelessness is her status as an expatriate. Laura has given up residence in and allegiance to her American homeland. She has renounced the Catholic faith of her childhood and is uprooted from her past. Porter writes, "Uninvited she has promised herself to this place; she can no longer imagine herself living in another country, and there is no pleasure in remembering her life before she came here." Laura seems to fit Cowley's description of a "homeless citizen of the world" perfectly, but in other ways she is an atypical figure of the "lost generation." First of all, all of the writers whom Cowley discusses are men, as are the main figures of alienation they create. Secondly, World War I and its aftermath are considered formative for the generation, with an essentially male experience of war figuring prominently as a source of alienation. In "Flowering Judas" Porter offers a different vision of modernist alienation by setting her story in Mexico and by making her protagonist female. Laura lacks a sense of belonging in the country of Mexico and in the revolutionary belief system, both of which seem compromised to her. Her alienation in each realm relates to her status as a woman. While Laura's feeling of being "not at home in the world" transcends any specific place, her discomfort in the Mexico setting—and, particularly, in the house where she lives—reflects the gender-specific nature of her alienation.

It is significant that the action of the story unfolds within Laura's home, rather than in any of the public places mentioned in the story—the school, the prison, or the May Day confrontation. Laura's sense of being entrapped in her own house with Braggioni's coercive presence permeates the story. For Laura, home is a site of struggle and anxiety rather than security. She works all day, teaching children whose love she does not understand and delivering messages to people she perceives as strangers, all out of commitment to a political struggle in which she no longer believes. At the end of the day she avoids coming home because she knows that Braggioni will be waiting for her and

What Do I Read Next?

- *Pale Horse, Pale Rider* (1939) is a set of three short novels based on Porter's autobiographical protagonist Miranda. The acclaimed title story is set in Denver in the midst of an influenza epidemic near the end of World War I, taking up themes of illness, war, and death.

- *When the Air Is Clearer* (1958), a novel by Mexican writer Carlos Fuentes, depicts the cynicism of post-revolution Mexico and explores the betrayal of revolutionary ideals by former revolutionary fighters.

- *Death Comes for the Archbishop* (1927), by Willa Cather, an author Porter greatly admired, tells the story of the confrontation between faiths and cultures set at a mission in the southwest territories of the United States.

- *A Farewell to Arms* (1929), by Ernest Hemingway, takes up themes of romance, idealism, and disillusionment in a love story between an American soldier and an English nurse set on the Italian front during World War I.

- *The Waste Land* (1922), a famous poem by T. S. Eliot, in many ways defined the ethos of the modernist movement. Eliot shares with Porter an interest in elaborate imagery and themes of spiritual desolation and the alienated individual.

- *A Curtain of Green and Other Stories* (1941), by Eudora Welty, offers animated portraits of characters in the modern South in a series of acclaimed short stories.

---

that her duty as a devotee to the revolution will continue in its most onerous form. "Laura wishes to lie down, she is tired of her hairpins and the feeling of her long tight sleeves, but she says to him, 'Have you a new song for me this evening?'" The male revolutionaries in the story act out their commitment through public acts of violence and martyrdom, while their private conduct reveals them as hypocrites. Laura understands that, as a woman, her role in the revolution lies largely within the private realm. She must flatter the powerful man without encouraging his improper advances. Though she sees this role as equally ignoble as the masculine forms of heroism in which she has lost faith, she complies, "like a good child who understands the rules of behavior." She is not at ease in this role but, because she sees no alternative, she conforms to it passively. "Sometimes she wishes to run away, but she stays." Her external actions are at odds with her inner feelings, leaving her perpetually at odds with the world through which she moves.

Braggioni draws parallels between his revolutionary love of mankind and his voracious sexual love for women. In his view, a woman's role in the struggle is as a lover of its male participants. His wife is an almost comically extreme figure of revolutionary/sexual devotion, begging Braggioni's forgiveness and washing his feet when he finally returns home to her. When Porter writes that Mrs. Braggioni's "sense of reality is beyond criticism," it is a way of saying that, despite her misery, she is not alienated, not detached from her place in her world. She is, in this sense, the perfect counterpart to Braggioni—the self-effacing mirror image of his self-love and the passive feminine version of his anti-heroism. Braggioni cannot understand why Laura "works so hard for the revolutionary idea unless she loves some man who is in it" because he sees women as incapable of revolutionary action or the abstract idealism from which it derives. But Laura wishes to adhere to ideals rather than to a man. The men around her are part of the flawed reality she rejects, even as she rejects the parts of herself that are drawn to them.

Like Braggioni, the serenading youth comes to Laura's home uninvited and sings to her. He is more benign than Braggioni, but the youth also encroaches on Laura's privacy and contributes to her feeling of

> **"** But Laura wishes to adhere to ideals rather than to a man. The men around her are part of the flawed reality she rejects, even as she rejects the parts of herself that are drawn to them."

uneasiness in her home. While Braggioni's advances are untoward, she interprets the youth's actions as the observation of a convention "with all propriety, as though it were founded on law of nature, which in the end it might well prove to be." This signifies that Laura's discomfort with his serenade goes beyond her ignorance of Mexican courting rituals and even her ambivalent sexuality. He reminds her of her disconnection from what she sees as the "laws of nature" governing love and romance between men and women. She knows that she does not fulfill the role of a proper revolutionary woman but she is, in fact, still deeply attached to the idea of propriety. However, she simply cannot believe in his ritualized courtship any more than she can believe in Braggioni's leadership. She feels no connection to him because his feelings are expressed through conventions that seem empty to her. Again, she can envision no alternative kind of connection, so she resorts to rejection and suffers continued isolation. Just as she cannot imagine experiencing security or belonging in the compromised revolutionary movement, she cannot imagine experiencing security or belonging within the compromised conventions of romantic love.

The last man to come to Laura's house is the ghostly figure of Eugenio, who visits her in a nightmare. In life, Eugenio symbolizes Laura's failure in the feminine role of comforter of revolutionaries—her soothing sleeping pills enable him to commit suicide. In her nightmare, he is an ambivalent figure, both seductive and accusatory, who pushes her beyond proper, passive actions. He represents a fluidity of roles, pitying her as a "poor prisoner" and offering her flowers to eat, then calling her a murderer and cannibal a moment later. Though he himself was a political prisoner, he

recognizes her as imprisoned in her house and in the reality from which he, as a suicide, has fled. He is the first man in the story to invite her out of the house, which he acknowledges as "strange." "What are you doing in this house?" he asks, and promises to show her a "new country." Because Eugenio is dead, he is not of this world, not part of the world in which Laura cannot feel at home. He suggests the possibility of escape from the walls of her home and from the compromised forms of connection associated with its worldly reality, even though the escape is still a lonely one—for he refuses to take her hand. But the hand she seeks and the flower she eats are the only examples in the story of Laura's desire for the comfort and sustenance associated with home. Laura is not so lost in her dreamlike vision of death as she is in the world to which she again awakens.

Source: Sarah Madsen Hardy, "This Strange House: Home and Alienation in 'Flowering Judas,'" for *Short Stories for Students*, The Gale Group, 2000.

David Madden

In the following essay, Madden studies Porter's use of "charged images" and their thematic content to portray the state of mind of the heroine of the story.

In *Writers at Work, Second Series*, The interviewer asked Katherine Anne Porter whether "Flowering Judas" began as a visual impression that grew into a narrative. "All my senses were very keen," Miss Porter replied. "Things came to me through my eyes, through all my pores. Everything hit me at once . . ." Without words or images, her stories began to form. Then she starts thinking "directly in words. Abstractly. Then the words transform themselves into images." On several occasions Miss Porter has testified to the potency of the real-life image that generated "Flowering Judas."

She chose this story for inclusion in an anthology called *This Is My Best* (1942). Commenting on the story at that time, she said: "All the characters and episodes are based on real persons and events, but naturally, as my memory worked upon them and time passed, all assumed different shapes and colors, formed gradually around a central idea, that of self-delusion. . . ." In the *Paris Review* interview some twenty years later, she elaborated:

> That story had been on my mind for years, growing out of this one little thing that happened in Mexico. . . . Something I saw as I passed a window one evening. A girl I knew had asked me to come and sit

with her, because a man was coming to see her, and she was a little afraid of him. And as I went through the courtyard, past the flowering Judas tree, I glanced in the window and there she was sitting with an open book on her lap, and there was this great big fat man sitting beside her. Now Mary and I were friends, both American girls living in this revolutionary situation. She was teaching at an Indian school, and I was teaching dancing at a girls' technical school in Mexico City. And we were having a very strange time of it (1965). . . . I had a brief glimpse of her sitting with an open book in her lap, but not reading, with a fixed look of pained melancholy and confusion in her face. The fat man I call Braggioni was playing the guitar and singing to her [1942]. . . . And when I looked through that window that evening, I saw something in Mary's face, something in her pose, something in the whole situation, that set up a commotion in my mind [1965]. . . . In that glimpse, no more than a flash, I thought I understood, or perceived, for the first time, the desperate complications of her mind and feelings, and I knew a story; perhaps not her true story, not even the real story of the whole situation, but all the same a story that seemed symbolic truth to me. If I had not seen her face at that very moment, I should never have written just this story because I should not have known it to write [1942]. . . . Because until that moment I hadn't really understood that she was not able to take care of herself, because she was not able to face her own nature and was afraid of everything. I don't know why I saw it. I don't believe in intuition. When you get sudden flashes of perception, it is just the brain working faster than usual. But you've been getting ready to know it for a long time, and when it comes, you feel you've known it always [1965].

As raw material for literature, this real-life image was already, implicitly, dynamically charged with feeling and meaning. The author's physical distance from her friend that evening was an analog to the objectivity that was necessary when she transformed the real-life image into the fictive image. And out of this actual image was to grow also the structural, stylistic, and technical conceptions of "Flowering Judas," a created, transcendent image with an organic life of its own. This story is one of the most lucid exemplifications I know of what Croce calls "the aesthetic image," compounded of "a tissue of images," and of what I call *the charged image*. Ezra Pound's definition of great literature as "language charged with meaning to the utmost possible degree" (to "meaning" I would add the word "feeling") suggests the source of power in "Flowering Judas." Before I feel out the anatomy of this charged image, I want to quote Miss Porter again.

Soon after *Flowering Judas*, her first book of stories, was published in 1930, Miss Porter wrote to a friend:

"In preparation for the public violence that is imminent, Laura, who so intensely fears violence to herself, oils and loads Braggioni's pistols; no more grotesque half-parody of Freudian symbolism can be imagined."

I can't tell you what gives true intensity, but I know it when I find it, even in my own work. . . . It is not a matter of how you feel at any one moment, certainly not at the moment of writing. A calculated coldness is the best mood for that most often. Feeling is more than a mood; it is a whole way of being; it is the nature you're born with, you cannot invent it. The question is how to convey a sense of whatever is there, as feeling, within you, to the reader; and that is a problem of technical expertness.

Mr. Hagopian's response to Miss Porter's statement reflects my own conviction: "Thus, from the beginning, Miss Porter knew what she was doing—embodying the *true intensity* of experience into literary form with *technical expertness*." Mark Schorer, writing about technique in general, describes what Miss Porter does most brilliantly in "Flowering Judas": "When we speak of technique, then, we speak of nearly everything. For technique is the means by which the writer's experience, which is his subject matter, compels him to attend to it; technique is the only means he has of discovering, exploring, developing his subject, of conveying its meaning, and, finally, of evaluating it." Technique "objectifies the materials of art." The forms of the finest works of fiction, Schorer argues, are "exactly equivalent with their subjects," and "the evaluation of their subjects exists in their styles." He cites Miss Porter's work as exemplary. "The cultivated sensuosity" of Miss Porter's style has not only "charm in itself" but "esthetic value . . . its values lie in the subtle means by which sensuous details become symbols, and in the way the symbols provide a network which is the story, and which at the same time provides the writer and us with a refined moral insight by means of which to test it. Some readers may cite Miss Porter's phrase "a calculated coldness" to explain the coldness her technique and her sensibility instill in some of her stories. But that phrase and her comments in *Writers at Work* suggest her attitude about technique as a means of discovery; although she testifies that she knew the ending of "Flowering Judas" before she began to write (as she *usually* knows the ending before she begins to write a story), the powerful final stroke came unconsciously (but was made possible, most probably, by her habitual consciousness of technique). "I knew that the vengeful spirit was going to come in a dream to tow her away into death, but I didn't know until I'd written it that she was going to wake up saying, 'No!' and be afraid to sleep again." Although, as friends and critics have observed, one must regard Miss Porter's comments on her own work with almost the same caution with which one regards Faulkner's self-scrutiny, it is no contradiction of our image of Miss Porter as a conscious craftsman that she claims to write her stories in single spurts of energy. "I always write a story in one sitting. I started 'Flowering Judas' at seven p.m. and at one-thirty I was standing on a snowy windy corner putting it in the mailbox" (*Writers at Work*). Miss Porter glimpsed a girl and a man through a window in Mexico City and two years later, in a few hours in Brooklyn, recaptured and transformed that image into a work of art.

In her introduction to *The Selected Short Stories of Eudora Welty* (1954), Miss Porter describes the kind of story she prefers: one in which "external act and the internal voiceless life of the human imagination almost meet and mingle on the mysterious threshold between dream and waking, one reality refusing to admit or confirm the other, yet both conspiring toward the same end." Magalaner and Volpe declare that "Flowering Judas" is "from the first word of the title to the last word of the text" a model of that kind of story. They go on to say that it "is a sensitive and discerning philosophical statement of human relationships, made universal by the mythic elements which intrude as early as the hint in the title." But more than that, it is a remarkable aesthetic achievement to which we may return again and again, just as we return to Keats's "Ode on a Grecian Urn"; for long after we have absorbed its universal philosophical and psychological truths, "Flowering Judas" remains a "thing of beauty," a "joy forever," embodying Keats's declaration that "Beauty is truth, truth beauty."

In some ways "Flowering Judas" resembles literary form less than it resembles dance, mother of all the arts, especially of poetry and of the most contemporary of the arts—cinema (I use these analogies simply for their suggestiveness). The dynamic imagery of dance, the compression and the expressive juxtapositions of poetry, and the montage effects of Eisenstein's cinema are transmuted by Miss Porter, unconsciously, I imagine, into fictive techniques that produce what interests and moves me most in this story—the charged image. The omniscient author's psychological analysis of and philosophical reflections about Laura's predicament and the self-delusory processes that follow from her predicament are everywhere in the story, suffusing the very style that creates the tissue of images. But overwhelming her own overt interpretations when they threaten to intimidate the life of the story, the images embody Miss Porter's meaning with expressive vitality; ultimately, of course, this vitality cannot be separated from the vitality of Miss Porter's meditations about Laura. The story exfoliates from a tight intermingling of showing and telling. And that story, were it not for the author's technique of dramatically juxtaposing tableaux, is so rich and multi-faceted as to require the scope of a novel.

As the elements of Laura's exterior and interior worlds intermingle, they cohere in a developing pattern of images which expands from the charged image that inspired Miss Porter in life and that she sets forth in the beginning of her fiction:

> Braggioni sits heaped upon the edge of a straight-backed chair much too small for him, and sings to Laura in a furry, mournful voice. Laura has begun to find reasons for avoiding her own house until the latest possible moment, for Braggioni is there almost every night. No matter how late she is, he will be sitting there with a surly, waiting expression, pulling at his kinky yellow hair, thumbing the strings of his guitar, snarling a tune under his breath. Lupe the Indian maid meets Laura at the door, and says with a flicker of a glance towards the upper room, "He waits."

This central, most potent image is the hub, and all other images spoke out from it, and the author's meditating voice is the rim, and (to complete the metaphor) the reader's active participation is the energy that makes the wheel turn. Paralyzed, Laura is locked into this image, as though in a small box stage set, and we see her at a distance, as though through the original real-life window. With each image that Miss Porter shows us, we feel that Laura is withdrawing more and more deeply into herself, that her will is becoming more and more paralyzed.

The controlling image (Laura and Braggioni sitting opposite each other by the table) is a simplified visual and thematic expression of the entire story; this image recurs at strategic points in the pattern, creating that sense of simultaneity that makes a work of art cohere and seem inevitable. Laura's posture varies only slightly; and though Braggioni is singing and playing his guitar, the tableau virtually does not move—it vibrates from within, sending its electrical charge in a radial fashion out into the other images connected to it.

In 1961 at Centre College in Kentucky, I discussed ''Flowering Judas'' with my two classes of freshman students. Mystification over my charged image concept only compounded their boredom with the story itself. To enable them to see Miss Porter's story, and my point, more clearly, I arranged a demonstration with the Drama Department. Using multi-level space staging and lighting as a means of isolating one acting area, one scene, from another, we mounted a series of tableaux in pantomime, while a young woman read the story over a public address system. The images enacted were these (following the sequence in the story):

> Laura and Braggioni sit opposite each other by the table. In the first image that is juxtaposed, montage-fashion, to this hub image, we see Laura sitting in church. Cut to Braggioni at the table in Laura's house again, singing, playing the guitar. Fade to Laura in the classroom with Indian children. Fade to a composite image: Laura at a union meeting; Laura visiting prisoners in cells; Laura meeting men in dark doorways with messages; Laura meeting with Polish and Roumanian agitators in cafes. Fade to another composite image: Laura riding horseback with the Captain; Laura and the Captain at a table in a restaurant; Laura in the classroom responding to a floral design and message of affection to her drawn on the blackboard; Laura at her window responding to the youth who serenades her. Fade to another composite: Laura and the children again; Laura at the doors of fugitives again. Cut to Laura and Braggioni at the table again; he talks of love; her response is negative. Superimposed image of Braggioni in the streets. Fade to a composite: Braggioni's wife weeping on the floor in her room; Eugenio's body lying on the floor of his cell. Cut to Laura with Braggioni again; she cleans his pistols; Braggioni puts his gun belt on. Fade to Laura in the street on errands again, meeting strange faces. Fade to a composite: Braggioni and his wife; she washes his feet; they eat; they lie in bed together. Cut to composite image: Laura in white in bed; Laura at dark doors; Laura with children in classroom; Laura with prisoners. Fade to Laura with Eugenio in a nightmare, as he leads her away, offering her the blossoms of the Judas tree to eat. Cut to Laura awake, crying No! She is afraid to sleep again.

To this day, students tell me that this dramatic enactment of the story's charged image structure was one of the most electrifying theatrical experiences they have ever had. Re-reading the story itself, they were able to come closer to the kind of experiences the story offers readers who are more aesthetically responsive.

Miss Porter's technique of creating a dynamic interplay among images that are strategically spaced in an unfolding pattern is appropriate for the rendering of Laura's state of mind—self-delusion producing paralysis of will. Not only does she move very little in the recurrent scene set in the present, but her recent, habitual past life as well is presented in terms of static images. The reader feels the tension between these static images and Laura's impulse within the images to flee. From a positive standpoint, the static quality of the pictures is expressive of Laura's desire for stasis. The energy of the story is transmitted in the kinetic juxtaposition of one charged image to another. A few similes may make my simple point even clearer: reading the story is like watching a single photograph, simple in outline but rich in detail, yield more and more auxiliary images each time it is redeveloped and enlarged (I am thinking of the experience the photographer has in the movie *Blow-Up*); or the images are superimposed, causing a cumulative density of texture; or reading the story is like watching a cubist painting being painted, from the first stroke, the title, to the last word, No.

The contrast between the static quality of the images and the immediacy of the historical present tense generates a tension that enhances the effect of Miss Porter's basic image technique. She declares that not until someone asked her why she used it did she realize she had employed the historical present tense. In any case, it is clear that the present tense keeps the images themselves alive while they portend the incipient moribundity of Laura, the character who is at the center of each (even when, in the scene in Braggioni's hotel room, she isn't physically present). Miss Porter's technique resembles the early montage techniques of the European movies of the late Twenties and anticipates cinematic methods used by Resnais in *Hiroshima, Mon Amour* and *Last Year at Marienbad*. She shows us one scene, stops the camera, goes on to another scene, goes back to an earlier scene, holds, then goes further back to an even earlier scene, then leaps far ahead. But the image technique is also similar to one used long before the birth of the cinema—Spenser's tableau juxtapositions in *The Faerie Queen*.

Laura has just come from the prison and "is waiting for tomorrow with a bitter anxiety. . . . but time may be caught immovably in this hour, with herself transfixed, Braggioni singing on forever, and Eugenio's body not yet discovered by the guard." The result of Miss Porter's charged image technique is that the reader is left with this timeless image of Laura sitting opposite Braggioni at the table, transfixed in fear and accidie, all the other images clustered around her like spokes in a hub. Laura's one act in the present tense of the story comes toward the end: "The presence of death in the room makes her bold," so she "holds up the [gun] belt to him: 'Put that on, and go kill somebody in Morelia, and you will be happier!'" This is a futile gesture. In numerous little ways, Laura herself, we have seen, has already killed various kinds of generous human impulses toward love, including Braggioni's. So at this point, the recurrent static picture at the hub of all the other images moves, but to no purpose: Braggioni leaves, Laura goes to sleep.

Along with her use of present tense, Miss Porter's frequent use of questions—"Where could she go?"—is another technique for enlivening her overt thematicizing and the progression of static images. And the routineness of Laura's life is another element that makes Miss Porter's technique of repeating the same images in a pattern effective.

Laura has dehumanized herself by encasing herself "in a set of principles derived from early training, leaving no detail of gesture or of personal taste untouched." Miss Porter's attitude toward people like Laura is suggested in her comment on a certain kind of writer: "By accepting any system and shaping his mind and work to that mold, the artist dehumanizes himself, unfits himself for the practice of any art" (quoted in Magalaner). Braggioni tells Laura that they are more alike than she realizes; she sees the possibility of her being as "corrupt, in another way, as Braggioni . . . as callous, as incomplete," but rather than do something about these faults, she prefers "any kind of death." Figuratively, Laura and Braggioni reveal two perspectives on a single person; each exhibits aspects of the other. They also contrast with each other. But finally, Laura's personality embodies many aspects of Braggioni's, carrying them to a negative extreme. It is appropriate, then, that Miss Porter employs a modified omniscient point of view, favoring Laura, but shifting, strategically, to Braggioni near the end.

Braggioni, "a professional lover of humanity," who began as a "hungry world-savior," but who will never die of this love (one of many suggestions that he is a false Christ), tells Laura his true feelings about the common men who follow him: any of them might easily turn Judas (as, in spirit, Laura already has). In many instances, Laura is a Magdalene to one man, a false Magdalene or a Judas to others. Loyalty to one group necessitates Laura's betrayal of trust in other groups; thus "she borrows money from the Roumanian agitator to give to his bitter enemy the Polish agitator"; through her, Braggioni *uses* these people.

"Flowering Judas" delineates a maze of ambiguity of roles, beginning with Laura and Braggioni, going on down to the minor characters. Everyone seems to be both a savior and a Judas to everyone else. Braggioni is both a false and, in a purely human way of course, a real Christ to various people; but he is also a Judas. So is Laura both secular savior and betrayer of the same people. The author conceives of these complex savior-Judas relationships paradoxically and ironically and enhances them with a controlled atmosphere of ambiguity; this nexus of savior-Jesus analogies extends from the inner psychological realm of Laura and Braggioni out into the public realm and up to a symbolic level. Many kinds of service and betrayal are depicted and implied in the story; but Laura, by denying sex, love, meaningful purpose, and action, inclines too far toward betrayal, as the climactic nightmare scene stresses.

Miss Porter shifts scene and point of view deliberately for a dramatic contrast to Laura. Returning to his wife, who is still weeping, Braggioni is glad to be back in a familiar place where the smells are good and his wife does not reproach him, but offers to wash his feet (she is a genuine Magdalene to his Christ-role). We see that Braggioni is in many ways a more creative person than Laura. Out of remorse, he weeps, saying, "Ah, yes, I am hungry, I am tired, let us eat something together." His supper with his wife contrasts with Laura's devouring of the Judas flowers. His wife asks his forgiveness for failing to be sufficient to all his needs, and her tears refresh him—she weeps *for* him as well as because of him. At least with one other person, Braggioni experiences a rich sexual and affectionate relationship. He is lonely, soft, guilt-ridden, we see now, though we've sensed this all along; but because of his external public role and because of her rigid demeanor, Braggioni and Laura were unable to meet. Rilke says that "Love consists in this, that two solitudes protect, and touch and greet each other." If nothing more, Braggioni and his wife experience this touching of solitudes.

Now Miss Porter shifts point of view back to Laura as she "takes off her serge dress and puts on a white linen nightgown and goes to bed." Her virginal uniform of white mocks her sterility. She thinks of her children as prisoners who bring their jailor flowers. Numbers tick in her brain, turning her mind into a clock, a machine. Within her own solitude of mind and flesh, Laura cries out in anguish that "it is monstrous to confuse love with revolution, night with day, life with death," and invokes Eugenio's spirit "—ah, Eugenio!"

The midnight bell seems to be a signal she can't understand. Miss Porter handles the intermingling of interior and exterior worlds so adroitly that the dream passage comes with a controlled abruptness, and the change in tone does not jar, but seems inevitable. Without warning the reader, Miss Porter has Eugenio speak to Laura—without quotation marks, for his voice is pure expression, like an object. Echoing Christ's command to his followers, he tells Laura to get up and follow him. He asks her why she is in this strange house (in Mexico, in the world, in her own mind; one thinks of Lucifer's "The mind is its own place, and in itself/Can make a Heav'n of Hell, a Hell of Heav'n."). Here Miss Porter, though she is describing a dream that is happening now, shifts into the past tense to enhance our feeling that Laura's life, insofar as its capacity for responding to possibilities, is over, whether literally she dies soon after the story ends or not.

Eugenio calls Laura a murderer (she is *his* Judas, but the charge covers all her crimes of the body, the mind, and the spirit, for they affect *other* bodies, minds, and spirits, including his own.) But even to his offer to take her to a new country, death, Laura says, "No," fearing anything more than the fear to which she has grown accustomed and from which she is unable to imagine a separate identity for herself.

Miss Porter gives the reader a sense of the fluid, surrealistic changes of the nightmare landscape as Laura clings to the "stair rail, and then to the topmost branch of the Judas tree that bent down slowly and set her upon the earth, and then to the rocky ledge of a cliff, and then to the jagged wave of a sea that was not water but a desert of crumbling stone." All this suggests again Eliot's mental-physical Waste Land, and "The Love Song of J. Alfred Prufrock," and, as one critic has pointed out, "Gerontion," as well.

The ambiguous title of the story interprets all its images. The Judas tree gets its name from the belief that from such a tree Judas hanged himself. Abundant purple flowers appear in the spring before the leaves. A certain elder is called a Judas tree because it bears "Jew's ear," an edible, cup-shaped flower, resembling an ear, which is cherished as a medicine. So the tree itself and Miss Porter's title ultimately have both positive and negative connotations, and the story depicts in its charged images the gestures of both betrayers and betrayed; the reader feels his way through an ambiguity that deliberately makes it difficult to distinguish with any final clarity one from the other. Thus, Eugenio, who has qualities of Christ, as one betrayed offers *Judas* flowers to Laura, the betrayer; and thus, in eating of the body of Christ cannibalistically she is also eating of the body of Judas, for Eugenio, too, is a kind of Judas, betraying Laura. But the "flowering Judas" is Laura.

Eugenio offers her the flowers of the Judas tree, and as she devours them, he calls her "Murderer!" and "Cannibal!" "This is my body and my blood. Laura cried No! and at the sound of her own voice, she awoke trembling, and was afraid to sleep again." She wakes, but not to enlightenment (although one may argue that it is perhaps enlightenment that makes her afraid to sleep again), for the dominating idea in her life, as in the nightmare, is denial, and with this No, Miss Porter appropriately ends the story. By now the No (in contrast to the Yes with which Molly Bloom ends *Ulysses*) is both a strong auditory image and an object. Just as Eugenio's eyes, unlike Christ's, do not bring light, the dream does not result in self-revelation for Laura, and her self-delusion persists at the end, along with the paralysis of her will (reminiscent of Gabriel Conroy's predicament at the end of "The Dead," a story that concludes with a similar elegiac vision). When we discover Laura sitting at the table in the initial, persistent charged image, she has already lost in her conflict between ideal aspiration and actuality. What self-knowledge she has she fails to employ in an act of self-discovery.

While "Flowering Judas" is not concerned with religion in itself, suggestive religious terms and motifs recur throughout the story. The images are almost like black parodies of religious icons or such tapestries as the Bayeux, or scenes in church panel paintings, frescoes, and mosaics (scenes of worship, charity, love, and betrayal). Miss Porter's frequent use of paradox in style and characterization suggests her purpose in employing religious motifs—as analogies to patterns of human behavior and relationships on secular levels.

While politics is closer than religion to Miss Porter's concern with her characters as people alive or dying in the secular world, politics, too, functions almost expressionistically. Braggioni tells Laura about the May-day disturbances soon to occur. On the same day on which Catholics hold a festival in honor of the Virgin (a parallel to Laura, whose virginity is neither spiritual nor quite natural), the Socialists will celebrate their martyrs, and the two processions, coming from opposite ends of town, will clash. Thus, rather neatly, Miss Porter summarizes in a composite dialogue image the two conflicting public contexts (religious and political) of Laura's private despair. There is almost no sustained dialogue in the story until this scene; the fragments of dialogue are verbal parallels to the series of charged visual images. On Laura, Braggioni's voice has the same hypnotic effect it has on crowds; and as he expresses his vision of a world completely destroyed so that a better world of "benevolent anarchy" can be built upon the ruins, Laura feels he has forgotten her as a person. He will create a physical Waste Land (an objective correlative to the spiritual Waste Land of which Laura is a major exemplification). All separate identity will vanish, and "no one shall be alive except the elect spirits destined to procreate a new world" (that excludes Laura).

Institutionalized religion and political ideals, perverted in revolution, are escapes from ordinary love. Laura refuses not only Braggioni but the Captain and the youth as lovers; more crucial to her general dilemma is her failure even in non-sexual ways, for she cannot even love the children she teaches, nor Eugenio, the man to whom she offers release from the world in which she herself must continue to suffer. Failure to distinguish illusion from reality in the conflict between ideal aspiration and brutal actuality produces Laura's self-delusion and the "No" with which she arms herself against the world. Thus, she waits in fear; a sense of overwhelming futility paralyzes her.

In preparation for the public violence that is imminent, Laura, who so intensely fears violence to herself, oils and loads Braggioni's pistols; no more grotesque half-parody of Freudian symbolism can be imagined. Laura peers down Braggioni's "pistol barrel and says nothing." The barrel's sexual connotation is reinforced by the literal lethalness of its purpose. Corresponding with this double-barreled significance Laura feels "a long, slow faintness"

rising and subsiding in her, while Braggioni "curves his swollen fingers around the throat of the guitar and softly smothers the music out of it." This juxtaposition is the most powerful of several in which Miss Porter makes the guitar an analogy to Laura's body.

A psychological examination of Laura will reveal the organic unity of the story more closely. One may look at Laura in light of six forces that, simultaneously, dominate her life: 1) Laura's predominant state of mind is denial: No. Her general negativity as she waits in fear is the frame for everything else we discover about her. 2) rejects sex; she evades love; she substitutes a grim charity; she radiates a deadly innocence. 3) She gives everything (though it is not enough) to revolutionary politics, while refusing social fellowship and religious transcendence. 4) She fails to distinguish between illusion and reality. 5) Denying everything, overwhelmed by a sense of futility, she waits in fear of violent death. 6) These dominant elements in the story suggest a missing element: self-realization. But the reader sees what Laura fails to see. If one examine the story from beginning to end keeping in mind the pattern of images delineated earlier, one may see how each of these aspects of Laura's psychological and physical predicament is embodied in charged images that recur and cluster. I have suggested the thematic content that Miss Porter's images embody. In his introduction to *The Nigger of the Narcissus*, Joseph Conrad said: "A work that aspires, however humbly, to the condition of art should carry its justification in every line." "Flowering Judas" realizes that aspiration to an uncommon degree.

Source: David Madden, "The Charged Image in Katherine Anne Porter's 'Flowering Judas,'" in *Studies in Short Fiction*, Vol. VII, No. 2, Spring, 1970, pp. 277–89.

Dorothy S. Redden

In the following essay, Redden argues that Porter does not present a unitary view of life through her character but a view of life in tension between the way one lives life and the way life should be.

Katherine Anne Porter's "Flowering Judas," an unusually cryptic, complex, and challenging story, has been variously interpreted. Of the two best-known and most complete readings, that of William L. Nance maintains that Miss Porter follows "the principle of rejection," while Ray B. West, Jr., argues that she "embodied an attitude that demonstrated the necessity for the application of the ancient verities of faith and love as a fructifying element in any human existence." Though contradictory, both conclusions are right; each underestimates the presence of the other—an equally forcible opposite "principle," or opposite "attitude"—in the story. The paradoxes of Miss Porter's fiction, it seems to me, are insufficiently illuminated by tacit reliance on the assumption that this author holds a strictly unitary view of life. If, however, one explores the hypothesis that Miss Porter's outlook is essentially and irrevocably dual, many things fall into place, including the basic role of tension in her work.

"Flowering Judas" is perhaps her most remarkable story of tension sustained, threatened, and reestablished. Its protagonist is enduring an inner war between two contradictory attitudes, neither of which she can wholly accept or reject. Although "the desperate complications of her mind and feelings" must have a long history, or she would not be as troubled as she is, the story gives very little of this background, and remarks of Laura's past only that it was one of "many disillusions" and unspecified "afflictions" which she prefers to forget. To her present situation, on the other hand, Miss Porter devotes all but the final paragraph of the story in a probing analysis of the statement that Laura "cannot help feeling that she has been betrayed irreparably by the disunion between her way of living and her feeling of what life should be."

I should like to examine these two poles separately, starting with Laura's strange and painful "way of living," itself a clash of the opposing forces, seen in terms of fear. For Laura is "afraid of everything." That she fears death, even that she finds it evil, may be considered unexceptionable, at least in our civilization. An important part of her, however, feels the same way about life, and especially about its vital component of human relationships. To this part of Laura, life is not only a stifling emotional tyranny of love and sex, but a kind of death, equally vicious and sinister, equally terrifying.

Although she goes on living, she fears and hates life. At the same time, although she is drifting toward it, she fears and hates death. Obviously, these two attitudes create an insoluble dilemma. Because Laura's warring forces are evenly matched, their unresolving antagonism generates an almost overpowering tension. She feels herself mired in a

> The whole affective power of this story results from its balance, as well as its quality, of feeling--from the high pitch of equally disposed forces."

perpetual waking nigthmare, and for twelve pages of exposition the reader is held, with her, violently immobilized, suspended in a wild, frozen trance.

She is, in fact, barely alive. Life is motion; like wheels, human beings remain erect so long as they move ahead. They are (in our culture) propelled from behind by a fear of death, and drawn forward by a desire for life. The negative and positive forces work together to keep the organism upright and moving. Laura, however, is almost static. She is held erect not by her barely discernible motion, but by the pressures of two contradictory forces. The negative fear of death propels her from behind, it is true; but there is almost no positive force working with it to draw her forward. On the contrary, she is blocked by another negative, the fear of life.

The result is a horrible transfixion in which she feels that she must, at all costs, avoid losing her balance. As long as the two forces exert more or less equal pressure, she remains upright between them, safe. This, of course, is another delusion, for safety, if there is such a thing, lies in movement, in living, and not in a rigid stasis, which is dangerously close to extinction. But, allowed her premises, Laura is right. She cannot give up her defenses because to her they are justified; she believes that she knows the "truth" about life, what "reality" really is. If she were to relinquish her fear of life, she would have no love or hope or faith to put in its place. There would be only a vacuum, and she would topple.

Therefore, she feels that she can do nothing but try to keep the opposing pressures equal. And there is no way to do this except by complete negation. If she repudiates in one direction, she must repudiate in the other; she must deny "everything." *No* is the "one holy talismanic word which does not suffer her to be led into evil."

Laura's stance, then, is one of an almost unbearable equilibrium maintained by total denial. All of her strength is harnessed to preserving that uncertain balance, with its demand for unremitting vigilance. Fortunately, she has astonishing self-control, at least temporarily equal to the strains put upon it; it is no less impressive for being negative, and she needs every jot of it. It is her only defense against "that disaster she fears, though she cannot name it."

In a general sense the revolutionist leader Braggioni is the symbol of all that Laura hates and fears, the "reality" that seems to dominate her existence. Specifically, his characteristics are those that she finds typically human (which is to say animal), and as such they amply justify her rejection of human relationships.

These traits, overwhelmingly repellent and menacing, center around Braggioni's vastly bloated ego. Chief among them is his sensuality, for bursting out of his binding orchid-colored clothes he resembles nothing so much as a huge tumescent phallus, the opposite of everything romantic, sentimental, and "harmless." His handling of his guitar suggests what he has in mind for Laura: he scratches it familiarly, curves his swollen fingers around its throat, rips a thumbnail across its nervous strings. Sex Laura will resist to the end; her knees cling together under her heavy "nun-like" attire. But Braggioni can wait; she will drop into his lap finally "like an overripe pear."

Why does Laura not flee while she can? Although she knows what is in store, "violence, mutilation, a shocking death," she stands immotile, waiting. There is no place for her to go; since Braggioni comprises all of "reality," there is nothing to escape to. She is an alien not only in this country, but in this world. And although her fear of death is intense, it is offset by her fear of life; in her inability to choose between them, the tension is nearly insupportable. So far as Braggioni will put an end to this terrible indecision, he is, as he insists, her "friend." If only she can do nothing long enough, the choice will be taken out of her hands.

To avoid blurring the essential issues involved, I have temporarily isolated the fears on which Laura's "way of living" is based. Actually, her attitude toward life is ambivalent, and contains an important, albeit shackled, counterforce, as the fact that she stubbornly retains a "feeling" of "what life should be" implies. This element, although in a sense allied with her fear of death, is not itself grounded in terror.

On the contrary, something in Laura yearns for an entirely different kind of life, a positive existence including faith in God and confidence in human beings both in the aggregate and individually—in short, a life rich in love, the opposite of the smothering "reality" to which one side of her make-up is committed. This other part of her instinctively needs and longs for human contact; Laura's "feeling" is the involuntary cry of her half-drowned self.

But the idea of a love which is not oppressive and threatening is too alluring, with its suggestions of impossible joy and order and freedom. Since all of what Laura considers real is ugly and frightening to her, this element which does not fit into her scheme of things must be, by definition, illusive. She has had too many disappointments to dare to hope; she cannot really believe in her own insistent urge toward life. Neither can she put it aside.

In a general sense the jailed revolutionary Eugenio is the symbol of all that Laura vaguely hopes for in spite of herself. (It is not surprising that in her dream he takes on the attributes of a Christ-figure, associated with man as well as with God, with love and with life.) Specifically, Eugenio is one human being Laura might have—but has not—loved.

It is significant that Miss Porter does not mention him until late in the story, and then only briefly, to establish the fact that he is already dead. He has been much on Laura's mind, however. While solid, paunchy, callous, greasy, corrupt "reality" flourishes in her life, the pale insubstantial "ideal" seems hardly to exist there—but its tenacity will be demonstrated, for she senses that Eugenio stands for something which can bring her relief, and she will dream that.

If Braggioni and Eugenio are antithetical symbols personifying the tension between Laura's fear of and desire for life, the third and most important symbol in the story, the blossoming redbud tree, whose name expresses its divided nature, combines both of these attitudes in one emblem. It also shifts the emphasis to love (and sexuality, although this is sternly repressed). *Flowering* is a lovely word, and flowers are indeed associated with love in Laura's mind. But these are not just any flowers—they are Judas flowers; treachery is all that she can expect from love as her fears define it. Once again, Laura is simultaneously attracted and repelled.

The Judas tree (which, like all of the symbols in this story, is multiple and complex) has another function, for it embraces a further aspect of Laura's conflicting attitudes—her self-image. Laura's feelings about herself are directly related to her feelings about other people, and consist, like them, of two incompatible elements. On the one hand she respects and defends her self; on the other she undervalues and prosecutes it. In her own eyes she resembles the Judas tree—delicate, beautiful, perfidious. She feels not only that she has made a grotesque blunder in allowing her fears to drive her to negation, but that she is to blame for doing so. In other words, Laura has somehow learned to experience her private "revolution" against life and love as worse than simply mistaken—she sees it as morally reprehensible, a betrayal of herself as well as of others. Her sense of error is intensified by a sense of guilt, and she finds herself "wrong" in both of the meanings which our language gives to that word. ("It may be true I am as corrupt, in another way, as Braggioni." she thinks, "as callous, as incomplete.") As she drifts off to sleep, this repressed feeling of culpability, reinforced by her Christian training, begins to emerge from the unconscious, and she accuses herself harshly with "it is monstrous to confuse love with revolution, night with day, life with death—ah, Eugenio!"

With this, the long, taut prelude of the story ends. Although nothing important has happened, Laura's state of paralysis and her feelings about it have been exposed with surgical precision. Now, in the final paragraph, where the entire action of the story begins, rises to its climax, and subsides, something is happening at last, if only in a dream.

It has to happen in a dream. Only in a dream can Eugenio appear as a savior, can Laura even momentarily believe in and reach out toward "life as it should be," an alternative to her deathlike "way of living."

With the tolling of the midnight bell, the signal for the dead to arise, the wraith of Eugenio appears. Come, he beckons, leave this "strange house" you have built for yourself; I will guide you to death—not to physical death (that belongs to Braggioni), but to the death which is rebirth.

Laura is irresistibly drawn after him, although the goal is distant and the way tortuous. Eugenio can no longer give her physical support, and anyway, there are some things one must do for oneself. There is no time to hang back, yet she cannot brave the journey alone; perhaps the vacuum caused by the removal of her defenses will not be filled, and she will lose her precarious balance fatally in the waste-land that stretches ahead. She is still the prisoner of her wretched fears.

As if he understood this, Eugenio responds with pity. Poor creature, he seems to say, this will give you the strength you need; and he strips the pulsing flowers from the Judas tree and holds them to her lips. In promising this new life which is also the death of the old life, Eugenio seems forgiving, compassionate, Christ-like. He offers the life-bringing nourishment with Christ's words; and the flowers themselves, like the bread and wine which satisfy spiritual hunger and thirst, are warm and bleeding, suggesting Christ's corporeal being. Laura accepts them, crushes them eagerly into her mouth, for she is starving for love in all of its forms.

But these are still Judas flowers: not even in a dream can Laura wholly overcome her profound distrust. The act of acceptance makes her vulnerable to her pervasive sense of guilt, her feeling that she is unworthy of love and forgiveness. She feels responsible for Eugenio's death not because she brought him drugs, but because she has closed off in herself the springs of compassion. Laura has been taught to believe that self-betrayal is also a betrayal of others, and thus of Christ. It is a mortal sin. Eugenio turns from a figure of mercy to one of vengeful justice, the personification of her own relentless conscience.

"Murderer!" he calls her, and "Cannibal! This is my body and my blood." The ritualistic words touch a buried nerve in Laura, for they evoke the whole of her religious upbringing. It is true that she has intellectually repudiated her childhood faith, but that does not mean that it does not still have immense power over her; the "set of principles derived from her early training," in which she has rigidly "encased herself," is an iron load of moral accountability.

In this context, Laura feels that she is subverting the sacrament which is a remembrance of and a participation in Christ's atoning death and resurrection, the visible sign of an invisible grace. When one has committed a mortal sin, one must cleanse one's soul in repentance and confession before receiving the Host. Laura has not been able to do so, and she feels that she is committing another and greater sin in taking communion unworthily. This is an act of murder and cannibalism; like Judas, she has betrayed Christ to his death and yet feasts on his symbolic flesh and blood. It is to her a false communion, a desecration of the Host. Eugenio, she dreams, is pointing out to her the visible sign of her invisible damnation; she is on the brink of horrifying self-knowledge.

But Laura cannot consciously confront her mistakes, ensnarled as they are with a guilt-laden concept of ''her own nature''; to do so would undermine her resistance to death and collapse the personality she is holding together by sheer will. She must negate *everything*. Recoiling in fright from the threat of disintegration, she reacts with a final ''No!'' and the shattering revelation goes underground again.

With this her balance is restored—but it is again a balance of tension, rather than of resolution. On one side, the secret burden of self-accusation, with its moral overtones, is heavier, for Laura stands in her own court doubly condemned—guilty first of transgression, now of refusing to confess. On the other side, the instinct of self-preservation still operates; she is ''determined not to surrender her will to such expedient logic.'' And there is something strong and admirable about Laura's fierce resistance to annihilation. She does not go to pieces. She is not insane. She holds on.

Her future is not spelled out. So far as this story shows, Laura will remain in her private limbo indefinitely, afraid to live or to die. (As Braggioni says of the coming May-day disturbances, ''There will be two independent processions, starting from either end of town, and they will march until they meet, and the rest depends. . . .'') The rest depends. Possibly her two embattled forces will gradually crush her between them, but more likely Laura will survive her civil war; one feels somehow that she will never die of it, however joyless her days.

The significance of her moving and terrifying experience is, I take it, that it is impossible to break the deadlock between inner needs and inculcated precepts—at least when those precepts are founded on conventional Western ideas of moral responsibility. Miss Porter records the conflict—not dispassionately—but with her passions tightly in rein and equitably divided.

One voice in her concurs in Laura's self-condemnation, on the familiar grounds that good and evil (however hard to identify) exist, that the individual possesses—or should possess—the means (however rudimentary) to discriminate between them, and that his decisions (however well-intentioned) are subject to inexorable review. Laura has been trained in this school; she knows—or ought to know—right from wrong; she has somehow chosen

the latter; and to her, the infallible sign of her guilt is her ineradicable feeling of guilt. At the same time, another voice in Miss Porter, while not directly contesting these assumptions, concurs in Laura's self-acquittal, as it were. The author clearly understands and respects her heroine's torment, and silently cries ''Bravo!'' to her spirited refusal to yield. Whether one chooses to consider Miss Porter half-persuaded or half-skeptical of both verdicts, ''Flowering Judas'' is, in my opinion, ''the testimony of a mental attitude'', and that attitude is dual.

The contention that Miss Porter, like her protagonist, takes a double view in this story may not be subject to any concrete ''proof.'' It is impractical to adduce here the evidence of her other work, which (again in my opinion) reflects a similar duality. Still, the reader may speculate about the effect on ''Flowering Judas'' if Miss Porter were presumed to take a single view of its dominant character and her dilemma. (It is a tribute to the authenticity of Laura that she elicits and supports such speculation.)

But which view? It would be naive to label Miss Porter either simple moralist or simple individualist; she is too perceptive and experienced to be either, and hardly simple in any case. The only viable possibility is that she is fully aware, as Laura is not, of the nature of an estrangement such as this character feels: its origins, its symptoms, its remedy.

Suppose for a moment that Miss Porter meant to show that her protagonist is the victim of feelings she can neither understand nor control, much less trace to their source. Yet from her present situation one unmistakably infers a certain kind of past. The details cannot be guessed, but ''the desperate complications of her mind and feelings'' clearly indicate that Laura is following a typical neurotic pattern forced on her by early emotional deprivation, which she experienced as a betrayal of love. In such cases, the unloved child usually assumes that it is *prima facie* unlovable, somehow a ''bad'' rather than a ''good child who understands the rules of behavior.'' Out of the resultant feelings of guilt and fear such a child develops a defensive personality marked by negation of the moralistic relationships that are the source of its disappointment and pain, and, by extension, of all human relationships. This movement, of course, involves a misapprehension, not of the nature of the child's experience, which it reads accurately, but of the nature of life outside of its experience—of, for example, the unconditional quality of love.

Laura has obviously constructed a large part of her existence around some such misapprehension. Irony piles upon irony. Her "reality" is not real; her "truth" is not true. There are times when people are savage, when sex does destroy, when "love" does suffocate. But she has mistaken these qualified facts for the whole fact; human relationships are not by definition hostile to her individuality, and one cannot dismiss them without incurring the ache of loss, as she has learned.

Suppose further that Miss Porter were also showing that mistakes are not "sins," that evil, as Socrates put it long ago, is simply error. From this standpoint, Laura's mistakes were inevitable, her only protection when she was too young to question the price of survival. She could not have done other than she did. Her most self-destructive error was the assumption of guilt in the first place, but this too was a mistake she could not help making. As for her dream, Laura's refusal to confess is not at all an act of moral cowardice, but evidence that a vital spirit of independence still persists in her, still fights tenaciously for its life. She is no more treacherous than the flowering Judas tree, a pretty bush to which, because of its name, she has attached some unfortunate connotations. Her feeling that she is self-betrayed might better be replaced with self-forgiveness—or rather (for it is gratuitous to forgive oneself for trying to survive), with self-acceptance.

If this were Miss Porter's unitary view, it would cap the story with a final ironic twist—that far from being either guilty or not guilty, Laura need not be on trial at all. "Flowering Judas" would be a different—not a better—story, and its gist that human beings are seldom given enough light to see by.

But this is not the story Miss Porter wrote, and I am not misguidedly trying to improve on it; it is a superb achievement just as it stands: a study in irreconcilables, a portrait of stress. As such, it cannot easily be the product of a single undivided viewpoint. If Miss Porter did not stand in the same relation to both of her heroine's attitudes, one or the other would exert less force, and a disequilibrium between them would make itself felt. The whole affective power of this story results from its balance, as well as its quality, of feeling—from the high pitch of equally disposed forces. The double outlook, moreover, is integral to the success of the story, for it increases the tension which is also its subject. This reinforcement of theme extends to even the smallest details, and creates an almost

electric intensity, an emotional impact of impressive voltage.

Another telling indication of the dual point of view of the story is that one cannot imagine Miss Porter relaxing her allegiance either to the felt rights of the instinctual identity or to the fundamental moral strictures of our culture. Concerning individuality, she is as passionate as Hawthorne (and shows much the same cast of mind) in resenting any intrusion upon the inviolable soul. As for morality, her very language, which is scrupulously exact protests a loyal adherence to what she has elsewhere called "some very old fashioned noble" values. For example in saying, as she has, that this story coalesced around a central idea of "self delusion," she selects a term which, like *betrayed* and *Judas*, bows under a weight of implicit moral judgment.

This does not mean that Miss Porter accepts her heritage without qualification, however. She is also in continual, if incomplete, revolt against it. "Flowering Judas" is (to borrow her description of another first-rate story of her own) "a story of the most painful moral and emotional confusions." The extent to which Laura reflects a widespread state of mind cannot be investigated here, but her tangling of the moral and the emotional is deeply relevant to at least some of the more painful confusions of modern man in the detritus of his civilization. While Miss Porter is not inclined to parry the thrust of the entire Judeo-Christian tradition, she effectively questions one basic aspect of it in this story, and provokes conjecture about the nature and validity of the sense of guilt, as well as of guiltiness itself.

Source: Dorothy S. Redden, "'Flowering Judas': Two Voices," in *Studies in Short Fiction,* Vol. VI, No. 2, Winter, 1969, pp. 194–204.

Sources

Bogan, Louise. In *The New Republic*, Vol. 64, No. 829, October 22, 1930, pp. 277-78.

Cowley, Malcolm. *Exile's Return: A Literary Odyssey of the 1920s,* New York: The Viking Press, 1934.

Review of "Flowering Judas," in *New York Times Book Review*, September 28, 1930, p. 6.

Richardson, E. R. In *Bookmark*, Vol. 72, October, 1960, p. 172.

Tate, Alan. In *Nation*, Vol. 131, October 1, 1930, p. 352.

Welty, Eudora. *The Eye of the Story,* New York: Random House, 1978.

West, Ray B. *The Art of Modern Fiction*, New York: Rinehart, 1949.

Further Reading

Bloom, Harold, ed. *Katherine Anne Porter*, New York: Chelsea House, 1986.
   A collection of critical essays on Porter's fiction.

Givner, Joan. *Katherine Anne Porter: A Life*, New York: Simon & Schuster, 1982.
   This definitive biography of Porter sets the record straight on the flamboyant and enigmatic author's life and paints a detailed portrait of her times.

Hendrick, Willene, and George Hendrick. *Katherine Anne Porter*, Boston: Twayne Publishers, 1988.
   A concise critical introduction to Porter's fiction groups her stories according to theme, setting, and character, and offers a brief, lucid interpretation of each.

Lopez, Enrique Hank. *Conversations with Katherine Anne Porter: Refugee from Indian Creek*, Boston: Little, Brown and Company, 1981.
   A biographical study based on a series of taped conversations with Porter during the last years of her life offers a glimpse into Porter's fascinating personality, though the facts are subject to her fanciful fictionalization.

Walsh, Thomas F. *Katherine Anne Porter and Mexico: The Illusion of Eden*, Houston: University of Texas Press, 1992.
   A detailed scholarly study of Mexico's influence on Porter's art includes useful analysis of the political and historical background to Porter's stories as well as literary interpretations based on a psycho-biographical approach.

West, Ray B. *The Art of Modern Fiction*, New York: Rinehart, 1949.
   West focuses on religious symbolism, arguing that Braggioni is capable of redemption, while Laura, who is unable to love, is not.

The Garden Party

Katherine Mansfield
1922

Widely anthologized, "The Garden Party" is considered Katherine Mansfield's finest piece of short fiction. Such modernist authors as Virginia Woolf were profoundly influenced by Mansfield's stream-of-consciousness and symbolic narrative style. "The Garden Party" is a remarkably rich and innovative work that incorporates Mansfield's defining themes: New Zealand, childhood, adulthood, social class, class conflict, innocence, and experience.

Structured around an early afternoon garden party in New Zealand, "The Garden Party" has clear connections to Mansfield's own childhood and adolescence in New Zealand. The main character of the story, Laura, is an idealistic young girl who wishes to cancel the planned afternoon gathering when she learns of the death of a working-class laborer who lives down the hill from her parents' home. The story concerns Laura's alternating moments of resistance and conformity to her mother's idea of class relations. Like Laura, Mansfield was the daughter of a well-to-do businessman—Harold Beauchamp—and his wife, Annie Burnell Dyer Beauchamp. Like the Sheridans in "The Garden Party," the Beauchamps lived luxuriously, in grand houses in and around Wellington, New Zealand.

"The Garden Party" was first published in 1922 in a collection entitled *The Garden Party and Other Stories* and immediately became a classic example of the short story form. In an essay published in 1957, Warren S. Walker wrote, "The most

frequently anthologized of Katherine Mansfield's works, ''The Garden Party'' has long enjoyed a reputation for near-perfection in the art of the short story.'' In her time, Mansfield was seen as one of the prime innovators of the short story form. After Mansfield's death in 1923, Virginia Woolf would remark in her diary, ''I was jealous of her writing—the only writing I have ever been jealous of.'' Even though it has enjoyed a fine reputation, critics and readers alike have puzzled over what they see as an unsatisfactory ending—an ending that, as Warren Walker remarks, ''leaves readers with a feeling of dissatisfaction, a vague sense that the story somehow does not realize its potential.''

Author Biography

Katherine Mansfield was born Kathleen Mansfield Beauchamp to a wealthy family in Wellington, New Zealand, on October 14, 1888. She was educated in London, deciding early on that she wanted to be a writer. She studied music, wrote for the school newspaper, and read the works of Oscar Wilde and other English writers of the early twentieth century. After three years in London she returned to New Zealand, where her parents expected her to find a suitable husband and lead the life of a well-bred woman. However, Mansfield was rebellious, adventurous, and more enamored of the artistic community than of polite society.

Mansfield began publishing stories in Australian magazines in 1907, and shortly thereafter returned to London. A brief affair left her pregnant and she consented to marry a man, George Bowden, whom she had known a mere three weeks and who was not the father of her child. She dressed in black for the wedding and left him before the night was over. Upon receiving word of the scandal and spurred on by rumors that her daughter had also been involved with several women, Mansfield's mother immediately sailed to London and placed her daughter in a spa in Germany, far away from the Bohemian artists' community of London. During her time in Germany, Mansfield suffered a miscarriage and was disinherited. After returning to London, Mansfield continued to write and conduct various love affairs.

In 1911, Mansfield published her first volume of stories, *In a German Pension*, most of which had been written during her stay at the German spa. That same year she met John Middleton Murry, the editor of a literary magazine. Although they lived together on and off for many years, her other affairs continued. Together Mansfield and Murry published a small journal, the *Blue Review*, which folded after only three issues. However, the experience led to friendships with members of the literary community of the day, including D. H. Lawrence and Frieda von Richthofen Weekly. In 1918, Mansfield was granted a divorce from Bowden, and she and Murry married.

Stricken with tuberculosis in 1917, Mansfield became very ill. She continued to write, publishing her collections *Bliss and Other Stories* and *The Garden Party and Other Stories* in 1920 and 1922 respectively. The latter collection includes both ''The Garden Party'' and ''Miss Brill.'' The collections received favorable critical attention, and she continued to write even after her health forced her to move to Fontainebleau in France. Though she was separated from Murry for long periods towards the end of her life, it was he who saw that her literary reputation was established by publishing her last stories and her collections of letters after she died of a massive pulmonary hemorrhage in January, 1923, at the age of thirty-four.

Plot Summary

Katherine Mansfield's short story ''The Garden Party'' opens with frantic preparations being made for an afternoon garden party. The main character, Laura, is an idealistic and sensitive young girl. She is surrounded by her more conventional family: her sister, Jose, who, as the narrator tells us, ''loved giving orders to servants''; her mother, Mrs. Sheridan, a shallow old woman whose world consists of having enough canna lilies; her father, a businessman; and her brother, Laurie, to whom she feels most similar in feeling and ideals. As many critics have remarked, Mansfield's prose depicts an almost dreamlike world.

This atmosphere is compromised for Laura when she hears of the death of one of the laborers who lives in the cottages down the hill from her house. Struck by the inappropriateness of throwing a garden party when a neighbor has been killed, Laura immediately suggests that they cancel the party. The rest of the story is structured around Laura's reconciliation of her concern for the dead laborer and her family's reactions to his demise. Laura attempts to convince Jose of the necessity of canceling the party. Jose's response is indicative of the family's overall view of the impoverished laborers. She chastises Laura for her desire to cancel the party, saying, ''You won't bring a drunken workman back to life by being sentimental.'' The narrator's later description of the cottages reveals the family's general hostility toward their neighbors.

After Jose's rebuff, Laura attempts to convince her mother of the need to cancel the garden party. Laura's relationship with her mother is a significant aspect of ''The Garden Party.'' Earlier, in greeting the workmen who were to put up the marquee, Laura had tried to mimic her mother in order to prevent the workmen from perceiving her as a child: ''Good morning,' she said, copying her mother's voice.'' In the next moment of her conversation with the handymen, however, Laura attempts to distinguish herself from her mother's perception of the working class.

At first, Laura is aghast at her mother's reaction to the news of the dead laborer. Mrs. Sheridan worries only that the death occurred in the garden: ''Mother, a man's been killed' . . . 'Not in the garden?' interrupted her mother.'' Mrs. Sheridan reacts to Laura's suggestion like Jose does—she becomes annoyed and thinks that the idea of canceling the party is absurd. Giving her a black hat to wear for the garden party, Mrs. Sheridan hopes it will change her mind. At first Laura resists this appeal to her vanity, but once she's left her mother's room, she sees herself in a mirror and is soon overwhelmed by her own ''charm.'' Caught up in her mother's comfortable vision of garden parties and black hats, Laura now perceives the laborer as a distant object of curiosity—like a picture in the newspaper—and no longer a reason to cancel a lovely afternoon garden party.

The party itself is not fully described in Mansfield's story; the only impressions of it are given through snatches of conversation. From these moments it is apparent that the party has transpired as expected, with much made of Laura and her black hat: ''Darling Laura, how well you look!'' ''What a becoming hat, child!'' and so on. Soon afterwards, however, the dead laborer once again disturbs Laura's complacency. Mr. Sheridan brings up the ''beastly accident.'' Mrs. Sheridan suggests that Laura deliver some leftover food to the laborer's widow. At first Laura doubts the appropriateness of such an action, but she is soon convinced by her mother.

Katherine Mansfield

Almost perversely, Mrs. Sheridan insists that Laura go down to the cottages in her party garb.

Laura's journey to the cottages is described as a journey into an anti-world. Rather than the fresh, airy, and ethereal Sheridan atmosphere, Saunders Lane is characterized by darkness, shadows, half-dressed children, and a sense of oppression. ''Dark knots of people'' are seen to stand outside the widow's cottage. Laura soon feels the inappropriateness of her dress. She plans to quickly drop off the basket and rush from the disturbing scene.

Unfortunately for Laura, the widow's sister will not allow her to escape so quickly. Laura meets the sorrow-ravaged widow—''her face, puffed up, red, with swollen eyes and swollen lips.'' Although her mother has asked her not to look at the dead body, Laura allows the sister to take her to the corpse. Contrary to her expectations, she is struck by the peacefulness and beauty of the young man and by how inconsequential garden parties and lace frocks are to one who is caught up in a different and incomparable dream. Overwhelmed by the disparity between her world and this picture of peaceful death, Laura exclaims in a sob, ''forgive my hat.''

Laura runs out and encounters her brother, Laurie. Sensing that Laura might be disturbed by her visit, he asks, "Was it all right?" Laura tries to explain her impressions to Laurie but realizes that this momentary sight of the transcendent is unexplainable. Laurie, however, understands what Laura has seen and in response to Laura's unfinished exclamation "Isn't life—" answers, "*Isn't* it darling?" The story ends with the two sharing this impression of a world beyond parties.

Characters

Cook

The Sheridan's cook is a nurturing figure, allowing Laura and one of her sisters to indulge in eating rich cream-puffs that have been delivered for the garden party just after they finish breakfast.

Mother

See Mrs. Sheridan

Jose Sheridan

Jose is Laura's class-conscious older sister. She takes a dim view of Laura's wish to cancel the garden party when she tells Laura that she "won't bring a drunken workman back to life by being sentimental."

Laura Sheridan

Laura Sheridan is an idealistic and impressionable young person who struggles with her own and her family's perceptions of class difference. Learning that a working-class neighbor was accidentally killed, Laura wants to cancel the garden party planned for that afternoon. The narrative centers on Laura's vacillation between feelings of empathy for the dead laborer and her vanity and class elitism. She unsuccessfully tries to convince her mother to cancel the party. However, her mother distracts her with the gift of a new hat, and when Laura sees herself in the hat, she no longer presses for cancellation of the party. By the end of the story, however, Laura has made an attempt to relate to the lives of the family's working-class neighbors, although the conclusion to the story is ambiguous. It is not clear what, if anything, she has learned or if the experience has changed her.

Laurie Sheridan

Laurie is Laura's older brother and closest family member. After viewing the body of the laborer who died before the garden party, Laura is comforted by Laurie. The conclusion is ambiguous—it is not clear if either Laurie or Laura truly understand their own feelings at that moment.

Meg Sheridan

Meg Sheridan, another one of Laura's sisters, possesses a manner and attitude similar to that of Jose and Mrs. Sheridan. The reader first encounters Meg as she comes down to breakfast with her freshly washed hair wrapped up in a green turban and a "dark wet curl stamped on each cheek." She refuses to go and supervise the workmen assembling the party tent because her hair is wet, so that responsibility falls to Laura.

Mrs. Sheridan

Mrs. Sheridan is Laura's mother. Like Jose, Laura's older sister, Mrs. Sheridan will not consider canceling the garden party because of the death of a laborer living nearby. In an attempt to appease Laura, however, she does suggest that Laura take the party leftovers to the widow of the dead man. She declares early in the story that she intends to leave the party preparations entirely up to her daughters, but it becomes clear that she is closely monitoring—and managing—every step.

Themes

Innocence and Experience

"The Garden Party" traces the psychological and moral growth of Laura Sheridan. The story presents her adolescent confusion regarding the social values of her family and her awakening to a more mature perception of reality after her exposure to poverty and death at the carter's cottage.

Laura's self-consciousness regarding her own youth and inexperience is evident whenever she encounters members of the working class. When sent to supervise the workers who have come to set up the marquee, she regards them as "impressive" because they carry their tools and work in shirt sleeves. In her initial dealings with them, she attempts to play the role of her mother—the adult—but soon loses her composure: "Laura wished now that she had not got her bread and butter, but there was no place to put it and she couldn't throw it away. She blushed and tried to look severe and even a little shortsighted as she came up to [the workers]." Copying her mother's voice, Laura says greets the workmen but soon feels that she sounds "affected" and is ashamed.

This lack of assurance affects her at various moments in the narrative, particularly when she is called upon to make adult responses to events which are outside her childhood environment and experience. Her initial idealization of the workmen's natural camaraderie changes to feelings of unease and discomfort when she sees the real conditions of the working-class community—their poverty and their claustrophobic, dark kitchens. When she learns of the death of the carter and wants to cancel the party as an appropriate gesture, she is seduced by the hat her mother gives her and the privileged world the hat symbolizes. The sophistication of her more assured sisters and mother, who have no problem justifying the convenient pleasures of their lifestyle, contrasts sharply with Laura's awkward attempts to do the right thing by canceling the garden party.

Although Laura's responses are frequently childish, there are significant moments of growth in her character. She is always conscious, for example, of the limitations inherent in her class-conscious world and is open to alternate experiences even when she cannot always respond maturely to them. For example, she is genuinely concerned for the carter's widow. Her desire to cancel the garden party in order to spare the widow the sounds of revelry at her sad time is a sign of maturity in its consideration and empathy.

Journey

The theme of journey is used in this story to illustrate Laura's rite of passage from childishness to maturity. As the story progresses, Laura moves from the interiors of the Sheridan home, with its abundance of domestic detail, to the sunlit garden and, later, to a region beyond this enclosed and protective space of primary identity. This journey starts in gathering darkness as Laura crosses the

Media Adaptations

- "The Garden Party" was adapted as a film in 1974. It is now available on video through AIMS Multimedia.

road to where the lane becomes "smoky and dark." She enters the cottage, travels down a "narrow, dark passage" to the claustrophobic kitchen, past the grief-stricken widow with "swollen eyes and swollen lips," to look upon the calm beauty of the face of the dead carter at the culmination of the journey. At the end of the passage, Laura gains an insightful vision of life and death.

Dream and Reality

Illusion and reality are central themes in "The Garden Party." The world of the Sheridans is consistently characterized as part of a dream that suppresses and excludes the working-class world. The sorrows of the real world are present here only in the pretty song that Jose sings before the garden party.

Laura buys into these upper-class pretensions. When she endorses the rituals of the garden party, for example, the reality outside of the party seems to be an illusion to her: "She had a glimpse of that poor woman and those little children, and the body being carried into the house. But it all seemed blurred, unreal, like a picture in the newspaper." Even when Laura travels beyond the confines of the Sheridan garden, the dream continues as she carries the sensations of the party with her—"It seemed to her that kisses, voices, tinkling spoons, laughter, the smell of crushed grass were somehow inside her."

Style

Style

Katherine Mansfield's short story "The Garden Party" employs a style that is distinctly modern

Topics for Further Study

- Investigate the literary movement of Modernism in the 1920s. You may want to consult sources such as *A Homemade World: The American Modernist Writers*, by Hugh Kenner (Johns Hopkins University Press, 1989), and *The First Moderns: Profiles in the Origins of Twentieth-Century Thought*, by William R. Everdell (University of Chicago Press, 1997). What contributions did Katherine Mansfield make to the then literary avant-garde? What were some of other modernist innovations in poetry, in art and in music?

- Research one of the major historical topics of the 1920s and before: World War I, the rise of fascism, the spread of Marxism, British imperialism, the European and American stock markets, unionism, feminism, gay life. How did these events affect the rich? In what ways did they affect the poor differently?

- Investigate Katherine Mansfield's correspondence and journals. Consider the connections between their subjects of concern and the concerns of her fiction, especially "The Garden Party."

---

in its use of impressionistic detail and stream-of-consciousness narrative method. These stylistic features also characterize the works of Virginia Woolf, Dorothy Richardson, and other innovative writers of the 1920s and 1930s.

The narrative begins in "the middle of things"—in *media res*. The narrative voice describes the scene in a casual and immediate manner which at once establishes an intimacy with the reader—"And after all the weather was ideal. They could not have had a more perfect day for the garden party if they had ordered it." The almost confidential presentation of such objective facts establishes the narrative voice as the central consciousness of the story—one that perceives and interprets experience and that also, for most of the story, melds with the character of Laura. As the reader is made privy to

authorial confidences and interpretation, an appeal is made to identify with Laura's and the narrator's point of view. The reader is drawn into this "central" consciousness gradually, gaining access to Laura's sensibility through constant access to her perception and emotional responses. Most often, the alternation between a third-person narrative voice and Laura's own perception is demonstrated in single sentences, the transition occurring without narrative markers. A prime example of this happens before Laura meets the workmen who are to put up the marquee: "Away Laura flew, still holding her piece of bread and butter. It's so delicious to have an excuse for eating out of doors, and besides she loved having to arrange things," or "His smile was so easy, so friendly, that Laura recovered. What nice eyes he had, small, but such a dark blue!"

This technique of focusing on the thoughts of a central consciousness is referred to by literary critics as stream of consciousness. Using this method to achieve a more truthful presentation of reality, Mansfield, like other modernists, saw it not as something independent of one's perceptions but rather as constituted by each individual's particular perceptions. In the "The Garden Party," for example, Laura's perceptions are immediately made available, frequently overwhelming what few realities reach the reader through a different source than the main character. At the start of her journey down to Saunders Lane, for example, her thoughts are filled with "the kisses, voices, tinkling spoons, laughters, and the smell of crushed grass"—memories of the party which at first obscure the actual journey down to the carter's cottage.

Appropriately, the linear narrative of the events surrounding the Sheridan garden party leads up to the climactic conflict of Laura's consciousness. Again, her perceptions at this climactic moment are articulated by the narrative voice, which almost speaks for her, moving from a third- to a first-person point of view. "There lay a young man fast asleep—sleeping so soundly, so deeply, that he was far far away from them both. Oh so remote, so peaceful. . . . What did garden parties and baskets and lace frocks matter to him? He was far from all of those things. He was wonderful, beautiful. While they were laughing and while the band was playing, this marvel had come to the lane."

Symbolism and Imagery

Mansfield's descriptive language in this story presents a richly textured, suggestive world. Colors, shapes, and textures become a medium through which the scenes of the story acquire significance. The story begins with an impressionistic presentation of the interiors and gardens of the Sheridan home. The garden itself is presented as a space glowing with color and filled with the warmth of the roses, yellow karake fruits, and lilies. These fruits and flowers symbolize the mood of ethereal beauty that characterizes the Sheridan home. This sense of luminous calm is suggested perhaps most clearly by the following image: "And the perfect afternoon, slowly ripened, slowly faded, slowly its petals closed."

This scene of light and air visibly darkens as Laura leaves the brilliant garden to walk down the hill to the worker's cottages. The somber mood and lack of hope for the villagers is illustrated by the shade as Laura nears Saunders Lane. Similarly, the soft rustling breezes of the garden and the comfortable domestic chatter of the Sheridan house are replaced by silence and the ominous hum that Laura hears as she approaches the worker's neighborhood—"How quiet it seemed after the afternoon. . . . A low hum came from the mean little cottages. In some of them there was a flicker of light, and a shadow, crablike, moved across the window."

The shadows intensify as Laura approaches the carter's cottage and is led through a "gloomy passage" by a "woman in black." Within the obscured interior of the cottage, Laura is exposed to death in the form of the young laborer, and the epiphany that she experiences as she looks upon the calm beauty of the dead face suggests a radiant revelation in this final setting.

Historical Context

Katherine Mansfield's "The Garden Party" was written in 1922, during the period between the two world wars. In many ways it reflects the context of its creation. The 1920s saw enormous political and social disturbance throughout Europe. In the new Soviet Union, for example, the Marxist revolution was nearing completion. The Soviet Union's powerful leader, V. I. Lenin, had succeeded in wresting control from the Russian aristocracy and was establishing a system of agricultural collectivization in the rural parts of the Soviet Union. In parts of Europe, political groups were beginning to promote fascism—a philosophy that supports a government of unlimited power, often ruled by a dictator. These changes alarmed many and prompted people every-

where to discuss issues related to the class systems that existed during the period.

World War I and the political and social upheavals of the mid-war years had tangible effects on the arts and literature. Katherine Mansfield, like many others in England and elsewhere, felt the impact of the war, as her beloved brother was killed. Other writers and artists were similarly affected by the psychological and cultural fallout of the war. In his 1922 poem *The Waste Land*, for example, T. S. Eliot characterizes his sense of individual alienation and cultural uncertainty, having the poetic "I" of this poem remark, "These fragments I have shored against my ruins." The fragments to which Eliot alludes are those bits of Western culture and the humanist tradition that may be used as shields against the new cultural disruption and uncertainty. In nonfiction, Oswald Spengler, a German historian, predicted the end of the hegemony of Western humanist values and culture in his now-classic work, *The Decline of the West*. Rather than a decline of the West, "The Garden Party" may be understood to depict the end of caste-ridden "garden party" civilization—the carefree gentility of pre-World War I Europe—in its representation of Laura Sheridan's struggle between the worlds of her parents and her working-class neighbors.

Critical Overview

Critical attempts to interpret the story's conclusion have led to many analyses of its overall structure. In his article "Crashing the Garden Party, I: A Dream—A Wakening," Donald S. Taylor perceives the story as a narrative of Laura Sheridan's awakening from the comfortable but shallow existence that she has been living. Taylor thus views the lyrics of Jose's song as a foreshadowing of Laura's eventual awakening. Taylor attributes much of the responsibility for this dream-world to Mrs. Sheridan, who, he writes, "keeps the daughters in the dream by giving her daughters the illusion of maturity" in planning the garden party.

In the critical analyses that examine the story structurally—as a representation and negotiation of two worlds—Laura Sheridan is given much of the responsibility for her own growth or her own awakening. In this sense, "The Garden Party" is much like a *bildungsroman*—a story of individual growth and maturity. In his article "Crashing the Garden Party: The Garden Party of Proserpina," Daniel A.

Compare
&
Contrast

- **1920s:** With the advent of the modernist movement, writers, artists, and musicians struggled to express the alienation they felt toward Western culture.

  1990s: Cultural commentators are still drawing inspiration from the disconnection they perceive with their values and popular culture. A term ''Generation X'' has been coined to describe a whole generation of people that is thought to feel alienated from the rest of society.

- **1920s:** Stalin establishes himself as dictator of the Soviet Union and proceeds to purge his people of dissent.

1990s: The Soviet Union has deteriorated into a debt-ridden Russian Republic. Democratic institutions are weak but existent.

- **1920s:** Harold Ware demonstrates mechanized farming to the Soviets. He also takes volunteers and $150,000 of equipment and seed to a 15,000 acre demonstration farm near Moscow.

  1990s: America helps Russia avert a food shortage by loaning it money to buy American grain. The grain, which would otherwise have been dumped, is being bought at a price higher than its current market value.

Weiss likens Laura's journey of self-awakening to Proserpina's journey to the underworld. In his reading, Saunders Lane is the underworld of death that Laura must journey to and return from as part of her initiation into life's ultimate mystery—death—and away from the dream world of her family.

In mapping out the mythic and autobiographical aspects of ''The Garden Party,'' Anders Iversen compares Mansfield's story to a story written by Danish author I. P. Jacobsen. He sees the similarities between the two stories as structural; both deal with the contrasting worlds of rich and poor. These two worlds, Iversen argues, not only signify wealth and poverty but also life and death. While in Jacobsen's story there is no mediation between the two worlds, ''The Garden Party'' allows what Iversen calls a ''moment of contact'' between the world of life—the Sheridans—and the world of death—Saunders Lane. This moment of contact is made by Laura Sheridan, who alone ventures forth from what Iversen has characterized as her personal ''garden of Eden'' to what is beyond the garden—the world of the Scotts. Iversen understands this journey as a ''rite of passage,'' one of the fundamental ingredients of the *bildungsroman*.

Rather than analyzing ''The Garden Party'' through the lens of mythic archetype, feminist critics such as Kate Fulbrook take a more psychological and political view of the story and of the character of Laura Sheridan in particular. In her essay Fulbrook presents Laura's struggle with the class values of her parents as a struggle with her own identity. She views Laura as caught between a sense of herself as an outsider within her own family and her vanity—particularly after she has seen herself in her black hat, when she thinks it impossible to cancel the garden party. Interestingly, Fulbrook interprets Mansfield's representation of Laura's moral confusion as an indictment of ''the inadequacy of education of 'the daughters of educated men'''—an indictment, which, as Fulbrook notes, is ''deepened by the story's account of the suffering taking place below the Sheridan's privileged hill.''

Criticism

Jennifer Rich

Rich is an instructor of literature, composition, and gender issues at Marymount Manhattan Col-

---

Formal garden design with rectangualr middle with small shrub borders and grass in the center.

lege. In the following essay, she examines ways in which "The Garden Party" uses contrasts between social classes to illustrate how the classes define each other.

Most criticism of Katherine Mansfield's short story "The Garden Party" concentrates on the story as a truncated *bildungsroman*—a story of the growth and maturity of a young idealistic character. Critics such as Daniel S. Taylor in "Crashing the Garden Party: A Dream, A Wakening," for example, see Laura's initiation as a passage from the "dream world of her parents and social class to the real world of the Sheridan's neighboring working-class." As Taylor notes, describing the symbolic significance of the garden party, "The garden party epitomizes the dream world of the Sheridan women, a world whose underlying principle is the editing and rearranging of reality for the comfort and pleasure of its inhabitants. Its war is with the real world, whose central and final truth is death." Similarly, Clare Hansen and Andrew Gurr, in "The Stories: Sierre and Paris," discuss Laura's evolution into adulthood as taking place in the context of a gulf

What Do I Read Next?

- *Bliss and Other Stories* (1920), *The Garden Party and Other Stories*(1922), *The Doves Nest and Other Stories* (1923), *Something Childish and Other Stories* (1924) were all written by Katherine Mansfield. The collections of stories listed above are crucial to examine for Katherine Mansfield's narrative innovations and for the diverse number of subjects and characters that her stories concern. These are also prime examples of literary modernism in the 1920s.

- *The Tunnel*, a collection of twenty-four vignettes by Dorothy Richardson, was written in 1919. Dorothy Richardson was a great influence on Katherine Mansfield, especially in regards to Mansfield's stylistic innovations. While different in content and subject-matter, these pieces are interesting to read as examples of early twentieth-century female modernism.

- *To the Lighthouse*, Virginia Woolf's most famous novel, was published in 1928. Virginia Woolf and Katherine Mansfield were friends and were great influences on one another. After Mansfield died, Woolf noted that she was the only writer of whom she was jealous. *To the Lighthouse* is a masterpiece of stream-of-consciousness narrative, and, as such, it shares similarities to Katherine Mansfield's "The Garden Party".

- *Mrs. Dalloway*, by Virginia Woolf, was pub-lished in 1922. Similar to "The Garden Party," Mrs. Dalloway is structured around an evening cocktail party. It pairs Mrs. Dalloway, an upper-middle-class wife of a government official, with Septimus Smith, a mentally-ill veteran. The narratives of the two intertwine throughout and serve to comment upon the other. As such, it is a striking indictment of complacence and snobbery.

- *The Letters of Katherine Mansfield*, by Katherine Mansfield, was published in 1928. Katherine Mansfield was a prolific correspondent and many of her letters include commentary on her own fiction as well as other writers of her time.

- *The Journals of Katherine Mansfield*, by Katherine Mansfield, was published in 1927. These journals are an invaluable source for understanding Mansfield's political and social beliefs and the aesthetic and non-aesthetic influences upon her writing.

- *Women in Love*, by D. H. Lawrence, was published in 1920. One of the main protagonists of this novel, Gudrun, is based on Katherine Mansfield. The novel is structured around the friendships and marriages of two couples—as such it is loosely based on Mansfield's and John Middleton Murry's friendship with Lawrence and his wife, Frieda.

---

between rich and poor—a gulf that is indicated by the Mansfield's oppositional descriptions of the world of the Sheridans and the world of their less fortunate neighbors:

> Words such as "perfect," "delicious," "beautiful," "splendor," "radiant," "exquisite," "brilliant," "rapturous," "charming," "delightful," "stunning," convey the outward beauty of the Sheridan's life . . . In striking contrast are words describing the working people and Saunders lane: "haggard," "mean," "poverty-stricken," "revolting," "disgusting," "sordid," "crablike," "wretched."

Given that "The Garden Party" was written in 1922 at the height of Marxist movements across Europe and Russia—which, among other things, attempted to understand class structure and identity—it is necessary to explore the way in which "The Garden Party" presents a picture of class interdependence. Specifically, "The Garden Party" is interesting to investigate for the way it portrays families like the Sheridans as being dependent for their class—identity on their always nearby working—class neighbors. Thus, rather than conceptualizing the worlds of the Sheridans and the worlds of the Scotts as diametric opposites whose paths seldom cross, this essay will explore the way in which "The Garden Party" presents the two worlds as always meeting and clashing—defining one and the other through their continual juxtaposition.

"The Garden Party" is structured around the preparations for an early afternoon garden party. The sense of the Sheridans as inhabiting a dream-like world is set out in the very first lines when the narrator comments on the ideal weather conditions for the garden party. "And after all the weather was ideal. They could not have had a more perfect day if they had ordered it. Windless, warm, the sky without a cloud." The family, and particularly its female members, seem to derive their life-force from the carefree atmosphere in which they live. In the story's first scene, Meg, one of Laura's sisters, is seen sipping coffee, hair washed, wrapped in a green turban. Jose, another sister, is simply described as a butterfly who always "came down in a silk petticoat and a kimono jacket."

Mansfield, however, does not allow this sense of early morning luxuriance to go uninterrupted. Immediately, those upon whom the Sheridan sisters' luxury depends burst in upon this scene of lazy breakfast-taking. Their entrance is signaled by a break in the narrator's description of the garden and weather: "Breakfast was not yet over before the men came to put up the marquee." The now down-to-earth tone of this sentence connotes linguistically a clash between the lives of the Sheridan sisters and the men who must come at dawn to put up the marquee for the party. This interruption is further signaled when Laura, the main character who throughout the story attempts to bridge personally these two ever-present worlds, runs out to meet the workmen with breakfast—the signifier of her "Sheridan" life—in hand. Significantly, Laura feels embarrassed still holding the bread and butter when she comes to meet the workmen: "Laura wished now that she had not got the bread-and-butter, but there was nowhere to put it and she couldn't possibly throw it away."

The reason for this awkwardness is precisely that the bread and butter, the piece of Sheridan life which she has taken with her, defines her to the workmen as not one of them but as opposite from them, and upper class. Laura attempts to mediate that duality by playing both roles—taking a big workman-like bite from her slice of refined Sheri-

> Ironically, the hat—after the garden party—is a catalyst for a moment of understanding/connection between Laura's world and the world of the Scotts."

dan life while thinking of the "absurdity of class distinctions."

While Laura is exulting in her camaraderie with the workmen, one of them catches her attention. He seems somewhat apart from his compatriot—he does not share the general frivolity, and functions to once again remind Laura of their difference. Discussing the placement of the marquee, Laura remarks that there will be a band playing at the party. To this the workman replies, "H'm, going to have a band, are you?" After this remark, Laura notices that this workman "was pale," and with a "haggard look as his dark eyes scanned the tennis court." At this very moment, however, of a sense of mutual alienation, the workman picks and smells a sprig of lavender from the garden. Witnessing this, Laura feels their differences evaporate and "wonder(s) at him for caring for things like that—caring for the smell of lavender." Once again, then, a moment of antimony, of unmediated difference of "two worlds," is mediated by an action, this time on the part of one of the workmen rather than Laura.

This sense of similar class identities is short-lived, however, as the narrative continues with the continued clashing and jarring of the two worlds. In fact, during the rest of the story there is never a moment where Saunders Lane is forgotten. Even at the dreamiest point in the Sheridan world, Saunders Lane is suggested in some way or another. For example, after Laura has met the workmen, she settles down for a moment and listens to the sound of the house. As she listens she finds that the house is an airy delight, "every door seemed open . . . And the house was alive with soft, quick steps and running voices." Even this momentary enjoyment of the house's heavenly comfort is interrupted by Saunders Lane. The interruption comes in the form of "a long chuckling absurd sound. It was the heavy piano being moved on its stiff castors.'' Although we are told that Meg and Jose are involved in moving the piano, it is the servant Hans's physical labor that Laura undoubtedly overhears.

A more humorous (if not satirical) moment of potential mediation between the two worlds of the story is Jose's absurd song with which she tests her voice. Jose has been earlier described as a ''butterfly''—a girl of cream-puffs and linen dresses, and of course garden parties. Yet, the song that she sings is decidedly not of this type: ''This life is *Wee-ary*,/ A Tear—A Sigh./A Love that *Chan- ges/This* life is *Wee*-ary.'' Rather than the expected moment of unity between the Sheridan house and Saunders Lane, the absurd pairing of an emotionally calloused character like Jose with a song of sorrow and desperation serves instead to remind the reader that it is precisely the weariness of others that makes possible Jose's butterfly-like existence. This antithesis of expression and experience is punctuated by Jose's actions at the close of the song,

> But at the word ''goodbye'', and although the piano sounded more desperate than ever, her face broke into a brilliant, dreadfully unsympathetic smile, 'Aren't I in good voice, Mummy?'

This mismatch of expression and character is underscored by the fact that this song is preceded by Jose giving orders to the servant, Hans, to rearrange the tables and to sweep the rug.

The garden party is itself not fully described in the story. We are only privy to certain snatches of conversation—and these tell us that it has been a success, with Laura the center of much attention because of her black hat. Before the garden party, Laura's mother, Mrs. Sheridan, had distracted Laura from thinking about the dead laborer and her wish to cancel the garden party by enticing her with a black hat. Laura had at first resisted this appeal to her vanity, but once she leaves her mother's bedroom, she catches a glimpse of herself in the hat in her bedroom mirror. What she sees startles her, and serves to obliterate the image of the dead laborer.

> There, quite by chance, the first thing she saw was this charming girl in the mirror, in her black hat trimmed with gold daisies, and a long velvet black ribbon. Never had she imaged she could look like that. . . . Just for a moment she had another glimpse of that poor woman and those little children, and the body being carried into the house. But it all seemed so blurred, unreal, like a picture in the newspaper.

The hat thus functions at this moment to reinforce more than ever the division between the world of the Sheridans and the world of the Scotts. Suffused with vanity as a result of the hat's charm, Laura forgets the tragedy down the hill, and more than ever desires to continue with the garden party. Even when confronted with her brother, Laurie—the family member with whom she is most emotionally intimate—Laura decides not to tell him of Scott once he has complemented her on her hat.

Ironically, the hat—after the garden party—is a catalyst for a moment of understanding/connection between Laura's world and the world of the Scotts. After the party, Laura's mother suggests that Laura take a basket of party scraps down to Scott's widow. At first, Laura questions the appropriateness of this gesture, but is soon convinced. Mrs. Sheridan also insists that Laura ''run down just as [she is]''–in party dress and hat. Arriving at Saunders Lane, Laura soon feels awkward because of the way in which she is dressed. This awkwardness, I would argue, signals a moment of insight for Laura into the lives of the workers who live on this lane. She is disturbed because of the brightness of her frock and the extravagance of the famous hat: ''how her frock shone! And the big hat with the velvet streamer—if only it was another hat!'' Noting the difference between her dress and that of the laborers—tweed capped men and shawled women—Laura realizes the life absent of carefree happiness that the inhabitants of Saunders Lane must endure. A bright frock and an extravagant hat have no home here. Like the bread and butter episode, this piece of Sheridan life reveals to her the almost unsurmountable disjuncture between her life and the lives of these workers.

The hat also functions to create another moment of insight for Laura when she is alone with the body of the laborer. When Laura enters the Scott home, she is immediately confronted with the sorrow-ravaged face of the laborer's widow. Although Laura tries to escape as soon as it is possible, the widow's sister insists that she view the now-peaceful body of Mr. Scott. Laura is soon overwhelmed by the peacefulness of the expression on the laborer's face; particularly she is overcome by the remoteness of his appearance. ''He was given up to his dream. What did garden-parties and baskets and lace frocks matter to him? He was far from all those things. He was wonderful, beautiful. While they were laughing and while the band was playing, this marvel had come to the lane.'' Laura feels that she can not leave Scott without saying something that would indicate the affect that he has had on her— ''She gave out a loud, childish sob . . . 'Forgive my hat,' she said.''

Although her plea is undoubtedly comical and absurd, it also carries within it a significant moment of understanding. As we have seen, the hat has heretofore functioned as a prime signifier of the division between the two worlds—earlier, the hat had caused Laura to forget the tragedy just down the hill. By apologizing for her hat, Laura is also apologizing for what it represents—class snobbery, selfishness, and the almost unsurmountable psychological and social division between the world of the laborers and the world of the Sheridans. The hat, then, here facilitates a moment of connection—of class similarity—through its very significance as a symbol of division and antimony. The story concludes with Laura meeting her brother, Laurie, in Saunders Lane. Her demeanor with him indicates that she has been touched by the universality of death and life—both know neither class borders nor garden parties.

Source: Jennifer Rich, ''Overview of 'The Garden Party,''' in *Short Stories for Students,* The Gale Group, 2000.

Ben Satterfield

In the following essay, Satterfield discusses the importance of irony in ''The Garden Party.''

All of the writing on Katherine Mansfield's most anthologized story recognizes or implies that ''The Garden Party'' is a fable of initiation. The general interpretation argues that Laura goes from her Edenic world to one in which death exists, and that archetypally she loses her innocence, thereby acquiring knowledge and reaching a point of initiation. Laura has a great discovery, true; but because of her inability to make any kind of statement about it that would serve to clarify its meaning, critics disagree on whether she will go on to learn more about life and death or whether she will retreat into the sanctuary of the garden world. Much of the disagreement can be resolved, I believe, by a close examination of the irony—which has been largely ignored—and the function and effect of that irony upon the events of the story. Also, ''The Garden Party'' contains *two types* of initiation, a fact mostly overlooked, and the initiations are not compatible, as the details of the story make evident.

Irony is the keynote. The central character of ''The Garden Party,'' Laura Sheridan, is protected from the exigencies of life and is unable to view reality (even death) except through the rose-tinted glasses provided by a delicate and insulated existence. Laura's world is a world of parties and flowers, a pristine world of radiant, bright canna lilies

> That Katherine Mansfield could present two types of initiation, one profound and the other shallow, is a tribute to her consummate skill: the fact that the protagonist opts for the shallow in no way detracts from her art but serves to increase the poignancy of her tale and to mark its realism."

and roses, a precious and exclusive world. Laura's sister, Jose, is early described as a butterfly—and what creature is more delicate than a butterfly? That Jose chooses to sing a song about a weary life, obviously something she is unacquainted with, has to be ironic: in the Sheridan family, weariness and sorrow are merely lyrics to be mocked.

Mansfield's exquisite use of imagery is as telling as her irony. For example, the flower imagery throughout the story serves to keep the reader reminded of the delicacy of Laura's world. The flowers are splendid, beautiful, and—what is not stated—short-lived. Laura, too, is beautiful, radiant, flower-like. But even the afternoon is likened to a flower: ''And the perfect afternoon slowly ripened, slowly faded, slowly its petals closed.'' Laura, her vision attuned to the superficial, can see only the beauty and not the dying of the flower, and she cannot see that, in many ways, she is very much like a flower herself.

The symbolism of Laura's hat as well as her name (from *laurel,* the victory crown) is apparent. Marvin Magalaner adroitly sums up the significance of both: ''When the mother thus presents her daughter with her own party hat in typical coronation fashion, she is symbolically transferring to Laura the Sheridan heritage of snobbery, restricted social views, narrowness of vision—the garden party syndrome.'' Surely this is the case, although

Laura may not be aware of it. Hence here is an initiation that is true and subtle.

But the strong irony of this story results from the contrast between the way Laura sees herself and the way the reader is led to see her. Laura has very little—if any—insight, a fact made manifest throughout "The Garden Party." Her dealings with the workmen illustrate her lack of awareness: she sees them as "extraordinarily nice," apparently not realizing that their "niceness" is more than likely due to their roles as subordinates, mere hirelings. Laura does not even seem to realize that what to her is a delightful party is simply toil to the workmen. Self-absorbed and narcissistic, she takes the superficial at face value because both she and her perceptions lack depth. "She felt just like a work-girl" is stingingly ironic because the reader knows that Laura has absolutely no concept of the life of a work-girl, just as she has no idea of what lies behind the friendly veneer of the workmen. For her to imagine that she would "get on much better with men like these" rather than the "silly boys" who come to her parties is an indication of how little general comprehension and self-understanding she possesses.

The other obvious contrast in the story is between the gaiety on the top of the hill and the sorrow below. The death of a man intrudes upon Laura's affected sensibilities and she discusses the possibility of canceling the party, but, as we suspected, her conscience is easily assuaged (and by the symbolic hat, a distraction that serves to fix Laura permanently in her world). Nothing, positively nothing, is permitted to spoil the party; even the weather is described as "ideal"—a "perfect day for a garden-party."

In the Sheridan world, suffering and misery cannot take precedence over well-ordered but mundane social functions, and will not be allowed to interfere. Consequently, Laura, with uncommon self-centeredness, blots out the death of a common man until a more convenient time: "I'll remember it again after the party's over, she decided." But even then, for her to realize that she is actually going to the house of the dead man is difficult because "kisses, voices, tinkling spoons, laughter, the smell of crushed grass were somehow inside her. She had no room for anything else." Unmistakably she has room for little else than parties, and the closer she comes to the house of the dead man the more she realizes her mistake, for here is a reality she does not want to face: it is so much easier to commiserate

from the top of the hill—and then to go on with one's fun. When she actually views the dead man, she can see him only as she sees death, as something remote, far, far away. (In addition, she has no more understanding of why she is there than does the dead man's wife.) Death is so removed from Laura's insular life that it is unreal; it cannot really be experienced, much less coped with, so she sees it as she sees everything else, as something marvelous and beautiful. Just as Laura is unable to pierce the facade of the workmen, she is equally unable to see beyond the face of death, the stark reality of which is transformed into dream, and she sees the dead man as sleeping, happy, content.

Any initiation into the mystery of life and death is incomplete, whereas the installation of Laura into the Sheridan tradition is certain. That Katherine Mansfield could present two types of initiation, one profound and the other shallow, is a tribute to her consummate skill: the fact that the protagonist opts for the shallow in no way detracts from her art but serves to increase the poignancy of her tale and to mark its realism.

Laura is not without sensitivity, but her sensitivity is subordinated to the comforts and trappings of the Sheridan way of life. She is young and inexperienced, and she has been shielded from the harsher aspects of existence. Even after facing the reality of death, however, she is unable to view it realistically and transforms it into a dream, into something wonderful and happy, something that will fit into the tableau of her resplendent world. The ironic tone has been too clearly established for the reader to take Laura's encounter as profoundly affecting. In this regard, "The Garden Party" asserts itself as not just another story of the loss of innocence, but an alteration of a mythic pattern.

The intimations of mortality are only vaguely perceived, and the story closes on a final note of irony: Laura apparently thinks that she has discovered something new about life, not an awesome truth, but something deep and ineffable, something she attempts to explain to her brother, but cannot. Unlike the emperor Augustus, who would sometimes say to his Senate, "Words fail me, my Lords; nothing I can utter could possibly indicate the depth of my feelings," Laura seems more confused than moved, and her inability to articulate her feelings to her brother is a result of her failure to understand, her inability to grasp the full significance of what she has witnessed. "No matter. He quite understood." That is, he understood as much as Laura.

They both will in all likelihood remain in the refuge of their bright house on the hill and continue giving expensive, gay parties and toying with the surface of things until the petals of their own lives are closed.

Source: Ben Satterfield, "Irony in 'The Garden Party,'" in *Ball State University Forum*, Vol. XXIII, No. 1, Winter, 1982, pp. 68–70.

Clare Hanson and Andrew Gurr

In the following excerpt, Hanson and Gurr explore issues of class conflict in "The Garden Party."

Into her narrative, Katherine Mansfield weaves a series of contrasts and parallels which unobtrusively carry forward her theme at the same time as they unify the different elements of the story. "The Garden Party" is a great story and a complex one because in it . . . we are presented simultaneously with several distinct yet interlocking levels of meaning. There is the social meaning provided by the real-life framework; the emotional and psychological overtones of the events in which Laura plays a central part; and the broader, philosophical significance of the total experience Katherine Mansfield lays before us.

The fact that the rich can avoid (or attempt to avoid) the unpleasant realities of human existence, even summon up beauty and elegance at will, is conveyed in the very first paragraph of the story. This opening paragraph is redolent of the fullness and richness of life, indeed of birth, since the rose bushes are bowed down as if "visited by archangels" in the night. At the same time, there is an unreal, artificial quality to this beauty which the personification of the roses underlines. And so the scene is set for the contrast which is integral to the patterning of the narrative: the contrast between the essentially artificial, almost unreal world of the Sheridans and the quite different but real world of the Scotts. While the Sheridans' money brings them life in its fullness, the Scotts' lack of money confers on them only hardship and death.

The world of the Scotts dominates the ending of the story, the world of the Sheridans the first part. Rich and poor alike have their social rituals, and the ritual being celebrated by the Sheridans is the garden party, which at once allows them to display their wealth and fulfill the obligations of hospitality. Convention governs the attitudes, the behaviour and even the voices of the Sheridan women. Laura's conscious attempt to copy her mother's voice, fol-

> **Emphasising the gulf between the rich and the poor is the descriptive language of the story."**

lowed by her realisation that she sounds "so fearfully affected," indicates the artificiality of the Sheridan manner of talking. Laura, who despises "stupid conventions," cannot act a role; but her mother and sisters do. Jose, for example, delights in the artificial. She loves "giving orders to the servants" and making them feel that "they were taking part in some drama." Emotion is something she simulates but does not feel. Practising her song, "This Life is *Wee*-ary, / Hope comes to Die," Jose sings of a tragic feeling only to break into a "brilliant, dreadfully unsympathetic smile." Behaviour is learned, not something spontaneous, in this sheltered world of wealth; and the Sheridan reaction to events taking place outside the family circle is dictated by what is expected. Thus Laura's instinctive feeling that the garden party should be cancelled because a death is being mourned nearby is rejected by her mother and sister in virtually identical words. Jose tells Laura, "nobody expects us to," and this is echoed by Mrs Sheridan: "People like that don't expect sacrifices from us."

It is principally through Laura's perceptions that we glimpse the quite different world of the workmen. The distinguishing characteristic of these ordinary people is their naturalness and spontaneity. Whereas feelings are assumed, disguised, or restrained by the Sheridan women, they are expressed freely by the working class. Instinctively, Laura is attracted to the warmth and friendliness of the working men who come to erect the marquee; and the sensitivity shown by the man who smells a sprig of lavender makes her compare these men and the boys of her own social class. "How many men that she knew would have done such a thing," she thinks. "Why couldn't she have workmen for friends rather than the silly boys she danced with and who came to Sunday night supper?" Laura is searching for an identity of her own when she inwardly voices her dislike of the "absurd class distinctions" and "stupid conventions" which pervade the Sheridan world and prevent her from having friendships with such men. She tries to legitimise her attraction to the workmen by pretending to be "just like a work-girl." But the class barriers cannot be broken down, and it is with her brother, Laurie, that she shares her own warmth. "Suddenly she couldn't stop herself. She ran at Laurie and gave him a small, quick squeeze." Responding in a "warm, boyish voice," Laurie echoes the warm voices of the workmen.

Tension in the story is generated by the underlying conflict between Laura, who cannot fully accept the artificial Sheridan conventions, and her mother. Because she is close to the natural world, the girl empathises with the feelings of the working people who are themselves part of that world. With Laurie, Laura had explored the forbidden territory where "washerwomen lived in the lane. . . . It was disgusting and sordid. . . . But still one must go everywhere; one must see everything." If Laura is something of a rebel, out of tune with her mother and sisters because she needs to include knowledge of the real, outside world in her perception of life, she is also set apart because she is "the artistic one." So long as her imagination functions usefully in the context of the Sheridan life-style, all is well. But when she imaginatively experiences the horror of the working man's death and, forgetting the distinctions between the different social worlds, wants to stop the garden party, she is condemned as "extravagant."

Laura's inner division is central to the working out of "The Garden Party" On the one hand her naturalness draws her to find out about life as it is lived outside the confines of the Sheridan household; on the other her artistic temperament causes her not only to respond to beauty but to cast over it a special imaginative colouring. The world of illusion is as precious to her, although for different reasons, as it is to her mother and sisters. It seems to be Laura who feels that roses "understood that [they] are the only flowers that impress people at garden-parties," who registers the noise of the piano being moved as a "long, chuckling, absurd sound," who imagines that "little faint winds were playing chase" and that "two tiny spots of sun . . . [were] playing too." Knowingly, Mrs Sheridan appeals to the imaginative side of her daughter's personality when she cleverly distracts the girl by placing her own hat on her head. "I have never seen you look such a picture," she says admiringly. As Laura gazes at her own beauty in the mirror and decides to forget the death until after the party, the attractions of illusion triumph over the demands of reality. And for the duration of the party, illusion holds sway.

But the magical perfection of the garden party, indeed the whole story, is enclosed within a philosophic framework which reminds us that everything has its opposite. There is a hint of birth in the opening paragraph; in the final section death asserts its presence. In contrast to the frivolous party given by the Sheridans, the gathering at the Scotts' is for the funeral rite of death. Instead of the artificial drama enjoyed by Jose, a real-life drama must be endured in Saunders Lane. And, while sadness and deeply-felt emotion are kept at bay by the Sheridan women, the dead man's wife mourns, her face "puffed up, red, with swollen eyes and swollen lips."

Emphasising the gulf between the rich and the poor is the descriptive language of the story. Words such as "perfect," "delicious," "beautiful," "splendour," "radiant," "exquisite," "brilliant," "rapturous," "charming," "delightful," "stunning," convey the outward beauty of the Sheridans' life—and its artificiality. In striking contrast are words describing the working people and Saunders Lane: "haggard," "mean," "poverty-stricken," "revolting," "disgusting," "sordid," "crablike," "wretched." In the domain of the Sheridans, mutability can be warded off so long as the outwardly beautiful appearance of things is preserved. This unattainable ideal of permanence, or stasis, is symbolised by the word "picture." In their ordered perfection, the garden, the roses and the canna lilies resemble pictures. When Mrs Sheridan places her hat on Laura's head and says, "I have never seen you look such a picture," she is in effect framing the young girl's beauty, giving it the semblance of permanence. There is a different kind of picture which Laura briefly visualises: that of the poor woman in the lane and her dead husband. "But it all seemed blurred, unreal, like a picture in the newspaper."

Laura is the central character in "The Garden Party" from whose point of view the story is essentially told; and it is she who bridges the contrasting worlds of the Sheridans and the Scotts. Her personal dilemma is that she must reconcile a sympathetic understanding of the poor, and an awareness of reality, with an imaginative attachment to the almost unreal, magical beauty which sweetens the lives of the rich. Her ordeal comes at the end of the story when she must physically cross the boundaries between her house and Saunders Lane, and in doing so face up to that other, "blurred, unreal" picture. When she enters the cottage of the dead man, the story comes full circle. Just as she had done previously, the girl empathises emotionally with the working people and echoes their grief with a sob. Earlier in the day, her emotional identification with the workmen had been deflected towards her brother: again, it is Laurie who "put his arm round her shoulder. ''Don't cry'', he said in his warm, loving voice.'' Laurie, whose warmth links him with the workmen, helps his sister emotionally to transcend the barriers between the classes. The unchanging love of brother and sister, moreover, makes bearable the cruelty of life, the heartlessness of human beings, the ''Love that Changes'' of Jose's song, and the knowledge of mutability''; of the inevitable ending of a ''perfect afternoon,'' and the ending of life.

But the crucial philosophical problem in ''The Garden Party,'' the problem that Laura shares with all sensitive human beings, is how to encounter ugliness and death yet retain a personal vision of beauty and hope. In this closing scene, Katherine Mansfield contrives an answer. She brings together the contrasting pictures of beauty and ugliness in a picture whose beauty appears truly permanent, ''a marvel.'' The sister-in-law of the dead man tells Laura that '''e looks a picture''; and Laura, the artistic one, agrees that he is indeed ''wonderful, beautiful.'' Imaginatively, she is able to forget the suffering inflicted by his death and think only that, ''while they were laughing and while the band was playing, this marvel had come to the lane. ''In her writing, Katherine Mansfield, too, has come full circle. Nothing, in her youthful stories, tempered a young girl's initiation into the harshness of adult life. At the ending of ''The Garden Party'' she allows Laura to retain her illusions. If we are left with the uneasy feeling that she has let her character off too lightly, we nevertheless accept the emotional rightness of the ending. For there is a sense in which Katherine Mansfield has granted us, too, a reprieve; has assuaged both our guilt about social inequalities and our haunting anxiety about death.

Source: Clare Hanson and Andrew Gurr, ''The Stories 1921-22: Sierre and Paris,'' in *Katherine Mansfield*, St. Martin's Press, 1981, pp. 95-139.

Warren S. Walker

In the following essay, Walker examines the characterization and the conflict between characters in ''The Garden Party'' and concludes that the story's conclusion is vague and uncertain.

The most frequently anthologized of Katherine Mansfield's works, ''The Garden Party'' has long enjoyed a reputation for near-perfection in the art of the short story. Its characters are deftly drawn with quick Chekhovian strokes; its action moves along at a vigorous pace; its central situation, richly textured, suggests both antecedence and aftermath; its dialogue, especially the internal debate, is psychologically apt and convincing. And yet, for all its undeniable strength and beauty, ''The Garden Party,'' often leaves readers with a feeling of dissatisfaction, a vague sense that the story somehow does not realize its potential. The difficulty, I think, is a structural one: the conflict has a dual nature, only part of which is resolved effectively.

''The Garden Party'' is a story concerning the most common form of character development, if not the easiest to portray: the process of growing up. Viewing the changing reaction of the protagonist to an incident that threatens to upset an upper class social occasion, one is aware that throughout the whole story there is a groping toward maturity, and that at the end Laura is indeed more mature than she is at the opening. The incident is the accidental death of a relatively unknown man, but for Laura it brings the first real consciousness of the phenomenon of death. Shocked at first, she comes eventually to see life and death in a new perspective in which death is not as unlovely as she had imagined. One aspect of the conflict, then, and seemingly the more important one, is the struggle between fear of and acceptance of death. That death is different from what she had anticipated, that it is beautiful in one respect is the new awareness, and this, climaxing a story about a young person, can be considered a maturing experience.

But there is another aspect of the conflict that immediately engages the attention of the reader, one which is less fundamental but surely not unimportant: the clash of basic social attitudes represented by Laura and by her mother. This adds a dimension of irony to the story, for on the surface Laura attempts to ape her mother socially by taking charge of the arrangements for the party; she even affects the mannerisms of Mrs. Sheridan, ''copying her mother's voice'' when she first addresses the workmen and trying ''to look severe and even a bit shortsighted'' as she comes up to them. Beneath such trivia, however, there is a profound difference. The sensitivity of Laura for the suffering of others is set over against the callousness of Mrs. Sheridan, and the two attitudes struggle for dominance in the child's mind. What she strongly feels to be right is pronounced wrong by the person she imitates, and Laura wavers and is understandably perplexed. Open

> " Here at the climax of the story, then, a decisive stage has been reached in the respective struggles between two sets of opposing forces: 1) youthful fear of death vs. some kind of acceptance of death, and 2) Laura's social attitude vs. her mother's."

hostility between the two forces breaks out over the propriety or impropriety of going ahead with plans for the party after it is learned that a near neighbor has been killed. Laura insists that the noisy affair—a band has been employed for the event—must be cancelled. The mother, at first amused ("She refused to take Laura seriously"), finally loses all patience with her daughter. Mrs. Sheridan implies that Laura is being immature and calls her "child" in the argument that ensues. Here, then, is another criterion for maturity, one in the realm of human rather than cosmic considerations.

Whether it is maturity that is involved or something else, the reader, from the opening paragraphs, identifies himself with Laura, is sympathetic toward her point of view, and is himself antagonized by the values of Mrs. Sheridan. This is true even before the accidental death of Scott, a carter, brings the issue to a crisis. When, for example, Laura realizes that laborers are really fine people after all and remarks, in the internal dialogue, on their "friendliness" and on the "stupid conventions" that have kept her from seeing this before, the reader is less amused at the ingenuousness of her observations than annoyed at the parents responsible for a social orientation that would make necessary such an elementary discovery. It is even more true when mother and daughter argue, and the reader's passive agreement with Laura's humane stand turns into empathic support. Mrs. Sheridan is hopelessly alienated from the reader, and everything she says makes her appear worse. In an attempt to soften the incontrovertible fact that one of the indigent cottagers is dead, she remarks, with heartless logic, "'I can't

understand how they keep alive in those poky little holes.'" In refutation of Laura's statement that the party should be postponed out of deference to the bereaved survivors, she says, "'People like that don't expect sacrifices from us.'" It is with no surprise that we learn that the Sheridan children have been brought up to scorn the cottages of the laborers:

> They were the greatest possible eyesores, and they had no right to be in that neighborhood at all. They were little mean dwellings painted a chocolate brown. In the garden patches there was nothing but cabbage stalks, sick hens, and tomato cans. The very smoke coming out of their chimneys was poverty-stricken. Little rags and shreds of smoke, so unlike the great silvery plumes that uncurled from the Sheridans' chimneys.

The Sheridans, who see this rural slum adjacent to their estate as "disgusting and sordid," apparently never make any effort to alleviate the condition of the wretches living there, or even to extend moral support to them. Laura, on the other hand, overcoming the snobbery of her upbringing, is acutely concerned about their feelings.

A resolution of this second aspect of the conflict seems to be suggested obliquely by the use made of hats—hats in general, and one hat in particular. Hats are used functionally in the plot and acquire symbolic value within the framework of the story as they come to represent the whole social milieu of the Sheridan class with its leisure, its conspicuous consumption, and its caste distinctions. In an opening scene, "Father and Laurie stood brushing their hats ready to go to the office." Immediately after this mention of male headwear, Mrs. Sheridan tells Laura to ask Kitty Maitland, with whom Laura is talking on the telephone, to be sure "'to wear to the party that sweet hat she had on last Sunday.'" When Laura is badly upset by the death of the carter, Mrs. Sheridan diverts her attention from the tragedy by giving her a bright jewel from her glittering social world, a "black hat trimmed with gold daisies and a long black velvet ribbon." Laura is thus enticed, for the time being, from her better feelings. One last spark of humane concern flares up that afternoon when Laura encounters her brother Laurie, home from work now. Perhaps Laurie, who of all the family is the only one who even begins to understand Laura, will agree with her on the undesirability of going on with the party. In her confused state she relies on Laurie to provide an ethical touchstone for testing the validity of her opinion.

She wanted to tell him. If Laurie agreed with the others, then it was bound to be all right. And she followed him into the hall.

"Laurie!"

"Hallo!" He was half-way upstairs, but when he turned round and saw Laura, he suddenly puffed out his cheeks and goggled his eyes at her. "My word, Laura! You look stunning," said Laurie. "What an absolutely topping hat!"

Laura said faintly "Is it?" and smiled up at Laurie, and didn't tell him after all.

Her last resistance overcome now, the spell of society is upon her, and Laura does not escape its influence throughout the ritual of the party.

She is the official hostess, according to plan, thus assuming the position the mother would ordinarily have held, welcoming guests, helping them solicitously to refreshments, and receiving their compliments—for her hat. Finally, the party over and the guests departed, the Sheridans sit down to rest, and Mr. Sheridan contributes to the conversation what he mistakenly thinks will be news to the family: the information about the carter's death. His wife, secretly exasperated at the necessity for renewing a debate she had thought won, rallies with "one of her brilliant ideas." Still completely unmoved by the plight of the widow and her five children, Mrs. Sheridan realizes that now Laura will have to be placated on the issue, and so she suggests that they gather up a basketful of the left-overs from the party and send them to the grieving family, much as one might pick out scraps for a pet sow that had hurt its foot. Laura, quite appropriately, is appalled to think that this is the best they can do for people in trouble, but she goes along with her mother's suggestion, the only concession she has been able to gain. She starts for the cottage of the deceased with the basket, and only when it is too late to turn back realizes how inappropriate is her hat, which by now has become an emblem of the mother and her hard-shelled world. "If only it was another hat!" she admonishes herself. Then comes the incident in the Scott cottage, during which Laura sees something quite peaceful and serene in death. But, significantly, the only thing she says to the dead man is "'Forgive my hat.'" She has not, it seems, succumbed permanently to the enchantment of her mother's world after all.

Here at the climax of the story, then, a decisive stage has been reached in the respective struggles between two sets of opposing forces: 1) youthful fear of death vs. some kind of acceptance of death, and 2) Laura's social attitude vs. her mother's.

There is no doubt about the resolution of the first issue:

> There lay a young man fast asleep. . . . He was given up to his dream. What did garden-parties and baskets and lace frocks matter to him? He was far from all those things. He was wonderful, beautiful. . . . All is well, said that sleeping face.

About the second part of the conflict, however, there is considerable doubt, for the problem is suddenly dropped, and no further reference is made to it. Does Laura now switch to her mother's view of the matter, and does she now feel that her previous concern about the cotter's family was as unwarranted as the fear of death that accompanied it? Or has her plea "Forgive my hat" indicated her irrevocable commitment to a position opposed to that of Mrs. Sheridan? If so, will she not now have to reorient her feelings toward her family? We never find out, for no hint of an answer to this dilemma is to be found in the conclusion.

To make matters still more vague at the end, in comes Laurie, who she thinks will understand her. He had failed to sense her difficulty before the party, however, when she had depended on him to do so, for he too had made the social genuflection to the sanctity of the hat. Now Laura hopes that he will grasp intuitively the feelings she is unable to articulate. But does he? The scene at the cottage was "wonderful, beautiful. . . . this marvel" to her, but Laurie seems to think that it must have been otherwise. "'Was it awful?'" he asks. And then a moment later when she says, "'Isn't life . . .'" (mysterious, or surprising, or something else), he answers, "'Isn't it, darling?'" Does he really understand what she is talking about? One wonders. One wonders whether he even understands the significance of the death to her; one is morally certain that he never suspects the inner turmoil she has undergone in defending to herself, as well as to the family, her benevolent sensibility.

Source: Warren S. Walker, "The Unresolved Conflict in 'The Garden Party,'" in *Modern Fiction Studies*, Vol. III, No. 4, Winter, 1957, pp. 354–58.

Sources

Fulbrook, Kate. "Late Fiction," in *Katherine Mansfield*, Harvester Press, 1986, pp. 86-128.

Hanson, Clare, and Andrew Gurr. "The Stories 1921-22: Sierre and Paris," in their *Katherine Mansfield*, New York: St. Martin's Press, 1981, pp. 95-139.

Iverson, Anders. "A Reading of Katherine Mansfield's 'The Garden Party,'" in *Orbis Litterarum*, Vol. 23, 1968, pp. 5-34.

Taylor, Donald S. "Crashing the Garden Party, I: A Dream—A Wakening," in *Modern Fiction Studies*, Vol. IV, No. 4, Winter, 1958-59, pp. 361-62.

Walker, Warren S. "The Unresolved Conflict in the 'The Garden Party,'" in *Modern Fiction Studies*, Vol. III, No. 4, Winter, 1957-58, pp. 354-58.

Weiss, Daniel A. "Crashing the Garden Party, II: The Garden Party of Proserpina," in *Modern Fiction Studies*, Vol. IV, No. 4, Winter, 1958-59, pp. 363-64.

Further Reading

Fulbrook, Kate. "Late Fiction," in *Katherine Mansfield*, Harvester Press, 1986, pp. 86-128.
In this feminist critique, Fulbrook argues that Mansfield satirizes female ignorance in "The Garden Party,"

and that she attacks the "inadequacy of education" that fosters such calloused social perceptions.

Iverson, Anders. "A Reading of Katherine Mansfield's 'The Garden Party,'" in *Orbis Litterarum*, Vol. 23, 1968, pp. 5-34.
Iversen looks at the symbolic and mythological structure of "The Garden Party." He examines the way in which the story can be read as an allegory.

Taylor, Donald S. "Crashing the Garden Party, I: A Dream—A Wakening," in *Modern Fiction Studies*, Vol. IV, No. 4, Winter, 1958-59, pp. 361-62.
Taylor views "The Garden Party" as a story of Laura Sheridan's awakening from the false dream-like world of her family and their garden parties to the world of labor, sorrow and death.

Weiss, Daniel A. "Crashing the Garden Party, II: The Garden Party of Proserpina," in *Modern Fiction Studies*, Vol. IV, No. 4, Winter, 1958-59, pp. 363-64.
Weiss likens Laura's experience to archetypal myths about initiation and awakening. He particularly compares Laura's journey to the cottager's houses to Proserpina's journey out of Pluto's underworld.

The Grand Inquisitor

Fyodor Dostoevsky

1880

"The Grand Inquisitor" was originally published as the fifth chapter of the fifth book of Dostoevsky's novel *The Brothers Karamazov*, his last and perhaps his greatest work. Dostoevsky died just months after the novel was published, and he did not live to see the peculiar situation of his novel's most famous chapter being excerpted as a short story—something he did not intend. A further peculiarity arises from the fact that the story is not excerpted the same way every time, so that whole paragraphs of the novel may be included or excluded from the short story, according to each editor's sense of how best to make the part seem like a whole.

The legend of the Grand Inquisitor is a story within a story. Jesus returns to Earth during the Spanish Inquisition and is arrested. The Grand Inquisitor visits him in his cell to tell him that he is no longer needed on Earth. The Church, which is now allied with the Devil, is better able than Jesus to give people what they need. The story has often been considered a statement of Dostoevsky's own doubts, which he wrestled with throughout his life.

Throughout the novel the themes of the legend are repeated and echoed by other characters and in other situations. Ivan explains some of what is to come before he tells the story, and he and Alyosha discuss the story when he is finished telling it. In the excerpted form, it is more difficult for readers to determine who is speaking, whose story it is, and how it is to be taken.

Author Biography

Fyodor Dostoevsky was born in Moscow, the capital of Russia, on October 20, 1821. The son of a Russian family of moderate privilege and wealth, he was highly educated and raised in the Russian Orthodox religion. His father was a doctor and a member of the aristocracy, and his mother's family belonged to the merchant class. They had a house in town and a country estate with more than one hundred servants. Dostoevsky wrote in Russian, which has a different alphabet than English. Hence, his name may be spelled in English as Dostoevsky, Dostoevski, Dostoyevsky, among others, due to inconsistent transliteration and translation. His works also appear in English translation with slightly varying titles. As a child, Dostoevsky was an avid reader who hoped to become a professional writer one day. His first novel, *Poor Folk* (1846), was well received by the critics. It tells a story about poverty and compassion through a series of letters, which makes it an example of an epistolary novel. His second novel, *The Double*, concerns the mental breakdown of a poor clerk. Although this novel received almost unanimously bad reviews, Dostoevsky had established a modest reputation in Russia's literary world and easily found publishers for his work. At the same time, he began to show symptoms of epilepsy and developed a gambling habit that plagued him for the rest of his life. Dostoevsky belonged to a literary group that secretly met to read and discuss social and political issues of certain writings that were forbidden by Russia's tsarist regime. In 1849 Dostoevsky and others were arrested. He spent four years at hard labor in a Siberian prison camp under terrible conditions. The next twenty years were turbulent ones, but he wrote some of his greatest works during this period, including the novels *Crime and Punishment* (1866), *The Idiot* (1868), and *The Possessed* (1872). Dostoevsky achieved some recognition in Russia for his talent, but he was forced to leave. He wandered around Europe for five years to escape his debts. Many of his works from this period explore ideas about religion, faith, and sin, which increasingly concerned him as he aged. In the last two years of his life he wrote *The Brothers Karamazov* (1879-80), from which "The Grand Inquisitor" is taken. Dostoevsky died of a lung hemorrhage on January 28, 1881. Over the next ten years, his reputation dwindled, but he eventually became famous at home and abroad. Throughout the Western world he is considered one of Russia's greatest writers and renowned for his psychological and philosophical insights.

Plot Summary

"The Grand Inquisitor" begins with a set of opening quotation marks. An unidentified speaker says, "Fifteen centuries have passed since He promised to come in His glory, fifteen centuries since His prophet wrote, 'Behold, I come quickly.'" The uppercase "H" in the word "He" is used conventionally to indicate that "He" is the Christian God; in this case it is Jesus Christ, as is made clear later in the sentence when the speaker refers to the "Son" and the "Father." The story, then, takes place fifteen centuries after Jesus walked on Earth. In the intervening time, according to the speaker, there was a period of great faith and miracles, and then a period in which people began to doubt the miracles and doubt their faith.

Some time in the sixteenth century, in Seville, Spain, Jesus returns to Earth. He arrives during the Spanish Inquisition, a time from 1478 until 1834 when, under the orders of the Roman Catholic Spanish monarchs, Jews and Muslims who had forcibly been converted to Christianity were questioned and, in many cases, sentenced to death for insincerity. The day before Jesus's appearance, almost one hundred had been rounded up, and "in the splendid *auto-da-fe* the wicked heretics were burnt." *Autos-da-fe* (literally, "acts of the faith") were carried out by the non-religious authorities of Spain after a religious authority had pronounced a sentence. In this case, the victims had been sentenced by "the cardinal, the Grand Inquisitor," and killed "in the presence of the king, the court, the knights, the cardinals, the most charming ladies of the court, and the whole population of Seville."

When Jesus appears, he is recognized immediately by the people, although he makes no demonstration other than "a gentle smile of infinite compassion." He passes through the crowd blessing and healing people, and raises a child from the dead. When the Grand Inquisitor sees how the people love and follow him, he has Jesus arrested and led away. The crowd makes no protest, but "bows down to the earth, like one man, before the old inquisitor." Jesus is thrown into a dark prison. That night, the Grand Inquisitor comes to ask him why he has come back, announcing that he will have Jesus burned at the stake "as the worst of heretics."

Up to this point in the story, the speaker has not been identified. Suddenly the narrative is interrupted. "'I don't quite understand, Ivan. What does it mean?' Alyosha, who had been listening in silence, said with a smile." Ivan and Alyosha are not introduced; readers of the novel would already know who they are, but readers of the short story are never told. Ivan, apparently the speaker, explains that it is irrelevant whether it is actually Jesus or not. What concerns him is the cardinal's speech, and his insistence that Jesus has no right to "add to what has been said of old" with any new works or words. Ivan's point is that the Roman Catholic Church has its power consolidated as things are. With the Pope in place as Jesus's representative on Earth, Jesus himself is irrelevant.

Nearly all the rest of the story is a long monologue by the Grand Inquisitor, while Jesus makes no reply. He explains that the Pope and the Church have assumed responsibility for the freedom of the people; the people believe they are free, but they are actually slaves to the Church. This is to the people's benefit, because they could never be happy if they truly had free will. Jesus should have known this. He should have learned it when he was tempted by Satan.

The Gospels of Luke and Matthew tell the story of Jesus's temptation in the desert. As he wandered in the wilderness, Satan tempted Jesus to turn stones into bread, to perform a miracle to prove his divinity, and to look to earthly authority. Jesus refused each request. Referring to this incident, the Grand Inquisitor argues that in the temptation the entire nature and history of mankind was foretold. Jesus's mistake was in choosing badly. Satan urged Jesus to use his power to turn stones into bread to feed his people. Jesus made the famous reply, "Man does not live by bread alone." He chose to turn people's attention to God instead of to material things, to heavenly bread instead of to earthly bread. The Grand Inquisitor says that this was a mistake, because hungry people have no free will. The Church has been able to control people by feeding them. If Jesus had worked this great miracle, the people's faith would not have wavered.

The Church offers people security and mystery, which is what all people crave. Most people are too weak to find salvation through faith alone, so they have turned away from Jesus and given their loyalty to the Church. The Church, in alliance with the

Fyodor Mikhailovich Dostoevsky

devil, has power and strength so long as it can keep the people in slavery. Jesus's coming again threatens to interrupt their power-building, and so Jesus must be burned at the stake. Actually, says the Grand Inquisitor, their way makes more people happy, since only the strong could be saved Jesus's way.

When the cardinal stops speaking, he waits for Jesus to reply, eager to answer Jesus's angry objections. Jesus says nothing, but approaches him and softly kisses him on the lips. The Grand Inquisitor shudders, then opens the cell door and says, "Go, and come no more . . . come not at all, never, never!" He leads Jesus out into the alley, and Jesus walks away.

Characters

Alyosha

Alyosha listens to Ivan reciting the legend of the Grand Inquisitor, and twice interrupts the narrative to ask questions. He speaks only eight sentences in the story—all questions—but gives Ivan and Dostoevsky opportunities to explain and interpret for the reader.

Media Adaptations

- ''The Grand Inquisitor'' has not been recorded as a separate story. However, the entire novel from which it is taken, *The Brothers Karamazov* has been recorded as read by Walter Covell. The novel on tape runs 42 hours, and can be purchased from Books on Tape, Inc.

The Cardinal

See The Grand Inquisitor

The Grand Inquisitor

The Grand Inquisitor, a ninety-year-old cardinal of the Roman Catholic Church during the sixteenth-century Spanish Inquisition in Seville, Spain, speaks most of the lines in the story. He is among the crowd of people to whom Jesus appears, and he sees Jesus raise a child from the dead. But the Grand Inquisitor's own influence is so great that when he makes his presence known to the crowd, they bow before him rather than to Jesus. The Inquisitor has Jesus arrested, and comes to visit him in his cell, where he delivers the long monologue of condemnation that makes up most of the story. His speech is dense, with long complex sentences and ideas, and he uses language that is formal and old-fashioned. When he finishes his diatribe, and receives only a kiss from Jesus in return, he is flustered. He does nothing in reply except release his prisoner.

Ivan

Ivan is the supposed author of the legend of the Grand Inquisitor, a story in poem form that he is reciting to Alyosha. When Alyosha occasionally breaks into the narration to ask questions, Ivan gives vague answers. He tells his brother that the meaning of the Grand Inquisitor's words is less important than the fact of them, and invites Alyosha to interpret them any way he can. He does comment that ''the most fundamental feature of Roman Catholicism'' is its static quality, its refusal to adapt and grow. In the novel *The Brothers Karamazov* and in

some versions of the short story, Ivan introduces his legend at some length, and comments on it afterward.

Jesus

Jesus does not speak at all throughout the story. He appears on Earth for reasons that are never explained. He moves through an adoring crowd, raises a dead child, and then is arrested by the Grand Inquisitor. He sits silently through the Grand Inquisitor's long speech, making eye contact and listening intently but not replying. When the speech is over, Jesus goes to his accuser and kisses him on the lips. The Grand Inquisitor opens the cell door and lets him out. Jesus goes away.

The Old Man

See The Grand Inquisitor

The Prisoner

See Jesus

Themes

God and Religion

The fundamental tension in ''The Grand Inquisitor'' is between God, in the form of Jesus, and religion, in the form of the Roman Catholic Church. According to the Grand Inquisitor, the two cannot coexist in the modern world; one must give way because they require different things from their followers. Jesus refused to make things easy for his followers. He could have given them bread when they were hungry in the desert and satisfied in one gesture their need for material comfort and their need to see miracles. But he refused, demanding instead that his followers believe on the strength of their faith alone, without any proof. God will not force people to believe in him, or to follow him. Each person must be free to choose her own path. This road to salvation, says the Grand Inquisitor, is appropriate only for the very strong. Ordinary people are too weak to find this satisfying, as he explains: ''Thou didst promise them the bread of Heaven, but . . . can it compare with earthly bread in the eyes of the weak, ever-sinful and ignoble race of men?''

People seek ''to worship what is established beyond dispute, so that all men would agree at once to worship it.'' This is the reason for religious wars: people demand that everyone believe as they do, and ''for the sake of common worship they've slain each other with the sword.'' In placing the freedom to choose above all else, God has permitted this misery. And yet, ''man is tormented by no greater anxiety than to find someone quickly to whom he can hand over the gift of freedom.'' In short, says the Inquisitor, God does not understand the true nature of human beings.

To fill that need, the Church has stepped in. The Church offers the mystery and the community that people need, and so it has joined forces with the devil to deceive people and take away their freedom. The Grand Inquisitor knows that he is in league with Satan, and he accepts the damnation that will be his in the end, because he is making people happy—something Jesus refused to do. The Inquisitor once followed Jesus, but ''I awakened and would not serve madness.''

Critics have debated about Jesus's silence in the face of these accusations, and wondered whether the Grand Inquisitor speaks for Ivan, and whether Ivan speaks for Dostoevsky. Does Jesus stand silent because he has no answer, or because he is God and need not answer? Is the kiss he gives to the cardinal a kiss of loving forgiveness, or one of thanks? Dostoevsky was an adherent of the Russian Orthodox faith, and believed that the Russian Orthodox Church allowed people to come closer to God because it does not have a Pope whose powers are handed down. Ivan tells Alyosha that it does not matter whether the man in the cell was really Jesus or not; what matters is that the cardinal thinks he is and that the cardinal says what he says. In other words, Jesus's response is not really the issue. What is important is what the Inquisitor's words reveal about the position of the Roman Catholic Church.

Within the novel as a whole, the theme of God and religion is addressed in different ways by different characters, and Ivan's position as a doubter is clear. As a short story, ''The Grand Inquisitor'' presents only one character, the cardinal, who believes that God and the Roman Catholic Church are at odds, and that people can follow only one of them.

Free Will

Throughout his life Dostoevsky used his writing to explore the issue of free will. He believed that human beings are given free will, and that they must constantly choose between good and evil. It is not an easy choice, and God and the devil battle each other for the possession of every soul. Dostoevsky was conscious of this struggle all his life. He wished

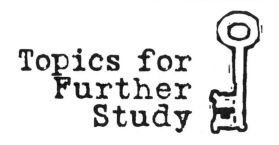

Topics for Further Study

- Look at the story of Jesus's temptation in the wilderness in either the Gospel of Luke (Luke 4:1-13) or the Gospel of Matthew (Matthew 4:1-11). Do you think the Grand Inquisitor is right in the way he interprets the significance of the temptations?

- Find out what you can about the Roman Catholic Church and the Russian Orthodox Church, especially their beliefs about earthly authority. Explain why Dostoevsky, an ardent Russian Orthodox follower, might think that the Roman Catholic Church had joined forces with the devil.

- Investigate socialism, especially as it was understood in Europe in the late nineteenth century. Find out what kinds of specific programs and policies socialists worked for. Do you agree that socialism is concerned only with the people's material needs?

- Read about the Spanish Inquisition. Why might Dostoevsky have chosen to set his confrontation between Jesus and a Church official in this time and place?

to believe, yet his intellect kept raising doubts. For him, the question of free will was central to his understanding of humans and society.

As the Grand Inquisitor states it, Jesus was tempted to offer his followers aids to faith, and Jesus chose instead to insist on free will. Had he followed the devil's suggestions and given the people food, or miracles, or an earthly structure such as an organized religion, the people would not be choosing freely. The Inquisitor claims that people are too weak to make a free choice. As Edward Wasiolek in *Dostoevsky: The Major Fiction* states, for the Inquisitor ''it is not a question of *what man would like to be* but *what he is and can be*. He argues logically about the human condition as he sees it, as history has proven it, and he can see no place for free will if people are to be happy.''

The Grand Inquisitor takes the position that faith and religion are intellectual issues, that the truth can be reasoned with the brain. His strategy is to try to reason with God, to persuade him by rational argument. Jesus's response is to sit in silence, listening intently but not engaging in argument. For Jesus, the issues are not intellectual or provable, and happiness on earth is not the goal. As Wasiolek explains, "What he offers them is the same as what he demands of them. He asks them to rise above their natures, to make over their natures in his image, and they can do that only as he had done it: in loneliness, terror, and anxiety."

Free choice and free will are only free if there are no conditions on them. To demand proof, or miracles, or a secure structure—or even happiness—are to put conditions on the choice. Do not think, says Jesus. Choose to believe. This freedom is what Jesus offered, and it is what the Grand Inquisitor rejects.

Style

Narrator

Perhaps the most important thing to keep in mind when reading "The Grand Inquisitor" is that the long speech is spoken by a character in a novel. It should be obvious, but it is easy to forget, that this is not an argumentative essay by Dostoevsky, in which the ideas expressed can be traced directly back to the mind of the author. Rather, a fictional character named Ivan tells a story, and within that story another fictional character called the Grand Inquisitor says what *he* thinks about God and man. The fact that there are multiple levels of narration does not mean that the ideas expressed by the Grand Inquisitor are not Dostoevsky's; it simply means that they need not be.

For the first several pages, the reader of the short story does not know who is speaking. The narrator states that God has come to Earth to visit "holy men, martyrs and hermits," and quotes the Russian poet Fyodor Ivanovich Tyutchev (1803-1873) as an authority who will verify that God has wandered through Russia. The narrator himself steps forward to add his own weight to the claim: "And that veritably was so, I assure you." Still, the reader does not know who is speaking, or why a poet and an unnamed speaker should be accepted as authorities on the conduct of God.

A few times in the opening pages the narrator steps forward to address his audience and reveal his role as storyteller. "My story is laid in Spain," he says as he begins the action. Several lines later he again refers to his own discourse. "Everyone recognised him. That might be one of the best passages in the poem. I mean, why they recognised him." As it becomes increasingly clear, the speaker is not actually telling a story, but talking *about* a story that he has created, moving the narrator still another step further away from the reader and from Dostoevsky.

When Alyosha interrupts for the first time ("I don't understand, Ivan. What does it mean?"), he clouds the issue of narration further. Who is quoting Alyosha's questions and Ivan's answers? There is another level of narration between Dostoevsky and Ivan, a narrator telling the story of Ivan telling the story of the Grand Inquisitor.

Ivan makes it clear that certain plot elements of his story are still negotiable. He does not care, for example whether Alyosha believes that the man in the cell is really Jesus. He says, "If you like it to be a case of mistaken identity, let it be so. . . . Does it matter to us, after all, whether it was a mistake of identity or a wild fantasy?" For Ivan, the plot is just a structure, a reason for the Inquisitor to make his long speech: "All that matters is that the old man should speak out, should speak openly of what he has thought in silence for ninety years."

Through the device of multiple levels of narration, Dostoevsky accomplishes two things: he puts extra emphasis on the Grand Inquisitor's speech by demonstrating that the plot surrounding it is relatively unimportant, and he makes it clear that the speech is a piece of fiction created by a character. The reader's charge, then, is not only to evaluate the wisdom of foolishness of the Inquisitor's speech and Jesus's response, but also to examine the mind of Ivan, who created them.

Didacticism

Connected with the issue of narration in "The Grand Inquisitor" is the issue of didacticism. A piece of writing is said to be didactic when its primary purpose is to instruct, especially about religious, moral, or ethical matters. Although writing that is openly instructional has always been able to find readers, modern critics have tended to look down upon this kind of writing when they have found that the message or lesson being delivered is stronger than the artistic quality of the work.

The long speech delivered by the Grand Inquisitor is openly and solidly didactic. To put it another way, when the Inquisitor gives Jesus the catalog of his complaints, he is concerned with what he is saying, not with how he is saying it. He speaks formally, and eloquently, as is appropriate to his station as a cardinal in the Roman Catholic Church, but his concern is with message, not with form. His speech is not intended to raise questions, but to cut them off, and give answers.

As creator of the Inquisitor's speech, Ivan is somewhat didactic, but he is also concerned with form. He has created the story to help himself think through the issues of God and religion and free will, and although his character the Inquisitor speaks didactically, the fact of Jesus's silent response raises the question: Is the Grand Inquisitor right? The story is able to raise the question only because Ivan has worked hard on form; although the story is a fantasy, he has created believable characters. The Grand Inquisitor's focus is on his message, while Ivan's focus is on his character who is delivering a message.

Dostoevsky is one step further back. His hope is that the reader will look at Ivan and wonder, not "Is the Grand Inquisitor right?" but "What kind of a man would make up a story like this?" "The Grand Inquisitor" is a useful story for coming to understand didacticism, because it presents shades or degrees of it. The Grand Inquisitor represents didacticism in the purest form, the form that critics have rejected most strenuously. Dostoevsky represents an ideal writer who writes artistic fiction that raises open-ended questions about important issues. Ivan represents the writer in the middle, who is perhaps so concerned with his message that it threatens to overpower his artistry.

Historical Context

The Russian Empire
Russia in the 1860s and 1870s was in a great upheaval. Its ruler, Tsar Alexander II, had negotiated the end of the Crimean War in 1856, ending four years of conflict between Russia and an alliance comprising England, France, Sardinia and Turkey. Russia, at the time one of the greatest powers in Europe, had wanted to seize control of the Balkans and other territory that had been controlled by

Turkey, but had been stopped temporarily by Turkey and her allies. Although the war was over, the "Eastern Question" still loomed over the region, and Russia still wanted to acquire access to the Mediterranean Sea, and to expand the influence of the Russian Orthodox Church. As part of the settlement that ended the Crimean War, Turkey agreed to enhanced tolerance for Christians within its borders.

In 1861, Alexander began a series of dramatic social reforms. Until that year, about one third of the population of Russia were serfs, or indentured servants who worked for a landowner. They were not slaves, but not entirely free either. Dostoevsky's father had almost one hundred serfs attached to his country estate; they received accommodations and a share of the land's yield in exchange for manual labor. Alexander issued the Emancipation Edict of 1861, abolishing the system of serfdom, freeing all the serfs, and requiring landowners to make land available for the serfs to purchase. Alexander also weakened his own power, introducing *zemstvo*, a modest form of self-government similar to a local assembly. The *zemstvo* organized and controlled local institutions including health care and education, and elected representatives to a regional body.

These reforms led to chaos and confusion, as well as to real improvements in the lives of many people. As the former serfs struggled to succeed in the new political and economic climate, the wealthy and the educated minority protested the destabilization and the erosion of their own influence. Fearful of losing his own power, Alexander II grew more conservative, causing further confusion.

Dostoevsky and others believed that autocratic rule, or government by one tsar (also spelled czar), was necessary and right. They called for a return to the old system of an established peasant class, a single authority, and a central role for the Orthodox Church. By the end of the 1870s, repression had grown and had been countered with the formation of terrorist groups whose goal was the assassination of Alexander. In 1880, dynamite was exploded in the Winter Palace where Alexander was expected to be. Alexander was not harmed, but dozens of others were hurt, and ten guards were killed. Other attempts followed.

It was in this climate that *The Brothers Karamazov* was written and published. In *The Russian Dagger: Cold War in the Days of the Czars*, Virginia Cowles quotes Dostoevsky telling the edi-

Compare & Contrast

- **1870s:** Dostoevsky is part of a political movement in Russia calling for the establishment of a great Greek Orthodox Empire with Russia as its leader and Constantinople as its capital. Non-Orthodox Christians, particularly Roman Catholics, were considered heretics.

   1990s: After a serious decline during the middle of the twentieth century, the Russian Orthodox Church has regained its position as the most important of the Eastern Orthodox Churches. Since 1962, the Eastern Orthodox and Roman Catholic Churches have had free dialogue as equals.

- **1870s:** Socialism in Europe and in Russia calls for the collective or government ownership and management of the means of production and distribution of goods. Dostoevsky believes that socialism is concerned with bread rather than with God.

   1990s: Socialist parties are still influential in Western Europe, and still relatively unimportant in capitalist countries like the United States. In 1999, one member of the United States House of Representatives, Bernie Sanders of Vermont, is a Socialist.

- **1880:** The Friends of Russian Literature is divided between those who praise the poet Pushkin as a great Russian and European, and those who believe being Russian and being European are mutually exclusive. Dostoevsky gives a great speech declaring that Pushkin's genius was in being able to use the best of other nations, and reunites Russia's literary community.

   1990s: Debates about the meaning of national literature and ethnic literature continue. In the United States, some writers identify themselves as Anglo-American writers or African American or Native American, while others wonder whether the term ''American literature'' has any useful meaning.

---

tor of the Russian *Times* ''that tragedy was in the air. 'You said that there had been some clairvoyance in my *Brothers Karamazov* . . . Wait till you have the sequel . . . I shall make my pure Aliosha join the terrorists and kill the Czar.''' Two months later Alexander was assassinated in another explosion at the Palace. Two more repressive tsars followed before the Russian Revolution overthrew tsarist government in 1917.

Critical Overview

When *The Brothers Karamazov* was serialized in the *Russian Herald* in 1879 and 1880, it won high praise, and finally earned Dostoevsky enough to pay off his debts for the first time. He considered the novel his greatest work, and critics have generally echoed this sentiment over the past century and more. Although Dostoevsky died just a few months after the completion of the novel, at the height of his acclaim, his reputation in Russia declined in the generation after his death, and his international reputation had to wait decades to become established. *The Brothers Karamazov* was first translated into English by Constance Garnett in 1912; other translations have since been published. The first English publication of ''The Grand Inquisitor'' as a separate short story did not appear until the 1930s.

The story has tended to divide critics sharply. The first important English-language piece of criticism of ''The Grand Inquisitor'' was by the British writer D. H. Lawrence, who had read the novel twice previously. His ''Preface to Dostoevsky's *The Grand Inquisitor*'' (1930) in *Dostoevsky: A Collection of Critical Essays*, finds in the story a ''final and unanswerable criticism of Christ.'' The antithesis is the view expressed by Jacques Catteau

Inquisition headquarters and the church of Santa Maria Minerva.

in *Dostoevsky: New Perspectives*. Catteau claims that "Dostoevsky's indictment of his Grand Inquisitor would indeed seem grave and without appeal."

Lawrence argues that in the confrontation between Jesus and the Inquisitor, the Inquisitor is wise and intelligent. At the end of the story, Lawrence says, "Jesus kisses the Inquisitor: Thank you, you are right, wise old man!" Robert Belknap disagrees in *Modern Critical Views: Fyodor Dostoevsky*, calling the kiss "obviously a blessing; it burns in the Inquisitor's heart as holy things do in this novel. . . . Here, in a single kiss, the most absolute and most appealing part of the Grand Inquisitor's exploit becomes an empty, unnecessary gesture." William Leatherbarrow describes the kiss in *Fedor Dostoevsky* as a "kiss of forgiveness."

Lawrence's view that Dostoevsky uses the story to explain Jesus's failings is widely echoed by Russian critics, including Leo Shestov and V. Rozanov. Edward Wasiolek asserts that "we know that Lawrence's interpretation is not what Dostoevsky intended," but he finds some delight in the fact that "the revolt of so many distinguished readers against Dostoevsky's conscious intention is, whatever else, a testimony to the force and persuasiveness with which Dostoevsky was able to state the other case."

An interesting third possibility is offered by Robert Lord in *Dostoevsky: Essays and Perspective*. He writes that "Dostoevsky never intended the reader to select one or the other alternative," and continues, "Dostoevsky is continually hinting that solutions are to be resisted at all costs. There are mere temptations; like Christ's temptations in the wilderness, so aptly described by Ivan Karamazov's Grand Inquisitor."

In addition to highlighting the central critical question of the story, Lawrence's preface also introduces the central difficulty with criticism of the short story. Even critics who attempt to discuss only the legend of the Grand Inquisitor tend to do so in the context of the novel as a whole, or to bring in material from Dostoevsky's other works. Lawrence, for example, answers the question "Who is the grand Inquisitor?" with "it is Ivan himself." He continues, "Ivan is the greatest of the three brothers, pivotal. The passionate Dmitri and the inspired Alyosha are, at last, only offsets to Ivan." Comments like these are meaningless to readers who encounter "The Grand Inquisitor" as a separate story.

Ralph Matlaw, in an introduction in *Notes from Underground and The Grand Inquisitor*, an edition of the extracted story, saw his own project as in some ways doomed. "To lift it from its context is to distort its meaning, for it too is a highly revealing confession by a character and is elsewhere in the novel balanced by other confessions, statements, attitudes and actions. . . . 'The Grand Inquisitor' is a much richer and fuller episode when read in the novel than it can be here.'' But whether or not they believe the story can be removed from the novel successfully, critics have agreed that, as Bruce Ward stated in *Dostoevsky's Critique of the West* (1986), the legend ''can be regarded as the culmination . . . of his religious and political thought—his 'final statement' concerning the question of human order.'' Perhaps the sign of Dostoevsky's genius is that there is still room for intelligent readers to disagree about the meaning of that ''final statement.''

Criticism

Cynthia Bily

Bily teaches English at Adrian College in Adrian, Michigan. In this essay, she discusses the meanings of speech and silence in ''The Grand Inquisitor.''

The central conflict in ''The Grand Inquisitor'' is between the Inquisitor himself and his prisoner, Jesus. On the surface, it is a one-sided battle. The Inquisitor does literally all the talking, making accusation after accusation while Jesus refuses to defend himself. Perhaps ''refuses'' is the wrong word, for it implies a level of engagement that does not seem to be there. Jesus does not refuse to speak in his own defense; he simply does not do so. He sits in silence, he listens intently; no one says the Grand Inquisitor refuses to be silent. The two ''speak'' different languages, one of talk and one of action, one of thinking and one of knowing.

As Jesus walks on earth he encounters many who speak the Inquisitor's language, but he will not speak it. The contrast from the moment he appears is sharp. Jesus comes softly: ''He moves silently in their midst with a gentle smile of infinite compassion. The sun of love burns in his heart, light and power shine from his eyes, and their radiance, shed on the people, stirs their hearts with responsive love. He holds out His hands to them, blesses them, and a healing virtue comes from contact with him, even with His garments.'' The people around him do not move softly, but remarkably loudly. They ''sing and cry hosanna,'' ''the crowd shouts,'' ''the mother

of the dead child throws herself at His feet with a wail'' before she ''cries'' out. Jesus responds by uttering the only words he speaks in the entire story: ''He looks with compassion, and His lips once more softly pronounce, 'Maiden, arise!''''

How seemingly alike and yet how different when the Grand Inquisitor arrives on the scene. He too is silent, and he too gets a strong reaction from the crowd. He merely ''holds out his finger and bids the guard take him. And such is his power, so completely are the people cowed into submission and trembling obedience to him, that . . . in the midst of deathlike silence they lay hands on Him and lead Him away. The crowd instantly bows down to the earth . . . before the old inquisitor. He blesses the people in silence and passes on.'' Both Jesus and the Inquisitor move among the people and bless them in silence. But only Jesus's presence ''stirs their hearts with responsive love''; only his blessing yields ''a healing virtue.''

Of course, there is no great insight in concluding that Jesus is divine and the Inquisitor is not. The tension that I find interesting is in the uses both make of silence and speech. Jesus is a man of action. He does not ask the people for anything, he does not tell them anything, he simply walks among them smiling and touching. Is this all he has come for? Yes. He has come to demonstrate Christianity as a robust, active faith, not as an issue for logical debate. His only words, ''Maiden, arise,'' are the words that are the action, that work the miracle.

Although like the crowd he cannot help talking to Jesus himself, the Inquisitor at first welcomes Jesus's silence: ''Don't answer, be silent. What canst Thou say, indeed? I know too well what Thou wouldst say. And Thou has no right to add anything to what Thou hast said of old.'' The Inquisitor comes back to this point again, insisting that Jesus has no right to speak. It is an odd thing to insist, as Ivan points out, especially since Jesus shows no sign of wishing to say anything. It is the technique of a debater, and perhaps one who is not sure he is right.

After a while, Jesus begins to make the Inquisitor nervous. He interrupts his long monologue three times to draw attention to Jesus's silence. ''Were we right teaching them this? Speak!'' But Jesus does not reply. ''And why dost Thou look silently and searchingly at me with Thy mild eyes? Be angry.'' Again, no response. ''Who is most to

What Do I Read Next?

- Dostoevsky's *The Brothers Karamazov* (1879-80) is the novel from which "The Grand Inquisitor" is taken. A man is murdered, probably by one of his four sons. As the crime is solved, the novel explores the political and intellectual ideas being debated in nineteenth-century Russia. Several fine English translations are available.

- *The Double* (1846) is a short fantasy novel by Dostoevsky. When a poor civil servant is unable to win the hand of his employer's daughter, his double mysteriously appears and succeeds where he has failed.

- *Dostoevsky, His Life and Work* (1967) is a translation by Michael Minihan of Konstantin Mochulsky's critical biography. A solid and insightful critical biography, especially valuable for its coverage of the end of Dostoevsky's life.

- "Ward No. 6" (1892) is a short story by Anton Chekhov, perhaps the finest Russian short-story writer. A doctor who operates a mental hospital himself slips into alcoholism and mental illness. He holds long philosophical discussions with one of the patients, before his condition erodes to the point where the doctor becomes one of the inmates in his own hospital.

- Flannery O'Connor is an American fiction writer whose work often deals with the struggle to find God. Her collection *Everything That Rises Must Converge* (1965) contains some of her finest short stories.

---

blame for their not knowing [the value of complete submission]? Speak!'' Nothing. Within his speech the Inquisitor has already anticipated Jesus's reply which is no reply. He reminded Jesus that he did not "come down from the Cross when they shouted to Thee, mocking and reviling thee." As the Inquisitor knows, Jesus does not respond to verbal bullying. The Inquisitor also knows that he is not persuading his audience, he knows he is only trying to convince himself, but he cannot stop talking. With the crowd, with his inferiors, he can use silence as a tool of power, but with Jesus he is as weak and babbling as those he despises. There is no sense throughout the monologue that Jesus is cowering. Clearly his silence is a sign of power.

The word "babbling" is appropriate here, because it echoes a favorite image of the Inquisitor's: the tower of Babel. The Old Testament book of Genesis tells the story of Noah's descendants, who wandered until they came to Babylonia. Skilled at brickwork, they set to building a great tower, the highest structure ever made. God saw this structure as a sign of arrogance, and to punish the people he created the different languages so that the people could no longer speak to each other, thus preventing the completion of the tower. The Grand Inquisitor states that men need structures, and that they cannot help but create chaos and confusion. He does not understand why Jesus did not step in when he might "have prevented that new tower and have cut short the sufferings of men for a thousand years."

"By their fruits ye shall know them," says Jesus in the Gospel of Matthew, and the fruit of the Grand Inquisitor is speech. Even the name by which he is known, "Inquisitor," means one who inquires, one who asks questions and gets answers and hopes to find the truth in the words. Dostoevsky chose the Spanish Inquisition for his setting because the Inquisition demonstrates most clearly how language and speech can be used wrongly to serve the Faith. It is not simply that the Grand Inquisitor is saying the wrong things; the fact that he relies on argument at all in the presence of his Lord is a sign that he does not understand what faith is.

This is what Ivan means when he says that it does not matter whether the Inquisitor was truly speaking to Jesus or not. The Inquisitor reveals himself by the *fact* of speaking, of thinking that rationality and argumentative speech are the ways

> "Jesus asks his people to give up speech and logic because they do not need it, because he wants them to have real faith, not because they should not dare to speak."

to reach God. Ivan says, "All that matters is that the old man should speak out, should speak openly of what he has thought in silence for ninety years." The content of his speech is not important. "All that matters is that the old man should speak out."

Nicholas Berdyaev, who claims that Dostoevsky "has played a decisive part" in his spiritual life, points to the importance of Jesus's silence in his 1957 book : "Christ is a shadowy figure who says nothing all the time; efficacious religion does not explain itself, the principles of freedom cannot be expressed in words; but the principle of compulsion puts its case very freely indeed. In the end, truth springs from the contradictions in the ideas of the Grand Inquisitor, it stands out clearly among all the considerations that he marshals against it. He argues and persuades; he is a master of logic and he is single-mindedly set on the carrying-out of a definite plan; but our Lord's silence is stronger and more convincing."

The Grand Inquisitor demands silence from his subjects, and they comply. But God does not want his people to be "cowed into submission and trembling obedience." Jesus asks his people to give up speech and logic because they do not need it, because he wants them to have real faith, not because they should not dare to speak. Jesus is silent before the Grand Inquisitor, but it is not a silence born of fear like the crowd's silence, and the Inquisitor knows it. The message of Jesus is beyond and above language: believe. Don't talk about it, don't reason it out logically. Words can fail you; they can deceive you. Have faith.

When the Grand Inquisitor runs out of words, he is desperate for Jesus to reply, but "his silence weighed down upon him. He saw that the Prisoner had listened intently all the time, looking gently in his face, evidently not wishing to reply. The old man

longed for Him to say something, however bitter and terrible." He still wants Jesus to argue, to be angry. It is the only language he knows. But Jesus stays silent, the man of action not of speech. He stands and delivers that soft kiss, and earns an emotional, human response from the Inquisitor: the old man shudders. His long monologue has not affected Jesus at all, but he has been touched by the simple gesture.

The Grand Inquisitor condemns Jesus because he has not provided "miracle, mystery and authority," the three things people need in order to believe. But in fact Jesus has shown all three to the Inquisitor himself: miracle in raising the child from the dead, mystery in his silence which the Inquisitor cannot understand, and authority in kissing his accuser and walking away. By his speech and his inability to control it, the Inquisitor demonstrates that he is less than God, and that he does not have faith in God. By his control of speech, by his using it only to save the girl and not to condescend to argue with the Inquisitor, Jesus demonstrates his divine power and authority.

Source: Cynthia Bily, for *Short Stories for Students*, The Gale Group, 2000.

Bruce K. Ward

In the following excerpt, Ward discusses "The Grand Inquisitor" as Dostoevsky's exposition of the his final Western formula—"The Pope—the leader of communism"—through the three temptations of Jesus in the Wilderness.

Dostoyevsky presents his definitive elucidation of the final Western social formula in "The Grand Inquisitor." This short writing, considered by him to be the "culminating point" of *The Brothers Karamazov*, can be regarded as the culmination also of his religious and political thought—his "final statement" concerning the question of human order. The importance which he attached to his critique of the West is perhaps most conclusively established by the fact that his final statement about human order is also his final statement about the West. The thought about human order contained in "The Grand Inquisitor" is of universal import. But clearly, for Dostoyevsky, this thought is at least initially inseparable from the consideration of the meaning of Western civilization. It can hardly be an accident that the universal themes of this writing, which represent the distillation of years of Dostoyevsky's thought about the "mystery of man," are expressed by a Western character. The Grand

Inquisitor is, with minor exceptions, the only attempt at a portrayal of a non-Russian figure in Dostoyevsky's art. Dostoyevsky's willingness thus to risk the aesthetic effect of his "final statement" bears eloquent testimony to the significance which the question of the West held for him. Our concern with finding in "The Grand Inquisitor" an elucidation of the social formula—"The Pope—leader of communism"—will bring us inevitably into the presence of Dostoyevsky's timeless thought. The same concern, however, will determine the limits of our consideration of this thought, for this chapter does not pretend to plumb all the "fathomless depth" of "The Grand Inquisitor" which, as Nicholas Berdyaev maintains, has "never yet been properly explored."

The exposition of the final Western social formula is the primary concern of the Grand Inquisitor's monologue. Apart from this monologue, the only constituents of the writing itself are Ivan Karamazov's brief "literary introduction," and the silent figure of Christ. Ivan's authorship of "The Grand Inquisitor," and the presence within it of Christ, both serve to integrate it within *The Brothers Karamazov* as a whole. Yet although it thus points, on the one hand, to Ivan's "rebellion" against God and, on the other, to the Christian teachings of Father Zosima, "The Grand Inquisitor" can be approached, at least initially, as an independent writing. Ivan himself maintains that, with regard to the Inquisitor's monologue, "the only thing that matters is that the old man should speak out, that at last he does speak out and says aloud what he has been thinking in silence for ninety years." This assertion is made in response to Alyosha's question concerning the meaning of that silent presence to which the "old man" addresses himself, and it could serve equally as a response to the question of Ivan's own relation to "The Grand Inquisitor." It is my intention to heed Ivan's assertion by examining the Inquisitor's monologue first in isolation from the thought either of Ivan or of Father Zosima.

Before consideration of what is said in the monologue, note should be made of who, precisely, is speaking. The Grand Inquisitor, as Ivan points out in his "literary introduction," is a cardinal of the Roman Catholic Church in sixteenth-century Spain "during the most terrible time of the Inquisition, when fires were lighted every day throughout the land to the glory of God. . . ." He therefore embodies Roman Catholicism, not at the time of its apogee in the twelfth century, but at the time of its desperately militant attempt during the Counter-Reforma-

> **"** The modern state, moreover, in consciously founding itself solely on reason, is bound up with a science which holds out possibilities for the control of human and non-human nature beyond anything dreamt of in the past. For these reasons, the modern Western state must be regarded as the most effective instrument of social order that the world has yet seen."

tion to preserve itself by means of the Spanish sword. The Inquisitor, close to death at ninety years of age, stands near the end of Roman Catholic civilization in the West, and at the beginning of the modern quest for a new order. Though rooted in a particular time and place, the old man's vision extends in both directions to encompass the entire history of Western civilization, from the ancient Roman Empire to the new Rome which he anticipates after the fall of modern liberalism and socialism. "The Grand Inquisitor" is meant to be a teaching about Western civilization as a whole. And beyond this, it is meant to be a teaching about humanity as a whole, for the Inquisitor's fundamental concern is to articulate the social order which most closely corresponds to human nature. In this endeavour he looks to the history of the West for evidence of the truth of his teaching, and for an answer to the question of its realizability.

The Inquisitor sets his account of the best social order within the framework provided by the biblical account of Christ's temptation in the wilderness (Matthew 4:1–10). He claims that the "prodigious miracle" of the story of the three temptations lies in the fact that the questions posed in them should have appeared among men at all, particularly at such an early date in human history, for the posing of these questions evinces an insight into everything which is most fundamentally at issue in the problem of human order, an insight arrived at prior to the centuries of historical experience which have since borne it out:

> If it were possible to imagine, for the sake of argu-ment, that those three questions of the terrible spirit had been lost without leaving a trace in the books and that we had to rediscover, restore, and invent them afresh and that to do so we had to gather together all the wise men of the earth—rulers, high priests, schol-ars, philosophers, poets—and set them the task of devising and inventing three questions which would not only correspond to the magnitude of the occasion, but, in addition, express in three words, in three short human sentences, the whole future history of the world and of mankind, do you think that the entire wisdom of the earth, gathered together, could have invented anything equal in depth and force to the three questions which were actually put to you at the time by the wise and mighty spirit in the wilderness? From these questions alone, from the miracle of their ap-pearance, one can see that what one is dealing with here is not the human, transient mind, but an absolute and everlasting one. For in those three questions the whole future history of mankind is, as it were, antici-pated and combined in one whole and three images are presented in which all the insoluble historical . . . contradictions of human nature all over the world will meet.

The Inquisitor's social formula is founded on his own interpretation of, and response to, the three ''everlasting'' questions posed to Christ in the wilderness. To him, each question reveals a funda-mental truth about human nature—or, more precise-ly—a fundamental human need which is actually present in people and verifiable in their historical experience. The only order which can be considered final is that order which satisfies the three basic human needs articulated in the temptations.

The Inquisitor's elaboration of his social for-mula proceeds in terms of the three human needs revealed in the temptations. This elaboration, how-ever, assumes his recognition of one primal human need, which determines his interpretation of the others. Note must be taken of this chief need, or ''torment,'' of humanity which constitutes the uni-fying theme of the Inquisitor's discourse. This need, of ''every man individually and of mankind as a whole from the beginning of time,'' is the need for order itself. We have seen that in Dostoyevsky's thought the need for order is tantamount to the need for a religion, in the broadest and yet most literal meaning of a ''binding together.'' This teaching is reflected in the Inquisitor's assertion that ''man's universal and everlasting craving . . . can be summed

up in the words 'whom shall I worship?''' The need for religion inevitably becomes, according to the Inquisitor, the yearning for a common religion, for the existence of differing reverences casts doubt upon all of them:

> It is this need for *universal* worship that is the chief torment of every man individually and of mankind as a whole from the beginning of time. For the sake of that universal worship they have put each other to the sword. They have set up gods and called upon each other, 'Give up your gods and come and worship ours, or else death to you and to your gods!' And so it will be to the end of the world, even when the gods have vanished from the earth: they will prostrate them-selves before idols just the same.

According to the Inquisitor, the primal human yearning for order has never enjoyed complete and permanent satisfaction because the great movers of humankind have not been unanimous in according it the recognition it deserves. Throughout history the Caesars have been opposed by the Christs, who have placed freedom higher than the need for order. In their sanctioning of the free individual in separa-tion from the mass, the preachers of freedom (en-compassed symbolically for the Inquisitor in the figure of Christ) have repeatedly encouraged disor-der. The Inquisitor accuses these preachers of be-having as though they hated human beings and wished to mock them, or, at best, as though they were blithely indifferent to the most elementary facts of human life. Surely those who truly love human beings would recognize and make provision for the fact that they suffer from disorder as from a disease—a disease which they are too weak to endure for the sake of freedom.

The Inquisitor interprets the entire history of the West in terms of the struggle between the advocates of order and the advocates of freedom, between those who take human beings as they actually are and those who estimate them too high-ly. According to his interpretation, the ancient world was just within sight of success in its Herculean attempt at a permanent solution to the problem of order when it was undermined by Christ's affirma-tion of personal freedom. It had been the enormous accomplishment of Roman Catholicism to salvage what remained of the ancient order, and on this basis to re-integrate the isolated individual within a ''Chris-tian civilization'':

> ''Was it not you who said so often in those days, 'I shall make you free?' But now you have seen those 'free' men,'' the old man adds suddenly with a pensive smile. ''Yes, this business has cost us a great deal,'' he goes on, looking sternly at him, ''but we've completed it at last in your name. For fifteen centuries

we've been troubled by this freedom, but now it's over and done with for good.''

For fifteen centuries the West had been in fragments, but it had finally become whole again thanks to the Roman Catholic reconciliation of Rome with Christ. This wholeness, however, was to be of short duration. Turning towards the future, the Inquisitor anticipates with foreboding the dissolution of Roman Catholic order in the series of events being initiated in his own time by the ''dreadful new heresy'' which had arisen in the ''north of Germany.'' He does envisage, beyond this period of chaos, a renewed attempt at order; but he prophesies that this attempt will be futile unless and until the variants of liberal-socialist thought which will inform it give way before his social formula. Although he considers his formula to be the best for all human beings at all times, he clearly thinks that its actualization is most likely in the modern West, in the aftermath of the internecine struggle between bourgeois liberalism and political socialism. Addressing in the figure of Christ all the teachers of freedom, he nevertheless proposes his formula particularly in opposition to the Christ who is the ''great idealist'' of Geneva thought.

It is evident that the Inquisitor's social formula is founded, not only on the conviction of the primacy of the human need for order, but also on the conviction that the satisfaction of this need is incompatible with the affirmation of freedom. The dissonance of freedom and order is sounded throughout his discourse. However, it is important to recognize (as Alyosha does) that the Inquisitor's opposition of freedom to order stems from a particular understanding of freedom. For the Inquisitor, as for Geneva thought, the affirmation of freedom is synonymous with the affirmation of the individual as a separate ''conscious will,'' as an isolated being endowed with reason and will. Yet the Inquisitor does not share the Geneva hope that the separate individual can be re-integrated within the social union through the mediatory power of love. Because freedom and social cohesion are ultimately antithetical, freedom is an intolerable burden for humanity: ''nothing has ever been more unendurable to man and to human society than freedom! . . . I tell you man has no more agonizing anxiety than to find someone to whom he can hand over with all speed the gift of freedom with which the unhappy creature is born.'' The Inquisitor maintains that freedom, though intolerable, is a fact of life which cannot simply be abolished. It can, however, be transferred into the hands of a few rulers who will

exact from the majority of humanity absolute obedience in all things large and small, thereby granting them the order for which they yearn. A final solution to the problem of order is possible for the Inquisitor only on the basis of the positing of a radical inequality among human beings. Dostoyevsky has him state this inequality most explicitly in the rough notes for the novel: ''But the strengths of mankind are various. There are the strong and there are the weak.''

The Inquisitor's attribution to human beings of a fundamental need for order is therefore subject to a decisive qualification: there are those, inevitably a minority, who are strong enough to renounce the satisfaction of this need. The existence of two sorts of human beings can militate against order when the strong demand comparable strength from the weak, as did the ''great idealist,'' Jesus. But when the strong are also compassionate, then the most complete order becomes possible. The ''millions and scores of thousands of millions'' of the weak, anxious to surrender the conscious will which alienates them from the spontaneous life of complete social integration, will be able to place their freedom in the hands of the ''great and strong'' who consent to ''endure freedom and rule over them. . . .'' The appeal to an evident inequality along human beings by way of justifying the absolute rule of a minority of free individuals over the mass of humanity, who are equal only in their slavery and free only because they gratefully accept the assurance of their rulers that they are free, recalls Shigalyov's scientific reinterpretation of the Geneva idea. Unlike the taciturn Russian, however, the Spanish cardinal is more than willing to elaborate his formula for the only earthly paradise possible for human beings.

The First Temptation

The first temptation to which Christ was subjected is interpreted by the Inquisitor as follows:

> And do you see the stones in this parched and barren desert? Turn them into loaves, and mankind will run after you like a flock of sheep, grateful and obedient, though forever trembling with fear that you might withdraw your hand and they would no longer have your loaves. But you did not want to deprive man of freedom and rejected to offer, for, you thought, what sort of freedom is it if obedience is bought with loaves of bread?

The rejection of the loaves constitutes a rejection of the first, and most self-evident, of the three principal means whereby individuals can be relieved of their burdensome freedom—for in this first temptation is revealed the truth that the weak will give up the prerogative of individual freedom to those who assure them that this prerogative is merely a chimera, that the real concern of human life is the multiplication and satisfaction of natural needs. According to the Inquisitor, "heavenly bread"—synonymous with such notions as the right to "freedom," or "moral responsibility," or the "spiritual dimension" of human life—cannot compare in the eyes of the weak with "earthly bread." This preference has its source in the fundamental need of human beings for at least the minimum satisfaction of their natural inclinations, for the minimum protection from hunger, cold, and the numbing hopelessness of material poverty. Despite the obviousness of this need, its strength has repeatedly been underestimated by the preachers of heavenly bread. Yet can the offer of heavenly bread have any impact upon people who are subject to the tyranny of unsatisfied natural desires? This is the question posed in the first temptation.

Those strong enough for the most inflexible disciplining of their inclinations by the conscious will may perhaps be able to contemplate virtue while suffering the pangs of hunger; but there still remain the weak, "numerous as the sand of the sea," who cannot ignore their pain. According to the Inquisitor, it is terribly unjust to add to the suffering of the majority of humanity the additional burden of moral guilt because of their preference for earthly bread. The "great idealists" are all too quick to condemn precisely where they should show compassion. Those who love human beings with a genuine love will not condemn them for a yearning too strong to struggle against, but will attempt to alleviate their suffering by satisfying this yearning. The Inquisitor thus stands with those who declare: "Feed them first and then demand virtue of them!" The meaning of this declaration is elaborated by Dostoyevsky himself in a letter in which he discusses explicitly the first temptation:

> Rather than go to the ruined poor, who from hunger and oppression look more like beasts than like men, rather than go and start preaching to the hungry abstention from sins, humility, sexual chastity, wouldn't it be better to *feed* them first? . . . give them *food* to save them; give them a social structure so that they always have bread and order—and then speak to them of sin—Command then that henceforth the earth should bring forth without toil, instruct people in such science or instruct them in such an order, that their lives should henceforth be provided for. Is it possible not to believe that the greatest vices and misfortunes

of man have resulted from hunger, cold, poverty, and the impossible struggle for existence?

Those self-styled teachers of humanity who have evinced an apparent indifference to the enormous suffering which material poverty has inflicted and continues to inflict upon the vast majority of their fellow beings are accused by the Inquisitor of exhibiting a dire lack of commonsense, or worse, a reprehensible severity.

Although the first temptation discloses a truth which is "absolute and everlasting," it anticipates also the "future history of mankind," for the issue which it raises was to be especially predominant in a certain epoch of history. The Inquisitor, present at the barely discernible incipience of this epoch, foresees the full course of its development:

> You replied that man does not live by bread alone, but do you know that for the sake of that earthly bread the spirit of the earth will rise up against you and will join battle with you and conquer you, and all will follow him, crying 'Who is like this beast? He have given us fire from heaven!' Do you know that ages will pass and mankind will proclaim in its wisdom and science that there is no crime and, therefore, no sin, but that there are only hungry people. 'Feed them first and then demand virtue of them!'—that is what they will inscribe on their banner which they will raise against you and which will destroy your temple.

The historical epoch anticipated here is that of the modern West. The allusion to Prometheus (whom Marx regarded as "the foremost saint and martyr in the philosophical calendar") indicates perfectly the Inquisitor's understanding of the spirit of Western modernity as a rebellion against the insubstantial, otherworldly notion of heavenly bread on behalf of the tangible, earthly need of those who suffer here and now. The traditional Christianity which the Inquisitor himself represents must face the consequences of its failure to accord sufficient recognition to actual human suffering: "we shall again be persecuted and tortured. . . ." After tearing down the Roman Catholic "temple," the modern rebels will embark upon the construction of an alternative order: "A new building will rise where your temple stood, the dreadful Tower of Babel will rise up again. . . ."

The builders of the new Tower of Babel are not named, but in the letter previously quoted Dostoyevsky specifies the historical movement alluded to by the Inquisitor:

> Here is the first idea which was posed by the evil spirit to Christ. Contemporary socialism in Europe . . . sets

Christ aside and is first of all concerned with bread. It appeals to science and maintains that the cause of all human misfortune is poverty, the struggle for existence and an oppressive environment.

Socialism is thus specified as the most effective historical embodiment of the Promethean attempt to alleviate the suffering of the "millions, numerous as the sand of the sea" who hunger for the earthly bread which has been denied them. According to Dostoyevsky, the compassion of socialism for human suffering is combined with an understanding of suffering as ultimately material in origin, as the consequence of "poverty, the struggle for existence and an oppressive environment." Despite the apparent nobility of its intentions, then, socialism inevitably develops into a form of political materialism. The modern Western rebellion against Roman Catholic order in the name of earthly suffering culminates in the materialism of communism and its rival, bourgeois liberalism. The Inquisitor thus anticipates, not only the destruction of Roman Catholic order, but also the overcoming of the Geneva idea by the appeal to earthly bread.

The ultimate insufficiency of any order which fails to protect the mass of humanity from "hunger, cold, poverty, and the impossible struggle for existence" is painfully demonstrated for the Inquisitor in the imminent breakdown of Roman Catholic civilization. The future practical success of modern political materialism will constitute an indisputable lesson concerning the crucial place which material need occupies in human existence. The final triumph of socialism over its liberal rival will indicate that it has learned this lesson more thoroughly and has demonstrated a superior capacity for distributing bread equitably and efficiently. Nevertheless, in the face of the lesson concerning humanity's need for earthly bread, the Inquisitor reaffirms the primacy of the need for order and, evaluating socialism in terms of this need, he finds it deficient. He certainly does not deny that materialism is capable of functioning as a religion; indeed, he acknowledges that earthly bread may well be the most incontestable object of worship which can be offered to humanity. What could be more evident to the perception, and the inclination, of the masses than natural satisfactions? The meaning of earthly bread is obvious, and it enjoins no troublesome chastisement of natural inclination for the sake of some obscure "spiritual destiny." Rather than setting the conscious will against natural impulses, the religion of earthly bread encourages human beings to exercise the will only insofar as it serves these impulses. The consequent atrophying of the conscious will can only facilitate the overcoming of isolation and the individual's re-integration within the social unit.

Yet despite his acknowledgment of the primal appeal of earthly bread, the Inquisitor judges it to constitute an inferior idea of life, ultimately incapable of satisfying the human need for order. The futility of the modern attempt to found a new order on the universal satisfaction of material needs will finally become inescapably clear: "No science will give them bread so long as they remain free. . . . They will, at last, realize themselves that there cannot be enough freedom and bread for everybody, for they will never, never be able to let everyone have his fair share." Those who would give humanity "fire from heaven" will be compelled to recognize that the universal and fair distribution of bread will never be realized in a society which has not completely overcome individual freedom. For inevitably there will be those who, unwilling to attune their desires to the collective, will demand more than their "fair share" of life's goods. What could induce these more strongly desiring individuals to "make a sacrifice" for the whole? The inadequacy of political materialism is manifest for the Inquisitor in its inability to furnish a conclusive answer to this question. The socialist argument that competitive individualism is itself a product of the socio-economic environment is ultimately no more than wishful thinking. For the available evidence concerning the "always vicious and always ignoble race of man" does not encourage hope for a flowering of human goodness within a more "rational" environment.

The inability of socialism to secure the compliance of every conscious will in the social union necessarily implies the failure, not only to distribute bread effectively among human beings, but also to give them the order which they desire above all. The Inquisitor thus adds a significant qualification to his initial declaration that human obedience can be bought with bread. In summoning up the spectre of the rebellious individual against the new Tower of Babel, he asserts that any renunciation of individual freedom called forth by the need for material satisfaction can only be temporary. To assume that the alienated individual will be reconciled to the collective through a certain transformation of external material structures is to fail to penetrate to the roots of humanity's attachment to the conscious will. The builders of the modern Tower of Babel do not grasp the significance of human freedom, and will thus never be able to possess it. They will break their hearts "for a thousand years" with their tower, without being able to complete it.

For the Inquisitor, the truth of modern political materialism lies in its profound appreciation of the need for earthly bread. Its fatal error lies in its disregard of the continuing need for heavenly bread. Communism is correct in inscribing on its banner—"Feed them first and then demand virtue of them!"—but its tendency to concentrate on the first part of this slogan to the exclusion of the second betrays an incomplete understanding of human nature. Thus, while castigating the "great idealists" for their failure to heed the teaching about human order expressed in the first temptation, the Inquisitor nevertheless acknowledges the ultimate validity of their refusal to uphold earthly bread as humanity's highest end:

> With the bread you were given an incontestable banner: give him bread and man will worship you, for there is nothing more incontestable than bread; but if at the same time someone besides yourself should gain possession of his conscience—oh, then he will even throw away your bread and follow him who has ensnared his conscience. You were right about that. For the mystery of human life is not only in living, but in knowing why one lives. Without a clear idea of what to live for man will not consent to live and will rather destroy himself than remain on the earth, though he were surrounded by loaves of bread.

Earthly bread is necessary, but it is not sufficient, for the final solution to the problem of order. Human beings can be finally relieved of the burden of their freedom only if the distributors of the loaves satisfy another human need—the need for a "moral enticement." This need and the means by which it can be met are explicated in the course of the Inquisitor's interpretation of the second temptation.

The Second Temptation

"Man is born a rebel." According to the Inquisitor, the primary source of this "rebelliousness" is the insistence of human beings on regarding themselves as something more than the product of nature. The striving to transcend the limitations of natural necessity expresses itself particularly in the tendency to measure human existence against an ultimate good. In spinning its fine web of necessity around human beings, socialism forgets their insistent need to know that what is necessary can also be called "good." And if they cannot affirm the goodness of the order which provides them with bread, then they will finally reject this order and its bread, whatever the consequences for their natural wants. Against the modern Tower of Babel, then, the Inquisitor asserts the human propensity for making moral distinctions. Whether or not human beings are in truth entirely a product of chance and necessity, they are in fact beings who insist on perceiving themselves as something more. This tendency seems so deeply rooted as to be impervious to any amount of re-education according to the laws of "utility" and "necessity." Insofar as people tend, not only to make moral distinctions, but to insist on making these distinctions for themselves, their propensity for moral judgment is intimately associated with the assertion of the individual conscious will. The "conscious will" can thus be more precisely designated the *"conscience."* For the Inquisitor the personal conscience is the mainspring of human freedom. Those who understand human freedom as directed primarily towards natural, rather than moral, ends will never be able to possess it.

According to the Inquisitor, the personal conscience has been no less important than the desire for earthly bread in inspiring that rebelliousness which has undermined human order throughout history. The nearly complete order of antiquity was doomed when the individual began to reject the "strict ancient law" in order to "decide for himself with a free heart what is good and what is evil" (a movement associated above all with the names of Socrates and Jesus). The ensuing moral chaos had been alleviated by Roman Catholicism's massive effort to establish a solid morality which defined good and evil clearly for all. But the Inquisitor perceives, in the "dreadful new heresy" of Luther appearing in his own time, a renewed assertion of the personal conscience which can only issue in another epoch of moral chaos. He knows that the personal conscience will resist the threat of fire with which the Roman Catholic order vainly defends itself, and he knows that it will finally resist also the offer of earthly bread with which the builders of the modern Tower of Babel will attempt to tame it. These builders ignore at their peril the depth of the human attachment to the conscience. Like the yearning for material goods, this attachment is an "eternal problem" which centuries of historical experience have made impossible to ignore, at least for those who are genuinely and intelligently concerned with human happiness.

This "eternal problem" does admit of a solution, according to the Inquisitor. Despite his appreciation of the obduracy of the personal conscience, he insists still on the primacy of the human desire for order. His conviction that human beings ultimately wish to be induced to give up their freedom remains unshaken. For him, the proper estimation of the personal conscience is merely the prerequisite for capturing it: "whoever knows this mystery of mankind's existence knows how to go about subduing him, and who can, subdues him." The "mystery" of the conscience is that "there is nothing more alluring to man than . . . freedom of conscience"; at the same time, "there is nothing more tormenting, either." In this paradox resides the possibility of relieving human beings of their freedom.

According to the Inquisitor, human beings strive for an ultimate good only in order finally to attain to a condition of happy repose. When the longed-for tranquillity eludes them and the moral quest becomes a perpetual striving, then the personal conscience becomes a torment—particularly for the "thousands of millions" of the weak who lack the spiritual capacity to sustain the arduous struggle for final peace of mind. If there is indeed an ultimate end to the moral quest, surely knowledge of it will be vouchsafed only to the few thousand of the strong, who are more like gods than human beings. For the weak, the freedom of conscience which they find so alluring issues only in "unrest, confusion, and unhappiness. . . ." To the Inquisitor this is demonstrable from the historical experience of the West just as surely as is the tenacity with which humanity upholds the prerogative of the personal conscience. Gazing into a distant future in which the Protestant conscience has been translated through Geneva thought into the right of each individual to decide independently "with a free heart" what is good, the Inquisitor predicts that the mass of humanity will come to rue the day that simple acquiescence in the given morality of the Roman Catholic order was rejected:

> They will pay dearly for it. They will tear down the temples and drench the earth with blood. But they will realize at last, the foolish children, that although they are rebels, they are impotent rebels who are unable to keep up with their rebellion. Dissolving into foolish tears, they will admit at last that he who created them rebels must undoubtedly have meant to laugh at them.

The Inquisitor does not claim that individuals will cease to be moral beings, for the need to make moral judgments is too deeply rooted. He thinks, however, that in the aftermath of the trials in store for them, human beings could be persuaded to relinquish the right to make such judgments *for themselves*, "with a free heart." Yet the sacrifice of personal conscience, which the modern individual will be only too willing to make, will be merely temporary unless it is accepted by those with the knowledge to hold it "captive for ever."

According to the Inquisitor, this knowledge is disclosed in the second temptation. The temptation, properly interpreted, not only reveals that human beings will surrender their freedom only to those who can fully appease their conscience, but reveals also the most effective means of appeasement:

> There are three forces, the only three forces that are able to conquer and hold captive for ever the conscience of those weak rebels for their own happiness—these forces are: miracle, mystery, and authority. You rejected all three and yourself set the example for doing so. When the wise and terrible spirit set you on a pinnacle of the temple and said to you: 'If thou be the son of God, cast thyself down: for it is written, He shall give his angels charge concerning thee: and in their hands they shall bear thee up. . . .'

The "rebels" have to be taught that the question of good is a "mystery" which must be believed rather than known, that it is not the "free verdict of their hearts nor love that matters, but the mystery which they must obey blindly, even against their conscience." Remembering the "horrors of slavery and confusion" to which a "free mind" brought them, they will gratefully accept the assurance that the ultimate good is inaccessible to human knowledge. The "authority" of those who preach the "mystery" will be confirmed, above all, by "miracles," or the appearance of miracles, for when freedom of conscience becomes too agonizing "what man seeks is not so much God as miracles." Human beings are ultimately unable to carry on without a miracle, so much so that even in the modern age which has banished miracles they will find new miracles for themselves and will worship the pseudo-miracles of the modern "witch-doctor."

The Inquisitor maintains that in Western history the preaching of "miracle, mystery, and authority" has come within the special province of the Roman Catholic Church. And he foresees no serious rival arising to contend with the traditional supremacy of Roman Catholicism in this matter. It would thus appear that when modern people begin to yearn for "miracle, mystery, and authority," they will have no choice but to return to that morality which they have spurned with such cavalier disregard for their own happiness. The Roman Catholic Church may again be compelled to hide itself in the catacombs; but the Inquisitor thinks it possible that the day will come when it will be sought out in its hiding place and asked to renew its possession of the human conscience. This time will come when humanity's striving after knowledge of good and evil becomes completely transformed into the directionless striving after knowledge for its own sake which is characteristic of modern science:

> Freedom, a free mind and science will lead them into such a jungle and bring them face to face with such marvels and insoluble mysteries that some of them, the recalcitrant and the fierce, will destroy themselves, others, recalcitrant but weak, will destroy one another, and the rest, weak and unhappy, will come crawling to our feet and cry aloud: 'Yes, you were right, you alone possessed his mystery, and we come back to you—save us from ourselves!'

The Inquisitor's social formula is based on his interpretation of the first two temptations. It can therefore now be stated in the following way: those who would rule over humanity for its happiness must be both distributors of "loaves" and preachers of "miracle, mystery, and authority." Properly interpreted, and regarded in the light of historical experience, the first two temptations reveal that people will ultimately consent only to an order which provides them with both earthly and heavenly bread. Only to rulers who simultaneously satisfy their physical and moral appetites will people relinquish forever their freedom for the sake of that social re-integration which is their most fundamental desire. Because it is based on two "eternal" or "everlasting" truths about human nature, the Inquisitor's social formula applies to human beings everywhere and always.

The very timelessness of the Inquisitor's formula, however, must inevitably render it more or less "abstract," despite his citing of concrete historical evidence for its validity. Yet "abstractness" implies a certain dissociation of theory and practice which the Inquisitor, of all people, must not admit. For he is concerned with the *actual* happiness of human beings, a concern which leads him to refuse to ask too much of them and to found his social formula on human beings as they actually *are* rather than as they *ought* to be. The Inquisitor cannot remain content with a teaching which is the best in theory, though it may never be realized in practice. For him, this would be equivalent to siding with the "great idealists," who do not love humanity sufficiently. His entire enterprise requires that his social formula be realizable. The confident assurance with which he does anticipate the realization of his formula has its source in his interpretation of the third temptation.

The Third Temptation

The third and last "torment" of humanity is the need for "universal unity," for the union of all in a "common, harmonious, and incontestable ant-

hill. . . ." The Inquisitor avers that the human yearning for order will not be satisfied by the idea alone of an ultimate good, even when this idea is provided in conjunction with earthly bread, for human beings need also to give a practical living expression to the object of their belief, and they need to do so in unity with others. The unity sought is ultimately universal, for the co-existence of differing ideas of life tends to undermine the certainty of those who live by them. For the Inquisitor the human need for a universal order is not to be satisfied by the appeal (which Christianity, for instance, has made) to a universality which is "spiritual" in nature. The universality for which humanity has always yearned is a visible universality; therefore, in the Inquisitor's thinking, "universal" is synonymous with "world-wide" (or "ecumenic," as first defined by the Roman historian, Polybius). According to the Inquisitor, then, human beings require an actual world-wide social order corresponding to the "miracle, mystery, and authority" which they obey—an order, moreover, which grants them at least the minimal satisfaction of their material wants. This is to say that human beings will ultimately settle for nothing less than the realization, not merely in a dream but in actuality, of the Inquisitor's social formula.

The Inquisitor interprets the offer of the "kingdoms of the world" in the third temptation as the offer of the most powerful instrument for satisfying the human need for universal unity—the universal state. The universal state is the prime vehicle for the actualization of the social order ruled by keepers of humanity's conscience who are also distributors of its bread. History for the Inquisitor is important chiefly as the realm of the appearance and progressive development of this vehicle. (Indeed, his ecstatic certainty concerning the future realization of his final solution to the problem of order makes his view of history reminiscent of that modern Western "philosophy of history" developed from Vico to Marx.)

According to the Inquisitor, the dawn of history coincides with the first tentative efforts towards the construction of a universal order. The persistence with which human beings have moved towards the universal state, even in its most rudimentary form, reflects at least a half-conscious awareness of its importance for their happiness:

> Mankind as a whole has always striven to organize itself into a world state. There have been many great nations with great histories, but the more highly developed they were, the more unhappy they were, for

they were more acutely conscious of the need for the world-wide union of men. The great conquerors, the Timurs and Genghis Khans, swept like a whirl-wind over the earth, striving to conquer the world, but, though unconsciously, they expressed the same great need of mankind for a universal and world-wide union.

The work of the Timurs and the Genghis Khans is a striking manifestation of the human impulse towards the universal state; but, in them, this impulse remained merely unconscious, and hence failed to bear fruit. The conscious aspiration towards the construction of the universal state first appeared in the ecumenic empires of Persia, Macedon, and Rome. The Inquisitor focuses upon the last as the culmination of ancient humanity's striving for universal unity.

Humanity had possessed, in the Roman Empire, a splendid and apparently "eternal" instrument for its happiness. Yet just when it seemed that the human struggle towards order had achieved final success, Rome was undermined by the rebellion of the personal conscience, which found its most effective vehicle in Christianity. Despite its aura of finality, the Roman state had failed to understand properly the moral dimension of human life. This failure condemned humanity to a thousand years of the disease of disorder. The external political and legal structures of Rome proved extraordinarily durable, however, even after the life had gone out of them; the "sword of Caesar" remained at hand for the use of new architects of world-wide order. In its attempt to have Christianity serve order rather than disorder, the Western church did not spurn this sword, and the accommodation which it reached with the remnants of the Roman state gave birth to that Roman Catholic order which was to define Western civilization for centuries. Although it evinced a more profound appreciation of the need for heavenly bread, Roman Catholic order was also to be finally undermined by the assertiveness of the personal conscience, and also by the attempt to alleviate the sufferings of material deprivation. But in its rejection of Roman Catholic civilization, the modern West has not repudiated the "sword of Caesar"; indeed, it apotheosizes the state—still fundamentally the universal state of Rome—and opposes it to any other instrument of human order. Because of its wholehearted adoption of the state, the modern West tends to overcome the divergence of loyalties once rendered inevitable by the uneasy compromise achieved in the Middle Ages between the Roman church and the Roman state. The modern state, moreover, in consciously founding itself solely on reason, is bound up with a science which

holds out possibilities for the control of human and non-human nature beyond anything dreamt of in the past. For these reasons, the modern Western state must be regarded as the most effective instrument of social order that the world has yet seen. The "sword of Caesar" could prove, in its modern embodiment, to be more powerful than it ever was in ancient Rome or in medieval Europe. But who will wield this formidable instrument?

As we have already noted, the Inquisitor predicts that it is socialism which will finally inherit Caesar's sword. We have also noted, however, his expectation that the triumph of socialism will be short-lived unless it can offer humanity something more than earthly bread. Among the socialists there will be those sufficiently "scientific" to realize that the full compliance of the individual in the socialist order will require a "moral enticement." In order to preserve itself, socialism will at last be compelled to seek out preachers of "miracle, mystery, and authority." The Inquisitor thus foresees that the socialist state, following those driven to despair by the "jungle" into which freedom of conscience has led them, will turn to the Roman Catholic Church as the most practised adept in the realm of "miracle, mystery, and authority." This time, however, the alliance between church and state will be more complete than the compromise of the past allowed. The two will enter into the indivisible union expressed in the formula—"The Pope—leader of communism"—which is the outward historical expression of the Inquisitor's social theory. When socialism surrenders its highly organized system for the satisfaction of material needs into the hands of Roman Catholicism, then the keepers of humanity's conscience will also be the distributors of its bread. The problem of social order will be at last solved in actuality. Human beings will finally come into possession of that yearned-for earthly paradise which has always eluded them:

> And then we shall finish building their tower . . . and we alone shall feed them in your name . . . the flock will be gathered together again and will submit once more, and this time it will be for good. Then we shall give them quiet, humble happiness, the happiness of weak creatures, such as they were created. . . . They will grow timid and begin looking up to us and cling to us in fear as chicks to the hen. They will marvel at us and be terrified of us and be proud that we are so mighty and so wise as to be able to tame such a turbulent flock of thousands of millions. They will be helpless and in constant fear of our wrath, their minds will grow timid, their eyes will always be shedding tears like women and children, but at the slightest sign from us they will be just as ready to pass to mirth and

laughter, to bright-eyed gladness and happy childish song. . . . And they will have no secrets from us. . . . The most tormenting secrets of their conscience— everything, everything they will bring to us, and we shall give them our decision for it all. . . . And they will all be happy, all the millions of creatures, except the hundred thousand who rule over them. . . .

Source: Bruce K. Ward, ''The Final Western Social Formula,'' in *Dostoyevsky's Critique of the West: The Quest for the Earthly Paradise*, Wilfred Laurier University Press, 1986, pp. 101–134.

Temira Pachmuss

In the following essay, Pachmuss discusses Dostoevsky's concept of the dual heavenly and earthly nature of humankind as it is reflected in the Grand Inquisitor's three reproaches against Christ.

In Seeking To Reveal the tragedy of man as a dual being, Dostoevsky portrays the abnormal states of the psyche, all phenomena of which he considers manifestations of higher metaphysical realities. And an understanding of Dostoevsky's metaphysics of evil is necessary for one to discern the primal tragedy, which comes to the fore in his more mature works, particularly *The Brothers Karamazov,* where evil is expressed both in metaphysical and psychological terms. ''The Legend of the Grand Inquisitor,'' an expression of Ivan Karamazov's rebellion against God, stands in close connection with Dostoevsky's earlier writings, for it discloses more of the concept of duality which underlies the works previously examined. It reflects Dostoevsky's lifelong study of man as a ''mixture of the heavenly and the earthly,'' the problem which tormented his mind even when he was at the Military Engineers' Academy.

After the portrayal of man with inherent egocentricity, vanity, and other facets of his creaturely being, Dostoevsky arranges a trial, as it were, at which the Grand Inquisitor points out to Christ that God created man as the least perfect of all creatures. He burdened man with an animal being and so condemned him to continual suffering. The Grand Inquisitor appears as the defense counsel for man, the victim of God, Who has endowed him with a dual nature which man is too weak to bear with dignity. He elaborates his defense by showing that in most cases man either becomes a prey to his creaturely being or revolts against God. In neither of these instances does man strive for spiritual and moral perfection as should a creature made in the divine image. In the name of mankind, the Grand Inquisitor brings against Christ three charges. First of all, he states, man has earthly needs and a natural impulse to satisfy them. Man's freedom of spirit and the exercise of his will are impeded by these natural needs. How is it possible, the Grand Inquisitor asks, to reproach man with his efforts to maintain natural existence, an existence which requires, first and foremost, that his hunger be allayed? He rebukes Christ that He did not take from men the worry over their daily bread. As freedom of spirit can scarcely be reconciled with the natural needs of human beings, they abandon this freedom and say, ''Make us your slaves, but feed us.'' The Grand Inquisitor says to Christ, ''They themselves will understand at last that freedom and bread, enough for all, are inconceivable together, for never, never will they be able to share among themselves.'' There are but few people who have enough strength to neglect their animal being for the sake of living for the spirit. ''And, if for the sake of the bread of Heaven, thousands will follow Thee, what is to become of the millions and tens of thousands of millions of creatures who have not the strength to forgo the earthly bread for the sake of the heavenly?'' the Grand Inquisitor proceeds. He believes that, had Christ freed men from the anxiety associated with their earthly needs, He would have lifted the burden of suffering which arises from the duality of human nature. Their question as to whom they should worship would then have been answered. Man, relieved of this anxiety, would no longer doubt his Creator, for ''man seeks to worship what is established beyond any dispute.''

Man as a spiritual being, the Grand Inquisitor continues, needs worship as an expression of belief in immortality; but even if he succeeds in worshipping something ''established beyond any dispute,'' he cannot be happy so long as he is devoid of the feeling of unity with humanity. This feeling of isolation deprives him of contentment with life. ''The craving for *community* of worship is the chief misery of every man individually and of all humanity from the beginning of time,'' the Grand Inquisitor insists. Man's worry about his natural existence, however, forces him to struggle against his fellow men. Man is turned against man because they stand in a relationship similar to that of one animal toward another, each trying to seize the other's food. The animal is not disturbed by the question of whether or not this lies in the nature of universal laws, but man suffers under the law of the jungle, for it conflicts with his conscience. Had Christ freed men from the worry about their daily bread, He would also have freed them from this primitive state, and consequently from a stricken conscience: "And behold, instead of providing a firm foundation for setting the conscience of man at rest forever, Thou didst choose all that is exceptional, vague and enigmatic; Thou didst choose what was utterly beyond the strength of man, acting as if Thou didst not love him at all." The Grand Inquisitor considers that Christ demanded too much of man, and that His love for humanity was too uncompromising; it was directed toward man as he should be, and not as he is.

The second reproach of the Grand Inquisitor is that Christ withheld "miracle, mystery, and authority." Christ did not cast Himself down the mountain, nor did He descend from the cross. He submitted His body to the natural laws, for He did not want "to enslave man by a miracle." Man, however, a rebel by nature, will try to conquer these natural laws and rise above them, and a significant part of the tragedy of Dostoevsky's heroes lies in this struggle, for such attempts lead only to inevitable failure and spiritual pain. Raskolnikov strove to become a superman, stronger than that nature which condemned him to cling to his "flesh and lust." The Underground Man tried to run against "the wall of the laws of nature," although he knew full well the utter futility of his endeavor. Kirillov wanted, through suicide, to initiate the transformation of man into superman; and Ivan Karamazov, too, thought that he could disregard the laws of nature. All these attempts resulted only in suffering.

The Grand Inquisitor says to Christ, "Thou didst hope that man, following Thee, could cling to God and not ask for a miracle." Had Christ left the possibility of a miracle—a gap in the wall of nature—men would have followed Him, for "men are slaves, of course, though created rebels." Since the causal laws of nature exclude the miracle, man's faith grows weaker. Raskolnikov, dissatisfied with the social structure of the community—which is for him the consequence of causal laws—rages against God's creation and feels himself justified in attempting to improve it. The Underground Man, too, driven to desperation, tries to smash "the wall of the laws of nature." He cannot, in his state, be reconciled with God's creation or believe in Christ's love for man. Kirillov, who admired Christ's martyrdom, does not recognize the causal laws as ordained by God. He intends to free himself from subservience to them, and thus to point the way for humanity through his suicide. In a determination to destroy God, he aims at making the world happy.

> Without the negative, destructive principle of the dual force, which represents one pole of duality-- 'the indispensable minus'--there would be no phenomena on earth. While ultimate harmony would be attained, it would mean simultaneously the end of earthly life as man knows it."

Dostoevsky considers the causal laws of nature to be an apparent antithesis to the spiritual aspect of God's creation. "The highest heavenly world," as Father Zosima terms it, or "the higher noble spirituality," in Dostoevsky's words, is in utter contradiction with the earthly laws to which all men are subjected, irrespective of their denial of God's existence. Therefore, the Grand Inquisitor tells Christ that while these causal laws prevail, a weak man believes his faith in God and his striving to "the higher spiritual world" to be futile. The Grand Inquisitor's fears are justified in the case of Raskolnikov, the Underground Man, and Smerdyakov, who are unable to accept the world—in which the scoundrel prospers and the righteous man perishes—as a creation of a kind and merciful God. From this viewpoint, the Grand Inquisitor maintains that a miracle or "a gap in the wall of the laws of nature" can give man a belief in God and immortality, a belief which is essential for his peace of mind. If Christ had left for man a belief in the possibility of a miracle, he would have acquired his faith undisturbed by doubt, he would have attained peace and happiness. The immutability of the causal laws not only reduces him to "the last and the least of creatures," but is also the reason that in the whole creation of God "the law of spiritual nature is . . . violated." The Grand Inquisitor raises this violation as his second charge against Christ. Duality in the structure of the world makes man a wretched slave of the relentless laws of nature, a plaything in the hands of some all-powerful force. Out of compassion for man, the Grand Inquisitor censures Christ for His failure to abolish through a miracle this painful duality.

As in the argument presented by Glaucon and Adeimantus in Plato's *Republic*, Dostoevsky's rebellious characters such as Raskolnikov, the Underground Man, and even Ivan Karamazov, are ready to worship and believe in God if they can be sure of a reward. The valet Smerdyakov is also prepared to revere God if he is to be rewarded for his faith. He arrives at the conclusion that, since he cannot bid his faith to move a mountain, Heaven will not esteem highly his religious feeling, "for since the mountain had not moved at my word, they cannot think very much of my faith in Heaven, and there cannot be a great reward awaiting me in the world to come. So why should I let them flay me alive as well, and to no good purpose?"; For Smerdyakov, thus, there is no virtue without a reward. Even old Karamazov is aroused at such an interpretation of the Christian faith. Raskolnikov has a similar view of Christianity. He believes Sonya actually out of her mind to worship God without a reward. He witnesses the ruin of her family and cannot understand that, regardless of this, she still entrusts herself to a God Who can permit such an injustice as her terrible and shameful position in the community. Raskolnikov asks himself, when he thinks of Sonya, the tragedy of her future and that of her family, "What is she waiting for? A miracle?" He believes she endures her hard life only in the expectation of a miracle, a reward from God for her firm religious faith.

On the death of Father Zosima, his followers also expect a miracle as recompense for his life of purity. When none takes place and his body begins to decompose in accordance with the laws of nature, even Alyosha is shaken and, through his sorrow, driven almost to sin. The followers have already forgotten Father Zosima's words on the pure act of faith: "Children, seek no miracles. Miracles will kill faith." The Underground Man, too, denounces virtue without reward, and the noble-minded Ivan Karamazov's menial ego says to him, "Only those who have no conscience gain, for how can they be tortured by conscience when they have none? But decent people who have conscience and honor suffer for it." In despair, Ivan can only reply, "How could my soul beget such a creature as you?" whereupon the devil explains to him that this creature is the author of "The Legend of the Grand Inquisitor," and that the latter is the advocate for all such weaklings. The Grand Inquisitor is prepared to give man a longed-for miracle, since "man seeks not so much God as the miraculous," whereas Christ, craving "faith given freely," refused "to enslave men by a miracle."

The pawnbroker in "The Gentle Maiden" desires his wife's love "given freely," not based on compulsion. In this he resembles Christ in "The Legend of the Grand Inquisitor." The pawnbroker's wife, however, is too weak to measure up to such demands; in order to gain her confidence and love, her husband would have had to give her proof of his love for her, just as in "The Legend" Christ would have had to come down from the cross in order to win the love and faith of man. When the pawnbroker realizes that he was wrong in his expectations, he also grasps his wife's weakness. He, too, had rated her too highly, whereas she was only "a slave, even though rebellious by nature." Similarly, she revolted against her husband because he was a coward and a weakling. He should have shown her his power, or bribed her with love and compassion. Virtue without a reward did not exist for her any more than it existed for Golyadkin, Raskolnikov, and Ivan Karamazov.

The third reproach of the Grand Inquisitor is that Christ rejected the sword of Caesar and bequeathed to man a freedom in his decisions and actions, a freedom which will lead him to ruin. The Grand Inquisitor bitterly attacks Christ for His love, which has become a burden rather than a blessing for humanity: He has given men freedom of conscience for which they are too weak. He therefore says to Christ, "Hadst Thou accepted that last counsel of the mighty spirit, Thou wouldst have accomplished all that man seeks on earth, that is, Thou wouldst have given him someone to worship, someone to entrust his conscience to, and some means of unifying all into one unanimous and harmonious ant-heap."

The thought that man tries to shun all responsibility for the sins and actions which weigh heavily on his conscience was expressed by Dostoevsky for the first time in *The Double*. Golyadkin, when he can no longer manage his double, is willing to sacrifice his personal freedom for peace of mind. When he fails to achieve power and authority over others, he attempts to avoid self-reproaches by disclaiming the responsibility for his actions: "I look upon you, my benefactor and superior, as a father, and entrust my fate to you, and I will not say anything against your decisions; I put myself in your hands, and retire from the affair." He seeks someone to whom he can transfer the heavy burden of his conscience. In his anguish, he visualizes some magician who comes to him saying, "Give a finger from your right hand, Golyadkin, and we shall call it quits; the other Golyadkin will no longer exist, and you will be happy, only you will not have your finger." "Yes, I would sacrifice my finger," Golyadkin admits, "I certainly would!"

Men long to obey the one who can shoulder this encumbrance for them. "They will submit to us gladly and cheerfully," the Grand Inquisitor observes, "and they will be glad to believe our decisions, for it will save them from the great anxiety and terrible agony they endure at present in making a free decision for themselves." He believes that since man is continually torn between his spiritual and creaturely being, a freedom to govern his own decisions can only result in suffering. As man is weak and afraid of suffering, he will always seek someone whom he can make responsible for his actions.

Man's fear of assuming responsibility for his deeds prompts the Grand Inquisitor to relieve man of his duality by denying him conscience, "the greatest anxiety and terrible agony in making a free decision for himself." Once man is unburdened of this "terrible gift that has brought him so much suffering," he will rejoice and be happy. Christ's way of life has proven to be only for "the strong and elect," those who can cope with their freedom of conscience. Troubled by the thought of the weak ones, the Grand Inquisitor asks, "Are they to blame because they could not endure what the strong have endured? . . . Canst Thou have come only to the elect and for the elect?" In their freedom of conscience, given to men by Christ, they are tormented by their sins, and, like Golyadkin, they would like to appeal to "a benefactor and superior," as if to a father who would free them from conscience and, by so doing, allow them to sin again. "Oh, we shall even allow them to sin; they are weak and helpless, and they will love us like children because we allow them to sin. We shall tell them that every sin will be expiated, if it is done with our permission," the Grand Inquisitor promises Christ. If there is someone to accept responsibility for man's sin, his conscience will no longer suffer. If laws allow man to succumb to sins, he must have no feeling of guilt.

The Grand Inquisitor warns Christ that there are few elect people who can bear responsibility alone. "And besides," he proceeds, "how many of those elect, those mighty ones who could have become elect, have grown weary waiting for Thee, and have transferred and will transfer the power of their spirit and the ardor of their heart to the other camp, and end by raising their free banner against Thee." Raskolnikov has the strength to shoulder the responsibility for his murder and its consequences. However, even though filled with genuine Christian compassion and sympathy for the suffering and oppressed, he directs his strength against Christ for the sake of his "flesh and lust." A further revolt against Christ is Raskolnikov's wish to change Sonya's Christian state of mind—all enduring and sacrificial—into hatred toward her tormentors. The Grand Inquisitor refers to this attitude of Raskolnikov's in speaking of those who could have become the elect, but turned their free banner against Christ.

Svidrigaylov, Kirillov, Stavrogin, Versilov, and Ivan Karamazov also could have become elect, but they end in laying hands either on themselves or on others, raising in this way their free banner against Christ. With the exception of Kirillov, they are all slaves to the "coarse veil" of earth and the causal laws of nature against which they clamor so loudly. Even Kirillov, in the last minutes before suicide, is transformed from a man-god into a weakling through his subjection to the "earthly veil of matter."

In his logically developed argument the Grand Inquisitor has, however, missed one important possibility. He does not take into consideration the fact that these same mutineers, if given the opportunity, can find their way back to Christ. Raskolnikov, who is prepared to suffer in atonement for his crime, finally becomes enlightened and, having won the battle against his base instincts, is now ready to raise the banner for Christ. As will be shown later, Dostoevsky implies that such conflicts in the human mind are necessary to determine the meaning of earthly life. The conflict between Raskolnikov's denial and Sonya's acceptance of divine justice is of this nature. But the Grand Inquisitor, even though he understands the purpose of these antitheses, refuses to accept them. This appears to be the reason that he can see only the dark side of the rebel's actions: his mutiny against God and Christ.

From the Grand Inquisitor's three charges against Christ, man's spiritual suffering is shown to have its roots in his freedom of conscience, and the only way of relieving man from the mental pain caused by his duality is to deny him this freedom, the Grand Inquisitor suggests, since freedom and happiness are for him incompatible. In freedom, man is a slave and a rebel at the same time; yet if he is deprived of freedom, he will remain only a slave, and the pain arising from his duality will be eliminated. Had the Grand Inquisitor succeeded in freeing man from his burden of conscience, he would have removed the main source of man's mental anguish and enabled those "millions of men," who are his chief concern, to live a quiet and peaceful life, without suffering, without the pricks of conscience, and without a struggle for existence. This condition can be achieved only by depriving man of his divine image and of his chance to live for the spirit.

"The roots of man's thoughts and feelings are not here, but in other worlds," insists Father Zosima. In taking from man freedom of conscience, the Grand Inquisitor would have also lost for him a connection with "other worlds." As Father Zosima maintains, "the spiritual world, the higher part of man's being, would then be rejected altogether and banished." This possibility does not perturb the Grand Inquisitor because he cannot believe in man's divine origin, as he does not believe in God. Alyosha Karamazov recognizes this clearly when he replies to Ivan, "Your Inquisitor does not believe in God, that's his whole secret!" But even the Grand Inquisitor himself fears that an animal existence will never suffice for man, since he admits. "The secret of man's being is not only to live, but to have something to live for. Without a steadfast faith in the object of life, man would not consent to go on living, but would rather destroy himself than remain on earth, though he had bread in abundance."

In order to satisfy man with an animal life, the Grand Inquisitor must delude him into a conviction of happiness. To achieve this, he intends to give man a purpose in life by supporting his inherent belief in immortality and God, and, with promises of heavenly and eternal reward, so lead him to a false sense of bliss. The exclusion of suffering, however, would mean the destruction of humanity, as Ivan himself explains to Alyosha: "One should accept lying and deception and lead man consciously to death and destruction; and yet one should deceive them all the way so that they may not notice where they are being led, that the poor blind creatures may at least, on the way, think themselves happy." Ivan himself, thus, admits that the happiness promised mankind by the Grand Inquisitor is only a deception, and in so doing he, even if involuntarily, sides with Christ. This is plain to Alyosha, who exclaims, "Your poem is to praise Jesus, not to blame Him!"

The Grand Inquisitor, in denying man a link with the spiritual world, is determined to destroy human spirit and thought. Deprived of his divine origin, man will lose—in spite of the spurious notions of happiness provided by the Grand Inquisitor—the idea of God and personal immortality. He will view his life only as "a meaningless flash." There will be no further point to a life now devoid of all meaning; therefore no satisfaction will be left save in self-destruction, as it was with Svidrigaylov and Stavrogin. Dostoevsky explains this condition more fully in *The Diary of a Writer*:

> If man loses his belief in immortality, suicide becomes an absolute and inevitable necessity. . . . But the idea of immortality, promising eternal life, binds man closely to the earth. . . . Man's belief in a personal immortality is the only thing which gives point and reason to his life on earth. Without this belief, his bond with the earth loosens, becomes weak and unstable; the loss of life's higher meaning—even if it is felt only as a most subconscious form of depression and ennui—leads him inevitably to suicide.

As Dostoevsky explicitly states, without a belief in personal immortality,

> People will suddenly realize that there is no more life for them; that there is no freedom of spirit, no will, no personality; that someone has stolen everything from them; that the human way of life has vanished, to be replaced by the bestial way of life, the way of cattle, with this difference, however, that the cattle do not know that they are cattle, whereas men will discover that they have become cattle. . . . And then, perhaps, others will cry to God, "Thou art right, oh Lord! Man lives not by bread alone!"

The Grand Inquisitor, therefore, who contemplates the elimination of what he believes to be the principle of evil in the structure of the world, admits that he sides with Satan. "Listen," he addresses Christ, "we are not with Thee, but with *him*—that is our secret!" His intention will lead man to absolute evil: to death and destruction. The Grand Inquisitor realizes this, but he believes that his substitution of an acceptable myth for painful conscience will be justified, for he will secure for man the happiness denied him by his inability to accept the idea represented by Christ.

Dostoevsky clearly distinguishes this evil from that manifested in Ivan's hallucination of the devil, who says, "I am the 'X' in an equation with one unknown." It appears from this formulation that evil ending in suffering is an integral part of life just as the "X" is of such an equation. Suffering, for Dostoevsky, is not only inherent in man, but it provides the only spur toward a greater consciousness of reality, which in turn engenders the assertion of man's personality. Complete harmony on earth, therefore, is excluded by the existence of suffering. The world, as it is, must have suffering, and man must have his duality, and yet it is possible to strive for harmony on earth.

A dual force, in Dostoevsky's view, is indispensable for the whole of earthly existence. Life on earth is an incessant striving and must be stimulated by the operation of the two opposite forces of good and evil, which manifest themselves also in man as a part of the universe. As Lebedev in *The Idiot* explains to Evgeny Pavlovich, "The laws of self-preservation and self-destruction are equally powerful in humanity. The devil will maintain his domination over mankind for a period of time which is still unknown to us." The hypothesis that these impulses of self-preservation and self-destruction are a part of the dual and fundamental law of the universe which divert man from his "spiritual world" induces Lebedev to ascribe this law to the realm of the devil. But the impulse of self-preservation must be given its due, since it preserves earthly existence, even though it is one of destruction when considered in relation to the "spiritual world."

According to Dostoevsky, since man's physical nature hinders his independent thoughts and distorts his "spiritual world," there can be no paradise and no harmony so long as man must live under earthly conditions. Kirillov expresses a similar viewpoint in his conversation with Shatov: "There are seconds . . . when you suddenly feel the presence of the eternal harmony perfectly attained. It is something not earthly—I do not mean in the sense that it is heavenly—but in that sense that man cannot endure it in his earthly aspect. He must be physically changed or die." This thought occurs again in the following note: "We do not know which form it [eternal harmony] will take, or where it will take place, . . . in which center, whether in the final center, that is, in the bosom of the universal synthesis—God. . . . It will be in general hardly possible to call men human beings; therefore we have not even an idea what kind of beings we shall be."

With the attainment of man's goal, Dostoevsky further claims, human existence will become static. Thus, it will no longer be necessary for man to develop himself, or to await the coming of future generations to attain his goal. The life hitherto known to man will cease to be a life based on perpetual motion. In the same way, Ivan's devil, who represents the principle of evil in human nature, assures Ivan that he, the devil, "in a simple and straightforward way demands [his] own annihilation," but is commanded to live further. "For there would be nothing without me," he says, "if everything on earth were as it should be, then nothing would happen. There would be no events without me, but there must be events." Without the negative, destructive principle of the dual force, which represents one pole of duality— "the indispensable minus"—there would be no phenomena on earth. While ultimate harmony would be attained, it would mean simultaneously the end of earthly life as man knows it.

The same result would be achieved if man could solve the mystery of life and find an ultimate answer to the eternal question "why?" so convincingly presented by Lebyadkin. The devil, referring to this mystery of life, says to Ivan, "I know, of course, there is a secret in it, but for nothing in the world will they tell me this secret; for then, perhaps, seeing the meaning of it, I might shout 'hosanna!'; the indispensable minus would disappear at once, and good sense would reign supreme throughout the world. That, of course, would mean the end of everything."

Thus, while the principle of evil which destroys the "spiritual world" of man is indispensable for the preservation of earthly existence, the complete transition to absolute evil, quite consciously aimed at by the Grand Inquisitor, would exclude the principle of good, resulting ultimately in death and destruction. Even Ivan Karamazov himself is convinced that his devil— "the 'X' in an equation with one unknown"—is not the Satan mentioned by the Grand Inquisitor, but "only a devil." Similarly, Ivan questions Alyosha in one of the drafts, "In what way is he Satan? He is a devil, simply a devil. I cannot visualize him as Satan." In a letter to N. A. Lyubimov, Dostoevsky reasserts his viewpoint by writing, "Please forgive me my devil. He is only a devil . . . not Satan with his 'singed' wings." It is strange that this important distinction escaped the attention of some scholars and critics. D. H. Lawrence, for example, in his article "Preface to Dostoevsky's *The Grand Inquisitor*," states forthrightly: "As always in Dostoevsky, the amazing perspicacity is mixed with ugly perversity. Nothing is pure. His wild love for Jesus is mixed with perverse and poisonous hate of Jesus: his moral hostility to the devil is mixed with secret worship of the devil." It is evident that D. H. Lawrence has overlooked the dichotomy so important for Dostoevsky between Satan and the devil. As has been shown, the Russian novelist equates the devil with "the 'X' in an equation with one unknown," and with "the indispensable minus" in the structure of the world.

The principle of evil is a prerequisite of earthly existence, but Dostoevsky, through Father Zosima, states his view that only the "spiritual world," the "higher part of man's being" can be the goal of human aspiration. The contradictions discussed above, which are characteristic of Dostoevsky's philosophy and are reflected in his fiction, the writer reconciles very forcefully and lucidly.

Source: Temira Pachmuss, "The Metaphysics of Evil," in *F. M. Dostoevsky: Dualism and Synthesis of the Human Soul*, Southern Illinois University Press, 1963, pp. 97–111.

Sources

Belknap, Robert L. "The Rhetoric of an Ideological Novel," in *Literature and Society in Imperial Russia, 1800-1914*, edited by William Mills Todd III. Reprinted in *Modern Critical Views: Fyodor Dostoevsky*, edited by Harold Bloom. New York: Chelsea House, 1989, pp. 136-37.

Berdyaev, Nicholas. *Dostoevsky*, translated by Donald Attwater, Cleveland: Meridian Books, 1957, p. 189.

Catteau, Jacques. "The Paradox of the Legend of the Grand Inquisitor in *The Brothers Karamazov*," translated by Francoise Rosset, in *Dostoevsky: New Perspectives*, edited by Robert Louis Jackson, Englewood Cliffs, NJ: Prentice-Hall, 1984, p. 248.

Cowles, Virginia. *The Russian Dagger: Cold War in the Days of the Czars*, New York: Harper & Row, 1969, p. 140.

Lawrence, D. H. "Preface to Dostoevsky's *The Grand Inquisitor*," in *Dostoevsky: A Collection of Critical Essays*, edited by Rene Wellek, Englewood Cliffs, NJ: Prentice-Hall, 1962, pp. 90, 91, 97.

Leatherbarrow, William J. *Fedor Dostoevsky*, Boston: Twayne, 1981, p. 157.

Lord, Robert. *Dostoevsky: Essays and Perspectives*, Berkeley: University of California Press, 1970, pp. 166-67.

Matlaw, Ralph E. Introduction to *Notes from Underground and The Grand Inquisitor*, by Fyodor Dostoevsky, New York: Dutton, 1960, p. xx.

Ward, Bruce K. *Dostoevsky's Critique of the West: The Quest for the Earthly Paradise*, Waterloo, Ontario: Wilfrid Laurier Press, 1986, p. 101.

Wasiolek, Edward. *Dostoevsky: The Major Fiction*, Cambridge, Mass.: MIT Press, 1964, p. 169.

Further Reading

FitzLyon, Kyril, and Tatiana Browning. *Before the Revolution: Russia and Its People under the Czar*, Woodstock, N.Y.: Overlook Press, 1978.

Contains over three hundred black and white photographs of cities and villages of Russia, taken between 1894 and 1917. Many of the scenes photographed would have been familiar to Dostoevsky, who died in 1881.

Frank, Joseph. *Dostoevsky*, Princeton: Princeton University Press.

Four volumes of this masterful biography have been published so far, covering Dostoevsky's life from 1821 through 1871. Widely considered the best literary biography available.

Jackson, Robert Louis, ed. *Dostoevsky: New Perspectives*, Englewood Cliffs, N.J.: Prentice-Hall, 1984.

Contains fourteen relatively recent essays providing critical analysis of Dostoevsky's most important works. Included are three essays on *The Brothers Karamazov* and one, by Jacques Catteau, that concludes that "The Grand Inquisitor" is tragic but ultimately hopeful.

Kornblatt, Judith Deutsch, and Richard F. Gustafson, eds. *Russian Religious Thought*, Madison: University of Wisconsin Press, 1996.

Provides an analysis of the major ideas of Russian religious philosophy, with their historical backgrounds and cultural contexts.

Peters, Edward. *Inquisition*, Berkeley: University of California Press, 1989.

A scholarly but accessible attempt to correct generally held misconceptions about the Inquisition, written by an important historian.

Waldron, Peter. *The End of Imperial Russia, 1855-1917*, New York: St. Martin's Press, 1997.

A historical look at the economic and social consequences of tsarist Russia and the opposition to it, of which Dostoevsky was a part.

Wellek, Rene, ed. *Dostoevsky: A Collection of Critical Essays*, Englewood Cliffs, N.J.: Prentice-Hall, 1962.

Contains eleven older critical essays about the major works, including D. H. Lawrence's famous Preface to "The Grand Inquisitor." Wellek's introduction traces the history of Dostoevsky criticism and influence.

How I Contemplated the World from the Detroit House of Correction and Began My Life Over Again

"How I Contemplated the World From the Detroit House of Correction and Began My Life Over Again" was first published in magazine form in 1969 and then collected in her 1970 volume of short stories called *The Wheel of Love*. Its sarcastic rendering of upper-middle-class suburban life is not only an accurate critique of that aspect of American life, it is also a true rendering of the adolescent world view that rings as true today as it did when the story was written.

The story's experimental form seemed lifeless to some early critics, but has proven to have given the story literary staying power. The full title, "Notes for an Essay for an English Class at Baldwin Country Day School; Poking Around in Debris; Disgust and Curiosity; A Revelation of the Meaning of Life; A Happy Ending . . . ," invites readers to compare the prediction for a happy ending with the story the narrator tells at the end. Given her gift for sarcasm, is she telling the truth when she claims to "love everything" once she's returned to the safety, if sterile, of her parents' large suburban home? In the case of *"How I Contemplated,"* ambiguity and incompleteness in the narrative add to rather than detract from the story's richness.

Author Biography

Joyce Carol Oates was born in Erie County in western New York in 1938. Her parents worked

Joyce Carol Oates
1969

hard throughout the great depression to support her and her two younger siblings, her father at the tool and dye shop and her mother keeping house. Although her working class Catholic beginnings could hardly predict the literary heights she would attain later in life, she was always a serious and high-achieving child and made the most of the educational opportunities that she was given.

Her early education was uneven at best. After attending a one-room schoolhouse, and junior high, in Lockport, New York, she finally found a school that had what she needed when she began riding a bus everyday to a high school outside of Buffalo. After graduation, she enrolled at Syracuse University on a scholarship and began a lifelong engagement with books and writing. By all measures she was an extraordinary student and graduated Phi Beta Kappa and first in the class of 1960. The next year she entered the University of Wisconsin at Madison to begin the graduate work to set her on the path to becoming an academic. Within a year she had met and married fellow graduate student in English, Raymond Smith, to whom she is still married. She earned her M.A. in 1961 and moved to Beaumont, Texas where her new husband had gotten his first faculty appointment. She was enrolled in the Ph.D. program at Rice University when she had an experience, the story goes, that changed the course of her life.

While doing research in the Rice library, she ran across a copy of *Best American Short Stories* and found one of her own stories mentioned in it. At that moment she decided to become a professional writer. Though she has held teaching positions throughout her career, Oates kept her pledge to make writing her main focus. For the past thirty or more years, she had been one of America's most prolific and significant writers. Her output is staggering: from 1963 to 1998 she has published thirty-eight novels, twenty-four volumes of short stories, fourteen books of poetry, nine works of non-fiction, and twenty-one plays.

Oates lives in suburban New Jersey and is on the faculty of Princeton University. Her husband runs a small publishing house, Ontario Review Press, that the two of them founded years earlier. Many critics and interviewers have noted the differences and similarities between her placid and stable life and the world she creates in her fiction. On the one hand she has always been able to capture the details and nuances of the American suburban landscape, and her academic satires are clearly the work of a keen inside observer. On the other hand, her depictions of violence and brutality lurking beneath suburbia's placid surface have shocked and disturbed some readers. Oates addressed these objections directly in an essay in the *New York Times Book Review* by explaining that the question about why she would include such violence in her writing ''is always ignorant.'' She goes on to explain that ''Since it is commonly understood that serious writers, as opposed to entertainers or propagandists, take for their natural subject the complexity of the world, its evils as well as its goods, it is always an insulting question; and it is always sexist. The serious writer, after all, bears witness.''

Oates continues her amazing production, despite her claim to ''spend an inordinate time doing nothing,'' as she said to interviewer Robert Phillips. Her recent non-fiction book on the sport of boxing, first published in 1987 and then expanded in a new edition in 1994, has garnered a lot of attention and praise. In August 1998 she published an autobiographical essay about her own visit to a New Jersey house of corrections (as a guest on a tour), called ''After Amnesia.''

Plot Summary

In a partial and disorganized set of notes for an essay for her English class at a private school, a sixteen-year-old girl tells the story of a set of events that lead her to a house of correction and to an opportunity to contemplate her life and begin over again. Though the details are not presented in chronological order, the full story does emerge upon careful reading.

At fifteen years old, the narrator, the child of wealthy parents in one of Detroit's most affluent suburbs, escalates her habits of stealing and vandalizing by shoplifting a pair of gloves from an ''excellent'' department store and gets caught. Her parents react by hushing everything up and smoothing it over, and she never gets whatever attention she was craving. Her mother just wants to know why ''if she wanted gloves, why didn't you say so?''. The narrator thinks, ''I wanted to steal, but not to buy,'' but she doesn't tell her mother. Consequently, her next act of rebellion is even more drastic. She walks out of school and runs away to downtown Detroit, where she is so out of place that she doesn't even know what a pawn shop is for. Alone, vulnerable, and still desperate for the affection her chilly parents deny her, she is easy prey for Clarita, a prostitute, and her pimp, Simon, a drug addict. After an unspecified period of prostitution and abuse, the narrator is eventually picked up by the police and turned over to a juvenile facility. There she clings stubbornly to her rebellious posture and refuses to give information that would allow her to be released to her parents. Acting tough, "she says to the matron *I'm not talking about anything*, not because anyone warned her not to talk, but because she will not talk." She tries to fit in with the other girls there and seems to take some pride and pleasure in thinking she belonged. She is sadly mistaken, however, as she discovers one night when two of the girls corner her in the bathroom and beat her savagely, just because she is rich and white and privileged. After a stay in the hospital she returns to her Bloomfield Hills "traditional-contemporary home" with her parents. By the time she composes these notes, she has returned to school at Baldwin Country Day and is in the care of a psychiatrist. She seems to be working out her desire toward self-expression and her quest for identity through her writing and her therapy rather than through desperate and self-destructive behaviors like the ones that landed her first in Simon's bed and then in the house of corrections.

Joyce Carol Oates

Characters

Clarita

A woman of indeterminate age (between twenty and thirty-five), she is an addict and a prostitute. She has "an odor of tobacco about her," and has "unwashed skin, gritty toes, hair long and falling into strands, not recently washed." She has been living on the streets since she was about thirteen years old.

Dr. Coronet

Isabelle Coronet is the psychiatrist that the narrator's parents send her to twice a week after her return from the house of corrections. The narrator describes her as "queenly," but surprisingly "normal for a woman with an I.Q. of 180 and many advanced degrees."

Dolly

A "white girl of maybe fifteen," Dolly is one of the two girls in the house of correction who beat the narrator in the bathroom.

Father

The narrator's father, whose name she does not provide, is a successful physician, a member of all the right clubs, a "player of squash and golf." He is a prominent member of the community of Bloomfield Hills and is able to use his social connections to smooth over his children's difficulties with the authorities, but he seems to be unable to show them the love and attention they need.

Mr. Forest

Though "not handsome," Mr. Forest, the English teacher, is described by the narrator as "sweet and rodentlike." It's for his English class at Baldwin Country Day School that these "notes for an essay" are being written.

Raymond Forrest

Raymond Forrest is the owner of the "excellent" department store from which the narrator

Media Adaptations

- "Where Are You Going, Where Have You Been," the companion story to "How I Contemplated," was adapted as a film, *Smooth Talk*, directed by Joyce Chopra and starring Laura Dern, Treat Williams, and Mary Kay Place. It was originally produced in 1985 for the "American Playhouse Series" on the Public Broadcasting System and is available from Live Home Video and Vestron Video.

steals the gloves. After she returns home from the hospital and the house of correction, she reads that his father has died of a heart attack and feels an impulse to send a sympathy note.

Mother

Like the father, the mother goes unnamed throughout the story. Also like the narrator's father, the mother belongs to all the right clubs. She attends lectures and art openings and drives a "Lincoln, long and black" like all the other wealthy matrons on Sioux Drive. Physically, she is always stylishly and perfectly dressed, and has "hair like blown-up gold and finer than gold, hair and fingers and body of inestimable grace."

Narrator

Only fifteen years old when she runs away and ends up in the house of correction, the narrator, who never gives her name, is sixteen when she tries to describe her experiences in notes for an essay for her English class. She lives in her parents' large and comfortable suburban home in the suburbs of Detroit, but her rebellious and self-destructive impulses lead her to shoplifting, prostitution, and ultimately the house of correction. She is ambivalent about her affluent background and describes her parents and all of Bloomfield Hills with scathing sarcasm. Nevertheless, her experiences with Simon and the beating she suffers at the house of correction sent her fleeing back to the protection and comfort

of her parents' wealth and privilege. She doesn't provide many details about her own physical appearance, except that she wears her "hair loose and long and straight in suburban teen-age style, 1968."

Princess

As the narrator describes her, Princess is "a Negro girl of eighteen." She is "shrewd and silent" and the narrator is fascinated by her. At first she seems to take an interest in protecting the narrator, but later she is one of the two girls who corner and beat her.

Simon

Simon is the drug addict and pimp who seduces and uses the narrator after Clarita brings her to him. He is "said to have come from a "home not much different" from the narrator's, but he has descended completely into the junkie's life of desperation and crime. Despite how badly he treats her, she craves his touch and affection. Even a year later, she confesses that she would go back to him. She also believes that Simon is the one who saved her by telling the authorities that she was a runaway.

Themes

Love

Love is the engine that drives all of the girl's behavior in "How I Contemplated." She may be misguided, self-destructive, and immature, but the narrator's actions all derive from her desire to be loved. Despite their generosity, the girl's parents seem unable to give her the attention and unguarded affection that she craves. She describes her mother as icy, distant, and artfully constructed and her father as powerful, distracted, and unavailable. As we learn through several references in the story, the narrator's older brother, away at college, engages in the same desperate attention-getting behaviors.

In the narrator's eyes, the mother possesses an other-wordly charm and poise that she feels she can neither live up to nor puncture. Her mother is "a lady . . . self-conscious and unreal." She has "hair like blown-up gold and finer than gold, hair and fingers and body of inestimable grace." She is, above all, too busy and too self-absorbed to pay attention when her daughter is caught stealing from the "excellent" store. The mother's awkward and ineffective way of showing affection for her daughter is to buy her things in the hope that she will transform herself from an awkward, sullen teenager to a polished artifact like herself. The narrator recalls shopping with her mother, listening to her urging "why don't you want this, try this on, take this with you to the fitting room, take this also, what's wrong with you, what can I do for you, why are you so strange . . .?" The narrator wants to tell her mother that she "wanted to steal but not to buy," but decides not to.

The narrator's father is described not so much in terms of his appearance (like the mother is), but rather in terms of what he does; he is defined by his actions. The narrator's father's reaction to problems is to fix them. He handles his daughter's shoplifting episode in the same clinical, pragmatic manner that he uses to treat patients. He gets in touch with the store owner and makes the problem go away. He is completely blind to the fact that his daughter's behavior is a cry for his attention, not his expertise. The narrator recalls poignantly that her father is out of town at a medical convention when she was arrested in the department store. She also wonders, "where he was when Clarita put her hand on my arm, that wintry dark sulphurous day in Detroit." It remains unclear at the conclusion of the story whether her father will ever show her the love she wants, but at least he drives her home and holds her while she sobs in his arms.

The narrator's most desperate act in her search for love and affection is clearly her liaison with Simon and Clarita. Young and confused, the narrator seeks in Simon the physical affection that is missing in the relationships with her reserved and distant parents. What she finds instead is abusive sex and drugs and prostitution. On some level, however, Simon does fulfill some need for her. Asking herself a year later "Would I go back to Simon again? Would I lie down with him in all that filth and craziness?", she has to answer, "Over and over again." Ironically, Simon does make one genuine gesture of affection toward the narrator. By turning her in to the authorities, as she suspects he has, he helps her by doing the very thing that both of her cold and overprotective parents had failed to do.

Class and Race Conflict

The contrast between Sioux Drive and Detroit on which the story depends points to a deep and troubling divide between white suburbia and the minority-inhabited inner city. The circumstances and inequities that created and sustain this division

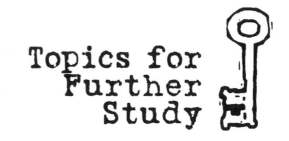

Topics for Further Study

- Although the narrator seems genuinely frightened by the beating she received and seems happy to be home, do you think she is sorry for her other offenses? Has she taken responsibility for her stealing and vandalism? What do you predict for the remainder of her teenage years?

- What do you think is attractive about Simon? Why does she say she would go back to him "over and over again."?

- What did the city of Detroit look like in 1968? Write a description of the scene the narrator would have encountered when she got off the bus?

- Could this story be written today? How would it be different? Is this story of teenage rebellion and isolation universal, or is it a story of the 1960s?

form the backdrop of the story (see below). The narrator's beliefs and behaviors also express her awareness of and ambivalence toward the racial and social conflict that simmers just beneath the surface.

The narrator's disdain for the affluent and protected world she and her parents live in is obvious in her scathing and sarcastic descriptions of life on Sioux Drive. She lists the number of rooms and architectural features of the houses in her neighborhood, on streets patrolled by "a private police force . . . in unmarked cars." On a Saturday night, the watch out for "residents who are streaming in and out of houses, going to and from parties, a thousand parties." Life on Sioux drive is so self-contained, so insular, she writes, that "when spring comes, its winds blow nothing to Sioux Drive, no odors of hollyhocks or forsythia, nothing Sioux Drive doesn't already possess." Like many teenagers, the narrator rebels against the lifestyle and values of her parents. In 1968, however, her rejection of her parents' way of life has a political dimension as well. She longs to be identified with the other world, Sioux Drive's opposite, Detroit and to be accepted by its inhabitants in order to take sides against her parents. This flawed reasoning leads her first to Simon's false arrest and then to her stubborn posturing in the house of correction. Finally, she is forced to confront the shallowness and pointlessness of her position when she is beaten up by Princess and Dolly who ''vent all the hatred of a thousand silent Detroit winters on her body.'' After the beating, the narrator rushed back to the safety of Sioux Drive, where there are ''sugar doughnuts for breakfast,'' and where ''sunlight breaks in movieland patches on the roof of our traditional contemporary home.'' The injustices and tensions between Detroit and Sioux Drive, between black and white, remain unchanged.

Style

Fragmentary Structure

Even many years after the story's publication, the structure of ''How I Contemplated'' is still striking and somewhat unsettling to readers. The experimental form Oates uses is fragmentary and full of gaps. Instead of writing the story of an affluent young girl's temporary descent into a life on the streets and in a house of corrections, she gives readers only the girl's own notes for an essay that she may or may not ever write.

What appears to be an orderly outline in twelve sections is really a random and partial arrangement of information recollected a year after the events. In the words of critic Sue Simpson Park, the sections are ''repetitive, disjointed, and dispersive . . . indicative of the state of mind of the sixteen-year-old protagonist, confused, questioning, attempting to make sense of the senseless, to impose order upon the chaos.'' Although the complete title removes any doubt the reader may have about whether the story has a ''happy ending,'' (she is writing a paper for a private school and has declared that she began her life over again), readers still have to piece together the narrative and read between the lines. One of the most significant gaps appears in the section titled ''People & Circumstances Contributing to This Delinquency.'' Under this heading is only the word, ''nothing,'' which suggests to the reader not that there are no contributing factors, but that the young narrator cannot see them or doesn't want to talk about them. In other words, the absence of reasons prompts readers to speculate and to supply reasons of their own to explain the girl's behavior.

Narration

The sixteen-year-old girl who composes these notes for an essay is what is known as an unreliable narrator. She's the only one who tells the story, but the version she offers is limited and possibly altered by her narrow point of view. The narrator's unreliability takes several forms. First, she is only sixteen and thus has the adolescent's limited and self-centered view of the world. In addition, only a year has passed since the events and she has not had sufficient time to gain perspective on what has happened. In fact, it seems like these notes for the essay represent a preliminary attempt (other than her visits to the psychiatrist) to organize her experience into a coherent pattern. Second, narrative features like blank spaces for names, series of questions (''A pretty girl? An ugly girl?'') and missing details cast doubt on her credibility. These missing details are especially noticeable because on other occasions she proves herself capable of remarkable candor and keen observation. For example, she's willing to admit to the other petty crimes she committed before getting caught shoplifting and she's able to render a nuanced and vibrant portrait of suburban life, complete with such vivid details as the car heavy enough '' to split a squirrel's body in two equal parts.''

The device of the unreliable narrator enhances the story's effect. It would be unreasonable and unrealistic to expect a sixteen-year-old to render a complete and objective account of such a traumatic set of events. The sketchy, uncertain and sometime evasive narrative structure is typical of an adolescent's (especially a troubled one's) world view and contributes to the story's authenticity and power. Finally, the narrator's unreliability makes the open-ended and ambiguous ending possible. It's impossible to be certain if she is being sincere when she claims that she will ''never leave home,'' and that she is ''in love with everything here.''

Historical Context

Urban Decay

The late 1960s and early 1970s in America was a period marked by huge and permanent economic and demographic changes. Particularly hard hit by these sweeping changes were many of the country's large industrial cities. Detroit became synonymous with urban decay and what soon came to be known as "white flight." As the narrator describes it, Detroit is "a large famous city that is a symbol for large famous American cities."

The trends had begun much earlier. In the years immediately following the end of World War II, veterans and their families enjoyed unprecedented prosperity and the high birth rate now known as the baby boom. As a consequence these families began to leave the inner cities for newly created suburbs and housing developments. This exodus from what had been thriving mixed-use neighborhoods in large cities set off a chain reaction that reached a crisis in the late 1960s and that continues to reverberate today. As families with at least modest means abandon urban neighborhoods, only those too poor to move remain. The poorer residents are unable to support the surrounding businesses and they in turn must move outward to the suburbs to be closer to their customers. Thus, the inner city loses the tax base that commercial property provides, further depleting the resources and degrading the services for the remaining residents. Public schools struggle to meet children's needs and to attract qualified teachers. Naturally, major employers soon find the suburbs more attractive and abandon the city's core as well. One of the most insidious aspects of this demographic shift is the racial segregation that it causes. The population that moves out to the suburbs is primarily white, while those that stay in the city are primarily people of color. Thus the cycle of poverty and lack of opportunity is reinforced and unequal and segregated school systems grow up within miles of each other.

Racial Tension and Violence

Not surprisingly, the demographic configurations and the economic and social disparities involved of major United States cities resulted in escalating tensions between the races. In the summers of 1967 and 1968 race riots erupted in major cities across the country. In several instances, the National Guard was called upon to restore order. These riots were sparked by a number of causes and found ample kindling in the deteriorating and minority-dominated inner cities. The civil rights movement in the south had awakened black radicalism in northern cities as well, and black power movements such as the Black Panthers gained considerable popular support among minorities and inspired fear and terror in most white people. The assassination of Dr. Martin Luther King, Jr. in the spring of 1968

initiated widespread protest, some of which became violent. In the summer of 1967 forty-three people were killed in race riots in the streets of Detroit. The images of this kind of violence further deterred white people from living or shopping in—or even driving through—the inner cities.

Women's Lib

The women's movement of the 1960s sought to liberate the suburban housewife. Almost exclusively a white, middle-class movement, women's lib, as this phase of feminism was known, exposed the myth of the happy consumer housewife and implored women to seek fulfillment in other areas of their lives. Betty Freidan's *The Feminine Mystique*, published in 1963 and the best-seller book of 1964, was the manifesto. In the words of *New Yorker* writer Daphne Merkin in a recent review of Freidan's biography, the book addressed "an amorphous malaise that afflicted college-educated American women, who smothered their children with attention, had unrealistic expectations of their husbands, and then sought to assuage their sense of quiet desperation by downing pills or having joyless extramarital affairs." Of course, many housewives and mothers resisted the radicalizing temptations and stuck firmly to the ideals they had inherited from their mothers. In the language of the movement, those who did so did not want to raise their consciousness and confront their dissatisfactions with their traditional, if comfortable, lives. One group, however, who would have found the rhetoric of women's lib impossible to ignore, is the daughters of these women. Young women rebelled against their mothers' examples, unsure of what they would become, but certain never to fall into the confinement of the unfulfilled housewife.

Critical Overview

When *The Wheel of Love* was published in 1970, Joyce Carol Oates was already an established writer of fiction and poetry. What was still open to debate was whether she was a serious "literary" writer or just a popular one. As she has often pointed out in interviews, this argument is based on the sexist premise that such a prolific *female* writer must have aspired to popularity instead of art. The stories in *Wheel of Love* continued to divide critical opinion, but in the decades since, several of them, including ''How I Contemplated,'' have taken their place among the best of American short fiction.

Writing in the *New York Times Book Review*, Richard Gilman noted that in some of the stories Oates created ''a verbal excitement, a sense of language used not for the expression of previously attained insights or perceptions but for new imaginative reality.'' Reviewer James A. Avant of the *Library Journal* singled out ''How I Contemplated'' as one of the stories that demonstrated Oates's ''striking expansions of the limits of fiction.'' Avant also goes on to concede that ''One must really go ahead and call her, at the outrageous age of 32, a great writer.'' On the other hand, Gilman also concludes that Oates's stories are full of ''a great deal of 'expressive' rumination about feeling [which] is accompanied by very little feeling itself.'' Similarly, critic R. E. Long wrote in the *Saturday Review* that the book is ''full of cleverness and nimble invention, but it lacks the sense of a deep involvement with life.''

Oates, who has written scores of stories for magazines, said in an interview with Robert Phillips for the *Paris Review*, that if she's ''serious about a story,'' she'll ''preserve it in book form.'' Otherwise she ''intends it to be forgotten.'' Since the early reviews of *The Wheel of Love*, some of the stories in the collection, including ''How I Contemplated,'' in the collection have become staples of American literature anthologies. Although somewhat over-shadowed by another story about adolescence in the volume, ''Where are your Going, Where Have You Been?'', ''How I Contemplated'' has continued to invite critical readings due to its innovative form and its portrayal of adolescent subjectivity.

Critical responses to the stories in *Wheel of Love* are typical of reactions to Oates work throughout her long and amazingly prolific career. In the first decades of her career she was often dismissed as just a ''woman'' writer, not a serious (male) writer. At the same time, however, she faced harsh criticism for writing about violent subjects that were considered off limits to female writers. Ironically, feminist critics who began the project in the 1970s of reconsidering and resuscitating American women writers never really gave Oates the attention she deserved. This has to do with Oates long-standing refusal to be identified as (just) a woman writer. In

the words of noted feminist scholar and fellow Princeton professor Elaine Showalter, ''feminist critics have sometimes taken Oates's insistence that the imagination has no gender as a denial of her social identity as a woman writer, . . . Oates's sense of herself as what she calls a '(woman) writer' has intensified during the 1980s. In the last two decades, Showalter claims, Oates has added a new dimension to her writing, ''an exchange with . . . [a] complex female literary heritage.''

Criticism

Elisabeth Piedmont-Marton

Elisabeth Piedmont-Marton teaches American literature and writing classes at the University of Texas. She writes frequently about the modern short story. In this essay she explains how ''How I Contemplated . . .'' is a subversion of the classic coming-of-age story.

In Mark Twain's classic American novel *The Adventures of Huckleberry Finn*, the protagonist, young Huck, is last seen preparing to ''light out for the territories.'' This story of Huck, poised on the brink of manhood, prepared to test his character and forge his identity on the frontier has become a master narrative for the American coming-of-age plot. Oates's ''How I Contemplated'' employs the elements of the coming-of-age story, but does so in an ironic, subversive fashion. At the heart of Oates's story is a female protagonist whose ''adventures'' represent regression rather than progress and whose experiences will not arrange themselves into the coherent pattern that the genre requires.

In the American coming-of-age tale, the hero—usually male—must leave the familiar landscape and civilizing influences of city or town life in order to test himself against nature. Even if he doesn't plan to light out for the territories permanently, like Huck, he must make at least a temporary excursion into a hostile or indifferent nature. In ''How I Contemplated'', however, Oates's female protagonist heads in what appears to be the opposite direction. In Oates's subversive use of the coming-of-age conventions, the city takes the place of the wilderness. The girl leaves behind the lush, green lawns of

Bloomfield Hills and Baldwin Country Day School and encounters the city as "wilderness." Ironically, the civilized territory she leaves behind carries an Indian name, Sioux Drive. To her the city's topography is alien, and its inhabitants predatory and sinister. The narrator describes Detroit as a place beset by hazards and warnings: "small warnings of frost, soot warnings, traffic warnings, hazardous lake conditions for small craft and swimmers, restless Negro gangs, restless cloud formations, restless temperatures aching to fall out the very bottom of the thermometer or shoot up over the top and boil everything over in red mercury." In comparison, on Sioux Drive, "There is no weather." These "territories" are no place to try to find yourself. As Clarita says to the narrator, "I never can figure out why girls like you bum around down here. What are you looking for anyway?"

What the narrator is looking for, like all protagonists in coming-of-age stories, is her self. What she finds instead is the wreckage of someone else who has tried to make the same pilgrimage, Simon, "who is said to have come from a home not much different" from her own on Sioux Drive. Simon is the subversive form of the mentor figure that is common to coming-of-age narratives. He had been down the same path before and is capable of acting as her guide, but in Oates's dark version of the genre he offers the very opposite of safe passage. He even acknowledges his role as failed guide when he says, "Once I was Huckleberry Finn, . . . but now I am Roderick Usher." By using the literary analogy to describe his decline and fall, Simon assures the narrator that they do come from the same world of good schools and good families. But the specifics of the comparison itself, spell out how far he has fallen from his original ambitions. Huck escapes an abusive father and overcomes all manner of obstacles, without losing his moral bearings, on the way to independence and manhood somewhere on the frontier (the "territories"). Roderick Usher (from Edgar Allan Poe's, "The Fall of the House of Usher"), on the other hand, is born into wealth and privilege, but descends into madness, addiction, and depravity and becomes so fearful and frail that he cannot leave the house. Whereas Huck's romanticism propels him outward and upward, Roderick's sends him inward and downward. Simon's search for identity and the frontier have become a primitive struggle just to survive. But the narrator remains powerfully attracted to her wayward mentor, and in probably the only heroic gesture he's capable of, Simon saves

Buildings in downtown Detroit.

her by turning her in, ironically sending her back to the safety of the "Indian territory" on Sioux Drive.

Another characteristic of coming-of-age narratives is the epiphany, or overwhelming moment of realization. Although many features of "How I Contemplated" lead readers to believe that the narrator is poised and ready for an epiphany, Oates leaves the matter very much in doubt. Even the short title implies that the narrator has experienced a powerful moment of self-realization, contemplation leading to a decision. The long title is even more explicit, promising to deliver "A Revelation of the Meaning of Life" and "A Happy Ending." By

What Do I Read Next?

- *Dubliners* (1914; rpt. 1949) by James Joyce is a collection of short stories that has become one of the classics of the coming-of-age genre. Joyce's protagonists struggle to find their identities and learn the meaning of life in vividly depicted Catholic neighborhoods of Dublin.

- "Where are You Going, Where Have You Been?" by Joyce Carol Oates is the companion story to "How I Contemplated" in which a young girl's sexual awakening occurs against a backdrop of potential violence.

- *This Boy's Life* (1989) by Tobias Wolfe is the successful college professor and writer's memoir of his childhood in an unstable family in a working-class town in the Northwest. The book, which was made into a film starring Robert De Niro and Leonardo De Caprio, is notable because the point of view never wavers from the child's perspective.

advertising these dramatic elements in the title, Oates is trying to call attention to the artificiality of the genre, pointing out how in real life our experiences do not conform so neatly to dramatic structures. The story's experimental notebook form also underscores this point as the narrator appears to layout all the elements she has learned belong in a story, and then struggles—unsuccessfully— to arrange her experiences into those categories.

Nevertheless, "How I Contemplated" does contain an ironic version of the moment of profound awareness found in classic narratives in the genre. The narrator experiences an epiphany, but it is a false one that leaves her with more questions and blank spaces than she had before. The false epiphany occurs "that night in the lavatory when everything was changed." Notice the passive construction in that sentence and how it relieves her from any responsibility or agency. She does not bring about change, nor does she acknowledge experiencing any essential change herself. Instead, it's every-

thing else that changes, she says. What happens in the lavatory that changes everything is that she is badly beaten by two of the other girls in detention. Turning points in coming-of-age narratives usually demand that protagonists act, that they imprint themselves on their circumstances, that they *do* something heroic. In this case, however, the narrator is robbed of all control and is viciously acted upon; she is the victim rather than the hero of her circumstances. Despite this inversion of the conventions of the coming-of-age story, however, the narrator in "How I Contemplated" does have the opportunity to use her experience as victim of assault to learn something. In other words, genuine self-revelation is available to her. But it appears that she's not capable of such self-reflection. Writing about "That Night" after nearly a year of twice-weekly visits to her psychiatrist later she still exclaims, "Why is she beaten up? Why do they pound her, why such hatred?" She doesn't have the courage to contemplate her identity in terms that would come close to explaining why Princess and Star would want revenge on her. She turns away from the revelation—painful though it is—that the beating offers her.

Because the narrator rejects, or is not prepared for, the lessons that her experiences in "the wilderness" have to offer her, she is destined to return unchanged to the safety of "civilization. By contrast, Huck, at the end of Twain's novel, has completely outgrown the possibility of "civilized" life with his Aunt Sally and knows he must seek challenges and opportunities on the frontier. Oates's narrator, however, returns to the insulating environment of her parents' house and swears that "never will she reconcile four o'clock in the morning in Detroit with eight o'clock breakfasts in Bloomfield Hills." Whatever dissatisfaction, restlessness, or desire drove her to Detroit and into Simon's arms has evaporated or is repressed." *I will never leave home, this is my home, I love everything here, I am in love with everything here,*" she says again and again.

If the narrator's breathless affirmations in the story's final section (titled "EVENTS") are any indication, then her journey has been as much a regression as a coming-of-age. If her objective had been to escape her parents' suffocating protectiveness, then she has absolutely failed. Like a child, she "burst[s] into tears and hysteria" and is "convulsed in Father's arms." The house appears to her as "like a doll's house." Readers no doubt share her joy at a safe return from such self-destructive behavior, but wonder if this is the "happy ending" they have been promised. Although it is possible to interpret her emotional return home as the beginning of her ability to accept herself and her parents' love. Oates's ending is ambivalent. The narrator describes herself in the last section as "saddened and converted." It makes perfect sense that she is saddened given what she has endured, but "converted" is more difficult to interpret. She may mean that she now prefers to see the world the way her parents do, satisfied to live their comfortable lives pretending that unpleasantness and injustice do not exist. She may also be suggesting that her weeks with Simon, whom she still fears and desires, have changed her permanently in ways that she has not revealed in these notes. She herself seems unsure, wondering as she sees her reflection distorted in the toaster, "is that my face?".

Source: Elisabeth Piedmont-Marton, for *Short Stories for Students*, The Gale Group, 2000.

Brenda O. Daly

In the following essay, Daly contends that the characters in Oates's writings (and therefore the author's imagination) do not transcend gender conventions.

When Joyce Carol Oates tells us that "most novelists divide themselves up lavishly in their novels," she implies that a writer's imagination enables her to transcend socially determined gender categories. Nevertheless, as I shall show, Oates's early fiction reveals a pattern of authorial self-division that conforms to gender conventions: her male characters, such as Richard Everett in *Expensive People* and Jules Wendall in *them*, assume the right to define themselves, whereas her female characters, Maureen Wendall and Nadine Greene in *them*, merely act out roles in some (male) author's fiction. This probably unconscious projection of Oates's authorial power upon male characters is symptomatic, I believe, of a certain anxious authorship in her fiction in the 1960s, an anxiety rooted more in gender than in social class. Indeed, in the final pages of *them* lower-class Maureen asserts herself more effectively than does her counterpart Nadine from the upper-middle class suburb of Grosse Point, a passive princess whose problems Oates also explores in "How I Contemplated the World."

We see, for example, that the unnamed narrator of "How I Contemplated the World" refers to herself only in the third person, as "the girl," whereas Richard Everett, as narrator of *Expensive*

> Because the narrator rejects, or is not prepared for, the lessons that her experiences in 'the wilderness' have to offer her, she is destined to return unchanged to the safety of 'civilization.'"

People, begins his memoirs with the bold, "I was a child murderer". Although both are children of wealth, only Richard readily assumes an authorial persona, speaking from the place of a violently preestablished, coherent authorial "I." By contrast, the girl, who has no preestablished I, illustrates Judith Kegan Gardiner's point that female identity is a process that does not conform to the Oedipal myth of a unique, whole, and coherent self. Moreover, though Gardiner suggests that women often define themselves through the act of writing, the girl does not. Although both of these privileged adolescents have been educated in elite private schools, only Richard writes well. Moreover, only Richard dares to criticize America. His highly polished memoirs are a savage satire of the values of a consumer society, the same values his parents uphold. Richard's confession that he has killed his mother, not his father, is even more sophisticated satire—an inversion of the Oedipal plot that functions as a critique of the model of identity promoted by the Freudian psychiatrists who, of course, fail in their attempts to "cure" him.

The socially determined personae adopted by both of these adolescents—the male "author" and the female "character"—are ultimately self-destructive. For example, it is apparent from the girl's essay, a disorganized outline of her experience of running away from home, that she is a character still in search of a (male) author, a lover to replace her father; whereas Richard, a mirror image of the girl, is already an accomplished author, but one whose I has been established by violence, by matricide. His satire reeks of aggression, not only against his parents but against most adults, including his anticipated readers. Helplessly acting out the script of the

> Yet the girl, as she calls herself, desires something. She is hungry for something. She opens her essay with a description of herself before the 'fall'. . . ."

passive female character and the aggressive male author, these adolescents clearly acquiesce to traditional gender roles. Like many other adolescents in Oates's early fiction, as Robert Fossum says, they feel as if they are "actors in a script written and directed by someone else." Both "How I Contemplated the World" and *Expensive People* also illustrate Fossum's point that "repeatedly, Oates's people crave an order associated with 'home' and the loving protection of the father. Repeatedly, this conflicts with the yearning for the 'road' and freedom from the father."

Of course, "lighting out for the territory" is hardly a new metaphor for the struggle for self-definition in American fiction. Huck Finn and Holden Caufield are well-known examples of adolescents who not only run away, but narrate their stories of flight with considerable insight. This male tradition may lead Fossum to conclude that the yearnings of adolescents in Oates's fiction, whether for home or for the road, are "expressions of a struggle to control their own lives against the forces of 'accident,' circumstances, [and] other people." Here Fossum minimizes the desire for relationship implicit in the metaphor of "home," perhaps because his unexamined model of identity formation is, in fact, based upon male experience. This romantic model of identity places emphasis on control and autonomy, almost to the exclusion of connectedness. Yet whether we are at home or in flight, we define ourselves only in relationship to others; even our declarations of independence must be acknowledged by someone, as Jessica Benjamin points out. In both her criticism and fiction Oates emphasizes, as does Benjamin, that the self is socially embedded, or "interconnected." Oates also shares with Bakhtin a belief in the relational nature of consciousness, a conception of the self constructed in and through language. And if we accept the notion

that identity is formed through both private and public discourses, it follows that, as Bakhtin says, language "ventriloquate[s]" us. It then becomes apparent why Bakhtin asserts that "we must all, perforce, become authors." If we do not author language, language authors us.

It is not surprising, however, that Oates's experiences as a woman make her more attentive than Bakhtin to the ways that gender complicates self-definition or self-authorship. In fact, the problem of self-authorship became an "obsession" for Oates, as she says in a 1973 comment about "How I Contemplated the World." She defines this story's theme—which, she states, "so obsessed me that I've treated it half a dozen times, perhaps more"— as the riddle of "why we leave home or make vain attempts to leave home, or failing that, yearn to leave home." She adds, "there are many ways of leaving." She intimates that one way of leaving home is literal; another is imaginative. Both ways pose considerably greater problems for young women, as Oates implies in this elaboration of her theme:

> While you're away, trying to map out another life, new parents or stray adults or simply anyone with an I.Q. one point above yours conquers you. They just walk up to you and take hold. That's that. The puzzle is, how do we become these people who victimize us? They are so charming, so much in control of their bitten-off part of the world; they are so very masculine.

This comment betrays a degree of autobiographical anxiety about how Oates herself is to leave home, how she is to leave the house of fiction the "masters" have built. How, for example, is she to use her own high I.Q.? How is she to claim authorial power without becoming one of those who victimize others, one of those "very masculine" authors who are "so much in control of their bitten-off part of the world"?

Yet Oates's remark about those who "just walk up to you and take hold" at least implies a democratic ideal. One might go further and assert that this image of over-aggressive masculinity suggests the need for a more maternal conception of authorial power, power that nurtures rather than controls. Oates also understands that such nurturant power— more a daughter's inheritance than a son's—lacks cultural authority, since it has, historically, been limited to the domestic sphere. As Lynda Boose and Betty Flowers point out, the authority a daughter inherits from a mother is not parallel to that which a son inherits from a father. Oates explores this power disparity in *Expensive People*. She lays bare the gender politics of the Oedipal myth of authorial power by creating a writer who is also Richard's mother. Thus Richard must "kill" his mother, rather than his father, in order to acquire authorial power. Imagining himself a character in his mother's fiction, a violent man in a short story called "The Sniper," Richard literally acts out the part of "the sniper." Eventually, having failed to win his mother's attention, he turns his gun against her, against the mother who is forever abandoning him because, as we learn, she is unhappy with the constraints of her social identity—as Mrs. Everett, wife and mother. Richard's psychiatrists, blinded by their belief in one plot, an Oedipal plot of course, assume that he has fantasized the matricide. Their own gender politics cause them to deny Richard's credibility, as he anticipates many of his readers will also.

But *Expensive People* is more than a satire of Oedipal plots and psychiatric theories of personality. It is also a satire of Joyce Carol Oates's previous fiction. Some of the titles written by Richard's mother, Natashya (Nada) Everett, are the same as those by Oates: "The Molester," for example, and "Building Tension in the Short Story." Why this self-satire? The fact is that, like Nada, Oates has written violent plot lines for her male protagonists. Her first two novels end in suicide—Shar Rule's in *Expensive People*, Swan Revere's in *A Garden of Earthly Delights,* and now Richard Everett's, as promised, at the end of his memoir, *Expensive People.* This pattern of violent closure explains why Oates perceives herself, like Nada, as sacrificing her heroes for aesthetic purposes: to "build tension" in her fiction. Significantly; in her next novel, *them,* both Maureen Wendall and her brother Jules physically survive, but they do not escape traditional gender scripts. Indeed, at the end of the novel, they seem fated to reenact old scripts, scripts that transform victims into victimizers.

How do we [not] become these people who victimize us? Oates returns to this question in *them,* once again exploring—through the creation of an alternate self—how to nurture the young. This time she portrays herself as a teacher, a "Miss Oates" who fails a student just as her counterpart, Nada Everett in *Expensive People,* failed her son. In particular, Miss Oates flunks a young woman named Maureen Wendall, a student who attended her English class at the University of Detroit night school. After leaving the class, Maureen writes a letter to Miss Oates which begins positively, "I think I am writing to you because I could see, past your talking and your control and the way you took notes care-fully in your books while you taught, writing down your own words as you said them, something like myself." But in a subsequent letter Maureen says bluntly, "You failed me," explaining that on the only paper she had handed in, Miss Oates had written "*Lack of coherence and development* " in blue ink, along with a failing grade. Like *Expensive People*, this novel illustrates the failure of an educated adult woman—writer, mother, or teacher—to nurture the young. Oates has yet to create an adult woman who uses her imagination, as Oates herself does, to move beyond powerlessness. Although her novels criticize the socio-economic system that destroys the human potential not only of "them" but also of "expensive people," they fail fully to elucidate—or transform—their own equally oppressive gender scripts.

In the Author's Note to *them,* however, Oates calls attention to this problem, as if after completing the novel she could finally see the gender issue more clearly. Although Joanne Creighton thinks that most readers will find the author of the Note "indistinguishable in any way from the 'real' author," herself at least as a co-creator, shaper of dreams, one who transforms images into art? Susan Gubar argues that this problem is common to female writers:

> Because of the forms of self-expression available to women, artistic creation often feels like a violation, a belated reaction to male penetration rather than a possessing and controlling. Not an ejaculation of pleasure but a reaction to rending . . . a painful wounding, a literal influence of male authority. If artistic creativity is likened to biological creativity, the terror of inspiration for women is experienced as the terror of being entered, deflowered, possessed, taken, had, broken, ravished—all words which illustrate the pain of the passive self whose boundaries are being violated.

Waller describes Oates in similar terms, as "almost passively open to the tortures and obsessions, the agonies of the particular place and time of America today." But in *them* it is not a woman but her hero Jules whom Oates describes as "torn apart" by his love for his family—"dragged to the bottom of the river by chains of love," just as, during the writing process, Oates herself is torn by contending voices. By contrast, Nadine doesn't want to be touched, doesn't want to "'get them mixed up with myself, everybody so close.'"

This gendered self-division occurs, I think, because Oates projects her authorial powers onto her male character, Jules, and her anxieties about loss of control onto her female characters, Maureen and Nadine. By the early 1970s, in *Marriages and Infidelities,* Oates escapes monologic (either male or female) gender archetypes by redefining this struggle for authority as both love *and* infidelity to the masters of fiction, both marriage *and* resistance to monologic authorial control; but in the 1960s, Oates had not yet satisfactorily defined her own authority, or that of her female characters. The difficulty is, as Sandra Gilbert and Susan Gubar argue, that defining the canon as shaped by Oedipal struggle—with the pen as phallus—creates difficulties for the female writer. Yet as Oates continued to seek a different self, and a new kind of authority, she resurrected ''the girl'' again and again. In ''How I Contemplated the World,'' for example, she gives a young woman the persona of author and the chance to author herself, but all her dreams lead her either back home or to her tyrannical lover Simon, both of which are ''evil'' choices. As Oates comments, ''It's a story with an evil ending because not only must you return home again (lacking the power, I mean the economic and physical power, to stay away), but while you're away, trying to map out a new life, new parents or stray adults or simply anyone with an I.Q. one point above yours conquers you.'' This comment may apply to either young men or women, but adolescent girls suffer more severely from lack of economic and physical power, as well as the habit of allowing others to dominate them. Men can assume the role of author, of conqueror, whereas women become anxious when they acquire power. If women are to become self-authoring, how should they redefine authorial power? Thus, the young writer of ''How I Contemplated the World'' enacts Oates's own struggle to leave home, a struggle to re-imagine both conventional characters and conventional endings.

The young narrator of ''How I Contemplated the World'' begins bravely, but she too is fated to act out the metaphysics of romance plots. She drafts an essay for Mr. Forest, a man she describes as ''sweet and rodentlike,'' who is nevertheless more powerful than she because, she writes, he ''has conferred with the principal and my parents and everything is fixed.'' According to their agreement, and according to convention, her identity is ''fixed,'' stable, already defined. Indeed, in the upper-class ''heaven'' of Grosse Point, her desire does not exist. In this materialistic world, even her actions, however ''bad,'' have no consequences. Her parents, the principal, and Mr. Forest agree to ''treat her as if nothing has happened, a new start, begin again, only sixteen years old, what a shame, how did it happen?'' Yet the girl, as she calls herself, desires something. She is hungry for something. She opens her essay with a description of herself before the ''fall'': ''The girl (myself) is walking through Branden's, that excellent store. Suburb of a large famous city that is a symbol for large famous American Cities. The event sneaks up on the girl, who believes she is herding it along with a small, fixed smile, a girl of fifteen, innocently experienced.'' She sees herself, in retrospect, as ''innocently experienced,'' someone who thinks she is in control of events but who suddenly finds herself stealing a pair of gloves. This theft, like leaving home, is a desperate attempt to resist the role of passive virgin. Like Alice in Wonderland, the girl desires experience, desires a fall. This necessary fall, this journey into the world below—to what she calls ''poking around in the debris'' of Detroit—appears regularly in the romance, usually as a pattern of descent experienced by the hero. Generally, of course, the role of heroine in a romance is more restrictive: she is more often a victim than an initiator of action, more often concerned with preserving her virginity than with gaining experience, sexual or otherwise.

The girl is striving, heroically, to break this pattern, a pattern that Oates also explored in the figure of Nadine in *them*. Nadine acts the part of a passive object to the questor Jules who, despite his lower class origins, has greater freedom to initiate action, and greater freedom of imagination as well. The girl, however, anticipates no response and no changes in her static world; she assumes that her parents and teachers won't hear her. Yet ''How I Contemplated the World'' also explores ways to alter gender roles in the romance plot, making the young woman the initiator of action, and providing her with a guide to the world below. Clarita, the young black woman who guides her in the world of ''them,'' says, ''I can never figure out why girls like you bum around down here,'' and asks, ''What are you looking for anyway?'' It is difficult for Clarita, who imagines herself moving up—as she watches television—to imagine someone wanting to move down. Yet Clarita and the girl are both victimized by Simon. A drug addict and a pimp, Simon might have played the part of romantic hero, but having escaped from a world very much like the young white woman's, he says, cynically, ''Once I was Huckleberry Finn . . . now I am Roderick Usher.'' If he is Roderick Usher, locked in his mad house, the young woman's fate should be obvious to her, and yet she can't seem to resist this mirror image of herself. Behaving like a sacrificial victim, she allows herself to be sexually abused by him and, she tells us, sold to other men for drug money when she was "too low for him." Even so, the girl confesses that she would go back to Simon, if she could. "Would I go back to Simon again? Would I lie down in all that filth and craziness? Over and over again." Like her author, Joyce Carol Oates, she is drawn back to a man like Simon, a man whose apparent capacity for conquest, for the heroic, fascinates her.

Oates tells of this fascination in her 1980 preface to *Three Plays*, plays she describes as rituals of sacrifice behind "a surface realism and a prose facade." In these plays it is men who become "mock-saviors and mock-playwrights," and "whose refusal to be mere third-person characters assures them victory." The problem for a female writer is how to be democratically both, how to be her own author while at the same time a character in the lives of others. Such traditional gendering of authorial power is a puzzle that Oates explicitly acknowledges in a 1982 discussion of her childhood reading of *Alice's Adventures in Wonderland* and *Through the Looking Glass*:

> I might have wished to be Alice, that prototypical heroine of our race, but I knew myself too shy, too readily frightened of both the unknown and the known (Alice, never succumbing to terror, is not a real child), and too mischievous. . . . Though a child like me, she wasn't telling her own story; that godly privilege resided with someone named, in gilt letters on the book's spine, "Lewis Carroll."

Having become Joyce "Carroll" Oates, she found the masculine authorial self a problem throughout the 1960s; she remained puzzled about how to be a female writer without victimizing others, without forcing them to act as characters in a script determined by someone with "godly privilege." Oates managed to solve this riddle, but not before experiencing a personal crisis.

This personal crisis was resolved, according to Joanne Creighton, by writing the story *"Plot."* Although *"Plot"* may be read as the story of a young man who commits suicide, it also tells the story of the character's author, who self-consciously identifies with her hero, but at the same time strives to differentiate herself from him. Oates solves her anxiety about authorial power by sharing it with readers, by fully disclosing the writing process, by demystifying it. As the first two lines of the story show, this self-disclosure requires graphic self-division:

> Given: the existence of X. / Given: the existence of myself. / Given: X's obsessive interest in me. / Given:

the universe we share together, he and I, which has shrunk into an area about two miles square in the center of this city.

The writer then hypothesizes that X "is on a mission of reclamation, a private detective hired by my father; he is a police agent." Here it becomes apparent that the character is "he," whereas the writer, the I, experiences the character, X, as a paternal agent. He = X = Paternal Agent = Author = Violence. The I imagines she has committed some offense. Could that offense have been to claim the right to be both woman and writer, and furthermore, to write as a woman? This graphic self-division marks the point at which Oates rejects the notion of a unified self—an I in competition with all others—consciously adopting, as part of her writing strategy, Gardiner's notion of identity as process. In "Plot," Oates makes this process visible, opening a space—on the same plane—for a writer's more democratic self-division into all her characters, regardless of gender.

Source: Brenda O. Daly, "'How Do We [Not] Become These People Who Victimize Us?': Anxious Authorship in the Early Fiction of Joyce Carol Oates," in *Anxious Power: Reading, Writing, and Ambivalence in Narrative by Women*, edited by Carol J. Singley and Susan Elizabeth Sweeney, State University of New York Press, 1993, pp. 235–52.

Sue Simpson Park

In the following essay, Park interprets the story's structure, imagery, motifs, and verbal echoes to show that the title reflects the protagonist's return to "a place that before had failed her miserably."

Joyce Carol Oates is a most prolific writer. Born in 1938, she has now published seven novels, five collections of short stories, two volumes of poetry, a collection of critical essays, and a number of uncollected stories, poems, and essays. Any reader who undertakes a critical study of Oates's production finds himself in very fertile but almost wholly uncultivated ground; the primary material is there, rich and teeming, but so far subjected to little serious analytical consideration. The short fiction particularly holds abundant possibilities for critical development: there are depths of mythic patterns, psychological probings, and structural complexities; however, only the shallowest spade work has been done. Indicative of the richness is the short piece of experimental fiction called "How I Contemplated the World from the Detroit House of Correction and Began My Life over Again."

> "An additional motif, not extensively developed but clearly in keeping with the protagonist's difficulty in discerning reality, involves romantic stories and fairy tales."

The title itself, with its seventeen words, suggests a departure from the conventional practice of relatively short titles. The headnote for the story provides a further hint as to the experimental quality of what is to follow: "Notes for an essay for an English class at Baldwin Country Day School; poking around in debris; disgust and curiosity; a revelation of the meaning of life; a happy ending. . . ." A prefiguration of the contrapuntal nature of the story is evident in these preliminaries: on the one hand, the abstractions of contemplation, revelation, the meaning of life, beginning life over again; on the other, the tangibility of the Detroit House of Correction and an English class at Baldwin Country Day School.

When the events of the story are arranged chronologically, what emerges is this: A fifteen-year-old girl from a wealthy family steals a pair of gloves from a department store, even though she has money—"bills, she doesn't know how many bills"—in her purse. The store detective stops her, someone notifies her parents, her physician father talks to the owner of the store, and no charges are filed. The girl's mother takes her shopping in an attempt to understand the actions; the girl is apathetic, thinking but not saying aloud, "I wanted to steal but not to buy." Weeks later, the girl leaves school in midafternoon and takes a bus to downtown Detroit. There she is taken in by a prostitute, lives with her and her lover Simon, participates in sexual relations with Simon and with men Simon brings in. Someone, she thinks Simon, turns her in to the authorities as a minor and she is taken to the Detroit House of Correction, where she is most uncooperative and refuses to give any information as to her past or her identity, vowing she will never return home. Then, one night, two girls beat her severely, she is hospitalized, and her father takes her home—back to school, with twice-weekly appointments with a female psychiatrist. Now sixteen, she sits in her pink room on Sioux Drive in Bloomfield Hills and makes notes for an essay for her English class.

The "notes for an essay" are presented in twelve divisions marked with Roman numerals. At first glance, one surmises from the form that this is the work of a careful student, arranging material in an orderly fashion (twelve sections, reminiscent of *The Aeneid*, *Paradise Lost*, and such novels as James's *The Ambassadors*, a year's installments) for the purpose of organizing experience into a coherent system. Such an assumption, however, is erroneous, for the divisions do not constitute a topical outline; neither are they chronological. Instead, they are repetitive, disjointed, and dispersive—in other words, indicative of the state of mind of the sixteen-year-old protagonist, confused, questioning, attempting to make sense of the senseless, to impose order upon chaos.

The major divisions are these:

I Events

II Characters

III World Events

IV People & Circumstances Contributing to This Delinquency

V Sioux Drive

VI Detroit

VII Events

VIII Characters

IX That Night

X Detroit

XI Characters We Are Forever Entwined With

XII Events

Three divisions are labeled "Events"—the first, the seventh, and the twelfth. Hence the story begins, centers, and ends in recollected action; and action at least is relatively unequivocal, however ambiguous the motives behind the action. Two other sections are linked to events—section III, "World Events," the total content of which is the single word "Nothing," and section IX, "That Night," a brief description (five sentences, two of which are short questions) of the beating which sent the girl to the hospital.

Three divisions are labeled "characters." Sections II and VIII follow immediately "event" divisions, and XI, with the amplified heading, "Characters We Are Forever Entwined With," immediately precedes the final "event" division. Section IV seems to link together the idea of characters ("people") and events ("circumstances"), but again the entire section consists of one word, "Nothing."

The remaining three divisions are basically descriptive: V, a picture of Sioux Drive, and VI and X, brief delineations of Detroit. Thus it appears that the girl is trying to organize her material around three points, possibly suggested by her English teacher. Events, Characters, and Places are the focal points of her outline, but there is no intrinsic order to the arrangement of points; it is random, apparently unpurposeful. What knits the scraps of information together into a movingly effective totality is not the protagonist's pathetic effort to establish meaningful continuity, but the artist's skillful interweaving of motifs and verbal echoes.

Basic to the ultimate unity of the story is a pattern of contrasts. The title and the headnote suggest this contrapuntal interplay; the story elaborates upon the suggestion. Bloomfield Hills is contrasted with inner-city Detroit, the girl's mother with the prostitute Clarita, the girl's father with the procurer-addict Simon. The differences are vast—and yet in each case the contrast is intensified by a curious and significant identity. But most important is the duality of the girl herself.

The pattern of contrasts is established by unlike settings. Bloomfield Hills is an exclusive suburb with "monumental houses" located on curving lanes with such names as Sioux Drive and Burning Bush Way and Du Maurier Drive and Lois Lane. There are no prosaic "streets" in Bloomfield Hills. The houses are Georgian and Colonial and French-Normandy, imitations of other cultures and other times, with columns and baywindows and "fireplaces in living room, library, recreation room, paneled walls wet bar five bathrooms five bedrooms two lavatories central air conditioning automatic sprinkler automatic garage door . . . a breakfast room a patio a large fenced lot fourteen trees a front door with a brass knocker never knocked." Detroit,

on the other hand, is a world that is "falling out the bottom." In Detroit there are streets and avenues, 12th Street, Fourteenth Street, Woodward Avenue, Livernois Avenue. Instead of the "heartbreaking sidewalks, so clean" of Bloomfield Hills, there is filthy pavement from which "scraps of paper flutter in the air like pigeons, dirt flies up and hits you right in the eye, oh Detroit is breaking up into dangerous bits of newspaper and dirt, watch out." While the Bloomfield Hills police are "quiet private police, in unmarked cars. Cruising on Saturday evenings with paternal smiles for the residents," the Detroit city police are hated "cops" who are not paternal: "It took three of them to get me in the police cruiser . . . and they put more than their hands on my arm."

Bloomfield Hills is characterized by stores with "many mild pale lights, easy on the eye and the soul . . . [and] women shoppers with their excellent shoes and coats and hair dos, all dawdling gracefully, in no hurry." The curving residential drives are "slow"; the policemen "quiet"; the rooms "lovely in the sunlight"; this is a world of "God in gold and beige carpeting, . . . and the miracle of a clean polished gleaming toaster and faucets that run both hot and cold water." Detroit is "pavement and closed-up stores; grillwork over the windows of a pawnshop." Instead of quiet and slow and heavy, Detroit is "hazardous," "restless"; it is a world that boils and shoots and aches. Instead of beige carpeting and chandeliers, Detroit rooms have "a mattress on the floor" and "wallpaper hanging in strips." Whereas the living room in a five bedroom Colonial house at 250 Sioux Drive is "thirty by twenty-five," Simon lives in a "six-by-six room."

The winds blow nothing to Sioux Drive, "no odors of hollyhocks or forsythia," nothing it does not already possess. Sioux Drive has everything it could desire. In Detroit, however, Simon longs for the "cold clean air . . . from Canada" which might bring a degree of purification to the dirty city streets. And in Bloomfield Hills, even weather vanes, "had they weather vanes, don't have to turn with the wind, don't have to contend with the weather. There is no weather." The suburban way of life is insulated, artificially cooled and heated and cleaned. As the girl "dreams along the corridors" of the Baldwin Country Day School, she "presses her face against the Thermoplex glass. No frost or steam can ever form on that glass." There is no such insulation, no such freedom from contention with the elements in the inner city; section VI, the first of the two sections describing Detroit, begins, "There is always weather in Detroit. Detroit's temperature is always 32°. Fast-falling temperatures. Slow-rising temperatures. Wind from the north-northeast four to forty miles an hour" and ends, "Detroit's temperature is 32°. Fast-falling temperatures. Wind from the north-northeast four to forty miles an hour." Inner-city life is cold, hovering on the point of freezing, with wildly fluctuating winds.

Bloomfield Hills and Detroit are so different that it seems hardly possible that they exist only a few miles apart. The same destructive force which the girl experiences in the Detroit House of Correction, however, is for her a terrifying interloper upon the insulated tranquillity of Bloomfield Hills. The two girls, one black and one white, who corner the protagonist in the lavatory on "that night" and beat her unmercifully are executing "revenge on the oppressed minorities of America! revenge on the slaughtered Indians! revenge on the female sex, on the male sex, revenge on Bloomfield Hills, revenge revenge." In Detroit "shoppers shop grimly, their cars are not parked in safe places, their windshields may be smashed and graceful ebony hands may drag them out through their shatterproof smashed windshields, crying, Revenge for the Indians!" Bloomfield Hills is the place where there is no weather, where the windshields shield residents from the wind, but if the locked locks and the nailed-shut doors of the Detroit House of Correction provide no safety, neither does suburbia; the shatterproof windshields can be smashed. Thus the "happy ending" of the headnote is more accurately a desperate retreat behind the Thermoplex glass, but with no real assurance of impregnability. The girl, as she makes notes for the assigned essay, shivers at the thought of Simon climbing in through her bedroom window to strangle her: "Why do I shiver? I am now sixteen and sixteen is not an age for shivering." Her teeth chatter at the irrational thought of being sued should she unintentionally divulge the identity of the famous automotive designer for whom her family's house was originally built. She even fears the maid who evidently has worked for the family for years; on her return home, the girl is "weeping, weeping, though Billie the maid is *probably listening*" and "Billie the maid is *no doubt* listening from the kitchen as I burst into tears and the hysteria Simon got so sick of." So Bloomfield Hills and Detroit, different as they are, are really two sides of one coin, a coin of insecurity and potential violence.

The mother-Clarita contrast also fits this pattern. Whereas the mother is a "lady [with] hair like blown-up gold . . . hair and fingers and body of inestimable grace," Clarita is a "woman" with "hair long and falling into strands, not recently washed." The expensive clothing which the girl's mother wears—coat, boots, gloves, a fur hat—provides protection against the cold of the Michigan winter and, symbolically, against the encroachment of the ugly in life. Clarita, in contrast, wears jeans, a sweater, "unwashed underclothes, or no underclothes," and there is no protection for this woman whose face is exhausted, over-wrought, from her experiences as a prostitute since the age of thirteen. "At the age when I was packing my overnight case for a slumber party at Toni Deshield's [shield, protection, insulation]," the narrator notes, "she was tearing filthy sheets off a bed and scratching up a rash on her arms." Too, Clarita tells her about tearing the wallpaper from the walls with her teeth, fighting for her life one night against a "barbaric tribe" of men "high from some pills." These events surely are foreign to the mother who drives a "heavy . . . big car, a Lincoln, long and black" in Bloomfield Hills where all the women drive "automobiles bought of Ford and General Motors and Chrysler, very heavy automobiles. No foreign cars."

Faithfully, diligently, the mother performs the proper rites to care for her body, her mind, and her civic obligations; she belongs to the athletic club and the golf club, to the "Village Women's Club at which lectures are given each winter on Genet and Sartre and James Baldwin, by the Director of the Adult Education Program at Wayne State University," to the country club and the art association and the Founders Society of the Detroit Institute of Arts. She is "in perpetual motion," while Clarita "lounges" by the highway, hitchhiking, or "slouches" on a counter stool in a diner. Clarita's "adult education" comes from the late movies on television, where she can experience vicariously "all those marvelous lives" she might have lived had her *pre*-adult education not been so explicit. Clarita knows nothing of Sioux Drive or Raymond Forrest; "Harvard Business School could be at the corner of Vernor and 12th Street for all she cares, and Vietnam might have sunk by now into the Dead Sea under its tons of debris, for all the amazement she could show."

Despite their differences, however, the mother and the prostitute are akin. Both are puzzled by the girl. The mother is first introduced as a voice—"earnest, husky . . . saying, 'If you wanted gloves [love?], why didn't you say so? Why didn't you ask for them?'" She later asks, on the abortive shopping trip, "What's wrong with you, what can I do for you, why are you so strange?" The girl first encounters Clarita as a voice on the streets of closed-down barber shops and diners and movie houses and faces: "Honey, are you looking for somebody down here?" and later, "I never can figure out why girls like you bum around down here. What are you looking for anyway?" Neither woman appreciates the younger girl's frustration; neither can answer the questions raised by her actions. And if Clarita is like the mother in her inability to understand the girl, the two are also similar in the inadequacy of what they do offer to her. The mother's attempts to buy things to fill the void in her daughter's life are rebuffed; Clarita's proffered sanctuary from the alien streets is accepted only briefly and then is rejected.

Of particular significance is the likelihood that the girl subconsciously considers both her mother and Clarita to be her rivals. Seemingly sensing that the competition with her mother is unequal, she associates her with grace and motion—and heaviness: "Heavy weighs the gold on the back of her hairbrush and hand mirror. Heavy heavy the candlesticks in the dining room. Very heavy is the big car, a Lincoln, long and black, that on one cool autumn day split a squirrel's body in two unequal parts." In this context the squirrel may be representative of the girl (note the rhyme) since the girl on more than one occasion mentions the *chattering* of her teeth and describes herself as wearing a close-fitted coat with a fur collar; thus she may see herself as being destroyed in the rivalry with the more powerful older woman. The girl, therefore, wants to hurt her mother; she says that "her mother's heart would break to see" the dirty yellow Kleenex in her purse; in the same purse is a lipstick called Broken Heart—and in the same sentence there are these words: "Her fingers are trembling like crazy; her teeth are beginning to chatter; her insides are alive; her eyes glow in her head; she is saying to her mother's astonished face *I want to steal but not to buy.*" Since the mother is not present at the moment being described, it is likely that the girl is vitalized by the thought of the shock on her mother's face, the

broken heart, should she tell her mother what she is feeling. And when the girl returns home after her hospital stay, there is only one sentence which reveals that the mother is even present—"Mother embraces me"—while it is the father in whose arms she cries. Clarita, too, must be a kind of rival to the girl, though a less formidable one. When the prostitute takes the girl into her apartment above a restaurant, Simon is the older woman's lover, but in a short time Simon has become the girl's lover—whether *also* or *instead* is not made clear. The girl supposes that it is Simon who turned her in to the police when he grew tired of her; she makes no conscious connection between her arrest and Clarita's saying "mournfully to me *Honey somebody is going to turn you out let me give you warning.*" Perhaps there is no connection; perhaps, however, her never knowing for sure that her arrest was Simon's doing is suggestive of a refusal on her part to admit another defeat at the hands of a competitor.

In a parallel fashion, Oates develops the contrasts between the girl's father and Simon. The father is a physician for the "slightly sick" and a "player of squash and golf." His name is never mentioned; he is Dr. ———. He evidently is a handsome man, for the girl describes him as "looking like a prince" when he takes her home from the hospital. Evidently, too, he is a busy man who does not have time for his daughter, at least not as much time as she wants from him. The fact that he is in Los Angeles at a medical convention when she steals the gloves suggests that she is thus demanding attention from him; evidently her ploy is successful, for her father talks to Raymond Forrest, the owner of the store, and gets her off. Where he is weeks later when she runs away from home is not indicated, but in her notes she writes, "And where was he when Clarita put her hand on my arm . . . and said, 'Honey, are you looking for somebody down here?'" She *is* looking for somebody, a father who will admit her importance, substantiate her self-worth, provide her with an identity so that she can answer her questions about herself: "A pretty girl? An ugly girl?"

Simon is a drifter, a parasite who lives off women. He sleeps mornings and afternoons, coming alive at night and only then with the stimulation of a pill or a cigarette. Physically he is tall, slightly stooped, with long blond hair in "spent languid curls." He describes himself thus: "Once I was

Huckleberry Finn, but now I am Roderick Usher.'' From a wealthy background similar to the girl's, he one day simply walked away and left it, perhaps with the spirit of adventure and the restless vitality that characterize Huck Finn; now he is a dweller in a haunted palace filled with Poe's ''Vast forms that move fantastically / To a discordant melody; / While, like a rapid ghastly river, / Through the pale door, / A hideous throng rush out forever, / And laugh—but smile no more.'' At first, he fills the void in the girl's life. He is old enough to be her father—thirty-five. He is Clarita's lover, and, if Clarita is a substitute mother, Simon is a substitute father. The sexual relationship between the girl and Simon is an acting-out of her Electra complex. In her notes she asks, ''Would I go back to Simon again? Would I lie down with him in all that filth and craziness? Over and over again.'' She has answered her own question. One must note, however, the typography:

> Would I lie down with him in all that filth and craziness? Over and over again. a Clarita is being betrayed as in front of a Cunningham Drug Store she is nervously eyeing a colored man who may or may not have money . . . .

The period after ''again'' completes a sentence, but the lower case ''a'' which follows and the spacing involved compel the reader to see an additional thought: ''Over and over again a Clarita [not simply Clarita, but *a* Clarita, *any* Clarita] is being betrayed.'' The betrayal is instigated by Simon, but the girl shares in it; her ambivalent feelings of guilt and desire are indicative of her sense of having betrayed Clarita, the mother who saved her from the street, and her sense of having achieved some sort of victory in capturing Simon-father, however briefly, for herself.

So Simon is a surrogate father whose whole attention the girl has managed to attain. The father-daughter analogy is further enhanced by Simon's words to her: ''*Ah Baby!* '' and ''*You are such a little girl.*'' One morning Simon ''forces her to give him an injection with that needle she knows is filthy, she has a dread of needles and surgical instruments and the odor of things that are to be sent into the blood, *thinking somehow of her father* '' (italics mine). But Simon too deserts her. He is displeased with her moods and when she is ''down too low for him,'' he loans her to a bearded friend of his for three days; on other occasions, he takes from her bills which are ''passed into her numb hands by

men.'' When he forces her to give him the injection, she is terrified that the drug may kill him, and yet she does what he asks, viewing her action as a gift she can give him, and the drug as a ''magic that is more than any woman can give him, striking the back of his head and making him stretch as if with the impact of a terrible sun.'' After the injection, when she tries to embrace him, he ''pushes her aside and stumbles to his feet. *Jesus Christ*, he says.''

She speculates that it is Simon who, ''tired of her and her hysteria,'' has the city police take her to the Detroit House of Correction. Even in the House of Correction, she will not talk about Simon, keeping him her secret while ''she aches still for Simon's hands and his caressing breath, though he gave her little pleasure.'' Then, when her real father takes her home, she once again has *his* attention; she is ''convulsed in Father's arms'' and vows she ''will never leave again, never, why did I leave, where did I go, what happened, my mind is gone wrong, my body is one big bruise.'' In her mind the events of the recent past are being replayed over and over, ''perpetually are Simon's hands moving across my body and adding everything up and so too are Father's hands on my shaking bruised back, far from the surface of my skin on the surface of my good blue cashmere coat.''

The contrapuntal pattern, omnipresent in the story, is ultimately traceable to the dichotomy within the girl herself. She has a desperate need for love, security, self-approbation. Her insecurity is revealed, for example, in the variety of substantives she uses to refer to herself. She never mentions her name; ''Honey'' is the only form of address anyone uses for her. Most frequently she refers to herself as ''the girl'' or with a third person feminine pronoun. Occasionally she shifts to first person, as in the first sentence of the story: ''The girl (myself) is walking through Branden's, that excellent store.'' The second division of the first section begins, ''The girl seated at home. . . . Someone is talking to me,'' and the third division of the first section describes ''Mother in her black coat, I in my close fitted blue coat. . . . The girl droops along in her coat.'' There are also first-person plural pronouns: ''We live on Sioux Drive'' and ''our maid Billie.'' Once in this first section, she refers to herself indirectly in the second person when she says, ''The strings draw together in a cat's cradle, making a net to save you when you fall''; obviously the net of connections she refers to is the net which "saved" her and brought her back to Sioux Drive. This same mixing of referents occurs through a large part of the story; only in the last two sections does she consistently refer to herself in the first person; here she has had forced upon her the decision to retreat into the pseudo-haven of suburbia and, at least for the time being, is trying to hold on to her identity through linking herself with material objects. She sees her face reflected, "distorted" in the shiny toaster, and wonders, "Is that my face?"

Moreover, she frequently insists that she makes her own decisions, and yet she knows she does not. When she steals the gloves—which she has the money to buy and does not even really want since she considers them "ugly"—the "event sneaks upon the girl, who believes she is herding it along." In the House of Correction she refuses to talk, "not because everyone has warned her not to talk but because, because she will not talk; because she won't say anything about Simon, who is her secret." She denies that there have been any "people and circumstances contributing to this delinquency," even while she is thinking of her brother, "remembering him unclearly," remembering that he at the age of ten had stolen "trick-and-treat candy from some six-year-old kids" and that he is not doing well at the Susquehanna Boys' Academy, an "excellent preparatory school in Maine." Recalling her own stealing which began at the age of eight, her smashing of a basement window "in her own house just for fun," and her failure to do "*work compatible with her performance on the Stanford-Binet*," she can still refuse to admit contributory influences. She summarizes "World Events" as "Nothing," attempting to shut out the world beyond the shaky security of Bloomfield Hills. Nevertheless, this self-sufficiency is illusory. It is akin to the names given to the teenage singing groups "of 1968 . . . *The Certain Forces, The Way Out, The Maniacs Responsible* ."

Typical of nearly every division of the notes is an ambivalence, revealed partially through the device of interrogatives. Of herself she has little certain knowledge, only that which can be measured empirically—her age; her height, "five feet five inches . . . ordinary height"; the color of her hair and her eyes. But value judgments she cannot make; she wonders whether she is a "pretty girl? An ugly girl?" Is Raymond Forrest "a handsome man? An ugly man? . . . who is Raymond Forrest, this man who is my salvation?" Is Clarita "twenty, twenty-five, . . . thirty or more? Pretty, ugly, what?"

Another device frequently employed to reinforce the pattern of contrasts is the paradox. The girl sees herself as "innocently experienced." She describes her home as "Classical contemporary. Traditional modern." The temperature in Detroit is "always 32°. Fast-falling temperatures. Slow-rising temperatures." Her father's "doctoring is of the slightly sick. The sick are sent elsewhere . . . the unsick are sent to Dr. Coronet (Isabel, a lady), an excellent psychiatrist for unsick people who angrily believe they are sick and want to do something about it."

The shoplifting incident, moreover, also illustrates the contrast of the worlds inhabited by the girl. She slips the gloves into her pocket; they are encased in a plastic bag, "airproof breathproof plastic bag," as insulated and lifeless as the rest of the Bloomfield Hills world. In her purse, in the billfold containing her money, are "snapshots of the family in clean plastic windows," protected from contamination. The rest of the purse's contents, however, is not so tidy: "a blue comb, not very clean," "a lot of dirty yellow Kleenex," hairpins, safety pins, a broken pencil, a stolen ballpoint. There, too, are a "compact of Cover Girl Make-Up, Ivory Rose," and the lipstick called "Broken Heart, a corrupt pink." The girl carries with her the paraphernalia for making herself superficially compatible with the pastel pink world of the suburbs—the covering, masking trappings. Pink is used to characterize the culture of Bloomfield Hills; "bloom" suggests pink; Harriet Arnold's, the shop where the mother takes the girl after the gloves episode, is decorated in pastel pink, with "graceful glimmering lights"; the most expensive mansion on Sioux Drive belongs to "himself, who has the C account itself, imagine that!" whose wife has a "bathtub of smooth clean glowing pink"; the girl's room is pink and she sits in it, making notes for her essay, looking around with "sad pink eyes." Pink, a color traditionally associated with an innocent baby girl, is also a tainted white and a diluted red, neither pure nor passionate; it is an appropriate color for the "innocently experienced" protagonist and her habitat.

The girl's association of herself and the squirrel, discussed above in another context, is an example of her use of animal imagery in descriptions of characters, suggestive of inability to perceive herself or anyone else as distinctly human. The store in which she steals the gloves is *Branden's* ; she *herds* her actions through the aisles; the strings of connections "draw together in a *cat's* cradle, making a *net* to save you." She leans against a window and a smudge of grease from her forehead appears on the pane; she wonders if "she could be boiled down to grease" as are cattle and sheep in a rendering plant. Her English teacher, Mr. Forest, whose "name is plain, unlike Raymond Forrest's, . . . is sweet and *rodent* like. Simon thinks of being chased over the "Canadian border on foot, *hounded* out in a blizzard of broken glass and horns." He is "always cold," perhaps like a reptile since he "uncoils" emotion in the girl. He "emerges from the cracks at dark" like a rat or a cockroach; he moves in "a feline cautious way, . . . always on guard." (All italics in this paragraph are mine.)

An additional motif, not extensively developed but clearly in keeping with the protagonist's difficulty in discerning reality, involves romantic stories and fairy tales. Her psychiatrist is Dr. Coronet (a crown); the doctor's first name is Isabel (Queen Isabella and a variant of Elizabeth); Dr. Isabel Coronet is "queenly, an elegant nicotine-stained lady." Princess, the black girl who attacks the narrator in the House of Correction, spends her spare time reading *Nancy Drew and Jewel Box Mystery.* Simon, who once thought of himself as Huck Finn, now thinks of himself as Roderick Usher. The girl's explanation that her "head hangs heavy as a pumpkin on my shoulders, and my hair has just been cut by Mr. Faye at the Crystal Salon" invokes images of Cinderella with the pumpkin and the crystal slipper, Rapunzel with long, heavy hair, and fay, a fairy or elf. The father who takes her home from the hospital is "a prince himself, come to carry me off," and on one occasion she speculates "that weeds might climb everywhere over that marvelous $180,000 house [as in "Sleeping Beauty"] and dinosaurs might return to muddy the beige carpeting, but never never will she reconcile four o'clock in the morning in Detroit with eight o'clock breakfasts in Bloomfield Hills."

Religious imagery, too, colors the story, but without evidence of serious commitment on the girl's part. The title and the headnote suggest contemplation, revelation, and rebirth, and indeed the girl leaves the hospital "bruised and saddened and converted." Mr. Forrest, the English teacher, vows to "treat her as if nothing has happened, a new start, begin again," and his essay assignment makes him a confessor in that "words pour out of me and won't stop. I want to tell everything." She thinks of Raymond Forrest as "this man who is my salvation"; when his father dies of a heart attack, she wants to "write Raymond Forrest a note of sympathy. I would like to thank him for not pressing charges against me one hundred years ago, saving me." She wants to write to him "telling of my love, or some other emotion that is positive and healthy. Not like Simon and his poetry . . . but when I try to think of something to say, it is Simon's language that comes back to me, caught in my head like a bad song." Simon, then, is presented as a sort of foil to Forrest and thus perhaps an inversion of a savior; there is, of course, his name; his hands bears wounds in the palms, "teeth marks from his previous life experiences"; his poetry, which will not leave her head, declares, "I am heading upward/. . . And I am going to dissolve into the clouds." And when she gives him the injection, she sees his "bright blood" as the drug enters his body, "making his face stretch as if with the impact of a terrible sun. . . . *Jesus Christ,* he says."

The story has made clear that Sioux Drive has not in the past provided a sense of security and self-worth for the girl, and it seems unlikely that it will begin to do so now. The "beginning again" of the title, as well as the "happy ending" of the headnote, is really a return to a place that before had failed her miserably. The house to which the girl returns is "a doll's house, so lovely in the sunlight," sunlight which "breaks in movieland patches" on the roof. This is not reality, but a make-believe world of games and movies; for the present, though, it offers at least a pretense of safety. Repeatedly the girl acknowledges her retreat into security, however tenuous it may prove. Nine times in time closing section of the story she uses "never" in connection with her intention never to leave home again; her insistence suggests that this is not a conscious decision to remain, but a desperate attempt to convince herself that this is her home, a place of safety where inner conflict ends.

This incredibly concentrated story, then, is developed in such a way that structure, imagery, motifs, verbal echoes work together to create for the reader the actual experience of the experiencing mind of the protagonist. The author's experiment can only be judged a success.

Source: Sue Simpson Park, "A Study in Counterpoint: Joyce Carol Oates's 'How I Contemplated the World from the Detroit House of Correction and Began My Life Over Again,'" in *Modern Fiction Studies*, Vol. 22, No. 2, Summer, 1976, pp. 213–24.

Sources

Avant, James A. Interview, in *The Library Journal*, September 1, 1970.

Gilman, Richard. Review of *The Wheel of Love*, in *The New York Times Book Review*, October 25, 1970, p. 4.

Long, R. E. Review of *The Wheel of Love*, in *The Saturday Review*, October 24, 1970.

Phillips, Robert. Interview, in *The Paris Review*, Fall, 1978, pp. 199-206.

Showalter, Elaine. "My Friend, Joyce Carol Oates: An Intimate Portrait," in *Ms. Magazine*, March, 1986, pp. 44-50.

Further Reading

Creighton, Joanne. *Joyce Carol Oates*, TUSAS, Twayne Publishers: Boston, 1979.
   Like all volumes in this series, this book provides an overview of the author's life and work to date. It also contains a thorough and easy to use bibliography.

Milazzo, Lee, ed. *Conversations with Joyce Carol Oates*, University Press of Mississippi: Jackson, 1989.
   A collection of interviews from 1969-1988, the book provides insight into the life and work of a dedicated and prolific writer.

In Another Country

Ernest Hemingway

1927

Ernest Hemingway is a legendary figure in twentieth-century American literature. His reputation stems not only from his body of written work, but from his adventurous and amorous lifestyle. His crisp, almost journalistic prose style, free of the long, sometimes flowery language common to much of the literature that appeared before him, has won him great acclaim and some of the highest literary honors: The Pulitzer Prize, which he won for his novella, *The Old Man and the Sea* in 1952; the Nobel Prize for Literature, which he received in 1954; and the Award of Merit from the American Academy of Arts and Letters, which he also received in 1954.

Despite these accolades, Hemingway is not without his critics. Some scholars complain that his tough, often violent subject matter is limited and without insight, and that his female characters, in particular, lack dimension. His devotees claim that behind his work's often tough, macho exterior lurks a complex world of wounded, complicated human beings. His short stories are among those most frequently studied and anthologized, especially ''The Snows of Kilimanjaro,'' ''A Clean, Well Lighted Place,'' ''The Gambler, the Nun, and the Radio,'' ''The Short, Happy Life of Francis Macomber,'' and ''In Another Country,'' which was first published in 1927 in Scribner's magazine. His novels include such American classics as *The Sun Also Rises*, *A Farewell to Arms*, *For Whom the Bell Tolls*, and *The Old Man and the Sea*. He has also

written several works of nonfiction, including *Death in the Afternoon*, about bullfighting, and *The Green Hills of Africa*, about big game hunting.

Author Biography

Ernest Hemingway was born in Oak Park, Illinois, into an upper-middle-class family. Although his childhood does not seem to have been particularly traumatic, in later years he often displayed bitterness towards his father, whom he saw as weak and ineffectual, and his mother, whom he felt was strict and domineering. By the time he was in high school he had developed an interest in literature, writing for his school newspaper and its literary magazine. During his family's summers in northern Michigan, he developed a love of hunting, fishing, and outdoor life. Upon graduation, he took a job at the *Kansas City Star*, where he honed the spare, objective style that would be his hallmark.

When the United States entered World War I, Hemingway volunteered as an ambulance driver for the Red Cross in Italy. Wounded, he recuperated in a Milan hospital among injured Italian soldiers, an experience that would provide the background for his 1927 story "In Another Country." This is also where he met nurse Agnes von Kurowsky, the inspiration for Catherine Barkeley in his novel *A Farewell to Arms*.

Upon returning to the United States in 1919, Hemingway wrote several short stories, but sold none. One year later, he met Hadley Richardson; they were wed the following year. They moved to Europe, settling primarily in Paris where their expatriate colleagues included important literary figures, such as F. Scott Fitzgerald and Gertrude Stein. During that time, Hemingway published two collections of short stories, followed by his acclaimed novel *The Sun Also Rises*, which featured characters based on his new circle of friends. Not long after, in 1927, he and Richardson divorced; Hemingway married Pauline Pfeiffer, a writer, less than two months later. In 1929, *A Farewell to Arms* was published, which cemented his literary reputation.

During the 1930s, Hemingway moved to Key West, Florida, yet spent much of his time traveling in Spain, where his fascination with bullfighting became the subject of his 1932 nonfiction work, *Death in the Afternoon*. He also pursued big game hunting, which he wrote about in *The Green Hills of Africa* (1935). Hunting figures prominently in many of Hemingway's stories, including "The Short Happy Life of Francis Macomber," first published in 1936.

In 1937, Hemingway went to Spain to cover the Spanish Civil War for the North American Newspaper Alliance and began a relationship with writer Martha Gelhorn, whom he had met in Florida. He received a divorce from Pfeiffer in November, 1940; Gelhorn became his third wife two weeks later. The same year, he published his novel about the Spanish Civil War, *For Whom the Bell Tolls*, another major success, and his play *The Fifth Column* was performed briefly on Broadway.

The 1940s found Hemingway working first as a war correspondent in China, then, along with Gelhorn, in Europe during World War II. However, their relationship deteriorated and they divorced in 1945. He began a relationship with Mary Welsh, another writer, whom he married in 1946. They lived in Cuba, as well as the United States and Europe. Hemingway continued to write, but did not have another major success until his 1952 novella, *The Old Man and the Sea*, which won the Pulitzer Prize in 1953. The next year he received the Nobel Prize for Literature, but did not attend the ceremony to accept the prize. In 1960, after suffering a mental breakdown, he entered the Mayo Clinic to undergo electrotherapy. He killed himself in his home in Ketchum, Idaho in 1961.

Plot Summary

"In the fall the war was always there, but we did not go to it anymore." So begins Ernest Hemingway's short story, "In Another Country." The war he refers to is World War I; the setting is Milan, away from the scene of the fighting. The narrator describes the city he passes on his way to the hospital to receive physical rehabilitation for the leg wounds he received while at the front. Though the narrator remains unnamed, scholars generally agree the young man is Hemingway's alter ego, Nick Adams.

At the hospital, the narrator, a young man, sits at a machine designed to aid his damaged knee. Next to him is an Italian major, a champion fencer before the war, whose hand has been wounded. The doctor shows the major a photograph of a hand that has been restored by the machine the major is using. The photo, however, does not increase the major's confidence in the machine.

Ernest Hemingway

Three Milanese soldiers, the same age as the narrator, are then introduced. The four boys hang out together at a place called Cafe Cova following their therapy. As they walk through the city's Communist quarter, they are criticized for being officers with medals. A fifth boy, who lost his nose an hour after his first battle, sometimes joins them. He wears a black handkerchief strategically placed across his face and has no medals.

One of the boys who has three medals has

> lived a very long time with death and was a little detached. We were all a little detached, and there was nothing that held us together except that we met every afternoon at the hospital. Although, we walked to the Cova through the tough part of town, walking in the dark, with the light singing coming out of wineshops, and sometimes having to walk into the street where the men and women would crowd together on the sidewalk so that we would have to jostle them to get by, we felt held together by there being something that had happened that they, the people who disliked us, did not understand. (Excerpt from "In Another Country")

Having all faced death and survived, the boys are linked in a way that the outsiders cannot understand. This special bond exists between them even though the narrator as an American, is otherwise more of an outsider to the soldiers than the unwounded Italians on the street who despise them.

They feel particularly connected at the Cova, where they drink and carouse with local girls.

The Italian soldiers change their manner toward the narrator when they realize he received some of his medals for being an American, and not for bravery, as they had. Though the narrator likes to imagine he would have been as brave as they had, he knows this is not true because he is indeed afraid to die. Despite their initial common bond, the Italian soldiers drift from the narrator due to this difference. Only the undecorated boy, without the nose, remains his close friend. This boy will not return to the war, so will never get the chance to find out if he also is afraid of death.

The major, the great fencer, is cynical about bravery, and so the narrator then feels a bond with him. As they sit at their respective physical therapy machines, the major helps the narrator improve his Italian.

One day when the narrator feels as hopeless about his machine as the major does about his, the major, usually poised and soldier-like, suddenly calls the narrator "a stupid impossible disgrace," who he had been "a fool to have bothered with." Standing upright to calm himself, the major asks the narrator if he is married. He answers, "No, but I hope to be." The major bitterly tells him, "A man must not marry," explaining that a man "should not place himself in a position to lose [everything] . . . He should find things he cannot lose." When the narrator counters this statement, the major angrily exclaims, "He'll lose it. Don't argue with me!," then demands his machine be turned off.

The major goes into another room for a massage, then asks for a phone, shutting the door for privacy. A short time later the major returns, composed. He apologizes to the narrator, then announces his wife has just died. The narrator feels sick for him, but the major remains controlled, saying, "It is difficult. I cannot resign myself." He then begins to cry. Quickly, however, the major stands erect, like a soldier, and fighting back his tears, exits.

The doctor says that the major's wife, a young, healthy woman, had died unexpectedly of pneumonia. The major returns three days later, wearing a black band on his sleeve to signify mourning, a symbol which further separates him from the narrator. Large framed photographs of healed hands have been hung to offer the major hope. However, the major ignores them; instead, he just stares out the window, knowing the machines cannot cure him of this different kind of injury.

Characters

American Soldier
See Narrator

Italian Major

The Italian major, a former fencing champion, is in the Milan hospital because his hand has been mangled in battle. A controlled military man, he is cynical about the machines that are used to rehabilitate his wounded extremity, and about the tales of bravery and heroism he hears from the young Italian officers. He befriends the narrator, who is also injured, and tutors him in Italian. The Italian major has recently married a young woman, something he would not do until he was injured—and therefore would not be sent into battle again. However, when his wife dies unexpectedly from pneumonia, the major loses his soldier-like composure, and weeps, not just for her death, but also, according to Earl Rovitt in his essay, "Of Human Dignity: 'In Another Country,'" for his understanding that he must now confront the meaninglessness of life, one that has shown him that his strict military code could not protect him from life's vulnerabilities.

Major
See Italian Major

Major's Wife

Though the major's wife never appears in the story (she is mentioned only in the second-to-last paragraph of the story), she plays a major role. A young, healthy woman, her sudden death from pneumonia leads the Italian major, her husband, to learn he cannot control life, a lesson which is also observed by the story's young narrator.

Narrator

The narrator is a young American in Italy during World War I. Though unnamed, the narrator's identity is assumed to be Nick Adams, an alter-ego for many of Hemingway's semi-autobiographical short stories. The narrator is in an Italian hospital receiving therapy for his injured leg. He befriends several other officers with whom he shares the experience of facing death and surviving, and of getting decorated for their efforts. When the other

soldiers learn that the narrator's other medals are merely for his being an American, and not for acts of heroism or bravery, he becomes an outsider to their circle. Realizing that his fear of death would make him an unlikely member of their group in the future, the narrator befriends an Italian major whose hand is wounded, a man whose cynicism toward bravery does not alienate the narrator from him. The narrator senses their connection is lost, however, when the major unexpectedly loses his young wife to pneumonia. According to Laurence W. Mazzeo in his "Critical Survey of Short Fiction," Nick comes to realize that "nothing of value can last in this world."

Signor Maggiore
See Italian Major

Themes

"In the fall the war was always there, but we did not go to it anymore." So begins Ernest Hemingway's short story, "In Another Country." The war he refers to is World War I; the setting is Milan, away from the scene of the fighting. The narrator is a young American man who is in the hospital to receive physical rehabilitation for the leg wounds he received while at the front. Sitting next to him is an Italian major, a champion fencer before the war, whose hand has been wounded and with whom the narrator speaks about life. At the story's end, having learned of his wife's death of pneumonia, the major must face the future knowing the machines cannot cure him of this different kind of injury.

Dignity and the Human Condition

In the story, the young narrator has faced death and survived. This is also true of the Italian officers who, like the narrator, come to the hospital each day to receive therapy for the wounds they have received while at the front. The narrator learns about dignity and the human condition primarily through his interaction with an Italian major. While the young narrator is fearful of dying on the battlefield, the major seems to have made peace with this possibility. He knows he must do his duty in the dignified manner consistent with being a professional soldier and, more specifically, an officer. He is uninterested in the bravado expressed by the young decorated officers. Bravery requires acting on impulse, making snap decisions based on one's

Media Adaptations

- *Hemingway's Adventures of a Young Man* is a film which assimilates the author's Nick Adams stories into a single narrative. Adapted by A. E. Hotchner, directed by Martin Ritt, starring Richard Beymer (best known as Tony in the film musical *West Side Story*) as Nick, produced by De Luxe, 1962.

- *The Killers* begins as a nearly word-by-word film adaptation of the Nick Adams story of the same name. In the story, Nick is in a diner as two killers come in looking for a man called Andersson. The film then segues into an original drama about Andersson. Nick is featured in one of these later scenes. Screenplay by Anthony Veiller, directed by Richard Siodmak (Academy Award nomination, best director), starring Burt Lancaster (film debut), Edmond O'Brien, and Ava Gardner. U-I, 1946.

- The film *In Love and War* chronicles 19 year-old Hemingway's recovery in an Italian hospital from the wounds he received driving an ambulance during World War I. The film focuses on his love affair with a 26 year-old nurse, the woman who is said to have inspired the character Catherine Barkeley in Hemingway's novel *A Farewell to Arms*. Chris O'Donnell plays the young Hemingway; Sandra Bullock portrays the nurse. Richard Attenborough directed. A New Line Cinema release, 1996.

- Hemingway's novel *A Farewell to Arms*, a fictional version of the same love affair featured in *In Love and War*, has been filmed twice, first in 1932 by director Frank Borzage, starring Gary Cooper and Helen Hayes, a Paramount Picture; then in 1957, starring Rock Hudson and Jennifer Jones, directed by Charles Vidor, a De Luxe release.

---

emotions. The major instead depends on control and precision. One day, however, the major breaks his composure; while sitting at the machine intended to heal his injured hand, he becomes angry with the narrator's hope to marry in the future, irately adding that the young American "should not place himself in a position to lose [everything]. . . . He should find things he cannot lose." The major then does the previously unthinkable; he breaks into tears. The narrator soon learns from a doctor that the major's young and, presumably, healthy wife has suddenly died from pneumonia. When the major returns to the hospital, three days later—his first break in his regime of daily visits—he is a more openly vulnerable man. He sits dutifully at his machine, stands in an erect, soldierly manner, but now his dignified stance is more hard won. He has learned that life cannot be controlled, that it is filled with arbitrary tragedies, even off the battlefield, for which one may be unprepared. The major may have been prepared for his own death, like any good soldier, but his wife's sudden passing leads him to confront life's meaninglessness, an aspect of the human condition he, who has survived, must now struggle to face with dignity.

Courage and Cowardice

Not unconnected is the theme of courage and cowardice. While many heroes, particularly in American fiction, especially American films, are portrayed as stoic and unafraid, "In Another Country" depicts a more complex and humanistic type of courage. Following the unexpected loss of his wife, the major's return to the hospital signifies his willingness to survive, even with his new awareness of chaos in the world and his inability to prevent being touched by it. His willingness to face life with this new and painful understanding can be seen as a definition of genuine courage, the kind of courage befitting a real hero. This truer, more human heroism even requires the initial shedding of tears, an act that is seen in some circumstances as a sign of cowardice.

This definition of heroism contrasts with the more traditional kind of heroics, the kind that wins medals, displayed by the brash young Italian officers. These men are seemingly proud of their naive bravado; however, because they have not dealt with the emotional consequences of the violence they have faced, they have become "a little detached" and withdrawn.

Alienation and Loneliness

This theme is expressed initially in the story's title, "In Another Country," which refers to being or feeling alienated from the comfort of the familiar, a circumstance which often leads to loneliness. In this story, the narrator is literally in another country, Italy, an ocean apart from his home, the United States; however, he is also apart in other ways. When he walks in the streets of Milan alongside the young Italian officers he is first accepted by, he knows the civilians who verbally abuse them do not understand what they, the officers, have faced. Though the officers and these native Milanese share the same streets, they are in "another country" from each other, separated by their differing life experiences. Once inside the warmth of the cafe, the narrator feels the loneliness this alienation causes disappear. Later, these same officers drift from him because they discover that some of his medals are for being an American, while theirs are for feats of bravery, acts the narrator knows his own fear of death would probably not permit him to perform. This leads to his being separate, in "another country," from his former friends. Out of loneliness, the narrator maintains a friendship with the only member of the group who has not received a medal and, since he is too injured to return to battle, never will. The narrator likes to pretend this friend would be like him in battle, cautious and a little afraid. The narrator insists on imagining he and this young man are connected in this way to alleviate the loneliness he feels now that he has become alienated from the others. At the end of the story, the narrator becomes alienated from his new friend, the major, after the major experiences a loss that the narrator has not, the death of a wife to pneumonia. The major's resulting understanding of life's cruel lack of meaning puts him in "another country" from the younger, still somewhat idealistic narrator. The mind set of the major is both alien to him and lonely, yet it is inevitable to all human beings. After all, the story suggests, attempts to avoid loss are only temporary.

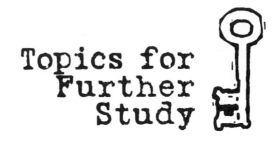

Topics for Further Study

- Explain the multiple meanings of the title of the short story "In Another Country."

- Write about a time when you were alienated from those around you because of a physical injury, language barrier, or other circumstances. Relate this to what the protagonist of "In Another Country" experiences.

- Read a book or short story about a soldier in the Vietnam War, such as *Dispatches* by Michael Herr or *In Pharaoh's Army* by Tobias Wolff. Compare the attitudes expressed by one of those writers toward the Vietnam war to Hemingway's as expressed in one of his works set during World War I, such as "In Another Country" or *A Farewell to Arms*.

Style

"In the fall the war was always there, but we did not go to it anymore." So begins Ernest Hemingway's short story, "In Another Country." The war he refers to is World War I; the setting is Milan, away from the scene of the fighting. The narrator is a young American man who is in the hospital to receive physical rehabilitation for the leg wounds he received while at the front. Sitting next to him is an Italian major, a champion fencer before the war, whose hand has been wounded and with whom the narrator speaks about life. At the story's end, having learned of his wife's death of pneumonia, the major must face the future knowing the machines cannot cure him of this different kind of injury.

Point of View

All of the events that occur in "In Another Country" are told from the point of view of the story's unnamed narrator, an American officer receiving physical therapy in a Milan hospital on his leg, which has been wounded at the front during World War I. The narrator is a young man, presumably about 19, the same age as the author when he also spent time in a Milan hospital, recovering from leg injuries received while working as an ambulance driver for the Red Cross. The events are filtered through the narrator's perspective, therefore the first person ''I'' is used throughout. How these events affect the narrator, particularly those which are written about in the greatest detail, like the major's disillusionment following the death of his wife, is not directly revealed. However, it is apparent that what he has witnessed has made a strong impact on him because he has chosen to recount the story so vividly. Readers may assume it is an older narrator who is telling the story, as it is written in the past tense.

Objectivity

One of the most distinctive aspects of this story, and most of Hemingway's literature, particularly his many stories about this same narrator—unnamed here, but known as Nick Adams elsewhere—is its objective tone. Though the story is told from the narrator's perspective, how they affect him is never made explicit. Instead, each of the events is described almost in the way a journalist reports a newspaper story, with as little subjectivity, or personal interjection, as possible. One way this is achieved is by using very few adjectives. This is done to avoid manipulating the reader's imagination. The specific details of each event are recorded in an objective way, leaving the readers to put the pieces together; this way readers can discover their own interpretation of what the events mean. This distinctive style, perfected by Hemingway, has been widely imitated and greatly praised, though it has its share of detractors as well.

Existentialism

Existentialism is a philosophy concerned with the meaning of existence. One of the aspects of this philosophy is the isolation of the individual, a condition all human beings must face at some time. The Italian major comprehends this after the unexpected death of his wife to pneumonia. When he returns to the hospital to continue the machine treatments on his hand soon after her passing, the narrator observes the major struggle to maintain his previous soldierly posture as he stares out the window. It has been implied by scholars that, having lost his innocent belief that loss can be minimized through discipline and precision, what the major sees out that window is life's vast emptiness. He is coming to terms with the fact that all connec-

tions are eventually lost, especially through death, and that life carries with it a sense of its own meaninglessness. This knowledge is one of the cornerstones of the existentialist philosophy, and it can be found in much of Hemingway's literature.

Symbolism

There are several examples of symbolism throughout the story. One such symbol is the window the major looks out of following the death of his wife. Previously, he looked at a wall while receiving his machine therapy. But, after his wife's death, he stares out the window instead. The major, at this point, is no longer emotionally walled in; he is open, vulnerable. The window symbolizes this opening inside him. The machines also have symbolic significance. Though utilized by the patients, the men know that they are probably ineffective; yet, they still return to them day after day, following the regime their use requires. Humans each follow their own daily regimes, hoping that they, too, are useful, purposeful. However, the story suggests, this is unlikely. The machines are an external symbol of life's probable futility, a condition which becomes apparent to the major after his tragic loss.

Irony

Irony occurs when the outcome of an event contrasts the intention of what has come before it. A particularly strong example of this can be seen with the Italian major. He has lived his life carefully, following a strict military code which has helped him maintain emotional control even while having to confront death, his own and that of others, nearly every day while at war. He depends on this, believes it will save him from being unprepared for great loss. Ironically, this man who believes he is in control of his life, soon learns, via the death of his wife, that his composure, his military precision worn like armor, cannot protect him from personal tragedy. This irony changes his life, and brings out many of the story's major themes.

Historical Context

Ernest Hemingway's story ''In Another Country'' takes place in a war hospital in Milan during World War I. The war began in 1914 when Archduke

Franz Ferdinand, a member of the Hapsburg family, the rulers of what was then known as the Austro-Hungarian empire, was assassinated while on an official state visit to the city of Sarajevo in Bosnia. His killer was a young Bosnian Serb, Gavrilo Princip, a member of a secret underground organization who protested the Austro-Hungarian empire's claim over their country. When the Austro-Hungarians demanded entrance to Bosnia so they could find and then bring to trial Ferdinand's assassin, the Bosnian government refused, insisting they would conduct their own investigation. The Austro-Hungarians then declared war on Bosnia. Quickly, Germany allied with the Austro-Hungarian empire, while Russia, France and Great Britain allied with Bosnia, with Italy soon to follow.

The United States joined World War I at the end of 1917. A German submarine had torpedoed a British passenger ship, the Lusitania, claiming it secretly carried American munitions aboard. The United States denied this, but joined the fray when the British and French requested their assistance. Most American soldiers were initially stationed on the Western Front, in France. Believing the American army to be inexperienced and, according to Hemingway, "overfed and under trained," the Germans immediately attacked. To much of the world's surprise, the Americans, despite being outnumbered and lacking experience, fought off the German army, solidifying their reputation as a world military power. The United States and its allies won the war in 1918. About 118,000 American soldiers were killed in action, more than double the 55,000 lost in World War II, a generation later.

Hemingway wrote "In Another Country" while residing in Paris in 1926. There he lived among a circle of writers and poets, many of whom would go on to be among the most prominent literary figures of the century. Expatriates like himself, these authors included F. Scott Fitzgerald, Sherwood Anderson, John Dos Passos, Thornton Wilder, Ezra Pound, e. e. cummings, and Hart Crane, along with Gertrude Stein and her lover, Alice B. Toklas, whose salon was a common meeting ground for the group. Coined "The Lost Generation" by Stein, these writers came to Paris in search of inspiration and a new understanding of the boundaries and purpose of art. Malcolm Cowley, one of their clique, wrote about this period in his book *Exile's Return*. A collection of Hemingway's anecdotes of this experience was published posthumously under the title *A Moveable Feast* in 1964.

Critical Overview

Hemingway's spare, objective style has been widely imitated and adapted by many other writers. His choice of material, and his stoic, masculine way of dealing with issues of life, death, and love in a troubled, often violent world has made him a controversial figure. Though many admire his sparse prose, suggesting it reveals the inner workings of his macho male heroes, a share of scholars, feminists in particular, have criticized his work, arguing that rather than illuminating and critiquing the he-men behavior of his characters, he is, instead, embracing, even sentimentalizing it. They also complain that his female characters have less dimension than his male characters, and that they generally fall into two stereotypical categories, the saintly and the whorish, showing an underlying dislike of women in general. Hemingway supporters counter that he adores the women he writes about, almost to the point of idealization.

His short story, "In Another Country" is one of his most popular; it is also one of his most anthologized. Like much of Hemingway's work, it has been written about at great length. Forrest Robinson in his article "Hemingway's Invisible Hero," published on *Essays in Literature* argues against the notion that the story's narrator is not "merely passive in his painful acceptance of his lack of bravery, and is respectful in his observance of the [Italian] major's resignation to despair." He goes on to say that the narrator is not really the story's protagonist, which many assume, but that the Italian major is.

"In Another Country" is widely considered to be one of Hemingway's serial, semi-autobiographical Nick Adams stories. In fact, when all the stories featuring Nick were published together as *The Nick Adams Stories* in 1972, "In Another Country" was included in the book. However, James Steinke, in his article "Hemingway's 'In Another Country' and 'Now I Lay Me,'" published in *The Hemingway Review* in 1985, argues that the story has been "mistakenly seen as one more contribution to composite of 'Nick Adams.'" He also writes that the Nick Adams stories are not "fictionalized personal history," as others claim. He uses a quote by the author himself to support his point: "When you first start writing stories in the first person, if the stories are made so real that people believe them, the people reading them nearly always think the stories really happened to you."

Ambulance and driver on a city street in Italy during World War I.

In addition to having his work labeled fictionalized autobiography, Hemingway's work has also led to the author being called such "critical classifying terms as Disillusioned Idealist, Realist, Naturalist, Existentialist and even—after *Old Man and the Sea*—Christian," according to Richard Irwin in his essay, "Of War, Wounds, and Silly Machines: An Examination of Hemingway's 'In Another Country.'" Irwin goes on to say that the author may be a Naturalist, but that he is not a true Naturalist. He feels Hemingway is a Naturalist "in the sense that for him human destiny is largely controlled by factors which lie beyond the individual will and choice, and those factors do not operate at the behest of an ultimately beneficent divine being." However, he feels that Hemingway can not be called solely a Naturalist because his work does not "reveal . . . sentimentality toward the hard aspects of the human condition . . . a belief in a benign, responsible creator [or] a keen awareness of the 'forces' which operate independently of man's conscious will." He also comments that Hemingway's writing does not "assume a universe indifferent to the suffering of human beings," and so does not fulfill the definition required to be considered a Naturalist.

Despite the vast array of opinions surrounding the work of Ernest Hemingway, his popularity and influence are still felt 35 years after his death. His position as one of the most distinctive and lauded writers of this century is assured, a title supported by a long list of devoted readers, the inclusion of his work in dozens of anthologies, and several of the most prestigious honors a writer can receive.

Criticism

Michael Zam

Zam has been an associate professor at Fordham College and New York University, as well as a writer for the Harvard Gay and Lesbian Review *and* Details *magazine. In the following essay, he examines Hemingway's sparse writing style, and compares that style to the early motion-picture technique of montage.*

One of the most often-discussed aspects of Ernest Hemingway's writing is his distinctive style. Whereas many writers of his day were still heavily influenced by the verbose, extremely descriptive style of English and American authors of the nineteenth century such as Charles Dickens, Jane Austen, and Herman Melville, Hemingway was not. His literature is free of the extensive use of adjectives common in the

What Do I Read Next?

- *The Nick Adams Stories* (1969) is a collection of all of Hemingway's stories, including ''In Another Country,'' featuring Nick Adams, some of which had been previously published in other collections. Eight stories had never been published, some of which are unfinished.

- *The Snows of Kilimanjaro and Other Stories* (1927) is a collection of short stories by Ernest Hemingway including ''In Another Country.''

- *Ernest Hemingway: A Life Story* (1969), by Carlos Baker, is a well-known biography of the author.

- *All Quiet on the Western Front* by Erich Maria Remarque is a classic anti-war novel chronicling the fates of several young German men who eagerly enlist in World War I. Originally published in the United States in 1929.

- *What We Talk About When We Talk About Love* (1980) is one of several short story collections by Raymond Carver. His stories, written primarily in the 1970s and 1980s, have often been compared stylistically to Hemingway's.

- *Exile's Return* by Malcolm Cowley (1934) recounts experiences of the expatriate writers, including Hemingway, in 1920s Europe by a writer who knew them intimately.

---

work of many earlier writers, and of many of his immediate contemporaries. As a result, his work has often been described as sparse, objective, and journalistic. It's also been called original, so much so that even readers who would not consider themselves scholars can immediately recognize a book, a story, or even a paragraph that he has written without knowing beforehand that he was its author. His style is so singular, in fact, that to this day there is an international writing contest held every year in which writers are asked to submit a short story in his style. Knowing full well that the results will most likely be second rate, the contest is called the ''Bad Hemingway Competition.'' The winner is awarded a free trip to Italy which includes a complimentary dinner at Harry's Bar in Venice, one of Hemingway's old hangouts.

The fact that Hemingway worked throughout his life as a journalist clearly influenced his spare prose style. In fact, before he had published any fiction, Hemingway, upon his graduation from high school, took a job as a junior reporter at the *Kansas City Star*. Only eighteen years old, and still developing his authorial voice, Hemingway was clearly inspired by the *Star*'s guidelines which demanded compression, selectivity and precision for their news stories. Though his background in news writing was an undisputed influence on his writing style, there is another strong influence that guided it as well: the movies. This is not too surprising; Hemingway was born just before the start of the twentieth century, the same time mass motion pictures were invented.

At the time that Hemingway began writing prose seriously, just at the end of World War I, in 1919, and up until the time he was considered an important writer some seven years later, movies were the most popular form of entertainment throughout the western world. This was more than three decades before television overtook motion pictures in popularity—in fact, television as a technology as we now know it had not yet been invented. Many people commonly went to the cinema several nights a week in the 1920s (even more so in the 1930s and early 1940s). The movies these large audiences were watching were, of course, silent movies.

Films with synchronized sound were not introduced to mainstream audiences until 1927, when *The Jazz Singer*, which included several musical numbers with synchronized sound, revolutionized the industry. That film's astronomical success led movie studios, within the year, to stop producing silent films. Because the sound technology was so

> " Many scholars and feminists have commented that Hemingway's work has embraced the stoic, unfeeling masculine stereotype."

new, these early "talkies" became more stage-bound, featuring longer scenes with actors clustered around flower vases and table lamps that hid strategically placed microphones. Movies had, for a time, lost their visual flair. The word overtook the image as the prime focus of filmmakers. Silent film, starting in the late 'teens, and up to 1927 (the same years Hemingway began seriously writing fiction), had matured; film language, dependent on the visual image to tell its story (with the exception of a few inter titles for important dialogue), had hit what many film scholars consider an artistic peak that was not found again for many decades to follow

One of the ways in which the best silent films of the time communicated their narratives and the emotions that they wanted their audiences to experience while watching them was through a technique called "montage." Montage is when several unrelated images are edited together to create a desired effect. For instance, if one sees an image of a man turning his head suddenly, then to one of a gun being aimed in his direction, to a shot of a tree falling in a nearby forest, the audience instinctively knows that the man has been shot, even without the sound of the gunshot. If we see several shots of an impatient crowd, followed by an image of a raised fist, we know that the fist represents the angry emotion of the mob without having to be told this. Hemingway makes subtle use this same montage technique in his writing.

An example of this can be seen clearly in the story, "In Another Country," especially the first paragraph. "In the fall the war was always there, but we did not go to it anymore. It was cold in the fall in Milan and the dark came very early. Then the electric lights came on, and it was pleasant along the streets looking in the windows." This establishes the setting and context of the story. Hemingway follows with a series of images which collectively create a mood and develop the story's themes.

"There was much game hanging outside the shops, and the snow powdered the fur of the foxes and the wind blew their tails. The deer hung stiff and heavy and empty, and small birds blew in the wind and the wind turned their feathers." We can feel the approaching winter through these details, and may start to subliminally sense that the details are also showing us, as opposed to telling us, that death, too, is approaching. Winter is the time when the life that bloomed in spring, thrived in summer, and weakened in fall, is taken away. We may also feel that a life-changing transition is also coming, and that, like the coldest of seasons, it will be a chilly reminder that the life we innocently enjoyed during the warmer months will be gone.

This montage technique is also prominently used in the story's important climactic sentences when the Italian Major returns to the hospital after hearing of his wife's sudden death from pneumonia. "Then he came at the usual hour, wearing a black band on the sleeve of his uniform . . . there were large framed photographs around the wall, all sorts of wounds before and after they had been cured by the machines. In front of the machine the major used were three photographs of hands like his that were completely restored." Hemingway then interjects his own equivalent of a silent film's inter title, "I do not know where the doctor got them. I always understood we were the first to use these machines." But the major, he tells us in the last sentences, is not moved by the photographs; instead, in the story's final, telling image we are told that the major "only looked out the window." Again, image builds upon image to create a final impression of existential despair, a message artfully expressed without being directly stated.

Is it any wonder, then, that Hemingway's works were quickly scooped up by movie studios? However, this did not occur until talkies were already in place and most of these adaptations, critics argue, lack much of the visual expressiveness present in Hemingway's writing. In fact, the film version that is considered most successful on an artistic level is the first, *A Farewell to Arms* of 1932. Though it has its share of characters sitting in rooms talking, like most films of its period, even these scenes are punctuated with what one critic called "a strange, brooding expressionist quality," which other adaptations of his writing lack.

It's important to note that Hemingway was clearly a filmgoer. According to his letters, published in a thick volume under the title, *Ernest*

Hemingway: Selected Letters: 1917-1961, the author writes many times about film stars, some of whom he had met, as well as discussing in some detail his involvement in casting choices and screenplay ideas he had contributed to several of the films made from his work. Films clearly played a role in his life and, to some extent, played a part in his work as well.

One of the things for which Hemingway has been criticized, particularly in the decades following his death, is his portrayal of macho characters. Many scholars and feminists have commented that Hemingway's work has embraced the stoic, unfeeling masculine stereotype. However, though his heroes are nearly always strong men who are not weepily sentimental, Hemingway has usually found a way to show the pain these men feel. In fact, part of his interest in writing about these characters is so he can use them to comment on their macho posturing. Again, "In Another Country" can serve as an example of this. Hemingway shows the story's narrator spending time with a group of young Italian officers who are proud of the masculine bravado they have demonstrated in battle. He writes, however, that they are emotionally "detached," unable to express their innermost feelings about the tragedies they have witnessed and experienced. He contrasts their behavior with that of the Italian major, a man who, in the end, is held up as a braver man for giving up his controlled facade, for coming to terms with the deep loneliness and isolation of death and the loss that it entails. Even when the major cries, that most unmacho of acts, the author does not criticize him; in fact, Hemingway seems to be rather approving, as long as the tears do not relate to cowardice.

Source: Michael Zam, "Overview of 'In Another Country,'" for *Short Stories for Students*, The Gale Group, 2000.

Forrest Robinson

Forrest Robinson is affiliated with Western Illinois University. In the following excerpt, he argues that the reader's revelation in Hemingway's "In Another Country" "can be seen only through the consciousness of the invisible first-person narrator who—in the creative act of giving a form and a focus to his own past experience—resolves a conflict implicitly disclosed in the process of narration."

Hemingway's "In Another Country" offers unusual evidence of the essentially heuristic and therapeutic nature of his storytelling. His thematic concern—that a person "find things he cannot lose"—

takes on considerable significance when the distinction between the protagonist and the first-person narrator is clarified. It is the protagonist who, along with the Italian major, faces the wall of despair and death after being wounded in Italy during World War I. It is the narrator, however, who epitomizes Hemingway's hero in this story. True heroism is not passive. True heroism is the action of the creative artist, the storyteller of "In Another Country" who discovers a "window" through which he can see beyond the "wall" facing those who suffer permanent wounds.

Confusion is understandable because Hemingway's narrator in this story is "invisible," that is, nameless, and he tells his own story. Moreover, he never calls attention to himself as narrator except indirectly in comments which establish a temporal distance between his past experience and his narration. Because of the narrator's "invisibility," readers can easily fail to see his formal function, therefore focusing their attention exclusively upon the narrator's younger self, the protagonist. Consequently, they see the young protagonist as one who is merely passive in his painful acceptance of his lack of bravery and is respectful in his observance of the major's resignation to despair. To overlook the formal function of Hemingway's invisible first-person narrator, however, represents a failure to apprehend the story as a total imaginative act. It is the narrator who looks back upon himself in a conflict which he, as protagonist, could not understand. As protagonist, he acted blindly, victimized as he was by his unrecognized responses to the world around him. "In Another Country," therefore, is not the protagonist's story, nor is it the major's. It is the narrator's, and the way into the story is through an effort to understand his concern in the conflict he recalls. The revelation of the story, then, can be seen only through the consciousness of the invisible first-person narrator who—in the creative act of giving a form and a focus to his own past experience—resolves a conflict implicitly disclosed in the process of narration.

That the narrator is an older man looking back over the years can be established in two ways. First, and more obviously, the narrator employs the past tense. Secondly, when he tells about the four soldiers with whom he used to walk in the streets of Milan, he offers an explicit statement about the temporal distance between his narration and his past experience. One of the young soldiers wears a black silk handkerchief to cover his horribly mutilated face. The narrator comments upon him in such a

> **If we realize that the narrator is 'meeting himself' in his remembered experience, then we can grasp his concern in his narrative. Incidents recalled express his concern in the present, and the end of his narrative becomes more significant if viewed from this perspective."**

way as to indicate a knowledge extending years beyond the action of the story:

> They rebuilt his face but he came from a very old family and they could never get the nose exactly right. He went to South America and worked in a bank. But this was a long time ago, and then we did not any of us know how it was going to be afterward.

The failure to consider the function of a narrator who is invisible is, I have said, understandable. All of his attention is focused upon himself as a young man in his encounters with therapeutic machines, "hunting hawks," and a major. Nonetheless, whatever the narrator's story discloses grows out of the way in which the machines, the hunting hawks (those men who were brave), and the major participate in the resolution of a conflict within the narrator's mind.

I

One way to focus the conflict is to examine the structure of the story. What the narrator remembers can be divided into five sections. With the possible exception of the last paragraph of the story, which is expository, sharp transitions help to set off each section. In the first two-paragraph section, the narrator begins to focus his attention in the process of recollection. Moving from his memory of specific sensations in the streets of Milan to the various routes he and his friends used to walk to the hospital, the narrator allows us to enter his consciousness, thereby enabling us to experience his sense of isolation as he walks to the new pavilions, which were beyond the old hospital and the courtyard where the funerals begin, and to "the machines that were to make so much difference." The machines which were to heal their wounds have not, of course, made much difference at all. If we think of the first section figuratively, as a recalled movement toward healing, we will have a way of conceptualizing each section of the story as a movement toward a healing which fails.

Before moving to the second section, let us return to the first sentence: "In the fall the war was always there but we did not go to it anymore." The fall is the season of nature's dying, and it is also the season for killing game, or hunting. Beyond the cluster of associations recalled by the narrator as he remembers his walks by the shops is the larger and seemingly interminable context of the war. That he says ". . . we did not go to it anymore" reveals the first element of separation. In other words, the narrator recollects that he and his four wounded friends are soldiers who are no longer participating in the action of the war. As we learn in section three, the protagonist is separated from more than the war; he is cut off from his "hunting hawk" friends who had earned their medals for bravery. Their only common ground lies in their having been wounded and in their efforts to recover from their wounds by going to the "healing machines."

The second section of the story, which begins with the, doctor's asking the protagonist what sport he played before being wounded, serves to emphasize a sense of the futility of the therapy. Both the protagonist and the major he encounters are damaged, and they realize that they are permanently damaged. Juxtaposed with their awareness of futility is the ineffectual but well-meaning effort of the doctor to persuade them that the machines are going to make them completely whole again. The language the doctor uses—"Did you practice a sport?" and "You will play football again like a champion"—implies a lack of knowledge about sports and calls into question his judgment about the protagonist's full recovery. When the doctor tells the protagonist that he will play football better than ever, the narrator conveys the impossibility of such restoration by simply stating that his calf had been completely shot away. Also played down is the intense pain which he must have felt when the machine lurched, indicating that its force met the resistance of the knee that would not bend. The major, moreover, is not under any illusions about his hand, which is reduced to the size of a baby's. His fencing days are over, and not all of the photographs in the world can convince him that he will recover fully from his wound. If the first section is seen as a movement toward the ineffectual healing machines, the second section can be seen as a movement away from false hope toward no hope.

By regarding the first two sections of the story as movements of consciousness, the narrator's concern—what he is seeking—becomes clearer. Each movement of consciousness happens against the backdrop of the "world" of the story—a world at war, a world of destruction and death. The narrator's concern is how to participate in a world that inflicts wounds from which there is no permanent recovery. His football and soldiering are behind him, and the first of three efforts to recover has failed. The healing machines cannot heal permanent wounds. And the narrator recalls that it is the major who faced head-on the fact of his condition.

Although the major is not mentioned in section three, this scene immediately follows his flat assertion that he has no confidence in the healing machines. The transition is so abrupt that we are likely to overlook how the major's honesty influences the narrator's recollection of relationships with the other wounded boys. In fact, the progression of the narrator's use of the first-person plural "we" to the singular "I" in this section is framed by the major's attitude toward the machines and his attitude toward bravery in the first sentence of section four.

In the first paragraph of section three, the narrator tells us about the sense of camaraderie which he and the other three boys experienced as they were ridiculed when they walked the streets of Milan. The narrator proceeds in the next paragraph to tell us that they had all received medals except the boy who wore the black silk handkerchief over his face. He had not been at the front long enough to get any medals. As the narrator focuses upon his relationships with the other young soldiers who had been wounded, he recalls his sense of alienation: "We were all a little detached, and there was nothing that held us together except that we met every afternoon at the hospital." The only bonds among the men were created by the dislike and discourtesy of the people in the streets and the universally understandable appetites that could be satisfied at the Cova, where in war or peace the girls were "patriotic." The narrator's comment that he believes the girls are still "patriotic" is a minor intrusion; however, it serves to establish further his distance in time from the past action.

The shift from "we" to "I" in the fourth paragraph of the third section reveals that the second method of participation within a context of struggle is unsatisfactory. Just as the therapy machines cannot fully restore wholeness of body, neither can other people be encountered in any satisfying relationship when the basis for human encounter is an ideal one cannot live up to. The narrator recalls that his failure to earn medals for bravery under fire had separated him from those who had. He had become a friend against outsiders, but he knew that he was not really one of the "hunting hawks." After the cocktail hour he could imagine he had been brave enough to earn citations; but in the cold air walking home he knew that he would never have been brave and that he was afraid to die. In other words, under the warming effects of alcohol he could, like the well-meaning doctor, avoid facing the fact of his estrangement. In the cold air of the street, however, he is like the major who coldly faces the fact of his condition.

We can now see that the narrator is recalling two aspects of his former condition of estrangement and despair; furthermore, we can realize that he is "meeting himself"—from the ground of a present crisis—in the events of his past. His process of focusing his consciousness upon these particular events implicitly discloses his concern about a present condition of estrangement and despair which is epitomized in his memory of the healing machines, the relationships with the other wounded soldiers, and, particularly, the major. The narrator first recalls wounds which cannot be healed by the products of modern science, the therapy machines. He then recalls his sense of being cut off from those men who embodied for him an ideal of selfhood which he felt—and continues to feel—incapable of attaining. At this point in the story, however, the ideal is not articulated. The narrator does this in the next paragraph.

In the fifth paragraph of section three, the image of the hunting hawk emerges in the consciousness of the narrator as a symbol for that capacity to function within a natural order characterized by struggle and death. The hunting hawk is a bird of prey, capable of sweeping down for the kill, swiftly and instinctively. The narrator remembers how the hawk had become for him an ideal of selfhood from which he had been hopelessly estranged. Significantly, his friend among the other boys was the one who had been wounded before he was tried under pressure.

II

The context of the war is only one of two contexts in the story. As we noted, the war serves as a metaphor for the natural order within which people struggle and die. The second context is the hospital, within which the issue at hand is the healing of those persons who have been wounded within the war-context. By extending these metaphors, we might suggest that the narrator's stake in his narrative is the resolution of how to be healed or how to be rejoined to a world characterized by destruction and death. The healing machines could not make him physically whole again, and he recalls that he could never be a hunting hawk; consequently, two of the three modes of survival in a destructive element failed to work.

Juxtaposed with the narrator's certainty that he was not a hunting hawk is his first comment about the major in section four: "The major, who had been a great fencer, did not believe in bravery." Bravery, that quality possessed by the hunting hawks, is of no importance to this man. What is important to him is what the narrator derives from him: precision and discipline. These qualities can no longer be exercised in fencing, but they can be in communication. In contrast with the doctor who uses false photographs to create the illusion of hope, the major calls things as he sees them and insists upon correct grammar. We might observe, then, that at this point in his narration the narrator remembers his initial regard for the major as a man of precision and authority.

By keeping in the foreground our primary effort to discover the narrator's stake in his re-enacted experience, we can see that he is groping for more than he has recalled thus far in his narrative. The major has given him a greater respect for precision and discipline in communication, but he has given him much more than this. In looking back, the narrator recalls that the major had also been engaged in finding a satisfactory mode of participating in the destructive element of life. He had acquired great competence as a fencer, and he had proved competent enough as a hunting hawk to become a major. Both accomplishments represent only partial and temporary modes of participation. The major had been deprived of his fencing skill by a wound, and the wound had forced him beyond "hawkery," as a mode of participation, to human love. Furthermore, the major had so valued the possibility of participation in life through human love that he waited until he knew he was permanently out of the war before he married.

Close to the end of the story the narrator recalls an incident which represents a turning point in his relationship with the major. Sensing that his young wife is going to die, the major tells the protagonist that he is a fool to hope to get married. Here again, the narrative perspective from which we are viewing this situation enables us to see more than a passive young man being instructed by an older man. We can now grasp what the major was trying to tell him: that there is no single way, once one has been wounded, to be rejoined in life—not by fencing, nor by hawkery, nor even by human love. The narrator learns that there are no things he cannot lose. And he also learns (when he recalls that the major had told him not to address him as "Signor Maggiore") that the possibility of death removes the distinction of rank, and there is now a common condition.

III

Thus, we can say that the ground upon which the narrator stands is similar to the major's at the end of the remembered experienced. Wounded by life, the storyteller recalls his earlier predicament as a young man physically wounded in the war. Struggling, also, for a way to heal his psychic wound— his sense of estrangement in the present—he recalls the context of healing in the new pavilions at the hospitals in Milan. Just as his body could not be restored to wholeness by the machines, neither could his estrangement as a young man be overcome by trying to be a hunting hawk. The death of the major's wife, therefore, is intensely relevant to the narrator's present condition. At the conclusion of his recalled experience, the death of a young woman seemed to seal off all avenues of recovery from the damage done to the major by life. Even human love cannot be relied upon as a way of re-entering the world.

All that can be done is what the major has done; what the major has done can easily be overlooked, however, because Hemingway's narrator forces each sentence in his story to carry heavy freight. For example, the major had earlier in the story sat at the machine and looked at the wall. At the end of the story, though, he sat at the machine and looked out the window. If we briefly retrace what the narrator recalls, we can see that the major's progression toward his particular end is similar to the boy's; and we can see that it is the narrator who welds both together in a story. The major who looks at the wall has gone through fencing and hawkery, and is facing the death of his wife. The young boy has gone through football, has failed at hawkery, and does not know where to go from here—except that he considers the possibility of marriage when he returns to the States. Although the narrator is distinct from the protagonist, he sees his present crisis epitomized in his earlier experience. If we realize that the narrator is ''meeting himself'' in his remembered experience, then we can grasp his concern in his narrative. Incidents recalled express his concern in the present, and the end of his narrative becomes more significant if viewed from this perspective.

The death of the major's wife shatters the major's rigid carriage and enables him to move outward toward the boy in a way that was not possible before. This last wound, the death of his wife, forces the major beyond the wall, that is, to the world beyond the confines of his personal and ineffectual therapy. All of these elements, of course, are remembered by the narrator. And not the least of these is what the major has gone through. The narrator's concern seems to be what can be done when nothing seems to assure complete recovery from the condition of being wounded. Once wounded, he realizes, one can never be the same; but perhaps the major points the direction for what can be done—in fact all that can be done. Instead of facing the wall, one would look out the window. The world lies out there to be seen, thought about, and then rendered into an art form—that activity which makes possible a maximum ordering of his life, a maximum association with others, beyond his personal condition of estrangement. The paradoxical truth, however, is that not until one is wounded does one see that world and become able to participate in it.

The narrator participates in the world by telling his story. We do not see this, however, if we focus upon the major as a figure of despair and the young boy as a passive witness. By focusing upon the invisible first person narrator who has relived his past, we can realize that he is no merely passive witness, and that he is the focal point in the story. For the narrator has turned to the only method of healing available to him, a method of healing which transcends that of the major's—the creative act of giving a form and focus to his own condition of estrangement, as honestly and precisely as possible. The narrator, at the end, is like the major in a figurative sense. He is no longer walled in by the impossible ideal of hunting hawkery, which excludes and therefore cuts off association and participation in the human community at a human level.

Like the major, at the end of the story, the narrator is not concerned with efforts, no matter how well-meaning, to create the illusion of hope for full recovery. Nor does human love, even, serve as a lasting mode of participation: love can be killed by any turn of the natural order.

The last word of this story is, significantly, ''window.'' And that window looking out upon the world offers the only release from the damage done by a permanent wound and the realization that there can never be a complete recovery. The world beyond the major's window is the common ground between the major and the boy, and it is the common ground between the narrator and the reader.

Source: Forrest Robinson, ''Hemingway's Invisible Hero of 'In Another Country,''' in *Essays in Literature*, Vol. XV, No. 2, Fall, 1988, pp. 237–44.

Colin S. Cass

Cass earned his doctorate in American literature at Ohio State University and has published critical articles on Hemingway, Fitzgerald, London, and James Gould Cozzens, as well as checklists for First Printings of American Authors. *In the following excerpt, he examines several aspects of* ''In Another Country,'' *including Hemingway's writing style, his allusion to Marlowe's* The Jew of Malta, *and his use of* ''window'' *and* ''looking'' *imagery.*

Ernest Hemingway's short story, ''In Another Country,'' is illuminated by three related observations: that the author shifts his attention from the American soldier to the Italian major midway through the story, that he exercises strict control over his title allusion to *The Jew of Malta*, and that he cultivates a very elaborate motif of images concerned with looking and windows.

The first two-thirds of the work is focused on the nameless [Although nothing in the published version warrants the assumption that the narrator is Nick Adams, many critics have suspected that he is.] young narrator convalescing in Milan. At the climax, however, when the major learns that his wife has died, the American becomes only an observer, and thereafter the major dominates. But the scheme is not as inept as it sounds. For the narrator, several ways of being in another country—for instance, as an American in Italy, a newcomer to the language, an officer among hostile civilians behind the lines, a patient with a serious handicap, and a frightened soldier among genuine war heroes—

> **❝** This brings us back to the windows. The second and third window images confirm the spatial equivalents implied by the first, but from the opposite point of view."

have already been explored. Hemingway is especially interested in kinds of experience that the American either lacks or underestimates. When the major emerges as the central character, it is because the story moves on to subjects beyond the American's experience, namely, love, despair, and death.

The opportunity for the American to witness the major's grief is so fundamental that Hemingway at the climax takes a big risk to secure it. Strictly speaking, the major's presence at physical therapy the day his wife dies is implausible. Hemingway tries to disarm this objection by saying, "She had been sick only a few days. No one expected her to die." But the major knows *before* the telephone call that she is either dead or dying, as his extreme agitation makes clear. He not only loves his wife; he has no confidence in the treatments. So in life he would have no reason to be present. Yet Hemingway must deliver the bereaved husband to the narrator. For the American to perceive the depths of love and despair, he must witness the effects of the wife's death. And there would be no justification whatever for the American's presence at the wife's bedside. In short, even at the expense of an implausibility, Hemingway is determined to make his point: the major, having experienced love and the loss of it, is in another country from the American.

Hemingway's title allusion to Christopher Marlowe's *The Jew of Malta* is well known. But because T. S. Eliot draws on the same passage for the epigraph to "Portrait of a Lady," and because Hemingway reuses the material himself in *The Sun Also Rises* and *Across the River and Into the Trees*, criticism has repeatedly been distracted from interpreting the lines in relation to the present story. As Philip Young says [in *Ernest Hemingway: A Reconsideration*, 1966], "Unless one knows the origin of this title its point is lost." Yet when he then explains

it as "a brutal allusion to the major's bereavement," he appears to have lost half the point himself. In Marlowe ["The Rich Jew of Malta"] the intention of the lines seems clear. Barabas, the Machiavellian Jew, having poisoned his own daughter along with a convent full of nuns, is trying to forestall the charge of murder by interrupting his accusers and confessing lesser sins:

> *2. Fryar.* Thou hast committed—*Barabas.* Fornication? but that was in another Country: And besides, the Wench is dead.

Correspondences between story and play seem obvious. The major's dead wife resembles the Jew's dead wench, and by extension, the major is counterpart to the Jew. The relationship is, however, patently ironic, not brutal. Hemingway alludes to the cynical, loveless Jew, who fornicated with some wench he cared nothing about, so that we will recognize by contrast the genuine article—love as the major knows it. The major's experience with love places him in another country from both the loveless Jew of Malta and the inexperienced American. One cannot shrug off such love as Barabas shrugs off the wench. Such a loss is desolating. The major cannot resign himself.

Having lost everything of consequence in his life, the major becomes an important exemplar of Hemingway's code of conduct. When, three days later, he returns "at the usual hour, wearing a black band," he has stoically resigned himself to the doubly hopeless situation and recovered his temporarily shattered decorum. But his new experience with loss leaves him utterly detached: "The photographs did not make much difference to the major because he only looked out of the window".

This reference to looking out the window is actually the last image in an intricate motif. Besides mentioning windows three times, Hemingway uses "to look" nine times. This, of course, is a common verb, yet nine occurrences in 2100 words seems unusual, a conclusion borne out by comparison with "A Way You'll Never Be" which, chosen at random, uses the verb eleven times in about 5000 words. The percentage for "In Another Country" (0.43%) is twice that for the control (0.22%). Moreover, after the first reference all the looking is done by the major:

> (1) it was pleasant along the streets looking in the windows. (2) The major held the photograph with his good hand and looked at it very carefully. (3) he sat straight up in his chair with his right hand thrust into the machine and looked straight ahead at the wall while the straps thumped. (4) He spoke very angrily

and bitterly, and looked straight ahead while he talked. (5) "He'll lose it," the major said. He was looking at the wall. (6) Then he looked down at the machine and jerked his little hand out from between the straps. (7) He looked straight past me and out through the window. (8) And then crying, his head up looking at nothing, carrying himself straight and soldierly, with tears on both his cheeks and biting his lips, he walked past the machines and out the door. (9) The photographs did not make much difference to the major because he only looked out of the window.

The looking must not be separated from the three references to windows. They occur precisely at the beginning, the climax, and the end of the story, and their main function is to emphasize the difference between the American's point of view and the major's. In the widely admired opening paragraph, "It was cold in the fall in Milan and the dark came very early. Then the electric lights came on, and it was pleasant along the streets looking in the windows." This looking in from the cold is an epitome of the lonely exclusion that the American suffers as an outsider. But it is also more. All the many images of death in the opening paragraph are outside—the fall, the cold, the darkness, the game hanging outside the shops, the snow, the wind, the carcasses "stiff and heavy and empty." The first window image creates spatial equivalents for the contrast between death outside and bright warm life within. From the narrator's inexperienced point of view, which dominates the beginning of the story, life seems the way the first paragraph depicts it: he is surrounded by frightening reminders of death and alienation, yet when he looks in the windows, life on the inside seems bright, warm, attractive.

The major, however, whose view prevails in the latter half, sees things differently. Several passages suggest that the unflinching manner of his looking is important. Twice he looks "straight ahead," once "straight past," once he looks "carrying himself straight and soldierly." But what he looks at is surely more informative. When he examines the photograph carefully, the first time he looks at anything, we see both what he would like to believe and what he is too realistic to accept. All the other looking occurs on or after the day his wife dies. Then he looks down on the machine and doesn't even bother to look at the faked photographs. But more eloquently, while his head is full of his wife's death, he is twice looking "at the wall" and once "looking at nothing." This last, in view of Hemingway's insistence on *nada* in "A Clean, Well-Lighted Place," probably means more than that the major is not looking at anything. He is looking at death, the blank wall, the nothing.

This brings us back to the windows. The second and third window images confirm the spatial equivalents implied by the first, but from the opposite point of view. The major—in every respect thus far an initiated character, an insider—sees through the windows from the inside out. The second occurrence falls precisely at the climax, and we know that his mind is full of death:

"I cannot resign myself."

He looked straight past me and out through the window.

The third occurs in the last line, neatly tying the beginning and climax to the end. The major by now has resigned himself, but the photographs that offered no hope the first time he looked still offer none, "because he only looked out of the window."

It is a deft move indeed, for this line, drawing together the imagery of looking and windows, also turns the structural peculiarity of a split perspective into an asset. Better yet, it discloses what is surely Hemingway's last and best reason for the Marlowe allusion. To the major, the fully experienced insider, life does not contain the brightness and warmth it seems to the American to have in the first paragraph. In gazing out the window, the major looks toward death, perhaps even with a lover's longing analogous to the American's feeling as he looked in. For, of course, the major is still thinking of his wife who, like Marlowe's wench, is in another country in the most final sense. Being in death, she occupies the one realm of experience from which the major himself has been excluded.

Source: Colin S. Cass, "The Look of Hemingway's 'In Another Country,'" in *Studies in Short Fiction*, Vol. 18, No. 3, Summer, 1981, pp. 309–13.

Sources

Baker, Carlos, ed. *Ernest Hemingway: Selected Letters, 1917-1961*, New York: Charles Scribner's Sons, 1981, 948 p.

Irwin, Richard. "'Of War Wounds, and Silly Machines': An Examination of Hemingway's 'In Another Country,'" in *The Serif*, Vol. V, No. 2, June, 1968, pp. 21-29.

Mast, Gerald. *A Short History of the Movies*, 2nd ed., Indianapolis: Bobbs-Merrill Educational Publishing, 1978, 575p.

Robinson, Forrest. "Hemingway's Invisible Hero in 'In Another Country,'" in *Essay in Literature*, Vol. XV, No. 2, Fall, 1988, pp. 237-44.

Rovit, Earl. "Of Human Dignity: 'In Another Country,'" in *The Short Stories of Ernest Hemingway: Critical Essays*, edited by Jackson J. Benson, Durham, North Carolina: Duke University Press, 1975, pp. 58–68.

Steinke, James. "Hemingway's 'In Another Country' and 'Now I Lay Me,'" in *The Hemingway Review*, Vol. V, No. 1, Fall, 1985.

Further Reading

Baker, Carlos, ed. *Ernest Hemingway: Selected Letters, 1917-1961*, New York: Charles Scribner's Sons, 1981, 948 p.
Collection of letters written by Hemingway to family members, friends, and colleagues including prominent literary figures as F. Scott Fitzgerald, Archibald MacLeish, and John Dos Passos, as well as his editor, Maxwell Perkins.

Rovit, Earl. "Of Human Dignity: 'In Another Country,'" in *The Short Stories of Ernest Hemingway: Critical Essays*, edited by Jackson J. Benson, Durham, North Carolina: Duke University Press, 1975, pp. 58–68.
Rovit argues that the Major in "In Another Country" represents "Hemingway's attempt to retain the ideal of dignity without falsifying the ignobility of the modern human condition.'

Steinke, James. "Hemingway's 'In Another Country' and 'Now I Lay Me,'" in *The Hemingway Review*, Vol. V, No. 1, Fall, 1985.
Steinke compares the two short stories in the title of his article, arguing that, despite external similarities, they are actually very different.

Waldhorn, Arthur. *A Reader's Guide to Ernest Hemingway*, New York: Farrar, Straus, and Giroux, 1972, 284 p.
A collection of essays discussing Hemingway's major works.

The Legend of Sleepy Hollow

Washington Irving

1820

The great American short story "The Legend of Sleepy Hollow" was written while Washington Irving was living in England, and it was published in England in a volume called *The Sketch Book of Geoffrey Crayon, Gent.* The *Sketch Book* was published in installments in the United States beginning in 1819, but the section that included this story was not issued until 1820. Readers on both sides of the Atlantic Ocean thus encountered the story at approximately the same time.

"The Legend of Sleepy Hollow" takes place in Sleepy Hollow, New York, a snug rural valley near Tarrytown in the Catskill Mountains. Constructed from German tales but set in America, it is a classic tale of the conflict between city and country, and between brains and brawn. Ichabod Crane courts Katrina Van Tassel, but is frightened away by his rival, Brom Bones, masquerading as the headless horseman. The story demonstrates the two qualities for which Irving is best known: his humor, and his ability to create vivid descriptive imagery.

Readers immediately took to "The Legend of Sleepy Hollow" and another tale from the *Sketch Book*, "Rip Van Winkle." Although little formal criticism greeted the arrival of the story specifically, the *Sketch Book* became wildly popular and widely reviewed both in the United States and in England. It was the first book by an American writer to become popular outside the United States, and helped establish American writing as a serious and

respectable literature. In 1864, ''The Legend of Sleepy Hollow'' was published as a separate illustrated volume for the first time, and there have been dozens of editions since. Today, most of Irving's work has been largely forgotten, but the characters of Ichabod Crane and the Headless Horseman have lived on as part of American folklore.

Author Biography

Considering that Irving's best-known fiction takes place in the countryside of rural upstate New York, it is perhaps surprising that he spent most of the first thirty-two years of his life in New York City, where he was born on April 3, 1783. He was the eleventh child of immigrant parents, and remained close to his family all his life. Irving's family had money and some influence in New York, and he received a solid education and then studied the law. He was only a mediocre student, and would probably not have made a good lawyer. Instead, he turned to a somewhat leisurely life as a man of letters, attending parties and the theatre, traveling around the state, and writing humorous newspaper pieces under a false name, Jonathan Oldstyle, Gent.

In 1807, Irving was part of a group that collaborated on a humorous periodical called *Salmagundi*, poking fun at the manners and customs of the day, describing the fashions, theatre and arts in wicked detail. The style of the pieces echoed essays written by the English writer Joseph Addison, but with determinedly American subjects. There were no important American literary influences for Irving to follow; the United States was still young enough that its artists had to look to Europe for their models. His first book was *A History of New York from the Beginning of the World to the End of the Dutch Dynasty* (1809), satirizing Dutch customs and manners, and also the pretentious writing style of historians.

He sailed to Europe in 1815, and lived there for the next seventeen years, finding acclaim as a writer and as a diplomat. His most enduring book, *The Sketch Book*, from which ''The Legend of Sleepy Hollow'' and ''Rip Van Winkle'' are taken, was published in America beginning in 1819, and in England in 1820. It was the first book by an American writer to reach a wide international audience, and proved to the world that America had subjects and themes that were of interest to Europeans.

Irving wrote many more books, but never wrote as well again as he had in the *Sketch Book*.

Back in his homeland, he traveled across the plains of the western frontier, and finally bought a large rural property in Sleepy Hollow, a valley near Tarrytown, New York, where he entertained the many people who wanted to meet the famous writer. He died on November 28, 1859, at the age of 76—a long life for the nineteenth century. He is buried in the Sleepy Hollow cemetery. Although in his own lifetime Irving was considered the most important writer America had ever produced, almost none of his books are read today. Only a few of his short stories live on, still loved for their vivid descriptions and humor.

Plot Summary

The story opens with a long descriptive passage offered in the first person by the narrator, who is revealed at the end of the story to be a man in a tavern who told the story to ''D. K.'' Irving's contemporaries, and readers of the entire *Sketch Book*, know that ''D. K.'' is Diedrich Knickerbocker, the fictional author of an earlier book of Irving's. The narrator describes the story's setting, creating images of a quaint, cozy Dutch village, ''one of the quietest places in the whole world,'' in a ''remote period of American history'' that seemed long-ago even to Irving's original readers. The village is not just far away and long ago; it is a magical place, ''under the sway of some witching power, that holds a spell over the minds of the good people, causing them to walk in a continual reverie.''

In this land lives Ichabod Crane, a schoolteacher and singing instructor who comes from Connecticut. His last name suits him. He is tall, lanky and sharp-featured, with clothes too small and ears too big. Crane is a serious and strict teacher, but liked well enough by his students and their families. He has apparently no real friends in the community, but is welcome as he passes from house to house eating whatever he can help himself to in exchange for doing light chores and entertaining the housewives with his stories and gossip. He is much admired for his intelligence, for, unlike the rest of the village, he has ''read several books quite through,'' and he is especially interested in tales of witchcraft and magic. Several local tales feature the ghost of a Hessian trooper, who was killed by a cannonball and who rides through the countryside each night looking for his missing head.

One of Crane's singing students, Katrina Van Tassel, has caught his eye, and he dreams of marrying her. Katrina is eighteen years old, plump and ripe, and "a little of a coquette." Crane desires her not because of her beauty or her personality, but because her father is wealthy and there is always wonderful food at the Van Tassel home. He fills his thoughts with images of roast pigs and pies and sausages, and imagines selling off the Van Tassel land to buy a homestead in the wilderness where he and Katrina "with a whole family of children" could go in a covered wagon. So Crane begins to court Katrina.

Because she is beautiful and wealthy, Katrina has other suitors. Chief among them is Brom Bones, a man who is everything Ichabod Crane is not: strong, rugged, handsome, humorous and clever. Katrina seems content to be courted by two men, and does not discourage either man's attentions. Brom's natural instinct is to fight with Crane, but since Crane will not fight Brom resorts to playing a series of practical jokes on Crane instead.

One evening, Mr. Van Tassel hosts a big party for everyone in the village. Crane dresses up in his finest and makes himself look as handsome as he can. He is so awestruck by the tremendous food-laden tables at the party that he decides to ask Katrina for her hand. After an evening of swapping ghost stories with his neighbors, he approaches his intended bride. Although the discussion is not recorded, a few minutes later he leaves the house "with an air quite desolate and chop-fallen." Feeling dismal, he begins the long ride home alone. Remembering all the ghost stories he has heard and told that evening, he gets more and more nervous.

Suddenly, he sees a large shadowy figure on the road ahead. It appears to be a headless man riding a horse, and Crane can just make out the shape of a head resting on the pommel of the saddle. Terrified, he races away, chased by the headless horseman. He is unable to escape. The last thing he remembers is the sight of the rider about to throw the head at him; struck by the flying object, he is knocked unconscious to the ground.

The next morning Crane does not come to school, and he is never seen in the village again. A search party finds his hat and a bundle of his possessions, and nearby on the ground a smashed pumpkin. Brom Bones marries Katrina, and for the

Washington Irving

rest of his life gives a knowing look and a laugh when the mysterious disappearance of his rival is mentioned. Though some in the village may suspect that Brom was responsible for Crane's disappearance, most of the women maintain that Crane was carried away by the headless horseman. Crane himself has become the subject of the kind of ghost story he so loved to tell.

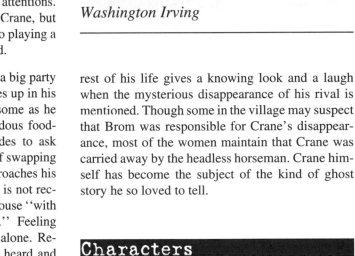

Characters

Brom Bones
See Abraham Van Brunt

Ichabod Crane
Ichabod Crane, the protagonist, is a stern schoolteacher and singing instructor who has come to Sleepy Hollow, New York, from Connecticut. He is lanky and sharp-featured, awkward and somewhat clumsy, but more educated and sophisticated than the native villagers. He is quite fond of food, and is well fed by the neighboring housewives, who share his delight in telling and re-telling ghost stories. When he sets his sights on marrying Katrina Van Tassel, it is not because of any feeling he has for her, but because her father is wealthy and Crane admires

Media Adaptations

- "The Legend of Sleepy Hollow" has been recorded by Donada Peters as part of a five-hour set of audiotapes titled *Rip Van Winkle and Other Stories*. The set is distributed by Books on Tape, Inc. The story is also available on audiocassette as a musical dramatization that has received excellent reviews. Produced by Reed Publishing USA in 1993, it is part of the Carousel Classics collection.

- The story is also available on videocassette. *Tales of Washington Irving* (1987) is a videocassette release of animated films made in 1970. Distributed by MGM/UA Home Video, the 48-minute tape contains "The Legend of Sleepy Hollow" and "Rip Van Winkle", and features the voice talents of Mel Blanc and other familiar stars. Another videotape, *The Legend of Sleepy Hollow by Washington Irving,* uses human actors and sets the story in a recreated early American-Dutch settlement. Published by Guidance Associates, it is designed to motivate students to read the story.

- Among the many film versions, two deserve special note. *Shelley Duvall's Tall Tales and Legends: The Legend of Sleepy Hollow* is a 52-minute film starring Ed Begley, Jr., and is distributed by Trimark. Scheduled for a November 1999 cinema release is a major motion picture, *Sleepy Hollow,* directed by Tim Burton and starring Johnny Depp as Ichabod Crane.

---

the food that is always displayed in the Van Tassel home. Katrina refuses him, however, preferring the manly and strong Brom Bones. In his disappointment Crane allows his imagination to run away with him. He is tricked by Brom into believing that he is being chased through the night by a headless horseman. In the morning he is gone, having left town without saying good-bye.

Abraham Van Brunt

Brom Bones is Crane's chief rival for Katrina's affections, and is in every way Crane's opposite. He is large, strong, rough, humorous, and good-natured, as well-known for his skill as a horseman as Crane is for his education. When he sees that Crane is paying attention to Katrina, Brom begins a series of practical jokes to humiliate him. Finally, he disguises himself as the headless horseman and chases the impressionable Crane through the darkness. When Crane leaves town, Bones marries Katrina.

Baltus Van Tassel

Old Baltus Van Tassel is a veteran of the American Revolution, and the patriarch of a wealthy Dutch farming family. He owns a large, well-kept home and barn, with livestock and fertile fields. Van Tassel is a warm and generous neighbor and an indulgent father. He does not interfere in his daughter's dalliances with the local young men.

Katrina Van Tassel

Katrina is the eighteen-year-old daughter of Baltus Van Tassel and his wife. She is beautifully plump and rosy-cheeked, and always dresses to enhance and emphasize her attractiveness. She is flattered by the attentions of the young men, and does nothing to encourage or discourage Ichabod Crane and Brom Bones from flirting with her. But when Crane presses for a commitment, she sends him away, and soon after marries Brom.

Themes

City versus Country

One of the great themes of American literature and American folklore is the clash between the city and the country, between civilization and the wil-

Topics for Further Study

- Find a few of the many illustrated versions of "The Legend of Sleepy Hollow" in the children's section of the library, or some of the video or filmstrip versions. Compare the pictures of Ichabod Crane in these versions with Irving's descriptions in the text. How precisely does Irving describe Crane? How closely do the pictures match your own vision of Crane's appearance?

- Find a copy of "The Castle of Indolence," a poem from 1748 written by the Scottish poet James Thomson. Why might Irving attached four lines of this poem to his own story? What do the two pieces have in common?

- Research the status of African Americans in New York during the end of the eighteenth century. Analyze Irving's casual disrespect for the "Negro" characters in his story in terms of how his contemporary readers would have responded to it, and in terms of how modern readers might respond.

- Closely examine the passages in which Irving describes food in lingering detail. Based on the modern food pyramid, how healthy was the diet of wealthy Dutch farmers in the late 1800s?

---

derness. As the theme is played out in literature around the world, it carries one of two interpretations: either the city is seen as beautiful, civilized, rich, clean and safe, and the country is ugly, dirty and dangerous, or else the city is dirty and dangerous, populated by swindlers who love nothing better than tricking the kind, gentle people from the beautiful country. American folklore from the nineteenth century tends to favor the second view. Settlers were proud of their wilderness, and excited by it, and their stories celebrated the skills and qualities one needed to survive on the frontier. The heroes from this period—Daniel Boone, Mike Fink, Paul Bunyan, John Henry, the Swamp Angel—are rugged, strong and clever. When supposedly educated city slickers venture into the countryside, they are outsmarted by these heroes every time.

Ichabod Crane, a native of Connecticut, is a typical scholar who wishes he were an outdoorsman. Irving points out that there are two types of men who come out of Connecticut, "pioneers for the mind as well as for the forest," who become "frontier woodmen and country schoolmasters." Crane is not completely out of place in the forest—he is able to help with the "lighter labors" on the farm—but thinks of himself and is considered by others "a

kind of idle gentleman-like personage, of vastly superior taste and accomplishments to the rough country swains." On Sunday afternoons, while he strolls about with the young ladies of the village, "the more bashful country bumpkins h[a]ng sheepishly back, envying his superior elegance and address."

Brom Bones, Crane's most formidable competitor for the hand of Katrina, is as unlike Crane as he could be, "burly, roaring, roistering." Where Crane is "esteemed by the women as a man of great erudition," Brom is "the hero of the country round, which rang with his feats of strength and hardihood." Crane is "tall, but exceedingly lank, with narrow shoulders," while Brom is "broad-shouldered" and has a "Herculean frame." Crane courts Katrina "in a quiet and gently insinuating manner," while Brom's "amorous toyings" are "something like the gentle caresses and endearments of a bear."

Irving sets up a confrontation between these two opposites, and any reader of American folklore knows how it will turn out. Crane's education is no match for Brom's native wit, his scrawny body and awkward riding are no match for Brom's strength and skill, and the woman chooses the rough and strong man over the refined and delicate one. Neither man is particularly unlikable, but in America, a young country with frontier to be tamed, the values of the country win out over those of the city.

Creativity and Imagination

"The Legend of Sleepy Hollow" is a story about stories and story-tellers, and a lesson in keeping the line clear between fiction and reality. The title is significant. Irving identifies this as a legend, a type of story that may be loosely based on truth but is clearly fiction, that may feature the supernatural, that is handed down by a people and that reflects the national character of that people.

This quality is captured in "The Legend of Sleepy Hollow" as the narrator reminds the reader again and again of the special nature of the valley where the story takes place. The name of the valley is no accident, for "a drowsy dreamy influence seems to hang over the land, and to pervade the very atmosphere." The place "holds a spell over the minds of the good people, causing them to walk in a continual reverie." Ichabod Crane is not immune to the influence, for even outsiders, "however wide awake they may have been before they entered that sleepy region," are sure to "inhale the witching atmosphere of the air, and begin to grow imaginative."

One function of imagination and story-telling is to bind a community together, as seen in the party scene. Most of the stories told are unverifiable and untrue: "Just sufficient time had elapsed to enable each story-teller to dress up his tale with a little becoming fiction, and, in the indistinctness of his recollection, to make himself the hero of every exploit." The exaggeration is just part of the fun, and so long as everyone understands this there is no harm.

Crane, however, does not understand the limits of imagination. His dreams are too grand; he tries to make them reality but he can never live up to them. When he sees the bounty at the Van Tassel home, he dreams "in his devouring mind's eye" of "every roasting-pig running about with a pudding in his belly" and every turkey and duck and pigeon becoming a meal for him. When he looks over the Van Tassel land, "his imagination expanded with the idea, how they might be readily turned into cash." And when he looks into the mirror as he prepares for the party, he sees a cavalier, where the narrator sees only a "grasshopper." No wonder Crane is bold enough to ask for Katrina's hand, and no wonder he is surprised when she refuses him.

This lack of discernment is Crane's downfall. Because he imagines himself to be a "knight-errant in quest of adventures," he humiliates himself in front of Katrina. Because he does not understand that the story of the headless horseman is just a story, he is easy prey for Brom. If only he were as wise as the story-teller in Knickerbocker's postscript, who says of his own story, "Faith sir . . . I don't believe one half of it myself."

Style

Narration/Narrative/Narrator

There is an almost dizzying number of levels of narration and narrators in "The Legend of Sleepy Hollow": a) Washington Irving is the author of *The Sketch Book of Geoffrey Crayon, Gent.* ; b) Geoffrey Crayon is the fictional author of the volume, the one responsible for collection or creating the stories and sketches; c) Diedrich Knickerbocker is the character who supposedly wrote down "The Legend of Sleepy Hollow," and in whose hand the postscript was "found," presumably by Crayon; d) the legend was told to Knickerbocker by a "pleasant, shabby, gentlemanly old fellow"; e) within the legend, the characters tell stories that they have heard or read, many of them concerning "a figure on horseback without a head." Ichabod Crane, then, is a man who is frightened by a story within a story within a story within a story.

The narrators are not only numerous, but also unreliable. Knickerbocker claims that he has repeated the legend "almost in the precise words in which I heard it related"—a ridiculous claim considering the length of the story, the amount of description, and the fact that he heard it only once. The "gentlemanly old fellow" makes a great pretense in the beginning of his narration of telling the truth, pointing out that he has heard an explanation for the name "Tarry Town," but he will not "vouch for the fact, but merely advert to it, for the sake of being precise and accurate." By the end, however, he admits that the legend might be a bit extravagant, and says, "I don't believe one half of it myself."

The inhabitants of Sleepy Hollow are subject to fits of imagination, "they are given to all kinds of marvelous beliefs,'' and they enjoy gatherings at which each story-teller is encouraged ''to dress up his tale with a little becoming fiction, and, in the indistinction of his recollection, to make himself the hero of every exploit.'' When the men are not telling stories of how they won the war single-handedly, they are telling ''tales of ghosts and apparitions,'' and finding the stories delightfully frightening. As narrators, they are as unreliable as Knickerbocker and his acquaintance.

The effect of all these unreliable narrators is to distance the reader from the action and from the characters. If nothing can be believed, empathy cannot develop, and the reader forms no strong feelings about Crane, either positive or negative. As a psychological study, ''The Legend of Sleepy Hollow'' falls short, because the reader never gets close enough to the characters to look inside their minds. Cardboard characters move through a humorous situation, and although there is some trickery afoot, no one really gets hurt. This emotional distance, created by the multiple levels of narration, focuses readers' attention on the humor, and it is the humor that has made ''The Legend of Sleepy Hollow'' an American favorite for almost two hundred years.

Imagery

One of the most striking features of the story is the long passages of rich descriptive detail. The narrator opens with a long reverie on the dreaminess of the landscape, but when the story shifts its focus to Crane and his thoughts, the description becomes more vivid. When Crane walks home in the evening, for example, the narrator lists every creature that frightens him: the whip-poor-will, the tree-toad, the screech-owl, the fire-flies, the beetle. When he looks over the Van Tassel barn, ''bursting forth with the treasures of the farm,'' Crane's gaze—and the reader's— lingers over every swallow, martin, pigeon, pig, goose, duck, turkey, guinea-fowl and rooster.

When he sees a farm animal, Crane imagines it as food, and the list of farm creatures is followed immediately by a longer list of the dishes they might yield. ''In his devouring mind's eye'' Crane sees the pigs roasted, the pigeons ''snugly put to bed in a comfortable pie,'' the ducks ''pairing cozily in dishes, like snug married couples, with a decent competency of onion sauce.'' Inside the Van Tassel home, Crane cannot keep his eyes still as he admires

the tools, the furniture, and most importantly the fruits of the earth: ''In one corner stood a huge bag of wool ready to be spun; in another, a quantity of linsey-woolsey just from the loom; ears of Indian corn, and strings of dried apples and peaches, hung in gay festoons along the wall, mingled with the gaud of red peppers.'' Where other men are attracted to Katrina because of her beauty, Crane sees her only as a stepping stone to ''the treasures of jolly autumn.''

William Hedges observes that ''the method of this story is to heap up images of abundance and contrast Sleepy Hollow's amplitude with the meagreness of Ichabod Crane's body and spirit.'' Mary Weatherspoon Bowden refers to the same images of ''glorious autumn days and autumn harvests, to food, food, and more food, to buxom lasses and merriment and pranks'' when she concludes that the legend is ''a celebration of the bounty of the United States.''

For Americans at the beginning of the nineteenth century, the United States was still the land of plenty, a country of endless resources. This was a source of pride for Irving and his American readers, and a subject of fascination and wonder for his British readers, whose national wilderness had been tamed centuries before. Irving uses lush imagery precisely for its lushness, to demonstrate and celebrate the endless resources of a new, unproven nation.

Historical Context

The Dutch in New York

In its earliest days as an outpost for Europeans, New York was settled by the Dutch, or people from the Kingdom of the Netherlands. Henry Hudson, referred to in ''The Legend of Sleepy Hollow'' as ''Master Hendrick Hudson,'' sailed in 1609 from present-day New York City to Albany up what the Dutch called the Tappan Zee, and what is now called the Hudson River; the Tappan Zee Bridge in New York City commemorates this today. Hudson was British by birth, but was working for the Dutch East India Company, and after his explorations the Netherlands claimed what is now New York as its

Compare
&
Contrast

- **1810:** Irving's home town, New York City, is a major metropolitan center with a population of 80,000. The population of the United States is 7,239,881.

  1990: The population of New York City is 7,322,564.

- **1810s:** Women's bodies are thought to be attractive if they are, like, Katrina Van Tassel's, "plump as a partridge." Many women think it is vulgar to be thin enough that the shape of their bones is revealed.

  1990s: Women are expected to be thin. Defined cheekbones are a mark of beauty.

- **1810s:** Few people in a rural village are educated enough to teach school. Most people are not able to read and write. Therefore, teachers come from outside, often from the cities.

  1990s: Adults who cannot read or write have great difficulties managing daily life.

- **1810s:** Veterans of the American Revolution are still alive, and enjoy telling true and exaggerated war stories at social occasions.

  1990s: Veterans of the Korean and Vietnam conflicts tend to keep quiet about their experiences.

---

own territory. The first Dutch settlers arrived at present-day New York City in 1624. Although the territory eventually came under British and then American control, the Dutch people were still numerous and influential throughout New York in Irving's day.

As with any ethnic group, stereotypes of the Dutch were abundant. They were said to be jolly, prosperous, well-fed, and foolish. Irving had poked fun at Dutchmen in *A History of New York from the Beginning of the World to the End of the Dutch Dynasty*, whose fictional author was Diedrich Knickerbocker. Knickerbocker is supposedly the source of this story as well, and the stereotypes are used to comic effect in the characters of Baltus Van Tassel, his daughter Katrina, and their superstitious and somewhat pompous neighbors. It should be said that there were also widespread stereotypical notions about Yankees, or people of Anglo-Saxon descent, who were considered—like Ichabod Crane—to be vain, overeducated, sophisticated and lacking in common sense.

Irving made use of the folklore about Dutch people, and in a minor way contributed to it. When he created the character of Diedrich Knickerbocker,

he made up the name "Knickerbocker" to sound funny and at the same time come close enough to a genuine Dutch name to be believable. With Irving's growing popularity, people began to associate the last name with the people. Dutch people were referred to as "knickerbockers," and later the baggy pants gathered below the knee that the men wore came to be known as "knickerbockers" and then "knickers." Knickers fell out of fashion after the 1930s, but the name is still used by the professional basketball team the Knickerbockers, or the New York Knicks.

The New American Fiction

Irving was alive and writing at the moment in American literary history when a true national literature was being called for and created. Previously, the writing coming out of the colonies and then out of the new nation was primarily religious or historical, and was scarcely different from the same kinds of writing coming out of Europe. Ichabod Crane's own favorite writer, Cotton Mather (1663-1728), was a preacher and a political writer of rational, stern treatises on subjects of the day. His books about witchcraft grew out of the Salem witchcraft trials, and they were neither imaginative, nor intended to entertain or to express the writer's experiences or emotions. Instead, in *The History of New England Witchcraft*, which Daniel Hoffman has identified as *Magnalia Christi Americana* (1702), Mather presented case histories of what he believed to be actual and Satanic events, for the purpose of informing his readers and arguing against the witch trials.

By the end of the eighteenth century, there was a demand for American characters and American themes, and plays filling this need had already begun to appear. The popularity of novels imported from England led to the beginnings of the American novel, and to serious discussions about what kinds of literature would best reflect the values of a democratic society. Irving was among the first American writers who had both the talent and the will to write American fiction, but he had no American models.

The Sketch Book, written in England, contains more than thirty sketches or stories, and nearly all of them have to do with English life and English characters. "The Legend of Sleepy Hollow" was unusual, though not unique, in being set in the United States. To create the story, Irving borrowed heavily from the German legends of Ruebezahl from the *Volksmaerchen der Deutschen*, transporting the basic action and characters to Upstate New York. It was a beginning. The *Sketch Book* became the first book by an American to sell well in England, proving that it could be done.

Historians and critics have debated for over a century whether Irving invented the short story when he wrote "The Legend of Sleepy Hollow" and "Rip Van Winkle." Some have argued that the two are not actually stories at all, but merely tales. Whether he was a creator or an adapter, a writer of stories or of tales, Irving expanded the possibilities of American writing, and helped make possible the explosion of new forms and idioms that would come along at the middle of the nineteenth century.

Critical Overview

Most early readers of *The Sketch Book* praised the volume for its humor and its graceful descriptive writing, but did not single out "The Legend of Sleepy Hollow" for special attention. Francis Jeffrey, in an 1820 review in *Edinburgh Review*, did note that the legend, along with "Rip Van Winkle," was among only five or six pieces in the collection of thirty-five that relates "to subjects at all connected with America. . . . The rest relate entirely to England." But other than pointing out its existence, he had nothing to say about the story. Jeffrey was clearly delighted with the collection, and astonished that Irving was able to produce it: "It is the work of an American, entirely bred and trained in that country. . . . Now, the most remarkable thing in a work so circumstanced certainly is, that it should be written throughout with the greatest care and accuracy, and worked up to great purity and beauty of diction."

More recently, critics have attempted to delineate just what is American about Irving's fiction. Terence Martin, writing for *American Literature* in 1959, focuses his attention on the newness of the United States as a nation during Irving's career, and the American tendency at the time to equate "the imaginative and the childish." Irving's struggling to control his appetite and to use imagination properly can be seen as mirroring the struggles of the new society to behave maturely. He concludes, "for Irving there is no place, or a very limited place, for the hero of the imagination in the culture of early America." In *The Comic Imagination in American Literature* (1973), Lewis Leary traces the influence Irving's work had on American humor, and claims that in "The Legend of Sleepy Hollow" and other early tales, Irving "opened doors which gave access to native varieties of the comic spirit."

Around the middle of the twentieth century, attention was turned toward finding the sources Irving used in crafting his tales. The most important work was done by Henry A. Pochmann in 1930. In articles in *Studies in Philology* and *PMLA [Publications of the Modern Language Association]*, Pochmann demonstrated that Irving had translated and adapted German stories to create "The Legend of Sleepy Hollow" and other tales. In a 1953 article in *PMLA*, Daniel G. Hoffman explored Irving's use of American folkloric sources, finding that Irving used great "originality in interpreting American themes," and he developed his ideas further in his 1961 book, *Form and Fable in American Fiction*.

In the last quarter century, some critics have examined the story from a feminist perspective, to

Ichabod Crane, fleeing on a horse from a ghost holding a head over its shoulders.

examine what the story reveals about Irving's ideas about the role of women. In her 1975 book *The Lay of the Land*, Annette Kolodny describes Sleepy Hollow as a feminine pastoral setting. She sees Ichabod Crane as a male aggressor who threatens this community and therefore must be driven away. In 1993, Laura Plummer and Michael Nelson again find that Crane is "an intrusive male who threatens the stability of a decidedly feminine place," as they explain in an article in *Studies in Short Fiction*. They describe the story as a conflict between male and female forms of storytelling, and point out its "misogynistic bent."

Other critics have seen Crane as threatening, but in different ways. Writing for *American Imago* in 1981, Edward F. Pajak explains how the legend is a variation of the myth of Narcissus, and describes Crane's "poorly integrated identity." Crane's attraction to Katrina and her father masks his unconscious attraction to Brom Bones, and he can find resolution only by "a rejection of the world." For Albert J. von Frank, Crane is more than paranoid and regressed. He finds in a 1987 article in *Studies in American Fiction* that "Irving's genial reputation largely obscures the evil that Ichabod represents." Crane's envy, avarice, sloth and gluttony, among other sins, threaten the community with "moral taint and eventual destruction," making it necessary to drive him from the village.

Criticism

Cynthia Bily

Bily teaches English at Adrian College in Adrian, Michigan. In this essay she discusses Irving's conception of Sleepy Hollow as an earthly paradise.

Irving's narrator opens "The Legend of Sleepy Hollow" with a brief description of Sleepy Hollow itself, "one of the quietest places in the whole world," a place of "uniform tranquillity." Before moving on to introduce his characters he concludes, "If ever I should wish for a retreat, whither I might steal from the world and its distractions, and dream quietly away the remnant of a troubled life, I know of none more promising than this little valley." In this opening, Irving establishes Sleepy Hollow as both of-this-world and not-of-this-world, an "enchanted region" of unparalleled beauty and fertility. Tapping a literary tradition that stretches back literally thousands of years, he sets his story in a comic American version of what is often called an Earthly Paradise.

A. Bartlett Giamatti explains in his book *The Earthly Paradise and the Renaissance Epic* that "the desire for a state of perfect repose and life eternal has always haunted mankind, and poets have forever been the spokesmen for the dream." Poets—and, more recently, prose writers—have created "idylls, eclogues, odes, epithalamia, epics, satires, romances, and occasional verses all [abounding] with descriptions of such an ideal life in an ideal landscape." These works of literature have tended to depict their landscapes using a traditional set of images and ideas, and Irving uses and adapts many of them in creating his own "enchanted region."

Stories set in an earthly paradise often take place in a Golden Age, a distant time and way of existence without strife and care. In the eighth century BC the Greek poet Hesiod outlined the five ages of man in his *Works and Days*; the five were the golden age, the silver age, the bronze age, the age of heroes, and the iron age in which we live now. The golden age was the first, the most simple and noble, and the yearning to return to the golden age has figured in ancient and more recent literature. As Giamatti writes, the image "never failed, or

fails yet, to evoke that time when the world was fresh with dew and man was happy." Even today, Americans look to the past ("those were the days") as a happier time, and tell themselves that "things were simpler then." In creating his earthly paradise, Irving comically sets his story in a new nation's version of ancient history, "in a remote period of American history, that is to say, some thirty years since."

The attractive thing about the golden age landscape is that it does not change. The narrator pines, "Though many years have elapsed since I trod the drowsy shades of Sleepy Hollow, yet I question whether I should not find the same trees and the same families vegetating in its sheltered bosom." Sleepy Hollow is the kind of place where "the population, manners, and customs remain fixed; while the great torrent of migration and improvement, which is making such incessant changes in other parts of this restless country, sweeps by them unobserved."

But it is the landscape, not the society, that makes an earthly paradise. One of the most common ways of depicting paradise is as a garden, for example, the Bible's Garden of Eden. Giamatti finds that "in a garden, meadow or field poets have always felt Nature most nearly approximates the ideals of harmony, beauty and peace which men constantly seek in some form or other." Another common depiction is the beautiful but somewhat wilder landscape used in pastoral poetry as a setting for love to bloom. Albert J. von Frank sees elements of both the garden and the pastoral in "The Legend of Sleepy Hollow." In a 1987 article in *Studies in American Fiction*, he writes, "Like other ideal settings, the larger Dutch community, Sleepy Hollow, and the Van Tassel farm are enclosed gardens, here concentrically frames, inviting, seductive, and as dangerous to itinerants as the island of the Sirens or the land of the Lotos-Eaters. The societies sheltered by these nested gardens are themselves closed and static . . . yet magically productive. Following pastoral convention, Irving describes the land."

One example will demonstrate the images that Irving is working with. Theocritus, the third century BC Greek poet who is credited with inventing the pastoral, wrote a series of "idylls," or brief poems about contentment in country life. In his seventh idyll is found this passage: Many an aspen, many an elm bowed and rustled overhead, and hard by, the hallowed water welled purling forth of a cave of the Nymphs, while the brown cricket chirped busily

What Do I Read Next?

- "Rip Van Winkle" (1819) is the second of the two stories for which Irving is famous today. Rip Van Winkle wanders off into the Catskill mountains to escape his wife's nagging, plays ninepins with a group of dwarfs, and sleeps for twenty years.

- "The Spectre Bridegroom, A Traveller's Tale" (1819) is another story from Irving's *Sketch Book*. A young girl is loved by two men, one from her own rural area and one from a far-away city. Although it is set in Germany, this story of competition, pranks and the supernatural is instructively like and unlike "The Legend of Sleepy Hollow."

- *The Life of Washington Irving* (1935) by Stanley T. Williams is a two-volume biography, notable for its thoroughness and for the strong sense Stanley creates of thoroughly disliking his subject.

- Davy Crockett's *Narrative of the Life of David Crockett* (1834) is a collection of tall tales, many of them about Crockett himself but also including stories of other rugged outdoorsmen outsmarting Eastern men from the cities.

- "The Man That Corrupted Hadleyburg" (1900) is a humorous tale by Mark Twain. A stranger uncovers the secret corruption of small-town America by promising unearned wealth to some of Hadleyburg's important citizens.

- *The Dark Way: Stories from the Spirit World* (1990), edited by Virginia Hamilton, contains twenty-five stories from Italy, Kenya, Russia, the United States and other countries, featuring the exploits of witches, devils, and tricksters.

---

amid the shady leafage, and the tree frog murmured aloof in the dense thornbrake. Lark and goldfinch sang and turtle moaned, and about the spring the bees hummed and hovered to and fro. All nature smelt of the opulent summertime, smelt of the season of fruit. Pears lay at our feet, apples on either side, rolling abundantly. And the young branches lay splayed upon the ground because of the weight of their damsons.

Although Irving's story takes place in the fertile harvest time of autumn instead of summer, he builds his descriptive passages out of nearly the same images, adding a comic twist here and there. The approach to the Van Tassel farm resembles the opening lines of the Theocritus passage, if a barrel can be asked to stand for the cave of the Nymphs: "A giant elm-tree spread its broad branches over it, at the foot of which bubbled up a spring of the softest and sweetest water, in a little well formed of a barrel." Where the Greeks had lark and goldfinch, here in America Irving boasts of a long catalog of birds, "taking their farewell banquets. In the fulness

of their revelry, they fluttered, chirping and frolicking, from bush to bush and tree to tree, capricious from the very profusion and variety around them." Even the tree-frog appears, not murmuring but giving a "boding cry."

And the food! The fruits of the American paradise are so much more than pears and apples and damsons (plums). There are apples, of course. Ichabod beholds "vast stores of apples; some hanging in oppressive opulence on the trees; some gathered into baskets and barrels for the market; others heaped up in rich piles for the cider-press." But there are also "great fields of Indian corn, with its golden ears peeping from their leafy coverts" and "yellow pumpkins lying beneath them, turning up their fair round bellies to the sun" and the "fragrant buckwheat fields breathing the odor of the beehive." Nearly every feature of Theocritus's poem is present in Irving's description.

One detail that is missing is the cricket, but Irving handles that in another way. In one of the most vivid images in the story, he shows Ichabod Crane riding off to meet his lady with "his knees nearly up to the pommel of the saddle; his sharp elbows stuck out like grasshoppers." Theocritus's cricket is brown, but Crane wears "rusty black."

This is not to say that Irving had read Theocritus (though he may have), but rather that Irving and Theocritus had read the same things, and had drawn from the same well of images. The earthly paradise often has other features, some of which Irving adopts or adapts: the landscape is situated on a high mountain (here it is "a little valley, or rather lap of land, among high hills"), there is a fountain (here the brook which seems to flow past every building in the valley), the west wind blows. In poems of the fourteenth century and later, the earthly paradise may be dangerous, the mountain may be in shadow, as Sleepy Hollow is. Giamatti describes a "beautiful-seeming earthly paradise where man's will is softened, his moral fiber unraveled, and his soul ensnared. It is the garden where insidious luxury and sensuous love overcome duty and true devotion."

The danger appears in a familiar form. Giamatti traces the idea of the danger to the fourteenth-century Italian poet Petrarch, in whose *Triondo d'Amore* "a man is tempted to let down his guard, to succumb to the desire for security and female domination which the garden promises. Man is weakened in such a place . . . in the arms of the woman who animates the place." Ichabod lets down his guard—loses his head—in the same way. The narrator claims that "he would have passed a pleasant life of it, in despite of the devil and all his works, if his path had not been crossed by a being that causes more perplexity to mortal man than ghosts, goblins, and the whole race of witches put together, and that was—a woman."

Irving's use of classical images and themes was not an accident of native talent and inspiration. He was adequately literate in several languages, and had read the important literature of Europe and the classical world. He was well acquainted with Sir Walter Scott, whose own novels and poems were based on legends and myths. As Daniel Hoffman argues in *Fame and Fable in American Fiction* (1973), Washington Irving was . . . something of an antiquary. His early *Knickerbocker's History of New York* reveals him to be enchanted with the very past he satirized. . . . Wherever Irving went he collected popular sayings and beliefs; he was prepossessed by a sense of the past, and recognized

> **"** Irving's use of classical images and themes was not an accident of native talent and inspiration. He was adequately literate in several languages, and had read the important literature of Europe and the classical world. **"**

the power—and the usefulness to a creative artist—of popular antiquities."

Irving knew the value of calling up old images. By echoing the ancients he borrowed some of their power, and claimed for his story—even if in a mocking way—a place among them. By adapting European imagery to use American details, he showed in a form of shorthand that America had as much to offer as the Europeans, and more. In this, he was not alone. But he was one of the first, one of the reasons Giamatti can state that "American literature is constantly read as a record of the quest for happiness and innocence in the great unspoiled garden."

Source: Cynthia Bily, for *Short Stories for Students*, The Gale Group, 2000.

Laura Plummer and Michael Nelson

In the following essay, Plummer and Nelson maintain that the women in Sleepy Hollow maintain their power through the tales that they tell. The tales of the women retain their strength as men measure their strength by defeating the evils in the women's tales and the women's tale of the Headless Horseman is a means of removing the aggressive Ichabod Crane from the maternally controlled Sleepy Hollow.

Discussions of Washington Irving often concern gender and the artistic imagination, but these topics are usually mutually exclusive when associated with the two most enduring stories from the *Sketch Book of Geoffrey Crayon, Gent.* (1819–20): "Rip Van Winkle" and "The Legend of Sleepy Hollow." Many readings of the former focus on gender, while discussions of the latter most often explore its conception of the artist's role in American society. "The Legend of Sleepy Hollow" does indeed address this second theme, but also complicates it by making art an issue of gender. Ichabod Crane is not only a representative of bustling, practical New England who threatens imaginatively fertile rural America with his prosaic acquisitiveness; he is also an intrusive male who threatens the stability of a decidedly female place. For Irving, the issue of art is sexually charged; in Sleepy Hollow, this tension finally becomes a conflict between male and female storytelling. A close look at the stories that circulate through the Dutch community shows that Ichabod's expulsion follows directly from women's cultivation of local folklore. Female-centered Sleepy Hollow, by means of tales revolving around the emasculated, headless "dominant spirit" of the region, figuratively neuters threatening masculine interlopers like Ichabod to ensure the continuance of the old Dutch domesticity, the Dutch wives' hearths, and their old wives' tales.

Although Irving often places the feminine in a pejorative light—the "feminine" in Ichabod is his unmanly, superstitious, trembling, and gullible side—he himself seems, in this tale, begrudgingly to acquiesce to the female sphere of Sleepy Hollow. And this sphere has none of the abrasiveness so blatant in "Rip Van Winkle." We have no shrewish wife, whose death in a "fit of passion" allows for Rip's carefree dotage upon his return to the village. Rather, we are left with a sense of relief at Ichabod's removal, at this snake's relegation to the mythology of the Hollow. Thus the tale presents a stark contrast to "Rip Van Winkle." In that story, women attempt and fail to confront men openly; in Sleepy Hollow, female behavior is much more subversive, and effective.

In "The Legend of Sleepy Hollow," Irving's conservatism subverts itself, since conservation of the existing power structure means the continuance of a female (though certainly not feminist) hierarchy. Irving's tale is one of preservation, then, of maintenance of the feminine, and the landscape is the predominant female. Sleepy Hollow lies "in the bosom" of a cove lining the Hudson, the valley is "embosomed in the great state of New York," and the vegetating families of Sleepy Hollow are rooted in its "sheltered bosom." Clearly the repose and security of the place rest in the maternal landscape—an assumption so pervasive that even our male narrator attests to it. For as he observes, in this tale of a Dutch Eden even the adamic act of naming

falls to women. "The good house-wives of the adjacent country, from the inveterate propensity of their husbands to linger about the village tavern on market days," have named the nearby "rural port" "Tarry Town"; the name and the power of naming thus operate as a gently sardonic means of reproaching unruly husbands and of preserving female dominance over the valley.

The narrator is not simply an idle observer, however. He comes to the Hollow to hunt:

> I recollect that when a stripling, my first exploit in squirrel shooting was in a grove of tall walnut trees that shades one side of the valley. I had wandered into it at noon time, when all nature is peculiarly quiet, and was startled by the roar of my own gun, as it broke the sabbath stillness around, and was prolonged and reverberated by the angry echoes. If ever I should wish for a retreat, whither I might steal from the world and its distractions, and dream quietly away the remnant of a troubled life, I know none more promising than this little valley.

The tale thus begins with a paradigm of masculine experience in the maternal bosom of Sleepy Hollow: an acquisitive, intrusive male both perpetuates female influence over the region and also acquiesces to constraints on male behavior. As the narrator remarks, the Hollow is his choice for "retreat" and security. But although the return to Sleepy Hollow is therefore a return to the womb, unfortunately, he is no longer welcome there.

For as he praises the soporific atmosphere of the Dutch valley, the narrator also admits it has repulsed him. It is clear that Mother Nature here produces a bower not to be disturbed by the masculine aggression of hunting, regardless of its tameness in the case of this "stripling." Hunting is not permitted, and trespassers will be startled into submission. Our gun-toting narrator is surprised not only by the roar of his own gun, his own masculine explosion into the place, but also by the sense that his behavior is inappropriate. This womb-like grove is for nurturing dream, not bloodsport; to be treated with respect due the sabbath, not rent asunder by blunderbuss ejaculations. Indeed, the "angry echoes" from the landscape suggest a rebellious reaction to such flagrant poaching. Indolent as the epigraph may make the place seem, Sleepy Hollow does not take kindly to intruders; hence the narrator is properly awed into acquiescence.

The youthful exploit of this opening scene is echoed by the actions of Ichabod and the Headless Horseman. For like the narrator, both Ichabod and "the dominant spirit" of Sleepy Hollow—"the apparition of a figure on horseback without a head''—are masculine, mercenary interlopers in this feminine place. The bony schoolmaster's desire to liquidate heiress Katrina Van Tassel's wealth, invest it ''in immense tracts of wild land,'' and take Katrina from the Hollow mirrors both the narrator's childhood intrusion and the former Hessian trooper's attempt to win Sleepy Hollow for Royalist forces ''in some nameless battle during the revolutionary war.'' They embody the essence of masculine imperialism: war, fortune hunting, and even squirrel hunting are all expressions of the same will to conquer. Gun, Hessian sword, or birch in hand, the narrator, the Horseman, and Ichabod all bear authority; and all three seek the spoils—political, material or sexual—of invading Sleepy Hollow.

Irving's bawdy imagery strongly suggests that all male intrusions in this female place are ultimately sexual. Ichabod, for example, is described in insistently phallic terms:

> He had, however, a happy mixture of pliability and perseverance in his nature; he was in form and spirit like a supple jack—yielding, but tough; though he bent, he never broke; and though he bowed beneath the slightest pressure, yet, the moment it was away—jerk!—he was as erect, and carried his head as high as ever.

The pedagogue's ''pliability and perseverance''—Ichabod is elsewhere accredited with possessing ''the dilating powers of an Anaconda''—suggest that he will not be as easily scared or awed as the narrator. It will take more than just the roar of his gun to frighten this persistent ''jack.''

Storytelling is also a part of male imperialism. Of the numerous tales that circulate through Sleepy Hollow, those told by men concern their own fictionalized exploits. ''The sager folks'' at Van Tassel's farm sit ''gossiping over former times, and drawling out long stories about the war''; ''just sufficient time had elapsed to enable each storyteller to dress up his tale with a little becoming fiction, and in the indistinctness of his recollection, to make himself the hero of every exploit.'' These stories are designed to increase the teller's status in the minds of his listeners by linking him to the heroic, historic, and masculine past.

True to this male practice of self-aggrandizing storytelling, Ichabod regales his female companions with scientific ''speculations upon comets and shooting stars, and with the alarming fact that the world did absolutely turn round, and that they were half the time topsy-turvy!'' Though fantastic in

> The narrator's sardonic comment that 'the old country wives . . . are the best judges of these matters' is clue enough to a rather disparaging attitude; resenting the authority of women is nothing new to Irving's fiction."

themselves, these stories are to Ichabod the height of learning and scholarly achievement. Even his tales of the supernatural show him as ''a perfect master of Cotton Mather's History of New England Witchcraft.'' Ichabod's familiarity with the subject attests to his book learning and his reliance on the great masters of American thought, not to his understanding of folklore. Boastfully displaying his knowledge of worldly matters, this ''travelling gazette'' brings word of the ''restless country'' of ''incessant change'' outside Sleepy Hollow. Part of the pioneer's repertoire, carried from town to town, his stories are meant to recommend him to each new audience by proving his erudition.

While male storytelling is a part of the will to compete and conquer, storytelling for the women of Sleepy Hollow moves beyond self-image to counter that male will. The ''witching power'' the narrator fails to define fully is a female influence that gently molds the inhabitants of Sleepy Hollow through the folklore that emanates from that exclusively female, domestic province, the hearth:

> Another of [Ichabod's] sources of fearful pleasure was, to pass long winter evenings with the old Dutch wives, as they sat spinning by the fire, with a row of apples roasting and sputtering along the hearth, and listen to their marvellous tales of ghosts and goblins, and haunted fields and haunted brooks, and haunted bridges and haunted houses, and particularly of the headless horseman, or galloping Hessian of the Hollow, as they sometimes called him.

Spinning, cooking, and spinning tales are simultaneous acts; the convergence of folklore and the domestic imbues everyday events with the supernatural.

The effectiveness of this domestication of the supernatural is clear from the extent to which folklore affects local inhabitants' behavior. At the tale's close, the bridge where the Horseman confronted Ichabod is no longer used, the schoolhouse is abandoned, and Ichabod's "magic books" have been burned in Hans Van Ripper's censorial flames; the community has accepted that the spirit world is larger than themselves, that despite their boasts and challenges, the lore of the place is still supreme and affects nearly every facet of their lives.

Perhaps the most convincing proof of the pervasiveness of female influence in Sleepy Hollow is that all the men have set themselves to challenging it. Accordingly, the narrator not only concedes the connection between women and spirits, but he also establishes women as the greatest source of fear for men:

> [Ichabod] would have passed a pleasant life of it, in despite of the Devil and all his works, if his path had not been crossed by a being that causes more perplexity to mortal man, than ghosts, goblins, and the whole race of witches put together, and that was—a woman.

Although this passage is supposed to be humorous, it nonetheless reveals Irving's characteristic misogyny and the male fear of disempowerment played out again and again throughout the tale. In contrast to Rip Van Winkle, however, the Hollow men displace this fear from women to characters of folklore. It is a misunderstanding that, as in the case of Ichabod, ensures men's continued thraldom.

Given the misogynistic bent of "The Legend of Sleepy Hollow," it is not surprising that despite the tale's narrative complexity, Irving suppresses actual female speech; in fact, the only narratives directly or indirectly related are spoken by men. This conspicuous absence of female narration underscores the way in which males both fear and resist the feminine. Thus, the narrator is at a loss to relate what Katrina says to Ichabod in their tete-a-tete after the frolic: "What passed at this interview I will not pretend to say, for in fact I do not know." The war stories told at the Van Tassel frolic, like the narrative as a whole, are told by men. And it is Sleepy Hollow *men* who tell ghost stories at the frolic. Tales from the female sphere must be validated by male retelling. That is, the story of the Headless Horseman originates in a tradition kept by women; storytelling sessions with women make Ichabod susceptible to local superstition; but men first reinforce, and then—as we shall see in the confrontation between Ichabod and Brom Bones—

capitalize on the fears and superstitions engendered by women.

The ultimate irony concerning gender and storytelling, then, is that the very female stories males debunk influence their lives, often through their own telling of them. The men who continually joust fictionally with the Headless Horseman not only inflate their prowess, but also repeatedly confront in narrative the threatening world formed, unbeknownst to them, by the alliance of female and spirit. Fighting mock battles in which they defeat what they mistakenly consider their greatest adversary, men actually strengthen the female hold on the community by reinforcing and perpetuating the narratives through which women maintain order.

Indeed, Brom Bones and Ichabod provide an example of males literally enacting these stories. In his role as the Headless Horseman, by means of which he intends to humiliate his rival, Brom unwittingly serves as the means to achieve the goal of the female community: the removal of Ichabod and himself as threats to Sleepy Hollow's quietude. Posing as the Headless Horseman of legend, Brom plays upon Ichabod's superstition and credulity to eliminate his opponent. And it is Ichabod's association of legend and place, engendered in his mind by the female-controlled mythology, that proves his undoing. Riding home alone from the Van Tassel farm at "the very witching time of night," "all the stories of ghosts and goblins that he had heard in the afternoon, now came crowding upon his recollection"; "he was, moreover, approaching the very place where many of the scenes of the ghost stories had been laid." Thus Brom Bones has at his disposal a carefully scripted and blocked drama with which to exploit Ichabod's credulity and superstitious fear.

The phallic language of this passage reiterates Ichabod's sexual threat and clearly indicates that the gullible pedagogue is essentially neutralized or neutered by figurative castration. Bones, masquerading as the Headless Horseman, appears as "something huge, misshapen, black and towering" "like some gigantic monster," while Ichabod flees in terror from the apparition "stretch[ing] his long lank body away over his horse's head, in the eagerness of his flight." Indeed, in this drama of competing masculinity, Ichabod's fear is of dismemberment. Ichabod, "unskilful rider that he was!" has trouble staying on his mount, slipping and bouncing from one side to the other "with a violence that he verily feared would cleave him asunder." Ichabod's fear is nearly realized when Brom hurls his pumpkin/head at the schoolmaster, "tumbl[ing him] headlong into the dust."

Brom Bones triumphs in this phallic contest of horsemanship and sexual potency—Ichabod is never seen in Sleepy Hollow again—but ironically this ejaculatory coup de grace effects his own emasculation. His impersonation of the Horseman prefigures his domestication: donning the garb of the dismembered spirit, and ultimately throwing away his head, Brom insures that his days as a "roaring, roystering blade" are numbered. The ultimate beneficiary of Brom's midnight prank is the Dutch community itself, the maintenance of whose dreamy repose and domestic harmony is the province of women.

The altercation between Brom and Ichabod and its inevitable outcome meet with tacit approval from the female sphere. Brom Bones, the "hero of the country round" with "more mischief than ill will in his composition," appears not to share the schoolmaster's desire to take Katrina and her wealth out of the Dutch community. Since marriage is a most soporific state for the men of Sleepy Hollow, it is more than likely that Brom, who "had for some time singled out the blooming Katrina for the object of his uncouth gallantries," will soon become as content and domesticated, and as plump and vegetable-like, as Katrina's father. Accordingly, there are no "angry echoes" to greet Brom's adventures; indeed, "the old dames" of the country, content with merely remarking "aye, there goes Brom Bones and his gang," indulge him in his revels and pranks. For Brom Bones would be a threat to Sleepy Hollow only if Ichabod should succeed in his suit, thus extending Brom's bachelorhood indefinitely (and enabling Ichabod to make off with the Van Tassel fortune).

Ichabod's expulsion from Sleepy Hollow, then, results from subtle manipulation of local folklore by women. "The Legend of Sleepy Hollow" thus provides a foil to the open male-female confrontation of "Rip Van Winkle"; the story is a darker, more paranoid vision of female power. Indeed, the narrative frame shows the lengths to which men go to find plausible alternatives to the female version of Ichabod's disappearance, which relegates him to the cosmos:

> The old country wives, however, who are the best judges of these matters, maintain to this day, that Ichabod was spirited away by supernatural means; and it is a favourite story often told about the neighborhood round the evening fire.

The male account asserts that Ichabod

had changed his quarters to a distant part of the country; had kept school and studied law at the same time; had been admitted to the bar, turned politician, electioneered, written for the newspapers, and finally had been made a Justice of the Ten Pound Court.

This version translates the jerky young man into the self-reliant American jack-of-all-trades and self-made success. Yet this story is also an import; it arrives via "an old farmer, who had been down to New York on a visit several years after." The ending is brought into Sleepy Hollow from New York, and by a man; it dismisses the supernatural perspective with a very plausible account of Ichabod's fear and mortification as impetus for his speedy removal, and places Ichabod in a respected occupation.

In similar fashion, Diedrich Knickerbocker attempts in the tale's postscript to lend credibility—a factual backbone—to his story, by placing it within a masculine sphere:

> The preceding Tale is given, almost in the precise words in which I heard it related at a corporation meeting of the ancient city of Manhattoes, at which were present many of its sagest and most illustrious burghers.

These wise old men are intended to lend credence and authority to a story that operates on a plane beyond that of burghers and business meetings. And, as Knickerbocker relies upon the authority of "precise words," we are reminded of the narrator's having told us early in the narrative that his aim is to be "precise and authentic." Something there is in these male storytellers that doesn't love a ghost.

The narrator's sardonic comment that "the old country wives . . . are the best judges of these matters" is clue enough to a rather disparaging attitude; resenting the authority of women is nothing new to Irving's fiction. Yet this remark does not alter the fact that the community listens to the women's stories. And this particular one is a favorite in Sleepy Hollow because it both warns and neutralizes threatening males. Ichabod becomes the community's most recent lesson by example, the shivering victim of his own acquisitive fantasies and proof positive of the truth of legend.

The postscript to the tale reiterates the gender conflict present in the story proper and the narrative frame. Diedrich Knickerbocker focuses on the confrontation between the narrator and a cynical listener that ends in the narrator's parodic syllogism and his ambiguous admission concerning his story that "I don't believe one half of it myself." Their verbal jousting is reminiscent of Brom's and Ichabod's own rivalry. And Diedrich Knickerbocker's description of the narrator is most telling: he is "one whom I strongly suspected of being poor, he made such efforts to be entertaining." This, too, allies the narrator with Ichabod and the men of the Dutch community; his performance stands as a final example of male self-aggrandizing storytelling. Indeed, the tale proper becomes the object of male desire and competition; it is the game our youthful narrator has waited the length of a "troubled life" to carry off. In turn, Diedrich Knickerbocker the antiquarian, and Geoffrey Crayon the sketch writer, extend this instance of storytelling as appropriation to fill the entire frame of the tale: its inclusion in *The Sketch Book*. The presence of gender as a central conflict is further buried under layers and layers of male acquisitiveness and competition.

But in "The Legend of Sleepy Hollow," stories, like wealth and game, are not exportable. It is the association of lore and place, of supernatural and practical, that gives the legend of the Headless Horseman its power and efficacy in controlling males within the Dutch community; the very title of the sketch reinforces the primacy of place in storytelling. Like the Horseman himself, the tale is powerless outside a circumscribed area. The ability to tell it in New York, where its supernatural elements are so easily debunked, attests not to the power of the male storyteller who does the debunking—as the postscript would have us believe—but to the element of female storytelling in Sleepy Hollow that insures the success of the female order: its subtle, self-effacing nature. Diffused throughout the folklore and the practical, everyday world of a particular place, the source of power in the Hollow—women—is disguised, making belief in the supernatural a matter of course, not compulsion. When the tale is told outside this female-controlled landscape of the naturalized supernatural, the effectiveness of the story dissolves, leaving only a Hollow husk.

Source: Laura Plummer and Michael Nelson, "'Girls can take care of themselves': Gender and Storytelling in Washington Irving's 'The Legend of Sleepy Hollow,'" in *Studies in Short Fiction*, Vol. 30, 1993, pp. 175–84.

Albert J. von Frank

In the following essay, von Frank explores the various aspects of the evil in Ichabod Crane's personality and actions that necessitates Ichabod's eventual expulsion from the community.

Washington Irving's reputation as a genial writer—as, indeed, America's *most* genial writer—has been firmly established for a century and a half, despite general agreement that his most enduring works are satires. *Knickerbocker's History* maintains its good humor largely by making its narrator appear foolish, but it is harder to say what keeps "The Legend of Sleepy Hollow" from seemingly overtly caustic, since in the portrait of Ichabod Crane Irving comes rather closer than in the *History* to adopting the controlling assumption of Augustan satire that the ridiculous and the evil are one. If Irving's genial reputation largely obscures the evil that Ichabod represents, it must also obscure the mythical structure of the story and, consequently, its formal relationship to such later works as "Young Goodman Brown," "The Man That Corrupted Hadleyburg," and a score of others. That Ichabod *is* evil needs all the more to be said since several modern readings of the story have made impressive moral claims on his behalf, or, alternatively, have transformed him into a pathetic hero, a figure more sinned against than sinning. One urges that he be taken "seriously as a symbol of man's higher aspirations," while another proclaims that "what he wants is simply a home, like anyone else." Even those who regard Ichabod as a threat to the Dutch community differ significantly in assessing the nature and seriousness of the problem he presents.

As Donald Ringe pointed out in 1967, the story is a work of regional satire, pitting Dutch New York against the restless spirit of New England; it is a story that "pleads in effect for the values of the settler and conserver over those of the speculator and improver." Irving's satire, however, works most significantly not at the sociological or political level, but—as all permanently valuable satire does—at the level of the underlying moral issues. The success of the satirical method in "The Legend of Sleepy Hollow" lies in Irving's ability to see the familiar Yankee character as only superficially comic while at the same time discretely ventilating the deeper moral disease of which that comedy is the not quite independently conceived mask. The complexity of tone arising from such a polarized treatment may be traced more specifically to the two uses that Irving makes of the setting. The world of the New York Dutch is something more and other than an ethnic region realistically sketched; it is, indeed, a mythically conceived community, unfallen and changeless, a place of perfect ripeness. Irving establishes the setting in precisely this light and locates Ichabod's mock-heroic chivalry in the most incongruous of all possible contexts, while at the same time raising that portentous central issue of American literature, the moral spoliation of the New World garden. Inasmuch as both the serious and the comic themes converge on the setting, Irving has made the recovery of *its* meaning a precondition for any interpretation.

The setting is not a frontier. Although Daniel Hoffman has persuasively argued that the portrait of Brom Bones owes a great deal to the type of the "ring-tailed roarer," it is not a point with which one can do much more than Hoffman himself has done. Irving indicates that Sleepy Hollow is in most ways the precise reverse of a frontier. Not only has it long been a settled region (a rural one, to be sure), but it is also emphatically a European community with European values. Those forces which on the frontier operate to break down imported cultures—like the rest of the "incessant changes" that Irving abhors—are outside, beyond the "high hills," and simply do not function in "such little retired Dutch valleys, found here and there embosomed in the great state of New York," where "population, manners, and customs, remain fixed." The true American frontier figures but once in the story and then only by way of the sharpest contrast with the Hudson Valley setting: knowing no more than Milton's Satan "to value right / The good before him," Ichabod proposes to exchange the "middle landscape" of the Van Tassel patrimony for a tract of wild land in "Kentucky, Tennessee, or the Lord knows where."

If the setting is not part of the frontier, it *is* a version of the American pastoral as Leo Marx has defined it, though ironically the distinction of Irving's version is that his innocent shepherds are all Europeans. They figure in this magic landscape as the stewards of their own abundant fruitfulness, which fertility takes on a sacramental character in the description of Baltus Van Tassel's farm, where architecture and institutions melt imperceptibly into the activity of farming, and that into a humanized version of the natural order, all under the benediction of an approving sun:

> Hard by the farm house was a vast barn, that might have served for a church; every window and crevice of which seemed bursting forth with the treasures of the farm; the flail was busily resounding within it from morning to night; swallows and martins skimmed twittering about the eaves, and rows of pigeons, some with one eye turned up, as if watching the weather, some with their heads under their wings, or buried in their bosoms, and others swelling, and cooing, and

> "Of the sorts of falls that such an agent as he might induce, consistent with Irving's fondness for his Dutch characters, there is the sort of pillow-soft, post-Miltonic fall of Brom, who, encountering evil without accepting it, passes from innocence to a knowledge of virtuous action and in the process gains his manhood."

bowing about their dames, were enjoying the sunshine on the roof.

This sequestered community is more than home to a company of Dutch farmers; in its sheltered resistance to change, its ungrudging fruitfulness, its feminine character, and, ultimately, its vulnerability, it is the fully elaborated symbol of home as a romantic moral concept.

Like other ideal settings, the larger Dutch community, Sleepy Hollow, and the Van Tassel farm are enclosed gardens, here concentrically framed, inviting, seductive, and as dangerous to itinerants as the island of the Sirens or the land of the Lotos-Eaters. The societies sheltered by these nested gardens are themselves closed and static (again, unlike the frontier), yet magically productive. Following pastoral convention, Irving describes the land in eminently hospitable feminine imagery, indicating in the first sentence that "in the bosom of one of those spacious coves which indent the eastern shore of the Hudson" lies the community named Tarry Town by the women of the region. Two miles away is the smaller village of Sleepy Hollow, likened to a "mimic harbour, undisturbed by the passing current," where one might find even yet "the same families vegetating in its sheltered bosom" In the description of the Van Tassel farm these gender-specific topological features recur: it "was situated on the banks of the Hudson, in one of those green, sheltered, fertile nooks, in which the Dutch farmers are so fond of nestling.'' Each specific location is a repetition of the others; each involves the feminine principle, repose, and water, so the ''small brook'' that glides through Sleepy Hollow ''with just murmur enough to lull one to repose'' is made to well up on Van Tassel's quiet Xanadu as ''a spring of the softest water'' that bubbled along ''among alders and dwarf willows.''

Whatever significance may finally attach to the dandy-and-squatter form of Ichabod's conflict with Brom Bones, the moral satire surely depends on seeing Sleepy Hollow less as the frontier setting of a memorable joke than as Irving's romantic notion of any man's true home. The tone of the story is at all points favorable to the settled and home-loving Dutch; it supports their sense of tradition, their security, their relation to the land, their repose and plenitude, and, most of all, their imagination, while the interloper, Ichabod, is point for point the destructive antithesis of all these traits.

Since the issue of the imagination has appeared to some to support a sympathetic view of Ichabod Crane, and since Irving himself indicates that Sleepy Hollow is an active abettor of the imagination, it is important to see how Irving discriminates between Ichabod and the Dutch on this point. ''It is remarkable,'' writes Irving, ''that the visionary propensity I have mentioned is not confined to the native inhabitants of the valley, but is unconsciously imbibed by every one who resides there for a time. However wide awake they may have been before they entered that sleepy region, they are sure, in a little time, to inhale the witching influence of the air, and begin to grow imaginative—to dream dreams, and see apparition.'' As an Arcadian environment, Sleepy Hollow is necessarily a source of inspiration, and yet those who dream under its influence do so according to their personalities and capacities. The genuinely inspired acts of imagination all belong to the Dutch: to Brom Bones most conspicuously, the Pan by whom Ichabod is panicked, and a poet not of words, certainly, but of virtuous action; to Yost Van Houten, the inspired architect of the schoolhouse locking system, modelled on ''the mystery of the eelpot,'' whereby, ''though a thief might get in with perfect ease, he would find some embarrassment in getting out''; or to Baltus Van Tassel, who monitors Ichabod's quixotic courtship of his daughter by recognizing and observing its appropriate symbol, that is, by ''watching the achievements of a little wooden warrior, who, armed with a sword in each hand, was most valiantly fighting the wind on the pinnacle of the barn.'' Ichabod's imagination

is a truly sorry thing in contrast, compounded, at worst, of Cotton Mather and simple credulity, and never, at its best, escaping the small shrewdness of his New England heritage. In his vision of the Van Tassel farm all its teeming life lies dead, served up as food for him alone, so that Irving's early description of Ichabod as ''the genius of famine'' comes finally to have a profounder point of reference than his gaunt and awkward appearance. He can easily imagine sacrificing all life to his own; the business of the story, however, is to force him to imagine his own death and ultimately to make that imagination feed and sustain the life of the community.

Nowhere is the difference between the Dutch imagination and Ichabod's more evident than in their respective superstitions. As the allusions to Cotton Mather suggest, Ichabod's superstitiousness is the vestige of a decadent Puritanism from which God and glory have departed equally. The schoolmaster is thus left with a system of infernal providences in which all of nature is supposed to have the power—even the purpose—of doing harm to Ichabod Crane. Never wholly secure, he is especially skittish after dark when ''every sound of nature . . . fluttered his excited imagination: the moan of the whip-poor-will from the hill side; the boding cry of the tree toad, that harbinger of storm; . . . or the sudden rustling in the thicket, of birds frightened from their roost.'' Ichabod is so radically disjoined from his environment that he and the natural world are fated enemies: nature frightens him, but, by the same token, he can and does frighten it. Put another way, the presence of death that he senses in nature, nature senses in him.

This development of the protagonist's character reveals an important aspect of Irving's method, because the frightening of the birds recalls the introduction of Ichabod as in appearance like a ''scarecrow eloped from a cornfield'' in a way that decisively alters its original comic application, just as the imagined devastation of the farm's teeming life recalled and deepened the earlier reference to Ichabod as the ''genius of famine.'' The thematic aptness of Irving's humor becomes increasingly apparent as this kind of transformation is several times repeated: the comic details are simply funny when first seen undeveloped or apart from a larger social or moral context (which is to say, from Ichabod's perspective); but when Irving then replants them in a more coherent universe (when he provides them, in effect, some of the morally settled quality of the Dutch perspective), the regional comedy darkens into moral satire.

It is, of course, the basic coherence of the Dutch imagination that prevents their very pronounced superstitiousness from having anything monstrous about it. They are on the best of terms with their ghosts, who are, like themselves and unlike Ichabod, intimately attached to life and the local scene. The Dutch women tell of "haunted fields and haunted brooks, and haunted bridges and haunted houses"; the men tell of "funeral trains, and mourning cries and wailings heard and seen about the great tree where the unfortunate Major Andre was taken" or "of the woman in white, that haunted the dark glen at Raven Rock." These manifestations are, in the way of folk mythology, so localized, so much a part of familiar nature, that to apply the term "supernatural" to them seems almost inappropriate. They tell of unexpected life in the landscape, not of death or threats of death. The Dutch, moreover, tell these tales artistically, neither as first-hand accounts nor as "extracts" from books, as Ichabod does, but as still living legends. The sole exception is Brom Bones' account of his match with the Headless Horseman, a tale combining a youthful irreverence for the mythology of his elders with a point that not even the supernatural is to be dreaded. Generically, the Dutch tales are poles apart from Ichabod's monstrous and unfriendly indication to his female hosts of the "fact that the world did absolutely turn round, and that they were half the time topsy-turvy!"

These unsettled and unsettling traits in Ichabod are manifestly related to, and yet go deeper than, the New England character that on one level is the object of Irving's regional satire. Not content merely to display and ridicule the social behavior of the type, Irving probes the character of his Yankee to give the most basic kinds of moral explanations for the comic inappropriateness of his outward actions. The nature of these explanations is determined by the structure of the story, which involves the penetration of an outsider into the very heart of an earthly paradise. Seen in this light, Ichabod's unsettling traits seem less significantly those of an awkwardly displaced regional character or even of a sinful individual than, at last, those of sin itself. Indeed, the characterizing details of the story seem clustered around the seven deadly sins, even though it is not certain that Irving consciously meant it to appear so.

Ichabod's envy is indicated in one way by his "large green glassy eyes" which are mentioned first as a part of a ludicrous physical description and then again with the moral implications more fully in evidence. His envy is indicated in another way, of course, in his whole attitude toward the domain of Van Tassel:

> As the enraptured Ichabod . . . rolled his great green eyes over the fat meadow lands, the rich fields of wheat, of rye, of buckwheat, and Indian corn, and the orchard burthened with ruddy fruit, which surrounded the warm tenement of Van Tassel, his heart yearned after the damsel who was to inherit these domains, and his imagination expanded with the idea, how they might be readily turned into cash, and the money invested in immense tracts of wild land, and shingle palaces in the wilderness."

This is not envy in the simple sense of wanting to own what others own but accords rather with the classic conception of the sin of envy in which, perversely, one seeks the annihilation of the object. The type of this sin is Satan's envy of the kingdom of God: he cannot hope to share in it, and so commits himself to its destruction. While it might be argued that merely *selling* the land would not destroy it, surely the point about these Dutch farms is that they never *have* been sold, never have had a "market value" or been held by strangers, and that what they represent would be forever lost if any of these conditions were to come to pass. Insidious as this threat is, however, it does not involve a passion that the Dutch, as the owners of the land, can directly be tainted with. In this sense, it is rather more disturbing that Ichabod has introduced envy in an altogether different way to people who seem never to have felt it before. While the schoolmaster escorts the village damsels about the churchyard on Sundays, "the more bashful country bumpkins hung sheepishly back, envying his superior elegance and address."

Ichabod's avarice is the concomitant of his envy and has already been suggested in the way his imagination is so casually dominated by the cash nexus. His plans for the Van Tassel-Crane estate show that he is interested not in the good life but in the immoderately wealthy life, which, for Ichabod, is the fiscal equivalent of never settling down. His "immense tracts" of frontier are for speculation, not for living on or farming, and reflect a characteristic desire that his wealth should come without labor.

Sloth ought to be a sin difficult to attain in this paradise, and yet Ichabod aspires even here. Aside from being a "flogger of urchins," he earns his bread not so much by the sweat of his brow as by assisting the Dutch "occasionally in the lighter labours of their farms." These labors comprise the sort of tasks then commonly assigned to women and children and include taking the horses to water and making hay. Even these he manages largely to avoid by becoming "wonderfully gentle and ingratiating" with the women: "He found favour in the eyes of the mothers, by petting the children, particularly the youngest, and like the lion bold, which whilome so magnanimously the lamb did hold, he would sit with a child on one knee, and rock a cradle with his foot, for whole hours together." Ichabod's almost systematic avoidance of productive labor is depicted mainly through his alliance with female society and through his adoption of the least consequential of the activities traditionally associated with women. Thus, for example, he is a major source of gossip in the community and would also "pass long winter evenings with the old Dutch wives, as they sat spinning by the fire, . . . and listen to their marvellous tales." However, his masculinity is most directly challenged by his being a "man of letters" in a community of farmers, where to work is perforce to have something to show for one's work. The women can appreciate his erudition, "for he had read several books quite through," though he was "thought, by all who understood nothing of the labour of headwork, to have a wonderfully easy life of it." It is a moral comment on Ichabod that a variety of his traits, including his problematic relationship to the world of work, divides a fundamentally coherent Dutch community along gender lines.

The subject of sloth appears to have been a complex and perhaps even a sensitive one for Irving, who, in the persona of Geoffrey Crayon, maintained a vested interest in the innocence of repose. The epigraph from Thomson's *Castle of Indolence*, a poem that successively celebrates the pleasures and indicts the decadence of indolence, contributes to the complexity of the issue by seeming to oblige the author to discriminate carefully in moral terms between the sloth he is condemning and the repose to which he is temperamentally and artistically committed. The distinction turns out, once again, to favor the Dutch, who never, throughout the course of the story, are shown at work. In the Van Tassel barn, "the flail was busily resounding . . . from morning to night," but workers neither work nor appear. The repose of the Dutch is simply prelapsarian, which means that they have, as the schoolteacher does not, something vital on which they *can* repose. Ichabod, who *is* shown working, who puts in his time at the schoolroom and performs his odd job, is nevertheless constantly preoccupied with schemes for rescinding the penalty of original sin in his own personal case, which is a large part of what Yankee ingenuity comes to in Irving's satire.

This fundamental difference parallels and at the same time further explains the qualitative distinction between the Dutch imagination and Ichabod's, the one effortless, natural, and supremely located, the other artificial, self-indulgent, and frenetic. From another point of view, Irving clearly had professional reasons for raising this issue, for if he was less personally concerned than Nathaniel Hawthorne with the public's perception of the value of the writer's vocation, he nevertheless knew that literature and scholarship in America were not always held in high esteem, that, indeed, they were often associated with idleness and self-indulgence. By creating in Ichabod a slothful character at whom such charges might be levelled with perfect justice, he shows that they are most appropriately brought against the poseur, the man of self-deluding pretensions to literature, and not against the true writer (or artist) at all. And by creating in his Dutch characters an imagination rooted in innocent, even blessed repose, he affirms the value and explains the virtue of his own art.

If, in Eden, sloth is difficult, gluttony is simply ungrateful. It suggests a certain doubt as to the extent and continuance of divine providence, and, as Irving shows, leads to envy:

> [Ichabod] was a kind and thankful creature, whose heart dilated in proportion as his skin was filled with good cheer, and whose spirits rose with eating, as some men's do with drink. He could not help, too, rolling his large eyes round him as he ate, and chuckling with the possibility that he might one day be lord of all this scene of almost unimaginable splendour.

Despite the narrator's gentlemanly imputation of thankfulness, the apparent fact is that Ichabod, having found heaven, aspires to *be*, not thank, its "lord." The appetite that prompts him is the sinister elaboration of the early, comic observation that "he was a huge feeder . . . though lank," while the transition from the physical fact to its spiritual implication has been prepared by Irving's intermediate use of the imagery of gluttony to describe Ichabod's mental processes. He is an intellectual gourmand: "His appetite for the marvellous, and his powers of digesting it, were equally extraordinary. . . . No tale was too gross or monstrous for his capacious swallow." After he is introduced to Katrina, it is, as the narrator says, "not to be wondered at, that so tempting a morsel soon found favour in his eyes," or that "his devouring mind's eye" could transform at a glance all the farm's life to food. If Ichabod's imagination is thwarted and traversed by his sloth, it operates ineluctably in service to his belly. Even as he goes for his last interview with Katrina, he is "feeding his mind with many sweet thoughts and sugared suppositions."

There are three moments in the story that shed light on Ichabod's tendency to the sin of anger, and they appear to form, as in the case of his gluttony, a pattern of deepening seriousness. His willingness to flog his students, and particularly the stronger, more threatening children, is consistent with his personal insecurity and impatience with "inferiors." Beneath the artfully dispassionate surface of his behavior ("this he called 'doing his duty by their parents,'" the anger is, though visible, well submerged and controlled, so much so that Irving is content merely to hint at it and at the same time to warn his readers against concluding too quickly that Ichabod is "one of those cruel potentates of the school, who joy in the smart of their subjects." That Ichabod takes no "joy" in it is sufficiently easy to believe. The second moment occurs at the Van Tassel farm where Ichabod, flush with food, contemplates the possibility of being "lord of all this scene." Here the surface parts to reveal how he contends emotionally with the prospect of success: "Then, he thought, how soon he'd turn his back upon the old school house, snap his fingers in the face of Hans Van Ripper, and every other niggardly patron, and kick any itinerant pedagogue out of doors that should dare to call him comrade!" With perfect ironic aptness, his idea of success involves becoming the niggardly patron he despises, but the more important point is that his greatest wrath is reserved for his own alter ego. This mounting sense of anger when he ought to be most satisfied and placid is concisely indicated in the succession of verbs, which points ultimately to the self-hatred at the heart of the sin of anger. In the third and final moment, Ichabod's social controls, along with his great expectations, collapse at the end of the party in his private interview with Katrina. Here the surface parts in a different way: "Without looking to the right or left to notice the scene of rural wealth, on which he had so often gloated, he went straight to the stable, and with several hearty cuffs and kicks, roused his steed most uncourteously from the comfortable quarters in which he was soundly sleeping, dreaming of mountains of corn and oats, and whole valleys of timothy and clover." The horse, sharing Ichabod's physical traits and innermost dreams, is another alter ego, though now the kicking has become actual.

In the sentence describing this outburst of passion, much of the humor centers on the word "uncourteously," which signals the whole issue of the ill-starred lover's chivalric self-image. The narrator's sarcastic allusion is to the ruins of what had been, from the start, the preposterous vehicle of Ichabod's conscious pride: his assumption that he was a bit too good for a community of bumpkins. In point of pride, he is the opposite of Baltus Van Tassel, who is "satisfied with his wealth, but not proud of it." Unlike the man he seeks to supplant, he is eager to misapply the social leverage of his prospective good fortune by—class-consciously—kicking itinerant pedagogues out of doors. But in perhaps the most telling revelation of all, Ichabod's pride appears at odds not with individuals but with sacred and communal values: "It was a matter of no little vanity to him to take his station in front of the church gallery, with a band of chosen singers; where, in his own mind, he completely carried away the palm from the parson." Appropriately, the profane Ichabod, the supercilious critic of the churchyard epitaphs, is avowedly the parson's self-anointed antagonist.

The treatment of lechery in "The Legend of Sleepy Hollow" is understandably circumspect, and yet it is very close to the effective center of the satire. The fact that Ichabod is a portrait of perverse and misdirected sexuality is arguably the author's final comment on his representative Yankee. Here Irving supplies two general contexts for Ichabod's behavior: one is the fertile feminine land that the schoolmaster threateningly lusts after, and the other is the prevailing sexuality of the Dutch, which is, for the most part, no sexuality at all. These are "general contexts" mainly in the sense that while they are rather inertly present all the while, they take on a heightened significance in conjunction with more particular details. For example, the first of these contexts is quickened when, on several occasions, Irving intimates that nothing is easier for Ichabod than to divert his sexual appetite into an appetite for food. After school he would sometimes follow students home "who happened to have pretty sisters, or good housewives for mothers, noted for the comforts of the cupboard." The change in the direction of this sentence, as the rest of the story goes to show, suggests a transformation rather than a competition of motives. By constantly pairing women and food in this metonymic way as objects of Ichabod's attention, Irving seems to imply that the gluttony is merely displaced lechery, and not, because food seems always to take precedence, that he is without lust.

Irving's favorite phallic symbols—on which so much of his early bawdy humor centers—are guns, swords, and noses. In "Rip Van Winkle" there is the "clean well oiled fowling piece" that in twenty years of disuse became rusty and dysfunctional; there is, too, among the men of Hendrick Hudson's crew playing at the masculine game of nine-pins, one whose face "seemed to consist entirely of nose, . . . surmounted by a white sugarloaf hat, set off with a little red cock's tail." This individual is singled out by the narrator from a group who carried "long knives in their belts" and of whom "most . . . had enormous breeches." The commander of this crew is further distinguished by having a "broad belt and hanger." In "The Legend of Sleepy Hollow" the "long snipe nose . . . that . . . looked like a weathercock" belongs to Ichabod, and Irving is even prepared to suggest, more directly than he ordinarily does, that this nose is a kind of reproductive organ: "There are peculiar quavers still to be heard in that church, and which may even be heard half a mile off, quite to the opposite side of the mill pond, of a still Sunday morning, which are said to be legitimately descended from the nose of Ichabod Crane." The final image in the story —that of a loitering ploughboy hearing these notes "among the tranquil solitudes of Sleepy Hollow"—seems in turn to allude to one of the very first images, that of the narrator breaking "the sabbath stillness around" by the startling "roar of [his] own gun," so that the story is framed by mutually defining instances of intrusion in which the virgin stillness of this enchanted feminine ground is symbolically violated by a foreign sexuality.

Another set of three images seems to work in much the same way, though it sheds a rather different light on the theme of Ichabod's lubricity. The transformation of the schoolhouse by the Dutch into an elaborate eelpot implicitly but quite directly casts Ichabod in the role of the eel. As though to underscore this impression, Irving shortly thereafter asserts, in one of the more surprising metaphors of the story, that Ichabod "had the dilating powers of an Anaconda." The effect of Irving's likening his protagonist to an eel becomes fully apparent only later, at the Van Tassels' harvest festival, where "the sons [appeared] in short square coats with rows of stupendous brass buttons, and their hair generally queued in the fashion of the times, especially if they could procure an eel skin for the purpose, it being esteemed throughout the country as a potent nourisher and strengthener of the hair." The schoolhouse, then, is explicitly an eel-trap constructed by a community that values eels as a source of male sexual potency. Apart from this

connection, it is difficult to see why either detail should be in the story. Read, thus connected, in the general context of the prevailing Dutch sexuality— that is, in the division of the Dutch characters into menopausal and pre-pubescent groups—it becomes necessary to look upon Ichabod as, in a manner of speaking, the serpentine source of sex in paradise or as the necessarily extrinsic agent, procured by Yost Van Houten in the name of Dutch folk wisdom, to help Brom Bones over the portal of maturity. In this event, Katrina's coquettishness takes its place as a single element in a much larger ritual, one that manages to include the whole community.

The husband-to-be is near to the point of escaping the socially useless boy-culture of "Brom Bones and his gang," but so long as his "amorous toyings" continue to be "like the caresses and endearments of a bear" he will clearly never pass muster with the blooming Katrina. His rite of passage, as it turns out, involves more than the simple conquest of a rival. It involves him in the first socially useful act of his life, his first act as a member of the whole community. The expulsion of Ichabod simply *is* the defense of that whole community from moral taint and eventual destruction, while, considered in relation to the marriage that ensues—the marriage that, indeed, it makes possible—it is the rejection or expulsion of "Yankee sexuality," of the perverse and aggressive lust of one who "in form and spirit [was] like a supple jack—yielding, but tough: though he bent, he never broke; and though he bowed beneath the slightest pressure, yet, the moment it was away—jerk! he was as erect, and carried his head as high as ever." It is to break *this*, once and for all, that the "Headless Hessian" at long last carries *his* head high, and, in the event, so frightens the hard-riding Ichabod as nearly to bring off the latter's castration "on the high ridge of his horse's back bone." Irving, though, is mercifully content with the symbolic castration of a blow to the "cranium," which is, appropriately yet problematically, the real seat of Crane's lechery.

To read "The Legend of Sleepy Hollow" in this way is to see its formal relation to an important sub-genre of American fiction that Roy Male, in defining it, called "the Mysterious Stranger story." This form is

> an inside narrative with an enclosed structure; its plot and characterization consist of the effect of a semi-supernatural and usually ambiguous stranger upon a crowd, a family, or an individual; its theme tends to center around faith and the contagiousness of good, or distrust and the contagiousness of evil and violence. . . .

The trickster-god appears unexpectedly, usually in disguise, tests or transforms a mortal, and disappears.

In Irving's Mysterious Stranger story all the elements are present, and yet, perhaps because he was more interested in the conflict than in its resolution and sequel, perhaps because he lacked the deeper ironic intelligence—certainly, in any event, because he made his devil too much the fool—Irving evades some central implications of the form, or, more particularly, has no use for the issue of "the contagiousness of evil and violence" that the structure of such a story raises. So far as the community is concerned, Ichabod is simply absorbed into the local mythology as the morally neutralized spectre that haunts the decaying schoolhouse. Death is absorbed into life. In a realm of such enchantment, there is no clear sign that Ichabod will have a lasting subversive effect on Sleepy Hollow or that anything serious will follow from the necessity that he himself created of expelling him by devious and forceful means. And if in the end there is no lurking worm of guilt, no paradise quite lost, yet it is to be remembered that Irving is attacking, not defending, the Puritan possibilities. Were he to insist that the expulsion of Ichabod is reflexively corrupting, it would be tantamount to giving the demonic mythology of New England precedence over the benign mythology of the Dutch. By refusing to give the devil his due, Irving in effect chooses to stress the preserving innocence which the recollection of home, safe from betrayal or violation, inveterately has in the memory.

Still, fictional forms have a force and a meaning of their own, built up of the uses to which they have previously been put by other writers. For this reason at least, Irving cannot quite escape the implication that Ichabod has forever changed Sleepy Hollow. Of the sorts of falls that such an agent as he might induce, consistent with Irving's fondness for his Dutch characters, there is the sort of pillow-soft, post-Miltonic fall of Brom, who, encountering evil without accepting it, passes from innocence to a knowledge of virtuous action and in the process gains his manhood. All that is shown of his life after marriage is that he would "look exceedingly knowingly whenever the story of Ichabod was related," and that some were led to "suspect that he knew more about the matter than he chose to tell," a sort of deviousness which, harmless enough in appearance, is certainly no longer an Arcadian simplicity.

Another kind of fall is suggested by the whole retrospective, memorial tone of the narration, augmented, perhaps, by a knowledge of the historic fate of these Dutch communities. The story is set in the past, but the wistfully receding perspective in which it is presented is a function mainly of the layered narration, a device which, as Irving handles it, tells its own story of declining prosperity and increasing sophistication. The first narrator is "a pleasant, shabby, gentlemanly old fellow . . . with a sadly humourous face; and one whom I [Dietrich Knickerbocker, the second narrator] strongly suspected of being poor. He tells his story—orally—in the same spirit in which the supernatural tales are given at the Van Tassel party, neither as "literature" nor as veritable history, claiming in the end not to "believe one half of it myself." Knickerbocker, who writes it all down, has literary aspirations and a sense of wider audiences, though as the *History* indicates, he is ultimately defeated by poverty. He figures at last as a deadbeat fleeing from a hotel, a wandering solitary man survived only by his papers. With the emergence of Geoffrey Crayon as the executor of this literary estate, the tradition has passed from the Dutch altogether, and the fall seems complete.

Source: Albert J. von Frank, "The Man That Corrupted Sleepy Hollow," in *Studies in American Fiction*, Vol. 15, No. 2, 1987, pp. 129–43.

Sources

Bowden, Mary Weatherspoon. *Washington Irving*, Boston: Twayne, 1981, p. 72.

Giamatti, A. Bartlett. *The Earthly Paradise and the Renaissance Epic*, Princeton, N.J.: Princeton University Press, 1966, pp. 3, 6, 34, 126-27.

Hedges, William L. *Washington Irving: An American Study, 1802-1832*, Baltimore: Johns Hopkins Press, 1965, p. 142.

Hoffman, Daniel G. *Form and Fable in American Fiction*, New York: Oxford University Press, 1961.

———. "Irving's Use of American Folklore in 'The Legend of Sleepy Hollow,'" in *PMLA*, Vol. 68, June, 1953, pp. 425-435.

Jeffrey, Francis. Review of *The Sketch Book*, in *Edinburgh Review*, Vol. 34, August, 1820, pp. 160-76.

Kolodny, Annette. *The Lay of the Land: Metaphor as Experience and History in American Life and Letters*, Chapel Hill: University of North Carolina Press, 1975, pp. 68- 70.

Leary, Lewis. "Washington Irving and the Comic Imagination," in *The Comic Imagination in American Literature*, ed. Louis D. Rubin. New Brunswick: Rutgers University Press, 1973, pp. 63-76.

Martin, Terence. "Rip, Ichabod, and the American Imagination," in *American Literature*, Vol. 31, May, 1959, pp. 137-149.

Pataj, Edward F. "Washington Irving's Ichabod Crane: American Narcissus," in *American Imago*, Vol. 38, Spring, 1981, pp. 127-35.

Plummer, Laura, and Michael Nelson. "'Girls Can Take Care of Themselves'; Gender and Storytelling in Washington Irving's 'The Legend of Sleepy Hollow,'" in *Studies in Short Fiction*, Vol. 30, 1993, pp. 175-84.

Pochmann, Henry A. "Irving's German Tour and Its Influence on His Tales," in *PMLA*, Vol. 45, December, 1930, pp. 1150-87.

———. "Irving's German Sources in *The Sketch Book*," in *Studies in Philology*, Vol. 27, July, 1930, pp. 477-507.

Theocritus. "Idyll VII," in *The Greek Bucolic Poets*, translated by J. E. Edmonds, Cambridge, Mass.: Loeb Library, 1938, lines 135-46.

von Frank, Albert J. "The Man That Corrupted Sleepy Hollow," in *Studies in American Fiction*, Vol. 15, No. 2, 1987, pp. 129-143.

Further Reading

Aderman, Ralph M., ed. *Critical Essays on Washington Irving*, Boston: G. K. Hall, 1990.

A survey of Irving criticism, with a selection of early nineteenth-century reviews as well as twentieth-century scholarly articles.

Bowden, Edwin T. *Washington Irving: Bibliography*, Boston: Twayne, 1989.

Volume 30 in *The Complete Works of Washington Irving*, this is the most complete and up-to-date bibliography available.

Bowden, Mary Weatherspoon. *Washington Irving*, Boston: Twayne, 1981.

The best introduction for the general reader, dealing chronologically with each of Irving's major works.

Hedges, William L. *Washington Irving: An American Study, 1802-1832*, Baltimore: Johns Hopkins Press, 1965.

Insightful literary analysis of Irving's major works, which Hedges believes are those written before his return to the United States.

Tuttleton, James W., ed. *Washington Irving: The Critical Reaction*, New York: AMS Press, 1993.

Sixteen critical essays about Irving's work. Three of the essays treat "Sleepy Hollow" directly, and two others help establish the context for the early work, including *The Sketch Book*.

Wagenknecht, Edward. *Washington Irving: Moderation Displayed*, New York: Oxford University Press, 1962.

An accessible biography and critical overview, emphasizing Irving's stature during his own lifetime as the United States' most significant writer.

The Lifted Veil

George Eliot

1859

George Eliot's novella ''The Lifted Veil'' was first published in 1859. Eliot had written ''The Lifted Veil'' between the publication of her first novel *Adam Bede*, and that of her second novel, *The Mill on the Floss*. Eliot's publisher was hesitant to publish the story, because it was nothing like *Adam Bede*, for which she had gained critical acclaim. He was concerned that this tale of horror would be bad for her literary reputation, but reluctantly published it in a literary journal, albeit anonymously.

''The Lifted Veil'' concerns themes of fate, extrasensory perception, the mystery of life and life after death. Eliot's interest in these themes stemmed partly from her own struggles with religious faith, as she was an extremely devout Christian as a child and young adult who later renounced Christianity completely. She also felt that she herself, like Latimer, the main character in ''The Lifted Veil,'' had extrasensory powers of perception, which she referred to as ''double consciousness.''

While Eliot came to be considered one of the greatest novelists of the 19th Century during her lifetime, ''The Lifted Veil'' is one of her lesser-known stories, probably because it is so different from the realist novels for which she is so well known. Yet, while is does not seem to match the rest of her *ouevre*, ''The Lifted Veil'' does fit squarely into the Victorian tradition of Gothic horror stories, which began with Mary Shelley's *Frankenstein* (1818) and included Robert Louis Stevenson's

Strange Case of Dr. Jekyll and Mr. Hyde (1886), as well as Bram Stoker's *Dracula* (1895). Such works of fiction were precursors of modern horror movies, such as *Psycho*, *Night of the Living Dead*, and *Nightmare on Elm Street*, as well as modern horror fiction, such as the novels of Stephen King.

Author Biography

George Eliot was born Mary Ann Evans in England on November 22, 1819. Her mother died when she was 16, and, apart from her time away from home in various boarding schools, she lived with her father as his housekeeper and caregiver until 1849, when he died. Her early schooling instilled in her a strong sense of Christian piety, and she was known to have dressed in rather severe, austere clothing. But exposure to free-thinking intellectuals eventually led Eliot away from her strict Christian faith, which resulted in a major conflict with her father in 1842. She eventually compromised by promising him that she would continue to attend Church in order to maintain a respectable appearance, although she would not be compelled to actually believe in the teachings of the church.

In 1851, Eliot moved to London to live as a freelance writer. There, she was further exposed to some of the leading intellectuals of her day, who maintained free-thinking attitudes about literature, politics, and religion. Through these connections, Eliot began to work as a journal editor and translator of some of the cutting edge essays and books emerging from this milieu. That year, Eliot was introduced to George Henry Lewes, a leading journalist and drama critic of the day. Lewes was married at the time, but his wife was notoriously unfaithful to him and had born two sons by another man. Although legal policies prevented Lewes from divorcing his wife, they eventually settled into a state of separation, during which time Eliot and Lewes became romantically involved. Although this was a happy union, which lasted over 20 years, Eliot suffered a loss of social status in maintaining a domestic partnership with a married man, including complete disaffection from her favorite brother, Isaac. Nevertheless, she and Lewes considered themselves to be husband and wife, living together in London and in Europe until his death in 1878.

Lewes was a strong influence in encouraging Eliot to write and publish essays, and it was he who first suggested she attempt to write fiction. In 1858, she began to publish under the pseudonym George Eliot. Although she published countless essays in contemporary journals, her most important literary legacy includes the novels *Adam Bede* (1859), *The Mill on the Floss* (1860), *Silas Marner* (1861) and *Middlemarch* (1871-72), universally agreed upon as her masterpiece. Eliot was widely recognized as a successful novelist by the late 1870s, which helped to make up for the loss of social status she incurred as a result of her unconventional relationship with Lewes, and the two of them became well known for their Sunday afternoon social gatherings.

In 1880, Eliot, still in a state of grief over the death of Lewes, married her banker, John Walter Cross, who was only 40 at the time, while she was 60. It was only upon this legal marriage that her brother Isaac reestablished contact with her. On December 22, less than a year later, Eliot died and was buried next to Lewes in Highgate cemetery.

Plot Summary

Latimer is the first-person narrator of "The Lifted Veil," as well as the main character. The story begins, as he informs the reader, exactly one month before his death. "Before that time comes," he explains, "I wish to use my last hours of ease and strength in telling the strange story of my experience." The story thus comes as the confession of a dying man who entrusts his lifelong secrets to the reader's sympathy. "I have never fully unbosomed myself to any human being," he says.

Through a flashback structure, Latimer tells his "strange story," beginning with childhood, when he first discovered that he had what he refers to as "superadded consciousness." A sickly, unscholarly and dreamy child, Latimer is dominated by his father's wish to expose him to all of the subjects he hates most: math, science, etc. At the age of 19, recovering from a long illness, Latimer finds that he is capable of envisioning an event before it actually occurs. He first experiences this "clairvoyance" moments before meeting his older brother, Alfred's soon-to-be fiancee, Bertha Grant. When, moments after his vision, the exact same scene is played out in reality, Latimer is so struck with the sight of Bertha that he faints.

As Alfred's impending marriage to Bertha grows more and more certain, Latimer becomes utterly romantically fixated on her. Bertha, for her part, seems to enjoy teasing and flirting with Latimer, while maintaining a cool distance from him. One day, Latimer has a vision many years into his own future, during which Bertha, now his wife, suggests, with hatred in her voice, that he commit suicide. Yet, despite this presentiment of a horribly doomed marriage, Latimer is not swayed from his desire for Bertha. When Albert fall off a horse and dies, Latimer is left to marry Bertha himself.

As Latimer had foreseen, he and Bertha, once married, develop a deep hatred of one another. Once Bertha's mystery has been dispelled, and Latimer sees that she is shallow, selfish and hateful, he completely looses interest in her. Bertha, for her part, no longer the object of Latimer's devotion, seeks the company of other men, spending most of her time socializing outside their home. Latimer, now completely alienated from all human society, spends these years alone in his house. Once Bertha's mystery is dispelled, Latimer's life no longer has meaning, and he spends his time anticipating with dread the encounter he had foreseen before their marriage, in which she suggests that he go ahead and kill himself. Yet, when this scene finally occurs, years later, Latimer finds that it is thoroughly anti-climactic, and not a turning point or crisis in his life at all, but merely one more in a lifetime of cruel and horrible encounters with his wife.

When Bertha hires a new maid, Mrs. Archer, to the household, Latimer senses that he is beginning to loose his power to perceive the thoughts of other people. Furthermore, Bertha and the new maid seem to be conspiring together over some secret endeavor. Eventually, however, Latimer perceives that Bertha and the maid have begun to hate one another. Yet, when the maid, an older woman, grows sick, Bertha maintains a solicitous vigilance over her sick bed.

One night, Charles Meunier, an old grade school friend of Latimer, whom he hasn't seen in years, pays a visit to the household. As it becomes evident that the maid is just hours from death, Meunier, a world renowned medical doctor, asks Latimer if he may try an experiment on the corpse, as soon as the old woman is dead. When the time comes, Meunier conducts a transfusion of his own blood to that of the newly dead Mrs. Archer. The corpse then comes to life, opens its eyes, points an accusatory finger at

George Eliot (Mary Ann Evans)

Bertha, and confesses that she had been hired by Bertha to poison Latimer. The corpse then falls back to its permanent death.

This revelation having been made, Latimer and Bertha go their separate ways, she to remain in England, and he to travel throughout Europe. During these years, Latimer, increasingly ill, is made to suffer with the foreknowledge of the circumstances of his own death. Upon completing the final pages of his story, Latimer gives himself over to "the scene of my dying struggle."

Characters

Alfred

Latimer's older brother Alfred is his opposite. Latimer describes him as "a handsome, self-confident man of 6 and 20 a thorough contrast to my fragile, nervous, ineffectual self." Alfred is their father's favorite, as he embodies all that the father desires in a son. When Latimer is introduced to Bertha as a probable future wife to Alfred, his natural dislike of his brother turns to envious hatred. Right before he is to be married to Bertha, Alfred

Media Adaptations

- George Eliot's novel *Silas Marner* was recorded on audiocassette by Recorded Books in 1988.

- George Eliot's novel *Adam Bede* was recorded on audiocassette by Books on Tape in 1994.

- George Eliot's novel *Middlemarch* was recorded on audiocassette by Blackstone Audio Books in 1994.

- George Eliot's novel *The Mill on the Floss* was adapted to the screen in 1939, directed by Tim Whalen and starring Geraldine Fitzgerald and James Mason.

- George Eliot's novel *Silas Marner* was adapted by BBC-TV in 1985, directed by Giles Foster and starring Ben Kingsley.

- George Eliot's novel *Middlemarch* was adapted as a 3-part mini-series by PBS in 1994, directed by Anthony Page.

---

dies from falling off a horse, leaving Latimer free to marry Bertha.

Mrs. Archer

Mrs. Archer is the new servant Bertha hires, a woman whose arrival Latimer dreads: "I had a vague dread that I should find her mixed up with the dreary drama of my life that some new sickening vision would reveal her to me as an evil genius." Latimer describes her as "a tall, wiry, dark-eyed woman, this Mrs. Archer, with a face handsome enough to give her coarse, hard nature the odious finish of bold, self-confident coquetry." Latimer remains wary of Mrs. Archer, as he perceives that she and Bertha share some dark secret from him. On the night of Mrs. Archer's death, Latimer allows Charles Meunier to perform a blood transfusion on her dead body. As a result, the body comes to life and points an accusatory finger at Bertha. In this brief moment of life after death, Mrs. Archer reveals that Bertha had hired her to concoct a poison to kill

Latimer. This revelation made, the body once again assumes the posture of death.

The Father

Latimer's father is cold, distant and disapproving of his sickly, unmotivated child. He hires a tutor to school the young Latimer in all of the subjects which he most dreads, and in which he is least capable. After Latimer's older brother Alfred, the favorite, dies, his father becomes more endeared to Latimer, who becomes sympathetic to his father, and is careful to please him as much as possible, as well as to care for him in his sorrow and old age.

Bertha Grant

Bertha is first introduced to Latimer as his brother's future fiancee. She is described as "no more than twenty, a tall, slim, willowy figure, with luxuriant blond hair." Because she is the only person whose mystery Latimer's powers of "double consciousness" cannot penetrate, Latimer becomes fixated on her as an object of his devotion. But after Arnold's death and their subsequent marriage, Bertha becomes for Latimer an object of hatred. Once Bertha's inner thoughts have been revealed to him, and she is no longer a mystery, Latimer finds that she is evil, heartless and shallow. Bertha, for her part, hates Latimer because of his unwillingness to maintain his former devotion to her. As their marriage develops into one of mutual hatred, Bertha seeks the company of other men. Years into their marriage, Bertha hires a new servant, Mrs. Archer, to poison Latimer. After Mrs. Archer dies, and is then momentarily brought back to life, she points an accusatory finger at Bertha, revealing Bertha's evil plan. Latimer and Bertha then separate for life.

Latimer

Latimer is the main character and narrator of "The Lifted Veil." He is a sickly child and a grave disappointment to his father. When Latimer is introduced to his older brother's soon-to-be fiancee, Bertha, he becomes hopelessly infatuated with her. At the same time, Latimer discovers that he has the mysterious power to foresee certain events before they happen. This supernatural power, which Latimer refers to as "double-consciousness," also gives him the ability to read the thoughts of those around him. After Arnold, his older brother, falls off a horse and dies, Latimer is left to marry Bertha. But already Latimer has seen a future incident which indicates that he and Bertha will come to despise each other. After their marriage, Latimer's powers of "double-consciousness" make the development of this mutual hatred between husband and wife that much more horrible to him. When it is revealed to Latimer that Bertha had been scheming to poison him, the two of them separate for life. At the story's end, Latimer is waiting for the dreaded moment of his own death, a moment he had perceived in exact detail a month earlier.

Charles Meunier

In the first half of "The Lifted Veil," Charles Meunier is the young Latimer's only childhood friend. Latimer describes the young Meunier as almost his opposite, one "whose intellectual tendencies were the very reverse of" his own. Of poor origins, Meunier pursues medical studies "for which he had a special genius." In the second half of the story, Meunier, now a renowned physician, comes to visit Latimer, whom he hasn't seen in years. One night of his visit, Mrs. Archer, the servant, is on her deathbed, and Meunier asks Latimer permission to perform an experiment on her corpse, the minute she is dead. He subsequently performs a blood transfusion from his own body into that of the dead servant. She instantly comes to life, opens her eyes, and points an accusatory finger at Latimer's wife, revealing a deadly secret which uncovers evil intentions. At the end of the story, it is suggested that this incident jolts Meunier into a contemplation of the spiritual, rather than the scientific; upon the corpse's revelation, "Meunier looked paralyzed: life for that moment ceased to be a scientific problem for him."

Themes

Science versus the supernatural

"The Lifted Veil," like many Gothic tales, interrogates the boundaries between scientific knowledge and the supernatural, between the rational and the irrational. This set of dichotomies is laid out in the differences between Latimer and his friend Meunier. Latimer describes their childhood friendship as an attraction of opposites, a meeting of minds between "the dreamy and the practical." As a doctor, Meunier is schooled in the field of science, the epitome of rational thought. Latimer, on the other hand, has no practical occupation, but possesses supernatural powers, associated with the irrational. Toward the end of the story, however, when Meunier performs the blood transfusion which brings Mrs. Archer momentarily back to life, this

distinction is put into question. It is through Meunier's scientific experimentation that this episode of life after death produces an effect which allows a glimpse into the supernatural or spiritual realm. Thus, for Meunier, "life ceased to be a scientific problem for him," upon witnessing this evidence of the spirit world.

Playing God

"The Lifted Veil" shares a similar theme to Mary Shelley's *Frankenstein*, in that it questions the morality of scientific inquiry which threatens the boundaries of the spiritual realm. Dr. Frankenstein "plays God" by endeavoring the create human life, using scientific methods. In "The Lifted Veil," Meunier's transfusion brings the dead Mrs. Archer momentarily back to life, bringing into question the morality of such an endeavor.

Clairvoyance

"The Lifted Veil" is about a man who suffers from his powers of clairvoyance. In the 19th Century, as now, many people believed that some humans may possess what we now refer to as "psychic" powers, to see into the future or past, or read the minds of other people. "The Lifted Veil" explores this theme in centering around a main character, Latimer, who possesses such powers. Yet, Latimer does not make good use of his clairvoyance. Rather, he only causes himself and those around him to suffer because of it. He does not use his powers to any creative or spiritual end, or to help people in any way. He is almost selfish in his "double consciousness." What he sees when the daily thoughts of those around him are revealed is a world of pettiness and selfishness.

The Mystery of Life

"The Lifted Veil" suggests that human beings are better off when kept from seeing beyond the "veil" of mystery which shrouds the human condition and the boundary between life and death. For Latimer, life becomes drained of almost all mystery. He is drawn to Bertha before their marriage because she is the only person who remains a mystery to him. After their marriage, when her selfish, petty thoughts are revealed to his supernatural powers of perception, she no longer holds any interest or romance for him. The poem at the beginning of the story comes in the form of a prayer to "Heaven" not to be granted extrasensory powers beyond those of common humanity. The story very clearly sug-

Topics for Further Study

- At the time of writing "The Lifted Veil," George Eliot was interested in various forms of supernatural experience, including mesmerism (hypnotism) and clairvoyance. Yet, she was not alone. Interest in the supernatural abounded in the 19th Century. Research and write about some of the trends in seeking out supernatural experiences during the 19th Century. Compare to current trends in extrasensory perception (ESP) and other forms of belief in the supernatural?

- George Eliot's "The Lifted Veil" can be categorized as Gothic fiction of the 19th Century, which was a precursor to the modern horror film, from *Psycho* to *Night of the Living Dead* to *Halloween* to the *Friday the 13th* to *Nightmare on Elm Street* and beyond. Watch a modern horror film and discuss what elements it has in common with Gothic fiction such as "The Lifted Veil." In what ways does the movie portray a different perspective on the phenomenon of the supernatural from the perspective portrayed in "The Lifted Veil."?

- In addition to George Eliot, a number of notable female novelists were successful writers during the 19th Century, such as Charlotte and Emily Bronte and Jane Austin. Research the biography and writing of one of these novelists. What were the conditions under which these women were able to achieve literary notoriety despite their position as women in Victorian society?

- George Eliot's life spanned a good portion of the 19th Century, referred to as the Victorian era in British history, because it was characterized by the reign of Queen Victoria. Research life in the Victorian era. Focus on one element of Victorian culture, such as advances in science, medicine, political reform, intellectual trends, the conditions of women or other trends in literature and art, such as Romanticism.

- Eliot's "The Lifted Veil" was published in 1859, the same year that Charles Darwin published *On the Origin of Species*, in which he put forth his theory of evolution. Find out more about the impact of Darwin's theories on Victorian ideas about science and religion.

- American writer Edgar Allen Poe wrote short stories in the genre of Gothic fiction during roughly the same era in which Eliot wrote. Read one of Poe's short stories for comparison.

---

gests that the powers of clairvoyance only drain the mystery from life, and do no earthly good.

Life after Death

In the climactic moments of "The Lifted Veil," Mrs. Archer, Latimer's maid, is momentarily revived from death by means of blood transfusion. In these brief moments of life after death, Mrs. Archer points an accusatory finger of Bertha, revealing that she had been hired by Bertha to poison Latimer. Latimer's exclamation at this point is telling: "Great God! Is this what it is to live again. . . . to wake up with our unstilled thirst upon us, with our unuttered curses rising to our lips, with our muscles ready to act out their half-committed sins?" This message simultaneously unburdens the soul of the dead woman of her sins, and exacts a revenge upon Bertha for drawing her in to such a deed. This story suggests that human beings are better off with a limited knowledge of what lies beyond the "veil" of death.

Fate

Fate is the idea that human destiny has been predetermined by some supernatural force and cannot be altered. "The Lifted Veil" explores the theme of fate because it questions whether or not Latimer would have been able to escape the painful events he foresaw in his own future. Latimer's suffering is in part focused on his vision of a moment in his marriage with Bertha during which she bitterly suggests that he commit suicide. Yet, despite this prevision of suffering, Latimer does nothing to alter his fate—he marries Bertha anyway, and spends years anticipating with dread this moment in their marriage. The reader is presented with the implied question: Would Latimer have been able to avoid this scene, had he tried? Or was it his fate to follow this course in life, and any effort to alter it would have failed anyway?

Style

Narration

"The Lifted Veil" is written in the first person, meaning that the story is told entirely from the perspective of one individual, the main character, Latimer. "The Lifted Veil" is Eliot's only story written in the first person. Because the reader sees the events of the story only through the eyes of the main character, the narrative creates the effect of an internal, psychological flow of ideas. Because the story is told as it is written by Latimer over the course of the month before his death, and recalls the events of his life, beginning in childhood, it takes on the form of an intimate confession, of a dying man's last effort to clear his conscience.

Narrative Structure

The story is structured in "flashback" form, as Latimer begins the story exactly one month before he knows he's going to die, then takes the narrative back to his childhood and adult experiences, and then ends the story once again in his sitting room, as he writes the last words of the story, before dying, as he knew he would. This flashback structure takes on another dimension, however, due to the fact that Latimer is a clairvoyant, who can see events in the future before they occur. In that way, several key events of the story are told in a "flash forward," as Latimer describes events which then occur in the future.

Setting

"The Lifted Veil" is set in Victorian England, in the early-to-mid 19th Century. Latimer's father's house, later his own, is a country estate. In his childhood, Latimer lives in Switzerland, and travels to Prague. After his separation from Bertha, he travels the world, staying in inns, but never too long in any one place. Latimer's visions of future events include scenes which take place in Switzerland, Prague and England.

The Epigraph Poem

Eliot attached an epigraph poem to the beginning of "The Lifted Veil" after she had completed the story. These four lines are written in the form of a prayer, "Give me no light, great Heaven," which essentially asks Heaven to grant the speaker no powers or knowledge beyond those of the everyday human world. In other words, it asks not to be granted the clairvoyant, or extrasensory powers with which Latimer is plagued, and which causes him such suffering. This epigraph is in some ways suggestive of the "moral" of the story, which is that perhaps it is better *not* to "lift the veil" of the mystery of life and death.

Gothic Horror

"The Lifted Veil" can be categorized as Gothic fiction, also referred to as Gothic horror. Gothic fiction is characterized by suggestions of supernatural occurrences, and often contains scenes of horror, including the appearance of ghosts and other forms of life after death. This literary genre, associated with 19th Century England, began with Mary Shelley's *Frankenstein*, and includes Robert Louis Stevenson's *Dr. Jekyll and Mr. Hyde*, as well as Bram Stoker's *Dracula*. The Gothic elements of "The Lifted Veil" include Latimer's supernatural ability to read the thoughts of others and to see into the future. The climactic scene in which Mrs. Archer's body is momentarily brought back from the dead is the key Gothic scene in the story, because it includes elements of Gothic horror such as the gory scene of the blood transfusion and the dead body coming back to life to point an accusatory finger at Bertha. These Gothic elements of the story are what caused Eliot's publisher at the time to hesitate in publishing it.

Historical Context

The Victorian Era

Alexandrina Victoria (1819-1901), Queen of the United Kingdom of Great Britain and Ireland (1819-1901) was born in the same year as George Eliot. Victoria's reign lasted from 1837 until her death. Because her life span and reign came to characterize this period in history, it came to be

Compare & Contrast

- **Victorian Era:** Experimentation and curiosity about the human mind and the supernatural lead to several trends of inquiry and experimentation in Victorian England. Mesmerism (now referred to as hypnotism) was thought to create alternate states of consciousness. Clairvoyance, the ability to read the thoughts of others, see into the future, or describe scenes of distant cities, etc., was also a subject of experimentation and general interest.

  1999: There is general interest in E.S.P., tarot cards, "new age" spirituality, astrology, etc. Hypnotism is now used in psychotherapy, as well as other, less scientifically accepted, practices, such as getting in touch with past lives or the dead. Clairvoyance, now commonly referred to as extrasensory perception, (ESP), or the people who have this power as "psychics," is doubted by many, but also believed by many, to be a real phenomenon. Police detectives have been known to call in psychics to help solve crimes.

- **Victorian Era:** Phrenology is the study of the external shape of the human head as a means of determining intelligence and character.

  1999: The study of phrenology has been completely debunked in the late 20th Century, and is associated with racist pseudo-sciences.

- **Victorian Era:** Gothic fiction, or Gothic horror, was developed as a literary genre in the 19th Century. Mary Shelley's *Frankenstein* is considered to be the first Gothic novel of note, followed by others, such as Robert Louis Stevenson's *Dr. Jekyll and Mr. Hyde* and Bram Stoker's *Dracula* .

  Late 20th Century: Gothic fiction in the late 20th Century has developed into two distinct genres. On one hand, the modern horror story flourishes, in both the novel form, with such prolific writers as Stephen King, and in film, with such films as *Psycho*, *Night of the Living Dead*, *Friday the 13th*, *Halloween*, and *A Nightmare on Elm Street*. On the other hand, the modern, mass-market paperback romance novel, often referred to as Gothic romance, is descended from the Gothic novel.

- **Victorian England:** In Victorian England, blood transfusion was a subject of scientific experimentation. Scientists experimented with animals, reporting that dead animals had momentarily sprung to life, following a transfusion. Blood transfusion was also used on women during pregnancy and after birth.

  1999: Blood transfusion is a standard medical practice during some surgeries and other medical procedures. Although it saves lives, it is not considered to be bring the dead back to life.

---

known as the "Victorian" Era. Victorian England is associated with restrictive moral attitudes and repressive standards of social behavior. There was, however, a strong element of criticism of these standards among many prominent writers and intellectuals of the time.

The Industrial Revolution

The 19th Century can now be seen as a period of transition from a pre-industrial economy to an industrial economy in most of the Western world. In England, the Industrial Revolution was accompanied by great political and cultural changes, as well as scientific advances. The development of railroads was seen by many to indicate a major change, while various reform bills marked a shift in the political, economic and social structure of the culture. These changes produced new class formations and a new class consciousness in England. The Great Exhibition of 1851, which brought visitors from all over Europe, showcased industrial machines by way of celebrating England's lead in the industrial revolution.

Charles Darwin, *On the Origin of Species* (1859)

In 1859 (the same year "The Lifted Veil" was published) Charles Darwin (1809-1882) published *On The Origin of Species by Means of Natural Selection*, in which he put forth his theory of evolution through natural selection, known as Darwinism. Theorizing that humans are descendants of apes, Darwinism was controversial, in that it posed a challenge to existing Christian ideas about the origin of life. However, among most scientists, Darwinism was readily received and quickly accepted. Herbert Spencer, a close friend of George Eliot, was an influential thinker and leading proponent of Darwinism.

Mesmerism, Phrenology and Clairvoyance

There were many areas of "pseudo-science" which piqued the interest of intellectuals and others in Victorian England. *Phrenology* was a theory that one could determine a person's character and ability based on a close examination of the shape and size of their head. (Phrenology has been debunked in the 20th Century as a pseudo-science, used to support racist ideas). *Mesmerism*, based on the practices of the physician Charles Mesmer, was the precursor to modern practices of hypnotism. *Clairvoyance* referred to having knowledge beyond that of everyday thought and perceptions, a phenomenon now commonly referred to as extrasensory perception (ESP).

Women in Victorian England

The rights of women in Victorian England were severely restricted. Women writers and novelists often chose a male penname, for fear that public knowledge of their sex would either restrict their publication options, negatively effect the response of critics or cause social disgrace. The rights of women were also severely restricted in terms of marriage laws. Divorce was difficult or impossible to obtain legally and looked down upon socially. A woman and man living together out of wedlock resulted in severe social stricture, often cutting off ties to family and friends. In the realm of higher education, women had few, if any, options.

Literary Trends

The mid-1850s saw two distinct trends in English literature—realism and Gothic romance. Eliot is widely considered to have mastered the realist novel through most of her works of fiction. Anthony Trollope, a contemporary of Eliot, is also known for his style of realist novel. The Gothic novel, meanwhile, was developed through such works as Mary Shelley's *Frankenstein*, Charlotte Bronte's *Jane Eyre*, and Emily Bronte's *Wuthering Heights*. Gothic fiction, which borrowed its name from the style of medieval architecture, was characterized by dark tales, often delving into the realm of the supernatural, and grotesque images. In the United States, Gothic fiction was mastered by Edgar Allan Poe, in such short stories as "The Fall of the House of Usher," and Nathaniel Hawthorne, in his collection of stories, *Twice-Told Tales*.

Critical Overview

After years spent as a journal editor, critical essayist and translator of the books of others, Eliot's unofficial husband, George Henry Lewes, encouraged her to try her hand at fiction. In 1857, she first assumed the penname George Eliot, and began to write her first novel, *Adam Bede*, which was published in 1859. *Adam Bede* brought Eliot immediate critical acclaim, suggesting to some critics that she posed a challenge in literary accomplishment even to the well-established Charles Dickens. Close on the heals of *Adam Bede*, Eliot published her second novel *The Mill on the Floss* in 1860. The following year, her third novel, *Silas Marner*, was published. Her masterpiece, *Middlemarch*, was published in 1871-72.

Publishing "The Lifted Veil"

Eliot paused between the publication of *Adam Bede* and completion of *The Mill on the Floss* to write her (long) short story, "The Lifted Veil." Blackwood, her publisher, was reluctant to publish the story, because it didn't fit in with her previous novel, and because he feared the controversial nature of its supernatural subject-matter would not be well received. Blackwood wrote her that, although it was "a very striking story, full of thought and most beautifully written," he "wished the theme had been a happier one." Eliot herself described "The Lifted Veil" as "a slight story of the *outre* kind[,] not a *jeu d'esprit*, but a *jeu de malancholie*." "The Lifted Veil" was, nevertheless, published anonymously in a literary journal in 1849. But Blackwood's opinion of the story remained negative, as he advised Eliot not to include "The Lifted Veil," as well as another of her stories, in his 1866 edition of her works.

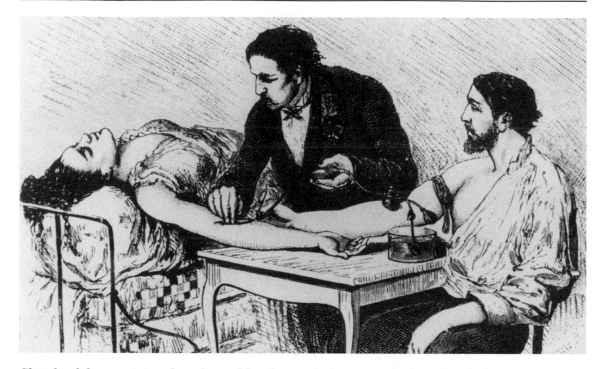

Sketch of donor giving first direct blood transfusion to patient, under doctor's supervision.

"The Lifted Veil" has remained to this day one of Eliot's lesser known works, perhaps because it is an anomaly among her more famous novels. As biographer Rosemary Ashton has remarked, "The Lifted Veil" is "indeed an uncharacteristic story for George Eliot to have written." Ashton explains that it was her only story written as a first person narrative, and the only one to include elements of the occult or pseudo-science. However, it's place in literary history fits snugly into the category of the Gothic tale of horror, published between Mary Shelley's *Frankenstein* (1818) and Robert Louis Stevenson's *Dr. Jekyll and Mr. Hyde* (1886), both of which integrate themes of scientific inquiry which, as in Eliot's story, borders on the edge of the supernatural.

The Height of Success

Biographer Frederick Robert Karl has stated that, by 1876, Eliot was "regarded as England's greatest living novelist." He goes on to say that "she was respected as a national treasure." Karl has stated that Eliot was "the voice of her century." According to Gordon S. Haight, by her contemporary critics she "was acknowledged the greatest novelist of her time." Biographer Elizabeth S.

Haldane notes that Eliot "indeed took her place among the great figures of the Victorian Era." Karl concurs that, "At the peak of her achievement, she was one of the three most famous women in England, along with Queen Victoria and Florence Nightingale."

Despite her socially unconventional domestic arrangements (living as husband and wife with a married man), Eliot's literary reputation by the 1870s had become so highly acclaimed that her position as a socially disgraceful woman was largely overlooked. She and Lewes hosted popular Sunday gatherings in their London home, and she was even privileged to dine with royalty.

Post-Humus Reputation

Eliot died at the height of her literary career. Karl states that, "At the time of her death, despite her detractors, Eliot was something of a cult figure, a legend." However, this reputation quickly declined in the years following her death. Although her funeral was attended by an impressive list of her surviving contemporary writers and intellectuals, her questionable social standing during life immediately came back to haunt her. Despite her widespread fame and recognition, she was denied

the right to burial in the "poet's corner" of Westminster Abbey, where the graves of many notable figures can be found. However, Eliot was
buried near her lifelong companion, Lewes, in
Highgate cemetery.

The first biography of Eliot to appear was
written by John Walter Cross, the husband of her
brief marriage at the end of her life. Cross's biography has since been widely criticized for its
disingenuousness in attempting to paint a picture of
Eliot which would leave her a respectable woman in
the eyes of posterity. Subsequent biographies have
revealed the more interesting and scandalous elements of her relationships with men, as well as the
less flattering but more psychologically complex
elements of her character. Despite, or perhaps due
to, Cross's efforts to normalize the story of Eliot's
life, her literary reputation went into rapid decline
after her death, and was not revived until over 40
years later.

By the turn of the century, Eliot had fallen out
of favor with literary scholars and critics, and,
according to biographer Ina Taylor, "by the end of
the century her work had become too *demode* (out
of fashion) to be read." But writers Virginia Woolf
and F. R. Leavis came "to recognize that her novels
ranked among the greatest in the language." They
were both instrumental in ensuring that "by the
middle of [the 20th] century George Eliot was
accorded the recognition and immortality she had
always sought." Thanks to the efforts of Woolf and
Leavis, Eliot's reputation as one of the greatest
novelists of the 19th Century has been, and continues to be, fully revived. In 1980, during the cen-
tenary celebration of her death, she was given
a monument in the Poet's Corner of Westminster Abbey.

Criticism

Liz Brent

*Brent has a Ph.D. in American Culture, with a
specialization in cinema studies, from the University of Michigan. She is a freelance writer and teaches
courses in American cinema. In the following essay,
she discusses the "curse" of clairvoyance in "The
Lifted Veil."*

The "Curse" of the Lifted Veil

The "veil" in George Eliot's novella "The
Lifted Veil" symbolizes the boundary between the

natural world and the world of the *supernatural*,
which in this story includes the realm of the spirit
and of death. The words "shroud" or "curtain"
also appear throughout the story as references to the
image of the "veil." Latimer's powers of clairvoyance, his ability to both see into the future and hear
the internal thoughts of people around him, is described in terms of his ability to see beyond the
"veil" which separates the natural world from that
of the spirit world. While these powers of clairvoyance would seem to be a gift, Latimer experiences
them as a "curse," which drains life of all pleasure,
bringing him only misery and suffering.

The "veil" or "curtain" which separates human beings with ordinary powers of perception
from foreknowledge of the future is lifted for Latimer,
allowing him to see events before they actually
occur. But this "superadded consciousness" which
allows him to see into the future deprives him of all
human pleasure in the present. He recalls his childhood, before the "curtain of the future" had been
lifted to him, as a happy one, "For then the curtain
of the future was as impenetrable to me as to other
children." For Latimer, the "hope" of his childhood was a result of possessing, like other children,
no knowledge of his own future, "I had all their
delight in the present hour, their sweet indefinite
hopes for the morrow." Once he has seen into his
own future, however, there is no basis on which to
harbor any sense of "hope." Also, because he
becomes preoccupied with these visions of the
future, he no longer experiences "delight in the
present hour."

Latimer describes his only pleasures in life as a
child, before acquiring his powers of clairvoyance,
in terms of *nature*, both in association with the
mystery of life and with his memories of maternal
love. Latimer's love of nature is specifically associated with his fond early memories of his mother,
who died when he was quite young. Although
generally a lonely child, Latimer describes his "least
solitary moments" as occurring in the presence of
nature, which he describes in terms of the "cherishing love" of his mother's embrace: "It seemed to
me that the sky, and the glowing mountain-tops, and
the wide blue water, surrounded me with a cherishing love such as no human face had shed on me
since my mother's love had vanished out of my
life." Latimer further describes his experience of
nature in terms of a spiritual, heavenly or godlike
quality, as "the sight of the Alps, with the setting
sun on them seemed to me like an entrance to
heaven." He goes on to describe his experience of

What Do I Read Next?

- *Middlemarch* (1871-72) is considered to be George Eliot's masterpiece of provincial life in Victorian England.

- *Frankenstein* (1818) by Mary Shelley is considered to be the first Gothic novel of note. Dr. Frankenstein creates a monster which he then seeks to destroy.

- *Strange Case of Dr. Jekyll and Mr. Hyde* (1886), by Robert Louis Stevenson, recounts how Dr. Jekyll concocts a potion which causes his person to split into one Mr. Hyde, a despicable creature who embodies all of the doctor's basest impulses.

- *Twice-Told Tales* (1837), by Nathaniel Hawthorne, contains some stories with Gothic elements in an American setting.

- *The Dead Zone* (1979), by Stephen King, portrays a man who is haunted by his ability to see into the future.

- *The Madwoman in the Attic* (1979), by Sandra Gilbert and Gubar, is a landmark feminist critique of the place of women authors in the canon of English literature.

- *George Eliot: A Life* (1886), by Rosemary Ashton, is a biography which discusses Eliot's life and work in the cultural and historical context of Victorian England.

- *The Lifted Veil: The Book of Fantastic Literature by Women, 1800-World War II* (1992) contains a collection of stories by women which explore the realm of the fantastic.

---

nature in terms which suggest religious fervor; he finds himself in a state of a "perpetual sense of exaltation," or almost religious awe "at the presence of nature and all her awful loveliness." Latimer's delight in the mystery and spiritual properties of nature are lost, however, when the "entrance to heaven" is in effect opened for him, in the form of his powers of clairvoyance. Once he is able to see beyond the realm of life and nature to the realm of death and the soul, this reverence for, and awe in the face of the mystery of nature is no longer a part of his experience.

Once both his future, or "destiny," and the thoughts and souls of other human beings are revealed to him by the lifting of the "veil" of life's mystery, Latimer no longer takes pleasure in the natural world. He thus comes to the conclusion that it is the *mystery* of life and of death which is the sole cause of pleasure in human life. In fact, he comes to believe that human beings thrive on that which is unknown to them.

> So absolute is our soul's need of something hidden and uncertain for the maintenance of that doubt and hope and effort which are the breath of its life, that if the whole future were laid bare to us beyond to-day, the interest of all mankind would be bent on the hours that lie between.

Because of Latimer's powers of clairvoyance, life for him contains nothing "hidden and uncertain" and is drained of any "interest," and therefore of any "doubt and hope and effort."

The Mystery of Bertha

Latimer's instant fixation on Bertha as an object of his adoration is thus due both to the fact that she is the only person whose inner soul remains a mystery to him, and because he associates her with images of nature. Latimer describes Bertha, upon his first introduction to her, as if she had emerged directly from the world of nature: "The pale-green dress, and the green leaves that seemed to form a border about her pale blond hair, made me think of a water-Nixie,—for my mind was full of German lyrics, and this pale, fatale-eyed woman, with the green weeds, looked like a birth from some cold sedgy-stream, the daughter of an aged river." In describing Bertha on their wedding day, Latimer again describes her in terms of nature imagery, which is also endowed with a spiritual element: "Bertha, in her white silk dress and pale-green leaves, and the pale hues of her hair and face, looked like the spirit of the morning." In Bertha, Latimer sees both the spiritual mystery and the maternal love he associates with his childhood experience of nature.

Latimer's fixation on Bertha is described most emphatically, however, in terms of the fact that she is the only person in the world who remains a mystery to him. Because Latimer is denied the human pleasures of *not* being able to see beyond the "veil" of life's mystery, of the spiritual world, Bertha, "my oasis of mystery in the dreary desert of knowledge," becomes the only source of pleasure in his life. It is what he *doesn't* know about Bertha that fascinates him. His fascination with Bertha is attributable to the fact that she is the only "enigma" left in his world, "amidst the fatiguing obviousness of the other minds around me." He explains that the overpowering "effect" Bertha had on him "was chiefly determined by the fact that she made the only exception, among all the human beings about me, to my unhappy gift of insight." Because Latimer's ability to see into the future spoils his sense of hope, Bertha's mysteriousness becomes his only source of pleasure in life, since "she had for me the fascination of an unraveled destiny."

He goes on to describe the "closed secret" of Bertha's face in terms of religious iconography; her face to him was the "shrine of a doubtfully benignant deity which ruled his fate." It's as if Bertha, being the only remaining mystery in Latimer's life, takes on all the power of the mystery of a "deity," or god, which Latimer had previously attributed to nature. She comes to represent for Latimer the realm of the unknown which, for him, is the source of all human delight in life. Bertha thus becomes for Latimer a mysterious godlike presence to which he blindly devotes himself.

In the beginning of their marriage, Bertha continues to be a mystery to Latimer, and therefore continues to capture his attention: "Bertha's inward self remained shrouded from me, and I still read her thoughts only through the language of her lips and demeanour." While her "inward self" is "shrouded" from Latimer, he is still able to "find in her alone among my fellow-beings the blessed possibility of mystery, and doubt, and expectation." Eighteen months after their marriage, however, upon the death of Latimer's father, the "veil which

> In other words, the 'speaker' of the epigraph sends up a prayer to 'heaven' to be spared the curse of supernatural powers of clairvoyance."

had shrouded Bertha's soul" from Latimer is lifted: "The terrible moment of complete illumination had come to me, and I saw that the darkness had hidden no landscape from me, but only a blank prosaic wall." Once this veil is lifted, and Bertha no longer a mystery to him, Latimer loses all interest in her, and she loses all power over him: "Before marriage she had completely mastered my imagination, for she was a secret to me. But now that her soul was laid open to me, now that I was compelled to share the privacy of her motives, to follow all the petty devices that preceded her words and acts, she found herself powerless with me"

Latimer's "curse of insight" into life's mysteries has the result of causing him such suffering that it has "annihilated religious faith within me." His only "deity" had been that which he imagined to have been enshrined in Bertha's face, and, once that shrine is shown to be empty, there is no longer any possibility of faith for him. Latimer spends the remainder of his life, after the revelation of Bertha's maid that she had been trying to poison him, fleeing from "my old insight" into the "Unknown Presence."

The Epigraph

Fifteen years after the initial publication of "The Lifted Veil" George Eliot added a short epigraph to the story.

> Give me no light, great Heaven, but such as turns
> To energy of human fellowship;
> No powers beyond the growing heritage
> That makes completer manhood.

This poem is written in the form of a prayer, whereby the speaker asks Heaven to give him "no light"—meaning, no knowledge or insight—"but such as turns to energy of human fellowship." In other words, the speaker asks to be granted no special powers of knowledge or insight (''light''), such as clairvoyance, which would turn his ''energy'' (thought or intention) away from ''human fellowship.'' The speaker asks to be granted only those ordinary powers of knowledge and perception which direct his ''energy'' toward ''fellowship'' with humans in the natural world. This clearly refers to Latimer's supernatural powers of clairvoyance—as if the heavens had granted him the ''light'' by which to see beyond the ''veil'' which shrouds the future, the spirit world and the realm of death from most human eyes. The poem goes on to pray for ''no powers beyond the growing heritage that makes completer manhood.'' The speaker asks to be spared any supernatural power beyond the wisdom endowed to a natural development of ''manhood,'' or human experience. In other words, the ''speaker'' of the epigraph sends up a prayer to ''heaven'' to be spared the curse of supernatural powers of clairvoyance.

Given that Eliot chose to add it fifteen years after original publication, it may be that the epigraph functions as a sort of ''moral'' to the story of ''The Lifted Veil.'' Because Latimer experiences his powers to see beyond the ''veil'' of life's mystery as a ''curse,'' the epigraph functions almost as a warning to the reader not to wish for such powers, but, rather, to turn the ''energy'' of his earthly knowledge and insight (''light'') to ''human fellowship,'' to the natural world of humanity, for it is the mystery itself of the ''Unknown Presence'' which gives meaning, ''hope'' and ''interest'' to human life.

Source: Liz Brent, for *Short Stories for Students*, The Gale Group, 2000.

Kevin Ashby

In the following essay, Ashby interprets ''The Lifted Veil'' in light of the ''transcendent ego'' standard of Blackwood's Edinburgh Magazine *as well as the magazine's treatment of such character types as the spasmodic poet and the uncertain scientist.*

How may ''The Lifted Veil'' throw light on the subject of regionalism and George Eliot? As Barbara Hardy has pointed out, the tale is, in part, about the intersection of the homely and the exotic. Half the action takes place during a fateful two months in Europe, half in the shires. In this case, however, the play between local and cosmopolitan experience is not one between embedded and enlarged sympathies. Latimer's imaginative ''gifts'' originate on the continent, but withdrawal and isolation are their result.

In fact, ''The Lifted Veil'' takes as its subject the *marginal* role played by centrifugal humanistic pursuits. In Latimer's discourse, traditionally central relationships are the site of comically squandered intellectual and emotional energies. Narrow-horizoned and ephemeral affairs predominate as fathers hunt for musical snuff-boxes, wives give dinner-parties and brothers recommend hunting as an existential cure-all. Grander discourses, representing human solidarity and progress, are also ineffective. Connubial love is roundly bemocked and education decided by a phrenologist. Latimer, sensitive, ''artistic,'' compassionate (he says), is a mere puzzle to his associates. Meunier, for all his ''European reputation,'' far-sighted interests and large-minded character, can make of life only a ''scientific problem.'' Even consciousness is a tissue of ''frivolities, ... suppressed egoism, ... puerilities ... and make-shift thoughts.''

This is a pessimistic picture. It depends, however, on reading the tale out of context. If we restore the story's originary frame of reading—the flagship Victorian periodical Blackwood's *Edinburgh Magazine*—some pertinent complications emerge. At one level, the pessimism is confirmed. The discourse of the magazine exposes more substantial problems of value with Latimer and Meunier than absorption by the *arriviste* families of provincial England. At another level, it provides a situation in which that pessimism may be partially reduced. There is no effective civilised activity in ''The Lifted Veil'' itself. There is in the kind of reading the story expects to receive.

The implied hermeneutic activity is signalled by adaptions of certain character types known in Blackwood's in the 1850s, namely, the Spasmodic poet and the unsound scientist and his experimental subjects. The context is important because the magazine attached a curious mixture of sympathy and mistrust to these cultural figures. Their epistemological status was ambiguous, their discourse full of partial insights but no overall authority; and Blackwood's recommended particularly self-conscious handling of them. One could enjoy a certain kind of interesting but unsolid figure while not deviating from the knowledge of its partial nature. This was a work at once of sustained intellectual clarification and strenuous moral resistance. For Blackwood's it was a kind of work which confirmed a person's essential and productive humanity, reflecting its central standard of the "transcendent ego." In evoking it, "The Lifted Veil" could be said to nurture not merely the surface reception of humanistic concerns, but their experiential investigation. The former would have been served by an omniscient narrator doling out careful moral disquisition—Eliot's more typical form. Here, readers are asked to identify Latimer *unaided,* actively making themselves a civilised community.

Let us examine these relations more fully, beginning with Latimer's connection to the so-called Spasmodic Poet. "Spasmodic" was an epithet coined by the magazine's main literary reviewer during this period, W. E. Aytoun. It covered the practitioners and products of a mode of poetry fashionable in the 1840s and 1850s, of which James Bailey's *Festus* (1839), Alexander Smith's *Life Drama* (1853) and Sydney Dobell's *Balder* (1853) were the most celebrated examples. Tennyson's *Maud* (1855) and Barrett-Browning's *Aurora Leigh* (1856) also show the influence of Spasmodic preoccupations. As Aytoun's epithet implies, commercial success did not bring critical acclaim in Blackwood's. The terms of the attack are illuminating.

According to the magazine, what is wrong with the Spasmodic poet is his mode of consciousness. This is realised throughout a Spasmodic work. Metric eccentricity, imagery, subject matter and the typical character of its hero all reveal the same problem: deficient intellectual and moral control over the streams of sensibility which are the materials of art. W. H. Smith, another regular contributor, called *Festus*, "poetic rant, a mere farrago of distracted metaphors, and crude metaphysics and bewildering theology." The terms are repeated. For Aytoun, *Maud* lacked "simplicity" of style—"when all false images and far-fetched metaphors" have been removed. Its politics were "ill-conceived . . . distorted and indistinct." Aytoun refers later to "hyperbole" and a "violent style of writing," words Smith had also used. The source of these faults, however, is not lack of talent. Bailey has "ardent imagination and . . . strong passion"; Tennyson, even in *Maud*, "such extraordinary rhythmical music, that the sense became subordinate to the sound." The difficulty is rather one of excess and lack of consideration. The poets have failed to exert their forming and clarifying intellectual powers. Tennyson "formerly bestowed great pains upon his style," according to Aytoun, to attain the "utmost degree of lucidity combined with energy." "Imagination ought not to be divorced from sense," said

> " There the problem is the lack in every character of that kind of self-possession. Latimer's incapacity for 'the sublime resistance of poetic production' is an index of his abandonment, as is Meunier's scientific obsession and the inability of father, brother and wife to see more than what boosts their own interests."

Smith. Bailey had better have "waited till his own opinions . . . had settled into something approaching consistency and harmony." Carelessness, not infacility, caused the "hideous cacophony" and "discord" of both poets' verse.

The poets' abandonment to the "torrent" of thought, sensation and image in their own minds, then, is the root of the matter. It is fixed by comparisons of Spasmodic verse to "monomania," "hypochondriacal brilliancy," or "maudlin imitations of passion, such as a tragedian . . . might utter, when the effects of [an] overdose of gin . . . were beginning to wear off." Delirium, staginess, inebriation, the terms add to the typology. They associate the "headlong career" of "unregulated," poetry-like thought with a risible delinquency. The same association with insipidity also connects the Spasmodic hero's turbulence and alienation. *Maud's* speaker is "morbid and misanthropical," by turns "abusive" or "silly" and "namby-pamby." The suicidal despair of the hero of *Life Drama* is premature and faintly ridiculous. Festus (that is, Faust), pouring out his cosmological vision, is a muddle-headed bore, while his Lucifer is "at one time the grand Personification of the Principle of Evil, . . . , at another, . . . a very slave to the passions of an amorous swain." The descriptions make the traits indivisible, mutually reinforcing. Indulging "poetic" trains of thought without a corresponding exercise of intellect means indulging extravagant, muddled, anti-social, sickly and weak-willed consciousness.

Latimer exemplifies this experience of consciousness and these traits. His timidity and lack of exertion is commented on many times. Misanthropy, however much disguised by later "pity," looms admittedly through his contempt for brother and father. The narrative begins with a global condemnation of human unkindness. Alienation and unhealthiness, though it is a "horror" to bemoan, is also something to pique oneself on. "I believe I was held to have a sort of half-womanish, half-ghostly beauty; . . . But I thoroughly disliked my own physique, and nothing but the belief that it was a condition of poetic genius would have reconciled me to it."

More important than these, however, are the general condition of alienation and "unregulated" imagination. The young Latimer enjoyed poetic "reveries." Rather than learn about water, he would watch it "gurgling among the pebbles and bathing the bright green water plants, by the hour together . . . [with] perfect confidence that there were good reasons for what was so beautiful." This experience of natural inspiration continues in Geneva. The whole condition is described in terms which verbally echo the strictures about Spasmodic poetry. Latimer has "the poet's sensibility without his voice" along with the attendant misery. He is "humiliated" by his dreams because they are "utterly disjointed and commonplace." When he tries to 'imagine' Venice "I was only colouring the Canaletto engravings that hung in my old bedroom at home; the picture was a shifting one, my mind wandering uncertainly in search of more vivid images." Imitation and lack of coherent form are familiar designations of a secondary mode of imagination.

The visions after his "terrible illness" also relate to the Spasmodic prototype. Latimer cannot control either the premonitions or the mind-reading. The insights are extraordinarily vivid, but either fragmentary—as in the case of Prague and the visions of Bertha—or reducible to no coherent form—as in the streams of others' thoughts which invade him. Later, after marrying Bertha, the visions—"of strange cities, of sandy plains, of gigantic ruins, of midnight skies with strange bright constellations etc."—are so frequent he "live[s] continually" among them. It is as if his consciousness is always full of the material of poetry, but he has no power to shape it. We already know he lacks "intellectual" capacity. This combination leads to his calling the condition at first an "intermittent delirium," "a diseased activity of the imagina-tion," then an "abnormal sensibility." As if to compound the associations, the second-sight begins during "the languid monotony of convalescence."

The combination of disease, alienation, negativity, feebleness and an untrammelled stream of poetry-like insight are all present. The reference is not an idle one. It alerts readers to a specific kind of hermeneutic activity. Says Smith of *Festus*: "Read it by all means, and with the pencil in your hand; for the probability is, that you will not work your way through it twice, and there are many things in it you will not be content to have caught a glimpse of only once." Aytoun on *Maud* clarifies the kind of attention required, when he tells us of the relief from it afforded by "Come into the garden." "[It is] the one passage we can read . . . with a perfect conviction that it is the strain of a true poet . . . we feel that our hands are bound, like those of Thalaba, when the enchantress sang to him as she spun." In effect, readers of Spasmodic verse must be productive. They cannot passively rely on a Spasmodic's discourse, but may not lazily reject it either. Sympathetic suspicion must be exercised instead. Alert for true poetic ore, one shovels away the "Sacramento mud" of rant and befuddlement.

This process, none other than what a successful poet would do while composing, has contradictory implications for Latimer's narrative. On the one hand, it casts doubt on the authenticity of his clairvoyance and exponentially degrades his character. The incessantly petty, egotistic voices in the poor man's head may be only his sickly, wretched, jaundiced projections. If this is so, the story is bleaker than we thought: there is no centrifugal voice at all. On the other hand, regardless of the hero's status as a seer, the reader's activity now quickly supplies what his discourse lacks. An unequivocally artistic—thus socially unifying—endeavour now shapes it. The reader progresses through the text, discarding as dross the narrator's weaklier judgements, retaining the purer and more clear-headed ones. For instance, we may question claims of paternal indifference. Latimer's father drops whatever his business was to be at his son's bedside when the latter falls ill—day after day, for months, in a foreign land—and does not leave him for the convalescence. We note, "My diseased consciousness was more intensely preoccupied with [my brother's] thoughts and emotions than with those of any other person," but that Latimer always envied and disliked his brother. Conversely, we applaud the son's eventual access of love and compassion for his father.

Two objections might be raised to the forego-
ing. Latimer dismisses his own capacities, exercis-
ing the self-recognition a Spasmodic did not. "I saw
in my face now nothing but the stamp of a morbid
disposition." This suggests that his reports of second sight, which "provisions of incalculable words
and actions proved . . . to have a fixed relation to
the mental processes of other minds," are not
consciously deceptive or unreflectively recorded.
"Morbidly sensitive," yes, but "self-distrustful"
enough to suspect himself "diseased." What evidence is there, besides, that the premonitions were
hallucinatory?

Another typology familiar to Blackwood's readers sheds some light. Investigations with supernatural implications were the subject of two articles of
the early 1850s, "What is Mesmerism" and "The
Night Side of Nature." The latter reviewed two
recent publications. In one, "Researches on Elec-
tricity, Magnetism etc. In Relation To The Vital
Force," translated by Dr. Gregory, Professor of
Chemistry at Edinburgh University, Karl, Baron
von Reichenbach, reported a series of experiments
made with magnets upon human subjects. The Baron claimed to have discovered a new force of
nature, the "odylic" force, which could produce
sensory effects at distance. While emphasizing his
thorough belief in Reichenbach's "good faith, perfect integrity and unwearied industry," the reviewer was sceptical. "All his deductions are founded on
certain vague, indescribable sensations, in persons
either morbidly sensitive or very peculiarly sensitive." (The more trustworthy witnesses are "artists.") All the effects arise from the mind's subjective effort, from "causes within the patient herself"
(sic). This psychological explanation was repeated
in the comments about Catherine Crow's "The
Night Side of Nature." This deals directly with
clairvoyance, which the reviewer equates with the
visions of sleep-walkers. Both clairvoyant and
somnambulist live inside an illusion which only
convinces them. The sleepwalker's world is particularly curious. One stage on from dreaming, it is a
vividly projected simalcrum which the victim tours
while simultaneously perambulating a real place
(his bedroom, house etc.). The former adapts itself
to the changes of the latter but the illusion is never
broken. Latimer, let us recall, says his visions are
dream-like but "more distinct" than dreams; and
while undergoing them he does not lose consciousness of the real place he is in.

The typology concerns willingness to take para-
normal experiences at their face value. It is the over-

sensitive and quasi-artistic who do so: but they find
themselves in a seductively life-like parallel reality
which is only a "coinage of the brain." In our
terms, they take off at a tangent from the common-
sense, consensual human world. The Mesmerism
article offers a more censorious version of the
paradigm. It is in the form of a letter, answered by an
editorial postscript. Eagles, the author, impersonat-
es an interested, concerned but inexpert reader of
the magazine who has investigated "mesmeric influence." His theory is that mesmerism, if it actually occurs, consists of a spiritual force, involving
omniscience, omnipresence and omnipotence in the
mesmeriser. It would be an objective effect, whereby the mesmeriser travels outside his own body,
causes inanimate objects to arrest people's movement and changes their moral natures. After complete initial scepticism, Eagles's character's observations lead to him to express horrified conviction
that at least some of the mesmerist's claims may be
true. The mesmerist can enter another mind, read it
and use it to be in two places at once. In the editorial
postscript, however, written by the then Professor of
Moral Philosophy at Edinburgh University, this
conclusion is reversed. As with the real Reichenbach,
the mythical correspondent's "candour and becoming gravity" are acknowledged. Nevertheless, mesmerism is decidedly a subjective phenomenon. The
mesmerist is a cunning charlatan; the mesmerised
"weak," "credulous" and "infatuated." The latter
self-indulgently wish to be deprived of their own
will and collude in "degenerate" fashion in hallucinatory experiences.

Whether clairvoyance, somnambulism or mesmerism is its source, claims to extrasensory perception cut no ice in the magazine. Even where an
investigator adopts the tones of a disinterested observer, no credence can be given. Experience of
these subjects itself signifies a reduced human centrality, "a *physique* and a *morale* greatly below the
average" (Ferrier's italics). What chance for Latimer,
then, who is decidedly interested and whose personality mirrors that of the experimental subject of this
unsound science? Even his great friend Meunier
may not be so admirable. *His* interest in resurrection
place him within the sphere of charlatan investigation, or at best that of the industrious but misguided
von Reichenbach and the "excellent" Eagles character, dabbling in the supernatural. His other great
interest, "the psychological relations of disease,"
also makes him suspect. In an article about the trial
of Edward Oxford, failed assassin of Queen Victoria, there was criticism of the medical evidence

presented by the defence. Lack of self control, of motive, eccentricity and involuntary giggling in the dock were given as symptoms of insanity, responsibility reduced by disease. They define criminal *ir*-responsibility, said Blackwood's. The medical profession had not fully considered the common-sense implications of its ideas.

We may now consider the internal evidence of the hallucinatory nature of Latimer's powers. Despite his own desperate belief, Latimer says of Prague only that it was "of a piece" with his premonition. The bridge in the vision was nightmarishly "unending" not the prosaic thing Latimer rushes across. A star-shaped point of light would not be difficult to find in a city's Jewish quarter. Similarly, it is significant that the premonition of Bertha occurs after Latimer has glanced out of his hotel window. Could he not have seen her and his father out of the corner of his eye? They enter only a few minutes later, so they must already be in the hotel's environs. We have only Latimer's word that the scene with a married Bertha is in fact repeated. As for the mind-reading, we have already pointed to the way it concentrates on a brother Latimer is peculiarly anxious about, reflecting his "antagonism." That Bertha is at first immune also questions the reality of the power: it only works to confirm what he wants to know. (Latimer deliberately denies his awareness that he and she are incompatible.) In addition, Latimer's self-pitying misanthropy is linked from the beginning with madness. He quotes Swift's epitaph as a mirror of his own case—but Swift is by no means a healthy precedent. One need not take all these signs as marks of delusion for the main point to be grasped. Latimer too may be a von Reichenbach—simply misguided. But there is enough in the text to make the reader's work of anti-credulity necessary. The further effect of that work is worth pondering. Speaking of a "terribly interesting chapter entitled 'Doppelgangers and Self-Seeing'" in "The Night Side of Nature," Blackwood's remarked "as a repertory of marvellous matter . . . read it through to the end," but do not take the reports as factual. Disbelief, in other words, does not preclude the extension of sympathy to the enjoyment of the impossible. As with a Spasmodic poem, the injunction seems to be—"Take whatever significance you can. Let such tales illuminate and extend your mind but never forget the boundaries of your own identity and your own standards."

If this is the case, the reader is meant to provide the civilising thrust ostensibly lacking in the tale in

more ways than one. It is not merely the epistemological matter we noted earlier. The reader is asked to avoid certain moral failures that the credulous Latimer or his scientist prototypes succumb to. The knowledge Eagles's correspondent, Catherine Crow and von Reichenbach proffer is suspect because its field is contaminated by self-indulgent, morbid natures. Some of that morbidity and lassitude rub off on the poor investigator, who lets his enthusiasm better his sobriety. Reichenbach should have rejected a line of observation "which can yield no satisfactory result." That he did not indicates a loss of will, a chasing of personal chimeras.

This is the same failure as that of the Spasmodic poet, led astray by "theories" and caprice from consideration of consensual truths. It is a moral question because it involves a damaging abandonment of the "transcendent ego" which I earlier identified as the core of the magazine's ideological project.

The theory of this object was set out in a series of articles by James Ferrier in the later 1830s, whose standards remained valid throughout the period we are concerned with. "Ego" here means the basic sense of identity, one's feeling of being an autonomous, independent, conscious self. It is created in an act of will that is also an act of knowing. Originally, it is the act of understanding the meaning of the word "I," says Ferrier. A baby's first use of the word is the founding act of will, a sheer decision to *be* an "I." As the founding act of will it is the basis of all active personality, all morality, all accountability and all human freedom.

This self-consciousness may be endangered in a number of ways. One may become absorbed in a particular state of mind—a passion, sensation or train of reason—and so lose the sense of self. This is dangerous because, no longer monitoring what is in one's head, one becomes enslaved, a mere "machine". The self can be nurtured, on the other hand, by detachment from the things which attract or affect one most. Freedom, responsibility and morality, then, the basis of "all that is good in or evil in man or society," depend on the denial of one's passionate interests.

In theory, such an ideal would reconcile a humanity with proliferating interests on the home ground of selfhood. Everyone would have to acknowledge the danger of absorption by their own pet theories and ideas. No doubt this is why it is the dominant concern of "The Lifted Veil." There the problem is the lack in every character of that kind of self-possession. Latimer's incapacity for "the sublime resistance of poetic production" is an index of his abandonment, as is Meunier's scientific obsession and the inability of father, brother and wife to see more than what boosts their own interests.

Yet Blackwood's readers are alerted to this condition by the constant references to other cultural figures with fallible egos. Spasmodic poets lost sight of their status as selves in passion. Mesmerised persons morbidly submitted to "prostration." Somnambulists were asleep. Such a person's discourse, unlike that of a "true poet," was not one a reader could lose themselves to. To be reminded of it was therefore to recall that it was *oneself* reading. Progressing at every point of Latimer's narrative with the pleasure due to a tale of the marvellous, one had to ask "Do *I* think this is meant to be true?" This is a morally self-confirming effort of sympathetic imagination. It is also a ground on which any reader could meet any other, whether they liked Latimer or not, whether they were Scot, provincial banker or metropolitan intellectual. Evoking in all readers an act of fundamental moral responsibility, however, "The Lifted Veil" also aligns itself rather well with the rhetoric of Blackwood's itself. This may be appropriate, for in many respects the periodical's cultural position was analogous to Eliot's. It spoke out of an "inferior" political position in the Anglo-Scottish Union, she out of an "inferior" gender position. Like her too, it was proud that its marginal origin masked attachment and contribution to national, even universal, culture. For instance, it supported the orthodox State Church, but without obscurantist rejection of new scientific and metaphysical discourses.

Blackwood's mix of intellectual elitism and common-sense Unionism was not entirely benevolent, however. The transcendent ego it theorised was, after all, rather a convenient excuse for inertia in the political domain. It eschewed Casuabonesque disdain for women's intellectual capacities, but in an article responding to the proposed Divorce Bill and Married Women's Property Bill, the transcendent ego was somewhat disturbingly deployed. "Pause," it warned in "The Laws concerning women," before you "break a lance upon the grand abstract tyrant, man." Judicious thought recognizes that "the law may be unnecessarily particular; but are its opponents on just ground?". It also saw a return to moral freedom in the nationalistic, bellicose prosecution of the Crimean War.

Perhaps we should question then, by way of conclusion, the success of Eliot's experiment in reader-response. In "The Lifted Veil" she deplores the parochialism of a self-obsessed mind (Latimer's), who hijacks the discourse of pity and sympathy. Simultaneously, she deplores the parochialism of the materialistic mind (Bertha's, Latimer's family), which sees no gain of prestige in humaneness. To do both at once, she relied on a peculiarly attuned reader. But there are other kinds of parochialism, not least historical parochialism, an attachment to tradition that could see in militarism and institutionalised material inequity a test of true selfhood. Perhaps for this reason Eliot did not repeat the experiment. In practice, the sense of identity her tale fostered was not cosmopolitan enough. The transcendent ego of Blackwood's was too complacently bound to its historical locality.

Source: Kevin Ashby, "The Centre and the Margins in 'The Lifted Veil' and Blackwood's *Edinburgh Magazine*," in *George Eliot—George Henry Lewes Studies*, Vol. 24–25, No. 2, 1993 pp. 132–46.

Anne D. Wallace

In the following essay, Wallace sees "The Lifted Veil" as demonstrating the "failures and delusions of memory," a challenge to "Wordsworth's assertion of recollection as the foundation of both poetry and human community."

Although *The Lifted Veil* is still little-read, influential critical evaluations by Terry Eagleton, Gillian Beer, and Sandra Gilbert and Susan Gubar offer us excellent points of access to this deeply pessimistic novella. Gilbert and Gubar, in particular, work to define the intersecting investigations of sexual and artistic identity that outline George Eliot's difficulties in being both woman and writer. All the extant treatments focus on Latimer's prescience and clairvoyance, and on the failures or dangers of his supernaturally enhanced perceptions. But Latimer has yet another mode of perception that lifts the veil of temporality, one commonly available to us all and one insistently identified as a crucial element of artistic vision during the nineteenth century: memory, the recollection and transformation of past experience. Most of Eliot's work appears to carry Wordsworth's assertion of recollection as the foundation of both poetry and human community steadily forward in the popular imagination.

Yet *The Lifted Veil* asserts not only the horrors of supernaturally acute perceptions of present and future, but the failure and delusions of memory as

View of Prague.

well. Through a narrator who aspires to be a Wordsworthian poet, a narrative which repeatedly calls attention to the failure of recollection in both life and art, and a structure which mimics the greater Romantic lyric but does not fulfill its expectations, *The Lifted Veil* runs explicitly counter to Wordsworthian poetics. Thus the novella constitutes a working-out of Eliot's artistic identity, not only in the terms already recognized by Gilbert and Gubar, but in terms of a direct and thorough contradiction of one of Eliot's "master voices."

Since the novella is seldom read, let me summarize what are, for our discussion, its most salient points. The entire story is told in first person by the protagonist. Beginning with the words, "The time of my end approaches," Latimer vividly describes his vision of his own death, noting the day, the time, the servants' indifference, the pain and terror of helplessness, and his final experience of "passing on and on through the darkness," his thought moving endlessly onward without sensation or sight. He then offers a memoir of his life from his childhood to the present, just a month before his death. Latimer describes a childhood happy only in its contrast to adulthood, lightened mostly by the memory of his mother's comforting love. While she still lives, he suffers an illness that temporarily blinds him; after

her death he is subjected to a regimen of mechanical and scientific training designed to balance what his father perceives as an oversensitive nature. But Latimer remains much as he was, an older version of the boy thrown into "mingled trepidation and delicious excitement" by the echoes of hooves and voices and barking dogs in the resounding stable near his home. He regards himself as a poet in sensibility, aware of his surroundings to the point of agony, but lacking the crucial power of expression. Even after three years of education in Geneva, which he passes in "a perpetual sense of exultation, as if from a draught of delicious wine, at the presence of Nature in all her awful loveliness," he is unable to describe the scenes around him or express the emotions he experiences:

> A poet pours forth his song and *believes* in the listening ear and answering soul, to which his song will be floated sooner or later. But the poet's sensibility without his voice—the poet's sensibility that finds no vent but in silent tears on the sunny bank, when the noonday light sparkles on the water, or in an inward shudder at the sound of harsh human tones, the sight of a cold human eye—this dumb passion brings with it a fatal solitude of soul in the society of one's fellow men.

In this state of continuing isolation, Latimer falls ill again and, as he recovers, has the first of four fully recounted episodes of presentiment or prevision: a vision of Prague; a vision of his first meeting with Bertha, whom he will fall in love with and eventually marry; a vision of the moment when he realizes Bertha's hatred for him and the cold shallowness of her soul; and the vision of his own death. Each of these is a true vision, later confirmed by his actual experience. He also develops clairvoyance or, as he calls it, ''insight'' into others' minds, into what he calls the ''naked, skinless complications'' of human thought. The only one immune to his capacity is Bertha, who temporarily becomes his ''oasis of mystery in the dreary desert of knowledge.''

With the sharp desire of beings that can imagine omniscience but cannot attain it, we humans long for Latimer's visionary gifts daily, almost involuntarily: ''if I had known then what I know now ...'' But Latimer's supernatural perceptions prove useless at best, curses at worst. His knowledge of the future does not enable him to avoid its sorrows; his knowledge of others only breeds contempt for the petty, disconnected consciousnesses that lie below the graceful drapery of social intercourse. Some of these incapacities and feelings, clearly, are due to Latimer's own natural passivity and misanthropy. But, the narrative asserts, the uselessness of vision derives mostly from the common human condition, one in which mystery and desire play an irreplaceable part. Here, in a voice that is unmistakably that of George Eliot teaching through her narrator's mouth, Latimer meditates on his inability to turn aside from the known horror of his future with Bertha:

> So absolute is our soul's need of something hidden and uncertain for the maintenance of that doubt and hope and effort which are the breath of its life, that if the whole future were laid bare to us beyond to-day, the interest of all mankind would be bent on the hours that lie between; we should pant after the uncertainties of our one morning and our one afternoon; we should rush fiercely to the Exchange for our last possibility of speculation, of success, of disappointment; we should have a glut of political prophets foretelling a crisis or a no-crisis within the only twenty-four hours left open to prophecy.... Our impulses, our spiritual activities, no more adjust themselves to the idea of their future nullity, than the beating of our heart, or the irritability of our muscles.

So it is with Latimer, who, in knowing terror, lives through his courtship, marriage, utter disillusionment, and, finally, death. In a few closing sentences, he returns the reader to his opening vision, now (the open-ended construction implies) actually occurring: ''It is the 20th of September 1850. I know these figures I have just written, as if they were a long familiar inscription. I have seen

> Not only does Bertha envision Latimer as a figure in a landscape, imagining his deficient psychology in terms of natural forms, but Latimer figures his expectation of Bertha's mind as an exterior, natural landscape, full and poetic and offering continued opportunities for exploration, only to discover a narrow interior scene bounded by 'blank prosaic walls.'''

them on this page in my desk unnumbered times, when the scene of my dying struggle has opened upon me....''

Following and expanding upon the commentary of U.C. Knoepflmacher and Rudy Redinger, Gilbert and Gubar detail the parallels between Latimer and Eliot herself. Their familial relations, defined by a dead angel-mother, a strong pragmatic father, and an irritatingly successful and conventional brother, place each in positions of emotional and economic dependence and inferiority. Both display an initial distrust of strangers; both dislike their bodies, which in each case deviate from the culture's sexual ideals, with the result that physical illness and weakness is an everyday affair. In each case, too, illness coincides with the onset of extraordinary visions which either promise or precede literary expression; and in each case that expression is deferred or denied.

These parallels suggest, as Gilbert and Gubar indicate, that Latimer's case is in some ways Eliot's: given an artist's extraordinary vision, each is thwarted in the expression of that vision, Latimer by an unsuitable mind and temperament, Eliot by the external and internal constraints imposed by cultural representations of sexuality. In each case, in fact, the problem might be abstractly rendered as a conflict between apparent and experienced gender, the comparison enforce by Latimer's inverted mirroring of Eliot's ''masculine'' mind in an ''unattractive'' woman's body: he is technically male, but both his mental and his physical characteristics are traditionally ''feminine.'' One of the primary issues of the *Veil*, then, is the interrogation of the conflicts between Eliot's gender and her artistry.

Gilbert and Gubar also thoroughly explore how the image of the veil traditionally functions in male representations of woman as angel/monster, noting that ''the recording of what exists behind the veil is distinctively female because it is the woman who exists behind the veil in patriarchal society, inhabiting a private sphere invisible to public view.'' This image, clearly, is crucial to our understanding of Eliot's novella, particularly because it acts as a nexus for sexual and artistic identities. Without diminishing their emphasis, let me analyze ''the veil'' in a slightly different way.

There are at least three veils (not unrelated to each other) which would, under normal circumstances, both isolate Latimer and shield him from the terrific and deadening vision that afflicts him: the veil of individuality, the veil of sexuality, and the veil of temporality. The first lifts for extended and agonizing periods of time, as Latimer is exposed to the thoughts of others. As we have already noted, the narrative asserts that Latimer's clairvoyance does little but give him pain; and since Latimer lacks or will not wield the power of poetic expression, his understanding remains entirely one-sided. Until he begins to write this last memoir, Latimer tells us, he has ''never fully unbosomed myself to any human being.''

The second veil, as his choice of terms here suggests, remains drawn despite sexually ambiguous characterizations that imply difficulty in drawing hard lines between the male and the female. Latimer's traditionally female sensitivity and intuition are unmixed with the masculine talent for artistic expression, and remain trapped in an ''effeminately'' weak, sickly, hysterical body which nonetheless is read as ''male.'' He cannot, indeed, unbosom himself, not only because he cannot shed his passivity but because he is not gendered female. His potential femininity and any possible advantage that might carry are short-circuited by the nominal appearance of masculinity, an appearance that causes people to expect rather different behavior from him. In one sense Latimer's very existence tears the veil

between man and woman, but neither he nor anyone else is freed from their gender roles by that involuntary act.

The last veil, that of temporality, is most clearly manifest as a veil of mortality, the ''dark veil'' of death. When this veil is drawn briefly aside, during the temporary resurrection of Mrs. Archer and in Latimer's vision of his own death, the results are once again active destruction or helpless pain: Mrs. Archer wakes only long enough to reveal Bertha's plan to poison Latimer, violently completing their growing disaffection and ending their married life together; and although Latimer sees his death, he can neither avoid it nor reconcile himself to it. Finally, the veil of death functions as the decisive limit to the narrative itself. Likewise, Latimer's foresight produces successful but inefficacious violations of the normal temporal bounds of knowledge. He does know the future, but often in unintelligible forms (as in his late visions of unknown places and persons), and can do nothing to alter even those aspects of the future he does fully comprehend.

But memory provides a third way to lift the veil of temporality (in this case the veil of the past), one naturally available to people, and which should, in Wordsworthian doctrine, stimulate individual moral growth, artistic expression and human community. Wordsworthian poetics, in formulas as familiar to Eliot as they are to us, establish memory as the foundation of poetic expression. Since ''all good poetry is the spontaneous overflow of powerful feelings,'' a poet must be ''possessed of more than usual organic sensibility'' (''Preface to *Lyrical Ballads* [1802]''. But he must also have ''thought long and deeply'':

> For our continued influxes of feeling are modified and directed by our thoughts, which are indeed the representatives of all our past feelings; and, as by contemplating the relation of these general representatives to each other we discover what is really important to men, so by the repetition and continuance of this act, our feelings will be connected with important subjects, till at length, if we be originally possessed of much sensibility, such habits of mind will be produced that . . . we shall describe objects, and utter sentiments, of such a nature and in such connection with each other, that the understanding of the being to whom we address ourselves, if he be in a healthful state of association, must necessarily be in some degree enlightened, and his affections ameliorated.

Thus poetry ''takes it origin from emotion recollected in tranquillity,'' the process of remembering the past experience gradually causing the disappearance of the present tranquillity and the production of "an emotion, kindred to that which was before the subject of contemplation . . . [which] does itself [that is, the kindred emotion] actually exist in the mind." The substance and form of Wordsworth's poems overtly enforce his declared poetics, as even a brief review of some of the best-known poems ("Tintern Abbey," "Michael," "The Ruined Cottage," the Intimations Ode, "I Wandered Lonely," and so forth) quickly reveals. Narrative recollection of past emotion re-presents that emotion and its original context, claiming to produce not only poetry but the achievement of or potential for the enlargement of the individual consciousness and of human community.

The most significant formal manifestation of Wordsworthian (and early Coleridgian) poetic is the development of the greater Romantic lyric, a form described to us by M. H. Abrams:

> [Greater Romantic lyrics] present a determinate speaker in a particularized, and usually a localized, outdoor setting, whom we overhear as he carries on, in a fluent vernacular which rises easily to a more formal speech, a sustained colloquy, sometimes with himself or with the outer scene, but more frequently with a silent human auditor, present or absent. The speaker begins with a description of the landscape; an aspect or change of aspect in the landscape evokes a varied but integral process of memory, thought, anticipation, and feeling which remains closely intervolved with the outer scene. In the course of this meditation the lyric speaker achieves an insight, faces up to a tragic loss, comes to a moral decision, or resolves an emotional problem. Often the poem round upon itself to end where it began, at the outer scene, but with an altered mood and deepened understanding which is the result of the intervening meditation.

In *The Lifted Veil*, Eliot offers us a narrator who aspires to be a Wordsworthian poet, communicating to us in a form which replicates the subjective circularity of a greater Romantic lyric but which completes itself with no alteration in the narrator's mood or understanding. Latimer's hyper-sensitivity, his intense emotional reliance on nature, and (as we shall see) his deliberate attempts to become a poet by the specific mechanism of recollection mark him not just as a poet, as he calls himself, but as a Wordsworthian poet. Certain telling details of his life buttress the theoretical identification. In Geneva, he finds his greatest solace in rowing his boat out into the center of the lake:

> it seemed to me that the sky, and the glowing mountaintops, and the wide blue water, surrounded me with a cherishing love such as no human face had shed on me since my mother's love had vanished out of my life. I used to do as Jean Jacques did—lie down

in my boat and let it glide where it would while I looked up at the departing glow leaving one mountain-top after the other . . . Then, when the white summits were all sad and corpse-like, I had to push homeward, for I was under careful surveillance, and was allowed no late wanderings.

Latimer directly identifies his experience with Rousseau, an allusion explored in Hugh Witemeyer's 1979 article on "George Eliot and Jean-Jacques Rousseau." But at least two other echoes are present. In another tale exploring gender and creativity, Victor Frankenstein floats in his boat on Lake Geneva, trying to find comfort in the peace of nature (an allusion Gilbert and Gubar miss, although they do connect the *Veil* with *Frankenstein*). More to our present point, Latimer's experience also recalls the famous row-boat passage in Wordsworth's *Prelude*; the lake surrounded with mountains, the movement from initial delight and liveliness to deathly sadness (though here rendered in more anthropomorphic terms) the sense of being watched and of being out of bounds all resonate with the boy-Wordsworth's account.

Notice, moreover, the date of Latimer's death, a date named in the second paragraph of the novella and repeated in its last paragraph: "the 20th of September 1850". Although the day and month seem random (the "20th" only mildly pointing to a possible "23rd"), the year is momentous—it is the year of Wordsworth's death, and of the publication of his master-work on the development of a poet's mind. Without context, one might dismiss this as an arbitrary choice. But this apparently slight link between Wordsworth and Latimer takes on substance in the context of the latter's obviously acceptance of Wordsworthian poetics and the failure of his attempt to practice them.

For Latimer, in fact, remembering almost never resurrects past experiences or enables the renovation of human feeling and community, but instead obscures original perceptions and deadens feeling. The one exception is his memory of his mother and her love, an exception which may, by its very isolation, further substantiate Gilbert and Gubar's identification of Latimer and Eliot. At every other point the narrative's overt insistence falls on the inefficacy of memory. When Latimer gains the power of clairvoyance, he describes the horrors of seeing in other people's minds "all the struggling chaos of puerilities, meanness, vague, capricious memories and indolent makeshift thoughts, from which human words and deeds emerge like leaflets covering a fermenting heap.'' Again, as Latimer strives to see what Bertha has been hiding in her cabinet (it is the poison with which she plans to kill him), he finds that memory obscures rather than preserves her experiences: ''[t]he recollections of the past become contracted in the rapidity of thought till they sometimes bear hardly a more distinct resemblance to the external reality than the forms of an oriental alphabet to the objects that suggested them.'' Not only does his insight reveal that memory, far from transforming present experience or preserving the past, drains the substance from what is remembered, but the terms of both metaphors suggest that verbal or written expressions based on recollection function either to obscure the truth, as in the deceptive leaflets covering the chaos of human minds, or to render them unintelligible, as in the translation of ''reality'' into an ''Oriental alphabet''—actually a system of characters, completely illegible to Westerners used to an alphabet.

Nor can his visions of the future grant power by means of his recollection of them. As Latimer relates his fascination with Bertha despite his knowledge of their future, he asks us to imagine ''this double consciousness at work within me, flowing on like two parallel streams which never mingle their waters and blend into a common hue'': ''my visions, when once they had passed into memory, were mere ideas—pale shadows that beckoned in vain, while my hand was grasped by the living and the loved.'' In every case, memory, this commonly human, canonically approved source of consciousness, knowledge and community functions to desubstantiate, to deaden, so that the veil of the past, too, remains unlifted.

A particularly telling case of the failure of memory appears in Latimer's recounting of his first vision, in which he sees Prague as a city

> unrefreshed for ages by the dews of night, or the rushing rain-clouds; scorching the dusty, weary, time-eaten grandeur of a people doomed to live on in the stale repetition of memories . . . urged by no fear or hope, but compelled by their doom to be ever old and undying, to live on in the rigidity of habit, as they live on in perpetual mid-day, without the repose of night or the new birth of morning.

In part, no doubt, it is Latimer's pessimism that darkens this vision. But the agent which he perceives as the deadening force here is ''the stale repetition of memories,'' the dead hand of a past that, in the process of recollection into the present, stifles new life.

Immediately after this, hoping that his vision is ''a picture that my newly liberated genius had painted in fiery haste, with the colors snatched from lazy memory,'' Latimer tries to perform an act of Wordsworthian recollection: ''I stimulated my imagination with poetic memories, and strove to feel myself present in Venice, as I had felt myself present in Prague.'' But this is a complete failure: Latimer can only recall, uncertainly, old engravings on his walls at home: ''It was all prosaic effort, not rapt passivity.'' He continues to perform this experiment for some time, always watching and hoping for the flowering of his poetic gifts under the stimulus of deliberate recollection, and always disappointed.

These overt narrative assertions of the failure of memory appear in a prose version of a poetic form designed to celebrate the power of recollection. The entirely first-person point-of-view, a most uncharacteristic choice for Eliot, has a plot-based explanation: Latimer has never before communicated his crucial experiences of prescience and clairvoyance to anyone, and so only he can tell his story and verify the truth of his visions. Formally, however, Eliot's choice follows the formula of the greater Romantic lyric, the speaker moved by a particular vision to recollection and expression. Latimer's narrative [is just] such a circular memoir, told in his own voice to the silent auditor, his readers, beginning with the vision of his death and ending with the death itself.

Classically, the scene the narrator of a greater Romantic lyric contemplates at the beginning and end of his story should be ''a localized, outdoor setting,'' so that the impressions of natural forms give rise to recollection. In this *The Lifted Veil* appears to deviate from our expectations. But I would argue that Latimer does contemplate a ''landscape'' here, the landscape of the mind. To think in such terms is, after all, most Wordsworthian: the whole point of contemplating a natural scene is not to explore that scene (although that is an analogous process to what follows) but to explore the landscape as it is remembered, the landscape in the mind and the ''landscape'' of the mind. In ''Tintern Abbey,'' for instance, the outdoor scene appears only briefly at the beginning of the poem, with the narrator then turning to descriptions of his own feelings as they are elicited by the landscape remembered, thus entering into a wholly psychological process. Latimer's account moves directly to that interior scene which is the primary concern of the greater Romantic lyric.

That Eliot's narrator thought in these terms, conceiving of mind as landscape, is signaled by his comments on the moment when Bertha's hatred and shallowness are revealed to him:

> I saw myself in Bertha's thought as she lifted her cutting grey eyes, and looked at me: a miserable ghost-seer, surrounded by phantoms in the noon-day, trembling under a breeze when the leaves were still, without appetite for the common objects of human desire, but pining after the moonbeams . . . The terrible moment of complete illumination had come to me, and I saw that the darkness had hidden no landscape from me, but only a blank prosaic wall: from that evening forth, through the sickening years which followed, I saw all round the narrow room of this woman's soul . . .

Not only does Bertha envision Latimer as a figure in a landscape, imagining his deficient psychology in terms of natural forms, but Latimer figures his expectation of Bertha's mind as an exterior, natural landscape, full and poetic and offering continued opportunities for exploration, only to discover a narrow interior scene bounded by "blank prosaic walls." With the mind or character understood as landscape, then, only two things are missing from this greater Romantic lyric: its "altered mood and deepened understanding," the quickening of moral sense in narrator and (by implication) reader, and the achievement of the poetry (as opposed to prose) which might bring this about. Although the form is fulfilled, the expectations set up, there is no transformation, no learning or shift, no renewal of the individual or of human community, and there is no elevation from the common understandings of prose into the sympathetic feeling of poetry. Despite memory, despite the representation of the past, all remains as Latimer first envisions it, bounded absolutely by the death of the individual consciousness.

There are many reasons for the increasing distrust of memory as an artistic and spiritual source in the Victorian period, most importantly the increasingly obvious permanence of the loss of agrarian life and values to industrialization, and that never lifting, always accelerating sensation of inevitable change. To look back in one's search for stable values becomes irrelevant, as the past itself becomes a series of changes. But for George Eliot, in particular, the search for value and verification in memory is dreadfully problematic. When a woman writer seeks her grounding in tradition, where will she find it? The influence of the Brontes and Mary Shelley, as Gilbert and Gubar demonstrate, is palpable. But when Eliot consciously thinks about her

antecedents, she must of necessity think mostly of men—of Shakespeare, of Milton, of Goethe, and most of all, of Wordsworth. One remembers her continual rereading of Wordsworth, and her comment to John Blackwood that she wonders that anyone other than herself will be interested to read *Silas Marner* "since William Wordsworth is dead". At this crucial moment, in the midst of writing her second novel and faced with increasing demands for the public revelation of her identity, Eliot must have felt the extreme pressure of Wordsworth's valorization of the past—which now included the traditions of his own writing—and needed a means by which to question its demands, even if she finally chose to accept them. I suggest, then, that *The Lifted Veil* not only investigates the common conflict between artist and woman, but confronts Wordsworth, Eliot's own master voice, and denies the fundamental premise of his power.

Source: Anne D. Wallace, "'Vague Capricious Memories': 'The Lifted Veil''s Challenge to Wordsworthian Poetics," in *George Eliot—George Henry Lewes Studies*, Vol. 18–19, September, 1991, pp. 31–45.

Marcia M. Taylor

In the following essay, Taylor re-evaluates Bertha Grant as the product of Latimer's creative interpretation of her as woman as subject."

In the conclusion of George Eliot's novella, *The Lifted Veil*, Bertha Grant's maid, Archer, is brought back to life momentarily by a blood transfusion. This revivication, brief as it is, is long enough for Archer to reveal in her second death-bed scene, that Bertha has plans to "poison" her husband. Archer's eyes meet Bertha's in "the recognition of hate" and she says in a gasping voice, ". . . the poison is in the black cabinet . . . I got it for you. . . ." Of the witnesses to the "poison" plot: Dr. Meunier is sworn to secrecy; Bertha is mute, forever silenced by Latimer's narrative; Archer is dead, presumedly for the last time. Latimer, the speaking subject, narrates the entire story from his first clairvoyant vision of a young woman he will later learn is Bertha, to his last scrawled words as he awaits his own foreseen death.

Criticism of *The Lifted Veil* in the past three decades has given primacy to the text's position within Eliot's canon, to her exploration of narrative structure, and according to individual analytic agenda, to the possibilities of conflicting ideology in the tale's extended metaphors.

> "It is my contention that it is Latimer who is incapable of love. Bertha remains at least partially an unknown, but she is capable of affection and sensuality."

Regardless of theoretic approach, when Bertha is mentioned at all, she holds the distinction of having more chilling adjectives affixed to her name than any other female character in fiction who comes to mind (with the possible exception of Lady Audley). For example: "evil," "wicked," "vampire-like," "sinister." Of course all of these quotes are used out of their context for my own purposes.

What is curious is that while critical evaluations of *The Lifted Veil* seek to find meaning hidden behind Eliot's multi-layered veil, Bertha Grant is most often given an analytic reading based on Latimer's creation of her. As narrator it is his story. But, also as narrator, he is empowered; Latimer and the critical enterprise surrounding the tale have glossed (or omitted) Bertha Grant. Charles Swann's compelling article, "Deja Vu: Deja Lu: 'The Lifted Veil' As An Experiment In Art," points to the story's "rather sideways look at some of the problems raised by determinism," but, more importantly, to Eliot's extended and often uncomfortable confrontation with her consciousness of what it means to be an author. Swann notes that Eliot experiments with the reader's expectations of narrative form and "challenges two of her dearest values: sympathy and memory as the bases of moral action." To do this, according to Swann, she creates an obvious fiction, and turns narrative form and Latimer's means of "Knowing" up-side-down, both reversing and questioning conventional modes of transmission.

In addition, Latimer's personal failures which he interprets and inscribes, such as his physical weaknesses, and his inability to voice his poetic impulses, are analogous to his failure to discern the larger issues, such as his lack of sympathetic feelings for human beings. This failure of insight (in the intuitive sense) into self and other also isolates him

from his own text. Bertha Grant is his fantasy: a fiction which he creates, reads and inscribes. Seen from this perspective, Latimer's creation of Bertha Grant as an evil enchantress invites a re-reading of his possible mis-reading.

The lengthiest and most thorough critical appraisal of Bertha Grant appears in Sandra Gilbert and Susan Gubar's *The Madwoman in the Attic*. This reading places Eliot in the role of a Miltonic "dutiful daughter," Bertha, a "Satanic Eve," and the poison in the cabinet a metaphor for the complicity of women, "offering the apple of death to their man". Whether the "poison in the cabinet" metaphor is interpreted as a complicitous and lethal injection of hemlock into the apple, as Gilbert and Gubar posit, or, in an anti-Edenic version, simply as Bertha's contempt for Latimer locked and seething within the "cabinet" of her body and mind, becomes immaterial seen in the light of subsequent event which Eliot dictates. What critical appraisals of Bertha Grant have appeared to overlook is that nothing happens. Bertha never actively unlocks the cabinet, either literally or metaphorically, although she has ample opportunity to do so. A vague span or suspension of time is indicated in Latimer's narrative between his notation of the "locking up of something in Bertha's cabinet" and the letter from Dr. Charles Meunier which announces that he will visit. If Bertha's release or activation of the "poison" is to be an actual event, this interim before Meunier arrives provides the temporal space in which to act. The "poison" in any sense, remains in suspension, deferred; a desire which may play the role of intent through the action of possessing and "locking," but remains unclear and lacks momentum.

My purpose is not to refute Gilbert and Gubar's reading, but to inject new blood into their resolution of Bertha as "fallen" in perpetuity: "doomed to live on in stale repetition." In short, I will attempt to give Bertha a transfusion that allows her the possibility of revivication, but without the necessity of re-creating her into a paragon. 'Granted,' both pernicious hatred or intent to "poison" are corruptive. Neither would function to justify valorizing Bertha. But, the weight that the "poison" metaphor carries with it has served to obscure other readings of Bertha which are counterpoint to Latimer's creation and narration of her. The severity of the charges which Archer makes against Bertha, in concert with what Latimer tells us about her all along, secure his reading and his control over her. Latimer's text has become yet another veil.

Entries into Latimer's creation and textualization of Bertha are numerous. Bertha's "birth" into Latimer's text as a "spectre of Romantic myth" and his consistent objectification of her as seen in the concluding passages of the story will serve. In addition, Eliot's provisions for Bertha, the fiction within the fiction, are of interest.

As Latimer's story begins by telling the reader how it will end, I will also begin (in the middle of this essay) with the end, and circle back to the beginning. At Archer's first deathbed scene, when Latimer tells us that Bertha wants Archer to die, without "lifting the veil" which would reveal the "secret," he appraises Bertha's appearance and attire. She was:

> fit to figure in a picture of modern aristocratic life: but I asked myself how that face of hers could ever have seemed to me the face of a woman born of woman, with memories of childhood, capable of pain, needing to be fondled?

Latimer's question is rhetorical; it may be seen as Eliot's ultimate irony and a transparent example of Latimer's inability to comprehend himself, Bertha or his text. Just as Latimer continues to objectify Bertha, this time into a picture, (and not even that; she is "fit to figure" in a picture) his authorship of her never allows her human birth, but creates an enchantress from his own fantasy. Bertha is never allowed a childhood or memories of it; if she suffers pain, Latimer silences it efficiently throughout his text; her touch is never returned, her sensuality never answered. What Latimer claims is his passion for her is "locked" within his own "cabinet" and replaced by his fear of her as subject.

At the onset of Latimer's first illusory experience, a vision of an unrefreshed dry city of Prague, doomed to repetition, he is recovering from a serious illness. When he "sees Bertha for the first time, in his second visionary episode, he has been looking from the window of a hotel suite in Geneva at "the current of the Rhone just where it leaves the dark-blue lake." What Latimer "sees" is a face without:

> a girlish expression ... the features were sharp, the pale grey eyes at once acute, restless, and sarcastic. They were fixed on me in half-smiling curiosity, and I felt a painful sensation as if a sharp wind were cutting me.

Bertha's gaze confronts Latimer directly, and he reads into her eyes both her subjectivity and her appraisal of him. The sharp wind that he feels cutting him, his terror of the other who demands subjectivity, demands his denial or figurative killing of the subject. It begins with his first illusion of Bertha.

Latimer's description of Bertha continues. Her image, he says,

> made me think of a Water-Nixie—for my mind was full of German lyrics, and this pale, fatal-eyed woman, with the green weeds, looked like a birth from some cold sedgy stream, the daughter of an aged river.

Bertha is not born from woman, but emerges from a cold stream, the daughter of an aged river. Carroll Viera and Jennifer Uglow, among others, have commented on the mythological, watery spirit of Bertha. Uglow writes that Bertha "represents the opposite of his loving, life-giving mother," but Bertha's watery entry "is one which contains the promise of death, not birth". At the same time Bertha may also represent an opposition to Latimer's first vision of the scorched and thirsty Prague with its people "doomed" to live on in a "stale repetition of memories." Latimer's earlier associations with watery images comprise his most pleasant memories. These textual recollections are immediately followed by his re-creation of his first illusion of Prague, "unrefreshed ... by ... the rushing rain-cloud. ..."

Gillian Beer in a footnote to her article, "Myth and the Single Consciousness: *Middlemarch* and "The Lifted Veil," attributes elements in both Bertha and Rosamond Vincy Lydgate to Friedrich de la Motte Fouque's *Undine*, published in 1811. This tale is of a beautiful and willful water sprite who marries a mortal in order to find love and gain a soul. The two women who vie for Huldbrand are Undine, the water sprite, and the selfish, spiteful Bertalda. What is problematic is that Undine, the water sprite, does gain a soul through her marriage to Huldbrand, and it is she who is the nurturing, life-giving woman. Mistreated and forsaken in favor of the scheming Bertalda, the water gods consign Undine back to the deeps, but she returns and is reconciled with her husband. Huldbrand, the waverer, recognizes his love for Undine, and drowns, as he knows he will, in her tears. If Latimer's head is full of German Water-Nixies as he looks from his window onto the Rhone, and if, as Beer states, *Undine* is a possible source, then Latimer from the beginning synthesizes the two fictional women, Undine and Bertalda, and creates a third fiction, Bertha Grant—in the image of the water sprite, Undine, but with the depraved soul of the calculating Bertalda.

As Gilbert and Gubar point out, Bertha has no voice. Neither does she have a history. Latimer reports that she is an orphan, adopted by her uncle and aunt, and that the uncle "means to provide for her ... as if she were his own daughter." This is Bertha Grant's personal history in its entirety. Nothing is ever told of her beginnings, her family, her memories. How can she, unlike Prague, be doomed to live in repetition of a past which doesn't exist? When Latimer asks how her face could have seemed to him the face of a woman with memories of childhood, the only possible response is that it never did.

As Eliot intended, a good case may be built for reading Latimer with sympathy. The second son of a capitalist, he has been raised without expectations as a physical weak and feminized "other." Though he blames his misfortune on seeing the evil within men's hearts, his foresight does not foster a raised consciousness which might allow him to see that he himself instigates his alienation from other people. He cannot penetrate Bertha's mind. He says that this mystery is the reason that drives his passion. U. C. Knoepflmacher states that "he has willfully deluded himself by loving a creature incapable of love," and that George Eliot implies that while Latimer's contempt for his fellow beings is excessive, "she also makes it clear that it is warranted by his unusual predicament."

It is my contention that it is Latimer who is incapable of love. Bertha remains at least partially an unknown, but she is capable of affection and sensuality. Early in the story on two occasions when they are alone, Bertha initiates physical contact, first by her arm slipped through his and then by grasping his wrist. Both times Latimer escapes by going into a trance. He gives her an opal ring and chides her for not wearing it. She draws a gold chain from her bosom. The ring hands upon it. She says, "it hurts me a little, I can tell you ... to wear it in that secret place...." Latimer can only blush like the opal and he can't ask her to keep it where it was.

Their marriage takes place "on a cold and clear morning in April, when there came hail and sunshine both together...." Latimer admittedly hurries through the rest of his story, "leaving ... feelings and sentiments to be inferred." Their life is a round of social engagements, a whirl which leaves their "solitary moments with hastily snatched caresses." Latimer is less reticent about the growth of his own wretchedness, despair, and passivity and Bertha's escalating coldness. What can be "in-

ferred" is that their marriage has sealed a bond of physical and mental alienation. Latimer can now "see" into her soul, and he sees "repulsion and antipathy harden into cruel hatred." The hostility which he had envisioned between them has become reality. Latimer continues to objectify her, and he tells the reader more than he himself knows. He says, "For Bertha too, after her kind, felt the bitterness of disillusion." He attributes her disillusionment to her failure to achieve mastery over him, and he claims that she had had mastery before their marriage because she was a secret to him, mastering his imagination.

Whose passions consume whose? Is Bertha a Water-Nixie seeking her soul through love? Is she a siren/enchantress, created evil without reprieve? What Latimer's text says is that she is curious and acute, aggressive and confrontational, affectionate and sensual. She is capable of selfishness, anger and hostility, of "hail and sunshine both together." She is, in Victorian terms, everything which is evil. She is woman as subject.

At the conclusion of my injection, I offer a textual citation which follows Archer's death-bed revelation.

> Since then Bertha and I have lived apart—she in her own neighborhood, the mistress of half our wealth, I as a wanderer in foreign countries, until I came to this Devonshire nest to die. Bertha lives pitied and admired; for what had I against that charming woman, whom every one but myself could have been happy with?

However we choose to read Bertha as metaphor: as evil; as a product of Latimer's created fiction; as a stand-in for Eliot's created fiction; subjectively as woman; or as all, with or without irony, George Eliot, who had experience in being self-created, jointly created, and as creator, leaves Bertha Grant admired by friends in her own neighborhood, wealthy, and free.

Source: Marcia M. Taylor, "Born Again: Reviving Bertha Grant," in *George Eliot—George Henry Lewes Studies*, Vol. 18-19, September, 1991, pp. 46-54.

Mary Carroll

In the following essay, Carroll describes the important character of Latimer as a masochist attempting to change by going "into the sadism" that dominates him.

> *Give me no light, great Heaven, but such as turns To energy of human fellowship; No powers beyond the growing heritage That makes completer manhood.*

Through her altruistic epigraph to a painful story, George Eliot suggests that the journey to greater human fellowship often requires a passage through suffering. In *The Lifted Veil*, Eliot explores the form of pain that shackles sado-masochistic relationships, and the roots of that pain—buried in the misperception that punishment is deserved. This paper will explore Latimer's attempt to change by moving through his masochistic stance into the sadism which has bound him.

The masochistic need for the sadist is captured by Eliot when she has Latimer moan:

> While the heart beats, bruise it— it is your only opportunity; while the eye can still turn towards you with moist timid entreaty, freeze it with an icy unanswering gaze; while the ear, that delicate messenger to the inmost sanctuary of the soul, can still take in the tones of kindness, put it off with hard civility, or sneering compliment . . .

Although Latimer's lament rings with self-pity, it also illustrates the tightness of the trap. Latimer's response at the onset of his heart attack represents a last resistance to change:

> I make great effort, and snatch at the bell again. I long for life, and there is no help. I thirsted for the unknown: the thirst is gone. O God, let me stay with the known, and be weary of it: I am content.

Latimer's cry for help is understandable, but surges through entrenched psychological or social structures usually have to be finalized in solitude. The courage to engage in the solitary completion of the journey arises from earlier accomplishments and future promises.

Eliot presents a bleak picture of Latimer's early experiences and his response to them. As a result of his eye complaint, his mother kept him "on her knee from morning to night." It is doubtful that an eye complaint would require such a symbiotic hold, but assertable that it would have a crippling effect on a child's growth. And it is in the crippling of the drive toward self-sufficiency that sadism finds its ready target. Bereft of his mother's knee and left with a father described as: "one of those people who are always like themselves from day to day, who are uninfluenced by the weather, and neither know melancholy nor high spirits" Latimer is helplessly alone.

Latimer's development is also blocked vocationally: "hungry for human deeds and human emotions," he is forced to study mechanical science. The murderous impulses emanating from such an environment and their self-destructive acceptance by the victim is captured by Eliot when she has

> " Death lies under the veil. The spiritual death of sado-masochistic relationships, and the death of the old that must be faced in change."

Latimer say: "my nature was of the sensitive, unpractical order, and . . . it grew up in an uncongenial medium which could never foster it into happy healthy development."

Away from the oppression of his home environment, Latimer forms a friendship with the orphan science student, Meunier. It is a friendship that arises from mutual isolation and develops into a spansion of poetry and science. Strengthened by his friendship with Meunier, Latimer falls ill:

> This happier life at Geneva was put an end to by a severe illness, which is partly a blank to me, partly a time of dimly-remembered suffering, with the presence of my father by my bed from time to time.

Latimer's prevision of Prague, as he recovers from his illness, may be taken as a metaphor for his life: "a city under the broad sunshine, that seemed to me as if it were the summer sunshine of a long-past century arrested in its course . . ." He emerges from the dream full of creative energy having focused on the rainbow light rather than the bleakness of the scene and recognizing that he has changed: "Was it that my illness had wrought some happy change in my organization—given a firm tension to my nerves—carried off some dull obstruction?"

Latimer has glimpsed a way out of his masochistic helplessness, but in order to turn his life around, he will have to understand his past from all sides. He will have to go into the sadism, if he is to leave his masochism. Latimer's journey begins with his response to his prevision of Bertha Grant: "I felt a painful sensation as if a sharp wind were cutting me." Upon meeting Bertha he faints at the prospect of the task ahead of him, but he continues.

Eliot gives Latimer clairvoyant abilities in order to demonstrate his mesmeric attraction to Bertha, and to show in conscious form the unconscious bond of sado-masochistic relationships. Latimer focuses on the negative as he enters the minds of others, and his pain increases as he proceeds from acquaintances to family members. He is blocked, however, from entering the mind of the woman he will marry. Externally, he perceives Bertha as:

> . . . keen, sarcastic, unimaginative, prematurely cynical, remaining critical and unmoved in the most impressive scenes, inclined to dissect all my favourite poems, and especially contemptuous towards the German lyrics which were my pet literature at that time.

Yet he describes each day in her presence as "delicious torment," thus capturing the sexual energy that swirls through sadism and binds the masochist. Eliot recognizes the nature of control in such relationships when she has Latimer state: "there is no tyranny more complete than that which a self-centred negative nature exercises over a morbidly sensitive nature perpetually craving sympathy and support."

Latimer's conscious perception of his bind clears as he views the painting of Lucrezia Borgia: "I felt a strange poisoned sensation, as if I had long been inhaling a fatal odour, and was just beginning to be conscious of the effects." He marries Bertha stating that: "The fear of poison is feeble against the sense of thirst."

The marriage follows a surge toward maturity. Prior to Alfred's death, Latimer had realized "my selfishness was even stronger than his—it was only a suffering selfishness instead of an enjoying one." And he is able to empathize with his father's feelings of loss at the death of Alfred.

Strengthened by his maturity, Latimer lifts the veil and penetrates Bertha's mind after the death of his father. His knowledge renders Bertha helpless, and Latimer grows increasingly sadistic toward her. He is not, however, able to leave the relationship:

> Towards my own destiny I had become entirely passive; for my one ardent desire had spent itself, and impulse no longer predominated over knowledge. For this reason I never thought of taking any steps towards a complete separation, which would have made our alienation evident to the world.

A public proclamation means there is no turning back, but it cannot be made until the essence of the tie is penetrated.

Bertha hopes Latimer will commit suicide, but that is not in his nature even though he is preoccupied with thoughts of his own death. As Latimer withdraws, Bertha shifts her focus to Mrs. Archer, a servant whose name implies a masochistic orientation. Latimer also obtains a new partner. Meunier,

the scientific man, arrives to visit Latimer, ends up caring for Mrs. Archer, and saving Latimer from Bertha's poison. Latimer penetrates Bertha's essence as she refuses to leave the sick room of her dying servant:

> The features at that moment seemed so preternaturally sharp, the eyes were so hard and eager—she looked like a cruel immortal, finding her spiritual feast in the agonies of a dying race. For across those hard features there came something like a flash when the last hour had been breathed out, and we all felt that the dark veil had completely fallen.

Death lies under the veil. The spiritual death of sado-masochistic relationships, and the death of the old that must be faced in change. The motivation of the sadist, unperceived by the masochist, is expressed by Mrs. Archer as she reveals Bertha's scheme:

> You meant to poison your husband . . . the poison is in the black cabinet . . . I got it for you . . . you laughed at me, and told lies about me behind my back, to make me disgusting . . . because you were jealous . . .

Eliot ends her story with Latimer and Bertha poles apart, but remaining as halves of a whole until Latimer dies of a heart attack.

A relationship between the blossoming of George Eliot's writing career and the story of *The Lifted Veil* has been clearly established chronologically, but dimly understood metaphorically. Perhaps an analogy can be drawn between Eliot's success with *Adam Bede* followed by her writing detour in *The Lifted Veil*, and Latimer's journey into pain after seeing the rainbow in Prague. The difference, however, lies in George Eliot's survival and triumph.

Source: Mary Carroll, "The Painful Challenge of George Eliot's Epigraph," in *The George Eliot Fellowship Review*, 1991, pp. 57–60.

Sources

Ashton, Rosemary. *George Eliot: A Life*, New York: Penguin Press, 1996, pp. 218-219.

Haight, Gordon S., ed. *Selections from George Eliot's Letters*, New Haven: Yale University Press, 1985, p. vii.

Haldane, Elizabeth Sanderson. *George Eliot and her Times: A Victorian Study*, New York: D. Appleton and Co., 1927, p. 5.

Karl, Frederick Robert. *George Eliot: Voice of a Century: A Biography*, New York: W. W. Norton, 1995, pp. 575, 643-644.

Taylor, Ina. *A Woman of Contradictions: The Life of George Eliot*, New York: William Morrow and Company, Inc., 1989, pp. 229-230.

Further Reading

Ashton, Rosemary. *George Eliot: A Life*, New York: Penguin Press, 1996.

A recent biography of Eliot which approaches her life through her personal psychology, her writing and the political, social and intellectual context of Victorian England. Each of her major works is examined in detail.

Beer, Patricia. *Reader, I Married Him: A Study of the Women Characters of Jane Austen, Charlotte Bronte, Elizabeth Gaskell, and George Eliot*, New York, Barnes and Noble, 1974.

Examines key female characters in the novels of prominent female writers of 19th Century England.

Dickerson, Vanessa D. *Victorian Ghosts in the Noontide: Women Writers and the Supernatural*, Columbia, Mo.: University of Missouri Press, 1996.

Examines Victorian Era fiction by women, such as Charlotte and Emily Bronte and George Eliot, which includes elements of the supernatural. Dickerson examines the relationship between the supernatural and issues of gender in the lives and work of these authors.

Haight, Gordon S., ed. *Selections from George Eliot's Letters*, New Haven: Yale University Press, 1985.

Haight has selected some of the most interesting excerpts from the thousands of Eliot's letters to create a single chronological narrative of her life and work. This selection includes the details of the writing and publication of her work.

Haldane, Elizabeth Sanderson. *George Eliot and her Times: A Victorian Study*, New York: D. Appleton and Co., 1927.

Haldane examines Eliot's ideas and writing in terms of larger intellectual and social trends in Victorian England. An intellectual history of the writer, which explains her life and work in its broader cultural and historical context.

Karl, Frederick Robert. *George Eliot: Voice of a Century: a Biography*, New York: W. W. Norton, 1995.

Karl examines Eliot's life and work in terms of her role as the "voice" of her century, the Victorian era. Eliot expressed the sentiments of a Victorian England undergoing many historical changes and cultural conflicts.

The Magic Barrel

Bernard Malamud

1954

Bernard Malamud's short story, "The Magic Barrel," was first published in the *Partisan Review* in 1954, and reprinted in 1958 in Malamud's first volume of short fiction. This tale of a rabbinical student's misadventures with a marriage broker was quite well received in the 1950s, and Malamud's collection of short stories, *The Magic Barrel*, won the National Book Award for fiction in 1959.

As Malamud attained a reputation as a respected novelist in the 1960s and 1970s, his short stories were widely anthologized and attracted considerable attention from literary students and scholars. A writer in the Jewish-American tradition, Malamud wrote stories that explore issues and themes central to the Jewish community. A love story with a surprising outcome, "The Magic Barrel" traces a young man's struggle to come to terms with his identity and poses the religious question of how people—Jews and others— may come to love God. Is human love, the story asks, a necessary first step to loving God? Malamud's "The Magic Barrel" is a story remarkable for its economy, using just a few strokes to create compelling and complex characters.

Author Biography

Bernard Malamud was born in Brooklyn, New York, in 1914 to Russian Jewish immigrants named

Max and Bertha Malamud. He later described his parents as "gentle, honest, kindly people." Max, the manager of a small grocery store, was the model for Morris Bober, the grocer protagonist of Malamud's second novel, *The Assistant* (1957). Malamud went to high school in Brooklyn and attended the City College of New York, graduating in 1936. In 1942 he received a Master of Arts degree from Columbia University.

Malamud did not begin writing seriously until after World War II, when the horrors of the Holocaust became known to the international community. The revelation seems to have made Malamud more actively aware of his own Jewish identity. "I was concerned with what Jews stood for," he recalled, "with their getting down to the bare bones of things. I was concerned with . . . how Jews felt they had to live in order to go on living."

In 1945 Malamud married Ann de Chiara. To the Malamud family, traditional Jews, Bernard's marriage to a gentile woman seemed an unforgivable act. After the wedding Max Malamud went through the rituals of mourning for his son—an act reminiscent of Salzman's actions in "The Magic Barrel." Ann and Bernard moved to Oregon in 1949, after Bernard accepted a teaching position at Oregon State University. There, Malamud recalled, "I was allowed to teach freshman composition but not literature because I was nakedly without a Ph.D." It was at Oregon State that Malamud wrote "The Magic Barrel" in the basement of the university library.

In 1952 Malamud published his first novel, *The Natural*, a poignant treatment of the American hero as baseball player. His second novel, *The Assistant* (1957), is the heartbreaking account of an impoverished grocer and the Catholic drifter who comes to work for him. In 1961 Malamud and his family moved to Vermont, where he took a job teaching creative writing at Bennington College—a position in which he would continue for almost twenty-five years.

A highly respected teacher, Malamud was himself skeptical of creative writing courses: "In essence, one doesn't teach writing; he encourages talented people whom he may be able to do something for. I feel that writing courses are of limited value although they do induce some students to read fiction with care." Malamud won the Pulitzer prize in fiction for his 1966 novel, *The Fixer*, and the American Library Association's Notable Book citation for *Dubin's Lives* in 1979. Malamud continued

actively to teach and write almost until his death in 1986.

Plot Summary

Part I

Leo Finkle has spent the last six years studying to become a rabbi at New York City's Yeshivah University. After hearing that he would have better job prospects if he were to get married, Leo decides to consult a matchmaker. Matchmakers, also called marriage brokers, were common in many European Jewish cultures, as well as in some Jewish immigrant communities in the United States. Leo's own parents were brought together by a marriage broker, and Leo is determined to find his bride through the same tradition. He contacts Pinye Salzman, a marriage broker who has advertised in *The Jewish Daily Forward*, New York's leading Yiddish newspaper. (Written in Hebrew characters and based on the vocabulary and syntax of medieval German, the Yiddish language was spoken by many European Jews and their American immigrant descendants.)

Salzman arrives at Finkle's apartment one day late in February and the two set about their task:

> Leo had led Salzman to the only clear place in the room, a table near a window that overlooked the lamp-lit city. He seated himself at the matchmaker's side but facing him, attempting by an act of will to suppress the unpleasant tickle in his throat. Salzman eagerly unstrapped his portfolio and removed a loose rubber band from a thin packet of much-handled cards. As he flipped through them, a gesture and sound that physically hurt Leo, the student pretended not to see and gazed steadfastly out the window. Although it was still February, winter was on its last legs, signs of which he had for the first time in years begun to notice. He now observed the round white moon, moving high in the sky through a cloud menagerie, and watched with half-open mouth as it penetrated a huge den, and dropped out of her like an egg laying itself. Salzman, though pretending through eyeglasses he had just slipped on, to be engaged in scanning the writing on the cards, stole occasional glances at the young man's distinguished face, noting with pleasure the long, severe scholar's nose, brown eyes heavy with learning, sensitive yet ascetic lips, and a certain, almost hollow quality to the dark cheeks. He gazed around at the shelves of books and let out a soft, contented sigh.(Excerpt from "The Magic Barrel")

Salzman boasts to Finkle that he has so many clients that he has to keep their cards in a barrel at his office. He summarizes the attractions of three young women to Finkle, listing their age, appear-

Bernard Malamud

ance, dowry, and the financial assets of their respective fathers. Finkle becomes embarrassed by the overtly commercial nature of the conversation and, wondering what role love might play in an arranged marriage, asks Salzman to leave.

Leo spends the next day restless and unsettled, wondering if he should try another matchmaker or if he should find a wife on his own. That evening Salzman returns to Leo's apartment, asking if the student has reconsidered any of the three women he described. Salzman particularly recommends one Lily Hirschorn, an unmarried schoolteacher. Finkle pretends to be ambivalent about the idea, but is intrigued; Salzman leaves the apartment confident that Leo and Lily will meet.

Part II

The next Saturday Leo takes Lily for a walk. She turns out to be "not unpretty," is *au courant* (or up to date) on a variety of topics, and talks easily and intelligently. Leo has the uneasy feeling that Salzman is hiding somewhere nearby, watching them. He pictures the matchmaker as "cloven-hoofed Pan" (in Greco-Roman mythology Pan is the god of nature, depicted as half man and half goat) sprinkling flower buds in their path to celebrate their union. Lily presses Leo for details about

his calling as a rabbi, and Leo realizes that Salzman has represented him to Lily as a passionately religious man. In a moment of unguarded honesty, Leo confesses to Lily: "I think . . . I came to God not because I loved him, but because I did not." Lily is disappointed in his answer and the afternoon ends with the understanding that there will be no match.

Part III

Leo returns home in despair. The conversation with Lily has made him realize some disturbing things about himself, in particular that he lacks the ability to love. Leo's religious vocation seems meaningless because he has lived an empty life. How can he love God if he does not love man? He considers leaving the university, then decides to continue his studies, but to find a wife to love on his own terms. When Salzman arrives the next day, Leo criticizes the matchmaker for having misrepresented the situation to Lily, and tells him that he will no longer require his services. Salzman departs, but leaves an envelope containing photographs of other women for Leo to consider.

After a few weeks, Leo opens the envelope. Inside are six photographs of women who are "past their prime." Disappointed, he returns the photographs to the envelope; at the last moment, a seventh photograph falls out. Leo looks at it a moment, then lets out a cry of love. The face in the photograph is beautiful, melancholy, and carries "an impression, somehow, of evil." Leo falls desperately in love with the image in the picture. He finds Salzman and presses him for the woman's name. Salzman hesitates, claiming that the picture was included in the envelope by accident, then bursts out: "This is my baby, my Stella, she should burn in hell." Salzman's daughter Stella, it is implied, has committed some terrible act of disobedience against her father and Jewish tradition. As punishment, she has been disowned.

Part IV

Leo cannot stop thinking of Stella. Finally, he resolves to find her and to "convert her to goodness, himself to God." He encounters Salzman in a Broadway cafeteria and insists that Salzman set up a meeting. Salzman agrees, and Leo suspects that Salzman had planned for him to fall in love with Stella from the beginning.

Part V

Shortly after, Leo finally meets Stella on a spring night. She stands smoking beneath a streetlight and he runs to her with a bouquet of flowers. We are then told that: ''Around the corner Salzman, leaning against a wall, chanted prayers for the dead.'' In Jewish tradition, a parent will say the *Kaddish*, or the prayer for the dead, for a living child only when that child has committed a sin of disobedience so grave as to cause a final separation from the parent.

Characters

Leo Finkle

Leo Finkle has spent the last six years studying to become a rabbi at New York's Yeshivah University. Because he believes that he will have a better chance of getting employment with a congregation if he is married, Leo consults a professional matchmaker. Leo is a cold person; he comes to realize that ''he did not love God so well as he might, because he had not loved man.'' When Finkle falls in love with Salzman's daughter, Stella, the rabbinical student must confront his own emotional failings.

Lily Hirschorn

Lily Hirschorn is introduced to Leo Finkle, the rabbinical student, by Pinye Salzman, the matchmaker. She is a schoolteacher, comes from a good family, converses on many topics, and Leo considers her ''not unpretty.'' It soon becomes clear, however, that the match between them will not work.

Pinye Salzman

Leo consults Pinye Salzman, who is a professional matchmaker. Salzman is an elderly man who lives in great poverty. He is unkempt in appearance and smells of fish. While Salzman works to bring couples together, Leo has reason to believe that the matchmaker, or ''commercial cupid,'' is occasionally dishonest about the age and financial status of his clients. Salzman seems greatly dismayed when Leo falls in love with Stella. Yet Leo begins to suspect that Pinye, whom he thinks of as a ''trickster,'' had ''planned it all to happen this way.''

Stella Salzman

Stella Salzman is the daughter of Pinye Salzman, the matchmaker. Salzman has disowned his daughter, evidently because she has committed some

grave act of disobedience. When Leo, who has fallen in love with Stella, asks her father where he might find her, the matchmaker replies: ''She is a wild one—wild, without shame. This is not a bride for a rabbi.'' When he finally meets Stella she is smoking, leaning against a lamp post in the classic stance of the prostitute, but Leo believes he sees in her eyes ''a desperate innocence.''

Leo consults Pinye Salzman, who is a professional matchmaker. Salzman is an elderly man who lives in great poverty. He is unkempt in appearance and smells of fish. While Salzman works to bring couples together, Leo has reason to believe that the matchmaker, or ''commercial cupid,'' is occasionally dishonest about the age and financial status of his clients. Salzman seems greatly dismayed when Leo falls in love with Stella. Yet Leo begins to suspect that Pinye, whom he thinks of as a ''trickster,'' had ''planned it all to happen this way.''

Themes

Identity

Malamud's Leo Finkle is a character trying to figure out who he really is. Having spent the last six years of his life deep in study for ordination as a rabbi, he is an isolated and passionless man, disconnected from human emotion. When Lily Hirschorn asks him how he came to discover his calling as a rabbi, Leo responds with embarrassment: ''I am not a talented religious person. . . . I think . . . that I came to God, not because I loved him, but because I did not.'' In other words, Leo hopes that by becoming a rabbi he might learn to love himself and the people around him. Leo is in despair after his conversation with Lily because ''. . . he saw himself for the first time as he truly was—unloved and loveless.''

As he realizes the truth about himself, he becomes desperate to change. Leo determines to reform himself and renew his life. Leo continues to search for a bride, but without the matchmaker's help: ''. . . he regained his composure and some idea of purpose in life: to go on as planned. Although he was imperfect, the ideal was not.'' The ideal, in this case, is love. Leo comes to believe that through love—the love he feels when he first sees the photograph of Stella Salzman—he may begin his life anew, and forge an identity based on something more positive. When at last he meets Stella he

Topics for Further Study

- When did Jewish people settle in large numbers in New York City? Describe the Jewish communities in New York City or in another large American city. In what way can ''The Magic Barrel'' be read as a story about the descendants of immigrants?

- In chapter twenty of the Book of Exodus in the Bible, Moses sets forth the Ten Commandments to the Israelites. Do the characters in ''The Magic Barrel'' follow the Commandments? What does this say about them?

- What does the story suggest about the relation between love and self-knowledge? What must Leo Finkle learn about himself before he is truly able to love?

''pictured, in her, his own redemption.'' That redemption, the story's ending leads us to hope, will be Leo's discovery through Stella of an identity based on love.

God and Religion

Central to Malamud's ''The Magic Barrel'' is the idea that to love God, one must love man first. Finkle is uncomfortable with Lily's questions because they make him realize ''the true nature of his relationship to God.'' He comes to realize ''that he did not love God as well as he might, because he had not loved man.'' In spite of the zeal with which he has pursued his rabbinical studies, Leo's approach to God, as the narrative reveals, is one of cold, analytical formalism. Unable fully to love God's creatures, Leo Finkle cannot fully love God.

Once again, the agent of change in Leo's life seems to be Stella Salzman. The text strongly implies that by loving Stella, by believing in her, Leo will be able to come to God. Just before his meeting with Stella, Leo ''concluded to convert her to goodness, him to God.'' To love Stella, it seems, will be Leo's true ordination, his true rite of passage to the love of God.

Style

Point of View

Point of view is a term that describes who tells a story, or through whose eyes we see the events of a narrative. The point of view in Malamud's ''The Magic Barrel'' is third person limited. In the third person limited point of view, the narrator is not a character in the story, but someone outside of it who refers to the characters as ''he,'' ''she,'' and ''they.'' This outside narrator, however, is not omniscient, but is limited to the perceptions of one of the characters in the story. The narrator of the story views the events of the story through the eyes of Leo Finkle even though it is not Leo telling the story.

Symbolism

Symbolism is a literary device that uses an action, a person, a thing, or an image to stand for something else. In Malamud's ''The Magic Barrel'' the coming of spring plays an important symbolic role. The story begins in February, ''when winter was on its last legs,'' and ends ''one spring night'' as Leo approaches Stella Salzman under a street lamp. The story's progression from winter to spring is an effective symbol for the emotional rebirth that Leo undergoes as he struggles to grow as a human being.

Idiom

Idiom may be defined as a specialized vocabulary used by a particular group, or a manner of expression peculiar to a given people. In other words, different groups of people speak in different ways. While the narrator and most of the characters in ''The Magic Barrel'' speak standard English, Pinye Salzman, the matchmaker, speaks Yiddish. Written in Hebrew characters and based on the grammar of medieval German, Yiddish was the common language of many European Jewish communities. A Russian Jew at the turn of the century (Malamud's father, for example) might read the Torah in Hebrew, speak to his gentile neighbors in Russian, and conduct the affairs of his business and household in Yiddish.

Since World War II, Yiddish has become less prevalent in Europe and in the immigrant Jewish communities of North America. In another generation, it may totally die out. Many of Malamud's characters, however, still use the idiom. When Salzman asks Leo, ''A glass tea you got, rabbi?''; when he exclaims, ''what can I say to somebody that he is not interested in school teachers?''; and when he laments, ''This is my baby, my Stella, she should burn in hell,'' the reader hears an idiomatic version of English seasoned with the cadences of Yiddish speech.

Historical Context

Malamud's ''The Magic Barrel'' was first published by the *Partisan Review* in 1954 and reprinted as the title story in Malamud's first volume of short fiction in 1958. The period between those two dates was an eventful time in American history. In 1954 the United States Supreme Court unanimously rejected the concept of segregation in the case of *Brown v. Board of Education*, which found that the practice of maintaining separate classrooms or separate schools for black and white students was unconstitutional.

In the same year Senator Joseph McCarthy was censured by the Senate for having unjustly accused hundreds of Americans of being communists. In 1957 the Soviet Union launched Sputnik, the first satellite to successfully orbit the earth, sparking concern that the Soviets would take control of space.

While the text of ''The Magic Barrel'' is almost entirely free of topical or historical references that might allow readers to place the events of the story at a particular date, one detail establishes Leo's encounter with Salzman as taking place roughly at the time of the story's publication in the mid-fifties. Finkle is about to complete his six-year course of study to become a rabbi at New York City's Yeshivah University. *Yeshivah*, in Hebrew, means a place of study. Yeshivah University is the oldest and most distinguished Jewish institution of higher learning in the United States. While its history goes back to 1886, the school was not named Yeshivah until 1945, when its charter was revised. At the end of the traditional six years of study to become a rabbi, then, Leo would probably be considering marriage sometime early in the 1950s.

By consulting a professional matchmaker to find a bride, Leo is acting more like his immigrant grandparents than an American Jew of the 1950s. In Yiddish, the secular language of many European and American Jewish communities, the word for ''matchmaker'' is *shadchen* (pronounced shod-hun). Before the seventeenth century, the *shadchen* was a highly respected person, responsible for the perpetuation of the Jewish people through arranged marriages. As European Jewish communities grew larger and as modern secular notions of romantic love became pervasive, professional matchmakers became less scrupulous in their dealings and were frequently the objects of satire and derision. Indeed a wealth of humor at the expense of the *shadchen* developed during the nineteenth and twentieth centuries; representative is the remark of the Yiddish writer Sholom Aleichem (1859–1916), who quipped that the *shadchen* was best defined as ''a dealer in livestock.''

Regardless, the *shadchen* tradition survived Jewish immigration to the United States. In his history of Jewish immigrant life on New York City's lower east side, *World of our Fathers*, Irving Howe describes the typical *shadchen* as similar to Malamud's Pinye Salzman: ''Affecting an ecclesiastic bearing, the matchmaker wore a somber black suit with a half-frock effect, a silk *yarmulke* (skullcap), a full beard.'' The matchmaker, according to Howe, ''customarily received 5 percent of the dowry in addition to a flat fee, neither one nor both enough to make him rich.'' Pinye Salzman is in many ways, then, a stereotypical figure who has stepped from the world of Jewish oral humor into the pages of Malamud's story. Leo, in seeking the *shadchen's* help in the 1950s, reveals himself not only as a formal, but as a very old fashioned young man.

Critical Overview

When Malamud's ''The Magic Barrel'' first appeared in *Partisan Review* in 1954, it provided a colorful glimpse into the world of American Jews. Fours years later, after his second novel, *The Assistant*, had been enthusiastically received, Malamud reprinted ''The Magic Barrel'' as the title story in a collection of his short fiction. The collection sold well, and was praised by reviewers for its honesty, irony, and acute perception of the moral dilemmas of American Jews. It won the National Book Award for fiction in 1959.

Between the publication of the collection in 1958 and his death in 1986, Bernard Malamud became one of America's most respected writers of fiction, publishing six more novels and numerous collections of short fiction. Malamud's writing has been the subject of critical debate for three decades. Writing in 1966, Sidney Richman examines the

Compare & Contrast

- **1950s:** Decades of immigration from Eastern and Western Europe have led to a considerable Jewish population in the United States. Strong and vibrant Jewish communities thrive in many American cities. Yet discrimination against the Jewish people exists.

  1990s: Through intermarriage and assimilation, many people in the Jewish community believe that Jewish culture is endangered. Unfortunately, discrimination still exists in the United States, but many groups fight misinformation and discrimination against Jews.

- **1950s:** The Jewish matchmaker, also known as the "shadchen," performs a vital function within the community. Arranged marriage, although losing popularity among Jewish families, is still a viable option for young Jewish men and women of age.

  1990s: Matchmaking is considered an antiquated tradition. It is mainly used in orthodox Jewish communities, as other networking opportunities allow Jewish men and women to meet and find possible marriage partners.

---

emotional sterility of the protagonist Leo Finkle. According to Richman, ". . . Finkle knows the word but not the spirit; and he makes it clear that in a secret part of his heart he knows it."

Theodore C. Miller, in 1972, compares "The Magic Barrel" to Hawthorne's *The Scarlet Letter*, pointing out that both stories explore "the love of the minister and the whore." Unlike Hawthorne's minister, Arthur Dimmesdale, however, Malamud's rabbinical student, Finkle, "comes to accept Stella for the reason that he accepts universal guilt." Miller also contends that Salzman has arranged the love affair between Leo and Stella because he wishes "to initiate Leo Finkle into the existential nature of love." When at the end of the story Salzman says *Kaddish*, the traditional Jewish prayer for the dead, he is "commemorating the death of the old Leo who was incapable of love. But he is also celebrating Leo's birth into a new life."

Both Richard Reynolds and Bates Hoffer offer interpretations of "The Magic Barrel" based on specific Jewish religious traditions. Reynolds's focus is on the role of *Kaddish*, maintaining that Salzman hopes that Leo will bring Stella, "the prodigal daughter," back to a moral life. In that case, reciting the *Kaddish* is particularly appropriate given the ancient prayer's emphasis on resurrection. Hoffer compares the five-part structure of the story to the Torah (the first five books of the Old Testament, the sacred text of Judaism) and claims that Leo has broken a majority of the ten commandments.

Finally Carmen Cramer maintains that Leo's story is a journey of emotional maturity. Rather, "The Magic Barrel" chronicles the rabbinical student's "Americanization," his gradual assimilation into American culture. Cramer asserts that Finkle "possesses few of the typical American traits—decisiveness, emotionality, action-orientation—but he melts into the American pot by the end of Bernard Malamud's polished piece of writing. . . ."

Criticism

Benjamin Goluboff

Goluboff has taught English at Lake Forest College in Lake Forest, Illinois. In the following essay, he places the story within the context of Jewish fiction of the 1950s and focuses on the theme of inter-generational relations.

Publishing "The Magic Barrel" in 1954, Bernard Malamud was at the beginning of his career, and near the beginning of a brief and remarkable period in the history of Jewish-American writing. For

What Do I Read Next?

- *The Jews in America*, a work by Arthur Hertzberg, is an accessible and entertaining history of Jewish people in the United States from colonial times to the civil rights movement of the 1960s.

- Anzia Yezierska's *Bread Givers* is a powerful novel about a family of Russian immigrant Jews on New York's Lower East Side.

- *The Assistant* is Bernard Malamud's second novel. Frank Alpine, a drifter and dreamer, works in the corner grocery of Morris Bober, an impoverished and hard working Jew. Through his friendship with Morris and his daughter Helen, Frank learns about Jewish culture and religion.

- *The Stories of Bernard Malamud*, published in 1983 several years before the author's death, contains stories of great wit and frightening insight.

---

perhaps a decade, from the mid-1950s to the mid-1960s, the American literary imagination seemed to have been captured by a series of books by and about Jews. In 1953 Saul Bellow published *The Adventures of Augie March*, a story of tragicomic misadventures set in Chicago's Jewish immigrant milieu. In 1957 Malamud brought out his second novel, *The Assistant*, the tale of an impoverished Brooklyn grocer who becomes a kind of Jewish everyman. 1959 saw the literary debut of Philip Roth, whose *Goodbye, Columbus* was the account of a doomed love affair between two Jewish young people divided by social class.

Goodbye Columbus won the prestigious National Book Award for fiction in 1960, as Bellow's *Augie March* had done in 1954, and as Malamud's collection of short stories, *The Magic Barrel*, had in 1959. Equally distinguished Jewish-American writers—such as Norman Mailer, Joseph Heller, and Chaim Potok—attracted attention on the literary scene during these years as well.

The novelists who made their reputations during this time didn't always have Jewish concerns as the focus of their fiction. Still, for a decade or so, Malamud's fiction seemed to be part of a movement of the American novel toward the lives and problems of Jews. Of course, Jewish-American fiction was not invented in the 1950s; novels by and about American Jews comprised a tradition of some significance and depth by the time Malamud began

his career. In one important respect—in its theme of change and conflict between generations—Malamud's "The Magic Barrel" is solidly embedded in the tradition of Jewish-American fiction.

The first important Jewish-American novel was Mary Antin's *The Promised Land* of 1912. Born in Russian Poland, Antin immigrated to Boston as a child in 1894 and became a social worker in the immigrant neighborhoods of that city. *The Promised Land* is based on Antin's own immigrant experience, contrasting the poverty and persecution of Jewish life in Eastern Europe with the freedom and economic opportunity available to immigrants in the United States.

The vision of America is not so happy, however, in *The Rise of David Levinsky* by Abraham Cahan (1917). Cahan was a Russian immigrant who found success in America as an editor and journalist. (He edited the *The Jewish Daily Forward*, the Yiddish newspaper in which Leo Finkle reads Pinye Salzman's ad.) Like his creator, David Levinsky encounters an America where opportunity is purchased at great sacrifice. As David rises in New York's garment industry, his success costs him love and personal integrity. Most of all, David's success results in his betrayal of those Jewish spiritual traditions that had sustained his ancestors in Russia. David ends the novel as a representative of an immigrant generation that has lost the integrity of its ancestors.

> Consequently, Finkle's transformed character would suggest that, unlike their ancestors, the younger generation is open to passion, to change, and to new beginnings exempt from the influence of tradition."

The theme of change and conflict among generations appears powerfully in Anzia Yezierska's 1925 novel *Bread Givers*. Yezierska's novel dramatizes the conflict between Sara Smolinsky, a lively young Jewish woman, and her dictatorial father, a Russian immigrant Rabbi. Rabbi Smolinsky has devoted his life to study of the Torah, and insists that his daughters work to support him as he continues his studies in America. Sara dreams of receiving a secular American education and becoming a teacher, but to do so she must defy the will of her father: "More and more I began to see that father, in his innocent craziness to hold up the Light of the Law to his children, was a tyrant more terrible than the Tsar from Russia." Sara eventually realizes her dream, becoming a teacher in the New York Public Schools, but only at the price of breaking off her relationship with her father. When the two reconcile at the end of the novel, it is because Sara has come to recognize that the drive and will that allowed her to finish her education came from her father.

As Leo Finkle and Pinye Salzman pursue each other through the pages of Malamud's "The Magic Barrel," the theme of generational conflict presents itself with rich ambivalence. It's as clear from his profession—an arranger of marriages in the way traditional to nineteenth-century European Jewish communities—as it is from his Yiddish-inflected speech that Pinye Salzman is the story's representative of an older generation of immigrant Jews. Leo Finkle, born in Cleveland and bearing a gentile given name, as clearly embodies a younger population—perhaps those second- or third-generation American Jews who came to maturity in the 1950s. What's less clear, however, is with which of the two generations the story encourages us to empathize.

Who has moral authority in the story, old Salzman or young Finkle?

It is tempting to read the story as favoring youth, especially in light of the emotional transformation that Leo Finkle undergoes. Leo enters the story as a cold and passionless young man. He requires a bride not because he is in love, but because he is about to be ordained as a rabbi and believes that he will find a congregation more readily if he is married. Leo praises Salzman's profession with chilly formalism; the matchmaker, he says, makes "practical the necessary without hindering joy." After his date with Lily Hirschorn, Leo comes to recognize and deplore his own passionlessness. Prompted by the matchmaker, Lily had expected Finkle to be a man of great human and spiritual fervor. Leo disappoints her, of course, and sees "himself for the first time as he truly was—unloved and loveless."

In the aftermath of this revelation, Leo appears to change. He tells the matchmaker, "I now admit the necessity of premarital love. That is, I want to be in love with the one I marry." Salzman's reply to this declaration seems to identify the matchmaker with the older generation: "'Love?' said Salzman, astounded. After a moment he remarked, 'For us, our love is our life, not for the ladies. In the ghetto they—.'" (Finkle interrupts here with more about his new resolve to find love on his own.) In his fragmentary response Salzman seems to say that for the older generation—those who had lived in the Jewish ghettoes of Europe—romantic love was a frivolous luxury. Survival was what mattered ("our life"), not "the ladies." With that remark, Salzman appears to inhabit a past whose dangers are no longer real to any but himself.

Finkle's transformation is complete when he falls in love with the photograph of Salzman's daughter, Stella, left accidentally among pictures of the matchmaker's other clients. Loving this fallen woman, and loving her only on the basis of her photograph, is just the passionate leap of faith of which Leo has been previously incapable. His eyes now "weighted with wisdom," Leo has learned at last the redemptive nature of passion.

Old Salzman, however, is more inflexibly than ever rooted in tradition. He considers his daughter dead because of her mysterious sin, and even Finkle's newfound passion for her can't restore Stella to the living in her father's eyes. In the story's mysterious final section, Finkle rushes to Stella with a bouquet of flowers while: "Around the corner, Salzman, leaning against a wall, chanted prayers for the dead."

If we interpret Salzman's *Kaddish*—the traditional Jewish prayer for the dead—as being for his daughter, then as representative of the older generation Salzman is so committed to tradition that he sees only death where life had just begun. Consequently, Finkle's transformed character would suggest that, unlike their ancestors, the younger generation is open to passion, to change, and to new beginnings exempt from the influence of tradition.

One problem with this interpretation is that the story more than once suggests that Finkle's sudden passion for Stella might not have been an accident, that it might have been planned by the wily Salzman. Finkle suspects that the old man is capable of intrigue. As he walks with Lily Hirschorn, Finkle senses Salzman "to be somewhere around, hiding perhaps high in a tree along the street, flashing the lady signals with a pocket mirror. . . ." Just before the story's conclusion, when Salzman has finally agreed to let Finkle meet Stella, Leo is suddenly "afflicted by a tormenting suspicion that Salzman had planned it all to happen this way." If Leo's meeting with Stella is part of the matchmaker's plan, then we would have to attribute to him, and to the older generation he represents, a knowledge of human frailty and passion superior to that of the formalistic rabbinical student.

What, then, do we make of the Salzman's saying *Kaddish* at the story's conclusion? If his plan has been all along to educate Leo in the necessity of passion, then it would be inconsistent with that plan for Salzman to mourn just when he has succeeded in bringing the lovers together. Critic Theodore C. Miller has suggested a persuasive way out of this dilemma: ". . . if Salzman has planned the whole episode, then the matchmaker through his *Kaddish* is commemorating the death of the old Leo who was incapable of love. But he is also celebrating Leo's birth into a new life." Viewed in this way, the matchmaker's prayer of mourning celebrates the success of his plan for Leo and Stella, the *"Yiddishe kinder"* (Jewish children).

Because Malamud's "The Magic Barrel" is a work of art and not a sociological study of intergenerational relations, it must remain a matter of interpretation whether the story privileges the older or younger generation. Because its central interpretive question involves this judgment between two generations, however, "The Magic Barrel" is a story

solidly grounded in the tradition of Jewish-American fiction.

Source: Benjamin Goluboff, "Overview of 'The Magic Barrel,'" for *Short Stories for Students*, The Gale Group, 2000.

Sidney Richman

In the following excerpt, Richman provides a plot synopsis and an examination of the major themes of "The Magic Barrel."

The impact of "The Magic Barrel" is, inexplicable—certainly as inexplicable, and for much the same reasons, as *The Assistant*. The story of the love and maturation of a young rabbinical student, it conspires like the author's second novel in a boundary world which pulsates now with the bright energy of a fairy tale, now with something of the somber tones of a depression tract. Both qualities are immediately apparent in the opening: "Not long ago there lived in uptown New York, in a small, almost meager room, though crowded with books, Leo Finkle, a rabbinical student in the Yeshivah University."

The key to Leo Finkle's rebirth, however, lies not alone in the protagonist, a poor and lonely student hurrying after six years of study toward his June ordination. A Frankie Alpine in a black fedora, Leo unites myth and anti-myth in his own person. Passionately interested in Jewish law since childhood, Leo is nonetheless Godless. Bound in his deceit, he throbs through the torment that washes over Malamud's love-hungry and God-hungry young Jews. Like Fidelman on Giotto, Finkle knows the word but not the spirit; and he makes it clear in every gesture that in a secret part of his heart he knows it.

But Leo Finkle's heart is too secretive, and his salvation depends upon another who can test all there is of humanity in the student. The "other" does not arrive, however, until the last page; in her place there comes a marriage broker whom Leo has summoned when he learns that a wife will help him win a congregation. But from the moment Pinye Salzman materializes, the student is on the way. For, reeking of fish and business, the broker seems only another Susskind. Half criminal, half messenger of God, Salzman whips from his battered portfolio a select group of feminine portraits, for "is every girl good for a new rabbi?"

As Pinye exalts his merchandise, however, Leo persists in positing reservations; and they are not alone a matter of distrusting Salzman's grossness (indeed, he seems *too* gross to be believed). When

> "It is impossible to tell for whom Pinye chants—for himself and his guilt (for even Leo had finally suspected 'that Salzman had planned it all to happen this way'), for Finkle's past or Finkle's future, or for all these reasons."

Pinye plays his trump card: "Ruth K., Nineteen years, Honor student. Father offers thirteen thousand cash to the right bridegroom," Leo, sick of the whole business, gives himself away: "But don't you think this young girl believes in love?"

Dismissing Pinye, Leo slides into misery; but the misery is only the signal of breaking ice. Trying to analyze his reactions, he wonders if perhaps "he did not, in essence, care for the matchmaking institution?" From this thought, slightly heretical, he flees throughout the day; and it is only at nightfall, when he draws out his books, that he finds any peace. But Pinye, like a haggard ghost—and he grows more desperate-looking with each meeting—is soon at the door, his presence thrusting Leo out of his books and threadbare composure. Bearing the vitae of Lily Hirschorn, high-school teacher and linguist, young (twenty-nine instead of the thirty-two of the night before), Pinye dispels Leo's lack of interest with a mournful imprecation: "Yiddishe kinder, what can I say to somebody that he is not interested in high school teachers?"

Despite the retiring young scholar's hesitancy, a meeting is arranged; and one Saturday afternoon he strides along Riverside Drive with Lily Hirschorn, oldish but pretty, hanging to his arm. From the beginning, however, Leo senses the presence of Pinye, somewhere in the background, perhaps "flashing the lady signals with a pocket mirror; or perhaps a cloven-hoofed Pan, piping nuptial ditties."

But if Pinye is directing the proceedings, he is after more than a quick profit; for about the walk there is strong suggestion of ritual indoctrination, a testing by question and answer that suddenly exposes Leo. Lily, having been primed by Salzman into the belief that Leo Finkle is the true anointed of God (or is Lily another Iris?) addresses herself as if to a holy image: "How was it that you came to your calling?" When Leo, after some trepidation, replies, "I was always interested in the Law," Lily's questions soar: "When did you become enamored of God?" In mingled rage at Pinye and himself, Leo finds himself speaking with shattering honesty: "I am not a talented religious person. I think that I came to God not because I loved Him, but because I did not."

After the smoke-screen of hatred for Pinye dissipates, there is a long week of "unaccountable despair" in which Leo's beard grows ragged and his books meaningless. Feeding on his confession to Lily, which had revealed "to himself more than her—the true nature of his relationship to God," Leo bounds to further revelations. He realized that, "apart from his parents, he had never loved anyone." Then, with a quick jolt, the two ragged ends of his lovelessness fuse: "Or perhaps it went the other way, that he did not love God so well as he might, because he had not loved man."

Made desperate by the unexpected image of himself, Leo contemplates leaving Yeshivah. "He had lived without knowledge of himself, and never in the Five Books and all the Commentaries—mea culpa—had the truth been revealed to him." The knowledge sends Leo scurrying into near hysteria, a state disagreeable and pleasurable at the same time, and then into a long swoon, a kind of moral way-station from which he "drew the consolation that he was a Jew and that a Jew suffered." The revelation, needless to say, represents a turning; and when Salzman returns—at precisely this moment—he must listen to a new Leo: "I want to be in love with the one I marry. I find it necessary to establish the level of my need and fulfill it." Discharged, Salzman disappears "as if on the wings of the wind"; but he leaves behind a manila packet.

The pattern of pursuit which dominates the first half of "The Magic Barrel" parallels also the early sections of "The Last Mohican"; moreover, like Fidelman's in the Italian story, Leo Finkle's redemption involves the reversal of the pattern, the quest of the once despised. Coincident with the arrival of March and the turning toward spring, Finkle remains closeted in his room, gloomy over the frustrations of his hopes for a better life; and so, finally, he is drawn to open the manila packet which had all the while been gathering dust. Within he finds more photographs, but all seem versions of Lily Hirschorn. But, as the scholar puts them back, he discovers another snapshot, small and cheap, which without preliminaries evokes a shout of love. Staring back at him is a composite of every heroine Malamud has yet written about, from Iris Lemon and Harriet Bird through Pauline Gilley and Helen Bober. In shreds of images, some mythic, some terrifyingly real, the face closes, like fate itself, over Leo's heart:

> spring flowers, yet age—a sense of having been used to the bone, wasted; this came from the eyes, which were hauntingly familiar, yet absolutely strange. He had a vivid impression that he had met her before, but try as he might he could not place her although he could almost recall her name, as if he had read it in her own handwriting. . . . *something* about her moved him she leaped forth to his heart—had *lived*, or wanted to—more than just wanted, perhaps regretted how she had lived—had somehow deeply suffered. Her he desired he experienced fear of her and was aware that he had received an impression, somehow, of evil.

Dashing into the streets, Leo rushes off in pursuit of Pinye Salzman, only to discover from his wife (and "He could have sworn he had seen her, too, before but knew it was an illusion"), that the matchmaker was nowhere about, that he "lived in the air." "Go home," she suggests, "he will find you." When the student returns to his flat, Salzman, standing at the door, asks, "You found somebody you like?" Without hesitation, Finkle extends the snapshot. But for his eager love the student must submit to the final horror. With a groan, Pinye tells him "this is not a bride for a rabbi. She is a wild one—wild, without shame." When Finkle presses Salzman for a clearer answer, the old man dissolves in tears: "This is my baby, my Stella, she should burn in hell."

Under the covers of his bed, a makeshift chapel perilous, Leo, beating his breast, undergoes the climactic test. "Through days of torment he endlessly struggled not to love her; fearing success he escaped it. He then concluded to convert her to goodness, himself to God. The idea alternately nauseated and exalted him." Though brief, the ordeal finally draws Leo from bed with a long "pointed beard" and "eyes weighted with wisdom." A mixture now of lover and father, he meets Salzman again (and the marriage broker seems unaccountably young) and, despite Salzman's pleas to desist, a meeting is arranged.

The rendezvous, held on a spring night, is Malamud at his ambiguous best. With flowers in hand, Leo finds Stella standing in the age-old posture of the prostitute, under a lamp post smoking: "She waited uneasily and shyly. From afar he saw that her eyes—clearly her father's—were filled with desperate innocence. He pictured, in her, his own redemption. Violins and lit candles revolved in the sky. Leo ran forward with flowers outstretched."

This paragraph, however, is the penultimate one: as if the mixture of goddess and prostitute, the promise of hope through a future of willfully chosen agony, were not sufficiently confusing, Malamud allows the final paragraph to focus on Pinye, who, leaning upon a wall around the corner, "chanted prayers for the dead." It is impossible to tell for whom Pinye chants—for himself and his guilt (for even Leo had finally suspected "that Salzman had planned it all to happen this way"), for Finkle's past or Finkle's future, or for all these reasons. In some ways, the last alternative—that Salzman chants for everything—seems only proper; for if Leo has graduated into saint and rabbi, it is only by succumbing to the terrors which the role prescribes. What better reason to chant when to win means to lose?

But such confusions, as demonstrated in *The Assistant*, are the only possible vehicles for Malamud's faith. If the ironies undercutting the story preserve it from a kind of mythic schmaltz, the myth preserves the story from the irony. The same strange tension is surely in the characters—in the infested goddesses, like Stella, who can only be redeemed by the hero as victim, and in those unstable ministers of God, now devils and now angels, the Pinye Salzmans and the Shimon Susskinds. In that inexplicable and indeterminate character, they signal, as Alfred Kazin has said, "the unforeseen possibilities of the human—when everything seems dead set against it." One finishes "The Magic Barrel" as one finishes *The Assistant*—not with the exaltation of witnessing miracles, but with the more durable satisfaction of witnessing possibilities.

Source: Sidney Richman, "The Stories," in *Bernard Malamud and the Critics*, edited by Leslie A. Field and Joyce W. Field, New York University Press, 1979, pp. 305–31.

Bates Hoffer

In the following excerpt, Hoffer identifies parallels between the first five books of the Old Testament and the structure of the story, arguing that Finkle is a "sinner" rather than a hero.

No synopsis is a substitute for ["The Magic Barrel"]. One is given here in case you have not read the story for some time.

Leo Finkle, a rabbinical student, hears that he may have a chance at a better position if he is married. He approaches Salzman, a poverty-ridden matchmaker who smells of fish, who wears old clothes, and whose suggested brides are not shall we say big winners. After rejecting the few suggested by Salzman, Leo finds a picture in the file of a different girl and immediately falls in "love." The picture is of Salzman's daughter and the story does not make clear whether the picture is there by mistake (as Salzman says) or by design (as Leo suspects). It is clear that Salzman has indeed disowned his daughter who has gone completely bad. Leo demands to meet her, no matter what her background and condition. As the story closes, Leo is rushing toward her with a bouquet while she is standing under a streetlight dressed in red and white. The last paragraph then reads:

> Around the corner, Salzman, leaning against a wall, chanted prayers for the dead.

As common in Malamud's stories, the closing picture is ambiguous upon a superficial reading. Salzman is chanting for whom? His daughter? Leo? The current state of Judaism? Someone even suggested to me that Salzman is singing in happiness because he is a Jew who is about to get his daughter married!

One example of a previous interpretation of the story is given by Rovit [in *Bernard Malamud and the Critics*, 1970]:

> The aesthetic form of the story—the precise evaluation of forces—is left to the reader. . . .

> In the best of his stories in The Magic Barrel, the same pattern of ultimate poetic resolution by metaphor is evident.

I assume that you will agree, after re-reading the quote, that Rovit does not provide an interpretation at all. In fact, he finds purposeful ambiguity, as evidenced by:

> The dramatic action of the story attempts to lead the characters into a situation of conflict which is "resolved" by being fixed poetically in the final *ambiguity* of conflicting forces frozen and united in their very opposition. (Italics added)

In other words, the answer to the question "Who is he chanting for?" is "Who knows?" That answer is only sufficient if there is no evidence at all for an answer. That there is abundant evidence is made clear below.

Another example is from Rahv's Introduction to *A Malamud Reader*:

> Of all Malamud's stories, surely the most masterful is "The Magic Barrel," perhaps the best story produced by an American writer in recent decades. . . .

> . . . Salzman contrives to leave one picture in Finkle's room by which his imagination is caught as in a trap. When tracked down, he swears that he had inadvertently left the fatal picture in Finkle's room. "She's not for you. She is a wild one, wild, without shame Like an animal, like a dog. For her to be poor was a sin. This is why to me she is dead now . . . This is my baby, my Stella, she should burn in hell." (Rahv then quotes the last two paragraphs of the story.)

> Thus the rabbinical student who, as he confesses, had come to God not because he loved Him but precisely because he did not, attempts to find in the girl from whose picture "he had received, somehow, an impression of evil" the redemption his *ambiguous* nature demands. (Italics added)

Rahv, then, sees the basic ambiguity in Finkle and does not worry about Salzman.

But worry we must. Where Rahv assumes Salzman "contrives" to leave Stella's picture, others feel that Salzman tells the truth when he swears it was an accident. Assumptions and feelings will convince no one who does not agree with us. Therefore we must look for evidence in the story for support of one view or another. Let us, then, turn to independent but mutually supporting arguments, based on the story itself, for a non-ambiguous interpretation. We should only accept ambiguity after exhausting all procedures and even then realize that someone else may find the key to clear up the ambiguity. . . .

We start by noting that Leo is a final year rabbinical student about to obtain a doctoral degree from Yeshiva, a highly prestigious university. As rabbi, as scholar deeply knowledgeable of the Pentateuch, the Law, he will be "master" and "teacher" of the Law to generations of Jewish children. We therefore begin our analysis of Leo by judging his thoughts, words and deeds in light of his vocation. Although we might go deeply into the Law—and the reader is encouraged to do so—in order to judge, here we will mainly use the "basic" part of the Law which most of us know, the Ten Commandments from Deuteronomy 5:6–21. (I use Monsignor Knox's translation for a variety of reasons. It is important to note that Catholics, Protestants and Jews often number the verses, and consequently the commandments, differently.) Surely we can expect a rabbi to support at least the fundamental parts of the law.

Deuteronomy 5

6 And thus he spoke: I am the Lord thy God, it was I who rescued thee from the land of Egypt, where thou

7 didst dwell in slavery. Thou shalt not defy me by

8 making other gods thy own. Thou shalt not carve thyself images, or fashion the likeness of anything in heaven above, or on earth, to bow down and

9 worship it. I, thy God, the Lord Almighty, am jealous in my love; be my enemy, and thy children, to the third and fourth generation, shall make amends;

10 love me, keep my commandments, and mercy shall be thine a thousand-fold. (Commandment 1)

11 Thou shalt not take the name of the Lord thy God lightly on thy lips; if a man uses that name lightly, he will not go unpunished. (2)

12 Observe the Sabbath day and keep it holy, as

13 the Lord thy God has bidden thee. Six days for drudgery, for doing all the work thou hast to do;

14 when the seventh day come, it is a sabbath, a day of rest, consecrated to the Lord thy God. That day, all work shall be at an end, for thee and for every son and daughter of thine, thy servants and serving-women, thy ass, too, and thy ox, and all thy beasts, and the aliens that live within thy city walls. It must bring rest to thy men-servants and thy maid-servants,

15 as to thyself. Remember that thou too wast a slave in Egypt; what constraining force the Lord used, what a display he made of his power, to rescue thee; and now he will have thee keep this day of rest. (3)

16 Honour thy father and thy mother, as the Lord thy God has bidden thee; so shalt thou live long to enjoy the land which the Lord thy God means to give thee. (4)

17 Thou shalt do no murder. (5)

18 Thou shalt not commit adultery. (6)

19 Thou shalt not steal. (7)

20 Thou shalt not bear false witness against thy neighbour. (8)

21 Thou shalt not covet thy neighbor's wife. (9)

Thou shalt not set thy heart upon thy neighbour's house or lands, his servants or handmaids, an ox or ass or anything that is his. (10)

The first three commandments pertain to God and the next seven to man. As we go through the story and compare Leo's behavior against the standards of the law, recall that the first three were summarized by Christ with the phrase from Deuteronomy 6:5, "Thou shalt love the Lord thy God with the love of thy whole heart, and thy whole soul, and thy whole strength," and the last seven from Leviticus 19:18, "Thou shalt love thy neighbor as thy self; thy Lord is his." Note, then, that love of God is the focus of all.

> I am convinced that they **believe** that breaking God's law, dropping religious beliefs, and doing anything your little ole heart desires are the marks of maturation."

So now we look to Leo. Instead of observing the Sabbath, he goes out on a date with Lily. On the date he mentions the name of God in ordinary conversation. . . . And on the date he says he "came to God not because I loved Him, but because I did not." Poof! The first three commandments disappear, not broken but evaporated! We begin to suspect we are not here reading of a dedicated religious leader.

Before turning to the other commandments, let us pause and look closely at the definition of love in the Law and compare it with Leo's version. In commandment number one we find that love of God includes keeping the commandments: "If you love Me, keep My commandments." "Love," then, is a commitment of the will to behave in a certain manner. It might be helpful to use an example here. In the commandment against adultery, the word "adultery" itself refers to an "adulteration" of the love of God by an illicit love of someone or something. Thus fornication or sex outside marriage, and sex when married, are both adulterations of the Divine love. Human love is a reflection of Divine love and, therefore, true love is always within the limits of the Divine will expressed in the commandments and elsewhere. Yet when we turn to Leo's version of love, we find that he has decided to throw away the divine definition:

> Love, I have said to myself, should be a by-product of living and worship rather than its own end. Yet for myself I find it necessary to establish the level of my need and fulfill it.

He changes "love" to "need" and seeks not God's will but his own: "my" need, he says. Recall here that Leo's great "love" for Stella all comes from a cheap picture. He has not yet met her or seen her in the story. "Who can love from a picture?" Salzman asks. "If you can love her, then you can love anybody." Then Leo confirms what we have suspected, that he has thoroughly confused "love" with sex, desires, needs and etc. "Just her I want," he murmurs. This bastion of Judaism has spent almost seven years in rabbinical preparation and still has the understanding of "love" of a sex-starved sophomore. There is no evidence in the story of any commitment to his religion or his vocation, no evidence of any real practice of his faith or any real knowledge of it. We find that his study has not been rewarding. You can find, if you look, the several other places which indicate that Leo is not what you would call your model rabbi.

Let us go on to the other commandments. Numbers 6 and 9 deal with sex. There is evidence that Leo does not understand the morality of sex at all. When he goes out with Lily, he thinks he sees Salzman as a "cloven-hoofed Pan, piping nuptial ditties" throwing flowers in their way. Note the pagan image for marriage. When he first thinks of using a matchmaker, he looks out the window and

> observed the round white moon, moving high in the sky through a cloud menagerie, and watched with half-open mouth as it penetrated a huge hen, and dropped out of her like an egg laying itself.

My judgement is that Leo is thinking primarily of the physical part of the marriage, to put it diplomatically. The last example here occurs when he discovers Stella's picture. You should re-read the whole paragraph, but in case you do not have a copy handy, here are some critical lines:

> It was not, he affirmed, that she had an extraordinary beauty—no, though her face was attractive enough; it was that *something* about her moved him. Feature for feature, even some of the ladies of the photographs could do better; but she leaped forth to his heart—had *lived*, or wanted to—more than just wanted, perhaps regretted how she had lived—had somehow deeply suffered: it could be seen in the depths of those reluctant eyes, and from the way the light enclosed and shone from her, and within her, opening realms of possibility: this was her own. Her he desired. His head ached and eyes narrowed with the intensity of his gazing, then as if an obscure fog had blown up in the mind, he experienced fear of her and was aware that he had received an impression, somehow, of evil. He shuddered, saying softly, it is thus with us all.

"Her he desired." He senses she is "evil" and shudders with excitement. Here at the 3/4 point of the story, the climax, he makes his decision to possess the evil. His desire must be attained. That she is evil is clarified by Salzman as he and Leo talk:

> "She is not for you. She is a wild one—wild, without shame. This is not a bride for a rabbi."
>
> "What do you mean wild?"

> "Like an animal. Like a dog. For her to be poor was a sin. This is why to me she is dead now."
>
> "In God's name, what do you mean?"
>
> "Her I can't introduce to you," Salzman cried.
>
> "Why are you so excited?"
>
> "Why, he asks," Salzman said, bursting into tears. "This is my baby, my Stella, she should burn in hell."

Ultimately, Leo chooses the wild animal, the dog, the disinherited Stella "dead" in sin. We can only conclude, following this line of reasoning, that eventually Leo consciously chooses evil and turns his back on God Whom he said he did not love anyhow. Leo is not, to put it mildly, thoroughly dedicated to the Law.

The other commandments are broken or ignored in less powerful ways. For example, Leo breaks the one against stealing when he refuses to give Salzman's picture of Stella back. The commandment against greed, avarice and envy of other's goods may be involved in the reason why Leo approached the matchmaker in the first place. Quite simply he wanted to "win" a better congregation. By which might be meant a bigger or more affluent one. The commandment against lying is broken when Leo turns down the lame girl; he tells Salzman, "because I hate stomach specialists," the profession of her father. The one against honoring mother and father is ignored when he decides to avoid the matchmaking institution. [At one point] he couples that institution with the honoring of his father and his mother. Indeed the only Commandment he does not overtly break is the one against murder—and my judgment is that he does indeed "murder" his own soul by choosing evil.

With all this evidence that Leo is precisely the worst possible rabbi—we have not time to note the other rules and laws he breaks—we must conclude that Leo is not a positive picture of a modern rabbi. He may be a picture of some modern rabbi, but Malamud does not give us a *positive* picture. Leo may even be a picture of one type of rabbi graduating today, one pursuing a "thrust for life" (to use Rahv's phrase) which is actually a grasp of spiritual death. At the story's close, Salzman is around the corner chanting prayers for the dead, which refers to Leo and Stella and their offspring to the third and fourth generation and to that part of Judaism which has a Leo, a great "lion" of God, as its master and teacher. . . .

There is a richer and deeper analysis of "The Magic Barrel" which carries us across the sweep of Jewish history and takes us into the heart of the

Pentateuch itself. For a few moments forget all you have read above and read this subsection independently.

In much great literature there is an underlying structure which borrows from religious and/or literary structure. James Joyce builds his *Portrait* on Dante's *Inferno*, Greene builds *End of the Affair* on John of the Cross' *Dark Night of the Soul*, Faulkner builds *The Sound and the Fury* on the New Testament through Revelations. Examples abound in any good survey of Western literature. To posit such a structure for "The Magic Barrel" is to suggest that some of the story's power derives from its allegorical structure.

The underlying structure begins to take shape when you see that the story is in five parts and that Leo has been studying the Pentateuch, the five parts of the Torah. Here is a brief version of each book . . . :

GENESIS: "In the beginning" the focal point is the fall of Adam which begins the redemption story.

EXODUS: "The going out" has Moses as the central figure. The deliverance by means of crossing the Red Sea is referred to throughout the Bible. The wandering in the desert and the manna from heaven are major points.

LEVITICUS: "The Levites" or Israelite priesthood discusses the ministry of the Levitical priesthood. This highly legalistic book demands perfect obedience and sets up the rites of the Day of Atonement in precise detail. Obedience will bring redemption.

NUMBERS: "In the wilderness" the Israelites are given final preparation for their entrance into the Promised Land. Numbers stresses that disobedience receives its due reward, but repentance results in pardon and restoration.

DEUTERONOMY: The "second law" describes the Israelites as they are about to enter the Promised Land. Moses will not be allowed to enter because of a sin. Moses exhorts the people to follow the law and describes the results of a lack of obedience. The concluding part is an added section on the death of Moses.

Before starting the broad outlines of the parallels between the Pentateuch and "The Magic Barrel," recall the simple point that allegories as defined in *Linguistics in Literature* are parallel structures. The story is divided into five sections overtly, that is, by spaces on the page.

"In the beginning" of the story Leo has his sexual image fantasy about the moon while Salzman is there talking about women.

In part two, parallel to Exodus or "the going out", he literally "goes out" with Lily. We notice the mention of his walking cane even as Moses carried a staff. This section contains an image that is extremely hard to explain except by reference to Exodus. The winged loaves of bread that Leo sees at the end of the story make perfect sense if we accept a parallel to the "bread from heaven" or *manna* which occurs in Exodus. The manna came down from heaven as if frost or snow in Exodus and of course just after the loaves of bread fly high overhead it snows in part two. Note also that part two ends with Leo still "out."

In part three Leo spends much time thinking of the priest hood (Leviticus), his reasons for his decisions, and so on. Leo seeks redemption for self in the sense of establishing the level of his need. The redemptive picture given by Salzman is the choice of good or evil, that is, he tells Leo that Leo should not choose Stella, "she should burn in hell."

In part four, parallel to Numbers in which the methods and choices in the redemption story become clear, Salzman offers Leo yet one more chance to avoid evil. "Who can love from a picture? . . . if you can love her, then you can love anybody."

Finally, again only in the broadest terms, in part five Leo rushes towards his serf-defined "promised land," Stella. Parallel to the funeral prayer for Moses, who could not enter the Promised Land, the section which concludes Deuteronomy, we find the prayers for the dead concluding this part.

Now let us pause for a while and reflect. The analysis above accounts for a whole potful of seeming aberrations in the story, for several occurrences which cannot be explained in an internally consistent way by any other analysis: loaves of bread flying overhead; a matchmaker who "appears" out of thin air, who is "transparent," almost "vanishing"; the prayers for the dead when no one is dead and so on. If, however, we had only the above parallels few would bother searching for the more particular parts of the parallel structure. Here I will give one extended parallel and drop a few hints for parallels you can have fun finding for yourself.

Let's look for a moment at the choice which Leo faces, Lily or Stella, coupled with a central choice which the priest has in Leviticus. In making an offering to God, the priest must choose only a *clean* animal, never an unclean. He must be able to distinguish them. We note here that the girl proposed by Salzman is named "Lily," surely a symbolic name for purity. The priest must also do something to the clean animal or the offering is not valid. That something is that it must be salted. Here we notice that Salzman (which means ''salt-man'') has disinherited his impure daughter. She is not only ''unclean'' but unsalted. Thus we find that the names of Lily and Salzman are perfectly suited to the parallel structure.

Let's go a little more deeply into Leviticus. Aaron's two sons mentioned in chapter 10 decide to honor the Lord more than their orders require by moving closer to the holiest place. They decided to do more; that is, they think they are choosing *good* when they decide to do it their own way. They are then consumed by fire from the Lord. Leo, too, wants to decide for himself and he decides Salzman's daughter is ''good'' despite all evidence to the contrary (100% of it). Now if I had written ''The Magic Barrel'' and had set up the parallel to this point, I would look for a girl's name which suggests purity or whiteness but which also suggests the fire which consumes her (''she should burn in hell'') and will, by extension, consume Leo. In fact, ''Stella'' does the job to perfection since it means ''star.''. . .

There are several other parallels you could track down. Part two ought to have a body of water (i.e. ''Red Sea''). It does. Leo ought to have other parallels to Moses. He does. There ought to be more examples of law and tradition breaking, since Leo is the great Law-Breaker rather than a Moses or Law-Giver. There are. Since Salzman appears and disappears on ''wings of the wind'' and has a relative who has fallen and burns in hell, it shouldn't be too difficult to relate them to the redemption story. (If you will permit me—if she indeed is *burning*, it is interesting to note that when Leo first sees her she is standing ''by the lamp post, smoking.''). . .

One last line of analysis must be given here to show clearly that what Leo thinks is a ''redemption'' process is precisely the opposite. We look at Leo at the end of each section and find how he had ''entangled himself'' to such an extent that he became suspicious of ''Salzman's machinations.'' He acted ''frenziedly'' in his craving for Stella, was ''afflicted'' with a ''tormenting suspicion'' and finally had ''prayers for the dead'' prayed for him. Leo looked upon evil, decided it was good, and ran to greet it with flowers outthrust.

I do not see how anyone could find the story ''ambiguous'' with respect to Leo's decision.

The analysis presented above uses a great deal of direct textual evidence (such as breaking of various rules) to show that Leo is the opposite of a high-level rabbi and it uses direct textual evidence for parallels between the story and the Pentateuch, that which Leo studied for years and that which he would be expected to teach as a rabbi. In the latter interpretation, Leo becomes the great Law-Breaker as contrasted to the author and ''hero'' of the Pentateuch, the Law-Giver, Moses. Leo seeks not the Promised Land offered by God, but the promised land of his own desires, union with a prostitute whom he does not even know, save from a cheap picture. Leo breaks God's laws, the Mosaic law, the natural law, the standards appropriate to a rabbinical student and to a Jew in general; he breaks the traditions of his religion, his race, his ancestors, his parents; he breaks the rules of common courtesy and kindness. He seeks that which makes him shudder, a picture of evil which he decides will become his good. From direct textual evidence, Leo is perhaps the greatest loser in the history of literature since *Lucifer's Fall.* . . .

You may disagree with the last sentence, but the point there was exaggerated for a particular reason. Over and over again the commentators on this story project Leo as a winner, as someone who has ''matured'' and seeks his redemption. Pinye Salzman is even seen as a ''criminal.'' How can anyone hold the idea that Leo is somehow ''maturing'' by choosing a hooker? Here I would like to attempt an answer, not by quoting endlessly, but by commenting on the type of criticism involved. Let us therefore begin by presenting a case for Leo as the good guy.

As we read ''The Magic Barrel'' we note that Leo is suspicious that Pinye *arranged* for him to find Stella's picture and that the whole story was *staged*. Leo is presented pictures of older or crippled girls so that Stella will seem better. Stella is condemned so as to make her more attractive to Leo. Pinye is a poor, undignified representative of the old, repressive system that must be broken through for true maturation to take place. (Maturation, in this interpretation, consists of doing exactly what one wants to do.) Leo runs toward his redemption to the tune of violins.

What precisely is it that is the key to the two polar opposite—and hence ambiguous?—interpretations? Clearly it is the interpretation of the role of the matchmaker. Is Leo right in his suspicion that the whole affair was staged or is Pinye right in denying any duplicity? If you side with Leo, then everything Pinye says is suspect because after all *lying* is breaking a commandment. If you side with the matchmaker, then you see Leo as having a guilty conscience, one that turns Pinye into a Pan or a liar or a fraud. How do we resolve the issue? We look closely at the story for evidence that one is presented as a positive character and the other as negative. Only if the evidence is mixed can we accurately say the story is *"ambiguous."* A close analysis shows Leo to be the consummate loser. The only evidence for Pinye as wrong comes from Leo's thoughts. No, Leo as hero simply will not hold up if you use the evidence of the story itself.

OK, you ask, but aren't we back where we started? How can someone cling to the view that Leo is the good guy? The answer is rather harsh, but I think the harshness is fully justified. My judgment, after some years of studying the issue, is that those critics actually *believe* that breaking all the rules and sleeping with a prostitute is a maturational experience. . . . Those critics must actually *believe* that "adult" movies are indeed adult, rather than mere adolescent sex fantasies. I am convinced that they *believe* that breaking God's law, dropping religious beliefs, and doing anything your little ole heart desires are the marks of maturation. They aren't, in the abstract, but the issue raised by their misunderstanding is a serious one. Let us spend a few lines on it. Leo may represent the "mature" modern rabbi who abandons his entire background and perhaps he may in a more general sense represent the Jew who has nothing of Jewishness left except his race. Certainly that interpretation fits with other Malamud Jews, especially Henry Levin (of "The Lady of the Lake") who changes his name to Henry R. Freeman and heads for Europe to escape and denies his Jewishness to one and all. But there is more to it than that, simply because Leo's story is more than abandoning his past values. Leo actually decides to treat what is shudderingly evil as a positive good through which to achieve redemption. The critics and commentators who find Leo a "model" for our youth must have absorbed the same reversal of values, which reversal after all so pervades American society. Leo, then, may also represent all of us who are faced with the profoundly spiritual question: which value system do I choose? We know Leo's choice and have clear and direct textual evidence that he chose wrong. The evidence from the story is clear, but we have come to the point in literary criticism where we may ignore the text, ignore the structure of the story, ignore anything that clashes with the interpretation we want to make. We have come to the point where the choos-ing of evil is considered a positive good—*just as Leo considered it.*

"The Magic Barrel" is a great short story. Its power is evident whether you seek a deeper level of meaning or not. It is anthologized widely and discussed by thousands of people every year. Analyses of it are still appearing. The point of this article is that Malamud has constructed his story of the student of the Pentateuch on the structural framework of the Pentateuch and that any interpretation which fails to take into account this integration of content and form is deficient. The conclusion of this analysis is that Malamud as master craftsman and Malamud as artist of vision has created for us a powerful short story which will stand the test of time as a classic of our century.

Source: Bates Hoffer, "The Magic in Malamud's Barrel," in *Linguistics in Literature*, Vol. 2, 1977, pp. 1–26.

Richard Reynolds

In the following excerpt, Reynolds investigates the meaning of the prayers for the dead that Salzman chants at the conclusion of "The Magic Barrel."

Published analyses of Bernard Malamud's "The Magic Barrel" praise the "richly ambiguous" conclusion. The consensus is that to reduce the story to specific meaning is to do the author an injustice. Perhaps, however, an interpretation may be sustained that points to a consistent moral thread.

Pinye Salzman is, as Professor Bellman suggests [in "Women, Children and Idiots First: The Transformation Psychology of Bernard Malamud," *Critique* (1965)], "almost supernatural." The title of the story supports that. What exactly is a magic barrel? Apparently Malamud did not have a specific analogue in mind, but the concept is quite clear; it is a barrel which produces surprises, usually inexhaustible quantities or unique qualities, or both. Plainly Salzman's briefcase is the magic barrel, providing first an endless number of possible brides for Leo Finkle, and then yielding, as if from a mysterious compartment, the special girl, Stella. There is thus an irreducible element of magic in the story; the narrative combines sheer fantasy with the idea that love and marriage are divinely supervised.

But Salzman also operates in the earthy sphere of gefilte fish, dingy tenements, and Broadway cafeterias. At this level, and at least in this one instance of Leo and Stella, Salzman is a superb manager, whose art is based on his understanding of Leo's character and situation. He gives Leo the

> " But Salzman also operates in the earthy sphere of gefilte fish, dingy tenements, and Broadway cafeterias. At this level, and at least in this one instance of Leo and Stella, Salzman is a superb manager, whose art is based on his understanding of Leo's character and situation."

chance to learn about himself by associating with people. The meeting with Lily Hirschorn brings Leo to the realization that "he had never loved anyone. . . . he did not love God so well as he might, because he had not loved man." The supposedly accidental appearance of Stella's picture from the magic briefcase leads to Leo's eager pursuit of her and to Salzman's evasions and assertions of his daughter's wild life. "If you can love her, then you can love anybody," Salzman tells Leo, apparently with scorn, but knowing this is exactly the challenge Leo wants. The image Salzman has presented of Stella contrasts sharply with Leo's own life. She has dared, sinned, suffered. She is the prodigal daughter. Leo has gone from a sheltered home in Cleveland to six years of intensive study in a small room. "Put me in touch with her . . . Perhaps I can be of service," Leo says to Salzman. He has learned that he will not reach God through books, that he needs to involve himself with mankind, and that he and Stella can assist each other.

Whether Stella is the fallen woman Salzman has suggested and Leo has visualized, is uncertain. She plays the part, standing by the lamp post smoking. But she waits for Leo "uneasily and shyly . . . her eyes . . . filled with desperate innocence." She is probably much less experienced than her father has indicated. That is of less importance than the revolution that Salzman has achieved in Leo's heart.

But what about the prayers for the dead, which Salzman is chanting at the end of the story? Does he do so because the meeting of Leo and Stella is a "disaster?" That hardly agrees with Leo's own notion that Salzman has been managing Leo's prospective marriage for some time. Is it [as Earl Rovit asks in his "Bernard Malamud and the Jewish Literary Tradition," *Critique* 6, No. 2] simply the matchmaker's "final dignified behavior," his part in the concluding tableau? Is it [as Sidney Richman asks in his 1966 *Bernard Malamud*] "impossible to tell for whom Pinye chants?" To decide, we must consider the nature of the *Kadish*, the prayers for the dead. [According to Meyer Waxman in *A Handbook of Judaism*, 1947:]

> [The *Kadish*] is not primarily a prayer for the dead. . . . It is not known definitely when the *Kadish* became the special prayers for mourners, and various reasons are advanced for this appropriation. The real reason seems to be that the Kingdom of God is so closely associated in the entire Talmudic and Rabbinic literature with the Messianic times when resurrection will take place, that a plea for its realization was considered indirectly a plea for the resurrection of the departed.

No one would appreciate this better than Leo Finkle, after six years' study about to be ordained. If, as one may well suppose from the story, Leo knows where Salzman is and what he is doing— reciting the *Kadish*—then the matchmaker is playing his part to the end: he has specifically told Leo that he considers Stella dead; Leo and love are to effect her resurrection. The understanding and art of Salzman have brought about a prospect of happiness.

Source: Richard Reynolds, "'The Magic Barrel': Pinye Salzman's Kadish," in *Studies in Short Fiction*, Vol. 10, No. 1, Winter, 1973, pp. 100–02.

Theodore C. Miller

In the following excerpt, Miller discusses the role of love in "The Magic Barrel."

Although Bernard Malamud has colored his short story "The Magic Barrel" with the language and the manners of the Jewish ghetto, he also makes use of a cultural past that has a closer relationship to Nathaniel Hawthorne and Blaise Pascal than to Sholem Aleichem.

Malamud, of course, is using the same motif that Hawthorne mined in *The Scarlet Letter*—the love of the minister and the whore. Hawthorne's Dimmesdale, the man of God, was destroyed because he could not accept Hester and her emblem of sexual transgression. In Malamud's story too, Leo Finkle, the young rabbinical student, is at first repelled when he senses the sexual history of Stella, the matchmaker's daughter. Although he does not yet know specifically that she is a whore when he first sees her picture, his attraction is stifled, for "then as if an obscure fog had blown up in the mind he experienced fear of her and was aware that he had received an impression, somehow, of evil." But Finkle, unlike Dimmesdale, comes to accept Stella for the reason that he accepts universal guilt. When Malamud adds that "[Finkle] shuddered, saying softly, it is thus with us all," Finkle is well on his way to becoming a Dimmesdale redeemed.

But Malamud's minister is ultimately quite different from Hawthorne's. For Leo Finkle does not fall in love primarily for a reason—but rather he loves for no reason at all. Malamud—who echoes Pascal in several other stories too—is suggesting that "Le coeur a ses raisons, que la raison ne connait point"—one must love even if all the evidence denies the emotion. Like Pascal, Malamud proposes that love is existential.

And if Salzman is Malamud's spokesman in the story, then he only appears to be the comic stereotype of the Jewish marriage broker. Although he has decided that his own daughter should be the bride of the young rabbinical student, he does not really believe in the matchmaker's ethic that love is the product of reason. Salzman is the sage who would initiate Leo Finkle into the existential nature of love—but that is a peculiarly difficult task since Finkle is the eminently rational young man committed to the life of reason. The student wants to marry for the solid cause that it will prove beneficial to his professional status. He has even turned to the rabbinate, not for love of God, but because he is interested in the Talmudic law—rules of reason. Therefore, in order to work his ends, Salzman must engage in a ruse—he initially enters into Finkle's system of thought, offering him several young women who should prove highly attractive according to all the rules of logic. One has a father, a physician, ready to give a handsome dowry; another has a regular teaching license—the reasons derive from the middle-class Jewish ethic.

But Finkle's rational world fails him, for despite all the logical good inherent in these young ladies, he cannot fall in love with them. Instead, he becomes filled only with existential despair as he realizes the emptiness of his life—and of his religious calling. Only after he has exploded Finkle's system can Salzman make sure that Finkle sees Stella's picture. But he must present her in a context so that it is absurd to marry her. And precisely because it is absurd, Finkle falls in love.

> " Salzman is the sage who would initiate Leo Finkle into the existential nature of love--but that is a peculiarly difficult task since Finkle is the eminently rational young man committed to the life of reason."

Several critics have accepted literally the description of Stella as a "carnal young lady" and a "girl of the streets." And indeed within the text, she evokes "a sense of having been used to the bone, wasted"; Finkle has that "impression of evil"; and Salzman, himself, describes his daughter as "a wild one—wild, without shame." But the accuracy of these characterizations is most ambiguous since they are all subject to double meanings. That Stella has been "used to the bone" may mean only that she has suffered. That she evokes "an impression . . . of evil" may be interpreted not in a sexual sense, but in Hawthorne's sense that all men bear human guilt. And Salzman's own statement may be part of his ruse to complete Finkle's initiation—and bring him to the marriage altar with his daughter. Just as Salzman only pretends to be a comic marriage broker who offers young women for rational cause, he must also pretend that his daughter is a whore, a girl whom there is no reason to marry. Near the end of the story Finkle himself recognizes that Salzman has perhaps planned this outcome from their first encounter.

When Finkle finally encounters Stella, her purity is suggested by the whiteness of her dress and furthermore by the explicit statement that Finkle sees a look of "desperate innocence" in her eyes.

But more important, her innocence clarifies the puzzling ending when the reader is told that Salzman is chanting a prayer for the dead. In the orthodox Jewish ritual, a parent may in extreme cases enact the ritual of mourning for a child who has broken a primary taboo. If Stella is really a trollop, her father, considering her and the rabbinical student to be a most unfit couple, is rejecting them both through his prayer. But if Salzman has planned the whole episode, then the matchmaker through his *kaddish* is commemorating the death of the old Leo who was incapable of love. But he is also celebrating Leo's birth into a new life. Salzman's remark to Leo about Stella "if you can love her then you can love anybody" is ironically not a statement disparaging his daughter as a social outcast. Rather Salzman is suggesting that if Leo can love Stella, he has unlocked his heart to mankind and God. He will have learned that the barrel in which Salzman keeps his pictures is then indeed a magic barrel, for love is a magic that cannot be explained by the normal laws of logic.

Source: Theodore C. Miller, "The Minister and the Whore: An Examination of Bernard Malamud's 'The Magic Barrel,'" in *Studies in the Humanities*, Vol. 3, 1972, pp. 43–4.

Sources

Antin, Mary. *The Promised Land*, first published 1912, reprinted, New York: Penguin, 1997.

Cahan, Abraham. *The Rise of David Levinsky*, first published 1917, reprinted, New York: Harper's, 1960.

Cramer, Carmen. "The Americanization of Leo Finkle," in *Cyahoga Review*, Vol. 1, No. 2, Fall, 1983, pp. 143–147.

Hoffer, Bates. "The Magic in Malamud's Barrel," in *Linguistics in Literature*, Vol. 2, No. 3, 1977, pp. 1–26.

Miller, Theodore C. "The Minister and the Whore: An Examination of Bernard Malamud's 'The Magic Barrel,'" in *Studies in the Humanities*, Vol. 3, 1972, pp. 43-4.

Reynolds, Richard. "'The Magic Barrel': Pinye Salzman's Kadish," in *Studies in Short Fiction*, Vol. 10, c. 1973, pp. 100–102.

Richman, Sidney. *Bernard Malamud*, Twayne, 1966.

Yezierska, Anzia. *Bread Givers*, first published 1925, reprinted, New York: Persea Books, 1975.

Further Reading

Astro, Richard and Jackson Benson, eds. *The Fiction of Bernard Malamud*, Oregon State University Press, 1977.
  Gives a comprehensive study of Malamud's short and long fiction.

Field, Leslie A. and Joyce W. Field, eds. *Bernard Malamud: A Collection of Critical Essays*, Prentice- Hall, 1974.
  Explores various aspects of Malamud's work.

Meeter, Glenn. *Bernard Malamud and Philip Roth: A Critical Essay*, Eerdmans, 1968.
  Examines the two writers in the context of Jewish fiction.

Pinsker, Sanford. "The Achievement of Bernard Malamud," in *Midwest Quarterly*, Vol. 10, July, 1969, pp. 379-89.
  Provides an assessment of Malamud's career.

Richman, Sidney. *Bernard Malamud*, Twayne, 1966.
  Gives a detailed survey of Malamud's life and works.

The Man to Send Rain Clouds

Written in 1967 and published two years later in the *New Mexico Quarterly*, ''The Man to Send Rain Clouds'' established Silko as a brilliant new Native American writer. The story brought her wide recognition as well as a grant from the National Endowment for the Humanities.

The story is based on an incident Silko had heard about in her hometown of Laguna, New Mexico: an old man had been found dead in a sheep camp and had been given a traditional Indian burial. The local Catholic priest resented the fact that he had not been called in to officiate at the service. Silko's story explores the Indians' blending of Catholic rituals with traditional Indian rituals during a funeral ceremony. The tension of maintaining traditional Pueblo practices and the co-opting of outside influences—in this case, the Catholic church—is a recurring interest of Silko's and appears in several of her stories.

As a story about Native Americans, ''The Man to Send Rain Clouds'' describes the quality of contemporary Laguna Pueblo life. The story is admired for Silko's masterful portrayal of the Indians' quiet acceptance of death and for its highly controlled narrative.

Leslie Marmon Silko

1969

Author Biography

Silko is one of the major authors to emerge from the Native American literary renaissance of the 1970s. Born in 1948 in Albuquerque, New Mexico, she grew up on the nearby Laguna Pueblo Reservation, where she was raised within a family of mixed Indian, Mexican, and white descent. Life on the reservation was a daily balancing act of Pueblo and Christian ways. Storytelling, or story-sharing, was an important part of Pueblo culture, and Silko grew up listening to stories of the Indians' struggles and their survival as a people. The stories lived on in her memory, and in later years she drew heavily upon her heritage in her writings.

She majored in English at the University of New Mexico because, as she put it, "I loved to read and write about what I'd read." Silko graduated *magna cum laude* in 1969, the same year she published "The Man to Send Rain Clouds." This short story would launch her career as a writer. She attended law school for a short time, but, disillusioned with the legal system, she left school after three semesters, having decided to seek justice for her people through the power of her imagination and stories. Since that time she has established herself as an important chronicler of American Indian life, though she hesitates to call herself a representative of the Pueblo, as she is but "one human being and one Laguna woman."

Silko's other works include the verse collection *Laguna Woman* (1974), the novels *Ceremony* (1977), *Storyteller* (1981), and *Almanac of the Dead* (1991), the autobiography *Sacred Water* (1993), and the essay collection *Yellow Woman and a Beauty of the Spirit* (1996). Also, in 1985 her letters to and from James Wright were published as *The Delicacy and Strength of Lace*. She has also written film scripts and given numerous interviews which provide insights into her works.

Silko has garnered much critical acclaim and numerous awards and grants for her fiction and poetry, including a Discovery grant for her short story "The Man to Send Rain Clouds" in 1969, a grant from the National Endowment for the Arts and a poetry award from *Chicago Review* in 1974, and the Pushcart Prize for poetry in 1977. In 1981 she was awarded a John D. and Catherine T. MacArthur Foundation grant.

Plot Summary

"The Man to Send Rain Clouds" is set on an Indian reservation in the American Southwest, with its wide mesas (plateaus) and arroyos (ravines). As the story opens, Leon and his brother-in-law, Ken, find an old man, Teofilo, dead under a cottonwood tree. They ritually paint his face and take his body, wrapped in a red blanket, to their home for a traditional Pueblo funeral ceremony. (The Pueblo people paint the faces of the dead so that they will be recognized in the next world. They also scatter corn and sprinkle water to provide food and water for the spirit on its journey to the other world. To the Pueblo, death is not the end of existence, but part of a cycle in which the spirit of the deceased returns to its source and then helps the community of the living by returning with rain clouds for the nourishment of the earth.)

On their way home, Leon and Ken encounter Father Paul, a young Catholic priest who expresses his sorrow that the old man had died alone. Teofilo's funeral is performed in the traditional Native American way until Leon's wife suggests to her husband that he should ask the priest to sprinkle holy water on the grave. At first, Father Paul refuses to use the holy water as part of an Indian burial ceremony. After reconsideration the priest, still confused about his role the ceremony, changes his mind and sprinkles the grave with the holy water:

> The priest approached the grave slowly. . . . He looked at the red blanket, not sure that Teofilo was so small, wondering if it wasn't some perverse Indian trick— something they did in March to ensure a good harvest—wondering if maybe old Teofilo was actually at the sheep camp corralling the sheep for the night. But there he was, facing into a cold dry wind and squinting at the last sunlight, ready to bury a red wool blanket while the faces of his parishioners were in shadow with the last warmth of the sun on their backs.
>
> His fingers were stiff, and it took him a long time to twist the lid off the holy water. Drops of water fell on the red blanket and soaked into dark icy spots. (Excerpt from "The Man to Send Rain Clouds")

Here the story ends, for now Leon is "happy about the sprinkling of the holy water; now the old man could send them big thunderclouds for sure."

Characters

Grandfather
See Teofilo

Ken

Ken is the brother-in-law of Leon and a minor character in the story. Like old Teofilo and Leon, he also believes in following Indian ways, and he helps his brother-in-law any way he can.

Leon

Leon is Teofilo's grandson. He manages to integrate American Indian ways and Christian ways; he is a Christian who still respects his roots and cultural heritage. He smiles as he paints his dead grandfather's face according to the Native American custom and believes that the old man's spirit will bring rain. He is a man of few words and has a calm, strong sense of dignity. After finding Teofilo's body, Leon does not talk about it. At home, Leon informs his family of Teofilo's death with few words. The fact that he is able to persuade the priest to sprinkle holy water at the grave site with a few well-chosen words—without argument—reveal his character.

Louise

Louise is Leon's wife. Efficient and capable, she plans Teofilo's funeral and suggests to Leon that it would be appropriate to use holy water to symbolically quench the thirst of the old man. Although her part is minor, it is her suggestion that triggers the culture clash in the story.

Father Paul

Father Paul is a young Catholic priest struggling to lead a parish on an Indian reservation. He has affection and respect for his parishioners, as seen in his concern for old Teofilo. He also understands that the spirit of the law is more important than the letter of the law. Although he is troubled by the persistence of Indian customs in his parish, he learns to adapt to them. When Leon asks him to use holy water at Teofilo's burial service, he at first refuses, but he later sprinkles the water on the grave.

Teofilo

Teofilo is ''the man to send rain clouds,'' the old man who is found dead under the big cottonwood tree. Teofilo is perhaps the most important character in the story, since the plot concerns the conflict that arises after his death between American Indian ways and Christian ways. A Native American living on a reservation in New Mexico, he was fiercely independent. He adhered to both the new and old ways: he wore mainstream American clothing, but also wore his white hair long in the

Leslie Marmon Silko

traditional Indian manner and still believed in the old ways. He made new moccasins for the ceremonial dances in the summer and was not keen on going to church. Teofilo was old and well respected, as evidenced by the affection shown him by Leon and his family.

Themes

Creativity

In her short story ''The Man to Send Rain Clouds,'' Silko perceives creativity as a source of strength for Native Americans, a theme that recurs in her later works. In particular, Leon's strength lies in his ability to creatively combine Indian rituals with Catholic rituals. He does not strictly follow the Indian ways, but adds a new element by asking the Catholic priest to sprinkle holy water on Teofilo's grave. Throughout the story, Silko emphasizes that the strength of Pueblo traditions lies in their ability to incorporate alien elements into their own way of life.

Custom and Tradition

Silko's story is concerned with the strength of the customs and traditions of the Native Americans,

Media Adaptations

- Although "The Man to Send Rain Clouds" has not been adapted to a multimedia version, the videotape *Running on the Edge of the Rainbow: Laguna Stories and Poems* (1979) offers readings from Silko's works and the author's commentary on Pueblo culture in Laguna, New Mexico.

and how to resolve a conflict between Native American customs and Christian customs. Leon asks the Catholic priest to participate in the community's Indian rites. Father Paul refuses at first, but later decides to sprinkle holy water on the grave, honoring the Native American belief that the spirit must have plenty of water in its journey to the other world. The story reveals how clashes over differences in customs and tradition can be avoided through a combination of customs.

Death

Related to the theme of custom and tradition in "The Man to Send Rain Clouds" is the theme of death, which is presented from a Native American perspective. Death is not an end, but part of a cycle wherein the spirit departs to return in time with rainstorms. As he finishes painting the dead face of Teofilo, Leon is not sad; instead he smiles and offers the conventional Pueblo prayer asking the dead man to send rain clouds.

Individual versus Community

Another theme in "The Man to Send Rain Clouds" is the struggle of the individual versus community. As the priest of a Native American parish, Father Paul must oversee the Catholics in his region. Yet after the old man dies, Leon does not inform the priest, though the rest of his parishioners have been informed. Father Paul is the last person to join his parishioners in the graveyard, and as he empties a jar of holy water on Teofilo's grave he, in a small way, joins the Native American community.

Appearances and Reality

"The Man to Send Rain Clouds" addresses the theme of appearances versus reality through the character of Father Paul. At one point excited and full of plans for his Native American parish, Father Paul finds the reality of working in an Indian parish very different from what he had expected. When Leon asks the priest to participate in the burial ceremony, Father Paul looks with tired, unseeing eyes at the "glossy missionary magazine . . . full of lepers and pagans" and refuses, but after a moment's reflection he decides to go with Leon.

Culture Clash

In "The Man to Send Rain Clouds," Leon and Father Paul belong to different cultures, and there is the moment of confrontation when, at Teofilo's burial service, Father Paul asks, "Why didn't you tell me he [Teofilo] was dead? I could have brought the Last Rites anyway." Leon replies, "It wasn't necessary, Father." The conflict is resolved with Father Paul agreeing to participate in an Indian ritual. Although it is not strictly a Christian burial, the dead man receives the blessings of both traditional and Christian cultures.

Style

Point of View

The story is told through an objective, third-person narrative, and unfolds in a rigidly objective tone. There is no hint of the narrator's personal voice as each character is presented. With the exception of the graveyard scene that concludes the story, the narrator does not explain the character's thoughts, but presents only the action of the story.

Setting

The story is set on the Laguna Indian Reservation in New Mexico. The landscape of the story with its arroyos and mesas is an integral part of the story. Silko captures the landscape very effectively in her narrative. For instance, "The big cottonwood tree stood apart from a small grove of winterbare cottonweeds which grew in the wide, sandy arroyo. . . . Leon waited under the tree while Ken drove the truck through the deep sand to the edge of the arroyo. . . . But high and northwest the blue mountains were still in snow. . . . It was getting colder, and the wind pushed gray dust down the narrow pueblo road. The sun was approaching the long mesa where it disappeared during the winter.''

Allusions

The title ''The Man to Send Rain Clouds'' alludes to the Pueblo belief that the dead are associated with rain clouds. The narrator makes several references to the Indian burial ceremony and the history of the Pueblo people. The story's title is taken from a traditional prayer in which the Indians pray for the spirit of the deceased to send rain clouds so crops will grow and the community will not starve. To the Pueblo, death is not the end of existence, but part of a cycle in which the human spirit returns to its source and then helps the community by returning with rain clouds. The Pueblo paint the face of the deceased so that he will be recognized in the next world. They also scatter corn and sprinkle water to provide food and water for the spirit on its journey to the other world. The reference to the Catholic church's ''twin bells from the King of Spain'' is important as it points to the history of the Pueblo's initial encounter with Christianity. In 1598, when the Pueblo swore allegiance to the king of Spain, Catholic missionaries arrived to convert Native Americans to Catholicism. Although Christianity was forced on them, the Indians continued to observe their traditional religious practices.

Humor

In this story, Silko uses humor as a double-edged tool. The encounter between the young priest, who is denied the opportunity to perform Catholic rites, and Leon, who insists that such rites are not necessary, is humorous. The exchange also provokes an awareness of intercultural conflict. One illustration of this is the following passage: ''The priest approached the grave slowly. . . . He looked at the red blanket, not sure that Teofilo was so small, wondering if it wasn't some perverse Indian trick— something they did in March to ensure a good harvest—wondering if maybe old Teofilo was actually at the sheep camp corralling the sheep for the night. But there he was, facing into a cold dry wind and squinting at the last sunlight, ready to bury a red wool blanket while the faces of his parishioners were in shadow with the last warmth of the sun on their backs.''

Irony

Irony is a literary device used to convey meaning to a phrase quite different than—in fact, often

Topics for Further Study

- Research the historical experiences of Native Americans by reading the introduction to Geary Hobson's anthology *The Remembered Earth* or portions of *Major Problems in American Indian History*, edited by Albert Hurtacto and Peter Iverson. Relate what you have learned to Leon's story.

- Study ''The Man to Send Rain Clouds'' within a larger context, specifically the spread of Christianity among other nations and cultures. For example, compare Father Paul's experience on the Pueblo reservation with the missionary's experience in India in Robin White's novel *House of Many Rooms*.

- Was Silko successful in creating the landscape of New Mexico in ''The Man to Send Rain Clouds?'' Discuss the importance of the story's geographical location and physical features and relate these features to the main themes of the story.

the direct opposite of—the literal one. Irony can be verbal or situational. Silko demonstrates a skillful use of irony in the story, notably in her depiction of the young priest, an authority figure who wants the Indians to follow Catholic ways but, in the end, himself uses holy water as part of a traditional Indian ceremony, participating in a non-Christian ceremony.

Description

Skillful use of adjectives and attention to detail are the hallmarks of Silko's descriptions. For instance, in ''The Man to Send Rain Clouds'' she uses such expressions as ''wide, sandy arroyo,'' ''low, crumbling wall,'' ''brown, wrinkled forehead'' and ''He squinted up at the sun and unzipped his jacket'' to enhance the beauty of her narrative.

Dialogue

Silko employs an interesting mixture of narration and dialogue. The dialogues between Leon and

Father Paul, and between Leon and Louise, present the characters to the readers directly. Readers are able to draw their own conclusions as to the characters' respective natures and motivations.

Historical Context

Silko wrote the story "The Man to Send Rain Clouds" in 1967 for a creative writing class, basing it upon a real-life incident in Laguna, New Mexico. In the late 1960s there was an interest in indigenous cultures in America. Many Indians moved off the reservations and into mainstream American culture, becoming more visible as a result. Peter Farb's *Man's Rise to Civilization* (1968) generated interest in Native Americans, while Scott Momaday, a Native American, won the 1969 Pulitzer Prize for fiction with his novel *House Made of Dawn*. Silko asserts, "It was a kind of renaissance, I suppose. . . . It is difficult to pinpoint why but, perhaps, in the 1960s, around the time when Momaday's books got published, there was this new interest, maybe it was not new, but people became more aware of indigenous cultures. It was an opening up worldwide." Native Americans were suddenly publishing books and Silko was one of the first published Pueblo women writers.

The story reflects life on the Laguna Indian Reservation in the 1960s. For more than 12,000 years the Pueblo had lived in the region and traditional religious beliefs permeated every aspect of life. Even when Christianity was introduced, it was incorporated into older Pueblo rites. Scholar A. LaVonne Ruoff maintains: "Silko emphasizes that these Pueblo Indians have not abandoned their old ways for Catholicism; instead, they have taken one part of Catholic ritual compatible with their beliefs and made it an essential part of their ceremony." The essence of the story lies in the "instance of cultural clash with the feelings and ideas involved."

The rituals in the story underscore the Pueblo concept of death. According to Per Seyersted, for the Indians, "man is a minute part of an immense natural cycle, and his death has nothing threatening in it because, after a life which contained both the good and the bad he goes back to where he came from, and in line with the communal thinking, it is hoped that his spirit will help the group he leaves behind by returning with the rain clouds."

Critical Overview

Michael Loudon maintains that "The Man to Send Rain Clouds" "testifies to the essential role of storytelling in Pueblo identity, giving the people access to the mythic and historic past and relating a continuing wisdom." In Silko's novel *Ceremony*, one character notes, "At one time, the ceremonies as they had been performed were enough for the way the world was then. But after the white people came, elements in this world began to shift; and it became necessary to create new ceremonies. I have made changes in the rituals. The people mistrust this greatly, but only this growth keeps the ceremonies strong. . . ." A. LaVonne Ruoff sees this theme as central to "The Man to Send Rain Clouds." Per Seyersted views the story as an example of Silko's ability to perceive life from a dual perspective: as a Pueblo and as a mixed-blood person who can perceive Laguna from the outside. Some critics believe that this story may become one of the classics of American literature.

Criticism

Angelina Paul

Paul is a doctoral candidate in English literature at the University of Hyderabad and currently is a Fulbright Visiting Researcher in South Asia Regional Studies at the University of Pennsylvania. She has published literary criticism American Literature Today and the Indian Journal of American Studies. In the following essay, she offers a general introduction to "The Man to Send Rain Clouds," including an overview of the story's reception by critics.

Her work widely anthologized, Leslie Marmon Silko is considered the preeminent Native American woman novelist, a legend in her achievements in the field of Native American literature. Her writings are included in the syllabus of various American literature courses in high schools and colleges. Raised on the Indian reservation in Laguna, New Mexico, she incorporates into her writing the stories, myths, and legends she heard as she grew up. Of Pueblo, Mexican, and white descent, she was both an insider and outsider in Laguna, and this makes her an interesting chronicler of stories about modern-day

Compare & Contrast

- **1960s:** Minorities, such as African Americans, Native Americans, and the Gay community, organize and fight the established system to gain equal rights in the United States. Women also struggle to obtain equal opportunity under the law. In several instances, violence erupts between groups; a national debate rages over the implications of racial and sexual discrimination.

  1990s: Affirmative action for many minority groups has been overturned in some parts of the country. Other legislation is under attack and congress refuses to pass a Federal hate crimes statute.

- **1960s:** Native American voices emerge to tell the Native American experience. Writers such as Leslie Marmon Silko are published to critical and commercial acclaim and become an important part of the American literary scene.

  1990s: Native American writers continue to offer insightful perspectives on American life. In many universities, the study of Native American literature and culture is an important part of the curriculum.

---

life on the reservation. In an interview she has stated: "Oral literatures of the indigenous populations worldwide contain (these) kind of valuable insights. . . . You can look at the old stories that were told among the tribal people here in a north country and see that within them is the same kind of valuable lessons about human behavior and that we need them still." In the Pueblo community, all education is achieved in a verbal, narrative form, and when Silko began writing at the University of Mexico, stories came naturally to her. She has said, "[The] professor would say, now you write your poetry or write a story; write the way you know, they always tell us. All I knew was my growing up at Laguna, recalling some other stories that I had been told as a child."

It was at the University of New Mexico that she wrote her first story, "The Man to Send Rain Clouds," which won her a Discovery grant from the National Endowment for the Humanities. The story is based on an incident she had heard of in Laguna, that an old man had been found dead in a sheep camp and had been given a traditional Indian burial, and that the local Catholic priest had resented the fact that he had not been called in. Having based her first work of short fiction on this incident, "The Man to Send Rain Clouds" brought Silko recogni-

tion and established her as a promising Native American author.

Silko claims that Pueblo narratives are lean and spare because so much of what constitute the stories is shared knowledge. Although the larger audience for "The Man to Send Rain Clouds" has no shared knowledge of the landscape or rituals, Silko still chooses to use the lean narrative mode, as the themes are universal and can be understood by any audience. But an understanding of the Pueblo burial customs gives an added dimension to an understanding of the story. In Pueblo culture, it is believed that neglect of tribal rituals can result in death and sickness, because the ghost returns without blessings, having been unable to enter the other world. To avoid this unhappy prospect, a prayer feather is attached to the hair of the deceased, and his face is painted so that the he will be recognized in the next world. These tasks are ordinarily performed by the village Shaman (religious priest), while corn meal is offered to the wind and water is sprinkled on the grave so that the spirit has nourishment on its journey to the other world. The ceremony concludes with the prayer, "Send us rain clouds." Familiarization with the landscape inhabited by the Pueblo Indians further enhances the reader's understanding of "The Man to Send Rain Clouds," for as

Native-American couple from Laguna Pueblo, hometown of Leslie Marmon Silko and setting for ''The Man to Send Rainclouds.''

Silko has written elsewhere, the landscape sits in the center of Pueblo belief and identity.

A character in Silko's later novel, *Ceremony*, says, ''At one time, the ceremonies as they had been performed were enough for the way the world was then. But after the white people came, elements in this world began to shift; and it became necessary to create new ceremonies. I have made changes in the rituals. The people mistrust this greatly, but only this growth keeps the ceremonies strong. . . .'' Scholar A. LaVonne Ruoff sees this theme as central to ''The Man to Send Rain Clouds.'' Leon's strength

lies in his creative combination of traditional Indian rituals with Catholic ritual. He does not strictly follow the Indian ways but adds a new element by asking the Catholic priest to sprinkle holy water at Teofilo's burial service, at his wife Louise's suggestion. Through this story, Silko emphasizes that the continuing strength of Pueblo traditions lies in the ability of the people to incorporate alien elements for their own purposes. Leon continues to follow the Pueblo rites and persuades the Father Paul to participate in them, as well. Per Seyersted sees the story as an example of Silko's dual vision as

What Do I Read Next?

- *Storyteller* (1981) is a collection of Silko's short stories, anecdotes, historical and autobiographical notes, poems, and folk tales.

- *Yellow Woman and the Beauty of the Spirit: Essays on Native American Life Today* (1996) is a collection of Silko's essays.

- *The Pueblo Indians*, Joe S. Sando's 1976 book on the history of the Pueblo, enhances the reader's understanding of the Pueblo community.

- *Redefining American Literary History* (1990),

edited by A. LaVonne Brown Ruoff and Jerry W. Ward, Jr., provides a context for the study of Native American literature in the United States.

- *House of Many Rooms*, Robin White's 1958 novel, chronicles the story of an American missionary in India. There Christians still follow Hindu customs, to the bewilderment of the missionary—who finally accepts their choices. This work provides an interesting thematic parallel to "The Man to Send Rain Clouds."

---

both a Pueblo and as a mixed-blood person who has the ability and freedom to see Laguna from the outside. Linda Danielson sees the sense of community in the story as central to understanding it, and views it in terms of Father Paul's entry into the community through the flexibility and power of Indian ritual, which assures the continuance of life.

In addition to these themes, the story also treats an indigenous community's encounters with Christianity. I use the word "indigenous" in the sense that Silko defines it in an interview. She says, "When I say indigenous people I mean people that are connected to the land for, let's say, a thousand or two thousands years." She further adds that one can see similarities in some of the struggles of indigenous peoples in Africa, in the Americas, and in Asia. This is exemplified in the part of the story in which Father Paul is depicted as bewildered by the incorporation of Catholic ritual in an Indian ceremony. Although the reservation Indians are Catholic, they retain pagan rituals and customs. In author Robin White's works one addresses a similar theme in her works about the American missionary experience in India. In White's novel *House of Many Rooms*, a missionary is at first bewildered by his reception by Christianized natives who use Hindu rituals. He refuses to accept the native Christian priest's hospitality, as his own Western notion of Christianity is offended. Later he ends up being a

good friend of the native priest and becomes part of the Christian community in India. Further parallels can be drawn between the history of Christianity in other indigenous cultures, in other literary and historical works.

The theme of death and time is also central to "The Man to Send Rain Clouds." Death is not an end or a frightening experience, but a fact of life to the Pueblo. The spirit returns to its source and returns bringing rain clouds to the community, staving off drought. A LaVonne Ruoff has written that the dead "are associated with cloud beings (storm clouds or Shiwana in Keres) who bring rain and who live in the six or four regions of the universe." Death is also, of course, associated with the notion of time. Silko has said that, for the Indian people, time is round, and not a linear string. Time in its historical dimension is unimportant as it is an endlessly repeating cycle in which man is but a minute part of the cycle. Because of these notions of time and death, Leon can accept old Teofilo's death in a calm, serene manner with the traditional prayer asking his spirit to send rain cloud. This is contrasted in the story with traditional Catholic thinking, which in Seyersted's words, "looks at (death) as one sinful mortal's final, critical meeting with his Maker, in which it is hoped that the blessing symbolized by the holy water will help.": Hence, for Father Paul, the sprinkling of holy water has a much

---

> " The theme of death and time is also central to 'The Man to Send Rain Clouds.'"

different significance than Leon's belief that it will simply quench the spirit's thirst on its way to the other world.

Apart from its thematic concerns and its cultural context, Silko's short story stands out as a technically masterful story. Skillful use of adjectives and attention to detail are the hallmarks of Silko's descriptions. For instance, she writes of a "wide, sandy arroyo," "low, crumbling wall," a "brown, wrinkled forehead" to enhance the beauty of the narrative. The skillful mixture of narration and dialogue also maintains the reader's interest. The dialogues between Leon and Father Paul, and between Leon and Louise, present the characters to the readers directly, thus enabling readers to draw their own conclusions as to the characters respective natures and motivations.

With this said, and because of the high accomplishment of the story itself, "The Man to Send Rain Clouds," a narrative of Pueblo life, deserves to be recognized as a classic Native American short story within the canon of American literature.

Source: Angelina Paul, "Overview of 'The Man to Send Rain Clouds,'" for *Short Stories for Students*, The Gale Group, 2000.

Linda L. Danielson

Danielson teaches English at Lane Community College in Eugene, Oregon. In the following excerpt, she offers a feminist interpretation of Silko's "The Man to Send Rain Clouds."

Over the last twenty years, the general development of scholarship about women's lives and art parallels an unprecedented flowering of creative writing by American Indian women. But in view of these parallel developments, American Indian women have shown little interest in the feminist movement, and conversely mainstream feminist scholarship has paid strikingly little attention to the writing of American Indian women.

Leslie Silko's *Storyteller* (1981), a product of this literary florescence, has remained virtually undiscussed as a whole by critics of any stamp. With its emphasis on women tradition bearers, female deities, and its woman author's personal perspective, *Storyteller* seems to ask for a feminist critical treatment. . . .

Particularly applicable to Silko's *Storyteller* are feminist critical strategies to reclaim as legitimate literary subjects, women's experience and female mythic power. Sandra M. Gilbert sees this strategy as a matter of *re-vision*, seeing anew: "When I say we must redo our history, therefore, I mean we must review, reimagine, rethink, rewrite, revise, and reinterpret the events and documents that constitute it." [*Feminist Criticism: Essays on Women, Literature, and Theory*, edited by Elaine Showalter, 1985].

Silko's *Storyteller* represents just such a re-vision of the world from her vantage point as a Laguna Indian woman. In fact, understanding her re-vision and reinterpretation of personal and tribal memory leads us past the easy impulse to call *Storyteller* a collage, a family album, or pastiche, on into a conception of its unity and significance as a literary work. In seeing anew, Silko expresses a deeply unified view of the world, reclaiming as central to her craft the tribe, the significance of ordinary women's and men's lives, and the set of values arising from the female power of the primary Keresan deities. . . .

Silko presents a highly personal view of tribal ways and at the same time a tribal slant on her personal memories, richly fed by the foremothers and forefathers whose words inspire *Storyteller*. Through the book she reclaims both personal and tribal traditions about men and women, animals and holy people, community and creativity. . . .

"The Man to Send Rain Clouds" returns to themes of creativity and community. In accordance with Keres tradition, Old Teofilo, even in death, is still a valued member of the community, for the people are looking to him to send them big thunderclouds. There is seriousness and ceremony, but no sorrow at his death. He is not lost, just redefined within the community as a Kat'sina spirit associated with the cloud beings who bring rain.

[A. La Vonne] Ruoff observes that the strength of Indian tradition for Silko is not in rigid adherence to old ways, but in creative incorporation of new elements [*MELUS*, 5, 4, Winter, 1978]. In "The Man to Send Rainclouds," modern Indian people not only create new ritual, but offer community to an outsider. The gift of water for the old man's spirit comes from the Catholic priest whom Leon induces to participate in the funeral, on Indian terms. But the priest remains an outsider, suspicious of "some perverse Indian trick—something they did in March to insure a good harvest". Nonetheless, his action brings him to the edge of the community: "He sprinkled the grave and the water disappeared almost before it touched the dim, cold sand; it reminded him of something—he tried to remember what it was, because he thought if he could remember he might understand this." The flexibility that can find needed ritual power and extend the hand of community to the outsider assures the continuance of life, like water and thunderclouds.

Source: Linda L. Danielson, "Storyteller: Grandmother Spider's Web," in *Journal of the Southwest*, Vol. 30, No. 3, Autumn, 1988, pp. 325–55.

Per Seyersted

In the following excerpt, Seyersted provides a thematic overview of Silko's "The Man to Send Rain Clouds."

In a sense [Leslie Marmon Silko] started to write in the fifth grade: "A teacher gave us a list of words to make sentences out of, and I just made it into a story automatically" (interview in Dexter Fisher, ed., *The Third Woman . . .*). But it was only at college in 1967 when she was forced to write a story in a creative writing course and found again that what was difficult for others came naturally to her, that she realized she was a writer. Back at Laguna she had just heard in headline form that an old man had been found dead at a sheep camp and had been given a traditional burial and that the priest had resented the fact that he was not called in. Unable to think of anything else, she decided to write about this incident and to try to imagine the scene and how the people had felt. The result was "The Man to Send Rain Clouds," which was quickly published in *New*

> 'The Man to Send Rain Clouds' returns to themes of creativity and community. In accordance with Keres tradition, Old Teofilo, even in death, is still a valued member of the community, for the people are looking to him to send them big thunderclouds."

Mexico Quarterly and also earned for her a "Discovery Grant."

In Rosen's 1974 anthology, Silko wrote about herself: "I am of mixed-breed ancestry, but what I know is Laguna. This place I am from is everything I am as a writer and human being." And she has also said (in *Laguna Woman*): "I suppose at the core of my writing is the attempt to identify what it is to be a half-breed or mixed blooded person; what it is to grow up neither white nor fully traditional Indian." It is as if she is saying that she is wholly a Laguna Pueblo and will write about the place where she grew up, but that at the same time she is a mixed-blood and therefore has been given the ability and the freedom to see Laguna also from the outside. Her first story exemplifies this double vision.

When Ken and Leon in their pickup come looking for old Teofilo, they already have with them what is needed to perform the preliminaries for a traditional burial, such as painting his face. When they have completed these tasks, Leon smiles and says, "Send us rain clouds, Grandfather." Returning to the pueblo with the body under a tarpaulin, they meet Father Paul, who is led to believe that Teofilo is alive and well at camp. Later at home, the funeral is performed with clanspeople and old men with medicine bags attending. While the others go to the graveyard, Leon acts upon Louise's suggestion that he ask the priest to sprinkle "holy water for Grandpa. So he won't be thirsty. Father Paul protests that a Christian burial would require the

> **What we have in the story are two different ideas of death, or rather, of our whole existence."**

Last Rites and a Mass, but in the end he reluctantly comes along, and when the besprinkled body is lowered, Leon is happy: "now the old man could send them big thunderclouds for sure."

Silko's interest in this story does not lie in the descriptions of the rituals themselves. She has said that while she has looked at anthropologists' reports on Laguna, she does not consult them. For one thing, she doubts that the informants (among whom were some of her own ancestors) always gave the scholars the true story, and more important, their reports are dead to her compared to the living reality of what she has heard and seen and felt herself. Also, she is an artist who wants to apply her imagination to the telling of tales, and to her, the essence of this particular incident is the story of this instance of cultural clash with the feelings and ideas involved.

To be sure, she does want us to see that these are Laguna rituals and attitudes. For example, she gives us such local details as that Leon ties a gray feather in Teofilo's hair and that he paints the old man's face with stripes of certain colors. But she does not tell us what the medicine men do at the important event of the funeral in Teofilo's home. Thus we have to guess that some of the things they all do, such as Leon's application of paints, may be part of the task of making "him so that he may be recognized" in Shibapu, and that others, such as Louise's sprinkling of corn meal and her concern that her Grandpa shall not be thirsty, are intended to make sure that he has "water . . . and also food for his traveling provisions" (Boas, *Keresan Texts*, 1928; rpt. New York: AMS Press, 1974 . . .).

What we have in the story are two different ideas of death, or rather, of our whole existence. The Indian, as Vine Deloria has reminded us, is wedded to place rather than time and to group rather than individual. On the one hand, as Ortiz has written,

"Indian traditions exist in, and are primarily to be understood in relation to, space; they belong to the place where the people exist or originated," their existence being likened metaphorically to that of a plant. And he adds: "time in its linear, historical dimension . . . is unimportant" compared to "cyclical, rhythmic time, time viewed as a series of endlessly repeating cycles, on the model of the seasons or, again, plants" (*Indian Historian*, Winter 1977 . . .). And on the other hand, as already suggested, pueblo societies see the survival of the group as more important than the existence of the individual. That is, man is a minute part of an immense natural cycle, and his death has nothing threatening in it because, after a life which contained both the good and the bad that all Pueblos brought with them from Shibapu, he simply goes back to where he came from, and in line with the communal thinking, it is hoped that his spirit will help the group he leaves behind by returning with rain clouds. This is of course wholly alien to Catholic thinking, which sees death in terms of the individual rather than the group and which looks at it as one sinful mortal's final, critical meeting with his Maker, in which it is hoped that the blessing symbolized by the holy water will help.

It is part of the mastery of this short story that Silko only lightly suggests all this in her spare, highly controlled narrative, in which she hardly enters into the protagonists' minds. Furthermore, as an objective writer, she does not take sides, but gives a balanced, sensitive presentation of the characters. In her depiction of the Pueblos she makes us feel what David B. Espey has termed "the mood of peace and simplicity, the quiet assurance with which [they] react to death," accepting from Catholicism only what they can use; and in her sympathetic picture of the priest we sense both his good will and his bewilderment. In the one riddle she leaves us with—Father Paul is reminded of something, but does not know what, when the water immediately disappears into the sand—she seems to suggest that he is on the verge of understanding the impossibility of Christianizing this proud, independent, "foreign" people who look to Mt. Taylor, looming up behind the graveyard, as a holy shrine and who have decorated most of the walls of the church in which he works with signs of thunder, clouds, and rainbows. In the quiet dignity of the telling of this moving tale, Silko makes it clear that she is an intelligent writer and a born storyteller.

Source: Per Seyersted, in *Leslie Marmon Silko*, Boise State University, 1980, pp. 15–18.

A. LaVonne Ruoff

At the time that this piece was published, Ruoff was affiliated with the University of Illinois/Chicago Circle. In the following excerpt, she asserts that the story gives an example of the strength and adaptability of tribal traditions.

For Leslie Marmon Silko (Laguna), the strength of tribal traditions is based not on Indians' rigid adherence to given ceremonies or customs but rather on their ability to adapt traditions to ever-changing circumstances by incorporating new elements. Although this theme is most fully developed in her recent novel *Ceremony* (1977), it is also present in her earlier short stories, ''The Man to Send Rain Clouds,'' ''Tony's Story,'' ''from Humaweepi, Warrior Priest,'' and ''Yellow Woman,'' included in the volume *The Man to Send Rainclouds: Contemporary Stories by American Indians* [edited by Kenneth Rosen, 1974].

The history of Silko's own Laguna Pueblo, influenced by many different cultures, provides insight into why she emphasizes change as a source of strength for tribal traditions. According to their origin legends, the Laguna tribe (in existence since at least 1300), came southward from the Mesa Verde region. Some versions indicate that after pausing at Zia, they were joined by the head of the Parrot clan, who decided to take his people southward with them. After wandering further, first southward from the lake at Laguna and then northward back to the lake, they settled Punyana, probably in the late 1300s. After founding Old Laguna (Kawaik) around 1400, they issued invitations to other pueblos to join them. Those which responded were the Parrot clan from Zia, the Sun clan from Hopi, the Road Runner and Badger clans from Zuni, and the Sun clan from Jemez. The tribe occupied the site of what is now called Laguna by the early 1500s. Additional immigration occurred during the 1690s, when the Lagunas were joined by Indians from the Rio Grande, probably fleeing both drought and the hostility of the Spanish after the Pueblo Rebellion in 1680 and the renewed uprising in 1696. These immigrants came chiefly from Zia, Cochiti, and Domingo, but a few came from Jemez, Zuni, and Hopi. Although some remained to join the Laguna tribe, others returned to their own pueblos when conditions improved. Over the years, a few Navajos intermarried with the tribe, bringing with them the Navajo Sun clan and kachina.

> " Thus, Silko emphasizes that these Pueblo Indians have not abandoned their old ways for Catholicism; instead, they have taken one part of Catholic ritual compatible with their beliefs and made it an essential part of their own ceremony. . . . "

The Spanish first entered the area in 1540, when Francesco de Coronado led an expedition to Zuni and two years later passed through the present site of Laguna on his way back to Mexico. Antonio Espejo, who commanded an expedition to New Mexico in 1582, visited the area in 1583. Between the appointment of Juan de Onate as New Mexico's first governor in 1598 and the Pueblo Rebellion in 1680, there is little historical data on Laguna. Although the pueblo was not subjected to as many attacks from the Spanish as the Rio Grande pueblos, it was forced to surrender in 1692 after an attack by the troops of Governor Diego de Vargas.

Concerning the mixture of people who settled at Laguna, Parsons comments that ''it is not surprising that Laguna was the first of the pueblos to Americanize, through intermarriage'' [Elsie Clews Parsons, *Pueblo Indian Religion*, 1939]. Around 1860 and 1870, George H. Pradt [or Pratt] and two Marmon brothers (Walter and Robert) came to the pueblo, married Laguna women, and reared large families. Silko indicates that her great grandfather Robert and his brother had a government contract to set out the boundary markers for Laguna. Walter, appointed government teacher in 1871, married the daughter of the chief of the Kurena-Shikani medicine men. The chief's son later took his place. According to Parsons, this group led the Americanization faction which was opposed by the pueblo hierarchy. The conservatives removed their altars and sacred objects from Laguna and moved to Mesita; around 1880, part of this group resettled in Isleta. While Robert Marmon served as governor, the two kivas of Laguna were torn down by the progressives and what was left of the sacred objects was surrendered. There were no kachina dances for some time after the Great Split and the laying of the railroad on the edge of the village. When a demand arose later for the revival of the dances, Zuni influences were introduced into Laguna rituals. Parsons closes her description of Laguna with the comment that although the ceremonial disintegration was so marked when she first studied it (around 1920) that it presented an obscure picture of Keresan culture, it now (1939) offered "unrivaled opportunities to study American acculturation and the important role played by miscegenation." Silko herself comments on these changes in her description of the impact of mixed-blood families on Laguna clan systems and the varying attitudes toward these families in the stories of that pueblo:

> People in the main part of the village were our clanspeople because the clan system was still maintained although not in the same form it would have been if we were full blood. . . . The way it changed was that there began to be stories about my great-grandfather, positive stories about what he did with the Laguna scouts for the Apaches. But then after World War One it changed. Soon after that there came to be stories about these mixed blood people, half-breeds. Not only Marmons but Gunns [John] and Pratts too. An identity was being made or evolved in the stories the Lagunas told about these people who had gone outside Laguna, but at the same time of the outsiders who had come in. Part of it was that the stories were always about the wild, roguish, crazy sorts of things they did [Lawrence Evers and Dennis Carr, *Sun Tracks*, III, Fall, 1976].

The continuing strength of Laguna traditions and the ability of her people to use alien traditions for their own purposes are strikingly portrayed in Silko's story "The Man to Send Rainclouds." The title alludes to the belief that the dead are associated with cloud beings (storm clouds or *shiwanna* in Keres) who bring rain and who live in the six or four regions of the universe (Parsons). The story deals with an Indian family's observance of Pueblo funeral rituals despite the local priest's attempts to cajole them into observing Catholic ones. Ironically, the young priest is trapped by the Indians into taking part in their ceremony. The importance of ritual in Pueblo Indian life is emphasized at the beginning of the story when Leon and Ken, after finding old Teofilo dead, immediately observe the first stages of the funeral rites. Neglect of burial or death ritual can result in death or sickness because the ghost returns (Parsons). Before wrapping the body in a

blanket, the men tie a gray prayer feather to the old man's long white hair (a custom similar to that of the Zuni) and begin to paint his face with markings so that he will be recognized in the next world—tasks ordinarily performed by a shaman. The face painting is interrupted by an offering of corn meal to the wind and is concluded with the prayer "send us rain clouds, Grandfather."

The pressure on Pueblo Indians to practice Catholicism is introduced when Father Paul stops Leon and Ken on their way home to ask about Teofilo and to urge them all to come to church. Using the age-old Indian technique of telling the non-Indian only what they want him to know, Leon and Ken answer the priest's questions about the old man's welfare ambiguously enough to keep him from learning about Teofilo's death. Only after the Indian funeral rites are almost completed does the family feel the need for the priest's services—to provide plenty of holy water for the grave so that Teofilo's spirit will send plenty of rainfall. Corn meal has been sprinkled around the old man's body to provide food on the journey to the other world. Silko skillfully and humorously characterizes the conflict between the frustrated priest, who is denied the opportunity to provide the last rites and funeral mass, and Leon, who doggedly insists that these are not necessary: "It's O.K. Father, we just want him to have plenty of water." Despite his weary protests that he cannot do that without performing the proper Catholic rites, Father Paul finally gives in when Leon starts to leave. Realizing that he has been tricked into participating in their pagan rites and half suspecting that the whole thing may be just a spring fertility ceremony rather than a real funeral, he nevertheless sprinkles the grave with a whole jar of holy water. Leon feels good about the act which completes the ceremony and ensures that "now the old man could send them big thunderclouds for sure." Thus, Silko emphasizes that these Pueblo Indians have not abandoned their old ways for Catholicism; instead, they have taken one part of Catholic ritual compatible with their beliefs and made it an essential part of their own ceremony. . . .

In all four of these stories, Silko emphasizes the need to return to the rituals and oral traditions of the past in order to rediscover the basis for one's cultural identity. Only when this is done is one prepared to deal with the problems of the present. However, Silko advocates a return to the essence rather than to the precise form of these rituals and traditions, which must be adapted continually to meet new challenges. Through her own stories, Silko demonstrates that the Keres rituals and traditions have survived all attempts to eradicate them and that the seeds for the resurgence of their power lie in the memories and creativeness of her people.

Source: A. LaVonne Ruoff, ''Ritual and Renewal: Keres Traditions in the Short Fiction of Leslie Silko,'' in *MELUS*, Vol. 5, No. 4, Winter, 1978, pp. 2–17.

Sources

Danielson, Linda L. ''Storyteller: Grandmother Spider's Web,'' in *Journal of the Southwest*, Vol. 30, No. 3, Autumn, 1988, pp. 325-55.

Krupet, Arnold. ''The Dialogic of Silko's *Storyteller*,'' in *Narrative Chance*, edited by Gerald Vizenor, University of New Mexico, 1989, pp. 55-68.

Ruoff, A. LaVonne. ''Ritual and Renewal: Keres Traditions in the Short Fiction of Leslie Silko,'' in *MELUS*, Vol. 5, No. 4, Winter, 1978, pp. 2-17.

Seyersted, Per. *Leslie Marmon Silko*, Boise State University, 1980.

Silko, Leslie Marmon. *Ceremony,* New York: Viking Press, 1977.

———. *Yellow Woman and a Beauty of the Spirit*, Simon and Schuster, 1996.

http://www.altx.com/interviews/silko.html. *An Interview with Leslie Marmon Silko*, by Thomas Irmer (Alt-X Berlin/Leipzig correspondent).

White, Robin. *House of Many Rooms,* New York: Harper, 1958.

Further Reading

Danielson, Linda L. ''Storyteller: Grandmother Spider's Web,'' in *Journal of the Southwest*, Vol. 30, No. 3, Autumn, 1988, pp. 325-55.

    An interpretation of Silko's ''The Man to Send Rainclouds,'' particularly with regard to themes of creativity and community, analyzed from a feminist perspective.

Ruoff, A. LaVonne. ''Ritual and Renewal: Keres Traditions in the Short Fiction of Leslie Silko,'' in *MELUS*, Vol. 5, No. 4, Winter, 1978, pp. 2-17.

    An analysis of the traditions at work in Silko's work, suggesting on pp. 2-5 that the story provides an example of the strength of tribal traditions through adaptability.

Seyersted, Per. *Leslie Marmon Silko*, Boise State University, 1980.

    Addresses Silko's biography, and provides a brief history of the Pueblo people and an analysis of Silko's works, in particular a study of the theme of culture clash in ''The Man to Send Rain Clouds'' on pp. 15-18.

The Masque of the Red Death

Edgar Allan Poe

1842

Edgar Allan Poe's short story ''The Masque of the Red Death'' was first published in 1842. In the original publication, the title was given the English spelling of ''mask,'' yet it was changed to ''masque'' in 1845. In this macabre tale, a Prince Prospero seals himself and a thousand of his friends into the abbey of a castle in order to protect them from a deadly pestilence—The Red Death—that is ravaging the country. But when the group indulge in a lavish costume ball in order to distract themselves from the suffering and death outside their walls, the Red Death, disguised as a costumed guest, enters and claims the lives of everyone present. The story is narrated in a manner which gives it the quality of a myth, allegory or fairy tale, exploring themes of man's fear of death, sin, madness, and the end of the world.

This tale is a prime example of Poe's Gothic horror fiction. Poe evokes a dark and eerie mood in a story that focuses on images of blood and death, while the personification of the Red Death lends an element of the supernatural. ''The Masque of the Red Death'' embodies Poe's mastery of the short story; in addition, it illustrates his literary philosophy. According to Poe, a short story should be tightly focused so that every word, from beginning to end, contributes to the overall effect. In ''The Masque of the Red Death,'' powerful imagery and an illusive narrative voice are tightly woven into a macabre tale of horror with insight into the human condition.

Author Biography

Edgar Allan Poe was born in Boston, Massachusetts, on January 19, 1809. The son of minor stage actors, Poe was orphaned at any early age, as his father abandoned him and his mother died of tuberculosis when he was still a very young child. He was then adopted by John Allan and Francis Allan, but Mrs. Allan, Poe's beloved foster mother, died of tuberculosis in 1829, when he was still a teenager. Although John never legally adopted him, Poe added the Allan surname to his own.

Poe spent his early adult life in and out of the army, engaging in an ongoing struggle over money with his foster father, and developing the notorious habits of alcoholism and debt. In 1835, at the age of twenty-six, he married his young cousin, Virginia Clemm, who was only thirteen. The exact nature of their relationship is unknown, although it is generally said that his treatment of her was more that of a father than of a husband. Virginia, however, died of tuberculosis in 1847, the third significant woman in his life to have died of the same disease.

Although a controversial figure during his lifetime, Poe's literary contribution to nineteenth and early twentieth century literature has been invaluable. His long poem, "The Raven," launched him into instant national, and eventually, international, success. The poem is perhaps the most famous and widely read of his works. His literary influence, however, derives largely from his numerous innovations in the art of the short story. Poe raised the short story to the status of an art form, solidifying a principle of short-story writing still in practice today: that the short story must be about one central idea or event, and one only.

He is considered to have single-handedly invented the modern detective story, of which the Sherlock Holmes stories are a direct descendent. Furthermore, Poe mastered the art of Gothic fiction in his tales of the macabre; his stories can best be characterized as "dark," focusing on death and taking place primarily at night. In this way, Poe developed the short story into a genre of fairy tales for adults, touching on the mystical and supernatural in stories which reach into the darkest corners of human psychology. Posthumously, Poe's work was also extremely influential on French and Russian literature.

One night in the fall of 1849, Edgar Allan Poe was found lying unconscious on a street in Balti-more. He was taken to a hospital, where he remained in a semi-coma for three days, after which he died. Although a life of heavy drinking certainly did not contribute to Poe's health, it is thought that his death was directly due to a brain lesion, complicated by other long-term illnesses. Obituaries appearing immediately after his death painted Poe's character in a rather unflattering light, a posthumous reputation that proved hard to remedy.

Plot Summary

Poe's story "The Masque of the Red Death" begins with a description of a plague, the "Red Death." It is the most deadly plague ever, as "no pestilence had ever been so fatal, or so hideous." The symptoms of the plague include "sharp pains, and sudden dizziness, and then profuse bleeding at the pores." The "scarlet stains" on the body, and especially the face, of its victims are the "pest ban" or first visible signs of the disease. Once the stains appear, the victim has only thirty minutes before death.

In order to escape the spread of the plague, Prince Prospero invites "a thousand hale and light-hearted friends from among the knights and dames of his court" to seal themselves "in deep seclusion" in an abbey of his castle, allowing no one to enter or leave. With adequate provisions, Prospero and his privileged guests attempt to "bid defiance to contagion," by sealing themselves off from the suffering and disease spreading throughout the rest of their country. The Prince provides for his guests "all the appliances of pleasure" to help them not to "grieve" or to "think" about the Red Death raging outside the walls of the abbey.

Toward the end of the fifth or sixth month, the Prince holds a masquerade ball for his guests, "while the pestilence raged most furiously abroad." The Prince takes elaborate measures in his decorations for the ball, which is to take place in "an imperial suite" of seven rooms, each decorated in its own color scheme. The only lighting in each room comes from a brazier of fire, mounted on a tripod, which is set outside the stained glass windows of each room, causing the color of the glass to infuse the entire room. The progression of rooms is from blue to purple to green to orange to white to violet to black. The seventh room, decorated in black velvet, is lit by the fire burning behind a red-stained glass window. But the effect of the red light

Edgar Allen Poe

is "ghastly in the extreme," and the seventh room is avoided by most of the guests.

In the seventh room is a "gigantic clock of ebony" which strikes at each hour. The sound of the clock striking is "of so peculiar a note and emphasis" that all of the guests, as well as the orchestra and the dancers, pause at each hour to listen, and there is "a brief disconcert in the whole company." But the revelers remain "stiff frozen" only for a moment before returning to their music and dancing.

At the stroke of midnight the guests, pausing at the sound of the clock, notice a mysterious "masked figure" in their midst. The figure wears "the habiliments of the grave" and the mask on its face resembles "the countenance of a stiffened corpse." The costume of the mysterious figure has even taken on "the type of the Red Death." Its clothing is "dabbled in blood" and its face is "besprinkled with the scarlet horror."

When Prince Prospero sees this mysterious figure, he orders his guests to seize and unmask it, so that he may hang the intruder at dawn. But the guests, cowering in fear, shrink from the figure. In a rage, Prospero, bearing a dagger, pursues the masked figure through each of the rooms—from blue to purple to green to orange to white to violet. The

figure enters the seventh room, decorated in a ghastly black and red, and turns to face Prospero. The Prince falls dead to the floor. But when the guests seize the figure, they find that, underneath its shroud and mask there is "no tangible form."

The guests realize that the Red Death has slipped into their abbey "like a thief in the night" to claim their lives, "and one by one dropped the revelers in the blood-bedewed halls of their revel." The last line of the story describes the complete victory of the Red Death over life: "And Darkness and Decay and the Red Death held illimitable dominion over all."

Characters

The Masked Figure

The "masked figure" that appears at Prince Prospero's costume ball is the most illusive "character" in the story. Upon the stroke of midnight, the guests first notice this "masked figure," who is "tall and gaunt, and shrouded from head to foot in the habiliments of the grave," and looks like the corpse of a body afflicted by the Red Death, its face "besprinkled with the scarlet horror." Prince Prospero orders that the figure be unmasked and hanged at dawn, but his guests refuse to unmask him. The figure then retreats through all seven rooms of the abbey, pursued by Prince Prospero. When the figure reaches the seventh room, it turns to face the Prince, who falls instantly to his death. When the guests rush to seize the figure, they find that, beneath the corpselike costume, there is no "tangible form." The masked figure turns out to be The Red Death itself. It had crept into the sealed abbey "like a thief in the night." The last line of the story indicates that the Red Death has triumphed over life: "And Darkness and Decay and the Red Death held illimitable dominion over all."

Prince Prospero

Prince Prospero is the central character of "The Masque of the Red Death." Despite the plague of the Red Death which rages throughout his country, the Prince ignores the suffering of others and invites "a thousand friends" from his court to seal themselves in an abbey of his castle in order to protect themselves from the pestilence. In order to distract them from the death and suffering outside their walls, the prince provides his guests with "all the appliances of pleasure," and holds a masquerade ball after the fifth or sixth month. In all of his arrangements, Prince Prospero's taste is extravagant and "bizarre." When the mysterious figure bearing the masque of the Red Death appears at his masquerade ball, the Prince demands that he be unmasked and hanged "at sunrise." Yet, while his guests shrink in horror from the figure, the Prince, carrying a dagger, pursues it through the first six rooms to the seventh. When he confronts the figure, the dagger drops from his hand and he falls to the floor, dead.

There is some indication that Prince Prospero may be a mad man, and that the entire story is his dream or delusional vision, and all its characters figments of his imagination.

The Thousand Friends

While a deadly plague devastates his country, Prince Prospero invites "a thousand hale and light-hearted friends from among the knights and dames of his court" to escape the plague by hiding in the abbey with him. While there are no individual characters among the Prince's guests, the "thousand friends" share a collective role as characters in the story. The prince holds a masquerade ball, at which his guests appear in outlandish costumes. As none of the guests, also described as "a multitude of dreams," are given any specific character traits, they could be interpreted as mere "fantasms" of the Prince's imagination, or imaginary projections of the Prince's psyche. When the mysterious masked figure appears at the ball, and Prince Prospero orders his guests to seize the intruder, they collectively shrink back in fear and, when the figure moves past the Prince, "the vast assembly, as if with one impulse" cowers in fear, allowing it to pass them without impediment. Yet they cannot escape the Red Death: "And one by one dropped the revelers in the blood-bedewed halls of their revel, and died each in the despairing posture of his fall." Like the Prince, his "thousand friends" cannot escape the inevitability of their own deaths.

Themes

Death

While this story is literally about a pestilence called the Red Death, it can be read at an allegorical level as a tale about man's fear of his own mortality. In the story, Prince Prospero and his "thousand friends" seal themselves into an abbey of his castle

Media Adaptations

- Poe's short stories "The Tell-Tale heart, And Other Terrifying Tales" were recorded on audiocassette by August House in 1995. The stories are read by Syd Liberman.

- "Poe Masterpieces" is a collection of Poe's short stories recorded on audiocassette by the Listening Library in 1987.

- Poe's detective stories are recorded on an audiocassette entitled "The Murders in the Rue Morgue" by Books on Tape in 1992.

- "The Best of Edgar Allan Poe" is a selection of Poe's short stories recorded on audiocassette by the Listening Library in 1987.

in an attempt to "defy contagion" and escape the clutches of the Red Death. The Prince employs "all the appliances of pleasure" in order to distract his guests both from the suffering and death outside their walls and from thoughts of their own vulnerability to the Red Death. The Prince's actions symbolize the ways in which all humans tend to focus on material pleasures in order to distract themselves from the knowledge that everyone, including themselves, eventually must die.

The fact that the Red Death slips in "like a thief in the night" to claim the lives of everyone present symbolizes the fact that no one, not even the powerful and wealthy, can escape death, which eventually claims all mortals. Just as everyone must eventually "face" the fact of their own mortality, the Prince dies the moment he literally "faces" his own Death, and can no longer deny its presence in his castle.

Time

The theme of time in this story is closely linked to the theme of death. Of course, the passage of time signals the approach of death; as the saying goes, each minute that passes brings us one minute closer to our death. Poe at one point capitalizes the word Time, as if it were a proper name, thereby personify-

Topics for Further Study

- Nathaniel Hawthorne was an American writer and a contemporary of Edgar Allan Poe. Hawthorne's short story collection *Twice-Told Tales* is considered to share similar elements of Gothic horror with the short stories of Poe. Read at least one of Hawthorne's stories from this collection for comparison with "The Masque of the Red Death." Discuss the similarities and differences.

- Discuss Poe's "The Masque of the Red Death" in terms of how it portrays a societal or group response to illness and plague. What is the attitude of the privileged guests of Prospero's castle toward those outside the castle who are more vulnerable to and afflicted by the Red Death? In what ways can this story function as a parable, or story with a moral, for understanding contemporary societal responses to the disease of AIDS and those infected with HIV?

- Poe's "The Masque of the Red Death" is, in some ways, a story about human and societal responses to the inevitability of death. In what ways do Prospero and his guests attempt to deal with, or not deal with, their own impending deaths? Research the psychology of death to learn more about how people in contemporary times attempt to deal with the deaths of others, and with their own mortality.

- During Poe's lifetime, tuberculosis was a very common disease, characterized most notably by the symptom of the coughing up of blood. As three of the most important women in Poe's life died of tuberculosis (his mother, stepmother, and wife), one could speculate that the "Red Death" in the story was inspired by his own experience of loved ones suffering from tuberculosis. Find out more about the disease of tuberculosis during the nineteenth century and today.

- After his death, Poe came to be a strong influence on the French poet Baudelaire and the Russian novelist Theodore Dostoyevski. Examine the work of one of these writers. In what ways is the influence of Poe apparent in their writing?

- The Black Plague (also known as the Bubonic Plague) was one of the worst plagues in human history. Learn more about the Black Plague, such as how societies responded to the problems caused by the plague, what "cures" were attempted. What was its historical impact?

---

ing it, which suggests that he is referring to time in a broader allegorical sense, rather than simply in a literal sense.

The connection of time with death is indicated by the placement of the "great ebony clock" in the seventh room of the abbey, which is the room associated with images of death. The passage of time marked by the chiming of the clock each hour symbolizes the limited time each person has to live. The guests at the ball are so disturbed by the sound of the clock's chime because it is a reminder to each person of their own encroaching deaths. With the passing of each hour, the guests at the ball are forced to think about their own mortality, despite all the distractions provided by their elaborate festivities, for "more of thought crept, with more of time, into the meditations of the thoughtful among those who reveled."

The hour of midnight, marking the end of the day, thus symbolizes the end of life. Indeed, the Red Death is first noticed among the guests at the ball shortly after the stroke of midnight, signaling the arrival of death for each partygoer. The death of the guests and breakdown of the clock are likewise simultaneous, for "the clock went out with the last of the gay."

Madness

"The Masque of the Red Death" can be interpreted as the interior monologue of a madman, and all its characters figments of his insane imagination. As G. R. Thompson maintains, Poe was "the master of the interior monologue of a profoundly disturbed mind." If this story represents the "interior monologue" of a mad Prince Prospero, the narrator must be Prince Prospero himself. The narrator first mentions the possibility that the Prince may be insane by attributing it to the opinion of others, stating that "there are some who would have thought him mad." But the narrator distances himself from this opinion by then stating that "his followers felt that he was not" mad.

If the entire story represents the figment of one man's mad imagination, then the guests are not real people, but merely characters in his own internal psycho-drama. Indeed, the guests at the masquerade ball are described as "a multitude of dreams" and even as "fantasms." In this sense the "masqueraders" at the ball are merely extensions of the narrator himself, just as the characters in dreams are extensions of the dreamer. It is the Prince himself who dresses his guests, for "it was his own guiding taste which had given character to the masqueraders." And the particular costumes are described as "delirious fancies such as a madman fashions." In other words, the mad Prince designed the costumes of his guests in accordance with his own "delirious fancies," or delusions. If the guests of the Prince are reflections of his own mad imagination, it also makes sense that even they are eventually referred to as "mad," in the phrase "mad revelers." And even the masked figure of the Red Death is described as taking on "mad assumptions."

Apocalypse

The use of language in "The Masque of the Red Death," as well as the nature of the tale, brings to mind a biblical story with apocalyptic implications. The story evokes images familiar from the Bible; the "pestilence" that has devastated an unnamed country described in the opening paragraph recalls images of God having sent a pestilence upon the land as a form of punishment to humans for their sins. Prince Prospero and his "thousand guests" seem like likely candidates for divine wrath, as they exhibit no sympathy for the suffering of their fellow countrymen, instead indulging in "all the appliances of pleasure."

As critic Patrick Cheney has pointed out in his article "Poe's Use of *The Tempest* and the Bible in 'The Masque of the Red Death,'" the final paragraph of the story take on a biblical tone, as "the language, rhythm and allusion are unmistakably Biblical." Most notably, the closing sentence evokes apocalyptic images of complete devastation: "And Darkness and Decay and the Red Death held illimitable dominion over all." Cheney, however, argues that, unlike the Bible, where God always ultimately triumphs, in Poe's story it is the forces of evil, "Darkness and Decay and the Red Death," which suggest an unholy trinity winning out over light and goodness and life.

Style

Allegory and Parable

"The Masque of the Red Death" is considered an *allegorical* tale; this means that the literal elements of the story are meant to be understood as symbolic of some greater meaning. *Britannica Online* explains that an allegory "uses symbolic fictional figures and actions to convey truths or generalizations about human conduct or experience." More specifically, this story may be read as a *parable*, a sub-category of allegory in which, according to *Britannica Online*, "moral or spiritual relations are set forth."

As a parable, "Masque of the Red Death" is symbolic of how humans respond to the knowledge of their own mortality. The reaction of Prince Prospero and his "thousand friends" to the presence of the Red Death is an attempt to use their material privileges in order to escape the inevitability of their own deaths. But the fact that the "masked figure" slips into their midst "like a thief in the night" is symbolic of the fact that no amount or wealth or privilege can exempt a person from death, no amount of entertainment or distraction can completely eliminate the fear of death, and no amount of security can keep death from arriving at one's doorstep. "The Masque of the Red Death" affirms the futility of man in his elaborate attempts to deny and defy his own mortality.

Imagery and Symbolism

The seven chambers of the abbey, according to critic H. H. Bell, Jr., in his article "'The Masque of the Red Death': An Interpretation," represent the seven decades of a man's life, so that the final chamber, decorated in red and black, represents death. Bell interprets the seven chambers as "an allegorical representation of Prince Prospero's life span." This view is supported by the fact that the first room is located in the East, which symbolizes birth, because it is the direction from which the sun rises, and that the last chamber is located in the West, which symbolizes death, as the sun sets in the West. Bell interprets each of the colors of the seven rooms—blue, purple, green, orange, white, violet— as symbolic of "Prospero's physical and mental condition in that decade of his life." The seventh room is the location of death, as it is eerily decorated in black and red—black being a color associated with death and night, and red being a color strongly associated with blood, and, in this story, the Red Death. Meanwhile, in the first six rooms "beat feverishly the heart of life."

Located in the seventh room, the clock can be read as a symbol of the limited time each person has to live. Thus, the stroking of the clock each hour is a reminder to the guests of the limited time left in their own lives. Midnight represents the hour of death, because it is at midnight that the "masked figure" is noticed by the guests. These allegorical details culminate in the death of the Prince, in the seventh room, shortly after the stroke of midnight, at the precise moment when he literally "faces" his own death. The clock as a symbolic representation of human life is also indicated in the closing lines, as "the life of the ebony clock went out with that of the last of the gay."

Narration

At the most literal level, this story is told in the "third person," meaning that the narrator is not a character in the story. However, as critic Leonard Cassuto has speculated, the narrator of the story may be the Red Death itself, since all of the people in the story are dead by the end, and the Red Death is the only one left to tell the tale. On the other hand, if the entire story is interpreted as the dream of a madman (the Prince Prospero), all its characters figments of his imagination ("dreams"), and his death not literal but psychological, then the narrator could be the Prince himself. Finally, because the story is told in the manner of a biblical morality tale, in which God punishes the evil by sending down a "pestilence" upon the land, it could be argued that the narrator is in fact a divine being.

Setting

The story takes place in an unnamed "country," in no specific time period or geographical location, which has been ravaged by a deadly "pes-

tilence." The ambiguity of the exact setting lends the story a "once upon a time" element, and places it in the realm of a parable or fable.

Personification

Personification is the use of metaphorical language that assigns a non- human object or animal human traits. Poe indicates the personification of certain concepts by capitalizing them, as one would a proper name. He thus personifies The Red Death, Time, Beauty, Darkness, and Decay. This lends the story an element of myth or fairy tale, as each term seems to be symbolic of broader concepts that refer to the human condition in general.

Gothic horror

Poe is considered one of the early masters of Gothic horror fiction. The genre was developed in the nineteenth century, originally in the literature of Great Britain, and is characterized by elements of the supernatural, gruesome scenes of horror, dark settings, and a preoccupation with death and madness. "The Masque of the Red Death" contains all of these elements.

Historical Context

Tuberculosis

Three of the most important women in Poe's life died of tuberculosis. Although the "pestilence" in the story "Masque of the Red Death" is not defined, it seems reasonable to assume that it is inspired in some ways by Poe's experience with tuberculosis. The distinguishing mark of the "Red Death" is profuse bleeding, just as the distinguishing sign of tuberculosis is the coughing up of blood. According to *Britannica Online*, tuberculosis, often referred to in literature as "consumption," is "one of the great scourges of mankind." The disease "reached near-epic proportions" in industrializing urban areas in the eighteenth and nineteenth centuries. During this time, it was "the leading cause of death for all age groups in the Western world."

Impressionism

Much of Poe's writing can be referred to as "impressionist," depicting the subtle details of a

Compare & Contrast

- **Nineteenth Century:** In the nineteenth and early twentieth centuries, tuberculosis (also commonly referred to as "consumption") reached epidemic proportions, particularly in developing urban and industrial areas. During this time, it was the leading cause of death in the West.

   Twentieth Century: Thanks to developments in sanitation and hygiene, the spread of tuberculosis was significantly curbed for most of the twentieth century. In the 1980s, however, the disease began to make a comeback in the West, and is still a threat in developing nations.

- **Nineteenth Century:** Gothic fiction, or Gothic horror, was developed as a literary genre in the nineteenth century. In England, Mary Shelley's *Frankenstein* (1818) was one of the first Gothic novels of note, followed by others, such as Robert Louis Stevenson's *Strange Case of Dr. Jekyll and Mr. Hyde* (1886) and Bram Stoker's *Dracula* (1895). In America, Edgar Allan Poe and Nathaniel Hawthorne were notable authors of Gothic fiction.

   Twentieth Century: Gothic fiction in the late twentieth century has developed into two distinct genres. On one hand, the modern horror story flourishes, in both the novel form, with such prolific writers as Stephen King, and in cinema, with such films as *Psycho*, *Night of the Living Dead*, *Friday the 13th*, *Halloween*, and *A Nightmare on Elm Street*. On the other hand, the modern, mass-market paperback romance novel, often referred to as Gothic romance, is also descended from the Gothic novel.

- **Nineteenth Century:** On the stage, tales of Gothic horror were depicted most notably in the style of the Grand Guignol, known for performances which emphasized graphic depictions of gory violence. Grand Guignol theater was performed primarily in France, although it enjoyed a brief popularity in England.

   Twentieth Century: The genre of Gothic horror has met with the greatest success in the twentieth Century in the cinema. Beginning in the 1960s, horror films showed increasingly graphic portrayals of blood, gore, and violence.

- **Nineteenth Century:** The HIV virus did not exist.

   1990s: Since the epidemic of the disease known as AIDS exploded in the early 1980s, the HIV virus that is believed to cause AIDS has spread throughout the world, reaching epidemic proportions. The spread of AIDS is thought to be the primary cause of the increased prevalence of tuberculosis in the West, as those suffering from AIDS are more vulnerable to infection with tuberculosis.

---

sensitive mind from a highly subjective perspective. *Britannica Online* describes an impressionist story as "a tale shaped and given meaning by the consciousness and psychological attitudes of the narrator." Impressionism—a school of thought in the world of painting—emerged primarily in France in the mid-1860s. The most notable impressionist painters were Claude Monet and Pierre August Renoir. Impressionist painters rebelled against the dominant values of painting at the time, which emphasized subjects taken from mythology. Instead, impressionism was, according to *Britannica Online*, "an attempt to accurately and objectively record visual reality in terms of transient effects of light and colour."

Gothic Fiction in England

Poe is considered one of the early masters of Gothic fiction. The term gothic was originally borrowed from architecture, but refers to a style of literature that developed in the late eighteenth century and throughout the nineteenth century, particularly in England. Gothic fiction is characterized by a dark, macabre atmosphere, focusing on themes of

---

death, horror, madness and the supernatural. Landmark works of Gothic fiction in England include Mary Shelley's *Frankenstein* (1818), Robert Louis Stevenson's *Strange Case of Dr. Jekyll and Mr. Hyde* (1886) and Bram Stoker's *Dracula* (1895).

The Short Story in Russia and France

It wasn't until the nineteenth century that the short story was developed into an art form and a respectable genre of literature. Poe was an early master of the short story, and a considerable influence in formulating a set of aesthetics for its unique form. The form of the short story was also developed around the same time in Germany, Russia and France. Great French short story writers included Alphonse Daudet and Guy du Masupassant, while many other writers, primarily known for their novels, also experimented with the form. In Russia, Nikolay Gogol, Ivan Turgenev, and Anton Chekov distinguished themselves as masters of the short story. Gogol, in particular, wrote impressionist stories on a par with Poe's. His 1842 story "Overcoat" was one of the most influential Russian short stories of the period.

The Grand Guignol

Poe's stories of Gothic horror contain the roots of modern horror fiction and the modern horror film. However, before the invention of cinema (about 1895), Gothic horror was enacted on the theater stage in a style referred to as Grand Guignol. Originally staged in England, but primarily successful in France, Grand Guignol performances depicted scenes of graphic horror, such as re-enactments of true-crime murders, with an emphasis on the special effects of blood, dismemberment and gore.

Critical Overview

By the time of his early death, Edgar Allan Poe (1809-1849) had written about 50 poems, 70 short stories, a short novel and over 50 essays. While his literary and personal reputation both during his lifetime and after death was controversial, today Poe is considered to be one of the most influential writers of the nineteenth century. He was a pioneer in the development of several literary genres and styles, including the short story, Gothic fiction, and

the detective/mystery story. In addition, critics assert that he mastered the art of the short story, still a relatively new form during his lifetime, and elevated it to the level of a high art.

Poe developed a theory for the art of the short story, asserting that a short story must be tightly focused on one event or duration of time (such as a single day), and that each element of a story must be symbolically and thematically central to its overall effect. According to G. R. Thompson, Poe's ideal for the short story "aimed at an almost subliminal effect through a carefully predesigned and unified pattern." Poe's own stories certainly achieved this ideal in that, as Thompson explains, they "exhibit an architectural symmetry and proportion and careful integration of details of setting, plot, and character into an indivisible whole."

In the realm of the newly developing genre of Gothic fiction, Poe was the American master, viewed as the counterpart to British writers such as Mary Shelley, whose *Frankenstein* signals the early success of the genre. Nineteenth-century Gothic fiction, or Gothic horror, was characterized by a preoccupation with death, madness, and the supernatural. Poe's literary sensibilities were well suited to the development of a Gothic style, as his stories are characterized by the morbid, the macabre, and the eerie. With his adept ability to create a dark, disturbing atmosphere, Poe effectively wrote from the perspective of a delusional narrator overcome with madness. According to Thompson, Poe was "the master of the interior monologue of a profoundly disturbed mind." In addition to "The Masque of the Red Death," "The Fall of the House of Usher" is one of his most famous stories in the Gothic style.

Poe's literary career was prolific but chaotic. He was periodically editor, co-editor and contributor to various literary magazines, controversial for his scathing literary reviews and tendency to feud with his editors or co-editors. Nevertheless, his 1844 poem "The Raven" won him instant national fame and recognition, with international notoriety soon to follow.

Poe, however, a notorious alcoholic and debtor during his lifetime, died in a certain degree of disgrace; his initial biographer, Rufus Wilmot Griswold, contributed to this public perception with his portrayal of Poe as an immoral drunk. While other authors attempted to counteract this image and redeem his reputation, their efforts were unsuccessful. Griswold, on the other hand, was at least tempo-

Death, standing and looking down upon suffering souls.

rarily successful in portraying Poe in the worst possible light.

One hundred and fifty years after his death, however, Poe's international influence on the literature of the nineteenth and twentieth centuries can hardly be underestimated. In Russia, he greatly influenced the novelist Fyodor Dostoyevski. His work was particularly influential in France, where the poets Baudelaire and Mallarme were strongly influenced by Poe in formulating the Symbolist and Surrealist movements. According to Thompson, "The vogue of Poe in France continues today with Poe's works holding special fascination for the

structuralist, post-structuralist, and deconstructionist cliques of avant-garde criticism." Interestingly, however, Poe, although a favorite among readers, is not necessarily considered to be a central figure in the tradition of English and American writers.

Criticism

Liz Brent
Brent has a Ph.D. in American Culture, with a specialization in cinema studies, from the Universi-

What Do I Read Next?

- ''The Raven,'' one of Poe's most famous works, is written from the perspective of a man remembering his love who has died.

- *Twice-Told Tales*, by Nathaniel Hawthorne, is a collection of short stories by a contemporary of Poe. These stories have elements of Gothic fiction, and are often compared to Poe's Gothic style.

- ''The Fall of the House of Usher'' is another of Poe's famous short stories, and is written in the Gothic style.

- *Edgar Allan Poe: Chelsea House Library of*

Biography (1992), by Suzanne Levert, presents a standard biography of Poe.

- *Twentieth Century Interpretations of Poe's Tales: A Collection of Critical Essays* (1971), by William L. Howarth, presents several diverse critical interpretations of Poe's work.

- *An Edgar Allan Poe Companion: A Guide to the Short Stories, Romances and Essays* (1981), by J. R. Hammond, offers an introduction to Poe's fiction and essays.

---

ty of Michigan. She is a freelance writer and teaches courses in American cinema. In the following essay, she discusses three possible interpretations of Poe's ''The Masque of the Red Death'' in terms of identifying the narrative voice of the story.

Edgar Allan Poe's short story ''The Masque of the Red Death'' may be interpreted variously as a parable for man's fear of death, a moral tale with biblical implications, or the delusional vision of a madman waging an internal battle for his own sanity. Depending on each of these interpretations, the narrator may be identified as a personification of Death, a divine being or an insane individual.

Death and Time

''The Masque of the Red Death'' can be interpreted as an allegorical tale about the folly of human beings in the face of their own inevitable deaths. If the Red Death symbolizes death in general, then the Prince's attempt to escape the pestilence, in ''defiance of contagion,'' is symbolic of the human desire to defy death. Prince Prospero attempts to create a fortress that will be impervious to the Red Death, providing his guests ''all the appliances of pleasure'' as a means of distracting them from the contemplation of death. The entire masquerade ball can be read as an allegory for the ways in which

humans attempt to distract themselves from thoughts of their own mortality by indulging in earthly pleasures. Yet, the ''masked figure'' who appears at the masquerade ball is the Red Death itself, which, despite all precautions, slips in ''like a thief in the night'' to claim the lives of everyone within, just as death eventually claims all mortals. As Joseph Patrick Roppolo has pointed out in his article ''Meaning and 'The Masque of the Red Death,''' the Red Death symbolizes ''life itself. The one 'affliction' shared by all mankind. Furthermore, because all of the people are dead by the end, and Death is the only one who survives to tell the tale, Leonard Cassuto, in his article ''The Coy Reaper: Unmasking the Red Death,'' has argued that the narrator of the story must be Death itself.

Thus, the masquerade ball may be interpreted as symbolic of human life, the hours during which the ball takes place as symbolic of the limited time each person must live, and the seven rooms of the abbey in which the ball is held as symbolic of the stages in a man's life, from birth to death. In his pursuit of the masked figure through the seven rooms of the abbey, Prospero metaphorically passes through all the stages of life. H. H. Bell, Jr. has pointed out in his article '''The Masque of the Red Death'—An Interpretation'' that Poe seems to represent these rooms as "an allegorical representation of Prince Prospero's life span." This is partly indicated by the fact that the first room is located in the Eastern end of the abbey and the last room in the Western end. Because the sun rises in the East and sets in the West, this arrangement is suggestive of the dawn and dusk of life. Bell explains that "these directions are time-honored terms which have been used to refer to the beginning and end of things—even of life itself." Furthermore, the seventh room is decorated in black, which is associated with night and death, and red, which the story strongly associates with the bloodiness caused by the pestilence of the Red Death. Out of fear, the guests avoid the seventh room, just as the living tend to avoid reminders of death. In the other six rooms, meanwhile, "beat feverishly the heart of life."

The placement of the great ebony clock in the seventh room connects the passage of time with the progression of the rooms from birth to death. The clock signifies the story's pre-occupation with Time as an instrument of death. That Poe chose to capitalize the word Time, personifying it by giving it a proper name, further suggests that he is referring to "time" not in a literal sense, but as in an allegorical sense. Extending the metaphor of a single day for a life span, as implied by the location of the seven rooms from East to West, the clock marks out the time remaining in the lives of the guests, ending at midnight.

While Prospero's guests dance and the orchestra plays, the striking of the clock each hour is a foreboding reminder that the passing of time brings them all closer and closer to the moment of their own deaths. Each time the clock strikes, and the music and dancing stops, everyone is reminded of their own impending death, the old more acutely than the young, for "it was observed that the giddiest grew pale, and the more aged and sedate passed their hands over their brows as if in confused reverie or meditation." Bell has suggested that "Poe meant for the clock to count off periods of life—not mere hours." So that when the revelers pause at the striking of the clock "they think not in terms of an hour having passed but rather in terms of just so much of their lives as having passed." While the ball is meant to distract them from thinking about death, the chiming of the clock inspires in the guests "meditation" on the limited time left in their lives.

The clock's chiming midnight signifies the end of life, as it coincides with the guests becoming "aware"

> **That these 'dream' guests may be mere reflections of the Prince's mind is further suggested by the description that 'these—the dreams—writhed about, taking hue from the rooms.'"**

of the presence of death amongst them. At the sight of the "masked figure," these thoughts become more persistent: "and thus it happened, perhaps that more of thought crept, with more of time, into the meditations of the thoughtful among those who reveled." The closing lines of the story again suggest that the clock measures the time limit placed on everyone's life, so that "the life of the ebony clock went out with the last of the gay."

Apocalypse

"The Masque of the Red Death" in told in such a way that its story takes on an almost Biblical tone, recounting a tale of sin, punishment by God and Apocalypse. The story opens with a description of a "pestilence," which, by the end, has wiped out all human life. Such a devastating "pestilence" evokes biblical implications, as plague or pestilence in the Bible is sent down by God to punish humans for their sins. As a parable reminiscent of a Biblical story, "The Masque of the Red Death" is a tale of a divine punishment of those who are oblivious to the suffering of others less fortunate than themselves.

The response of Prince Prospero to the pestilence of the Red Death which has "devastated" his country is one of decadence. In other words, he responds to the massive suffering of people less privileged and powerful than he by turning a blind eye to their plight and surrounding himself and his friends with extravagant distractions. While a deadly pestilence ravages his country, the Prince remains "happy and dauntless and sagacious," oblivious to the suffering of others. When "his dominions were half depopulated," his response is to retreat with his friends and distract them from "grieving" or "thinking" about the plight of their fellow countrymen by indulging them in lavish entertainment. The response of the general population to those afflicted by the Red Death is also portrayed as selfish and unsympathetic, for the "scarlet stains" which mark the bodies of those afflicted "were the pest ban which shut him out from the aid and from the sympathy of his fellowmen." Yet the Prince, with all his power, goes a step further in this response, as he contrives to "shut out" all those vulnerable to the plague, denying then any "aid" or "sympathy" in the process. The response of the Prince and his privileged friends to this massive suffering is harsh and unfeeling, their attitude being that "the external world could take care of itself."

The final line of the story is Apocalyptic in tone, written in a style reminiscent of the type of statements made in the Bible. As Patrick Cheney has pointed out in his article "Poe's Use of *The Tempest* and The Bible in 'The Masque of the Red Death,'" in the final paragraph, "the language, rhythm, and allusion are unmistakably Biblical." This is particularly so of the closing line: "And Darkness and Decay and the Red Death held illimitable dominion over all." As with the word Time, the fact that Poe chose to capitalize the words "Darkness" and "Decay" personifies these elements, thereby elevating them to a level of myth or parable. The personification of Darkness, particularly, calls to mind the Prince of Darkness, a name for the Devil. Cheney in fact refers to the Red Death as an "anti-Christ." Given this ending, it would be possible to conclude that, since evil has triumphed over the land, the narrator of the story may be the personification of evil. On the other hand, however, if this is to be interpreted as a morality tale of Biblical proportions, it could be argued that the narrator is in fact a divine presence, who has punished humanity for its sins.

Madness

G. R. Thompson, in *The Dictionary of Literary Biography,* has pointed out that Poe was "the master of interior monologue of a profoundly disturbed mind." "The Masque of the Red Death" may certainly be read on a psychological level as just such an "interior monologue," the delusional nightmare of a madman. The narrator suggests several times that there may be reason to believe Prince Prospero is insane, and that the entire story is his crazy dream. If this is the case, then the narrator of the story may be Prospero himself, describing his own mad vision. This would explain why the narrator distances himself from the statement that Prospero

may be "mad" by suggesting that it is only the opinion of "some" people, for he mentions that "there are some who would have thought him mad." However, the narrator just as quickly denies this assessment by calling forth the opinion of his "followers," who "felt that he was not."

Furthermore, the narrator specifically refers to the Prince's "friends" or "followers" as literally "dreams," as "To and fro in the seven chambers there stalked, in fact, a multitude of dreams." The guests are later referred to as "an assembly of fantasms." In other words, the "bizarre" figures which populate the Prince's masquerade ball may merely be figments of his mad imagination. That these "dream" guests may be mere reflections of the Prince's mind is further suggested by the description that "these—the dreams—writhed about, taking hue from the rooms." That is, the guests at the masquerade ball, referred to as "dreams" take their "hue" or color from the reflections of the glass in each room. This could serve as a metaphor for the way in which dreams take their form, or "hue" from their status as reflections of the dreamer's mind. In this case, the chiming of the clock is a reminder not so much of death in particular, but of reality intruding momentarily into the insane dream-world of the mad man, for, each time the clock chimes, the "dreams are stiff-frozen." At a literal level, the chiming of a clock is generally a sound which awakens people from a dream state. But, once the sound of the clock has died down, "the dreams live, and writhe to and fro more merrily than ever."

Eventually, the madness of the Prince is projected onto the "fantasms" which populate his mind; the "dream" guests are referred to as "mad revelers," indicating that they may be projections of the Prince's own mad mind. The masked figure of Death which appears at the ball even takes on the characteristic of madness, as his "mad assumptions" have the effect of evoking "awe" in the other guests. The madness of the Prince himself again emerges in response to the audacity of the masked figure, as the Prince "maddening with rage," pursues it to the seventh room.

In a psychological reading, the struggle between the masked figure and the Prince Prospero could be interpreted as the internal mental struggle between a man's sense of reality and his insane delusions. Thus, when the masked figure is revealed to have no bodily form, it is because it exists only as an imaginary "fantasm" with no physical existence in reality. In this case, the triumph of the masked figure over the Prince represents a triumph of insanity over sanity; the ''death'' of Prospero and his ''dreams'' could represent the death of the self when it is taken over by its own insanity.

Source: Liz Brent, for *Short Stories for Students*, The Gale Group, 2000.

Leonard Cassuto

In the following essay, Cassuto reasons that the narrator of the tale must be Death because he is the only one present at the festivity to survive to tell of the effects of the Red Death.''

Much has been written about Poe's narrators, and with good reason. Nearly always unnamed—and therefore seen as somehow unreliable—they also have disturbing tendencies that range from the unstable and the obsessed all the way to the insane. In *The Narrative of Arthur Gordon Pym* and several other tales, Poe himself even enters into the fiction, commencing the atmosphere of confusion that pervades throughout. All of this indicates that Poe wants us to pay attention to his narrators. If that is his goal, he has succeeded handsomely, but not completely. ''The Masque of the Red Death'' is a notable exception. The story has a narrator unique in the Poe canon. The teller of the tale is Death himself.

Substantiating such a claim must begin with locating a first-person narrator in the story. At first there does not appear to be one, but closer study reveals that an ''I'' is in fact relating the action. Perhaps no one has remarked upon his presence before because, unlike many of Poe's more overtly bizarre narrators, this one never steps up and introduces himself. For all of this seeming reticence, though, the raconteur of ''The Masque of the Red Death'' makes his presence known on three separate occasions.

The first of these comes after the description of the isolation of Prospero and his followers. After five or six months in the abbey that he has turned into a vault, Prospero has announced the masked ball, and all is being prepared. Here, the narrator steps forward for the first time:

> It was a voluptuous scene, that masquerade. But first let me tell of the rooms in which it was held.

Who is this ''me''? He must be someone who has seen the inside of Prospero's self-imposed prison, but it has been sealed ''to leave means of neither ingress nor egress.'' This fact points to the narra-

> Death is describing his own actions, but without telling us exactly what happens. His tone as a narrator is consistent with his character in the story: matter-of-fact, final, and anonymous."

tor's presence in the group inside the walls. One could argue that Poe is simply employing a casual reference, that ''me'' is simply a figure of speech, but the frequency of the narrator's direct intervention (three times in a seven-page story) precludes this assumption.

The story has a narrator, then, but this narrator may not be a character *in* the story. Perhaps Poe has adopted a familiarly omniscient first person narrator which would allow him to achieve a compromise between first-person involvement and third-person omniscience. This is not a new device, to be sure—Hawthorne, for one, employs it in many of his stories and romances. Maybe Poe does mean to have an ''I'' telling the story from without. The possibility certainly exists, but not to the exclusion of all others. Furthermore, such a narrator would be unique among Poe's tales of horror. On the few occasions when he does employ omniscient narration, it is always in the third person. All of his other first-person narrators live and breathe within their own fictional worlds; I submit that the teller of ''The Masque of the Red Death'' does so as well.

Given the presence of a narrator, it is clear that he can be nowhere else but present at the festivity. There would be no other way for him to describe a pause in the activity at midnight: ''And then the music ceased, as I have told; and the evolutions of the waltzers were quieted; and there was an uneasy cessation of all things as before.''

The narrator's comparison proves that he has been there since the beginning of the party. His reference to what he has already told hearkens back to a previous description of how the striking of the clock would stop the orchestra. The third and final time he refers to himself further confirms his presence amidst the merriment. He compares the Red Death figure to the other masqueraders at the party: "In an assembly of phantasms such as I have painted, it may be supposed that no ordinary appearance could have excited such sensation."

The Red Death is indeed extraordinary, but so must be the narrator, for he has somehow lived to tell us about it.

The narrator's survival thus presents a contradiction which allows for an alternate reading of the story, one that adds a new dimension to the grotesque scene which Poe describes. According to the narrator's own account, no one survives the Red Death's "illimitable dominion." How could the narrator be present at the ball and then be able to tell about it afterwards? The only one who "lives" is Death. The narrator must be Death himself.

This discovery adds a gruesomely ironic aspect to the entire tale. Death's storytelling is marked by a smooth, deliberate, almost deadpan calm. There is a sense of inevitability to the scene which precludes tension because the narrator already knows what will happen. The outcome is as dependable as the passing time, symbolized by the striking clock which governs the action in the story. No one escapes Death, so it is natural that Death should not perceive any suspense. Nor has Death any need for self-aggrandizement. We see the final confrontation between Death and the pursuing prince from Death's perspective, but description of the moment of truth is carefully avoided: "There was a sharp cry—and the dagger dropped gleaming upon the sable carpet, upon which, instantly afterward, fell prostrate in death the Prince Prospero." Only Death could have seen all of this; Prospero has run through six rooms while the other partygoers remain shrunk against the walls in fear. Death is describing his own actions, but without telling us exactly what happens. His tone as a narrator is consistent with his character in the story: matter-of-fact, final, and anonymous.

As Death remains masked to Prospero, so Death remains masked to us. The mockingly self-deprecatory way that he hides himself in both the action and the narration furnishes a humorous tinge to the macabre that is already present in the story, giving a uniquely grotesque turn to an already grotesque creation. Harpham has elsewhere pointed out various puns in the story's structure (e.g., the guests are "dis-concerted" when the clock stops). Another can now be added to the list: Death is the author of Prospero's fate in more ways than one.

Source: Leonard Cassuto, "The Coy Reaper: Un-masqueing the Red Death," in *Studies in Short Fiction*, Vol. 25, No. 3, 1988, pp. 317–20.

Patrick Cheney

In the following essay, Cheney argues that Poe's use of allusions to The Tempest *and the Bible reverse their theme of victory over sin, death, and time with the victory of Darkness, Decay, and the Red Death over humankind.*

In "The Masque of the Red Death" Poe's allusions to both *The Tempest* and the Bible have been widely recognized. Briefly, the allusions to *The Tempest* include Poe's use of "Prospero" for his hero's name; his use of the romance "masque" for his story's central event; and his borrowing of Caliban's curse of the "red plague" on Miranda for his story's central idea. Poe's allusions to the Bible include his remarks about the Red Death itself: that the Red Death "out-Heroded Herod"; that he "came like a thief in the night"; and that in the end he has "dominion" over all. As yet, though, no one has examined the relation between these two sets of allusions, as they contribute to the narrative and meaning of the story.

In this essay I suggest that Poe in "The Masque of the Red Death" uses Shakespearean and Biblical allusions to reveal a tragic and ironic reversal of a mythic pattern which *The Tempest* and the Bible have in common. Where the mythic pattern of both *The Tempest* and the Bible depicts man's victory over sin, death, and time, Poe's mythic pattern depicts the triumph of these agents of destruction over man. In Poe's "mythic parable" of man's role in the universe, Prince Prospero becomes an anti-hero, an image of man misusing his will as he attempts to shape reality; and the Red Death becomes an "anti-christ," an image of the cosmic force conspiring man's failure.

While admitting to the obvious differences between *The Tempest* and the Bible, we can also see that they have much in common. In the Bible, Adam is born into the Garden of Eden; he falls from this paradise when, tempted by Satan, he misuses his will; and finally, through the miraculous powers of the "second Adam" or Christ, he returns to a new Eden. The key to recovering Eden becomes Christ, who uses the miraculous powers of love to triumph over the old law of death, figured in his resurrection. Similarly, in *The Tempest* Prospero was originally the "right Duke of Milan"; but he lost his dukedom when he retreated into the private world of his study, to become the victim of Antonio, Alonso, and Sebastian; eventually, though, exiled on an island in the Mediterranean sea with his daughter, Miranda, he uses his magical powers to triumph over the "three men of sin." In his wedding masque, Prospero uses the spirit Ariel to present a vision of the world he is trying to create: a peaceful world of heaven on earth. Prospero interrupts his masque when he remembers the plot of his slave, Caliban, thus occasioning his famous speech, "Our revels now are ended," in which the "cloud-capped towers" vanish from the world "like the baseless fabric of this vision" (IV.i. 151–152). Despite this apostrophe to man's futile use of his will, Prospero goes on to regain for Miranda her lost inheritance, much as Christ regains for Adam his lost inheritance in the Bible. The mythic pattern of *The Tempest*, then, corresponds to that of the Bible by presenting a view of reality in which man uses his loving will to recreate a "brave new world," invulnerable to time and death.

In "The Masque of the Red Death" Poe's allusions to *The Tempest* and the Bible may suggest that he is responding to this mythic pattern. Like Shakespeare's Duke Prospero, Poe's Prince Prospero uses his will to confront the harsh reality of death, figured in the ghostly apparition of the Red Death itself. But Poe recasts the story so that Prince Prospero's primary action consists of retreating from the reality of the Red Death—the action of retreat being precisely what Shakespeare takes care to emend. Poe also takes away Prospero's magic powers, leaving his hero with an art that most closely resembles interior decoration—a mere "philosophy of furniture." As a consequence, Prince Prospero lacks the supernatural power that enables Shakespeare's Prospero to succeed. Taking refuge in a "castellated abbey," Prince Prospero uses his will to create an earthly paradise that parodies the "brave new world" of *The Tempest*—a world which, rather than transcending time, embodies the very instrument of time, the sinister "clock of ebony": Poe's Prospero, by building time into his abbey, ensures his own destruction. In the world of Prince Prospero, the governing force becomes not that of cosmic harmony and love but that of cosmic "disconcert," the musical instrument for which becomes the clock itself, that grim "sound" which hourly interrupts the dance. In hiding from death in the bosom of earthly pleasure, Poe's Prospero is like Shakespeare's Prospero if he had given up Ariel for Caliban; in a sense, Poe's story embodies Caliban's wish-fulfillment: "the red plague rid you," Caliban

> **Essentially, then, Poe in 'The Masque of the Red Death' reads Shakespeare and the Bible much as Marlowe's Dr. Faustus reads the Bible and Aristotle--out of context."**

says to Miranda, "For learning me your language" (I.ii.364–365). The story's subtitle appropriately becomes "Our revels now are ended"—a powerful overture to the vanity of human wishes. Prince Prospero's artistically inspired masque does not marry earth to heaven, but earth to death, so that the world of the abbey becomes, not a new Eden, but a "valley of the shadow of death."

Poe's use of Biblical symbolism does not become particularly noteworthy until the last paragraph, where the language, rhythm, and allusion are unmistakably Biblical:

> And now was acknowledge the presence of the Red Death. He had come like a thief in the night. And one by one dropped the revellers in the blood-bedewed halls of their revel, and died each in the despairing posture of his fall. And the life of the ebony clock went out with that of the last of the gay. And the flames of the tripods expired. And Darkness and Decay and the Red Death held illimitable dominion over all.

The sentence structure, with its repetition of the word "And," is like that in the Bible. The Red Death, Poe says, comes "like a thief in the night." The phrase is a direct quotation from 1 Thessalonians 5:2 and 2 Peter 3:10, which both refer to Christ. In Poe's mythology, the Red Death replaces Christ as the reigning force in the universe. Hence, the Red Death is said to have "dominion over all"—a reversal of Paul's statement in Romans 6:9, in which "death hath no more dominion" because of Christ's resurrection. Moreover, the halls of Poe's earthly paradise become "blood-bedewed"—suggesting a conflation of two familiar Biblical images, blood and dew: the blood of Christ's resurrection that redeems man, and the drops of dew that fall from heaven to save man from the harshness of nature. In Poe, the blood and dew of the Red Death replace the blood of Christ and the dew of heaven.

Poe may have in mind here the Pauline conception of baptism, in which man is baptized into Christ through being baptized into Christ's death—a conception that concludes, significantly, with Paul's remark that death will have no more "dominion" because of Christ's resurrection:

> Therefore we are buried with him by baptism into death: that like as Christ was raised up from the dead by the glory of the Father, even so we also should walk in the newness of life. For if we have been planted together in the likeness of his death, we shall be also in the likeness of his resurrection.... For he that is dead is freed from sin. Now if we be dead with Christ, we believe that we shall also live with him: Knowing that Christ being raised from the dead dieth no more; death hath no more dominion over him.

Poe inverts the Pauline conception of baptism by presenting his characters being "bedewed" in the unholy baptismal "blood" of the Red Death: "For he that is dead is freed from sin." Death becomes the grim "saviour" of this world; appropriately, the Red Death wears a "vesture dabbled in blood"—a grim inversion of Christ in the Book of Revelation:

> And he was clothed with a vesture dipped in blood: and his name is called The Word of God.

The Red Death joins Herod in denying Christ as the Messiah; but the Red Death "out-Herod[s] Herod" by spilling the blood, not merely of the innocent first born, but of everyone. The three figures presiding over the "blood-bedewed" halls—Darkness, Decay, and the Red Death—become an infernal triumvirate replacing the divine trinity as the ruling force of the world.

The Biblical counterpart to the romance "masque" or "mask" is the "veil." In the Old Testament, Moses wears a veil when he speaks in the name of Yaweh. In 2 Corinthians 3 Paul says that Moses' veil symbolizes the obscurity of man's knowledge of God given through the old law, which becomes for Paul the law of death. Hence, in wearing the veil, Moses is wearing the veil of death and blinding himself to the truth about man's relation to God. Paul goes on to say that the "vail is done away in Christ", that is, that Christ triumphs over the law of death through his resurrection. In John 20:6–7, the beloved disciple and Simon Peter go "into the sepulchre, and seeth the linen clothes, but wrapped together in a place by itself." The details draw attention to the success of Christ's resurrection: he has taken the veil of death away.

The prefiguration for this becomes Christ's raising of Lazarus from the grave: "And he that was dead came forth, *bound hand and foot with graveclothes*, and his face was bound about with a napkin. Jesus saith unto them, Loose him, and let him go."

Poe echoes the Lazarus passage when he makes his Red Death

> *shrouded from head to foot in the habiliments of the grave.* The mask which concealed the visage was made ... to resemble the countenance of a stiffened corpse.

But Poe rejects the notion that Christ takes the veil of death away by having his masquer, the Red Death, wear a veil that cannot be taken away:

> a throng of the revellers at once threw themselves into the black apartment, and, seizing the mummer ... , gasped in unutterable horror at finding the grave cerements and corpse-like mask which they handled with so violent a rudeness, untenanted by any tangible form.

In presenting an image of man helpless against the apparition of death, Poe suggests the inefficacy of Christ's triumph over death, thus delivering man into the world of the old law: the Red Death denies Christ his power of resurrection.

As such, the Red Death qualifies for what John calls an "antichrist": he who "denieth that Jesus is the Christ . . . is antichrist." John admonishes:

> Love not the world, neither the things that are in the world. . . . For all that is in the world, the lust of the flesh, and the lust of the eyes, and the pride of life, is not of the Father, but is of the world. And the world passeth away, and the lust thereof. . . . Little children, it is the last time: and as ye have heard . . . antichrist shall come.

Prince Prospero, who is "of the world" and suffers from "the lust of the flesh, and the lust of the eyes, and the pride of life," appropriately becomes the victim of an "antichrist," that figure who in the Bible temporarily replaces Christ as the ruling force of the world. That Poe is responding to Scripture here is further indicated if, as Thomas O. Mabbott says, the story has as one of its bases the clock at Strasbourg Cathedral,

> where, shortly before the stroke of the clock, a figure representing Death emerged from the center and sounded the full hour, while at the quarter and half hours the statue of Christ came out, repelling the destroyer.

Not surprisingly, Poe places his grim reversal of the Christian drama in an "abbey"—the Catholic bride of Christ, a holy sanctuary in which man uses religious ritual to commune with God. The abbey has seven rooms, each decked in a different color and having a "heavy tripod, bearing a brazier of fire" opposite a window of "stained glass." Critics have associated the seven rooms with the cycle of nature and the seven ages of man in Shakespeare. In the Bible, though, seven symbolizes fullness, completeness—man's oneness with God. The seven colors also correspond to colors of vestments worn in Catholic liturgy, as well as to the seven colors of the rainbow (Biblical symbol of hope and the new covenant between man and God). And the braziers, which use coals of fire, recall the "censer full of burning coals of fire from off the altar before the Lord" that is brought "within the vail" of the Old Testament temple in Leviticus 16:12, and the "seven lamps of fire burning before the throne" of God in Revelation 4:5. Hence, in the Red Death's destruction of the abbey, Poe seems to suggest the inefficacy of man's use of religious ritual to commune with God, as a means of transcending time and of triumphing over the law of death. Poe's story can be seen to have a basis in Ecclesiastes 6:2: "this is vanity, and it is an evil disease." The "Avatar" and "seal" of Prospero's world are not Christ, as in the Bible, but the "blood" of the Red Death. The shaping force of Poe's world becomes, not the Lamb of God, as in the Book of Revelation, but that type of antichrist in the fourth seal of God riding the "pale horse": "and his name . . . was Death."

Poe's use of *The Tempest* and the Bible to shape the mythic pattern of "The Masque of the Red Death" is not so much the product of a wild fancy as it is of an astute reading of western literature. For, as J. L. Borges has suggested in his story "The Gospel According to Mark,"

> generations of men, throughout recorded time, have always told and retold two stories, that of a lost ship which searches the Mediterranean seas for a dearly loved island, and that of a god who is crucified on Golgotha.

According to Northrop Frye, "Borges is clearly suggesting that romance, as a whole, provides a parallel epic" to the Bible; that, in fact, romance can be seen as a "secular scripture" whose mythic pattern mirrors that of the Bible. Hence, the allusions to *The Tempest* and the Bible in "The Masque of the Red Death" may suggest that Poe responds to the mythic pattern of the two kinds of stories which Borges and Frye suggest form the basis of western literature.

Essentially, then, Poe in "The Masque of the Red Death" reads Shakespeare and the Bible much as Marlowe's Dr. Faustus reads the Bible and Aristotle—out of context. He is attracted to the ideas in two speeches that are secular and sacred correlates of each other: Prospero's "Our revels now are ended" speech and the passage in the Bible about the victory of "antichrist" over man. Specifically, Poe inverts the romantic conventions of *The Tempest* and the religious tenets of the Bible. Prospero becomes, not the unifying force of love in the world, but the mere victim of a demonic opposite, the Red Death. And the Red Death replaces Christ as the shaping force of reality. In Poe's revision of the mythic pattern set forth in the secular and sacred mythologies, man is imprisoned in a world governed by the "law" of death. Hence, man's use of his will to link himself with heaven, as a means of triumphing over sin, death, and time, becomes a "masquerade"—a futile display of self-deception that culminates only in death. Man's final marriage is not with Milan or the Church, with home or heaven—but with the mere "shadow" of these: the Red Death.

Source: Patrick Cheney, "Poe's Use of *The Tempest* and the Bible in 'The Masque of the Red Death,'" in *English Language Notes*, Vol. 20, No. 3–4, May-June, 1983, pp. 31–39.

Patricia H. Wheat

In the following essay, Wheat argues that the prince attempts to prepare to meet death by assuming a mask of indifference to the effects of the Red Death and to death itself, but he fails to maintain this indifference in the ultimate meeting with death.

When Prince Prospero and his thousand carefree friends shut themselves up in a fortified abbey to escape the fearful Red Death and make merry, they also shut themselves off from the sympathies of critical opinion. Thomas Mabbot believes "one cannot run away from responsibility." Stuart Levine agrees, noting that "The nobles are fiddling while Rome burns; worse, they are fiddling in great style." David Halliburton suggests that Prince Prospero sins by trying "to supplant God's creation with a creation of his own." The Prince is viewed by Edward Pitcher as "arrogantly calculating," with character traits of "egotism, . . . pride, coldness, manic superiority and tyranny." H. H. Bell calls Prospero a "feelingless ruling prince." While it is difficult to entertain feelings of goodwill toward a monarch who deserts his people and stages a festive masked ball in the midst of their exposure to peril, negative attitudes toward Prince Prospero are to be found only in the writings of his modern critics and not in his story or in Poe's attitude toward him. Joseph Roppolo comes closest to Poe's meaning in "The Masque of the Red Death" when he discusses the isolation of man: "In the trap of life and in his death, every man is an island. If there is a mutual bond, it is the shared horror of death." The Prince and his friends have no desire to share death's horror. Poe, however, expresses no disapproval of his character's actions or of his apparent attitudes. Prince Prospero's supposed pride is best seen as a protective mask, a mask of indifference with which he tries to shield himself from death.

Commentaries on "The Masque of the Red Death" often, rightly, describe the story's action in terms of a battle. Walter Blair views it as a battle between death and life, between time and the "gaiety which seeks to kill time by forgetting it." In his comparison of Poe's story to several Hawthorne stories, Robert Regan comments that "the gaiety within is a psychological defense against a menacing antagonist. . . ." The battle is inevitable for all who live. However, from the introduction of the Prince in paragraph two, his defense is not an attempt to win the battle but an attempt to avoid it. He and the courtiers begin by retiring (literally, drawing back) into the "deep seclusion" of the abbey. A strong wall with iron gates surrounds the "amply provisioned" building, suggesting preparations for a siege.

Not only do the inhabitants make physical preparations as they take their stand against the coming onslaught, they must also be as mentally ready as possible. Mentally, as well as physically, the only defense is retreat. The retreat of the mind goes beyond mere forgetfulness or simple escape into "reality-denying fantasies." The Prince and his courtiers, in an unconscious defense mechanism, construct and maintain a pose of indifference to death. Gaiety, merry making, and all the joys of superficial pleasure are allowable under this pose; concern for self or others, serious thought, and strong emotion are forbidden, for they rankle the mind with the agonizing realization that when the battle comes it will certainly be lost. The only way to approximate success is to not let losing matter. The situation is something like that of the laboratory rat trained to run a maze for a food pellet. When an essential corridor is closed off, the rat will eventually stop trying to run the maze and will sit down in his hopelessness to starve. Prince Prospero differs only in that, as a human, he is able to use his inventiveness to make the best of his hopeless situation.

The weapon of indifference and its association with tightly controlled emotions are seen throughout the story. The victim of the disease is shut out "from the sympathy of his fellowmen." The bolts inside the abbey are welded shut not to keep the Red Death *out*, but to serve as a precaution against the courtiers' own "sudden impulses of despair or of frenzy." They let "The external world . . . take care of itself. In the meantime it was folly to grieve, or to think." Some critics have detected a note of authorial disapproval of the Prince in the first of these last two sentences. But the second invites a more sympathetic interpretation. Grief and thought are not only useless but are destructive, unwise, certainly not consistent with the character of the "sagacious" Prince. The external world here has the dual meaning of the worlds outside the abbey and outside the mind.

The movements of the masked ball, beginning in paragraph three, are dominated by the striking of the ebony clock in the ominous seventh apartment where "few of the company [are] bold enough to set foot." The dancers and musicians alternate between maintaining their pose of light laughter and gaiety and, when the doleful, deep-voiced clock chimes, becoming pale, uneasy, and thoughtful. The clock is the reminder of death, the enemy, and time, his companion. The musicians smile when the striking stops. They repent of their "nervousness and folly" and promise each other to let "no similar emotion" be evinced at the next sounding of the hour. It is foolish to be nervous or to give in to a despairing emotion.

One may ask, if the Prince and his friends truly have a need to feign indifference to an inevitable death, why do they bother to retreat to an abbey? Also, if the Prince wishes to forget the presence of death why has he surrounded himself and his courtiers with reminders of death and the grotesque—rooms strangely situated and lighted only by fiery torches glowing through tinted windows, bizzare masquerade costumes, and the coffin-like black room with its "blood-colored panes"? The answer to both questions lies in Prince Prospero's grand attempts to control his environment. A poor man who has just eaten can tell himself he is not concerned about food. In like manner, only within the relative security of the stone walls can the Prince and his friends act as though they are unconcerned about death. A control over their more hysterical emotions is possible only in the extremely artificial world designed and executed by the Prince. Pitcher believes Prince Prospero deliberately tries to frighten and disturb his guests with reminders of death ''to test the courage of his friends and to reveal their relative inferiority'' to himself. A more plausible explanation, I believe, is that he is trying to duplicate the outside world on a small scale and in a nontheatening manner. His seven rooms have been often compared to the seven stages of man's life. In an imitation of life's rooms, the apartments are situated so that ''the vision embraced but little more than one at a time.'' However, the rooms are much more fluid and accessible than are the stages of life, which cannot be retraced or explored in advance. Actual death is too horrible to be greeted with apathy, but a man-made black room, designed and furnished by the Prince himself, can be endured. Glass, even colored blood-red, can be tolerated. The clock is a constant mournful messenger of ''the Time that flies,'' but it is also a man-made device, and within man's control. Prince Prospero, like Mithridates, seems to be taking his poison a bit at a time. Ironically, he is so obsessed with death that all his efforts are aimed at showing how little death matters to him.

There are hints throughout the story that Prince Prospero is insane. Poe says, ''his conceptions glowed with barbaric lustre. There are some who would have thought him mad.'' The masquerade costumes ''were delirious fancies such as the madman fashions. . . .'' These and similar passages are often offered as additional evidence that Poe disapproves of the Prince. But these lines can also be interpreted as comments on society's view of him, as well as a reminder of the limitations of his power. To those outside the abbey, Prospero would seem mad because his actions and attitudes seem inappropriate for the situation at hand. On another level, his ''conceptions,'' or inventive ordering of the elements of the masquerade, are ''barbaric'' in that they are crude and simplistic. Prince Prospero has gained temporary control over his limited environment. But his power stops with the natural laws of the world, which are able to invade any man's plans and creations. It is necessary for the Prince to retreat to the abbey and feign indifference to the outside world—he becomes a madman with ''delirious fancies'' if he deludes himself that he has won the battle with death rather than avoided it.

Avoidance of death can only be temporary, as transitory as the parts of a play. The courtiers become not only guests at a masquerade, but also literally masquers, players in death's court. Before the masque and the assertion of the final royal authority belonging to the Red Death, the guests are

> **The Prince has been criticized for his apparent frivolity and lack of feeling. But it is evident that this frivolity, this pretended refusal to take death seriously, is all that separates the Prince from the horror of death."**

acting out a grimly comic anti-masque in a portrayal of ''the unruly, of the forces and elements royalty subdues.''

The real test—and the final failure—of the mask of indifference comes with the entrance of the mysterious masked figure dressed exactly like the corpse of a Red Death victim. The stranger becomes visible to the masquers just after midnight. The clock, the most powerful reminder of death in the Prince's world, is at its most powerful moment of the night, since it has twelve long, suggestive strokes to sound. The guests have too much time for thought—they slip irretrievably into meditation and become aware of the presence of the stranger who has haunted the abbey from the beginning. Death is no longer avoidable, and in its actual visitation the unfeeling gaiety must give way to feelings ''of terror, of horror, and of disgust.''

As the company becomes aware of the deathly figure, emotion quickly takes over. The mummer is ''beyond the bounds of even the prince's indefinite decorum,'' and the mask of indifference can no longer be retained. The challenge, the call to battle, is given in this central passage: ''There are chords in the hearts of the most reckless which cannot be touched without emotion. Even with the utterly lost, to whom life and death are equally jests, there are matters of which no jest can be made.'' The rooms and the costumes can be carelessly lived with. The chiming of the clock can almost be dealt with. But the appearance of a representation of the specific type of fatal illness from which Prince Prospero and his friends are physically and mentally trying to escape is too much. Even the Prince has not been hardened enough by his artificial surroundings to endure without emotion the taunting apparition. He has been heretofore ''reckless'' (literally, without concern). Life and death have been ''equally jests'' to him as he has convinced himself that he favors neither in his lack of interest. But the one matter which is not laughable has been introduced. The Prince's reaction is that of a man who prepares himself mentally for battle, as awakening emotions can no longer be restrained.

When Prince Prospero sees the intruder his initial reaction is that of the untried soldier going, at last, into a deadly serious battle after a long wait in the camp. He is ''convulsed . . . with a strong shudder either of terror or distaste.'' Like the untried soldier first meeting the enemy, he feels an overwhelming fear which no amount of preparation could forestall. The battle is already on its way to being lost as the Prince next grows red with anger. He is now moving to fight death on its home ground, but he makes several last vain attempts to avoid conflict. His statement, ''Who dares?'' is at once an acknowledgement of a challenge and impending fight, and an attempt to treat the stranger as merely another courtier, a foolish courtier who has overstepped the bounds of safety for all those in the abbey. He orders the guests to ''seize him and unmask him—that we may know whom we have to hang at sunrise, from the battlements!'' It is obviously fruitless to try to seize, unmask, and hang a personification of death. But if only this figure can be proven merely human, if only the court can ''know whom'' the tasteless mocker is, then it cannot be death. Prince Prospero's reluctance for conflict is reflected in his delegation of the seizure to his friends, and in the words ''whom we *have* to hang at sunrise.'' The hanging is unwanted but necessary. For the mask of indifference to be reassumed the impediment to indifference must be removed.

The Prince's attack upon the mummer is filled with references to intense emotions and hurried actions. He has lost his carefully nurtured self-control and foolishly attacked the unbeatable foe. He maddens ''with rage and the shame of his own momentary cowardice.'' He ''rushed hurriedly'' to the stranger, approaching him ''in rapid impetuosity.'' The stranger is, throughout, the challenger who need not fight. He approaches the Prince with ''deliberate'' step and later, when the Prince pursues, he simply turns and confronts him. Prince Prospero is dead before the Red Death can do its work. He is defeated in the quite literal face of death

by giving in to his emotions of terror and hysteria. The fear of death has become his master. The courtiers, who summon ''the wild courage of despair'' and attack the stranger's mask with ''so violent a rudeness,'' meet the fate of their leader immediately thereafter, submitting to the same lack of control over their emotions. Death's victory is complete—a victory over both the minds and bodies of the noblemen.

The Prince has been criticized for his apparent frivolity and lack of feeling. But it is evident that this frivolity, this pretended refusal to take death seriously, is all that separates the Prince from the horror of death. His personality and creations in the abbey provide an excellent illustration of Edward Davidson's description of horror as ''the total freedom of the will to function, at the same time that there is nothing to will 'for' or will 'against.' Its judgments are in a vacuum because it pretends to act in a world where no discoverable controls are operative.'' Prince Prospero can exercise his will freely within the vacuum of the abbey as long as he can deceive himself that his emotions, the world, life, and death can be controlled. When he allows his emotions to take control, the ''nameless awe'' of the unknown foe destroys him.

It is natural that Poe should have written a story such as ''The Masque of the Red Death'' in 1842. By this time he had lost his mother (1811); Jane Stanard, the inspiration of ''To Helen'' (1824); and his foster mother, Frances Allan (1829). He had experienced what David Sinclair in his biography of Poe calls a ''crippling sense of powerlessness in the face of death.''

Most critics of ''The Masque'' interpret it as an allegory and assume that, as such, it must point to a moral truth. But the truth in the story is existential, not moral. Poe as narrator presents characters who arm themselves against death through whatever means possible. Through his art, the author is a more formidable opponent to death than is Prospero. The Prince loses control and faces defeat, but Poe remains far removed. He voices no disapproval of the characters, but neither does he show sympathy for their fate. He maintains in his tone the superiority of what he portrays as the only, although feeble, defense against death—a perfect mask of indifference.

Source: Patricia H. Wheat, ''The Mask of Indifference in 'The Masque of the Red Death,''' in *Studies in Short Fiction*, Vol. 19, No. 1, Winter, 1982, pp. 51–56.

H. H. Bell, Jr.

In the following essay, Bell interprets time and the seven rooms in Prince Prospero's imperial suite allegorically as periods of a person's life.

If after reading it, one concludes that "The Masque of the Red Death" is nothing more than another of Poe's rather numerous explorations of the general theme of death, then there is little that may be said about its meaning other than that it is a rather good example of grim and ironic humor. However, to the student who inclines his attention toward the allegorical overtones of the work, other possibilities as to its meaning present themselves. It is the writer's belief that the story becomes more interesting, as well as broader in scope, when one concentrates on these allegorical elements.

Examining the text of the work, we discover that Prospero is a feelingless ruling prince. To the discerning reader there is also implicit within the text a strong suspicion that this man is probably insane, for we are told that "Prince Prospero was happy and dauntless and sagacious" even though half the people in his kingdom had been killed by the Red Death. This would hardly be the reaction of a ruler who is in contact with his environment. This same man, motivated by a morbid fear of death, selfishly decides to commit the Hawthorne-like sin of alienation by isolating himself from most of his subjects by retreating with a thousand light-hearted friends into a castellated abbey to escape the Red Death. Assuming that death, even the one that Prospero is trying to escape, is the wage of sin, there would be little allegorical objection to having Prospero seek refuge in an abbey—a monastery.

While in this stage of isolation, as it were, from the majority of his subjects, he entertains his carefully selected guests at a masked ball in the seven rooms of his imperial suite; and from the way that Poe treats these seven rooms, it may be gathered that he views them as the allegorical representation of Prince Prospero's life span. The fact that he does view them thus is further enhanced by his placing the first room in the eastern extremity of the apartment and the last room in the western extremity. These directions are time-honored terms which have been used to refer to the beginning and the end of things—even of life itself.

Since Poe appears to attach so much importance to these rooms, since he devotes so much time to describing them in general, and, furthermore, since he dwells in particular and at great length upon

> Enhancing the possibility of considering Prospero insane, Poe indicates that the rooms were filled with dreams such as those a man with a tortured mind might have."

their color and their lay-out within the abbey, a diagram of them as the writer imagines they might be situated is appended to this article with the hope that it may prove helpful to the reader.

As was noted above, the imperial suite consists of seven rooms, and if it is assumed that the entire suite allegorically represents Prospero's life span, then it is logical to assume that the seven rooms allegorically represent the seven decades of his life, which according to the Bible is the normal life span of man—three score and ten. It has also been noted above that there is a possibility that Prospero is insane, and some weight is given to this suspicion when one learns that this personage's life had been conditioned by his love of the bizarre, and when one learns that the seven rooms which represent his life present a different aspect from that of those rooms which would allegorically represent the life span of another—and perhaps normal—person.

Prospero's apartments were "irregularly disposed" and full of turns which prevented one's seeing from one end to the other. Despite the turns, however, one may infer from Poe's words that they were arranged more or less in a line. That they had a closed corridor on either side of them is definitely known. Likewise it is known that these closed corridors extended the full length of the apartments. In other words, the imperial suite or life span of Prospero is enclosed or embraced by two closed corridors or, if you will, by two unknowns. These two unknowns could very well be thought of as the unknowns of birth and death which in effect enclose or embrace the life of any man.

Poe is careful to point out that in many such palaces "such suites form a long and straight vista" with nothing to hinder one's view from one end to the other; and he is equally careful to point out that this is not true of Prospero's apartments. These he says are crooked and winding with a sharp turn every twenty or thirty yards that prevented one's seeing very far into or through them. By emphasizing the fact that Prospero's apartments differ from similar apartments owned by other people, Poe may well be trying to indicate that Prospero's life differed from that of most people—that it is more crooked and winding, more tortured and stress ridden than the lives of others which are straighter and perhaps calmer.

Each of the seven rooms, with the exception of the last one, has two Gothic windows and two doors. It does not appear that the seventh room—the room of death—would need two doors. An entrance way alone would be sufficient for this one. As for the Gothic windows, each of them has a fire brazier behind it in the closed corridor, and the effect of the fire shining through the colored glass of the windows was productive of "a multitude of gaudy and fantastic appearances." Since the only light in any of the rooms was that of the fires sifted through the stained glass windows, the effect would very likely be an eerie one indeed, productive of "delirious fancies such as the madman fashions." Prospero then perhaps comprehends his life only in terms of the glimmerings of light (knowledge) that emanate from the unknowns of birth and death, and he sees his life as something of a mad drama. At least this line of reasoning provides a *raison d'etre* for the closed corridors and the fire braziers. Otherwise they may just seem to be there as extraneous and more or less irrelevant items.

Poe has so much to say about the colors found in the seven rooms that it is difficult, if indeed not impossible, to think that he meant nothing by them. It has been suggested above that the seven rooms probably represent the seven decades of Prospero's life, and proceeding on this assumption, it is logical to conclude that the color in any given room may be related to Prospero's physical and mental condition in that decade of his life.

Admitting that color symbolism can be rather vague at best, there nevertheless appears to be enough evidence in the text of the story to warrant certain pertinent conclusions concerning Poe's use of such symbolism here. The first room, for example, is located in the eastern end of the apartments, and it is colored blue. The symbolism regarding Poe's use of the direction east here is rather obvious, and the color blue may be related to the same

beginnings and origins that "East" stands for by thinking of it in the sense that it is the residence of the unknown or the unexpected—i.e., such as when we speak of something coming as a bolt out of the blue. Since blue may thus be associated with the unknown, by extension of meaning it may reasonably be associated in this instance with the beginning of life, which is unknown also.

The second room, says Poe, was purple—a color worn by those who have achieved something in the world or in society. Again, by extension of meaning, one may think of this color as being representative of that period in Prospero's life when he has accomplished a little something in life—perhaps moving into maturity.

The third room is colored green, and the writer doesn't think that it requires too much imagination to associate this color with that which is verdant, with that which is full of life and vigor—indeed with a man who is in the prime of his years.

The fourth room is orange and quite easily suggests, at least to the reader focusing on color symbolism, the autumn of life. Prospero could well be considered here to be beyond his prime, but by no means old yet.

The fifth room is white, and if we follow the same train of thought it would suggest the silver or hoary haired period of old age.

The sixth room is violet, a color that is emblematic of gravity and chastity. It appears that it would not be too much to assume that this room then represents the gravity and the soberness of extreme old age as well as the more or less enforced chastity that goes along with it.

Poe tells us that the seventh room is black, a color easily and most often associated with death; but, as if this were not enough, he tells us that this room is the most westerly of all, and the association of conclusions, ends, and death itself with "West" are too numerous to mention.

Most of the dancing and gaiety in the apartment took place in the first six rooms, for as Poe says "in them beat feverishly the heart of life." We are also told that "there were few of the company bold enough to set foot within" the seventh room—the room of death. Also it is to be noted that in the seventh room was to be found the great black clock, which seemed indeed to be more than a clock and to do more than a clock does. It would appear from the way he writes that Poe meant for the clock to count off periods of life—not mere hours. It is perhaps for this reason that he capitalizes the word "Time" at this point in the story and thus personifies it. This is also very likely why all the maskers stop when the clock strikes off the hour. They think not in terms of an hour having passed but rather in terms of just so much of their lives as having passed. Lastly, let it be noted that the clock of death, though it is heard in all the rooms, is heard best in the seventh or room of death.

Enhancing the possibility of considering Prospero insane, Poe indicates that the rooms were filled with dreams such as those a man with a tortured mind might have. He says that in the rooms "there was much of the beautiful, much of the wanton, much of the bizarre, something of the terrible, and not a little of that which might have excited disgust." Amid these revelers and amid these fantastic dreams there appears at the stroke of midnight a masked figure representing death. That there may be no mistaking its identity, Poe clothes it in the "habiliments of the grave" and causes it to wear a mask which resembles the face of a corpse.

Prospero is very angry at the intrusion and asks, "Who dares insult us with this blasphemous mockery?" He also commands his guests to "seize him [the figure] and unmask him—that we may know whom we have to hang at sunrise from the battlements!" It should be noted that Prospero was standing in the blue room when he uttered these words—in that youthful period of life when a man is braver toward death than he is later on, when it is closer upon him.

In his anger Prospero rushes toward the figure of death with the intention of stabbing him to death—irony of ironies! In doing so he runs through every room in the apartment—through every period of life—only to be stricken dead in the seventh room when he catches up with his intended victim. Since Prospero is standing in the blue room when he sees the figure representing death, and since one knows that it is impossible to see very far into this apartment because of its windings, one may conclude that the figure of death is in either the first or second room. Allegorically this could very well mean that one becomes aware of death at a very early age.

Lastly, it might be pointed out that Prospero in his last fateful, headlong rush at death is probably acting from a self-destructive urge—attracted to that which he at the same time mortally fears. In any event, with Prospero's death comes the death of all in the apartment and the tale ends with the morbidity that is so typical of Poe—the victory of death over all.

Source: H. H. Bell, Jr. "'The Masque of the Red Death'—An Interpretation," in *South Atlantic Bulletin*, Vol. 38, No. 4, 1973, pp. 101–5.

Joseph Patrick Roppolo

In the following essay, Roppolo both reviews many previous interpretations of Poe's tale and offers his own interpretation of the Red Death figure as an allegory of life itself.

Those who seek guidance in interpreting Edgar Allan Poe's "The Masque of the Red Death" are doomed to enter a strange world, as confused and confusing as a Gothic Wonderland and in some respects as eerie as the blighted house of Roderick Usher. Their guides will be old critics, New Critics, scholars, biographers, enthusiasts, dilettantes, journalists, hobbyists, anthologists, medical men, psychologists, and psychoanalysts. From these the seekers will learn that Prince Prospero is Poe himself and that "The Masque" is therefore autobiography; that Poe never presents a moral; that "The Masque" is an allegory and must therefore teach a lesson; that there is indeed a moral; that there are unnumbered morals; that there is no message or meaning; that there is a message; that the message is quite obvious and understandable; and that the meaning of the message transcends human understanding. In the pages that follow I should like to tour, briefly, the tangled world of the critics of "The Masque of the Red Death" and then to explore "The Masque" with the best of all possible guides—Poe himself.

I

A representative of the psychological guide and of the group which sees no meaning in "The Masque of the Red Death" is Albert Mordell, whose book, *The Erotic Motive in Literature*, widely read since 1919, was reissued in 1962 with a new section on Poe. Mordell writes blithely of Poe's "Loss of Breadth" and of a character named Roger Usher who, "like Poe, had been disappointed in love, and probably also drank." To Mordell, Poe was not only a frustrated lover and a drunkard; he was also a sadist and a masochist, a man who suffered from "a damming of the libido" and who was "so absorbed in his dreams that he never tried to take an interest in reality. Hence," Mordell concludes, "we will find no moral note in Poe's work"—with the single exception of "William Wilson."

> ❝ 'Let there be light' was
> one of the principles of
> Creation; darkness, then, is
> a principle of Chaos. And to
> Poe Chaos is synonymous with
> Nothingness, 'which, to all
> finite perception, Unity
> must be.'"

In sharp contrast, Vincent Buranelli argues that Poe "was no sadist, no masochist, no pervert, no rake," but was instead "the sanest of our writers"—that he was, in fact, "America's greatest writer, and the American writer of greatest significance in world literature." Yet, oddly, Buranelli finds himself aligned with Mordell when he, too, asserts sweepingly that "Poe does not touch morality"; and he finds himself involved in something of a contradiction when he describes "The Masque of the Red Death" as "an allegory representing Death itself as one of the dramatis personae." Allegory, typically, is meaningful and moral, but Buranelli does not elaborate upon his statement; nor does he reconcile Poe's well-known detestation of allegory with Poe's use of it in one of his acknowledged masterpieces.

Joseph Wood, Krutch, who saw Poe as incompetent, sexless, and mad, but nevertheless marked by genius, dismissed "The Masque of the Red Death" as "merely the most perfect [*sic*] description of that fantastic *decor* which [Poe] had again and again imagined." Edward H. Davidson remarks on the paucity of "fact and information" in the piece and reveals that "tone and movement are all." Commenting at greater length, David M. Rein summarizes the narrative and adds that

> The prince, of course, represents Poe, once again as a young man of wealthy and distinguished family. Here Poe dreamed of escape from the harsh world, where such evils as the plague were dominant—escape into a secluded place of pleasure he himself designed. But like so many of Poe's fantasies, this dream world would not remain intact; the imaginary refuge, in spite of all precautions, was invaded by Death, whose merest look destroyed him. It may be significant, too, that all in this company fell back to avoid encounter-

ing the gruesome figure. The prince alone, unwilling to await the stranger's pleasure, went forth to pursue him. Does not Poe here once again, in fantasy, impatiently seek a danger that seems inescapable?

Avoiding the pitfall of imagining Poe's ratiocinative mind losing control of a carefully imagined dream world, Killis Campbell, among others, contented himself with seeking sources and with attempting to ground the fantasy of "The Masque of the Red Death" in fact. *In The Mind of Poe and Other Studies*, Campbell points out that Poe was "pretty clearly indebted to William Harrison Ainsworth's *Old Saint Paul's*" and then cites an account by N. P. Willis in the *New York Mirror* of June 2, 1832, in which Willis describes a Parisian ball featuring "The Cholera Waltz," "The Cholera Galopade," and, most pertinently, a masked figure representing the cholera itself. Willard Thorp, in *A Southern Reader*, makes the identity of Poe's Red Death positive: it is, Thorpe says, "undoubtedly the cholera, newly arrived in America"; Poe colors it red to distinguish it from the Black Death—the bubonic plague. In a more literary vein, numerous scholars have pointed out the use of the words "red plague" by Shakespeare in *The Tempest* (I.ii.364), without, however, making useful applications to Poe's "Masque."

Arthur Hobson Quinn is among those who believe that "The Masque of the Red Death" contains a moral or a message (he uses the terms interchangeably). "With a restraint that is one of the surest marks of genius," Quinn says, "Poe gives no hint of the great moral the tale tells to those who can think. For the others, he had no message." Whereupon Quinn leaves his reader to place himself among the thinkers or, unhappily, among the nonthinkers, disdaining to make explicit or even to suggest the "great moral" which Poe shields behind his "Masque."

Patrick F. Quinn agrees that "The Masque of the Red Death" is "one of the few serious moral tales that Poe ever wrote," but he, too, spares the reader the embarrassment of having the moral or morals pointed out to him. Others are less reticent, and their interpretations tend to fall into the familiar pattern of the *memento mori*. Typical are Frances Winwar and Norman Foerster.

To Frances Winwar, "The Masque of the Red Death" is "a compelling fantasy in scarlet and black where every effect stresses the inevitability of final dissolution. . . ." Foerster notes that red is "Poe's most frequent color" and sees in it "the horror of blood." To Foerster "The Masque of the

Red Death'' is a richly vivid contrast between life and death. Setting dominates, and "magnificence and voluptuousness heighten the sense of worldly pleasure till the heart of life beats feverishly—and stops." The clock symbolizes the processes of time—both life and death.

Three critics, Walter Blair, Harry Levin, and Marie Bonaparte, go far beyond the routine. To Blair, as to many others, there is "allegorical significration" in the seven rooms, which, "progressing from east to west—from blue to black—connote the seven ages of man from the blue of the dawn of life to the black of its night." The clock is, of course, Time; the masked figure is the Red Death; and the revelers are the living, "who seek to bar out and forget death by being gay and carefree," only to discover that death must inevitably conquer all humanity. So far, the critic is in the mainstream of interpretation. But Blair, more perceptive than most, refuses to confine "The Masque of the Red Death" to this moral. The closing note of the last paragraph is "inconsistent with such a meaning"; and Poe, a lover of ambiguity, would probably argue, Blair says, that "The Masque" is "suggestive of implications which cannot be made explicit this side of eternity." Harry Levin makes the venture. "The closing note, echoed from the pseudo-Miltonic last line of Pope's *Dunciad*," Levin says, "predicates a reduction of cosmos to chaos"—a challenging and, I hope to show, a fruitful bit of speculation.

It is left to Princess Bonaparte to lift "The Masque of the Red Death" from the limited realm of allegory to the expansive kingdom of myth. But, having placed "The Masque" among "typical" Oedipus stories, along with "The Cask of Amontillado," the Princess bogs down in a morass of conflicting Freudian symbols. The Prince, of course, is Oedipus, the son. The masked figure is the father. The castle of seven rooms is the body of the mother. The uplifted dagger is a phallus. The dropped dagger is the castrated phallus. And the Red Death—whether father-figure or something beyond that—is both death and castration. We are back in the weird and wonderful world of Albert Mordell, who, not surprisingly, admits owing a great debt to Princess Bonaparte.

Of all the critics mentioned, Blair is the most detailed and in many ways the most convincing. Foerster's brief statement, too, almost compels belief. But I should like to suggest that neither goes far enough. Foerster evades consideration of Poe's final paragraph. Blair acknowledges that paragraph—

vitally important because of its position—but leaves all attempts at its clarification to the other side of eternity. If Foerster's evasion is justified (and Levin' remark indicates that it is not), then Poe has failed to follow one of his own precepts, that "In the whole composition there should be no word written, of which the tendency, direct or indirect, is not to be the one pre-established design." And if Blair is correct, then Poe must have sprinkled his page with more than a grain of salt when he wrote that "Every work of art should contain within itself all that is requisite for its own comprehension." I do not believe that Poe was less than a remarkably skilled craftsman, nor do I believe that his critical dicta were deliberate jests. I should like to take Poe at his word in both quoted statements and, with both steadily in mind, study "The Masque of the Red Death" to see what it yields.

II

In Poe's imaginative prose, beginnings unfailingly are important. "The Masque of the Red Death" begins with these three short sentences:

> The "Red Death" had long devastated the country. No pestilence had even been so fatal or so hideous. Blood was its Avatar and its seal—the redness and horror of blood.

On one level, the reader is introduced to a disease, a plague, with hideous and terrifying symptoms, a remarkably rapid course, and inevitable termination in death. But Poe's heaviest emphasis is on blood, not as sign or symptom, but as avatar and seal. A seal is something that confirms or assures or ratifies. The appearance—the presence—of blood is confirmation or assurance of the existence of the Red Death or, more broadly, of Death itself. As avatar, blood is the incarnation, the bodily representation, of the Red Death. It is, further, something god-like, an eternal principle, for in Hindu myth, the word "avatar" referred to the descent of a god, in human form, to earth. Further, "avatar" can be defined as "a variant phase or version of a continuing entity." A second level thus emerges: blood represents something invisible and eternal, a ruling principle of the universe. That principle, Poe seems to suggest, is death.

But is it? The Red Death, Poe tells us, "had long devastated the country." And then: "No pestilence had ever been so fatal"—surely a remarkable second sentence for a man so careful of grammar and logic as Poe. Is or is not the Red Death a pestilence? And does the word "fatal" permit of comparison? I should like to suggest that here Poe is being neither ungrammatical nor even carefully ambiguous, but daringly clear. The Red Death is not a pestilence, in the usual sense; it is unfailingly and universally fatal, as no mere disease or plague can be; and blood is its guarantee, its avatar and seal. Life itself, then, is the Red Death, the one "affliction" shared by all mankind.

For purposes of commenting on life and of achieving his single effect, Poe chooses to emphasize death. He is aware not only of the brevity of all life and of its inevitable termination but also of men's isolation: blood, the visible sign of life, is, Poe says, "the pest ban which shuts him out from the aid and sympathy of his fellow man." In the trap of life and in his death, every man *is* an island. If there is a mutual bond, it is the shared horror of death.

Out of the chaos that has "long devastated" his dominions, Prince Prospero creates a new and smaller world for the preservation of life. A kind of demigod, Prospero can "create" his world, and he can people it; but time (the ebony clock) exists in his new world, and he is, of course, deluded in his belief that he can let in life and shut out death. Prospero's world of seven rooms, without "means [either] of ingress or egress," is a microcosm, as the parallel with the seven ages of man indicates, and its people are eminently human, with their predilection for pleasure and their susceptibility to "sudden impulses of despair or frenzy." In their masquerade costumes, the people are "in fact, a multitude of dreams," but they are fashioned like the inhabitants of the macrocosmic world. Many are beautiful, but many also are bizarre or grotesque. Some are wanton; some are "arabesque figures with unsuited limbs and appointments"; some are terrible, some are disgusting, and some are "delirious fancies such as the madman fashions" (and Prospero, the demigod, for all his "fine eye for colors and effects," may indeed be mad). But all of them are life, and in six of the seven apartments "the heart of life" beats "feverishly". And even here, by deliberate use of the word "feverishly", Poe links life with disease and death.

The seventh apartment is not the room of death; death occurs in fact in each of the rooms. It is, however, the room in which the reminders of death are strongest, and it is the room to which all must come who traverse the preceding six. Death's colors, red and black, are there; and there the ebony clock mercilessly measures Time, reminding the revelers hour after hour that life, like the course of the Red Death, is short.

When the clock strikes the dreaded hour of twelve, the revelers become aware suddenly of the presence of a masked figure which none has noted before:

> The figure was tall and gaunt, and shrouded from head to foot in the habiliments of the grave. The mask which concealed the visage was made so nearly to resemble the countenance of a stiffened corpse that the closest scrutiny must have had difficulty in detecting the cheat. And yet all this might have been endured, if not approved, by the mad revelers around. But the mummer had gone so far as to assume the type of the Red Death. His vesture was dabbled in *blood*— and his broad brow, with all the features of the face, was besprinkled with the scarlet horror.

Poe does not indicate in which room the awareness of the masked figure occurred first, but Prince Prospero sees this blood-sprinkled horror in the blue, or easternmost, room, which is usually associated with birth, rather than with death The figure moves then through each of the apartments, and Prospero follows, to meet his own death in the room of black and red.

Not once does Poe say that the figure is the Red Death. Instead, "this new presence" is called "the masked figure," "the stranger," "the mummer," "this spectral image," and "the intruder." He is "shrouded" in "the habiliments of the grave," the dress provided by the living for their dead and endowed by the living with all the horror and terror which they associate with death. The mask, fashioned to resemble "the countenance of a stiffened corpse," is but a mask, a "cheat." And all this, we are told, "might have been borne" had it not been for the blood, that inescapable reminder to life of the inevitability of death. The intruder is, literally, *"The Mask* of the Red Death," not the plague itself, nor even—as many would have it—the all-inclusive representation of Death.

There is horror in the discovery that "the grave-cerements and corpse-like mask" are "untenanted by any tangible form," but the horror runs more deeply than the supernatural interpretation allows, so deeply in fact that it washes itself clean to emerge as Truth. Blood, Poe has been saying, is (or is symbolic of) the life force; but even as it suggests life, blood serves as a reminder of death. Man himself invests death with elements of terror, and he clothes not death but the terror of death in garb of his own making—"the habiliments of the grave"—and then runs, foolishly, to escape it or, madly, to kill it, mistaking the mummer, the cheat, for death itself. The fear of death can kill: Prospero attempts to attack the masked figure and falls; but when man's image of death is confronted directly, it is found to be nothing. The vestments are empty. The intruder in ''The Masque of the Red Death'' is, then, not the plague, not death itself, but man's creation, his self-aroused and self-developed fear of his own mistaken concept of death.

Death is nevertheless present, as pervasive and as invisible as eternal law. He is nowhere and everywhere, not only near, about, and around man, but in him. And so it is, at last, that, having unmasked their unreasoning fear, the revelers acknowledge the presence of the Red Death. One by one, the revelers die—as everything endowed with life must; and, with the last of them, time, which is measured and feared only by man, dies, too.

Poe might have stopped there, just as he might have ended ''The Raven'' with the sixteenth stanza. The narrative is complete, and there are even ''morals'' or ''lessons'' for those who demand them. But, as Poe says in ''The Philosophy of Composition,''

> in subjects so handled, however skilfully, or with however vivid an array of incident, there is always a certain hardness or nakedness, which repels the artistical eye. Two things are invariably required—first, some amount of complexity, or more properly, adapation; and, secondly, some amount of suggestiveness— some undercurrent, however indefinite, of meaning.

To achieve complexity and suggestiveness, Poe added two stanzas to ''The Raven.'' To ''The Masque of the Red Death'' he added two sentences: ''And the flames of the tripods expired. And Darkness and Decay and the Red Death held illimitable dominion over all.''

''Let there be light'' was one of the principles of Creation; darkness, then, is a principle of Chaos. And to Poe Chaos is synonymous with Nothingness, ''which, to all finite perception, Unity must be.'' Decay occurs as matter ''expels the ether'' to return to or to sink into Unity. Prince Prospero's world, created out of a chaos ruled by the Red Death, returns to chaos, ruled by the trinity of Darkness and Decay and the Red Death. But, it will be remembered, Prince Prospero's world came into being *because of* the Red Death, which, although it includes death, is the principle of life. In Chaos, then, is the promise of new lives and of new worlds which will swell into existence and then, in their turn, subside into nothingness in the eternal process

of contraction and expansion which Poe describes in ''Eureka.''

There are ''morals'' implicit and explicit in this interpretation of ''The Masque of the Red Death,'' but they need not be underlined here. Poe, who had maintained in his ''Review of Nathaniel Hawthorne's *Twice-Told Tales*'' that ''Truth is often, and in very great degree, the aim of the tale,'' was working with a larger, but surely not entirely inexpressible, truth than can be conveyed in a simple ''Poor Richard'' maxim; and in that task, it seems to me, he transcends the tale (into which classification most critics put ''The Masque of the Red Death'') to create a prose which, in its free rhythms, its diction, its compression, and its suggestion, approaches poetry.

The ideas that were haunting Poe when he published ''Eureka'' were already haunting him in 1842, when he published ''The Masque of the Red Death,'' and what emerged was not, certainly, a short story; nor was it, except by the freest definition, a tale. For either category, it is deficient in plot and in characterization. Instead, ''The Masque of the Red Death'' combines elements of the parable and of the myth. Not as explicit or as pointedly allegorical always as the parable, ''The Masque of the Red Death'' nevertheless can be (and has been) read as a parable of the inevitability and the universality of death; but it deals also with the feats of a hero or demigod—Prospero—and with Poe's concepts of universal principles, and it has the mystery and the remoteness of myth. What Poe has created, then, is a kind of mythic parable, brief and poetic, of the human condition, of man's fate, and of the fate of the universe.

Source: Joseph Patrick Roppolo, ''Meaning and 'The Masque of the Red Death,''' in *TSE: Tulane Studies in English*, Vol. 13, 1963, pp. 59–69.

Sources

Bell, H. H., Jr. '''The Masque of the Red Death'—An Interpretation,'' in *South Atlantic Bulletin*, Vol. 38, No. 4, 1973, pp. 101, 104.

Britannica Online [database online], Chicago, Ill.: Encyclopaedia Britiannica, Inc., 1999- [cited August 1999], available from Encyclopaedia Britiannica, Inc., Chicago, Ill., s.v. ''Allegory,'' ''Impressionism,'' ''Infection,'' ''Parable,'' ''Short Story,'' and ''Tuberculosis.''

Cassuto, Leonard. ''The Coy Reaper: Un-masque-ing the Red Death,'' in *Studies in Short Fiction*, Vol. 25, No. 3, 1988, pp. 317–20.

Cheney, Patrick, ''Poe's Use of The Tempest and the Bible in 'The Masque of the Red Death,''' in *English Language Notes*, Vol. 20, No. 3-4, March-June, 1983, p. 34.

Roppolo, Joseph Patrick. ''Meaning and 'The Masque of the Red Death,''' in *TSE: Tulane Studies in English*, Vol. 13, 1963, pp. 59–69.

Thompson, G. R., *Dictionary of Literary Biography*, Vol. 3: *Antebellum Writers in New York and the South*, edited by Joel Myerson, Gale Research, 1979, pp. 249-97.

Further Reading

De Shell, Jeffrey. *The Peculiarity of Literature: An Allegorical Approach to Poe's Fiction*, Madison, New Jersey: Fairleigh Dickenson Presses, 1997.

Discusses both Poe's detective stories and his horror stories in terms of their allegorical meaning.

Deas, Michael. *The Portraits and Daguerreotypes of Edgar Allan Poe*, Charlottesville: University Press of Virginia, 1989.

A picture book of daguerreotype portraits taken of Poe.

Silverman, Kenneth. *New Essays on Poe's Major Tales*, New York: Cambridge University Press, 1993.

Diverse critical interpretations on the short fiction of Poe.

Smith, Don. *The Poe Cinema: A Critical Filmography of Theatrical Releases Based on the Works of Edgar Allan Poe*, 1999.

Lists film and videos based on Poe's works. Includes plot descriptions and themes, mostly in the horror genre.

Mateo Falcone

Prosper Merimee

1829

Prosper Merimee's "Mateo Falcone" (1829), originally subtitled "Les moeurs de Corse" ("The Ways of Corsica"), chronicles the killing of a ten-year-old boy by his father. The story, Merimee's first, is provocative in spite of the detached narrative voice of his unnamed narrator. This laconic, disconnected voice heightens the shock value of the event and at the same time demands the reader to interpret the story objectively. Such contemporaries as Stendhal (Henri Beyle), Henry James, and Walter Pater admired Merimee and praised him for his craft. Pater called "Mateo Falcone" "the cruellest story in the world."

"Mateo Falcone" is a brief, but complex story. It features at least five points of view and at least four "ways of life" (the "moeurs" of the original subtitle). Merimee's themes include betrayal and honor, savagery and civilization, vendetta and law, and custom and morality. Most importantly, "Mateo Falcone" exemplifies the art of storytelling at its most concentrated and allusive. Most critics consider the story disturbing and unforgettable.

Author Biography

Prosper Merimee was born in Paris in 1803 to a moderately successful painter, Leonor Merimee, and his wife, Anne. Merimee's mother was a painter as well as the granddaughter of Madame Leprince

de Beaumont, who had written and published a version of the popular children's story ''Beauty and the Beast.''

Merimee began attending the Lycee Napoleon at the age of eight. He showed promise in Latin and a few other subjects, but was generally considered an average student. He developed a strong interest in art and archeology, however, and from an early age became infatuated with members of the opposite sex. Although Merimee did not become a painter, he valued the skills of drawing and sketching and made much use of them in later life. He taught himself Serbian, Russian, and Greek, and he had learned English at home from his parents.

After graduation from the Lycee, Merimee entered law school; after receiving his degree, he embarked on a lifelong career as a civil servant. Most significantly, he became Minister of Historical Monuments in 1834. With his position he is credited with salvaging much of the French Gothic architectural legacy. He had a strong sense of history, and he strove not only to preserve important sites and buildings but to instill a popular appreciation of them.

Merimee began writing as a young man. He knew Stendhal and other writers of the day and received valuable advice from them. His earliest published works were two ''hoaxes:'' a collection of supposedly Spanish plays and a volume of ''Illyrian'' (Albanian) ballads. Merimee also wrote travel books and journalism, and he translated the Russian poet Pushkin into French for the first time. While not prolific as a fiction writer, Merimee produced a respectable body of work. In 1870, the year that Merimee died, composer Georges Bizet adapted a Merimee story with a Spanish setting as an opera. Probably because of the enormous success of that opera, ''Carmen'' (1845) is Merimee's best-known work.

Plot Summary

''Mateo Falcone'' is set in Corsica in the seventeenth century in the region of Porto-Vecchio, which is midway between the town of Corte and the maquis, the wild country of the Corsican highlands where outlaws and misfits find refuge from law and authority. Mateo Falcone, a forty-eight-year-old father of three married daughters and one ten-year-old son, is a successful sheep rancher. He sets off to gather his flock one afternoon. His wife, Guiseppa, accompanies him, and they leave their son, Fortunato alone.

Fortunato daydreams in the autumn sun. He anticipates going into town in a few days to have dinner with his uncle, a local notable, or ''corporal.'' Suddenly, gunshots echo from nearby. On nearby path, a wounded man appears. He has been shot in his thigh. Seeing Fortunato, he asks whether the boy is the son of Mateo Falcone. He introduces himself as Gianetto Sanpiero, the implication being that he has a tie to Falcone and thus a right to expect asylum. Fortunato at first declines to hide Gianetto, but when the bandit offers a piece of silver, the boy conceals him beneath the hay.

Six soldiers arrive, led by adjutant Tiodoro Gamba, who addresses Fortunato as ''cousin,'' once again implying a tie to the Falcones. Tiodoro wants to know whether Fortunato has seen a man on the trail. Fortunato evades Tiodoro's questions, and Tiodoro suspects that the boy is in complicity with Gianetto. He threatens to beat Fortunato, but the boy only replies that he is Mateo Falcone's son, and the lieutenant understands that he dare not harm Fortunato for fear of angering the father. The soldiers search the property but find nothing. Finally, Tiodoro attempts to bribe Fortunato with a shiny new watch:

> As he spoke he brought the watch closer and closer until it was almost touching Fortunato's pale cheek. The child's face clearly showed the struggle between cupidity and the claims of hospitality that was raging within him. His bare chest was heaving, and he seemed to be fighting for breath. And still the watch swung, twisted, and occasionally bumped against the tip of his nose. At last his right hand slowly rose towards the watch; his fingertips touched it; and he felt its full weight in his palm, though the adjutant still held the end of the chain. The dial was pale blue, the case newly furbished; in the sunshine it seemed ablaze. . . . The temptation was too great. (Excerpt from ''Mateo Falcone'' translated by Nicholas Jotcham)

Fortunato accepts the bribe and silently nods in the direction of the haystack. The soldiers discover Gianetto, who curses the boy. Fortunato throws the silver back at Gianetto. The prisoner accepts his capture; the soldiers treat him with respect, even though he has killed one of them and wounded another.

Mateo and Guiseppa return from the pastures. Tiodoro advances cautiously and explains to Mateo what has happened. The soldiers leave with their prisoner. When Mateo ascertains the facts, he tersely asks his wife whether the boy is really his child. Fortunato collapses in tears, sobbing and crying, and the wife becomes hysterical. Mateo commands Fortunato to leave with him into the high country.

As Mateo and Fortunato climb into the mountains, Guiseppa prays inside the house to an icon of the Virgin Mary. In a ravine, Mateo commands Fortunato to kneel and say his prayers. When he finishes praying, Fortunato begs for mercy, but Mateo gives none. He raises his rifle and shoots.

Characters

Fortunato Falcone

Fortunato Falcone is Mateo's ten-year-old son. His father regards him as ''the hope of the family.'' The name Fortunato, meaning ''the fortunate one,'' reflects his father's pride. Before the wounded Gianetto appears at the family home, Fortunato had been daydreaming about the meal that he is to eat with his wealthy uncle in Corte in a few days. Fortunato shows little human feeling towards the hunted Gianetto and agrees to hide him only when bribed with a piece of silver. When Tiodoro offers him a watch in exchange for information about Gianneto, Fortunato eyes it ''just as a cat does when a whole chicken is offered to it'' and gives away the bandit's hiding place. On the other hand, once he has divulged Gianetto's hiding place, Fortunato returns the silver.

Giuseppa Falcone

Giuseppa is the wife of Mateo Falcone and the mother of Fortunato. Merimee discloses few details about her. She has borne four children to Mateo, whom she married after a rival had been shot dead, presumably by Mateo himself. She is thus implicated in the Corsican cycle of violence. She begs for mercy for Fortunato when Mateo takes the boy to the mountains to kill him and prays to the Virgin Mary when her husband refuses.

Mateo Falcone

Mateo Falcone, aged fifty when the narrator knew him, was ''a comparatively rich man for that country—Corsica—where he lived.'' Falcone owns a large, one-room house of the peasant type halfway between the nearest town (Corte) and the wild maquis, or cane-fields, where outlaws take refuge from the law. He excels in the Corsican art of

Prosper Merimee

shooting; his acquaintances consider him an excellent marksman. The narrator implies that Falcone married his wife, Giuseppa, after dispatching his rival with a single rifle shot from long distance. The three daughters that Giuseppa bore ''enraged him.'' At last she bears a son, which pleases him.

Those in the region of Porto-Vecchio, in which Falcone lives, consider him either a ''a good friend'' or ''a dangerous enemy.'' Admired and feared, ''he lived at peace in the district.'' Readers understand Falcone as a man entirely devoted to the Corsican code of vendetta, or blood-feud. Protecting family and friends is a priority; the family bond transcends any abstract idea of law. Falcone, having married off his girls, knows that he ''could count in case of need on the daggers and rifles of his sons-in-law.'' The wounded bandit who seeks asylum in Falcone's house when he is absent tells Falcone's reluctant son, Fortunato, that his father will say that the son ''did right'' in hiding him from the pursuing soldiers.

Falcone adheres to the concept of machismo. His wife and children are hardly more than chattel. His wife, for example, must carry burdens from the field, ''for it is considered undignified for a man to carry any other burden but his weapon.'' After Falcone kills his son, he goes looking for a spade ''without throwing a single glance back at the body.''

Tiodoro Gamba

Tiodoro Gamba is an adjutant (an officer) of the local militia and, as such, a representative of the law. He regards himself as a relation of Mateo, as indicated by his use of the term "cousin" in addressing Fortunato. Tiodoro is wary of Mateo and, out of fear of angering him, does not beat Fortunato to get information, as he contemplates doing at one point during the interrogation. Tiodoro demonstrates psychological acuity when he determines to bribe rather than coerce Fortunato; he can understand Fortunato better than Fortunato can understand Tiodoro. He also approaches Mateo with calculated circumspection because he knows Mateo to be volatile and violent. Tiodoro differs from Mateo and all the other characters in that he no longer belongs to the vendetta world of the mountains. Like Gianetto Sanpiero, however, Gamba carries out his duty without letting personal feelings enter into it. He metes out decent treatment to the wounded captive. He also seems remarkably unconcerned over the death of one of his men in the pursuit: "That is not of great consequence, for the dead man was only a Frenchman."

Gianetto Sanpiero

Gianetto Sanpiero is a fugitive from the law. One of his crimes is that he stole a milch-goat from the Falcones. Gianetto has apparently been in town to buy powder for his rifle so that he could protect himself and hunt game where he has been hiding. Merimee gives him dignity; he shows no personal animosity towards the soldiers who pursue and capture him. He shows understandable spite towards Fortunato after the boy reveals his hiding place to the soldiers.

Themes

Culture Clash

"Mateo Falcone" concerns the cultural clash between savagery and civilization. The French, in particular, developed these themes, beginning with the work of Jean-Jacques Rousseau, whose *Essay on the Origin of Inequality Among Men* (1854) presented the notion that primitive people were uniquely free and true to themselves in their existence, while civilized people, on the contrary, led corrupt, hypocritical lives. Health and simplicity were associated with the savage, according to Rousseau, and neurosis and complexity to the "civilized" human being.

Merimee was not a follower of Rousseau, however, even though he was interested in Rousseau's philosophy. Merimee's idea of savagery was actually grounded in classical literature. Thus the Corsican ways described in the tale resemble those of the Cyclopes in Homer's *Odyssey*. The Cyclopes, like Merimee's Corsicans, are island-bound pastoralists; the Cyclopes understand a basic and brutal code of vengeance.

Law and Order

In "Mateo Falcone," vendetta assumes the role of law and authority instead of the traditional legal system. With vendetta, the response to acts of violence is always another act of violence. For example, if one man kills another's brother, the deceased's brother then kills the killer, and then the kin of the second dead man seek to kill his killer, and so on. Violence breeds more violence, and the founding principle of the system is not justice but revenge. Under an established legal system, those accused of a crime—say, of a killing—come under the jurisdiction of established authorities, whose loyalty is to an abstract system rather than to clans or to individual persons. The accused receives a trial in a court where evidence influences the discussion. Vendetta belongs to the countryside, law to the town. (Corte, the name of the town in Merimee's story, means "law-court.")

Vendetta is a custom, an unwritten rule acted on out of ancient habit and the pressure of conformity. A custom is a "lifeway," in the language of anthropology, and the original subtitle of "Mateo Falcone" was "The Ways of Corsica."

Honor and Betrayal

Honor, in the Corsican context, is the local custom of cultivating and appreciating loyalty among family and friends. Betrayal is the failure to recognize the bonds of loyalty, as when Fortunato gives up Gianetto for the sake of a shiny watch. Yet it is not a betrayal, according to the rules of vendetta, for Mateo to kill Fortunato for having revealed Gianetto for a price.

Natural Law

In this story, the sacrifice of Fortunato is considered obedience to the natural law. Fortunato must die in order to avenge the betrayal of someone in the community; the boy's death will guarantee the tenuous peace in the region. Otherwise, Gianetto's partisans might have come after someone in Mateo's family, whereupon Mateo would have been obliged

Topics for Further Study

- Read Part I of Jean-Jacques Rousseau's *Essay on the Origin of Inequality*, paying particular attention to the theory of "the noble savage." Compare Rousseau's idea of the primitive and the pre- or non-civilized with the depiction of Corsican montagnard life presented by Merimee in "Mateo Falcone."

- Discuss the concept of justice both in the abstract and as it relates to Merimee's "Mateo Falcone." Pay particular attention to Mateo's killing of Fortunato. If the killing strikes you as intuitively unjust, what then is the precise definition of justice? What is the just punishment in this case?

- Research the history and ethnology of Corsica. Use an encyclopedia and other sources, if they are available. Does Merimee give a generally

accurate picture of Corsican life? If not, where does his depiction diverge from reality?

- Read the "Exordium" and the "Eulogy on Abraham" in Soren Kierkegaard's *Fear and Trembling* (1843), in which Kierkegaard discusses the test of Abraham and Isaac that is related in the Old Testament. Compare the story of Abraham and Isaac and Kierkegaard's commentary with Merimee's story of Mateo and Fortunato Falcone.

- From the Chicago mobsters of the 1920s to today's drug cartels and street gangs, the ideas of "honor" and "treachery" have been used to justify brutal acts. Compare the code of the mobsters and drug cartels to the code of the Corsican montagnards as depicted by Merimee.

---

to retaliate, and so on. It ought to be noted that Mateo's killing of Fortunato resembles Abraham's aborted sacrifice of Isaac in the Old Testament. There, however, God intervenes to substitute a lamb for the child.

Violence and Cruelty

Violence is the eternal human problem. Cain killed Abel; the Egyptians oppressed the Hebrews; the Romans permitted the execution of Jesus. Wars are waged over boundaries and devastate vast civilian populations. Revenge leads to new wars. Civilization and religion address the problem of human violence and to this day try to find solutions to eliminate or lessen the violent impulses of man.

Style

Romanticism and Realism

"Mateo Falcone" (1829) illustrates the cruel toll exacted on a Corsican family by the code of vendetta, or feud. Falcone kills his own son,

Fortunato, because the son has betrayed a man to the authorities. Two concerns govern Merimee's style in "Mateo Falcone." The first is geographical and ethnological verisimilitude; the second is narrative minimalism, so that, for most of the story, Merimee's style can be described as spare and laconic.

It is useful to know that before he wrote the sequence of short stories that make up the collection *Mosaic*, in which "Mateo Falcone" appears, Merimee had written two literary hoaxes, the second of which, *La Guzla* (1827), exploits stylistic conventions associated with romanticism. Briefly, *La Guzla* (the word refers to the national instrument of the Albanian "bards," or poets) pretends to be a translation of native ballads of the mountagnards of "Illyria" (Albania), collected and translated into French by an Italian traveler familiar with the region. *La Guzla*, comes complete with scholarly notes on the sources of the poems and the character of the montagnards. In his mid-teens, Merimee had been deeply impressed by James MacPherson's *Ossian*, offered as translations into English of actual (but in truth fictitious) Celtic originals from the Middle Ages. Merimee also admired Byron's *Don*

Juan, which includes many vignettes in exotic settings. The three opening paragraphs of ''Mateo Falcone'' reflect—perhaps ironically—features of romanticism.

Romantic and Realistic Syntax

The long opening paragraph of the story stretches out its sentences. It guides us from Porto-Vecchio, a coastal town of Corsica, ''northwest towards the center of the island,'' where the ground becomes hilly and is ''strewn with large boulders and sometimes cut by ravines.'' The maquis itself is a type of underbrush ''composed of different types of trees and shrubs mixed up and entangled thickly enough to please God.'' Merimee explains that ''if you have killed a man, go into the maquis of Porto-Vecchio, with a good gun and powder and shot, and you will live there in safety . . . . The shepherds will give you milk, cheese, and chestnuts, and you will have nothing to fear from the law. . . .''

Such a wild place, outside the long arm of the law, is a romantic convention. In fact, the effect of the first three paragraphs of the story is to lull readers into romantic expectations.

By the fifth paragraph, Merimee omits the standard long periods of the scene-setting introduction. Much of the action is expressed in concise dialogue. Consider the killing:

> ''Oh, father, have mercy on me. Forgive me! I will never do it again. I will beg my cousin the corporal to pardon Gianetto.''
>
> He went on talking. Mateo cocked his rifle and took aim.
>
> ''May God forgive you!'' he said.
>
> The boy made a frantic effort to get up and clasp his father's knees, but he had no time. Mateo fired, and Fortunato fell stone dead. (Excerpt from ''Mateo Falcone'')

Merimee reduces everything to the minimum. In French, ''Mateo fired'' reads ''Mateo fit feu.'' The tri-syllable followed by the two monosyllables has tremendous finality. Merimee also deploys ambiguity in the tale. Who is the ''he'' who says ''May God forgive you!''? Is it Fortunato or Mateo? Or does it matter?

Merimee's two styles in ''Mateo Falcone'' do not contradict each other or disrupt the unity of the text. On the contrary, they work together to force upon the reader the difficult ethical questions posed by the tale.

Historical Context

Napoleonic France

By the time of Merimee's birth in 1803, Napoleon, a Corsican who had made himself Emperor of France, was at the height of his power. By 1814, when Merimee was eleven years old, Napoleon's wars had devastated Europe. Napoleon finally was beaten at the hands of an allied force led by the Duke of Wellington at Waterloo in Belgium. The island of Corsica became part of France in the eighteenth century and was retained by the French nation even after Napoleon's defeat.

France after Napoleon

After Napoleon, Louis XVIII became king. His supporters began to persecute anyone that had been associated with the Napoleonic regime. Louis attempted to assuage the extremists, but he was unable to control his supporters. In 1830, the year of ''Mateo Falcone,'' political discontent among the increasingly powerful middle classes (the bourgeoisie) erupted in revolution.

The vendetta, portrayed so shockingly in ''Mateo Falcone,'' was a significant part of French politics in the first three decades of the nineteenth century.

Romanticism

During these tumultuous years, romanticism gained prominence as a literary and artistic movement. Romanticism appeared, almost simultaneously, in England and in the German-speaking states of Central Europe (there was no united Germany until 1870). It was the philosopher Jean-Jacques Rousseau (1712–1778), a Frenchman whose *Essay on the Origin of Inequality Among Men* (1754), *The Social Contract* (1762), *Emile* (1762), and *Reveries of the Solitary Walker* (1778) signaled a return to emotionalism and primitivism in Europe and the United States. ''Man is born free,'' Rousseau claimed in *The Social Contract*, ''and everywhere he is in chains.'' Savages led noble lives; civilized men and women suffered from the repression of their natural impulses.

Influenced by Rousseau's ideas, young artists in Great Britain and Germany took up the cause of spiritual liberation. For example, William Wordsworth preached the innocence of childhood, the salvation offered by wild nature, and the corrup-

Compare & Contrast

- **Nineteenth Century:** The vendetta is perceived as a viable and ancient method of justice in many communities. The interest in Rosseau's theory of primitivism, with its implied rejection of the established legal system, somewhat legitimized traditional methods of justice and punishment.

  Twentieth Century: The vendetta still exists in different forms throughout the world. In the United States, revenge killings and drive-by shootings take thousands of lives every year. The perceived failure of the established legal system has led to vigilantism, as frustrated citizens take matters into their own hands to settle their own alleged vendettas.

- **Nineteenth Century:** France is a world power, despite its often turbulent domestic and foreign politics. After the overthrow of the monarchy in 1789, the country is a republic for many years before the ascension of Napoleon. France then waged war against the rest of Europe (1796–1815) until Napoleon was finally defeated in the battle of Waterloo. With Napoleon exiled, the monarchy was restored, but eventually overthrown in a violent revolution in 1848.

  1990s: France has enjoyed a relatively stable political and social situation for several decades. The country is considered an important part of the European community and an important trading and political friend to the United States.

tion of great cities, in his poems. Mozart celebrated "natural man" in the person of Papageno, the birdcatcher, in the opera *The Magic Flute* (1783). Johann Wolfgang von Goethe gave the world, in his *Faust*, Parts I and II, the archetypal Man of Will who yearns for the infinite and cannot be satisfied by the narrow confines of logic or propriety. In France, Goethe enjoyed great popularity, as did George Gordon, Lord Byron, another British poet, whose *Don Juan* and *Childe Harold* influenced a young Merimee. The great poet of French romanticism was Victor Hugo, also an advocate of will and imagination.

Realism and Naturalism

By 1830, the fascination with romanticism began to fade. Artists and writers turned from the primitive began studying the psychological and social customs of people in natural settings. They started to show things as they really were, not a romanticized version of it.

"Mateo Falcone" certainly has romantic elements, particularly in its description of settings. Yet it also reflects the blossoming interest in realism, as it describes the action in the story in concise terms. "Mateo Falcone" represents, in this sense, a crucial moment not only in the development of Merimee but in the larger development of nineteenth-century French and European thought.

Critical Overview

Merimee had the good fortune to be appreciated by critics and readers. Many commentators throughout the years have praised the great economy of Merimee's narrative style, his intense evocation of locale through few words, and his ability to create stark and powerful action. These traits appear in "Mateo Falcone" and endear the story to its earliest critics.

Walter Pater, an English critic writing around 1880, called Merimee's fiction "intense, unrelieved, an art of fierce colours." "Mateo Falcone" has, in particular, provoked admiration. Pater, for example, thought it quite possibly "the cruellest story in the world," intending the description as a compliment.

Map of Italy and surrounding countries, including the islands of Corsica and Sardinia.

Critics have cited the classical qualities of ''Mateo Falcone,'' as in A. W. Raitt's 1970 comment that the story ''obeys the unities as strictly as any classical tragedy.'' For Maxwell H. Smith (1972), the story represents Merimee's ''first dazzling success'' and constitutes a ''brief tale condensed into a dozen pages . . . sufficient to confirm the literary reputation'' of its creator.

Smith's reading of the tale exemplifies the typical interpretation, for Smith refers to ''the tragic loneliness of Mateo after the sacrifice of his beloved son,'' a remark which subtly justifies the killing, at least, so to speak, in its context. The typical reading is thus one that discusses the social code depicted in the story, particularly the role of vendetta. One might call this recurrent reading the ''ethnological reading'' in that it takes the position of a non-involved and non-judgmental observer of a particular ethnic ''way of life.'' Merimee's original subtitle, ''Les moeurs de Corse,'' or ''The Ways (or Manners) of Corsica,'' perhaps influences critics to take this stance.

Some critics have examined the detached and alienated narrative voice of the narrator in the story. Raitt and Albert J. George, for example, both com-

ment on the narrator's detachment, a trait noted previously by Hippolyte Taine and Pater in the nineteenth century.

Criticism

Thomas Bertonneau

Bertonneau is a Temporary Assistant Professor of English and the humanities at Central Michigan University, and Senior Policy Analyst at the Mackinac Center for Public Policy. In the following essay, he examines the roles of treachery and vendetta in ''Mateo Falcone'' and contrasts them with rational justice that prevails in civilized urban communities.

Prosper Merimee's short story ''Mateo Falcone'' (1829) culminates in the killing of a ten-year-old boy by his father; the killing—the question needs to be posed whether it is a murder—takes place in a ravine in the rugged hills of Corsica, and its victim bears the ironic name of Fortunato. The father and killer, Mateo Falcone, bears a surname which, in the Italiote dialect of Corsica, means ''falcon,'' a bird

What Do I Read Next?

- Merimee's story "Colomba," like "Mateo Falcone," features a Corsican setting; it can also be found in Merimee's collection *Mosaique*.

- Merimee's story "The Taking of the Redoubt," also in *Mosaique,* is a study of the violence of war, which Merimee considers different from the violence associated with feuds or criminality.

- Jean-Jacques Rousseau's *Essay on the Origin of Inequality among Men* (1754) maintains that civilization is corrupt and full of injustice, whereas primitive culture is "naturally just." Since "Mateo Falcone" can be read as a riposte to Rousseau's popular theory of savage nobility, Part I of the *Essay* makes good comparative reading.

- Jorge Luis Borges's story "The South" concerns the fate of a civilized, sophisticated librarian from Buenos Aires who journeys into the southern provinces of Argentina hoping to explore what seems to him to be the romantic life of gauchos and other colorful characters. What he finds is a world of machismo and brutality. This is an excellent contrast between the civilized and uncivilized, between law and vendetta.

---

of prey; in addition, just before the climax, Merimee endows Falcone with "lynx eyes," yet another indication of his predatory nature. Mateo believes himself justified in the terrible act of killing his own son and does not even glance backward as he turns from the bloody scene to fetch a spade for the burial.

Fortunato's crime, in the eyes of his father, is that he has betrayed Gianetto Sanpiero, a thief and outlaw who has ties to Mateo and the right to seek asylum with him if pursued; he had come to Mateo's house, chased by the militia, only to find Mateo absent and the house under the charge of Fortunato, who hid him for a price and then revealed him to the militiamen for a higher price. "Is this my child?" Mateo asks his wife, Giuseppa, when he learns of the facts. The dissolution of the filial tie comes abruptly and completely: "All I know is that this child is the first member of his family to commit an act of treachery." And under the code of vendetta, which is the prevailing custom in Corsica, treachery summarily incurs a capital sentence. Fortunato must die.

It would seem that this is the prevailing custom. The original subtitle of "Mateo Falcone" "Les moeurs de Corse" ("The Ways of Corsica"), indicates that, cruel as the unwritten law might be, this is how things are done in Corsica, whose people

cannot be judged by imported standards or dogmatic notions of moral rectitude. The lack of commentary by the author bolsters this supposition. Given the prevailing Romanticism of the early nineteenth century, with its celebration of primitive and non-European peoples and its Rousseau-derived assumptions that civilization is inherently corrupt and corrupting, one might guess that "Mateo Falcone" is simply one more vote for the uncomplicated authenticity of cultural taboos and ethnic traditions. But is Merimee really suspending judgment? Are his readers really intended to suspend judgment along with him? Consider not the end but the beginning of the tale.

The first two paragraphs of "Mateo Falcone" present a picture postcard of Corsica. According to Merimee (who would not in fact visit the island until seven years after writing about it), Corsica is civilized along its coast, where the cities lie, and increasingly uncivilized as one penetrates towards the interior:

Coming out of Porto-Vecchio, and turning northwest towards the center of the island, the traveller in Corsica sees the ground rise fairly rapidly, and after three hours' walk along tortuous paths, strewn with large boulders and sometimes cut by ravines, he finds himself on the edge of a very extensive *maquis,*

> **''**That vendetta is a lower order of existence than mercy is suggested by the animal qualities with which Merimee endows Mateo. He is an ignoble savage; compared with mercy, vendetta is sub-human.''

or open heath. This heath is the home of the Corsican shepherds, and the resort of all those who come in conflict with the law. . . .

If you have killed a man, go into the *maquis* of Porto-Vecchio, with a good gun and powder and shot, and you will live there in safety. . . . The shepherds will give you milk, cheese, and chestnuts, and you will have nothing to fear from the hand of the law, nor from the relatives of the dead man, except when you go down into the town to renew your stock of ammunition.

Corsica lies divided into two major regions mediated by a transitional region. There is the ring of cities and towns along the coastline, where people feel ''the hand of the law,'' and there is the thick chaparral of the maquis, home to pastoralists living in a type of prehistoric world and to men of violence flying from the law. Finally, between them there is the no-man's land where, not coincidentally, Mateo Falcone lives.

In an economic sense, Mateo has ties with civilization, since his wealth derives from his flocks, the produce of which is sold in Porto-Vecchio or Corte; sociologically, he belongs to the pre-urban world of the montagnards, a world governed not by law (and by all that implies) but by vendetta, a concept which contains the sub-concepts of honor and treachery. In the world of vendetta, peace is established not through the endorsement of impersonal justice decided rationally in courts by judicial officials but by the threat, and sometimes by the act, of violence. Mateo, for example, ''lived on good terms with everybody in the district of Porto-Vecchio,'' but this is partly because he is known as ''a dangerous enemy.'' Mateo gained his wife, Giuseppa, by eliminating a rival for her affections.

''He was a Corsican and a man of the mountains, and there are few mountain-bred Corsicans who, if they delve into their memories, cannot find some little peccadillo, a gunshot, a knifing, or some such trifling matter.'' The illusory peace of the mountains is thus purchased at the price of those shots or dagger-thrusts, the victims of which serve as reminders that trespass will incur personal vengeance from parties who consider themselves injured.

Once dead, the exemplary victims of this unwritten law are reduced in a rhetoric of memory to ''trifling matters.'' One remembers the victims and what their death portends for anyone who breaks the unwritten law, but one also reduces them by thinking of them as of no importance. The mental gesture is in complicity with the practical and lethal act. In such a world, immediate familial and personal ties, governed by the ideas of honor and treachery, overwhelm any larger or more abstract obligations, including those embodied in the word ''law.'' These same ties can disrupt family from within, as they do in the case of the Falcones, resulting in Fortunato's death. It is in flight from the law that Gianetto Sanpiero stumbles, wounded, into the Falcone property, where young Fortunato has been daydreaming about a forthcoming dinner at his uncle's in Corte. To which world does Fortunato belong? The answer is: to none. Although he is probably destined to inherit the vendetta world of his father, at present Fortunato is simply an immature creature motivated by childish greed. At first he refuses asylum to Gianetto and hides him only when offered a bribe—one piece of silver.

When his ''cousin,'' Tiodoro Gamba, an adjutant of the militia, arrives with a posse, Fortunato reveals Gianetto for the price of a shiny new watch, which Tiodoro promises him. This is the crime, the ''treachery,'' that infuriates Mateo and leads to Fortunato's killing. In geographical terms, the killing is outside the law, for according to custom or not, it takes place beyond the Falcone property, in the hills, towards the no-man's-land of the maquis. Also, when Giuseppa divines Mateo's intentions, she pleads mercy (not given) and then prays before an icon of the Virgin. The killing is not only outside the law, it violates the Judaeo-Christian notion of mercy. It is an impious deed.

At this point, one begins to notice certain tangential but important allusions in Merimee's text. Instantly determined to exercise maximum punishment for the act, Mateo ''struck the ground with the butt of his gun, then shouldered it, and set off again on the path leading to the maquis, calling on Fortunato to follow him. The child obeyed." The image of the father leading his only son into the mountains with the purpose of killing him brings to mind the story of Abraham and Isaac in the Old Testament. Merimee tells us that Giuseppa, to Mateo's fury, had first borne three daughters but at last bore a son, "the hope of the family." Here again, Mateo and Fortunato resemble Abraham and Isaac, for Isaac was the only son of elderly parents and Fortunato is the only son of Mateo. Abraham is willing to sacrifice Isaac at the behest of God. In the Biblical story, however, God stays the sacrifice at the last second by substituting a lamb for Isaac. From then on, human sacrifice is forbidden, and a new moral dispensation appears.

Giuseppa's devotion to the Virgin links her to that new moral dispensation, and her inclination to mercy, contrasted with Mateo's brutality, shows that there is an alternative to the unwritten rule of age-old custom. Indeed, in his description of the maquis, Merimee wrote that it was "thick enough to please God." Merimee was perhaps not a believer in any orthodox sense (it is known that his parents were agnostic), but neither was he a partisan of violence. Although the phrase "to please God" is a figural commonplace, it nevertheless suggests a presence, a concept, which Giuseppa recognizes and Mateo does not. And while not identical with the law, as represented by Tiodoro Gamba and the militia, this principle, like the law, stands in explicit opposition to vendetta.

The principle is mercy, which demands that men acknowledge the humanity of other men so as not to sacrifice them to idols and false causes—for example, the illusory honor of the Corsican "way." "Father, father, don't kill me!" shouts Fortunato, kneeling in prayer. But Mateo merely instructs him to say his prayers; "the child recited the Lord's Prayer and the Creed, stammering and sobbing." (The Lord's Prayer asks God to "forgive us our trespasses as we forgive those who trespass against us"—an injunction which Mateo docs not heed.) Mateo intones an "amen" each time Fortunato concludes, but the act seems empty given the circumstance. Fortunato then says the *Ave Maria*, reminding us that his mother is at that very moment praying to the Virgin. Then someone—Merimee's calculatedly ambiguous syntax makes it uncertain who—says, "May God forgive you!" (English translations that attribute these words to Mateo resolve an ambiguity without warrant to do so.) Mateo fires. Fortunato dies. In the very last line of

the story, Mateo tells his wife to "send word to my son-in-law Tiodoro Bianchi to come and live with us," making the dead Fortunato merely a replaceable commodity—something already reduced to a trifle.

Yet how does one justify this interpretation given the lack of any narrative judgment in Merimee's text? One starts by acknowledging the vast difference between the mentality that permits Mateo to kill his own son over a matter of "honor" and the mentality that regards that act as inexcusable. If readers of Merimee's time and our own instinctively rebel over Mateo's deed and immediately find apologies for Fortunato (his youth, his parents' failure to instill in him a moral sense, the manipulative cleverness of Tiodoro Gamba), this in itself is significant. Readers rebel because they belong to an order conditioned by notions of impersonal law and Judeo-Christian mercy, an order which can only come into being through explicit rejection of an earlier order based on the endless sacrificial violence of the vendetta. That vendetta is a lower order of existence than mercy is suggested by the animal qualities with which Merimee endows Mateo. He is an ignoble savage; compared with mercy, vendetta is sub-human.

If modern readers thus instinctively believe that the killing of Fortunato is a murder and not an act of "justice," as Mateo claims, this is because they have a more refined notion of justice, tempered by mercy, than the implacable montagnard. Not for nothing does Merimee stress the unchanging antiquity of the Corsican interior, which reflects classical concepts of barbarism, as in the depiction of the Cyclopes by Homer in the *Odyssey* . The Cyclopes, like the Corsican montagnards, are an island people without written laws and with no permanent institutions; they live by herding, and their only principle of organization is family solidarity and a code of vengeance. Merimee's observation that the maquis is a region where obliging pastoralists provide one with milk, cheese, and chestnuts needs to be balanced against the acknowledgment of what it costs to sustain that idyllic condition. The cost is that one gives up the protection of the law and submits to violence without mercy. A man is safe only as long as he has weapons and ammunition. Fortunato has none; all he has is a shiny new watch. So Fortunato dies, an Isaac whom God cannot rescue.

Source: Thomas Bertonneau, "Overview of 'Mateo Falcone,'" for *Short Stories for Students*, The Gale Group, 2000.

A. W. Raitt

In the following excerpt, Raitt examines the narrative style of Merimee's "Mateo Falcone," maintaining that the lack of moral judgment by the narrator contributes to the impact of the story.

Which of the tales is most effective is ultimately a matter of personal choice. Certainly none makes a more powerful impact than "Mateo Falcone." The story itself is not new; a good half-dozen versions were already in print. Nor can Merimee be given much credit for the details of local colour, since he had culled them all from various guide-books and historical works about Corsica (after he had himself visited the island in 1839, he corrected some of the more glaring inaccuracies and removed the subtitle of *Moeurs de la Corse* (*Corsiscan Manners*) which in the meantime had become sadly dated). But if Merimee's imagination invents little it excels at the selection and rearrangement of given materials and the vivid immediacy of "Mateo Falcone" is utterly convincing. Hastening through a series of linked crises—the arrival of the hunted bandit, the vain search by the troops, the bribe and its acceptance, the return of Mateo, the shooting of the boy—it maintains an almost unbearable tension. Few lines in French literature deliver a more stunning blow with simple means than the famous sentence relating the boy's death: 'Mateo fired and Fortunato fell stone dead.' The total absence of moral comment or inner psychological analysis concentrates attention exclusively on the action itself, but that is so carefully prepared and so full of emotive force that further explanations could only seem superfluous. The exact adjustment of outward deed or gesture to inward states of mind is always one of the great strengths of Merimee's art. Here the contrast between the awfulness of the killing and the author's rigid refusal to capitalise on it conveys a sense of icy sobriety which fully justifies Walter Pater's description of "Mateo Falcone" as 'perhaps the cruellest story in the world' [*Prosper Merimee*, in *Studies in Modern European Literature*, 1900].

Source: A. W. Raitt, "Story-Teller," in *Prosper Merimee*, London: Eyre & Spottiswoode, 1970, pp. 120–36.

Albert J. George

In the following excerpt, George asserts that the bare narrative style of Merimee's "Mateo Falcone" underscores the theme of family honor.

To be sure, "Mateo Falcone" (1829) came primarily from an article in the *Revue trimestrielle* of July, 1828, which contained the story of a Corsican shot by his relatives for betraying two deserters. Merimee also turned to the abbe Gaudin for details on a land he had not yet visited, but to this basic material he brought the skill that would make him one of France's greatest storytellers.

"Mateo Falcone" is related like an anecdote, in a clean style, stripped to essentials, lacking even the colorful adjectives so dear to the romantics. The plot is handled with a sure sense of the dramatic, all elements united to produce a single effect. Merimee thus produced a narrative that fits perfectly Poe's later definition of the formal short story.

Merimee introduced the reader to the *maquis* with a fine sense of visual appeal, then fell back on the direct approach: "Si vous avez tue un homme . . ." To heighten the exoticism, he gave advice on how to prepare for a stay in these wilds. Then, abruptly, he presented Mateo as though he had known him personally: "Quand j'etais en Corse en 18—. . ." Mateo lived on the edge of the heath, a good friend and an implacable enemy, famed for his marksmanship. He had three daughters, which infuriated him, and a ten-year-old son, ironically named Fortunato, upon whom he doted.

Most of the story happened in Mateo's absence, although he dominates the action. One fall day he left with his wife to inspect the flocks, leaving Fortunato to mind the house. The subsequent plot is articulated almost like a four-act play. Act I introduces an escaping bandit, Gianetto Sanpiero, wounded and hotly pursued by gendarmes, who bought refuge in a haystack from Fortunato for five francs. Act II revolves around Fortunato's betrayal for a silver watch offered by Sergeant Tiodoro Gamba. In a scene forecast by Fortunato's bargaining with Gianetto, the sergeant tempts the child, thrice subjecting him to bribery before the boy turns Judas. Act III brings Mateo back, and when he appears the stage is set for an explosion. Characteristically, he thinks the soldiers have come for him, then finds himself in a dilemma when Gamba reveals Fortunato's treachery. Mateo faces his problem in Act IV. He smashes the watch the sergeant had given Fortunato and marches the child into the glen. Patiently he hears the boy recite his prayers, then shoots him. Without a glance at the corpse, Mateo orders his wife to send for a relative to replace his son.

Using the appeal of the exotic, Merimee constructed the story around a point of honor, a subject dear to the romantics. For the sake of plausibility Merimee interjected himself into the introduction, but once the story began he let the characters shape their own tragedy. Events slip by rapidly, their passing noted in phrases which indicate that Merimee organized his material to keep psychological and reading time as close as possible to plot time. The action does not begin until Mateo has been absent a few hours, then Gianetto appears and is hidden in a matter of moments. "Quelques minutes apres" the police appear, Fortunato succumbs in about the same time, and Mateo arrives as the bandit leaves on a stretcher. For ten minutes he ponders and, after about the same time, Fortunato dies.

The narrative ostensibly revolved around the Corsican code of honor. Fortunato occupied the stage most of the time but only to prepare the dilemma, as important to the plot as the wounded bandit. At this point Merimee's ironical mind came into full play. Mateo was created according to the accepted recipe for the primitive but he failed to conform to the tradition of the "good" savage. Unlike the rational creature so dear to the eighteenth century, he never examined his own code. Family "honor" took precedence over all else and no transgression could be pardoned, even for a child. Mateo took all of ten minutes to decide on the murder of an only son who had informed on the killer of a policeman. Far from being a natural democrat, the good savage was an egotist who dared not challenge the local tabus. . . .

Source: Albert J. George, "Stendhal, Balzac, Merimee," in *Short Fiction in France 1800–1850*, Syracuse University Press, 1964, pp. 65–134.

Sources

George, Albert J. "Introduction" and "Stendahl, Balzac, Merimee," in his *Short Fiction in France: 1800-1850*, New York: Syracuse University Press, 1964, , pp. 1-9, 106-09.

Jotcham, Nicholas. "Introduction" and "Mateo Falcone," in his *The World's Classics: Prosper Merimee: Carmen and Other Stories*, Oxford: Oxford University Press, 1989, pp. vii-xxxiii, 54-66.

Raitt, A. W. *Prosper Merimee*, London: Eyre & Spottiswoode, 1970, pp. 9-10, 120-36.

> **Mateo was created according to the accepted recipe for the primitive but he failed to conform to the tradition of the 'good' savage."**

Smith, Maxwell A. "*Mosaique*," in *Prosper Merimee*, New York: Twayne Publishers, 1972, pp. 98–116.

Further Reading

Bowman, F. P. *Prosper Merimee: Heroism, Pessimism and Irony*, Berkeley and Los Angeles: University of California Press, 1962.
　Considers Merimee's fiction as a running autobiographical account of his life and a continuous commentary on his times.

Garraty, John, and Peter Gay, eds. *The Columbia History of the World*, New York: Harper and Row, 1972.
　Overviews developments in France during the period of Merimee's life.

George, Albert J., "Stendhal, Balzac, Merimee," in *Short Fiction in France 1800-1850*, Syracuse: Syracuse University Press, 1964, pp. 65-134.
　Comments on the verbal economy of Merimee's story and analyzes the themes of honor and betrayal.

Lyon, Sylvia. *The Life and Times of Prosper Merimee*, New York: Dial Press, 1948.
　A detailed biography which establishes the vital context for Merimee's literary activity.

Taine, Hippolyte. *Essais de critique et d'histoire*, Hachette: Paris, 1874.
　A valuable nineteenth-century critical reference on Merimee by a contemporary and acquaintance of the author.

Mrs. Bathurst

Rudyard Kipling

1904

"Mrs. Bathurst" is perhaps Rudyard Kipling' most popular short story. Although his career began as a journalist, it is Kipling's prose sketches and verse that earned him widespread respect as an author at an early age. Henry James considered Kipling the most complete man of genius he had ever known. Authors such as T. S. Eliot and C. S. Lewis acknowledged his influence on their own work.

Kipling's reputation as an author, however, has been under almost constant revision in the twentieth century. Lionel Trilling perceived him as a mere curiosity of the past, a man whose conservative politics eclipsed his literary status. George Orwell was equally dismissive of Kipling. After receiving the Nobel Prize in literature in 1907, critics agree that Kipling's subsequent career suffered in comparison with the achievement of such early novels as *Kim* and the two volumes of *The Jungle Book*.

"Mrs. Bathurst" incorporates central aspects of Kipling's fiction, including his use of dialect, his complex structure of composition, and his fascination with the sea. The critical reception of the story was enthusiastically positive, though critics have been confused by certain elements. Nonetheless, the story has fascinated readers and critics alike for more than ninety years, and has been at the center of the debate concerning Kipling's reputation as an author.

Author Biography

The son of English parents, Rudyard Kipling was born in Bombay, India, on December 30, 1865. He and his sister Alice ("Trix") were sent to England for their schooling at an early age, residing with a foster family at Lorne Lodge, a place later immortalized by Kipling in the *House of Desolation*. Kipling's separation from his parents might account for his later interest in children's stories. He attended the United Services College (boarding school) until 1882. He returned to India in 1882 and began to write stories for two newspapers, the *Civil and Military Gazette* and the *Pioneer*. His initial success inspired him to return to England and launch a literary career.

In London, Kipling met Wolcott Balestier, a literary agent from America, and eventually married Balestier's sister Caroline (who was given away at the wedding by the author Henry James). Her estate in Vermont served as the couple's first home and as the site where Kipling wrote the two *Jungle Books* and the critically acclaimed *Kim* (which was finished in 1901). The couple returned to England in 1896 and settled in Sussex. Kipling visited South Africa several times during the Boer War (1899–1902). It was during these trips that Kipling became acquainted both with South African culture and nautical life, important features of "Mrs. Bathurst," which was published in 1904.

On the basis of his successful career as a novelist and poet, Kipling was awarded the Nobel Prize in 1907, becoming the first Englishman to receive that honor. The advent of World War I as well as the death of his only son, John, (who was reported missing on his first day in action with the Irish Guards and never found) in 1915 adversely affected his writing. The stories "Mary Postgate" and "Sea Constables," among others, reflect these traumatic experiences.

Some critics contend that his literary interests were secondary to his political beliefs, specifically his support of imperialism. When he was buried in Westminster Abbey in 1936, the pallbearers included politicians, but no writers. Nevertheless, Kipling was a prolific writer who produced a great number of short stories, sketches, and poetry in addition to his four novels. By the time of his death, he was already acknowledged as a major influence on the fiction and poetry of such literary masters as Henry James, Thomas Hardy, T. S. Eliot, and W. H. Auden. Kipling's influence also stretches to later

Rudyard Kipling

authors like Albert Camus, Umberto Eco, and Gabriel Garcia Marquez.

Plot Summary

"Mrs. Bathurst" takes place in Glengariff, South Africa, in the years following the Boer War (1899–1902). The main story is told through a conversation between three men and the narrator; the four men discuss the tragic tale of Mrs. Bathurst, a hotel owner in New Zealand, and her lover, Mr. Vickery (also known as "Click"). The preface to the story is an excerpt from a mock-Jacobean tragedy written by Kipling entitled *Lyden's "Irenius"* that narrates a dialogue between a prince and one of his subjects. The themes of the epigraph—disinterested fate and accidental providence—carry over into the story.

The story begins with the narrator running into his friend Mr. Hooper, who is an inspector for the Cape Government Railways. The two men hitch a ride down the tracks on a chalk-car that is being repaired. Mr. Hooper starts to take something out of his pocket to show the narrator, but is interrupted by the shouts of Mr. Pyecroft, an old friend of the narrator's. With Pyecroft is his bulky companion,

Sergeant Pritchard. These two visitors climb into the car and introduce themselves to Mr. Hooper.

The conversation turns to the legendary story of "Boy Niven," who lured seven or eight sailors into the woods of British Columbia from port in Vancouver in 1887, promising to give them land. The group of sailors, which included Pritchard and Pyecroft, was court-marshaled for desertion. Sergeant Pritchard then mentions Spit-Kid Jones, a sailor who was also a member of the group and who later married a so-called "coconut-woman" and eventually deserted the ship *Astrild.*

The topic leads Pritchard to make reference to Mr. Vickery, nicknamed "Click" because of his noisy false teeth. Mr. Hooper asks about Click's infamous tattoos. Wary, Pritchard suspects that Mr. Hooper is an agent for the law and begins to leave, remaining only on account of entreaties from all three of the men. The narrator vouches for Mr. Hooper's honesty, and Pritchard apologizes for his suspicion.

Settled once again, the narrator asks why Vickery deserted the navy. Pyecroft replies, "She kep' a little hotel at Hauraki—near Auckland [New Zealand]," implying that the source of Click's departure was a woman. Pyecroft describes the woman, Mrs. Bathurst, as a widow who kept a hotel and wore black silk. Pritchard interrupts to give a personal account of Mrs. Bathurst's generosity of spirit, telling how she often let the sailors rent rooms on credit and how she once reserved four bottles of beer for him during a visit by cutting off a piece of her own hair ribbon and wrapping it around the necks of the bottles. To sum up her character, Pritchard proclaims, "She—she never scrupled to feed a lame duck or set 'er foot on a scorpion at any time of 'er life," indicating a mixture of charity and courage in her personality.

Pyecroft and Pritchard agree that, of all the hundreds of women they have been "intimate" with in their lives, Mrs. Bathurst is one of the most memorable. Pyecroft explains, "'Tisn't beauty, so to speak, nor good talk necessarily. It's just It. Some women'll stay in a man's memory if they once walk down a street, but most of 'em you can live with a month on end, an' next commission you'd be put to it to certify whether they talked in their sleep or not, as one might say."

The conversation returns to the subject of Mr. Vickery, and Pyecroft relates his most recent encounter with him on the ship *Hierophant,* from which he has just returned. While in port at Cape Town, Pyecroft recalls, Vickery had asked him to go to the cinema at Phyllis's Circus. On the way to the theater, Pyecroft felt strange because of the look on Vickery's face, which reminded him of "those things in bottles in those herbalistic shops at Plymouth. . . [w]hite and crumply things—previous to birth you might say."

At the cinema, Vickery told Pyecroft to pay special attention to the "Home an' Friends" portion of the movie, which showed news footage from Europe.

> Then the Western Mail came in to Paddin'ton on the big magic lantern sheet. First we saw the platform empty an' the porters standin' by. Then the engine come in, head on, an' the women in the front row jumped: she headed so straight. Then the doors opened and the passengers came out and the porters got the luggage—just like life. Only—only when any one came down too far towards us that was watchin', they walked right out o' the picture, so to speak. I was 'ighly interested, I can tell you. So were all of us. I watched an old man with a rug 'oo'd drooped a book an' was tryin' to pick it up, when quite slowly, from be'ind two porters—carryin' a little reticule an' lookin' from side to side—comes out Mrs. Bathurst. There was no mistakin' the walk in a hundred thousand. She come forward—right forward—she looked out straight at us with that blindish look which Pritch alluded to. She walked on and on till she melted out of the picture—like—like a shadow jumpin' over a candle, an' as she went I 'eard Dawson in the tickey seats be'ind sing out: 'Christ! There's Mrs. B!' (Excerpt from "Mrs. Bathurst")

Mesmerized by Bathurst's image, Vickery urged Pyecroft to return to the theater for five consecutive nights to watch the scene again. When Pyecroft pauses in his story, Mr. Hooper asks Pyecroft what he thinks of the whole thing. Pyecroft replies that he hasn't quite finished thinking yet, but one thing he knows is that Vickery was a "dumb lunatic" since he was convinced that Mrs. Bathurst was in England looking for him. But, Vickery remained very reserved about the whole affair, in Pyecroft's memory. Pyecroft feared for his own safety, thinking that Vickery would turn violent when the cinema left town and he no longer had access to the "stimulant" of seeing Mrs. Bathurst on film.

Pyecroft concludes the tale: after an hour-long meeting with the Captain, Vickery was sent on an errand to take over naval ammunition left after the war in Blemfontein Fort. The real reason for Vickery's journey, however, was to see the movie image of Mrs. Bathurst once more, since the cinema moved away from Cape Town to Worcester. Pyecroft escorted Vickery to shore and as they parted for the last time, Vickery said cryptically, "Remember, that I am *not* a murderer, because my lawful wife died in childbed six weeks after I came out." The rest of Vickery's story is "silence," as Pyecroft says, echoing Hamlet's dying words.

Vickery apparently reported to Bloemfontein, oversaw the loading of the ammunition, then disappeared. After the men have thought in silence about Pyecroft's story for a few minutes, Hooper speaks up to tell the group of a curious piece of railway line on the way to Zambesi that runs through a solid teak forest for seventy-two miles without curving. He explains that a month ago he was relieving a sick inspector on that line when he discovered two tramps who had been living in the forest. There had been a thunderstorm and they had been turned into "charcoal" by lightning. The man standing up had false teeth and tattoos on his arms and chest, including one with a crown and an anchor, and the letters "M.V." above.

Pritchard is overcome at the horror of the description. Mr. Hooper brings his hand out of his pockets (perhaps to show his companions the false teeth?), but it is empty. Pyecroft exclaims that, after seeing Vickery's eerie face five nights in a row, he is thankful that the man is dead.

Characters

Mrs. Bathurst

Mrs. Bathurst is one of the central characters in the story. She is the subject of a story told by Mr. Pyecroft and Sergeant Pritchard to Mr. Hooper and the narrator. Her name does not appear until almost midway through the story. She is the manager of a hotel and restaurant in Auckland, New Zealand, where she earned a reputation for beneficence toward sailors like Pritchard and Pyecroft. She is the main subject of fascination, however, for Mr. Vickery ("Click"), who (again, as told through the story of Pritchard and Pyecroft) has an affair with her and deserts his ship when he sees her a fleeting image of her in a movie.

Click

See Mr. Vickery

Mr. Hooper

Mr. Hooper is an inspector for the South African railway who meets the narrator in Simon's. Mr. Hooper fingers an unknown object in his pocket throughout the story; some readers have believed it to be the false teeth of Mr. Vickery, whose charred corpse he discovered along the railway line.

Narrator

Little is known about the narrator except that he is a friend of Mr. Hooper and Mr. Pyecroft. He acts as a peacemaker between Pritchard and Mr. Hooper.

Pritchard

Pritchard is the immature friend of Mr. Pyecroft who interjects small details into the story of Mrs. Bathurst, based on personal contact with her in Auckland. He is suspicious by nature.

Mr. Pyecroft

Mr. Pyecroft tells the story about Mr. Vickery and his relationship with Mrs. Bathurst. He and his companion, Sergeant Pritchard, surprise Mr. Hooper and the narrator in Glengariff Bay. Mr. Pyecroft is a talkative man with much sailing experience who often uses malapropisms in the telling of elaborate tales. He is the last one to have seen Mr. Vickery.

Mr. Vickery

Like Mrs. Bathurst, Mr. Vickery is a character who never appears in person; instead, he is the central character of the story told by Mr. Pyecroft and Sergeant Pritchard. Pyecroft describes Vickery as a "superior man," reticent and a bit creepy. Mr. Vickery has earned the nickname "Click" because of four false teeth that rattle in his mouth. Vickery's infatuation with the movie image of Mrs. Bathurst, and his subsequent search for her, indicates an obsessive single-mindedness in his disposition.

Themes

Art and Experience

"Mrs. Bathurst" explores, among other things, the relationship between experience and its artistic representation through language. The central story of the tale is told second-hand, by Mr. Pyecroft, with help from Sergeant Pritchard. Readers must evaluate the relative positions of all of the narrators in the story in order to understand that each of their

Topics for Further Study

- Research the history of film from its development in France and America to its popularity before World War I. How did movies affect the lives of the general public?

- Identify as many missing details in the story as possible and fill in these gaps, based on evidence from the text, historical context, and what you think may have happened.

- In the late nineteenth century, Britain was a major empire, with colonies all over the world. Research the Boer War (1899-1902), using history textbooks or historical books in your library. In what ways did that war affect the British empire?

- Research either the realism or modernism movements, using encyclopedias available in your school's library. Write down the major features of the movement you select. Which features are evident in "Mrs. Bathurst" ?

Appearances and Reality

Closely related to the theme of art and experience in the story is that of appearance vs. reality. Early on in the story, for instance, a local girl throws a Bass beer over a wall to Sergeant Pritchard because she mistakes him for someone else. Mr. Pyecroft jokes that, "Its the uniform that fetches 'em, an' they fetch it," emphasizing the importance of Pritchard's appearance.

Perhaps the central image that expresses this theme is the cinematic footage of Mrs. Bathurst. The cinema was a relatively new artistic medium at the time when "Mrs. Bathurst" takes place (1904) and the power of the projected movie image was regarded as, in some ways, uncanny and mysterious. Vickery's fascination with the cinema and its ability to reproduce an image of Mrs. Bathurst leads him to go to Phyllis's Circus, where the movie is showing, and then to desert his ship in order to see it an additional time.

The story's conclusion also reinforces the theme of appearances and reality, as Mr. Hooper tells the other three men how he has recently discovered the charred corpses of two tramps, and how one of the corpses had false teeth. This same corpse had tattoos on his arms and chest, which Mr. Pyecroft verifies were on the body of Mr. Vickery. Though this would seem to confirm that the corpse was that of Mr. Vickery, readers are by no means certain that it is.

perspectives on the story is only one of many. Mr. Pyecroft addresses this issue when he says, "I used to think seein' and hearin' was the only regulation aids to ascertainin' facts, but as we get older, we get more accomodatin.'" In other words, he realizes that his narrative, like many, relies on lived experience reconstructed through language, and that there is always room for discrepancy between what actually happened and how events are later remembered.

Moreover, since details of the central plot in "Mrs. Bathurst" are provided by three of the four characters who are actually present in the story—Mr. Hooper, Mr. Pyecroft, and Sergeant Pritchard—the plot becomes the product of a collective effort, one which does not always come together seamlessly to form a coherent whole. The identity of the two corpses found by Mr. Hooper, for instance, is left uncertain and ambiguous, as is the actual outcome of the story of Mr. Vickery's and Mrs. Bathurst's affair.

Love and Passion

Mr. Vickery's and Mrs. Bathurst's affair is the central subject of the narrative. The love and passion that they share is not conventional, however, since Mr. Vickery is already married. Mr. Vickery believes that Mrs. Bathurst has come to search him out in England when he sees her image on a movie screen in Cape Town, South Africa.

Less is known about Mrs. Bathurst's behavior and motivations since most of the story concerns Mr. Pyecroft's knowledge of Mr. Vickery. Some critics view Mr. Vickery's desertion of his ship, and his search for Mrs. Bathurst (or at least her image), as a sign of his undying love for her. Others perceive his actions as evidence of a guilty conscience or tormented soul, perhaps based on his cryptic admonition to Mr. Pyecroft that "I am *not* a murderer, because my lawful wife died in childbed six weeks after I came out." Nevertheless, there is clearly more to the relationship between Mr. Vickery and

Mrs. Bathurst than is revealed by Mr. Pyecroft's narrative.

Fate and Chance

"Mrs. Bathurst" raises many important questions about fate and chance. Accidents and coincidence pervade the story, from the chance encounter of the narrator and Mr. Hooper, to the random image of Mrs. Bathurst that captures the fascination of Mr. Vickery. Other coincidences include the meeting of the narrator and Mr. Hooper by Mr. Pyecroft and Sergeant Pritchard, who happen to be on the same deserted bay in South Africa at the same time, as well as Mr. Hooper's accidental discovery of the charred corpse of Mr. Vickery. These episodes seem random and accidental, but become part of a larger order when combined together. The abundant mistakes and coincidences in the story make the reader question the role of fate in literature and life.

Alienation

It is possible to talk about the theme of alienation in relation to "Mrs. Bathurst" from a number of perspectives. To begin with, the story takes place on a single brake-car that is resting on an isolated beach in South Africa, making the physical setting of the story difficult to locate. Moreover, all four of the men who converse are in some way absent from the place they should be—Mr. Hooper must repair a broken railway car, the narrator has missed his rendezvous with the ship he is supposed to visit, and Mr. Pyecroft and Sergeant Pritchard are either deserters from their ship or waiting for it to be repaired.

Furthermore, Mr. Vickery and Mrs. Bathurst are separated, yet engaged in the futile but passionate pursuit of one another. The cinematic image of Mrs. Bathurst, which Mr. Vickery watches in Cape Town, is an important symbol of this alienation, since the image itself must stand in for Mrs. Bathurst. In broader terms, Kipling's story points to the alienation not only of a society that is recovering from war, but also to that of the modern world in general, where larger urban populations and advances in technology tend to alienate individuals from various social structures.

Style

Setting

"Mrs. Bathurst" is set in an isolated railway car on a beach in Glengariff Bay, South Africa, where the narrator has gone after missing his ship. It is somewhat surprising, then, that Mr. Pyecroft and Sergeant Pritchard stumble onto the brake-car by accident and proceed to tell the story of Mrs. Bathurst and Mr. Vickery to the narrator and Mr. Hooper. It is relevant that the story takes place near the ocean, since it revolves around sailing and sailors. Moreover, the story takes place immediately after the Boer War (1899–1902) and the circumstances of this war provide a constant subtext to the story (such as when Vickery goes to collect ammunition for the Navy). The Boer War was a conflict between the Dutch colonists in South Africa and the countries of the British Commonwealth, including England and Australia.

Structure

The story of "Mrs. Bathurst" is told by a first-person narrator, but mostly contains dialogue between the four principal characters. For this reason, there is little narrative description in the story that is not part of a conversation. Moreover, the conversation that the narrator (and, in turn, the reader) overhears is sometimes in dialect, particularly those portions spoken by Mr. Pyecroft and Sergeant Pritchard. The effect of this is to make their phrases more realistic when read aloud, and also more difficult to understand.

The central structure of the narrative involves a story within the story, since the tale of Mrs. Bathurst and Mr. Vickery is told by two characters other than the narrator. There are two time frames in the story as well—that of the present tense in which the narrator meets up with three other characters in Glengariff Bay, South Africa, and that of the past tense, in which the love affair between Mrs. Bathurst and Mr. Vickery takes place.

Point of View

The reader is told the story via the unnamed narrator. Yet, the central or core story of the relationship between Mr. Vickery and Mrs. Bathurst is revealed through the narration of Mr. Pyecroft and Sergeant Pritchard. Therefore, the reader's point of view about the central narrative is filtered through two other narratives—that of Mr. Pyecroft and that of the narrator himself, who speaks in the first person. The various layers of narration in the story account for its complexity and the story's indeterminate, or fragmentary, style.

Symbolism

There are few traditional symbols in the story, since most of "Mrs. Bathurst" consists of dialogue. Moreover, the symbols that might be interpreted in the story seem to be not fully formed. The object in Mr. Hooper's pocket, for instance, which might be the set of false teeth that he has taken from the burnt corpse of Mr. Vickery, never appear. The image of Mrs. Bathurst on the movie screen is another image that is not fully materialized, since a movie image stands in for the real person, and because Mrs. Bathurst is possibly already dead at the time Mr. Vickery and Mr. Pyecroft observe her image at the cinema in Cape Town.

Historical Context

Science and Technology

The end of the nineteenth century brought many developments in science and technology that had a direct impact on the everyday lives of millions of people in Europe and America. The telegraph, photograph, and cinema were all products of the time. These inventions and others changed in fundamental ways how people communicated with each another, especially in urban centers. The rise of photography and cinema, in particular, produced new art forms that were capable of communicating the themes usually addressed by literature in less time and to a wider audience than ever before.

Novelists and painters reacted in varying ways to the development of these new media. Kipling's "Mrs. Bathurst" includes a scene in which the image of Mrs. Bathurst is projected onto a movie screen in Cape Town. The effect of this image on Mr. Vickery is one of the central episodes of the story, since it leads him to desert his ship in pursuit of the object of his desire. The effect of Kipling's story can be related to the movie itself, since both are primarily composed of dialogue and because the reader of Kipling, like a cinema viewer, is thrust into the midst of the scene, without abundant narrative background, and must make sense of the story largely by overhearing the dialogue of others. The story itself is constructed with the same unconnectedness, among its parts, as a newsreel.

Colonialism

Though you would be hard pressed to find concrete evidence of the colonization of South Africa in Kipling's South Africa, it is nevertheless a constant subtext of the story. The Dutch first settled the land that later became known as South Africa, but their claims were challenged by (among others) the British Commonwealth, giving rise in part to the Boer War. The British Navy was the preeminent maritime power in the nineteenth century. The mass colonization of Africa and other colonies could not have been achieved without it. When Mr. Hooper suspects the Malay boys of making noise around the railway car, the reader gets a glimpse of the natives of the colony, but one of very few. In general, one might argue that Kipling has successfully suppressed the colonial context of his story. Widely regarded as a supporter of British imperialism, Kipling's deliberate omission of colonial issues in "Mrs. Bathurst" must be balanced with such works as *Kim*, where these issues are brought more clearly into focus.

Modernism

Rudyard Kipling's fiction has been associated with the modernist movement in literature. Though there is no single modernist creed that unites all of the authors associated with the movement, many of the writers were reacting both to social and literary changes, in particular the urbanization and social decay of the time. Modernism was considered a radical break with the past, especially with what authors like T. S. Eliot and Ezra Pound saw as a late nineteenth-century poetic style that needed new blood.

Critical Overview

By 1889, Rudyard Kipling was considered as one of the leading writers of his day. The publication of "Mrs. Bathurst" (1904) was an important event in his career. Favorable critical response to the story reinforced his reputation as a writer of the highest order, a designation that was acknowledged by the European intellectual community with the Nobel Prize in 1907. Numerous critics deem "Mrs. Bathurst" as one of the finest examples of Kipling's work as a short-story writer. For example, Walter Allen selected the story as an example of the very best literature, and placed Kipling near the top of the pantheon of short-story writers in English. T. S. Eliot praised Kipling's "pagan vision" in the introduction to a volume of Kipling's poetry, entitled the *Choice of Kipling's Verse*.

Compare
&
Contrast

- **1904:** South Africa, initially colonized by the Dutch, is ruled by the British Commonwealth. The British Navy is the preeminent maritime power, and the mass colonization of Africa and other colonies could not have been achieved without it. Native peoples are persecuted and discriminated against, and kept in poverty while colonizers exploited the land's natural resources.

  Late 1990s: South Africa is now a republic, free from the colonial influence of England. Apartheid, the legal discrimination against the African people, is now illegal and native groups are achieving opportunity and equal rights under the law.

- **1904:** Realism is a popular literary style, reflecting changing American and European concerns in the twentieth century. Short stories gain widespread popularity as a literary genre.

  1990s: Short stories remain popular, and American and European literature are rich with fine

examples of the short fiction genre. With the advent of the twenty-first century, realism also remains a viable literary style.

- **1904:** Technological innovations change the way people communicate and live. The telegraph, photograph, and cinema were all products of the time. Photography, radio, and cinema provide a new way for politicians and artists to convey themes and images and offer a myriad of entertainment possibilities for citizens.

  1990s: Technology continues to advance, providing faster and more efficient ways to communicate and relay information. The Internet offers access to information and images to anyone with a modem and other necessary equipment. The VCR allows an individual to play movies in the privacy of his or her home; the video camera is a way for individuals to record their own movies. Science continues to refine and improve the way people communicate.

Not all of the reaction was favorable, however. Angus Wilson and Kingsley Amis regarded "Mrs. Bathurst" as pretentious. In more recent years, Norman Page has noted the story's "obscure power" over the reader.

"Mrs. Bathurst" was first published with ten other short stories in a collection entitled *Traffics and Discoveries*. It shares with many of the stories in the compilation (e.g. "Wireless") a reliance on personal experience. Kipling made many visits to South Africa during the Boer War, and drew from this experience when he wrote his stories.

"Mrs. Bathurst" features extensive use of dialect as well as a framing device and a series of narrators; these elements became trademarks of his short fiction. Kipling was known as an artist who used the utmost economy in his writing and some critics have observed that "Mrs. Bathurst" is almost a parody of concision. So much is left out of

the story that what remains has to possess an enormous amount of narrative weight in order for the tale to succeed. It is a little ironic that Kipling earned his reputation as a novelist for concealing as much as possible from his readers.

Criticism

Andrew Mercy

Mercy is a freelance writer and a doctoral candidate at the University of California–Berkeley. In the following essay, he suggests that the key to understanding Kipling's "Mrs. Bathurst" lies in its structure.

If you have come away from "Mrs. Bathurst" more than a little confused and frustrated by its complexity, then rest assured that you are neither the first nor

Aerial view of a forest in South Africa, perhaps the setting for part of the action of "Mrs. Bathurst."

the last to do so. Since its growing popularity as one of Kipling's most complex stories, "Mrs. Bathurst" has received a barrage of critical response, most of which takes for granted that the story is at once "obscure and puzzling," filled with "misinformation," "uncrackable," and, as though Kipling were pleased by his audience's frustrations, "teasingly ambiguous."

In fact, even those most familiar with Kipling's art have chosen to summarize "Mrs. Bathurst" before venturing to interpret its meaning, as though describing "what happens" is, in itself, an interpretive feat. Those who have refused to search out some meaning in the story have done so on the grounds that it is cryptic to the point of incomprehensibility, or even downright pretentious. For one scholar, the problem of the story's meaning "will remain unanswered" because it "probably never had much meaning."

One possible explanation for the difficulty we find in "Mrs. Bathurst" may have to do with Kipling's own preoccupation with questions of literary *construction*. In the autobiography printed after his death, Kipling writes of his fiction: "I made my own experiments in the weights, colours, perfumes and attributes of words in relation to other words, either as read aloud so that they may hold the ear, or scattered over the page, drew the eye" (*Something of Myself*).

With Kipling, we have the image of one who combines words the way a chemist combines chemicals, seeking some new reaction that might change the manner in which we experience the world through language. Elsewhere, in a letter to a young reader, Kipling offers this interesting advice: "read and reread [books] until you pass from mere reading to criticism and begin to see how they are put together and what means the author uses to produce certain effects." It behooves the reader to return to the story time and time again—not despite its complexities, but *because* of them.

Seeing how the story is "put together" is, perhaps, most central to understanding "Mrs. Bathurst." For it is precisely the story's construction, its manner of unfolding, that so often baffles readers. Take, for instance the insertion of what appears to be a series of *non sequiturs* into the story, ranging from the short tale of Boy Niven's circuitous misguidance, to the anecdote of how Pritchard receives a beer from a woman who apparently has *mistaken* him for someone else.

We might also note that the story begins with a mistake, as the narrator tells us: "The day I chose to visit HMS *Peridot* in Simon's Bay was the day that the Admiral had chosen to send her up the coast. She was just steaming out to sea as my train came in. . . ." From the very start, the story is fraught with mistimings, misrecognitions, disruptions, and unexpected detail; it is constructed like a building with hidden hallways and unfinished staircases. Precisely because Kipling fills lines with so much detail, with vivid "weights, colours, perfumes and attributes," we find ourselves confused, feeling more ignorant than informed. But only by acknowledging this as part of the story's strategy—this feeling of disorientation that we immediately get—can we really understand Kipling's narrative method and the "means the author uses to produce certain effects."

It should come as no surprise that the "production of effect" means a great deal to Kipling, especially if we consider the dominant subplot in "Mrs. Bathurst," namely the story of the cinema's effect on Mr. Vickery, leading to his eventual insanity and death. We may take for granted, as postmodern viewers accustomed to sophisticated visual technologies, the experience of watching film. However, we cannot pass too quickly over the importance of Vickery's experience watching Mrs. Bathurst on the movie screen. Indeed, his experience calls to our attention the difficulty of encountering new forms of representation, new visual and aural productions, such as the cinema, at the turn of the twentieth century. "I'd never seen it before," says Pyecroft about the new technology, "but the pictures were the real thing—alive an' movin'." Hooper, who is listening to this description and who seems to understand the difference between an image on the screen and one that is actually "alive and movin'," offers a correction: "I've seen 'em . . . Of course they are taken from the very thing itself—you see."

As a result of film's verisimilitude, it is easy for viewers, particularly those who have never confronted such technology, to confuse the "thing itself" with the representation of the picture on the screen; and this seems to be Vickery's and Pyecroft's confusion. "Why, it's the woman herself," says Pyecroft to Vickery, when he sees Mrs. Bathurst exit the train.

Of course, it's not the woman herself at all. To think that, is to mistake representation for reality,

What Do I Read Next?

- Rudyard Kipling's novel, *Kim* (1901), chronicles the story of a young Irish boy growing up in India during the waning years of British imperialism.

- Joseph Conrad's *Heart of Darkness* (1899) is the story of one man's journey to the interior of Africa in pursuit of a tyrannical madman named Kurtz. The story "Mrs. Bathurst" has been compared to this novel.

and potentially to go mad in the process, much as Vickery does. He cannot sort through the spatial tricks that appear on the "big magic lantern sheet" of the cinema; for example, that the representation of Mrs. Bathurst appears on a screen in Cape Town despite the fact that she is getting off a train in London's Paddington station. This confuses Vickery enough to make him look into bars every three minutes, expecting to see her. To the two men, when the image of Mrs. Bathurst passes the camera it appears as though she "melt[s] out of the picture" and phantasmically disappears, "like a shadow jumpin' over a candle." There is something haunting about the image on the screen. Nor can Vickery understand the temporal tricks played by film. Some critics have suggested that, at the time when Vickery and Pyecroft are watching Mrs. Bathurst on the screen, she is dead. Such an argument helps to explain why Vickery is so disturbed by her repeated "arrival" in London. "She's lookin' for me," he says, "stopping dead under a lamp."

At this point, we might suggest that the experience of reading "Mrs. Bathurst" is confusing to us in similar ways, and that our inability to piece together all of the details is a kind of interpretative madness. As readers, we are given no explanation of the narrator's business with the ship at the beginning of the story; we only know that, like Vickery, he wants to be where he is not. We never even learn the narrator's name or history. Likewise, Mr. Pyecroft and Sergeant Pritchard appear in the story as if out

> In one sense, Kipling anticipates modernist writers who defamiliarize their narrative styles--make them obscure and cryptic--in order to emphasize the distance between narrative and reality."

of nowhere, phantasmically to the narrator who has drifted off into a beer-induced sleep. Moreover, the abundance of unfinished sentences and, as I have already mentioned, *non sequiturs* make the story tough to visualize. In regard to many of the story's episodes, we as readers might say with Mr. Hooper, "I don't see . . . somehow." The information on the page does not conform easily to a mental picture in our imaginations.

Finally, we might ask why Kipling would construct a story that mimics, by its temporal and spatial shifts and its confusing narrative, the effects of the cinema. What is there for Kipling to gain by making his readers into disorientated viewers, who resemble Vickery in this regard and who must return again and again to the story, obsessed to find answers to many questions? In one sense, Kipling anticipates modernist writers who defamiliarize their narrative styles—make them obscure and cryptic—in order to emphasize the distance between narrative and reality.

One problem that faced many modernists was the public's willingness to collapse the boundaries separating artistic representation from reality. The film, the most "realistic" of new modes of representation, amplified this problem by glorifying its ability to mimic reality and to make representations appear, as Pyecroft says, "alive an' movin'." Some critics have even suggested that "Mrs. Bathurst" exemplifies literary realism, that the dialogue and the anecdotes in the story are strange precisely because they so closely resemble reality. Certainly, when four men sit in a circle and reminisce over beer, the conversation often takes strange, incomprehensible turns.

But this should not rule out the opposite assessment, namely that Kipling is reacting against literary realism by showing the dangers of assuming that representations *are* reality. "Mrs. Bathurst" moves away from clearly visible reality. We never know what happens to Vickery, because Hooper never pulls from his pocket the missing clue, which we assume he has. And we never see the title character of the story with clear eyes. What does she really look like? Where has she gone? In the end, it is left for our imaginations, not for our eyes to discern. "Yes," we remember Pyecroft saying, "I used to think seein' and hearin' was the only regulation aids to ascertainin' facts, but as we get older we get more accommodatin'."

Source: Andrew Mercy, "The Effect of 'Mrs. Bathurst' on the Reader," for *Short Stories for Students*, The Gale Group, 2000.

David Lodge

In the following excerpt, Lodge discusses the themes of love, death, and guilt in Kipling's "Mrs. Bathurst."

That is what Mrs Bathurst does when she appears on the screen: 'She walked on and on till she melted out of the picture.' And it is, metaphorically speaking, what Vickery does: he steps out of the frame of Pyecroft's perception at Simonstown station.

In this remarkable passage Kipling manages vividly to convey the disconcerting effect of the cinematic image—at once lifelike and insubstantial—when it was still a novelty, and to turn this experience into a poignant symbol of both the pain of disappointed desire and the mystery of human motivation. To Vickery, watching the newsreel, Mrs Bathurst is both present and absent, near and far. He can see her, but she, peering out of the screen with her 'blindish look,' cannot see him. From her expression, Pyecroft infers that she is looking for someone, and Vickery affirms that she is looking for him. This motif of interpreting someone's intentions from their countenance is repeated when Pyecroft and the cox, Lamson, scrutinise the captain's expressions after the latter's interview with Vickery. 'Mrs Bathurst' is, indeed, in one sense a story about the difficulty of interpretation, and Pyecroft challenges us as well as the other characters in the brake-van when he concludes his account of Vickery's strange behaviour with the question, 'How do you read it off?'.

How *do* we read it off? There is no difficulty in saying what 'Mrs Bathurst,' in a general sense, is about: it is about the tragic and destructive consequences that may ensue when a man becomes infatuated with a woman who, though morally blameless, is so powerfully attractive to the man that he will abandon all scruples, honour and material security on her account. Like other tales of Kipling, this one suggests that very ordinary humble people may enact tragedy. That Vickery's last recorded words are Hamlet's, 'The rest is silence,' makes this point. So does Vickery's remark to Pyecroft, 'What' ave *you* to complain of?—you've only 'ad to watch. I'm*it*,' irresistibly recalling Faustus's words, 'Why this is hell, nor am I out of it.' So does the densely obscure epigraph to the story—a fragment of an old play, in actuality written by Kipling himself, describing the death of a groom or clown which, it is said, would have excited more attention if it had been suffered by a prince.

'Mrs Bathurst' is a tragedy of love and death, but its details are obscure and ambiguous. It seems safe to infer that Mrs. Bathurst and Vickery were lovers, that he deceived her about the fact that he was married, that she came to England with the intention of meeting him. What we cannot ascertain is whether Vickery discovered that she came to England only when he saw the newsreel, or whether, after the moment recorded on the newsreel, they actually did meet in England. If the latter is the case, she would, presumably, have discovered that he was married, and, given her character, have broken off their relationship—perhaps, it has even been suggested, have died as a result of the shock, so that her apparition on the screen affects Vickery as a kind of ghost, 'looking for him' in an accusing, haunting fashion. If the former is the case, then Vickery is presuming that she will have found out that he was married, either before or after his wife died in childbirth. (Could the shock of the revelation have brought on the wife's death?)

The indeterminacy of the story is partly due to the indeterminacy of its chronology. It would seem that Vickery and Pyecroft saw the newsreel in December 1902, since we are told that it was just before Christmas, and shortly afterwards Vickery is sent to recover some ammunition 'left after the war in Bloemfontein Fort.' The Boer War ended in May 1902. The newsreel, however, seems to have been filmed while the war was still going on, since it includes a shot of a troopship 'goin' to the war.' We don't know when Vickery left England—whether it was before or after Mrs Bathurst discovered he was

" 'Mrs Bathurst' is a tragedy of love and death, but its details are obscure and ambiguous."

married. Perhaps his ship was steaming out to sea as her train was coming into Paddington station. But when he sees her on the screen, he must know, or have inferred, that there is no possibility of their union, either because she is dead or because of an irreparable breach between them. Otherwise, why should he desert, within a few months of his pensioned retirement, when he is free to marry her because of the death of his wife? Evidently Vickery is harrowed by guilt in relation to Mrs Bathurst, and feels he is on the verge of going mad and murdering someone, and persuades his captain to connive at his desertion by sending him up country, alone. He may, of course, be quite mistaken about Mrs Bathurst's reaction. The epigraph hints at this: 'She that damned him to death knew not that she did it, or would have died ere she had done it. For she loved him.'

It has been suggested by some readers that Vickery and Mrs Bathurst were united—that the mysterious figure found dead beside Vickery by Hooper is Mrs Bathurst. It is true that Pritchard seems to leap to this conclusion, covering 'his face with his hands for a moment, like a child shutting out an ugliness. ''And to think of her at Hauraki!'' he murmured,' and Hooper's description of the second figure as Vickery's 'mate' is nicely ambiguous as to sex. But this must be one last false clue put in by the implied author to tease the reader. There is no logical reason why Vickery and Mrs Bathurst should have met in this way and lived like tramps. It is in character for Vickery to have picked up some companion in his wanderings, as he picked up Pyecroft in Cape Town; and I am inclined to agree with Elliott L. Gilbert that this second corpse is introduced to indicate by its crouching posture that Vickery invited the fatal lightning stroke by standing upright beside the rail in the storm [Elliot L. Gilbert, *The Good Kipling: Studies in the Short Story*, 1972]. Thus his death is a kind of *liebestod*, comparable to Hamlet's leap in Ophelia's grave and subsequent expiatory death. The rest is silence.

I suggested earlier that there is in 'Mrs Bathurst,' as well as a discourse about the story, a story of the discourse—a suspense story in which the most obvious narrative question raised is, *What will Hooper produce from his waistcoat pocket*? In the classic detective story we should expect the answer to this question to coincide with the mystery in the core story. In 'Mrs Bathurst' this coincidence both does and does not occur. We have every reason to believe that Hooper has in his pocket the false teeth which constitute incontrovertible evidence that the corpse in the teak forest was in fact Vickery's, and it is entirely natural that he should refrain from producing the gruesome relic out of respect for the feelings of Vickery's friends. There is no logical ground to doubt this testimony—Pyecroft has already confirmed the complementary evidence of the tattoo. Yet on the symbolic level the long-delayed gesture of Hooper's bringing his hand away from his waistcoat pocket—*empty*, can only have the effect of generating doubt and uncertainty in the reader's mind, and emphasising the indeterminacy of the text.

Source: David Lodge, "'Mrs. Bathurst': Indeterminacy in Motion," in *Kipling Considered*, edited by Phillip Mallett, The Macmillan Press, Ltd., 1989, pp. 71–84.

Elliot L. Gilbert

In the following excerpt, Gilbert examines stylistic aspects of Kipling's "Mrs. Bathurst," asserting that the story's unorthodox narrative structure underscores the themes of chance and accident.

It would be useful for us, at this point, to consider what it is that happens in "Mrs. Bathurst." A warrant officer named Vickery, within eighteen months of his pension, has deserted his duty under peculiar circumstances in the back country of South Africa. Four men gather by chance in a railroad car and after some rambling discussion undertake to piece together Vickery's story from the fragments that each of them has. It seems that Vickery was a devoted family man until the day he met and fell in love with the fascinating Mrs. Bathurst, a widow who ran a small hotel for sailors in New Zealand. Many sailors, among them married ones, have casual affairs with women—Pyecroft and Pritchard have had more than they can remember—but Vickery, described somewhat ironically as a superior man, has apparently fallen deeply under Mrs. Bathurst's irresistible spell. And if the epigraph is to be taken as shedding any light on the story, the phrase "for she loved him" suggests that Mrs. Bathurst was equally serious. At any rate, Pyecroft says, "There

must 'ave been a good deal between 'em, to my way o' thinkin'." The epigraph also suggests, in astrological terms, the passionate nature of the relationship, speaking as it does of "Venus, when Vulcan caught her with Mars in the house of stinking Capricorn." (Vulcan is, of course, the classical artificer of lightning bolts.)

What the exact nature of that "good deal between 'em" was we are never certain, and there are those who feel that Kipling was wrong to apply his technique of calculated obscurity, which we shall see was quite valid elsewhere, to the story's central relationship. Information about Vickery and Mrs. Bathurst, the argument runs, is no substitute for a picture of the two of them together, for a confrontation that might have drawn the reader more personally into the story, engaged his sympathy, illuminated Vickery's fate and made it more poignant. It is difficult to defend Kipling and his reticence on this point, but mistaken or not he chose to keep the germinal experience of his story on the very edges of the narrative and to make us struggle to discover even the few facts he thought it necessary for us to have: that Vickery met Mrs. Bathurst, that his life became deeply entangled with hers so that to put his affairs in order would have taken more courage and strength than he had in the world, and that in the end he deserted her.

From that time, apparently, from that failure, dates the beginning of the madness which Pyecroft says must have been going on for years and which characterizes Vickery's last months. But the madness does not reach a crisis until Vickery attends a moving picture show one night in Cape Town and sees Mrs. Bathurst walking out of the screen toward him. We can imagine how he must have felt at the sight. The pictures, we are told, were extremely lifelike—"just like life"—and so realistic that when an engine headed straight at the audience, the ladies in the first row of the theatre jumped. To Vickery, burdened with his guilt, that enormous figure of Mrs. Bathurst bearing "blindishly" down on him must have been terrifying. Perhaps it made him think of a grim and now far-off domestic scene, the long-feared confrontation of husband, wife and lover to which that detraining had led. Perhaps, on the other hand, there had been no confrontation at all. Kipling does not offer enough information for us to be certain about what happened in London, and we can only conclude that he did not think it important for his readers to know the details; the merest suggestion of disaster was enough. The details he did want his readers to have however, he made extraordinarily graphic: the looming figures on the cinema screen, Vickery's guilty terror, and the chance fact that Mrs. Bathurst, hurrying one day from a railroad car, blundered blindly and unwittingly into range of a camera and thus was made the accidental tool of fortune, damning Vickery to death from thousands of miles away and never knowing she had done it. Hence the irony in Pritchard's repeated, almost panicky requests for assurance, ''Say what you please, Pye, but you don't make me believe it was any of 'er fault.''

The effect of the motion picture—ironically titled ''Home and Friends''—on Vickery is overwhelming and complex. On the one hand it awakens again all of his passionate infatuation for Mrs. Bathurst, drawing him back to the show night after night and leaving him, at the end of each performance, counting the minutes till the next. On the other hand it intensifies his sense of guilt and of inadequacy and contributes further to the disorder that will in the end destroy him. This effect manifests itself physically in Vickery's mad wanderings over Cape Town and in his suicidal urge, once the movie has completed its run and is about to move on, to abandon his duty and follow the film up-country.

What he says to the captain to win release from duty we are not told. All we know is that the two men speak for an hour, that Vickery comes away from the meeting in good spirits, and that the captain emerges a moment later shipping his court martial face, a face he had last worn on the day some of his men had dumped the ship's gunsights overboard. It is significant that gunsights, like the gyroscope mentioned earlier in the story as having been deliberately damaged, are instruments designed to keep men on target and on course, and as such are absolutely indispensable aboard a war ship. The captain thus reacts to indications of instability in one of his officers as he had done once before to the deliberate destruction of essential guidance equipment. It also is significant that in the description of the ship during Vickery's interview with the captain, there appear in the space of seven lines the words ''execution of 'is duty,'' ''my lawful occasions,'' ''as a general rule,'' and ''my duties,'' all emphasizing that ordered aspect of navy life which Vickery's madness is forcing him to flee. In the end, he is ordered off by himself on special assignment to Bloemfontein, an assignment from which he will never return.

Just before he leaves he encounters Pyecroft for the last time and tries to unburden himself a little of

> **The whole narrative may, in fact, be considered an extended example of aposiopesis.''**

his guilt. ''I've one thing to say before shakin' 'ands,'' Pyecroft recalls his words. ''Remember that I am *not* a murderer, because my lawful wife died in childbed six weeks after I came out. That much at least I am clear of.'' This is a cryptic speech but it comes a little more into focus when we realize that Kipling restored the word ''childbed'' to the passage when he was preparing the magazine version of the story for book publication [C.A. Bodelsen, *Aspects of Kipling's Art*, 1964]. Vickery clearly feels responsible for his wife's death—elsewhere he speaks of himself as capable of murder—and physically, of course, he *is* responsible. His real guilt, however, has to do with his sense of having killed her by betraying her with Mrs. Bathurst. Furthermore, there is the sense of having, in his weakness, betrayed Mrs. Bathurst with his wife. This compound treachery leads to such self-loathing that, like the groom in the epigraph, Vickery ''must e'en die now to live with myself one day longer.'' Certainly he desires nothing more, in his weariness with the burden of his own thoughts, than ''to throw life from him . . . for a little sleep.''

It is in this desperate state of mind that Vickery, having fulfilled his commission at Bloemfontein, drops from sight, embarking on an aimless life as just another one of the many wandering tramps who people the back country. For Vickery is not unique in his inability to confront the world. ''Takes 'em at all ages,'' says Pyecroft of another man who'd left his duty, and ''We get heaps of tramps up there since the war,'' Hooper explains, suggesting that men trained in destruction or shaped by it must use their talents somehow, if only on themselves. Death is what Vickery is seeking, then, as he drifts from place to place, and he is not long in finding it. One day he and another tramp take refuge beside a railroad track during an electrical storm and there, beneath the teak trees, the two are struck by lightning and are burned to charcoal. It is easily established that one of the two is Vickery, for Hooper happens coincidentally to be there, in his capacity as railroad inspector, to see the tattooed initials M. V. etched in white on the blackened corpse and to take from the crumbling jaws an undamaged dental plate identifiable as Vickery's. In fact, he has the plate in his waistcoat pocket but delicately refrains from showing it out of consideration for Pritchard's obvious distress. Vickery's death is bizarre, certainly, although it is based on a real incident with which Kipling was familiar. But what is really most striking about it is its appropriateness. The man who had been unable to cope with life's disorder achieves, at a stroke, by the accident of lightning, the final disorder of death. When Hooper tries to move the scorched body from its position beside the track it literally crumbles to dust. . . .

In "Mrs. Bathurst," Kipling is dealing with what Beckett calls "the mess," and while we have a right to expect that he will give some kind of shape to his particular vision of life, we are wrong to require that shape to appear necessarily on the narrative level of the story. It is precisely on this level that we should expect, instead, to find all the craziness of life, all its meaninglessness. And a meaningless death may, after all, be thematically significant. Nor is it begging the question to say that "Mrs. Bathurst" has a form imposed upon it by its theme, the persistence of accident, the multiplications of what an existentialist might call the absurd. It is, in fact, just this reiteration of absurdity that is meant to satisfy our craving for form.

Vickery's story ends spectacularly, then, in the back country of South Africa, but some of the questions raised by that story still remain unanswered. Indeed we have still to consider what, for some reason, has always been the most controversial of all the "Mrs. Bathurst" problems, the identity of the second tramp. It was in *The Colophon* that J. Delancey Ferguson, in February, 1932, published an article which took for granted the fact that the tramp found beside Vickery in the teak forest was Mrs. Bathurst herself. Since that time this theory has gained great currency among readers who feel that the story would not be as good if Mrs. Bathurst were not the tramp, who feel that for a satisfying plot it is required that the two central figures be brought together at the close. Kipling was, however, constructing anything but a neat plot here; his central point was, of course, the untidiness of the universe. Mrs. Bathurst is not the conventional heroine of romantic fiction, hurrying to the side of her destitute lover and casting in her lot with his. In the light of the rest of the story this conception is difficult to accept. She is, rather, the unwitting agent of blind chance who dooms Vickery to death without even knowing she has done it. She is far away when the man dies and she knows nothing of what has happened to him, for the fates do not know or care what they have done and they do not die with their victims. It is in just these facts that the great sadness of the story lies, in just this failure of communication.

Pritchard's last speech accents the blind impersonality of Mrs. Bathurst's power.

> Pritchard covered his face with his hands for a moment, like a child shutting out an ugliness. 'And to think of her at Hauraki!' he murmured—with 'er 'air-ribbon on my beer. "Ada," she said to her niece . . . Oh, my Gawd!' . . .

It has been suggested that this outburst could only be Pritchard's horrified reaction to the news that Mrs. Bathurst had been burnt to charcoal in the teak forest. But the speech has a different and perhaps greater significance. Throughout the narrative, Pritchard is presented to us as having himself fallen under Mrs. Bathurst's spell. He lovingly recounts his experience in the hotel bar at Hauraki and at each suggestion that Mrs. Bathurst may have been even remotely responsible for what happened to Vickery, Pritchard protests vehemently—protests almost too much—that the lady could not have had anything to do with it. He seems to have a great stake in her innocence, and all through the story he rejects the truth which is dawning slowly on the others. But the horrible image of Vickery, totally consumed by his passion, finally breaks through his defenses and lets the truth pour in all at once. And the realization overwhelms him—he is, as we have seen, naturally emotional anyway—that Mrs. Bathurst, for all her innocence, has been profoundly involved in Vickery's fate. In his horror, Pritchard recalls what, up to that moment, had always been one of his pleasantest memories, the harmless flirtation in the Hauraki hotel. And understanding now the true nature of that blind, corrosive, impersonal attraction he had felt and himself almost succumbed to, he "covers his face with his hands for a moment, like a child shutting out an ugliness." Outside the office car, waiting for their train, the picnickers sing of romance in conventional, sentimental terms, offering an ironic contrast to Pritchard's belated revelation about the true nature of woman's love.

> On a summer afternoon, when the honeysuck-
> le blooms,
> And all Nature seems at rest,
> Underneath the bower, 'mid the perfume of
> the flower,
> Sat a maiden with the one she loves the best.

It makes a properly bitter conclusion to a story which might equally well have ended with Kurtz's despairing words, "The horror, the horror!"

What happens in "Mrs. Bathurst" is, in the last analysis, a function of the work's structure. All his life Kipling experimented with techniques for drawing readers into the heart of a story, for forcing them, if possible, to participate in the creative process itself. In "Mrs. Bathurst," among other stories, he succeeded in a way which was to damage his popularity and earn him a reputation for trickiness. But it was in just such stories as this that he was most brilliantly the innovator, most startlingly the stylist ahead of his time. Of "Mrs. Bathurst" it can accurately be said that the structure is inextricably bound up with the content. "Mrs. Bathurst" is a story about a group of storytellers who are trying to put together a story and discover its meaning. The story they are constructing is also the one the reader must construct, so that the two activities go on simultaneously. The group of four men gathered in the railroad car to spin yarns is, like the cinema and the episode of Boy Niven, a metaphor for Kipling's vision of life: the irrationality of the universe and man's need to find some order in it. When the four come together, each of them, unknown to the others, has certain disordered fragments of a story, quite meaningless in themselves. (It would be more accurate to say that three of the members of the group have these fragments. The fourth member, the writer, will one day record the incidents.) They begin to chat idly, in a random way, and slowly, as they talk, a story begins to emerge a little haltingly from the anecdotes and the broken images that each contributes to the general store of information.

Even when all the fragments have been assembled it is plain that significant information is missing. But it is also plain that with just the pieces available to them they have made an important discovery which leaves them silent and disturbed. They have, in fact, discovered the theme of their own story, and though that discovery is never discussed in so many words, the same fragments of information which led the four narrators to their understanding are available to guide the reader to the same conclusions. Indeed, it is because what the storytellers do is so much the model for what Kipling would have his readers do that such emphasis is placed on the "picture-frame" elements in "Mrs. Bathurst." The process of telling the story is as important to an understanding of the whole as the incidents of the story themselves.

In order to tell his story in the way he wanted to, Kipling had to abandon certain of the conventions of prose fiction, most notably the convention of redundancy. . . .

The trouble with conventional dialogue is, in the first place, that people do not really talk in exposition. They say just enough to make themselves understood by the people they are addressing and do not behave as if they were aware of a large, unseen audience requiring to be kept informed. More important, such dialogue stands between the reader and the narrative, rejecting the reader's cooperation by assuring him that he will learn all there is to learn about the story without any effort on his part. In Kipling's dialogue there are few independently meaningful lines; meaning emerges from the total organization of what has gone before and what is to come. Description here is something more than decoration; it is a background against which individually obscure lines take on significance. A gesture will often finish a sentence. This kind of dialogue stretches the mind, requires, in Miss Tompkins' words, "a full participation of the imagination" [J. M. S. Tompkins, *The Art of Rudyard Kipling*, 1959] by readers who, like Pyecroft, recognize that seeing and hearing are not the only regulation aids to ascertaining facts.

There are many examples of this sort of dialogue in "Mrs. Bathurst." One toward the end of the story is representative. Hooper, speaking of his journey up-country on railroad business, says

> "I was up there a month ago relievin' a sick inspector, you see. He told me to look out for a couple of tramps in the teak." "Two?" Pyecroft said. "I don't envy that other man if—"

Pyecroft's aposiopesis, out of context, would be meaningless. It is probably meaningless, in any case, to casual readers of the story who have forgotten about Vickery's lunacy and murderous threats and Pyecroft's fear of being alone with the man. Those who have not forgotten are in a position to reconstruct the end of the sentence and so to participate, with the author and the four men in the railroad car, in the creation of the story.

The whole narrative may, in fact, be considered an extended example of aposiopesis. Hooper brings his hand to his waistcoat pocket, presumably to remove Vickery's teeth, but the hand comes away empty. Pyecroft seems on the verge of learning from Vickery's own lips the story of his affair with Mrs. Bathurst, but Vickery breaks off, saying, "The rest is silence." We are left to guess what exactly happened between Vickery and the captain, what Vickery did as a tramp up-country, and who his companion was. The tale of "Mrs. Bathurst," like Kipling's irrational universe, mocks our desire for reasonable explanations. Yet in the end, the theme of the story emerges clearly out of the calculated obscurity of the style. . . .

The symbol in "Mrs. Bathurst" is the story-teller, representing man's eternal quest for the meaning concealed in random events. And the art of the story is aposiopesis, the device of classical rhetoric which seeks, on every level of the narrative, to withhold the ultimate secret. . . .

Source: Elliot L. Gilbert, "The Art of the Complex," in *The Good Kipling: Studies in the Short Story*, Ohio University Press, 1970, pp. 76–117.

Sources

Bodelsen, C. A. "The Hardest of All the Stories: 'Mrs. Bathurst,'" in *Aspects of Kipling's Art*, Barnes & Noble, 1964, pp. 124-54.

Gilbert, Elliot. "The Art of the Complex," in *The Good Kipling: Studies in the Short Story*, Ohio University Press, 1970, pp. 71- 84.

Lodge, David. "'Mrs. Bathurst': Indeterminacy in Modern Narrative," in *Kipling Considered*, edited by Phillip Mallet, Macmillan Press, 1989, pp. 71-84.

Seymour-Smith, Martin. "Mrs. Bathurst," in *Rudyard Kipling* , Queen Anne Press, 1989, pp. 305–24.

Further Reading

Bodelson, C. A. "The Hardest of All the Stories: 'Mrs. Bathurst,'" in *Aspects of Kipling's Art*, Barnes and Noble, 1964, pp. 124–54.

Bodelson examines the cinematic footage in "Mrs. Bathurst" as a key element in the story, particularly with regard to how it advances the theme of haunting guilt. He also discusses the relationship between the characters Mrs. Bathurst and Vickery.

Brock, P. W. "'Mrs. Bathurst': A Final Summing Up," in *The Kipling Journal*, Vol. 31, September, 1964, pp. 6-10.

Comments on the chronology, symbolism, and action of the story.

Carrington, Charles. *Rudyard Kipling: His Life and Work*, Macmillan and Co., 1955, 549 p.

Explores connections between Kipling's life and his works.

McClure, John A. *Kipling and Conrad: The Colonial Fiction*, Harvard University Press, 1981, 182 p.

Offers an in-depth look at colonial themes in Kipling's stories written in the 1880s and 1890s.

Seymour-Smith, Martin. "Mrs. Bathurst," in *Rudyard Kipling* , Queen Anne Press, 1989, pp. 305–24.

Comments at length on the ambiguity of " Mrs. Bathurst."

Stinton, T. C. W. "What Really Happened in 'Mrs. Bathurst'?" in *Essays in Criticism*, Vol. XXXVIII, No. 1, January, 1988, pp. 55-74.

Compares "Mrs. Bathurst" to other Kipling stories.

A New England Nun

**Mary E. Wilkins
Freeman**

1891

When "A New England Nun" was first published in *A New England Nun and Other Stories* (1891), Mary Wilkins Freeman was already an established author of short stories and children's literature. Her first book of short stories, *A Humble Romance and Other Stories* (1887), had received considerable critical and popular attention, and she published stories in such notable journals as *Harper's Bazaar*, *Harper's Monthly*, and the *New York Sunday Budget*.

Mary Wilkins Freeman is often classified as a "local color writer." This means that she attempted to capture the distinct characteristics of regional America. Other well-known local colorists were Sarah Orne Jewett (with whom Freeman was often compared) and Harriet Beecher Stowe (author of the novel *Uncle Tom's Cabin*). As in the work of other local color writers, a recognizable regional setting plays an important part in most of Freeman's stories. However, she differed from writers such as Jewett and Stowe in that she rarely engaged in the meticulous description of places and people that they favored. The details in her stories tend to have symbolic significance, and most critics agree that her themes are more universal than those commonly found in much local color writing of the time. She is admired for her simple, direct prose and her insight into the psychology of her characters. "A New England Nun" has a very simple, perhaps even contrived plot. Yet Freeman manages to depict skillfully the personalities involved in this small drama and the time in which they lived.

Author Biography

Born in 1852, Mary Wilkins Freeman spent the first fifty years of her life in the rural villages of New England. It was an area suffering severe economic depression. The combination of fatalities from the Civil War (1861–65), westward expansion, and industrialization in the cities had taken large numbers of young men from the countryside. What remained was a population largely female, elderly, or both, struggling to earn a living and to keep up appearances. Freeman became famous for her unsentimental and realistic portrayals of these people in her short stories. She wrote, ''A young writer should follow the safe course of writing only about those subjects she knows thoroughly.'' This is exactly what she did, exploring the often peculiar and nearly always strong-willed New England temperament in short stories, poems, novels, and plays.

Freeman is best known for her short stories. She began writing short stories for adults in her early thirties when faced with the need to support herself and an aging aunt after the death of her parents. She had already had considerable success publishing children's stories and poems. Her first stories were published in magazines such as *Harper's Monthly* and *The New York Sunday Budget* in the early 1880s. She quickly made a name for herself and published her first collection of short stories, *A Humble Romance and Other Stories*, in 1887. A prolific writer, Freeman published her second collection—*A New England Nun and Other Stories*—only four years later.

Many of her stories concern female characters who are unmarried, spinsters or widows, often living alone and supporting themselves. It was a situation she knew well. She herself did not marry until the age of fifty, and her marriage was an unhappy one. She separated from her husband and spent the last years of her life with friends and relatives.

Although Freeman found popular success writing in many different genres, including ghost stories, plays, and romance novels that appeared in serial form in magazines, it is for her short stories that she is most highly regarded by critics. Most critics concur that her first two volumes of short stories contain her best work. She was awarded the William Dean Howells Medal in 1925 and in 1926 was elected to the National Institute of Arts and Letters. She died in 1930.

Plot Summary

''A New England Nun'' opens with Louisa Ellis sewing peacefully in her sitting room. It is late afternoon and the light is waning. We see Louisa going about her daily activities calmly and meticulously; she gathers currants for her tea, prepares a meal, feeds her dog, tidies up her house carefully, and waits for Joe Dagget to visit. Joe and Louisa have been engaged for fifteen years, during fourteen of which Joe has been away seeking his fortune in Australia. Louisa has been waiting patiently for his return, never complaining but growing more and more set in her rather narrow, solitary ways as the years have passed.

During his visit, both he and Louisa are described as ill-at-ease. Joe sits ''bolt-upright,'' fidgets with some books that are on the table, and knocks over Louisa's sewing basket when he gets up to leave. He colors when Louisa mentions Lily Dyer, a woman who is helping out Joe's mother. Louisa becomes uneasy when Joe handles her books, and when he sets them down with a different one on top she puts them back as they were before he picked them up. Once he leaves, she closely examines the carpet and sweeps up the dirt he has tracked in.

Despite their awkwardness with each other, Louisa continues to sew her wedding clothes while Joe dutifully continues his visits. One evening about a week before the wedding date, Louisa goes for a walk. As she is sitting on a wall and looking at the moon shining through a large tree, she overhears Joe and Lily talking nearby. It quickly becomes apparent that they are in love and are saying what they intend to be their final good-byes to one another. Lily has decided to quit her job and go away. After they leave, Louisa returns home in a daze but quickly determines to break off her engagement. The next evening when Joe arrives, she musters all the ''meek'' diplomacy she can find and tells him that while she has ''no cause of complaint against him, she [has] lived so long in one way that she [shrinks] from making a change.'' They part tenderly. Although that night Louisa weeps, by morning she feels ''like a queen who, after fearing lest her domain be wrested away from her, sees it firmly insured in her possession.''

Characters

Caesar

Caesar is the old yellow dog Louisa Ellis keeps chained securely to his hut in her yard. "Fat and sleepy" with "yellow rings which looked like spectacles around his dim old eyes," Caesar "seldom lift[s] up his voice in a growl or bark." The pet of Louisa's cherished dead brother, Caesar bit someone when he was a puppy and has been restrained ever since. Although he has become, over the years, just as placid as Louisa herself, his reputation as a ferocious, bloodthirsty animal has taken on a life of its own. He has become something of a village legend and everyone except Joe Dagget, Louisa's fiance, firmly believes in his ferocity.

Joe Dagget

Joe Dagget, Louisa Ellis's fiance for the past fifteen years, has spent fourteen of those years in Australia, where he went to make his fortune. He has returned and he and Louisa are planning to marry. Good-humored, honorable, and hardworking, Joe is awkward and uncomfortable in the meticulously ordered, domesticated world Louisa has built for herself over the years. He has already announced his intention to free Caesar, Louisa's old dog, who has been chained up ever since he bit someone while still a puppy. During the visit to Louisa, described in the story, Joe tracks in dirt, fidgets with the books on her table, and knocks over her sewing basket. Nonetheless, his sense of honor is so strong that even though he has fallen in love with Lily Dyer, a younger woman who has been helping his ailing mother, and although he realizes that he and Louisa are no longer suited to one another after a fourteen-year separation, he intends to go through with the marriage.

Dog

See Caesar

Lily Dyer

"A girl full of a calm rustic strength and bloom, with a masterful way which might have beseemed a princess," Lily Dyer is "good and handsome and smart," and much admired in the village. She is pretty, fair-skinned, blond, tall and full-figured. She works for Joe Dagget's mother and—as we and Louisa eventually discover—she and Joe have fallen in love when the story opens. A better match for

Mary E. Wilkins Freeman

Joe, Lily is full of life and vitality and just as good-natured and practical as he is. She also shares his strong sense of honor, declaring she wouldn't marry him even if he broke his engagement because "honor's honor, an' right's right."

Louisa Ellis

At the beginning of the story, Louisa Ellis has been engaged for fifteen years to Joe Dagget, who has spent fourteen of those years working in Australia. He has been back for some time, and he and Louisa are to be married in a month. All this time, Louisa has been "patiently and unquestioningly waiting" for her fiance to return. On her own since her mother and brother died, she has been living a serene and peaceful life. Her daily activities include sewing quietly, raising lettuce, making perfumes using an old still, and caring for her canary and her brother's old dog. Meticulous and tidy, she does everything with care and with the precision of old habit. She has "almost the enthusiasm of an artist over the mere order and cleanliness of her solitary home."

Known for her sweet, even temperament and her "gentle acquiescence," Louisa has "never dreamed of the possibility of marrying anyone else" in all the long years Joe has been away, and

Media Adaptations

- "A New England Nun" is available on audio tape from Audio Book Contractors (1991), ISBN: 1556851812.

- "A New England Nun" is also available on microfilm from Research Publications (1970-78), Woodbridge, CT. Wright American Fiction; v. 3.

has always looked forward to his return and to their marriage as the "inevitable conclusion of things." Just the same, she has, by the time the story opens, gotten so in the habit of living peacefully alone inside her "hedge of lace" that Joe's return finds her "as much surprised and taken aback as if she had never thought about" their eventual marriage at all. When Joe stops by for one of his regular visits, she becomes uneasy when he moves some books she keeps on a table, and as soon as he leaves she carefully checks the carpet and sweeps up any dirt he has tracked in. Without really noticing the change, she has become as much a hermit as her old yellow dog, Caesar.

Caesar, chained placidly to his little hut, and Louisa's canary, dozing quietly in his cage, parallel her personality. Her life is serene but also narrow, like that of an "uncloistered nun." Like the canary, who flutters wildly whenever Joe visits, Louisa fears the disruption of her peaceful life that marriage to Joe represents. After discovering that Joe is secretly in love with Lily Dyer, who has been helping to care for his ailing mother, Louisa breaks off her engagement to him with diplomacy, and rejoices that her "domain" is once again safe.

Themes

Choices and Consequences

One important theme in Mary Wilkins Freeman's "A New England Nun" is that of the conse-quences of choice. Louisa is faced with a choice between a solitary and somewhat sterile life of her own making and the life of a married woman. She has waited fourteen years for Joe Dagget to return from Australia. During this time she has, without realizing it, "turned into a path, smooth maybe under a calm, serene sky, but so straight and unswerving that it could only meet a check at her grave, and so narrow that there was no room for any one at her side." If she marries Joe, she will sacrifice a great deal of her personal freedom, her quiet way of life, and many of her favorite pastimes. On the other hand, if she chooses to remain single, she faces the disapproval of the community for rebelling against custom (women were expected to marry if they could); the villagers already disap-prove of her use of the good china on a daily basis. She also faces the probability of growing old alone with no children to care for her. In the end, when Louisa discovers Joe is in love with Lily Dyer and breaks off the engagement, she feels more relief than regret. She sacrifices her "birthright" in favor of her independence; she chooses to remain alone, in "placid narrowness."

Courage and Cowardice

Another important and related theme in "A New England Nun" is the relationship between courage and cowardice. Mary Wilkins Freeman shows us that it is often difficult to make decisions. For example, it takes all the "meek" courage and diplomacy Louisa Ellis can muster to break off her engagement with Joe Dagget; and she shows more courage than he, perhaps, in being able to broach the subject. Furthermore, it is courageous for a woman of her time to choose to remain single given the social stigma of being an old maid or spinster. Yet it is her fear of marriage and the disruption it repre-sents that prompts her to find this courage. Joe Dagget demonstrates courage, too, in his willing-ness to go ahead with the marriage. He knows he is in love with another woman but is willing to sacri-fice his own happiness for what he believes is the happiness of the woman who has waited fourteen years for him to return from Australia. Yet, there is something cowardly about Joe, too. He is unable to tell Louisa the truth about his feelings even when she has told him she no longer wishes to get married.

Search for Self

Louisa Ellis moves toward greater self-knowl-edge through the course of the story's action. In the

Topics for Further Study

- Mary Wilkins Freeman is known for her accurate portrayals of rural New England life during the late nineteenth century. Research urban life during the same time period (roughly 1880 to 1900) and compare the two. You may wish to read a few of her other short stories from her collections *A Humble Romance and Other Stories* and *A New England Nun and Other Stories* in order to get a more complete picture of rural life.

- Most historians consider the major forces that shaped the nineteenth century in America to have been the Civil War and Reconstruction, urbanization and industrialization, European immigration, and the expansion westward, including the building of the intercontinental railroad and the gold rushes of 1849 through 1899. Pick one of these factors and research its impact on American life. Can you find evidence of this impact reflected in "A New England Nun" or other stories by Mary Wilkins Freeman? Are we still feeling the impact of this factor today?

- Mary Wilkins Freeman claimed that one of the things she was interested in exploring in her short stories was the legacy of Puritanism in New England. Do some research on Puritanism, perhaps on the impact of the Great Awakening, the Puritan revival that swept New England in 1740-42. You may read one or two Puritan sermons, such as the famous *Sinners in the Hands of an Angry God*, by Jonathan Edwards. What traces of Puritanism can you find in "A New England Nun," other stories by Mary Wilkins Freeman, or works by other New England writers such as Nathaniel Hawthorne or Emily Dickinson? If you are familiar with New England culture today, what traces of Puritanism still remain?

- Since the 1970s, feminist historians have been interested in Mary Wilkins Freeman's short stories for their portrayal of women's lives in rural post-Civil War New England. Do some research to find out what kind of lives women led in New England and in other parts of the United States, such as the South and the West, in the latter part of the nineteenth century. What kinds of attitudes about women prevailed? What regional differences do you find? What differences between urban life and rural? How much have women's lives or attitudes about women changed today?

---

beginning we see a person who, while sweet and serene, is the very model of passivity. She agreed to marry Joe Dagget because her mother advised her to do so. She waited patiently for him for fourteen years without once complaining or thinking of marrying someone else. And when he returns and she discovers she does not love him and does not want to get married, she plans to go through with it anyway because she doesn't want to hurt Joe. She finally breaks off the engagement a week before the wedding; but even then she does so because she finds out Joe is in love with Lily, not because she decides to assert her own will. However, she does realize, after coming so close to sacrificing her freedom, how much she cherishes her "serenity and placid narrowness." While it is true Louisa has only

returned to the passive life she has been leading all these years, she returns to it as a result of active choice—perhaps the one active choice she has made in her whole life. In making this choice, she has chosen her self and her own "vision" of life.

Duty and Responsibility

Duty and responsibility are important themes in "A New England Nun" and they were important issues for the New England society Freeman portrays. People were expected to be self-sacrificing and to put responsibility, especially to family or community, ahead of personal happiness. Freeman shows us, however, that too rigid a definition of duty can be dangerous. Both Louisa and Joe are willing to go through with a marriage neither of them really wants any longer because of a sense of duty. It is to this same notion of duty that Lily refers when she says "Honor's honor, an' right's right." Adhering to this rigid notion of duty and responsibility would make three people miserable and accomplish nothing worthwhile.

Flesh vs. Spirit

The conflict between flesh and spirit is a theme that runs through "A New England Nun" and is depicted through a variety of striking images. Louisa's solitary life is largely a life of the spirit, or, as she says, of "sensibility." It is contrasted with the life of the flesh as represented by marriage which, of course, implies sexuality. Throughout the story we find pairs of images that stand for the conflict between the two. The sexually suggestive "luxuriant" wild growth, all "woven and tangled together," where fruit is ripening, is contrasted with Louisa's carefully clipped and controlled little vegetable garden where she grows cool lettuce that she cuts up daintily for her meals. The "order and cleanliness" and "purity" of her home are contrasted with the "disorder and confusion" she imagines represent married life. Indeed she actually sweeps away Joe Dagget's tracks after he has been in her house, symbolically trying to keep at bay all that he represents. And finally, we have Louisa sitting placidly once again at her window sewing at the end of the story while Lily Dyer walks past outside. Louisa is as contained as her canary in its cage or her old yellow dog on his chain, an "uncloistered nun" who "prayerfully" numbers her days. Lily is outside with the "busy harvest of men and birds and bees" and she is "erect and blooming" in the "fervid summer afternoon." Lily has, of course, embraced the very life Louisa has rejected. She will marry Joe in Louisa's place.

Style

Setting

This story about a woman who finds, after waiting for her betrothed for fourteen years, that she no longer wants to get married, is set in a small village in nineteenth-century New England. Critics have often remarked that the setting is particular but also oddly universal as are the themes Freeman chooses to treat. This village is populated with people we might meet nearly anywhere in rural America.

Point of View

"A New England Nun" is told in the third person, omniscient narration. That is, the narrator is not one of the characters of the story yet appears to know everything or nearly everything about the characters, including, at times, their thoughts. For example, the narrator tells us that, after leaving Louisa's house, Joe Dagget "felt much as an innocent and perfectly well-intentioned bear might after his exit from a china shop."

Symbolism

In general terms, a symbol is a literary devise used to represent, signal or evoke something else. For example, a fading red rose might be used to symbolize the fading of a romance. Like Nathaniel Hawthorne, to whom she has been compared, Freeman was adept at using symbolism in her short stories; but her touch is lighter than Hawthorne's.

There are many symbols in "A New England Nun." For example, the chained dog Caesar and the canary that Louisa keeps in a cage both represent her own hermit-like way of life, surrounded by a "hedge of lace." The alarm the canary shows whenever Joe Dagget comes to visit is further emblematic of Louisa's own fear of her impending marriage.

There is a great deal of symbolism associated with nature and plant life in this story. The evening Louisa goes for a walk and overhears Joe and Lily talking it is harvest time—symbolizing the rich fertility and vitality that Lily and Joe represent. Louisa, however, feels oppressed by the sexually suggestive "luxuriant" late summer growth, "all woven together and tangled;" and she is sad as she contemplates her impending marriage even though there is a "mysterious sweetness" in the air. The tumultuous growth of the wild plants reminds us of and contrasts with Louisa's own garden, which is tidy, orderly and carefully controlled.

Louisa sits amid all this wild growth and gazes through a "little clear space" at the moon. The moon is a symbol of chastity; Diana, the Roman goddess of the moon, was a chaste goddess. Louisa will later choose to continue her solitary and virginal, but peaceful life rather than tolerate the disorder and turmoil she believes married life would bring. Lily, on the other hand, embraces that life; and she is described as "blooming," associating her with the fertile wild growth of summer.

Realism

Freeman's work is known for its realism—a kind of writing that attempts to represent ordinary life as it really is, rather than representing heroic, fantastic, or melodramatic events. Realism, as a literary movement, began in America following the Civil War. The disruption of the war, followed by the Reconstruction of the South and widespread urbanization and industrialization greatly changed the way America looked at itself and, in turn, altered literary models. The romantic approach of the earlier generation of writers, represented by Hawthorne, Melville and Poe, gave way to a new realism. Prominent writers of the Realist movement were Mark Twain, Henry James, and William Dean Howells. Freeman can be further classified as a local color writer along with Bret Harte, Sarah Orne Jewett, and Kate Chopin, who wrote about life in California, Maine, and Louisiana respectively.

Writing Style

Mary Wilkins Freeman has frequently been praised by critics for her economical, direct writing style. She uses short, concise sentences and wastes little time on detailed descriptions. Her characters are sketched with a few strong, simple strokes of the pen. For example, the reader never really learns what Louisa Ellis looks like, but it does not matter to the story. We know what we need to know to keep us interested and to keep the story moving. Freeman is also known for her dry, often ironic sense of humor. One critic has called it "pungent." It is the kind of subtle humor that makes us smile rather than laugh aloud. Freeman's portrait of Caesar, the sleepy and quite harmless old yellow dog that everyone thinks is terribly ferocious, is a good example of her humorous touch. Freeman tells us "St. George's dragon could hardly have surpassed in evil repute Louisa Ellis's old yellow dog." It doesn't matter that Caesar has not harmed anyone in fourteen years. The mere fact that he is chained makes people believe he is dangerous. "Caesar at large might have seemed a very ordinary dog" she writes, "chained, his reputation overshadowed him, so that he lost his own proper outlines and looked darkly vague and ominous."

Historical Context

Religion and Economics

Mary Wilkins Freeman wrote most of her best-known short stories in the 1880s and 1890s. They provide a unique snapshot of a particular time and place in American history. The small towns of post-Civil War New England were often desolate places. The war itself, combined with urbanization, industrialization, and westward expansion, had taken most of the young able-bodied men out of the region. The remaining population was largely female and elderly. Women like Louisa Ellis, who waited many years for husbands, brothers, fathers and boyfriends to return from the West or other places they had gone to seek jobs, were not uncommon. The area was suffering from economic depression and many were forced to leave to support themselves and their families. There were many widows from the war, too, often living hand-to-mouth and trying to keep up appearances. Also common were the New England spinsters or old maids—women who, because of the shortage of men or for other reasons, never married. They were numerous enough that they contributed to the making of a stereotype we all recognize today.

Freeman knew these New England villages and their inhabitants intimately, and she used them as material for her many short stories. She said she was interested in exploring the New England character and the strong, often stubborn, New England will.

New England was settled by the Puritans during the early years of colonization in America. Vestiges of Puritanism remained in New England culture in Freeman's day and still remain today. Freeman often said that she was interested in exploring how people of the region had been shaped by the legacy of Puritanism. This is another question she examines in many of her short stories. In "A New England Nun" we can see traces of Puritanism in the rigid moral code by which Louisa, Joe and Lily are bound. Even if it makes them unhappy, Louisa and Joe both feel obligated to go through with their marriage because of a sense of duty. Lily echoes this same sense when she says she would never marry Joe if he went back on his promise to Louisa.

Women in the Nineteenth Century

Another aspect of nineteenth-century culture—not just in New England, but throughout the United States—that we find reflected in Mary Wilkins Freeman's short stories is that culture's attitude toward women. While contemporary readers may find Louisa's extreme passivity surprising, it was not unusual for a woman of her time. "Calm docility" and a "sweet, even temperament" were considered highly desirable traits in a woman. We can see

Compare & Contrast

- **1890s:** Women are faced with limited political, legal, and social options.

  1990s: Women are an important part of the political process. Candidates struggle to attract the female vote, and women's issues are central to many political platforms.

- **1890s:** Realism is a popular literary style, reflecting changing American concerns in the twentieth century. Short stories gain popularity as a literary genre.

  1990s: Short stories remain popular, and American literature is rich with fine examples of the short fiction genre. With the advent of the twenty-first century, realism also remains a viable literary form.

- **1890s:** Since in many areas of the United States women outnumbered men, spinsterhood was not uncommon. The declining male population can be attributed to the Civil War, other armed conflicts, and westward expansion. To remain single was a serious social stigma for women, as it was believed that a woman's primary duty was to marry and have children.

  1990s: Although marriage remains a goal of most young American men and women, many females in the late twentieth century often choose not to marry. A myriad of social and financial opportunities have lessened the stigma of remaining single. Divorce rates have skyrocketed in the past few decades, making marriage a less desirable option for many men and women.

that Louisa has learned these traits from her mother; and in fact, many parents raised their daughters to be much like Louisa.

Although things were beginning to change in larger towns and cities in America, in rural areas there were not many occupations open to women. As a result, while marriage was considered the most natural and desirable goal for women, it was often economically necessary as well. The skills a woman like Louisa acquired—cooking, sewing, gardening—from her own mother rather than from formal education, were intended to prepare her for a role as wife and mother. For many women like Louisa, the idea of not marrying was almost too outlandish to consider. Like Louisa they had been taught to expect to marry, and there were few if any attractive alternatives available to them. To turn down a chance to marry was considered both unnatural and foolhardy.

Realism

One important artistic influence on Freeman's work was realism. The same turbulent forces that shaped much of nineteenth-century American culture—the Civil War, the Reconstruction of the South, the industrial revolution—also affected literary tastes. Readers no longer liked the fanciful and heroic works of romanticism. Instead they wanted literature that reflected life as it truly was. William Dean Howells was one of the important novelists in this country to champion realism. Others were Henry James and Mark Twain. Howells was a friend and mentor to Mary Wilkins Freeman. However, it is possible Freeman would have been a realist even if she had not known Howells. Realism was in vogue and realistic short stories were what sold.

Critical Overview

Freeman's reputation was built upon her unsentimental and realistic portrayals of the rural nineteenth-century New England life. She was known for her ironic sense of humor and the idiosyncratic and colorful characters who populate her stories. Writing for *Harper's New Monthly Magazine* in

September of 1887, William Dean Howells, a life-time friend, mentor, and fan of Freeman, praised her first volume of short stories, *A Humble Romance and Other Stories*, for its "absence of literosity" and its "directness and simplicity."

An anonymous critic who reviewed *A New England Nun and Other Stories* for the *Atlantic Monthly* in 1891 noted Freeman's "short economical sentences, with no waste and no niggardliness," her "passion for brevity, her power for packing a whole story in a phrase, a word," and her "fine artistic sense." This critic found the short story "A New England Nun" particularly remarkable for its realism and praised the "novelty, yet truthfulness" of Freeman's portraiture. Later critics have tended to agree with Howells and the *Atlantic Monthly* critic, lauding Freeman's economy of prose, her realism, and her insight into her characters.

In this century, most critics have continued to deem "A New England Nun" as one of Freeman's best works, but they have valued it for new reasons. Since the 1920s, psychoanalytic criticism, based on the theories of Sigmund Freud, has become popular. With their revealing character sketches, her short stories have lent themselves well to this type of criticism. Perry Westbrook, in his book *Acres of Flint*, declared that Freeman's work reveals a "psychological insight hitherto unknown in New England literature with the exception of Hawthorne." "A New England Nun" and the character of Louisa have attracted a great deal of attention from psychoanalytic critics. Most of them tend to read Louisa as a person who has repressed her sexual side. Larzer Ziff, Jay Martin, and Perry Westbrook, for example have all read "A New England Nun" as a psychological study of a woman who has become so narrow as to be unfit for normal life.

Beginning in the 1970s, feminist critics and historians began to take an interest in Freeman's work for its depiction of the lives of women in post-Civil War New England. As a result, "A New England Nun" has been reevaluated and a debate has arisen between feminists, represented by the critic Marjorie Pryse, and more traditional critics such as Martin, Edward Foster, and Westbrook, over the interpretation of the character of Louisa. Pryse takes issue with these critics for seeing Louisa as a portrait of sterility and passivity. Pryse interprets her instead as a heroic character who dares to reject the traditional role society offers her—that of wife and mother—for a life she has defined for herself, albeit within the narrow range of choices

Priscilla Alden, leaning against a wooden fence and sewing on material, presenting a picture similar to Louisa Ellis in "A New England Nun."

available to a woman of her class in the nineteenth century.

Criticism

Deborah M. Williams

Williams is an instructor in the Writing Program at Rutgers University. In the following essay,

What Do I Read Next?

- Other short stories of note by Mary Wilkins Freeman include ''Sister Liddy,'' a story about women living in the poorhouse, ''A Conflict Ended,'' in which a stubborn parishioner refuses to enter the church, sitting on the steps instead, because he disagrees with the hiring of the new minister.

- Kate Chopin's short novel *The Awakening* (1899) chronicles the story of a young mother in Louisiana who leaves her husband and children in search of her own identity and later commits suicide. Like Freeman, Chopin has caught the attention of feminist critics and historians for her depiction of women's lives at the end of the last century.

- Carolyn Chute's novel *The Beans of Egypt, Maine* (1985) is an example of a recent work that continues the local color realist tradition. It tells of the poor and eccentric inhabitants of a small rural town in north-central Maine.

- Charlotte Perkins Gilman's social analysis, *Women and Economics* (1898), contends that the sexual and maternal roles of nineteenth-century women were overemphasized and their true potential neglected.

- Thomas Gray's 1751 poem ''An Elegy Written in a Country Church Yard'' meditates on the unrealized potential of the rural people buried in a cemetery. Many, he suggests, may have possessed artistic talent or other gifts stunted by ignorance or lack of opportunity. Critics have noted that the opening to ''A New England Nun'' seems to echo the opening to this poem.

- Sarah Orne Jewett's collection of short stories *The Country of the Pointed Firs* (1896) is regarded by most critics as her finest work. A local colorist and a contemporary of Mary Wilkins Freeman, Jewett wrote about aging Maine natives trying to preserve the values of the past in a dying small town. Critics often compare Freeman and Jewett.

---

she views Louisa as a woman who has made the most of the limited opportunities open to her and has channeled her creative impulses into the everyday activities of her simple life.

A number of critics have noted that the opening paragraph of Mary Wilkins Freeman's ''A New England Nun'' very closely echoes the first stanza of English poet Thomas Gray's famous ''Elegy Written in a Country Churchyard'': The curfew tolls the knell of parting day, / The lowing herd wind slowly o'er the lea, / The plowman homeward plods his weary way, / And leaves the world to darkness and to me. In Gray's poem, written in the eighteenth century, the speaker wonders if the rural churchyard might contain the remains of people who had great talents that became stunted or went unrealized and unrecognized because of poverty, ignorance and lack of opportunity. He muses that ''some mute inglorious Milton'' might be buried there—someone who possessed the talent of seventeenth-century poet John Milton, but who remains ''inglorious'' (or without glory) because lack of education made them mute. Freeman closes her story in the same way she opens it. Louisa Ellis is sewing peacefully at her window in the late afternoon light. Thus the opening and closing passages, with their allusions to Gray's elegy, stand as a sort of frame for the story itself, giving us a key to one possible interpretation.

As Marjorie Pryse has demonstrated in her essay ''An Uncloistered 'New England Nun,''' Louisa Ellis is a woman with artistic impulses. She has ''almost the enthusiasm of an artist over the mere order and cleanliness of her solitary home'' and has polished her windows ''until they shone like jewels.'' Even her lettuce is ''raised to perfection'' and she occupies herself in summer ''distilling the sweet and aromatic essences from roses and peppermint and spearmint'' simply for the pleasure of it. Louisa might have been an artist had her society provided her with the tools and opportunity. Lacking these, she has funneled her creative impulse into the only outlet available to her. She has made her life her life's work. Lacking paints, she has made her life like a series of still-life paintings of ''delicate harmony.'' Before the artist can begin to create, however, she needs a blank canvas or a clean sheet of paper.

As Perry Westbrook has noted, Louisa's life is symbolized by her dog, Caesar, chained to his little hut, and her canary in its cage. She has become a hermit, surrounded by a ''hedge of lace.'' Her canary goes into a panic whenever Joe Dagget visits, representing Louisa's own fears of what marriage might bring; and Louisa trembles whenever she thinks of Joe's promise to set Caesar free. Like her dog and her bird she does not participate in the life of the community. Instead, she watches from her window. We might interpret Louisa's life, her dog's chain, and her canary's cage as emblems of imprisonment, as does Westbrook; but they are also defenses. Caesar's ominous-looking chain keeps the outside world away more than it restrains the dog since the dog has no desire to go anywhere. And the canary's cage gives it a safe place to live. Likewise Louisa has found freedom in her solitary life. Just as she finds a ''little clear space'' among the tangles of wild growth that make her feel ''shut in'' when she goes out for her walk that fateful evening, Louisa has cleared a space for herself, through her solitary, hermit-like existence, inside which she is free to do as she wishes. The space-clearing gesture is a prerequisite to her creativity.

Although conditions were changing slowly, women in the nineteenth century did not have many vocational options available to them. Many of them received only a grade school education and then learned the rest of what was deemed necessary for them to know from practical experience in the home. Louisa, like her mother before her, learned to sew, cook, and garden in preparation for what was supposed to be her vocation as wife and mother. She was not taught to be a painter or musician. Hence, she channels her creative impulses into these other activities instead.

Critics have made much of the ''narrowness'' of Louisa's life. Some see it as the very emblem of sterility and barrenness; yet these interpretations surely overlook the fact that the community itself is

> **Critics who have seen Louisa's life as sterile are perhaps making the sexist mistake of assuming that the only kind of fertility a woman can have is the sexual kind.''**

narrow. Here is a town that disapproves of even so much individuality as Louisa's use of her good china. A rigid code of ethics is in operation here— one that dictates that Caesar must be chained for life because of one reckless act. Lily and Joe, for all their vitality and vigor, show themselves to be bound by this same narrowness. Joe determines to go through with a marriage to a woman he no longer loves because he is bound by a rigid sense of duty. Lily vows that she will not marry Joe even if he breaks off his engagement to Louisa because ''honor's honor, an' right's right.'' Without Louisa's intervention three people would be made miserable for the rest of their lives—all for the sake of duty. Louisa is the one who proves herself capable of stepping outside the narrow code. She alone is able to improvise an ending other than the ''inevitable conclusion'' the others see and a life for herself other than the one prescribed by her community. Her artistic sensibility allows her to provide a subjective, personal answer to what the rigid Puritan code of behavior sees as an objective question of right and wrong.

Furthermore, narrowness is not the same thing as sterility—or it need not be. Critics who have seen Louisa's life as sterile are perhaps making the sexist mistake of assuming that the only kind of fertility a woman can have is the sexual kind. Because Louisa chooses not to marry and reproduce, she is then deemed ''barren.'' These critics have overlooked the richness inherent in Louisa's deliberate life. She meditates as a nun might. She distills ''essences,'' which, as Pryse has noted, implies extracting the most significant part of life. Louisa ''would have been loathe to confess how often she had ripped a seam for the mere delight of sewing it together again.'' When she sets her table for tea, it takes her a long time because she does it "with as much grace as if she had been a veritable guest to her own self." She uses the good china, not out of ostentation (there's no one to impress, anyway), but out of a desire to get the most out of what she has. She has learned to value the process of living just as highly as the product. All her movements are "slow and still" and careful and deliberate and she savors every moment "prayerfully."

Critics have also made much of Louisa's passivity. We need to be careful about using twentieth-century values to judge a nineteenth-century heroine. In the nineteenth century, passivity, "calm docility," and a "sweet even temperament" were considered highly desirable traits in a woman. Parents raised their daughters to be this way; and we can see that Louisa has learned these traits from her mother (who "talked wisely to her daughter") just as she has learned to sew and cook. Louisa is passive because that is what her society has made her. She is not, however, completely without volition. She does choose not to marry, even if only to continue her placid and passive life. The choice is an act that, as Marjorie Pryse rightly points out, sets her at odds with her community and requires some bravery on her part. Louisa would surely have been aware of the social stigma associated with being an old maid.

While we can not know Mary Wilkins Freeman's intentions in writing "A New England Nun," we do know she understood what it meant to be a single woman and an artist in nineteenth-century New England. She herself did not marry until the age of fifty. And while we can not know how Freeman really felt about Louisa's placid and narrow life, we can note the tone of the story itself. Louisa's life is narrow, partly by her own choice and partly because her culture leaves her few options. Yet she has managed to craft a rich inner life within this tightly circumscribed space. Like Thomas Gray's "mute, inglorious Milton," Louisa's artistic gifts are somewhat stunted by her lack of education and largely unrecognized by her community; but they are not entirely unrealized.

Source: Deborah M. Williams, "Overview of 'A New England Nun,'" for *Short Stories for Students,* The Gale Group, 2000.

Marjorie Pryse

Pryse offers a feminist reading of "A New England Nun," interpreting Louisa Ellis's rejection of marriage—a conventional, expected role for a woman of her era—as a positive, self-affirming choice to make for herself a way of life that ensures her the greatest personal happiness and freedom.

In his biography of Mary Wilkins Freeman [*Mary E. Wilkins Freeman,* 1956], Edward Foster writes that "'A New England Nun' . . . has been considered Miss Wilkins' definitive study of the New England spinster." Yet because the spinster has traditionally carried such negative connotations, critics and historians have either phrased their praise of Freeman as apologies for her "local" or "narrow" subject matter, or deemed her depiction of Louisa Ellis in "A New England Nun" as ironic. Jay Martin views her as "an affectionately pathetic but heroic symbol of the rage for passivity." He judges that protagonists like her "have no purpose worthy of commitment. . . . Lacking a heroic society, Mary Wilkins' heroes are debased; noble in being, they are foolish in action" [*Harvests of Change: American Literature, 1865–1914,* 1967]. Foster concludes that "it is precisely the absence of desire and striving which is the story's grimly ironic point." Pathetic, passive, debased, foolish, lacking in desire or ambition: such a portrait, they imply, invites the reader to shun Louisa Ellis. Definitive study though she may be, we are not to admire or emulate her.

When Louisa Ellis reconsiders marriage to Joe Dagget, she aligns herself against the values he represents. Her resulting unconventionality makes it understandably difficult for historians, themselves the intellectual and emotional products of a society which has long enshrined these values, to view her either perceptively or sympathetically. For Louisa Ellis rejects the concept of manifest destiny and her own mission within it; she establishes her own home as the limits of her world, embracing rather than fleeing domesticity, discovering in the process that she can retain her autonomy; and she expands her vision by preserving her virginity, an action which can only appear if not "foolish" at least threatening to her biographers and critics, most of whom have been men.

In analyzing "A New England Nun" without bias against solitary women, the reader discovers that within the world Louisa inhabits, she becomes heroic, active, wise, ambitious, and even transcendent, hardly the woman Freeman's critics and biographers have depicted. In choosing solitude, Louisa creates an alternative pattern of living for a woman who possesses, like her, "the enthusiasm of an artist." If she must sacrifice heterosexual fulfillment (a concept current in our own century rather than in hers) she does so with full recognition that she joins what William Taylor and Christopher Lasch have termed "a sisterhood of sensibility" ["Two 'Kindred Spirits': Sorority and Family in New England, 1839–1846," *New England Quarterly*, 36, 1963]. For all of her apparent sexual repression, her "sublimated fears of defloration" [David H. Hirsch, "Subdued Meaning in 'A New England Nun,'" *Studies in Short Fiction*, 2, 1965], she discovers that in a world in which sexuality and sensibility mutually exclude each other for women, becoming a hermit like her dog Caesar is the price she must pay for vision. "A New England Nun" dramatizes change in Louisa Ellis. A situation she has long accepted now becomes one she rejects. The story focuses on what she stands to lose, and on what she gains by her rejection.

Although Louisa's emotion when Joe Dagget comes home is "consternation," she does not at first admit it to herself. "Fifteen years ago she had been in love with him—at least she considered herself to be. Just at that time, gently acquiescing with and falling into the natural drift of girlhood, she had seen marriage ahead as a reasonable feature and a probable desirability of life. She had listened with calm docility to her mother's views upon the subject . . . She talked wisely to her daughter when Joe Dagget presented himself, and Louisa accepted him with no hesitation." Wilkins implies in this passage that the "natural drift of girlhood" involving eventual marriage does require gentle acquiescence as well as wise talk from her mother, and that in taking Joe Dagget as her lover, Louisa has demonstrated "calm docility"—as if she has agreed to accept a condition beyond her control. When Joe Dagget announces his determination to seek his fortune in Australia before returning to marry Louisa, she assents "with the sweet serenity which never failed her"; and during the fourteen years of his absence, "she had never dreamed of the possibility of marrying any one else." Even though "she had never felt discontented nor impatient over her lover's absence, still she had always looked forward to his return and their marriage as the inevitable conclusion of things." Conventional in her expectations as in her acquiescence to inevitability, however, she has yet placed eventual marriage "so far in the future that it was almost equal to placing it over the boundaries of another life." Therefore when Joe Dagget returns unexpectedly, she is "as much surprised and taken aback as if she had never thought of it."

Given the nature of Joe Dagget's departure, and that of other men of the region after the Civil War who went West or moved to the cities, individually enacting the male population's sense of manifest destiny, Louisa Ellis chose a positive course of action in making her solitude a source of happiness. For Joe Dagget would have stayed in Australia until he made his fortune. "He would have stayed fifty years if it had taken so long, and come home feeble and tottering, or never come home at all, to marry Louisa." Her place in such an engagement, in which "they had seldom exchanged letters," was to wait and to change as little as possible. Joe Dagget might return or he might not; and either way, Louisa must not regret the passing of years. Within such a narrow prescription for socially acceptable behavior, "much had happened" even though Joe Dagget, when he returns, finds Louisa "changed but little." "Greatest happening of all—a subtle happening which both were too simple to understand—Louisa's feet had turned into a path, smooth maybe under a calm, serene sky, but so straight and unswerving that it could only meet a check at her grave, so narrow that there was no room for any one at her side." In appearing to accept her long wait, she has actually made a turn away from the "old winds of romance" which had "never more than murmured" for her anyway. Now, when she sews wedding clothes, she listens with "half wistful attention" to the stillness which she must soon leave behind.

For she has no doubt that she will lose, not gain, in marrying Joe Dagget. She knows, first, that she must lose her own house. "Joe could not desert his mother, who refused to leave her old home. . . . Every morning, rising and going about among her neat maidenly possessions, she felt as one looking her last upon the faces of dear friends. It was true that in a measure she could take them with her, but, robbed of their old environments, they would appear in such new guises that they would almost cease to be themselves." Marriage will force her to relinquish "some peculiar features of her happy solitary life." She knows that "there would be a large house to care for; there would be company to entertain; there would be Joe's rigorous and feeble old mother to wait upon." Forced to leave her house, she will symbolically have to yield her world as well as her ability to exert control within it.

She will also lose the freedom to express herself in her own art. She possesses a still with which she extracts "the sweet and aromatic essences from roses and peppermint and spearmint. By-and-by her still must be laid away." In Perry Westbrook's view, this still symbolizes "what her passivity has done to her." In distilling essences "for no foreseeable use," she "has done no less than permit herself to become unfitted for life" [*Mary Wilkins Freeman*, 1967]. Such an interpretation misses the artistic value, for Louisa, of her achievement in managing to extract the very "essences" from life itself—not unlike her fellow regionalist's apple-picker ("Essence of winter sleep is on the night/ The scent of apples . . . "). Her art expresses itself in various ways. "Louisa dearly loved to sew a linen seam, not always for use, but for the simple, mild pleasure which she took in it." Even in her table-setting, she achieves artistic perfection. Unlike her neighbors, Louisa uses her best china instead of "common crockery" every day—not as a mark of ostentation, but as an action which enables her to live "with as much grace as if she had been a veritable guest to her own self." Yet she knows that Joe's mother and Joe himself will "laugh and frown down all these pretty but senseless old maiden ways."

She seems to fear that the loss of her art will make her dangerous, just as she retains "great faith" in the ferocity of her dog Caesar, who has "lived at the end of a chain, all alone in a little hut, for fourteen years" because he once bit a neighbor. Louisa keeps him chained because "she pictured to herself Caesar on the rampage . . . she saw innocent children bleeding in his path. . . ." In spite of the fact that he looks docile, and Joe Dagget claims "'There ain't a better-natured dog in town,'" Louisa believes in his "youthful spirits," just as she continues to believe in her own. Louisa fears that Joe Dagget will unchain Caesar—"'Some day I'm going to take him out,'" he asserts. Should he do so, Louisa fears losing her vision rather than her virginity. Caesar, to Louisa, is a dog with a vision which, as long as he is chained, he retains, at least in his reputation: "Caesar at large might have seemed a very ordinary dog, and excited no comment whatsoever; chained, his reputation overshadowed him, so that he lost his own proper outlines and looked darkly vague and enormous." Only Louisa senses that setting the dog free would turn him into a "very ordinary dog," just as emerging from her own "hut" after fourteen years and marrying Joe Dagget would transform her, as well, into a "very ordinary" woman—yet a woman whose inner life would be in danger. Louisa "looked at the old dog munching his simple fare, and thought of her approaching marriage and trembled."

In addition, because the name Caesar evokes an historical period in which men dominated women, in keeping Caesar chained Louisa exerts her own control over masculine forces which threaten her autonomy. David Hirsch reads "A New England Nun" as Louisa's "suppression of the Dionysian" in herself, a Jungian conflict between order and disorder, sterility and fertility. He concludes that Caesar's continuing imprisonment "can be viewed as a symbolic castration," apparently of Louisa herself. To a point, the story appears to justify Hirsch's assertions, for Caesar's first entrance in the story visually evokes phallic power: "There was a little rush, and the clank of a chain, and a large yellow-and-white dog appeared at the door of his tiny hut, which was half hidden among the tall grasses and flowers." Yet Caesar emerges from his hut because Louisa has brought him food. If the image involves castration, it portrays Louisa intact and only masculine dominance in jeopardy.

Ambiguous images of sexuality abound in this story, sedate as Louisa's life appears to be. When she finishes feeding Caesar and returns inside her house, she removes a "green gingham apron, disclosing a shorter one of pink and white print." Shortly she hears Joe Dagget on the front walk, removes the pink and white apron, and "under that was still another—white linen with a little cambric edging on the bottom." She wears not one but three aprons, each one suggesting symbolic if not actual defense of her own virginity. When Dagget visits, "he felt as if surrounded by a hedge of lace. He was afraid to stir lest he should put a clumsy foot or hand through the fairy web, and he had always the consciousness that Louisa was watching fearfully lest he should." The visual image of clumsy hand breaking the "fairy web" of lace like the cambric edging on Louisa's company apron suggests once again that Louisa's real fear is Joe's dominance rather than her own sexuality. Joe, when he leaves, "felt much as an innocent and perfectly well-intentioned bear might after his exit from a china shop." Louisa "felt much as the kind-hearted, long-suffering owner of the china shop might have done after the exit of the bear." In Joe's absence she replaces the additional two aprons, as if to protect herself from his disturbing presence, and sweeps up the dust he has tracked in. When she imagines marrying Joe, she has visions of "coarse masculine belongings strewn about in endless litter; of dust and disorder arising necessarily from a coarse masculine presence in the midst of all this delicate harmony."

Taylor and Lasch discuss the nineteenth-century myth of the purity of women in a way which explains some of Louisa's rejection of Joe Dagget and marriage itself.

> The myth itself was yet another product of social disintegration, of the disintegration of the family in particular. It represented a desperate effort to find in the sanctity of women, the sanctity of motherhood and the Home, the principle which would hold not only the family but society together.

When Louisa waits patiently during fourteen years for a man who may or may not ever return, she is outwardly acceding to the principle by which women in New England provided their society with a semblance of integration. However, as Taylor and Lasch continue,

> the cult of women and the Home contained contradictions that tended to undermine the very things they were supposed to safeguard. Implicit in the myth was a repudiation not only of heterosexuality but of domesticity itself. It was her purity, contrasted with the coarseness of men, that made woman the head of the Home (although not of the family) and the guardian of public morality. But that same purity made intercourse between men and women at last almost literally impossible and drove women to retreat almost exclusively into the society of their own sex, to abandon the very Home which it was their appointed mission to preserve.

Louisa Ellis certainly repudiates masculine coarseness along with domesticity—for while within her own home she maintains order with the "enthusiasm of an artist," in Joe Dagget's house, supervised by a mother-in-law, she would find "sterner tasks" than her own "graceful but half-needless ones." In rejecting Joe Dagget, then, in the phrasing of Taylor and Lasch, she abandons her appointed mission.

Freeman goes farther than Taylor and Lasch, however, in demonstrating that Louisa Ellis also has a tangible sense of personal loss in anticipating her marriage. One evening about a week before her wedding, Louisa takes a walk under the full moon and sits down on a wall. "Tall shrubs of blueberry vines and meadow-sweet, all woven together and tangled with blackberry vines and horsebriers, shut her in on either side. She had a little clear space between them. Opposite her, on the other side of the road, was a spreading tree; the moon shone between its boughs, and the leaves twinkled like silver. The road was bespread with a beautiful shifting dapple of silver and shadow; the air was full of mysterious sweetness." As she sits on the wall "shut in" by the tangle of sweet shrubs mixed with vines and briers, with her own "little clear space between them," she

herself becomes an image of inviolate female sexuality. However, what she looks at "with mildly sorrowful reflectiveness" is not physical but imaginative mystery. Within the protection of the woven briers, Louisa's ability to transform perception into vision remains intact. What might be described as embattled virginity from a masculine point of view becomes Louisa's expression of her autonomous sensibility.

Therefore when she overhears Joe Dagget talking with Lily Dyer, "a girl full of a calm rustic strength and bloom, with a masterful way which might have beseemed a princess," and realizes that they are infatuated with each other, she feels free at last to break off her engagement, "like a queen who, after fearing lest her domain be wrested away from her, sees it firmly insured in her possession." Freeman writes, "If Louisa Ellis had sold her birthright she did not know it, the taste of the pottage was so delicious, and had been her sole satisfaction for so long." In rejecting marriage to Joe Dagget, Louisa feels "fairly steeped in peace." She gains a transcendent selfhood, an identity which earns her membership in a "sisterhood of sensibility."

In the story's final moment, she sees "a long reach of future days strung together like pearls in a rosary, . . . and her heart went up in thankfulness." Like Caesar on his chain, she remains on her own, as the rosary's "long reach" becomes an apotheosis of the dog's leash. Outside her window, the summer air is "filled with the sounds of the busy harvest of men and birds and bees" from which she has apparently cut herself off; yet inside, "Louisa sat, prayfully numbering her days, like an uncloistered nun." Freeman's choice of concluding image— that Louisa is both nun-like in her solitude yet "uncloistered" by her decision not to marry Joe Dagget—documents the author's perception that in marriage Louisa would have sacrificed more than she would have gained. If the ending of "A New England Nun" is ironic, it is only so in the sense that Louisa, in choosing to keep herself chained to her hut, has thrown off society's fetters. The enthusiasm with which Louisa has transformed "graceful" if "half-needless" activity into vision and with which she now "numbers" her days—with an aural pun on poetic meter by which Freeman metaphorically expands Louisa's art—would have been proscribed for her after her marriage. Such vision is more than compensatory for Louisa's celibacy. Louisa's choice of solitude, her new "long reach," leaves her ironically "uncloistered"—and imaginatively freer, in her society, than she would otherwise have been.

In looking exclusively to masculine themes like manifest destiny or the flight from domesticity of our literature's Rip Van Winkle, Natty Bumppo, and Huckleberry Finn, literary critics and historians have overlooked alternative paradigms for American experience. The very chaos which the challenge of the frontier for American men brought to the lives of American women also paradoxically led these women, in nineteenth-century New England, to make their own worlds and to find them in many ways, as Louisa Ellis does, better than the one the men had left. The world Louisa found herself inhabiting, after the departure of Joe Dagget for Australia, allowed her to develop a vision stripped of its masculine point of view which goes unnoticed—both in her own world, where Joe returns to find her "little changed," and in literary history, which too quickly terms her and her contemporaries sterile spinsters. Yet Louisa Ellis achieves the visionary stature of a "New England nun," a woman who defends her power to ward off chaos just as strongly as nineteenth-century men defended their own desires to "light out for the territories." The "New England nun," together with her counterpart in another Freeman story, "The Revolt of 'Mother,'" establishes a paradigm for American experience which makes the lives of nineteenth-century women finally just as manifest as those of the men whose conquests fill the pages of our literary history.

Source: Marjorie Pryse, "An Uncloistered 'New England Nun,'" in *Studies in Short Fiction*, Vol. 20, No. 4, Fall, 1983, pp. 289–95.

Jay Martin

In the following excerpt, Martin discusses prominent symbols in "A New England Nun" and asserts that the character of Louisa Ellis is meant to be a symbol of quiescent passivity.

In her best stories Mary Wilkins has an admirable control of her art. . . . Her best story is undoubtedly "A New England Nun." Louisa Ellis, the "New England Nun" who has been waiting fourteen years for her lover, Joe Dagget, to return from making his fortune in Australia, is shocked by his masculine presence—which now seems crude to her—when he finally comes back to claim her hand. For, in the intervening years, she has "turned into a path . . . so straight and unswerving that it could only meet a check at her grave": unwittingly she has become another in the tradition of New England solitaries. Her path is described by the adverbs modifying her unconscious modes of action—"peacefully sewing," "folded precisely," "cut up daintily.". . . Into this delicately ordered world, Joe comes bumbling and shuffling, bringing dust into Louisa's house and consternation into her heart. Whenever he enters her house, Louisa's canary—the symbol of her delicacy as well as of her imprisonment—awakes and flutters wildly against the bars of his cage. Joe's masculine vigor is symbolized by a great yellow dog named Caesar, which Louisa has chained in her back yard for fourteen years, and fed corn mush and cakes. Joe threatens to turn him loose, which suggests to Louisa a picture of "Caesar on the rampage through the quiet and unguarded village." At last, accidentally overhearing Joe and Lily Dyer confess their love for each other—while yet Joe sadly but sternly remains true to Louisa—she gently rejoices that she can release him, and herself, from his vows. In contrast to the wild, luxuriant fertility—the fields ready for harvest, wild cherries, enormous clumps of bushes—surrounding the scene between Joe and Lily stands the gently passive sterility of Louisa's life, who looks forward to "a long reach of future days strung together like pearls in a rosary." In contrast to the fervid summer pulsating with fish, flesh, and fowl, is Louisa's prayerful numbering of days in her twilight cloister.

Beginning with the comic stereotype in New England literature of the aging solitary . . . Mary Wilkins transmutes Louisa into an affectionately pathetic but heroic symbol of the rage for passivity. . . .

Source: Jay Martin, "Paradise Lost: Mary E. Wilkins," in *Harvests of Change: American Literature 1865–1914*, Prentice-Hall, Inc., 1967, pp. 148–52.

Abigail Ann Hamblen

In the following excerpt, Hamblen comments on the naturalistic detail of Freeman's first two books of short stories and explores her place in American local color fiction of the New England region.

Mary Wilkins' first two books of adult fiction, *A Humble Romance and Other Stories* and *A New England Nun and Other Stories* do much to establish her place in American literature. For these early collections are actually source material for anyone interested in early nineteenth century American life and thought, giving concrete and vivid details of a way of life that, presumably dead, still has noticeable repercussions.

It is true that a good many writers have concentrated on rural New England: Sarah Orne Jewett, Rose Terry Cooke, Margaret Deland, Alice Brown are only the most nearly typical of these, and perhaps the best known. They had their vogue for a time, Miss Jewett's delicate art earning special (and lasting) respect. And yet Mary Wilkins achieved something more. Granville Hicks explains: "Neither [Rose Terry Cooke nor Sarah Orne Jewett]," he says, "made any effective recognition of whatever was ignoble or sordid or otherwise unpleasant in the life of New England. . . . Mary Wilkins Freeman . . . at least saw that the small town had sometimes warped its inhabitants . . . she had an eye for varieties of character and types of experience her contemporaries ignored, and her stories made the record of New England more nearly complete" [*The Great Tradition: An Interpretation of American Literature Since the Civil War*, rev. ed., 1935].

Source: Abigail Ann Hamblen, in *The New England Art of Mary E. Wilkins Freeman*, The Green Knight Press, 1966, 70 p.

Sources

"New England in the Short Story," in *The Atlantic Monthly*, Vol. 67, No. 6, June, 1891, pp. 845-50.

Foster, Edward. *Mary E. Wilkins Freeman*, Hendricks House, 1956.

Hirsch, David. "Subdued Meaning in 'A New England Nun,'" in *Studies in Short Fiction*, Vol. 2, 1965, p. 131.

Howells, William Dean. "Editor's Study," in *Harper's New Monthly Magazine*, Vol. 75, No. 448, September, 1887, pp. 638-42.

Martin, Jay. "Paradise Lost: Mary E. Wilkins," in *Harvests of Change: American Literature 1865-1914*, Printice-Hall, Inc., 1967.

Pryse, Marjorie. "An Uncloistered 'New England Nun,'" in *Studies in Short Fiction*, Vol. 20, No. 4, Fall, 1983, pp. 289-95.

Westbrook, Perry. "The Anatomy of the Will: Mary Wilkins Freeman," in his *Acres of Flint: Sarah Orne Jewett and Her Contemporaries*, Scarecrow Press, 1981, pp. 86-104.

———. "Mary Wilkins Freeman," in *Dictionary of Literary Biography*, Gale Research, Vol. 78, 1989, pp. 159-73.

———. *Mary Wilkins Freeman*, Twayne Publishers, 1988.

Ziff, Larzer. "An Abyss of Inequality: Sarah Orne Jewett, Mary Wilkins Freeman, Kate Chopin," in his *American 1890s: Life and Times of a Lost Generation*, Viking Press, 1966, pp. 275- 305.

Further Reading

"New England in the Short Story," in *The Atlantic Monthly*, Vol. 67, No. 6, June, 1891, pp. 845-50.
    Anonymous review of Freeman's second collection of short stories which praises their realism and her "economical" writing style.

Donovan, Josephine. "Mary Wilkins Freeman," in her *New England Local Color Literature: A Woman's Tradition*, Frederick Ungar, 1983, pp. 119-38.
    A feminist/psychoanalytic interpretation of some of Freeman's short stories. Of particular note is Donovan's theory that the death of a mother figure is a major recurring theme in Freeman's works.

Foster, Edward. *Mary E. Wilkins Freeman*, Hendricks House, 1956.
    A meticulously researched and fairly straightforward biography, considered an important work by Freeman scholars.

Hicks, Granville. "A Banjo on My Knee," in his *The Great Tradition: An Interpretation of American Literature since the Civil War*, Macmillan Publishing Co., 1935, pp. 32-67.
    Marxian-influenced commentary upon Freeman's place in the local color tradition.

Hirsch, David. "Subdued Meaning in 'A New England Nun,'" in *Studies in Short Fiction*, Vol. 2, 1965, p. 131.
    A psychoanalytic appraisal that views Louisa as an example of sexual repression and sublimation.

Howells, William Dean. "Editor's Study," in *Harper's New Monthly Magazine*, Vol. 75, No. 448, September, 1887, pp. 638-42.
    Praises Freeman's first collection of short stories for their "directness and simplicity."

Westbrook, Perry. "The Anatomy of the Will: Mary Wilkins Freeman," in his *Acres of Flint: Sarah Orne Jewett and Her Contemporaries*, Scarecrow Press, 1981, pp. 86-104.
    Discussion of Freeman's "psychological insight" by a noted Freeman scholar.

———. *Mary Wilkins Freeman*, Twayne Publishers, 1988.
    A biographical and critical study in which Westbrook argues that Louisa's narrow lifestyle has made her unfit to live in normal society.

Ziff, Larzer. "An Abyss of Inequality: Sarah Orne Jewett, Mary Wilkins Freeman, Kate Chopin," in his *American 1890s: Life and Times of a Lost Generation*, Viking Press, 1966, pp. 275-305.
    Offers a psychoanalytical reading of "A New England Nun," arguing that Louisa is an example of "sexual sublimation."

Redemption

John Gardner

1977

John Gardner's story, "Redemption," was first published in the *Atlantic Monthly* in May, 1977. Gardner later included the story in his collection of short stories, *The Art of Living*, published by Knopf in 1981. "Redemption" chronicles the story of a young man named Jack Hawthorne who accidentally kills his seven-year-old brother in a farming accident. The accident takes place in the first paragraph, and the rest of the story reveals how Jack and the members of his family deal with the loss.

The central event in the story is autobiographical. As a young man, Gardner accidentally killed his younger brother; the circumstances of that tragic event are nearly identical to those described in the story. Gardner's recurring themes are present in this piece of short fiction: the relationship between art and experience, the consequences of death for survivors, the redemption from guilt, and the struggle between the forces of order and disorder.

Author Biography

The son of farmer John Champlin Gardner and his wife Priscilla Jones Gardner, John Gardner was born on July 21, 1933, and grew up on a farm. His mother had been an English teacher, and his father, like the father in "Redemption" was an avid reader of poetry, Shakespeare, and the Bible. As a result, Gardner was exposed to a myriad of literature and

popular culture during his childhood. When Gardner was in early adolescence, he was responsible for the accidental death of his brother, Gilbert, who was crushed beneath a cultipacker young Gardner was driving home. The tragedy became an important motivation for Gardner's writing in later years.

After graduating from high school, Gardner attended De Pauw University. When he was nineteen, he married Joan Patterson. Gardner finished his undergraduate career at Washington University in St. Louis in 1955, before earning an M.A. and a Ph. D. at the State University of Iowa. In addition to creative writing, Gardner studied medieval literature. After completing his Ph.D., Gardner taught at a number of colleges and universities. From 1959 to 1962, he taught at Chico State University in California; one of his students during this time was Raymond Carver, the short story writer.

Starting in the mid-1960s, Gardner published an enormous number of works, including critical essays, a biography of Chaucer, medieval studies, novels, short stories, plays, and poetry. In 1971, he published *Grendel*, the story of *Beowulf* told by the monster. In Gardner's version, the monster is depicted as an existentialist philosopher. In 1977, the year he first published ''Redemption'', he won the National Book Critics Circle Award for Fiction for *October Light*. During the same year he published *The Poetry of Chaucer* as well as *The Life and Times of Chaucer*, and underwent surgery for cancer.

In 1978, Gardner published his most controversial book, *On Moral Fiction*, a treatise in aesthetics and the purpose of fiction. He also married his second wife, Liz Rosenberg, whom he divorced in 1982. During the next few years following 1978, he traveled the country, debating the ideas introduced in the book. In 1981, he published a collection of short stories titled *The Art of Living and Other Stories*. The book includes the short story ''Redemption.''

In 1982, John Gardner died in a motorcycle accident, days before his planned marriage to Susan Thornton. The manuscripts he was working on at the time of his death were published in 1986 as *Stillness and Shadows*.

Plot Summary

''Redemption'' is set in a small farming community in upstate New York. The story opens abruptly with

John (Champlin) Gardner, Jr.

the announcement that, ''Jack Hawthorne ran over and killed his brother, David.'' Jack was driving a tractor and towing a cultipacker when his brother fell off the large machine. Jack is unable to act quickly enough to stop the accident, and David is crushed by the large machine.

The accident affects each member of the family in different ways, and the rest of the story is about how the family, especially Jack, finally come to terms with the death. Jack's father, Dale, takes the death very hard. A kind and genial man, Dale often recited poetry to groups at local churches and schools. After the accident, Dale begins to engage in a series of self-destructive actions, including riding his motorcycle at high speeds, smoking cigarettes, and engaging in a series of affairs with women. He vacillates between a hatred for God and despairing atheism.

Jack's mother, Betty, hides her grief from her children, crying only when she is alone. She concentrates on getting her two children through their grief. A religious woman, she has many friends who provide her with support. During this period, she also requires that her children take music lessons— Phoebe on the piano, and Jack on the French horn.

Although many people reach out to Jack, he withdraws from human contact. He isolates himself from family and friends, and even considers suicide. During the long hours he spends alone, the accident replays over and over again in his mind. He finds some solace doing his farm chores. One day, a year and a half after the accident, his sister brings him his lunch out in the field. When he did not say grace, she is distraught. Jack comforts her by lying, contending that he had said grace to himself earlier. This moment is an important one for the story, because for the first time since the accident, Jack shows concern for someone other than himself.

Meanwhile, Jack's father returns after three weeks away. When Jack comes into the house, he finds his father crying, asking his wife for forgiveness. Although Jack hugs his father, he is angry and resentful, presumably because after running away from his responsibilities to the family, his father can find solace when he returns.

Jack's father never leaves the family again. Jack, on the other hand, remains isolated, retreating into music. On Saturdays, he takes the bus to Rochester to take music lessons from an elderly Russian musician, Arcady Yegudkin, who had narrowly escaped the horrors of the Russian Revolution.

During one of Jack's lessons, Yegudkin plays a French horn, and Jack is transfixed. When he asks his teacher if he thinks that he will ever be able to play that well, Yegudkin laughs, clearly amazed that Jack would even think that such a thing were possible. Although Yegudkin's laughter moves Jack to tears, there is no indication that Jack will not continue with his lessons. Further, Yegudkin's response somehow provides a release for Jack, an acknowledgment that he does not have to be perfect. The story closes with Jack rushing for his bus, starting for home. The implication is that, like his father before him, Jack is starting the long journey toward healing.

Characters

Betty Hawthorne

Betty Hawthorne is Jack's mother. She grieves for her son in secret; the outward manifestation of this grief is a significant weight gain. Betty struggles to keep her family together through a very difficult time. Fortunately she is comforted by her supportive friends and is able to find the strength she needs to keep going. Betty is the one who introduces the children to music, and her insistence on French horn lessons makes possible Jack's eventual recovery.

Dale Hawthorne

Dale Hawthorne is Jack's father. The death of his younger son nearly destroys him, and he struggles to deal with the tragedy. He leaves his family, has several love affairs, and generally shirks his responsibility. However, he comes home at last, asking for forgiveness and searching for his own redemption.

Jack Hawthorne

Only twelve years old, Jack accidentally kills his brother by rolling him over with a cultipacker, a large machine used for farming. He blames himself for the accident and isolates himself from his family. Jack reviews the incident over and over again. Concerned about his increasing isolation, his mother insists that he take French horn lessons. Surprisingly, it turns into an effective therapy for the young man. In fact, it is through the French horn that Jack eventually finds redemption.

Phoebe Hawthorne

Phoebe Hawthorne is Jack's younger sister, the baby of the family. Only five years of age at the time of the accident, she copes with the loss by making cakes, doing household chores, and taking food to the men in the field. She believes that her family will be reunited in heaven and that God will heal her father.

Arcady Yegudkin

Arcady Yegudkin is Jack's music teacher. Like Jack, he is a survivor of a traumatic incident. He and his wife escaped from Russia during the Revolution after being shot and left for dead by soldiers. In Europe, he became a famous musician, and coped with his bad memories by burying himself in his music.

Themes

God and Religion

Gardner chooses God and religion as one of his central themes in ''Redemption.'' More specifically, Gardner chooses to explore theodicy, the defense of God's omnipotence and goodness in the face of evil. The central question of theodicy is, of course, if God is good and all-powerful, why does God allow evil in the world? How is it that a beneficent and omnipotent God would allow a small child to be crushed to death under the wheels of a cultipacker?

Dale Hawthorne represents the paradox of God's goodness and God's omnipotence in his response to David's death. His mind "swung violently at this time, reversing itself almost hour by hour, from desperate faith to the most savage, black-hearted atheism. . . . He was unable to decide, one moment full of rage at God's injustice, the next moment wracked by doubt of his existence." Often, when presented with unbearable pain, a human will either blame God or deny God's existence. Before the accident, Dale is "aloof from the timid-eyed flock, Christ's sheep." However, after returning to the family after an absence of three weeks, Dale begs for forgiveness. It is as if he finds redemption in bending to what he sees as God's will. Jack feels scorn for his father, now "some mere suffering sheep among sheep. . . ."

Betty Hawthorne represents a different response to the tragedy. She neither blames nor questions God. Rather, it is through her religious faith as well as the support of her friends that she is able to survive the disaster. This is vitally important for the family, because ultimately, she is the one who "keep[s] her family from wreck."

The character of Phoebe Hawthorne provides another insight into God's role in disaster. When she brings the lunch to Jack and he refuses to say grace, she is upset. To placate her, Jack lies and tells her that he has already said grace. He realizes later that Phoebe must depend on her religious faith; her survival requires the belief that God will heal her father and her brother, and that her family will be reunited in heaven. Phoebe finds solace in serving others; in many ways she is reminiscent of the "suffering servant" of Christian iconography.

Art and Experience

Certainly the most important theme in this story is that of art and its role in understanding life's experiences. Kent Thompson in his review in *Books In Canada* writes that virtually "every story in the collection is equally concerned with the various relationships between life and art." Gardner often claimed that art "made my life, and it made my life when I was a kid, when I was incapable of finding any other sustenance, any other thing to lean on, any other comfort during times of great unhappiness."

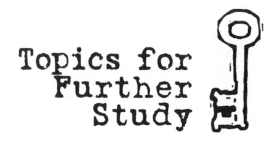

Topics for Further Study

- Investigate the number of farm accidents involving children in the 1940s and in the 1990s. What has happened to the number of reported accidents? To what can you attribute the change in the statistics?

- Read portions of Gardner's *On Moral Fiction*. According to Gardner, what is the role of fiction? Describe his philosophy regarding fiction and morality. How do Gardner's stories fulfill his goals? In what ways are they lacking?

- Listen to several recordings of French horn music. Reread the section of the story describing the music. How would *you* describe the music you hear? Try to be as creative as possible, using concrete images.

Art, for Gardner, had great redemptive powers. Indeed, only after writing the story did Gardner stop having flashback memories of his brother's death. Likewise, the story ends with the hope that Jack has found redemption through his music.

Furthermore, Gardner maintains that art has an important role to play in human experience. Literature should be moral, providing models for the way life should be lived. For example, although the characters in the story contemplate suicide, they all reject it as an appropriate response to their grief. Rather, each character finds a way to redeem him or herself through God, through work, or through art. As Thompson writes, for Gardner, "art is first of all an act of love."

Style

Images/Imagery

Several images recur throughout "Redemption." Skulls, for example, appear three times to remind Jack of David's death. At one point, Jack is alone, driving the tractor in the fields, thinking about the accident and his own guilt, his "sore hands clamped tight to the steering wheel, his shoes unsteady on the bucking axlebeam—for stones lay everywhere, yellowed in the sunlight, a field of misshapen skulls." Jack's identification of the stones with skulls is connected to his memory of his brother's crushed skull in the field. He then recalls his father's story of Lord Byron and Shelley's skulls, another indirect reference to what he saw happen to his brother's head.

A few pages later, he has a flashback of his brother's death, and this time, he does not see stones that look like skulls, nor Shelley's skull, but rather the cultipacker "flattening the skull of his brother." Moreover, the adjective "yellowed" suggests the aging of the skulls, and the time passing since his brother's death. Ironically, when Jack climbs down from the tractor because his memories overwhelm him, he fixes his eyes on "some comforting object, for instance a dark, smooth stone." The stone becomes a comforting image that brings him momentary peace.

Images of birds also figure prominently in the story. Each time, they seem linked to Jack's feelings. When he is alone on the tractor, his emotions threaten to overwhelm to such an extent that he must get off the tractor and calm down. The "birds crazily wheeling" overhead suggest the painful emotions inside. Later, in a peaceful moment, he hears birdcalls, and a "cloud of sparrows . . . explode[s] into flight." These birds are in search of safety. Likewise, Jack is looking for a safe place to work through his emotions.

A final bird image occurs in the closing pages. When Yegudkin begins to play the French horn, "it was if, suddenly, a creature from some other universe had appeared, some realm where feelings become birds and dark sky and spirit is more solid than stone." The sound grows until Jack likens it to "an enormous trapped hawk hunting frantically for escape." The repressed feelings threaten to tear him up. Suddenly, it seems as if Jack understands that through his music, his feelings can take wing like birds.

Antithesis

Anther important narrative device used by Gardner in this story is antithesis, a word that means oppositions or contrasts. The story opens with the most striking antithesis of all. It is a beautiful spring day, a time of year associated with birth. On this lovely day, David dies. Thus, birth and death are juxtaposed in a paragraph that begins, "One day in April. . . ." In so doing, Gardner associates the time of planting with death.

Midway through the story, Gardner opens another paragraph with the line, "One day in August, a year and a half after the accident, they were combining oats. . . ." The similarity between the two lines is striking and provides yet another antithesis. August is the time for harvesting. Harvest time is a time of death for crops, yet Jack begins to move away from his thoughts of death and toward his obligation to the living.

Historical Context

Post-War World

John Gardner, born during the Great Depression, reached adolescence in the years immediately following World War II. The accident that killed his brother took place in 1947, just two years after the end of the war. During this time, much of America was still rural and agricultural. With the advent of the nuclear age, American society began to change as they responded to the communist threat from Eastern Europe. The tension between the United States and the Soviet Union is known as the "Cold War."

In Europe, the aftermath of the World War II was very difficult. Much of Europe lay in ruins, the result of years of conflict. The realization of what happened at Nazi extermination camps shocked the public. In addition, the specter of Communism loomed as Eastern Europe found itself shrouded under what Winston Churchill called "The Iron Curtain."

Post-War Philosophy and Art

In 1947, Albert Camus published his book, *The Plague*. The horrors of the war had convinced many people that there was no God, for certainly God would not allow such evil to exist in the world. Existentialists such as Camus and John Paul Sartre believed that humans are alone in the world, that existence is unique and unrepeatable. In addition, they maintained that humans are free to choose their own path in the world. This freedom is both awesome and awful, in the philosopher Soren Kierkegaard's terms. Pushed to the extreme, existentialism becomes nihilism, the belief that there is no meaning in the world.

Compare & Contrast

- **1940s:** Many families live on farms, providing food and dairy products for the nation. Farmers were excused from the draft because they were essential to the health of the nation.

  1990s: Fewer and fewer families live on farms. Instead, most agriculture is conducted by large-scale industrial farms.

- **1940s:** Farming is one of the most dangerous occupations in the United States. In addition, many children who work on family farms suffer injury or death.

  1990s: While fewer children work on farms, the occupation is still a dangerous one. Injuries still occur to children working on their family farms.

- **1940s:** World War II draws to a close and veterans return home. Many attend college on the GI Bill. Women who have been filling factory jobs during the war are encouraged to return home to make room for returning soldiers.

  1990s: American soldiers are called up to fight in the Gulf War, and then in the bombing of Serbia. The United States is blessed with a low unem-ployment rate and qualified men and women have little problem finding a job.

- **1940s:** Existentialist philosophers such as John Paul Sartre, Albert Camus, and Soren Kierkegaard attempt to make sense out of the world devastated by the war. Sartre, a member of the French resistance, tries to recover from torture he suffered at the hands of the Nazis.

  1990s: The work of postmodern philosophers such as Jacques Derrida and Michel Foucault continue to influence the way that writers depict culture and reality.

- **1940s:** The end of World War II marks the beginning of the powerful Soviet Bloc. America and the Soviet Union struggle to gain supremacy over the other.

  1990s: The Soviet Bloc no longer exists, and communism is no longer considered the greatest threat to American security. However, the devolution of the Eastern Bloc leads to potentially dangerous situations in the former Soviet Union and Yugoslavia.

In 1947, Alfred Whitehead, the English mathematician and philosopher died. Whitehead and his philosophy had a great impact on Gardner; in fact, it was through Whitehead's philosophy that he was able to reject the existential position taken by most philosophers of the day.

The Cold War

During the 1950s, the United States engaged in a serious cold war with the Soviet Union. The explosion of the atomic bomb made further ''hot'' war unthinkable; the annihilation of the entire planet was possible with the new weapons. Nevertheless, the major powers rushed to build nuclear arsenals, and the decade saw confrontation after confrontation, the world teetering on the edge of nuclear disaster. In a world such as this, Gardner looked to art to provide the moral foundation that seemed to be so lacking in the modern world.

During the 1960s, the Cold War continued. At the same time, the United States became involved in the Vietnam War, a conflict that many young people viewed as immoral and wrong. The assassinations of John F. Kennedy, Robert Kennedy, and Martin Luther King, Jr., along with increasing violence in the nation's cities, led many to question the future of the nation.

Experimentation in literature and art occurred during the 1950s and 1960s. Richard Brautigan, William Gass, Thomas Pynchon, John Barth, and John Fowles experimented with fiction. Roland Barthes and Jacques Derrida in France began examining language and culture, which led to the concept of deconstruction. John Gardner, while a literary experimenter himself, often found himself in opposition to the trends of his day. For these reasons, he felt compelled to detail his aesthetic and moral philosophy in a number of essays and interviews. By the 1970s, Gardner was well known as a cultural and literary commentator, contending that good art is also moral art.

Critical Overview

"Redemption" was first published in the *Atlantic Monthly* in May, 1977. Gardner later included the story in his collection of short stories, *The Art of Living*, published by Knopf in 1981. Gardner was a writer who generated considerable critical controversy, in part from his prodigious writing output. Between the completion of his doctoral dissertation in 1958 and his death in 1982, according to Dean McWilliams in his book, *John Gardner*, the author produced "eight novels, two collections of short stories, an epic poem, a volume of lyric poetry, eight scholarly or critical books, five children's books, and five volumes of plays and opera libretti."

Although *The Art of Living* did not generate much critical commentary, the book was generally well-received. For example, Douglas Hill in *Maclean's Magazine* wrote, "Gardner is the master of the economical opening: he gives a reader just enough setting and background to slip him effortlessly into the world of each tale. . . . There's humor in these stories, and a full measure of graceful, unstudied prose. . . . There's considerable expertise in this book, and courage and joy."

Nevertheless, because the book followed Gardner's *On Moral Fiction*, a book-length essay discussing the role of fiction, reviewers noted that Gardner used the stories to illustrate the points he made in his earlier books. Kent Thompson, for example, wrote in *Books in Canada* in 1981, that the stories are "illustrations of ideas. Their consequent value is therefore not in what they are, but in what they lead us to talk about. They seem to be written for professors and students. . . ."

It seems notable, however, that few of the early reviews singled out "Redemption" for comment. This may very well be, ironically, because the story demonstrates strong writing, filled with vivid image and compelling moments. Such writing does not square with critics who want only to see the book as an illustration of *On Moral Fiction*. Certainly, later scholars returned to the story, noting in it a number of important ideas, themes, and images for the understanding of the corpus of Gardner's work. These same scholars, however, while concentrating on the philosophical nature of the story, admired the strength of the writing as well.

In recent years, "Redemption" has appeared in several anthologies of short stories and has received notable attention from scholars, a sure indication that the story inspires debate and commentary. Ronald Grant Nutter in his 1997 book *A Dream of Peace: Art and Death in the Fiction of John Gardner*, for example, spends his first chapter establishing the importance of "Redemption" as part of Gardner's work. He discusses autobiographical aspects of the story, and relates it to the work of Robert Jay Lifton, a famous psychiatrist.

Gregory L. Morris contends that "The theme of art as redemptive force comes through most clearly and most intensely in . . . "Redemption," which is Gardner's personal attempt to redefine a particularly painful part of his memory."

As an illustration of Garner's philosophy, as an autobiographical story providing insight into Gardner's life, or as a gripping and moving tale, "Redemption" is likely to garner study and critique in the coming years. Certainly, any student interested in the body of Gardner's work ought to carefully read the story for an exploration of what Morris calls "the magic of art."

Criticism

Diane Andrews Henningfeld

Diane Andrews Henningfeld is an associate professor at Adrian College and has written extensively for a variety of educational and academic publishers. In the following essay she examines the autobiographical and thematic importance of "Redemption" and relates it to the rest of Gardner's work.

At the time of his death in 1982, the result of a motorcycle accident, John Gardner was considered one of the most prolific, talented, and controversial writers of his generation. His output was prodigious, spanning genres and ideas with ease. Not content to write only fiction, he also produced literary criticism, children's books, plays, poetry,

Tractor and farm plow, 1981, suggesting both the power and potential dangerousness of farm machinery.

and biography. He was insistent on the role that fiction should play in the world, and made these claims explicit in books such as *On Moral Fiction*, *The Art of Fiction*, and *On Becoming a Novelist*, and in the scores of interviews he granted. By placing his assertions about fiction in front of academics and critics, in bold, vivid, and highly opinionated terms, he generated critical interest and controversy. Although most scholars agree that Gardner was not always successful in achieving the high goals he set for his fiction, most would also agree that his was an important literary and philosophical voice.

Put simply, as Julian Moynahan writes in *The New York Times Book Review*, Gardner steadfastly argued "that all good art, including prose fiction, should be moral. By this he means it should be life-enhancing, protecting human existence from the dark forces of chaos . . . pressing in from all sides and coming up from below, seeking whom they may devour." This statement seems particularly apt for any discussion of "Redemption."

A number of writers have suggested that Gardner reached this philosophical understanding of art as the result of an accident that occurred in his childhood. In an incident nearly identical to the one described in "Redemption," Gardner was responsible for the death of his younger brother, Gilbert. Although Gardner did not write of the incident in the thirty years between the accident and the composition of the short story in 1977, it seems clear that the trauma was at the heart of his writing and aesthetic theory. Certainly, one can hear the echoes of this accident in some of Gardner's statements such as this from *The Art of Fiction*: "To write with taste, in the highest sense, is . . . to write so that no one commits suicide, no one despairs."

One scholar who makes much of the significance of the accident for Gardner's life and of "Redemption" for Gardner's writing is Ronald Grant Nutter. In his book, *A Dream of Peace: Art and Death in the Fiction of John Gardner*, Nutter summarizes the story and the actual event. He finds the story important for two reasons. First, of course, is the autobiographical element in the story. Second, the story presents themes of death, guilt, religion, community and the redemptive nature of art. To explore these themes, Nutter turns to the work of John Howell, who in an important essay, "The Wound and the Albatross," discusses the connection between the wound and the creation of art; and to the work of Robert Jay Lifton, a psychiatrist who

What Do I Read Next?

- *Grendel* (1971) is perhaps Gardner's most famous novel. The story is a retelling of the Anglo-Saxon epic, *Beowulf*, from the monster's perspective.

- *Beowulf* is considered a masterpiece of medieval literature. It is a tale of heroes and monsters, life and death. Anyone reading *Grendel* should also read *Beowulf*.

- Gardner's book of advice for young writers, *The Art of Fiction: Notes on Craft for Young Writers*, offers insight into his ideas about art and life. Also included are a number of exercises designed to motivate writers.

has studied survivors and post-traumatic stress syndrome.

It is possible to expand Nutter's reading of ''Redemption'' by exploring an important critical approach, trauma theory. Although a complicated theory, it is possible to understand the basic principles. First, trauma theory hypothesizes that traumatic knowledge is a different kind of knowledge. As Geoffrey H. Hartman argues in *New Literary History*, traumatic knowledge is ''one that cannot [be] made entirely conscious, in the sense of being fully retrieved or communicated without distortion.'' That is, traumatic knowledge enters the mind in different way from knowledge in general. It bypasses the conscious mind and embeds itself directly in the unconscious. There is a direct and swift inputting of information deep within the victim's mind. The knowledge itself cannot be recalled directly by the conscious mind. At the same time, as Hartman explains, the trauma creates a ''kind of memory of the event, in the form of a perpetual troping of it by the bypassed or severely split (dissociated) psyche.'' In other words, the memory of the event, deeply embedded in the subject's unconscious mind, continually replays itself in the subject's conscious mind. Thus, while the knowledge of the experience is hidden in the person's mind, the memory of the event replays itself in the form of dreams, flashbacks, and hallucinations.

There is a gap, then, between the experience of the event and an understanding of the event itself. Recovering from trauma requires that the victim of the trauma must somehow bridge this gap. For Gardner, literature and art offer the possibility of such healing. He writes, ''Art begins in a wound, and is an attempt either to live with the wound or to heal it.'' Likewise, trauma theory, according to Hartman, ''helps us to 'read the wound' with the aid of literature.'' Thus, the psychic wound caused by trauma can serve as the impetus for the creation of art or literature. Moreover, the act of creation of art or literature is a life-affirming process, bridging the gap between experience and understanding.

That Gardner himself was the victim of traumatic stress seems clear. Gregory L. Morris in his book *A World of Light and Order* cites an interview from *The Paris Review* in which Gardner states,

> Before I wrote the story about the kid who runs over his younger brother . . . always, regularly, every day I used to have four or five flashes of that accident. I'd be driving down the highway and I couldn't see what was coming because I'd have a memory flash. I haven't had it once since I wrote the story. You really do ground your nightmares, you *name* them.

Obviously, Gardner and the characters he creates for his story all suffer from psychic wounds. Each character attempts to heal wounds in different ways, trying to fill the space that the loss of David creates. Dale Hawthorne, according to the story, was ''as much Romantic poet-hero as his time and western New York State could afford.'' Before the accident he was known for his vivid recitations of lines from plays and poetry. It may be significant that Dale read the works of others, rather than creating works of his own. Before the accident, Dale had seemed above the crowd to his son Jack, somehow different from the ''sheep'' of his audience. With David's death, however, Dale found himself suddenly empty, and no longer above the crowd. Although he contemplates suicide, he understands that suicide would only make greater the gaping hole the rest of his family is trying to fill. Thus, he turns to other women in his attempt to make himself whole again, as if by filling their sexual needs he could fill his own psychic gap. Only when he returns to his family and creates the tableau of penitence does he begin to heal. He returns to his recitations, but as a ''mere suffering sheep among sheep.''

Betty Hawthorne understands the need to hold her family together. To do so, she must repress her own grief. Although she has "considerable strength of character," she nonetheless turns to food, as if by filling her stomach, she can mend her heart. While the overeating does not lead to any healing, the act of writing does. Although she does not create art, so to speak, she connects her trauma to words in the letters she writes to her friends. The written dialogue that they establish moves her "step by step past disaster. . . ."

Jack, however, grows increasingly more isolated. As the central figure in the family tragedy, the one who created the moment after which all existence changed, he finds it hard to bridge the gap between his knowledge of the event and his understanding of it. He behaves as a survivor of trauma, the memory of the event replaying itself during every waking hour. He attempts to fill the gap first by creating dramas while riding the tractor, imagining himself as an actor on a stage. Eventually he turns to his French horn and his music for solace. It is when he begins taking lessons in Rochester from Arcady Yegudkin, however, that the healing begins.

Yegudkin, like Jack, has survived a trauma. With his wife, he had been shot at and left for dead by soldiers during the Russian Revolution. Yegudkin, a brilliant musician, fills the loss of his country and of his youth with music. For the purpose of the story, Yegudkin is more than a teacher of music, however. He models for Jack one way one can survive trauma. When he plays the new horn that he has ordered for a graduate student, the music completely fills the room. When Jack asks Yegudkin if he thinks that Jack might someday be able to play like him, the teacher laughs, causing an important moment in the story: "Jack blinked, startled by the bluntness of the thing, the terrible lack of malice, and the truth of it. His face tingled and his legs went weak, as if the life were rushing out of them." This description brings the reader back to the first paragraph of the story, when the life rushed out of David's legs. For Jack, this moment serves as a symbolic death, and a rebirth. When he leaves the studio, his horn and music under his arm, the crowd parts for him, receives him, and he begins his return to home. It is as if he understands that music must join him with his family, not separate him from them. Through his art, he is redeemed, the guilt over his brother's death washed clean by his own symbolic death. There is not a conclusive ending to the story, just the suggestion that Jack is beginning to

> "For the purpose of the story, Yegudkin is more than a teacher of music, however. He models for Jack one way one can survive trauma."

bridge the gap between the knowledge of the experience and the understanding of it.

Finally, while "Redemption" seems to make clear that suicide is not an appropriate response to trauma, and that trauma can be survived, it does not suggest that this is an easy, or quick process, nor does it suggest that there can ever be a return to the days before the trauma. Indeed, each of the characters of the story are markedly changed and transformed by the experience. Likewise, although Gardner survived his childhood and moved into adulthood, using his art to help bridge his own gap, he was a transformed individual. That he once again returned to the story of the accident and included it in a novel he was working on at the time of his death suggests that the wound could never be wholly healed. Nevertheless, Gardner devoted himself to the creation of a kind of art that he believed would persuade people to go on living in spite of the horror of contemporary life. As Nutter quotes Gardner, "Good artists are the people who are, in one way or another, creating, out of deep and honest concern a vision of life-in-the-twentieth-century that is worth pursuing." For Gardner, good art leads to life, to healing of the wound.

Source: Diane Andrews Henningfeld, for *Short Stories for Students*, The Gale Group, 2000.

Per Winther

In the following excerpt, Winther discusses reasons for reading "Redemption," including the forcefulness of Gardner's writing, the autobiographical nature of the writing, and the opportunity to see the effect of Gardner's personal tragedy on his writing.

"Redemption" also belongs to this group of stories which describe and explore the vulnerary function of art. The theme of this story differs somewhat from that of the other three, but the subject matter is the same: the protagonist seeks consolation in the world of music after the death of his brother. Jack Hawthorne, the protagonist, was driving a tractor when his younger brother, David, fell off and was run over and killed by the cultipacker the tractor was hauling. Driven by guilt and self-hatred, the young boy tries to deal with his confusion caused by the accident by perfecting his skills on the French horn; he uses the horn as a means of escape into self-imposed isolation, withdrawing from his family and any other company.

He is brought out of his isolation when he suddenly realizes that he will never reach the level of mastery of his teacher Yegudkin, a seventy-year-old Russian exile who has played with famous orchestras around the world. Yegudkin now teaches music but also has a set of arrogant values, constantly deriding ''the herd'' for failing to appreciate music at his own level. When Jack asks Yegudkin if he thinks that he, the student, will ever be able to play like the great master, the Russian scoffs at this foolish presumption. Thus, John Howell points out, Yegudkin, '''beatific and demonic at once,' has paradoxically saved [Jack] from the artistic self-absorption and isolation he has chosen.'' After the crucial lesson in which he is forced to recognize his own limitations, Jack's reintegration into society is described in symbolic terms. Rushing to catch his bus back home, he finds that ''the crowd opened for him and, with the horn cradled under his right arm, his music under his left, he plunged in, starting home.'' The young boy has to recognize his own limits; that is, he has to reconcile himself to the fact that the ideal (his aspirations of becoming a great musician) and the real do not always match up. Only by accepting his own fallibility and imperfections can he deal with his own guilt, become reintegrated into the community and be reunited with his family. Jack's clutching of the instrument and musical score in that symbolical final scene suggests that music will still be an important part of his life, but now more in the manner of the other three stories we have been discussing, and not as a means of alienating himself from the community.

''Redemption'' warrants close attention for several reasons. The early pages in particular contain some of the most gripping lines that Gardner ever committed. The opening paragraph, describing the accident which killed Jack's brother, is unique in its control and vividness. The ensuing study of the boy's self-loathing and his estrangement from his family moves as if by its own momentum, wholly logical and with considerable intellectual and emotional authority. Part of the story's attraction, then, lies in the sheer force of the writing that went into it. But even more important are the ways in which it suggests a key to some of the chief motivating factors behind the thematic direction of Gardner's fiction. The story also helps to explain why art has become such an all-encompassing concern for this writer. These points need to be elaborated on at some length.

The centrality of ''Redemption'' has to do with the fact that it is one of Gardner's most strongly autobiographical pieces of writing, exploring artistically an event which left an indelible mark on him as a person and as a writer. The key event—the accident—is lifted straight from Gardner's personal history, with only a few changes of incident and names. The scene was to play itself over and over again in his mind several times a day up to the writing of the story. (It was first published in the *Atlantic Monthly* in May 1977; the accident involving the death of Gardner's brother took place in 1947.) After he had written about the accident, Gardner stopped having the flashbacks, he says, confirming D. H. Lawrence's dictum that one sheds one's illnesses in art. The suicidal feelings Jack develops in the story are also true to Gardner's own experience, as witnessed, for instance, by the strongly autobiographical ''Stillness'' section of the posthumous work *Stillness and Shadows*, and the reason that the boy's father gives for not taking his own life—''the damage his suicide would do to his wife and the children remaining''—is the same one Gardner himself has offered for not giving in to his own suicidal inclinations. Like Jack, Gardner played the French horn, and the Eastman School of Music that Jack attends on Saturday afternoons is the one Gardner went to for his music lessons.

But the main impulse behind ''Redemption'' is not strictly autobiographical. We know that Gardner used writing much the same way that Jack Hawthorne used his horn, as a means of escape and as a way to combat confusion and despair. Art ''made my life,'' Gardner has said, ''and it made my life when I was a kid, when I was incapable of finding any other sustenance, any other thing to lean on, any other comfort during times of great unhappiness.'' It seems obvious, therefore, that when Gardner claims that art has the power to console, his prime authority is his own personal history; one of his chief purposes in writing these stories must clearly have been to awaken others to the potentially beneficial effects of art.

What is of greater interest to us here, however, is the extent to which the excruciating experience of accidentally killing his brother has affected his own writings. One should tread cautiously here and resist the temptation to establish the kind of relationship between Gardner's life and his art that Phillip Young sought to set up in the case of Hemingway, arguing that the direction of Hemingway's art, in terms of theme as well as of artistic technique, was determined by his continuous struggle to cope with the psychic effect of the physical wounds he received in the course of a turbulent personal history. Nevertheless, there is surely a large degree of truth to Edmund Wilson's claims about the relationship between the artist and his works:

> The real elements, of course, of any work of fiction, are the elements of the author's personality: his imagination embodies in the images of characters, situations, and scenes the fundamental conflicts of his nature or the cycle of phases through which it habitually passes. His personages are personifications of the author's various impulses and emotions: and the relations between them in his stories are really the relations between these.

Gardner has himself insisted on the close relationship between the art product and the personality of the artist: "The tensions we find resolved or at least defined and dramatized in art are the objective release of tensions in the life of the artist." One is therefore perhaps justified in pursuing the Hemingway parallel at least part of the way. The tensions that his childhood experiences engendered in Gardner evidently never lost their grip on him. As late as 1979 he stated: "You keep violently fighting for life, for what you think is good and wholesome, but you lose a lot. I think all my struggles toward anything worthwhile are pretty much undermined by psychological doubts. But you keep trying." Thus Heraclitus's old maxim—"the way up is the way down"—truly holds for Gardner. This is a fact to bear in mind when assessing the existential seriousness of his life affirmation. There is nothing facile about the basic optimism that controls his books. Gardner was intimately acquainted with personal despair, and as we shall see, his affirmations take into account a number of the major arguments that are traditionally advanced to support a pessimistic view of reality.

The paradigmatic nature of "Redemption" can hardly be exaggerated. Jack Hawthorne's self-hatred is generalized into a hatred of the total creation, man and animal. This attraction toward an absurdist view of the world (the motivating force behind Jack

> "Gardner was intimately acquainted with personal despair, and as we shall see, his affirmations take into account a number of the major arguments that are traditionally advanced to support a pessimistic view of reality."

Hawthorne's and—presumably—Gardner's suicidal inclinations) is explored again and again in Gardner's fiction. It is usually yoked with an absolutist approach to man and life, a failure to reconcile the discrepancy between the real and the ideal, and the failure to accept human fallibility, which characterizes Jack Hawthorne's initial response to the death of his brother. I am, of course, not suggesting that in everything Gardner writes lurk the shadows of his brother's death. But the frequency with which Gardner returns to situations and characters which allow him to explore this kind of tension attests to the biblio-therapeutical nature of his writings, as well as to the formative importance of the accident described in "Redemption." This is not to say that Gardner's fiction is narrowly confessional, representing a constant and obsessive picking of the scab over the wound caused by his brother's death; that would in the end have rendered his novels and stories trivial. What saves his fiction from triviality (in the sense of it being overly private) is the fact that in his personal traumas Gardner has discovered a paradigm, or a metaphor, for what he regards as the central illness of recent Western culture: the inclination to keep peering into the abyss, "counting skulls," losing oneself in a fashionable attraction toward despair.

In these four stories the answer offered to this type of dilemma is of a very general kind: art has the power to console provided one is receptive. It is probably no coincidence that for his exploration of this very general idea Gardner chose to focus on music, an art form which is almost totally abstract, speaking primarily to our emotions rather than to our intellect. But any art will not do for Gardner. When art moves into the sphere of ideas, for instance in the form of literature, it has to meet certain requirements in order to have the life-giving effect that Gardner thinks it can and ought to have. This is where his concept of moral fiction comes in, and a central axiom of this theory is the idea that *art instructs*. . . .

Source: Per Winther, ''Life Follows Fiction,'' in *The Art of John Gardner: Introduction and Exploration*, State University of New York Press, 1992, pp. 9–30.

Gregory L. Morris

In the following excerpt, Morris recommends ''Redemption'' for its expression of Gardner's belief in the power of art to console, redeem, and transform.

This theme of art as redemptive force comes through most clearly and most intensely in the second story, ''Redemption,'' which is Gardner's personal attempt to redefine a particularly painful part of his memory. The story is based on the tragic death of Gardner's younger brother Gilbert in a farming accident in the home-fields of Batavia, New York. Gardner talked of this memory in an interview in *The Paris Review*, and explained how the story served as a deliberate exorcism: ''Before I wrote the story about the kid who runs over his younger brother . . . always, regularly, every day I used to have four or five flashes of that accident. I'd be driving down the highway and I couldn't see what was coming because I'd have a memory flash. I haven't had it once since I wrote the story. You really do ground your nightmares, you *name* them.'' Guilt, it should be clear by now, is an integral part of Gardner's universe, and in ''Redemption'' Gardner attempted a reconciliation with his own private nightmares and misplaced responsibilities.

Death is typically most brutal in its effect on the living, and the tragedy of David Hawthorne's death is felt most clearly by his family. Dale Hawthorne, the father, is profoundly affected, is in fact ''nearly destroyed by it'':

> Sometimes Jack would find him lying on the cow-barn floor, crying, unable to stand up. Dale Hawthorne . . . was a sensitive, intelligent man, by nature a dreamer. . . . He loved all his children and would not consciously have been able to hate his son even if Jack had indeed been, as he thought himself, his brother's murderer. But he could not help sometimes seeming to blame his son, though consciously he blamed only his own unwisdom and—so far as his belief held firm—God. Dale Hawthorne's mind swung violently

at this time, reversing itself almost hour by hour, from desperate faith to the most savage, black-hearted atheism. Every sickly calf, every sow that ate her litter, was a new, sure proof that the religion he'd followed all his life was a lie. Yet skeletons were orderly, as were, he thought, the stars. He was unable to decide, one moment full of rage at God's injustice, the next moment wracked by doubt of His existence.

This disparity, as Nimram calls it, between the real and the ideal hits at Hawthorne as it hits at every person blasted by tragedy and the world's illogic. His mind turns, at times, to suicide and a sort of metaphysical escape, but he ultimately settles on literal physical escape, becoming a fugitive from his family and home. He abandons responsibility, leaves his son, daughter, and wife to mourn their loss among themselves, to survive as *he* hopes to survive.

His wife, Betty, survives in her changedness. She weeps alone at night, and embraces her children ''whenever new waves of guilt swept in.'' She is the emotional center who through her strength of character and sense of love keeps ''her family from wreck.'' Phoebe, the daughter, survives through an abiding child's belief in a God whose wisdom outruns his logic and justice; she sticks unthinkingly, as a girl her age would do, to her faith, tested for the first time by the world's unpredictability.

Jack Hawthorne, too, survives, through a long ordeal of doubt and guilt and sorrow. He doubts his own ability to love and to feel for anyone or anything: ''He'd never loved his brother, he raged out loud, never loved anyone as well as he should have. He was incapable of love, he told himself. . . . He was inherently bad, a spiritual defective. He was evil.'' Jack plummets to the depths of philosophical despair, damning himself for the accident of his brother's death. Like his father, Jack eventually comes to doubt the necessity of his existence, bemired as he is in the certainty of his own damnation: ''The foulness of his nature became clearer and clearer in his mind until, like his father, he began to toy—dully but in morbid earnest now—with the idea of suicide.'' The facticity of death, as Gardner has illustrated before, is the ultimate moral test. It drives us down, sinks us, and challenges us to submit or to respond. If we submit, we become nihilists; if we respond heroically, we rise to love and to believe once again.

Dale Hawthorne responds by returning to his family, who surround him in a tableau of forgiveness: the prodigal father come home. He is a man much changed by his experience; the luster has left his eyes and his body seems empty of its old energy. There is a new sobriety about him that tells you he has faced down tragedy and survived—not necessarily prevailed, but survived. Jack does not immediately perceive the agony his father has suffered, and so rages at him with a censorious sort of hatred. He isolates himself from the family, refuses the consoling, healing influence of those who love him, and turns to his music and to his French horn for solace and some sort of intuitive philosophical comfort.

At the end of the story, Jack visits his horn teacher in Rochester, Arcady Yegudkin, "the General." Yegudkin is an old man, an artist and a sufferer and, with his misshapen wife, a survivor. He is pathetically human—"In his pockets, in scorn of the opinions of fools, he carried condoms, dirty pictures, and grimy, wadded-up dollar bills"—but when he plays the horn, he becomes a god, a transformer of matter into spirit:

> In that large, cork-lined room, it was as if, suddenly, a creature from some other universe had appeared, some realm where feelings become birds and dark sky, and spirit is more solid than stone. The sound was not so much loud as large, too large for a hundred French horns, it seemed. . . . As if charged with life independent of the man, the horn sound fluttered and flew crazily like an enormous trapped hawk hunting frantically for escape. It flew to the bottom of the lower register, the foundation concert F, and crashed below it, and on down and down, as if the horn in Yegudkin's hand had no bottom, then suddenly changed its mind and flew upward in a split-second run to the horn's top E, dropped back to the middle and then ran once more, more fiercely at the E, and this time burst through it and fluttered, manic, in the trumpet range, then lightly dropped back into its own home range and, abruptly, in the middle of a note, stopped. The room still rang, shimmered like a vision. . . . Jack Hawthorne stared at the instrument suspended in space and at his teacher's hairy hands.

On the outer limits of art exists a transmogrified world, a world "suspended in space" and time, a world that Jack Hawthorne longs to know and to explore. For now, however, he can only cry, like Stephen Dedalus, at the beauty and the elusiveness of his vision, and fall once more into the arms of the world around him: his family, his art, his ability to love. There is much to suffer and to enjoy before he can transform the world as Yegudkin can, to take someone soaring and dipping as this artist has taken him. There is always the promise, though, that one's art can and will redeem, will erase the guilt and assuage the pain, will return one's faith and peace-in-sleep. That is the magic of art. . . .

> " The facticity of death, as Gardner has illustrated before, is the ultimate moral test. It drives us down, sinks us, and challenges us to submit or to respond. If we submit, we become nihilists; if we respond heroically, we rise to love and to believe once again."

Source: Gregory L. Morris, "The Art of Living and Other Stories," in *A World of Order and Light: The Fiction of John Gardner*, University of Georgia Press, 1984, pp. 184–205.

Sources

Allen, Bruce. "From Gardner, Short Stories Dimmed by Abstractions," in *The Christian Science Monitor*, June 24, 1981, p. 17.

Caruth, Cathy. *Unclaimed Experience: Trauma, Narrative, and History*, Baltimore: The Johns Hopkins University Press, 1996.

Hartman, Geoffrey H. "On Traumatic Knowledge and Literary Studies," in *New Literary History,* Vol. 26, No. 3, Summer, 1995, pp. 537-63.

Hill, Douglas. "Between the Moral and the Possible," in *Maclean's Magazine*, Vol. 94, No. 23, June 8, 1981, pp. 51-2.

McWilliams, Dean. *John Gardner*, Boston: Twayne, 1990.

Morris, Gregory L. *A World of Order and Light: The Fiction of John Gardner*, Athens: University of Georgia Press, 1984.

Moynahan, Julia. "Moral Fictions," in *The New York Times Book Review*, May 17, 1981, pp. 7, 27-28.

Nutter, Ronald Grant. *A Dream of Peace: Art and Death in the Fiction of John Gardner*, New York: Peter Lang, 1997.

Thompson, Kent. "Intimations of Morality," in *Books in Canada*, Vol. 10, No. 7, August-September, 1981, pp. 9-10.

Winther, Per. *The Art of John Gardner*, Albany: State University of New York Press, 1992.

Further Reading

Christian, Ed. ''An Interview With John Gardner,'' in *Prairie Schooner*, Vol. 54, No. 4, Winter, 1980-81, pp. 70-93.
Important interview for any student interested in Gardner's fiction. The writer discusses his creative process and philosophy of fiction.

Cowart, David. *Arches and Light: The Fiction of John Gardner*, Carbondale: Southern Illinois University Press, 1983.
Views Gardner as moral artist.

Morace, Robert A. *John Gardner: An Annotated Secondary Bibliography*, New York: Garland Publishers, 1984.
Lists interviews, articles, reviews and criticism. Morace also offers helpful annotations to the sources.

Residents and Transients

Bobbie Ann Mason

1982

Bobbie Ann Mason's short story, "Residents and Transients," initially appeared in the *Boston Review*, and was then included in her first collection of short stories, *Shiloh and Other Stories*. The book received nominations for a variety of awards and earned the Ernest Hemingway Foundation Award in 1983. While not as widely anthologized or reviewed as the title story, "Shiloh," "Residents and Transients" is an important story in the collection. Critics and readers praise the story for its tension between past and present, country and city, and childhood and adulthood.

Mason sets "Residents and Transients" in a region she is very familiar with—rural western Kentucky, the area she grew up in and the site of many of her short stories. As in her other work, she writes with a lean, spare style. Her characters speak in the cadences of western Kentucky, and often find themselves bemused by their situations.

"Residents and Transients" is the story of a woman, Mary, caught in a moment of transition. After a long absence, she has returned to live in the home of her parents who have since moved to Florida. Her husband, a salesman, is in Louisville, searching for a new house. She is supposed to sell the house and move to Louisville, but there is a part of her that wants to remain in her hometown. In addition, Mary finds herself caught between two men: her lover, Larry, and her husband Stephen.

She vacillates between two different lives, unable to choose her future.

War. The novel was made into a movie in 1989, starring Bruce Willis and Emily Lloyd.

Author Biography

Bobbie Ann Mason was born in rural Kentucky in 1940. Her father was a farmer, and Mason grew up on the dairy farm he owned. She attended the University of Kentucky and graduated in 1962. Immediately after graduation, Mason moved to New York City where she took a job writing for fan magazines. She earned both a master's degree from the State University of New York-Binghamton in 1966, and a doctoral degree in English from the University of Connecticut in 1972. After a number of years of writing literary criticism and nonfiction, she began to write short stories.

Her story "Offerings" was published in the *New Yorker* in 1980. "Residents and Transients" first appeared in the *Boston Review* in August of 1982 before being included in Mason's first collection of short stories, *Shiloh and Other Stories*. The volume received nominations for a PEN-Faulkner award and the National Book Critics Circle Award. The collection won the 1983 Ernest Hemingway Foundation Award.

The defining characteristic of Mason's fiction is change. Most of her stories are set in rural Kentucky, a region losing its distinctive flavor. Often, her protagonist is a woman at some moment of transition in her life. In the case of "Residents and Transients", her protagonist is at a moment of choice; either she will stay in her childhood home in the countryside, or move to Louisville to live with her "Yankee" husband.

In a conversation with Lila Havens in 1985, Bobbie Ann Mason confirms that one of the themes in her work is that of "residents and transients." She continues, "Some people stay home and others are born to run." Certainly, this describes the situation in the short story, "Residents and Transients."

Since the publication of *Shiloh and Other Stories*, Mason has produced a number of other works. In addition to the short story collection *Love Life: Stories*, Mason has also written a number of well-received novels. Perhaps her most famous is *In Country*, the story of a young woman's search for identity and for truth in the aftermath of the Vietnam

Plot Summary

"Residents and Transients" is set in western Kentucky. The protagonist, Mary, narrates the story in her own voice. She announces in the first paragraph, "Since my husband went away to work in Louisville, I have, to my surprise, taken a lover." From this surprising opening, Mary explains how she finds herself back in Kentucky, living in her former family home.

Three years before the story opens, Mary had returned to Kentucky (after an absence of eight years) in order to care for her ailing parents. Shortly after returning to Kentucky, she married Stephen, a word processor salesman. At the time of her marriage, she agreed to the frequent transfers his job would require, but now, she is not sure that she wants to move away from home again. Nevertheless, Mary herself feels like an outsider in her home community; her long absence has given her an understanding of the world that the local residents do not have.

Before the story opens, Mary's parents have moved to Florida. At the time of the story, Stephen is in Louisville, looking for a house for them to buy. Mary stays in her parents' house because she is responsible for selling the home. She loves the house and is not sure she wants to move to Louisville. Mary spends her days caring for the eight cats her parents left and visiting with her lover of three weeks, Larry, the dentist.

Larry and Mary have known each other since they were children, having both grown up in the same area. Larry is content with his life, and he wants Mary to stay with him. Mary seems ambivalent about both her husband and Larry.

Stephen calls Mary regularly, urging her to come to Louisville to see the house he has picked out, but she is not enthusiastic. She discusses financial transactions and visits to financial planners instead of her feelings.

In an important passage, Mary tries to explain to Larry the difference between residents and transients in the cat population. Although she is ostensibly discussing cats, it is clear that she is really trying to say something about her own status as a resident or a transient. She is not truly a resident, because of her long absence. However, neither is she a transient, at least while she is here in her parents' home.

After eating at a restaurant in Paducah, Larry and Mary are driving home in Larry's truck. In the road, Mary sees a rabbit with its hind legs smashed, trying frantically with its front legs to get off the road. The sight leaves Mary near hysteria. When the couple get back to the house the phone is ringing, and Larry answers without thinking. It is Stephen. Mary tells him she will be coming to Louisville; but instead of hearing her, he lectures her on the need for flexibility. This lecture upsets her, and she rushes outdoors.

Outside, Mary sees one of her cats walking up the drive. The cat's eyes shine red and green. The story ends with this image, the eyes like the image of a traffic light both red and green.

Bobbie Ann Mason

Characters

Larry

Larry is Mary's dentist. A friend of Mary's from childhood, he has never moved away. He is a gentle, quiet man, he is quite content with his life. In addition to his dental practice, he owns his own home and a truck. In contrast to Stephen, Larry is slow and relaxed. Although he is sensitive to Mary's moods and wants to make her happy, he believes that he bores her. He tells Mary that he does not want her to go to Louisville, but wants her to remain in town.

Mary

Mary is the narrator of the story. As the story opens, she announces that she has taken a lover. It is revealed that Mary returned to Kentucky about three years before to take care of her sick parents. Since that time, she has married Stephen and her parents have moved to Florida.

Mary is uncertain what she wants in life. She thinks she wants to settle on the farm; however, the farm is for sale. Stephen, her husband, has gone to Louisville to find them a new home. While her husband is away, Mary begins an affair with her dentist, Larry. The affair leaves her paralyzed with inaction; should she pursue the dentist, or move to Louisville with her husband? As the story ends, she is still waiting for something to happen that will help her decide.

Mary Sue

See Mary

Stephen

Stephen is Mary's husband. He met Mary when he came to Kentucky to sell word processors. As the story opens, he is in Louisville, looking for a new house. He is a salesman, but he does not seem to be doing a very good job of selling Mary on their future together. Furthermore, he does not seem to understand Mary's needs and desires, and often tells Mary how she should feel. Contending that her attachment to her family home is "provincial," he urges her to be more "flexible."

Themes

Change and Transformation

In an interview with Albert Wilhelm, Bobbie Ann Mason maintains that "Literature is principal-

Topics for Further Study

- Mason, Raymond Carver, and Anne Beattie have been called "K-Mart realists." Read several stories by each writer and a few definitions of realism. Do you think the label "K-mart realists" fits each of these writers? Why or why not?

- Research the changing rural landscape of the United States. How much farmland was lost in the 1980s and 1990s? What was built on this land? How do you think this changed the lives of the people who lived there? If possible, interview someone who currently lives on a farm or someone who has moved from a farm to find out more about their lives.

- Read the Dylan Thomas poem, "Fern Hill." What is the subject of the poem? Why does Bobbie Ann Mason allude to the poem in her story?

---

ly about textures and feelings, not themes and symbols, which are sort of like lead weights on the bottom of a shower curtain. They hold it in place and give it shape, but they aren't the curtain itself." Certainly, the textures and feelings in "Residents and Transients" are ones of uncertainty and change. While there is potential for transformation, it is unclear at the end of the story what that transformation may or may not be.

The main character, Mary, finds herself in the middle of both emotional and cultural changes. These are signaled, first, by her return to Kentucky, and second, by her reluctance to move to Louisville with her husband. Although she has been a transient for eight years, and agreed to continue this lifestyle when she married her husband, she seems to reject this lifestyle now. In addition, her surprise at having taken a lover suggests that this is not normal behavior for Mary. Her infidelity must be a symptom of a much bigger problem.

Mason presents a larger cultural change in her story as well. Mary tells the reader that Stephen "is one of those Yankees who are moving into this region with increasing frequency, a fact that disturbs the native residents." Furthermore, Stephen sells word processors. The influx of outside influences—technology, transient lifestyles, northerners—will surely bring with it concomitant cultural change to the quaint region.

Although it is clear by the end of the story that the area is undergoing change and transformation, it is difficult to determine how this ultimately will affect Mary. She is receiving (and sending) conflicting signals, the red and the green lights blinking simultaneously. She is neither resident nor transient, Stephen's nor Larry's. At the conclusion of the story, Mary is still unsure of her future.

Love and Passion

This is a story of a woman who has both a husband and a lover, yet there is little love or passion evident in the story. There is little proof that Mary loves her husband; the closest she comes to even expressing affection for him is when he calls to tell her he has found a house, and she muses, "His voice is so familiar I can almost see him, and I realize that I miss him."

In addition, Mary cannot remember how her affair with Larry began. "I can't remember what signals passed between us, but it was suddenly appropriate that he drop by," she reports. This scarcely seems like the start of a passionate affair. Although "Larry wears a cloudy expression of love," Mary seems to feel only pity for him. Mary's response to the affair is one of surprise, not love or passion. When Larry asks if she wants to stop seeing him because he thinks she is bored, Mary does not reassure him. Although it is clear she does not want to go to Louisville, it is unclear if this has anything to do with Larry.

The only love Mary seems to feel is for the cats, the corn growing in the field, and her mother's canning kitchen. The conclusion of the story is ambiguous. Although Mary tells Stephen she is coming to Louisville to see the house, she seems to retreat from this position when Stephen tells her how to feel. "'You've got to be flexible,' he tells her breezily. 'That kind of romantic emotion is just like flag-waving. It leads to nationalism, fascism—you name it; the very worst kinds of instincts. Listen, Mary, you've got to be more open to the way things are." Mary's response is to rush out of the house, and watch her cat come up the lane.

Style

Images and Imagery

Generally, images are defined as figures of speech that appeal to the senses of the reader. Therefore, there can be visual, auditory, olfactory, tactile, taste, or kinesthetic images. By appealing to the readers' senses, images help make the literature more immediate and visceral. Images often take the form of metaphors or similes, and are symbolic in nature.

Although Bobbie Ann Mason uses simple language in her stories, her images are nonetheless vivid and clear. Early in the story, she uses visual imagery to establish a clear contrast between the house Mary grew up in and the house her husband Stephen wants to buy. Mary says of the old homestead, "I loved its stateliness, the way it rises up from the fields like a patch of mutant jimsonweeds. I'm fond of the old white wood siding, the sagging outbuildings." When Stephen describes the house he has found, it sounds like anyone one of a hundred tract homes one would see in any suburb: "it's a three-bedroom brick with a two-car garage, finished basement, dining alcove, patio . . ."

Mason contrasts concrete images of the natural world with abstract metaphors of the financial world. For example, she makes several references to the corn growing in the field in front of the house. Stephen, on the other hand, speaks in terms of liquid assets and maximizing their potential. The two images coalesce in Mary and Larry's Monopoly game. Mary says, "I shuffle my paper money and it feels like dried corn shucks. I wonder if there is a new board game involving money market funds."

Perhaps the most terrible—yet most important—image in the story is the rabbit in the road. Mason writes, "In the other lane I suddenly see a rabbit move. It is hopping in place, the way runners will run in place. Its forelegs are frantically working, but its rear end has been smashed and it cannot get out of the road." The image is disturbing to Mary, who experiences it as a "tape loop." The image is also disturbing to the reader who realizes Mary's identification with the rabbit.

Barbara Henning asserts that "When a scene ends in Mason's work, it almost always ends with a focus on a specific image." This is certainly true in "Residents and Transients." The final scene of the story is of Brenda the cat, her eyes shining red and green in the porch light. Although readers are uncer-

tain what Mary will decide, the after-image of the cat's eyes is a haunting one.

Allusions

Allusions are references to other works of literature, pop culture, historical events, or fictional or historical characters. Sometimes writers allude to music, drama, or television to give their works immediacy and cultural currency. Mason is noted for her use of allusions from popular culture. In *In Country*, for example, Sam and Emmett watch reruns of the television show *M.A.S.H.* and the characters from the television show almost seem to become characters in the novel. What is notable in "Residents and Transients" is the absence of such allusions. Instead, Mason includes an important allusion to a famous poem by Dylan Thomas. The allusion is an important one for readers to grasp, because it reveals the heart of Mary's anxiety.

In the poem, the poet recalls the days of his youth. "And I was green and carefree, famous among the barns / About the happy yard and singing as the farm was home . . ." Like the poet, Mary longs to return to the days of her childhood. Furthermore, Thomas reflects on the way youths do not care about time and change, although by the last stanza it is clear that he regrets both. As a youth, he did not care that he might "wake to the farm forever fled from the childless land." This is, however, the concern of an adult. Likewise, Mason's use of this allusion suggests that Mary herself has deep anxieties about the sale of her family farm, and that she is leaving the land childless, with no progeny of her own to take over the farm.

Historical Context

A Changing Landscape

Bobbie Ann Mason sets "Residents and Transients" in a rural landscape to underscore the changes both the countryside and her characters are experiencing. Mary's parents have retired and moved to Florida, leaving her to supervise the sale of the farm and the auction of their belongings. The house will soon be lost, and it is likely that the new owners will not farm the land. Such situations were common throughout the 1980s and 1990s across the rural areas of Kentucky. More and more acres, formerly dedicated to farming, were converted to housing

Compare & Contrast

- **1980s:** Unemployment is at 10.8 percent in 1982, a record high since the Great Depression of the 1930s. High inflation rates inhibit economic recovery.

  1990s: The last half of the decade sees low employment rates, low inflation, and a booming economy. In some sectors, notably technology, corporations struggle to attract qualified workers.

- **1980s:** The divorce rate peaks in 1981 at 5.3 divorces for every 1000 people, before falling off slightly in the next few years.

  1990s: While the divorce rate drops slightly, it is still generally thought that one out of every two marriages ends in divorce. The marriage rate continues to drop throughout the decade.

- **1980s:** Many industries move South to take advantage of lower salaries and more favorable tax laws. This leads to a boom across the South and a corresponding slump across the Northeast and Midwest.

  1990s: The rush to the South slows, and there is a recovery in Northern industrial states. However, the population of Southern states continues to rise as aging baby boomers begin to retire.

- **1980s:** A recession slows the housing market and makes it very difficult for sellers, prospective buyers, and real estate companies to do business.

  1990s: Home mortgages reach post-World War II record low rates. Because financing a house is relatively easy, new home construction thrives.

and shopping malls. In Graves County, Kentucky, for example, forty-two percent of all the homes in the county have been built since the 1970s.

Likewise, the demographics of the region are changing at the time of the story. Stephen represents the influx of businessmen from the North; in his case, he is a salesman, selling new technology that brings about further progress. With word processors, modems, Internet access, and electronic mail, no area is too remote, no area remains untouched by technology.

Mary is unlike other Mason female characters who are generally blue-collar, working-poor women. Moreover, Mary does not fit the demographic pattern of the area, emphasizing her role as an outsider. For example, only eleven percent of Kentuckians had been to college in 1980. The implication is that Mary has had at least four years of higher education, and perhaps more than that. In addition, Mary's family, while not wealthy, own land and a farm. Her parents have enough money to retire to Florida. Given that the per capita income in Graves County, Kentucky (Mason's home county),

was only $10,900 in 1985, Mary's financial situation is far better than most of the people around her.

While Stephen and Mary's financial situation seems to be secure, their marriage is not. The divorce rate in the United States peaked in 1981 at 5.3 divorces for every 1000 people. In addition, in the years since Mason wrote her story, the marriage rate has steadily dropped. These figures are in contrast to people the age of Mary's parents who generally married younger and stayed married longer.

In her deft portrayal of the changing countryside, Mason has accurately and poignantly captured a Kentucky in transition. The cultural and social changes provide a rich milieu for Mason's characters.

Critical Overview

After initially appearing in the *Boston Review*, Mason's short story, ''Residents and Transients,'' was collected in her first collection of fiction, *Shiloh and Other Stories*, published in 1982. The volume was favorably received by critics and readers and earned nominations for a National Book Critics Circle Award, an American Book Award, and a PEN/Faulkner Award. Mason also won the 1983 Ernest Hemingway Foundation Award. "Residents and Transients" is considered an important story in the collection.

Reviewers noted Mason's understated prose; her characters speak in convincing dialogue, and it is possible to hear the rural Kentucky dialect in their speech patterns. However, some reviewers disliked this style, suggesting that Mason's characters and stories are both unconvincing and insignificant.

Both Gene Lyons and Anne Tyler offered praise for Mason. Lyons found Mason's simple prose to be a positive characteristic of her work, while Tyler deemed Mason "a full-fledged master of the short story. . . ." She also wrote that although *Shiloh and Other Stories* was Mason's first book of fiction, "there is nothing unformed or merely promising about her."

As noted above, Mason's work was not without detractors. Some critics derided the lack of character development in the stories. Patricia Vigderman suggested that the stories end with "a closeness that seems tacked on. . . ." She also charged that "Mason takes us into her characters' new Kentucky homes and then runs a made-for-TV movie. Her people's emotions come across merely as dots on the screen."

In addition, some reviews faulted Mason for the similarity among her stories. Robert Towers, for example, in *The New York Review of Books* wrote, "Individually effective as they are, there is a degree of sameness to the collection. . . ."

In the years since its publication, the collection continues to generate critical interest. John W. Aldrich, in his book, *Talents and Technicians: Literary Chic and the New Assembly-Line Fiction*, concedes that "one encounters in her work such traditional fictive materials as genuine social environment, characters who take on substance through the complex interacting relationship that is created when people actually inhabit an environment." However, he faults Mason for not giving her characters greater depth and significance. "But what she somehow does not bring to life is their significance, the manner in which their experience tells us something fundamental about the human condition. . . ."

Mason's stories more frequently inspire praise for their portrayal of characters caught in moments of cultural and personal change. Albert Wilhelm writes in *The Southern Literary Journal* that "culture shock and its jarring effects on an individual's sense of identity" is the theme that "dominates the sixteen pieces in *Shiloh and Other Stories*." Maureen Ryan, in an essay in *Women Writers of the Contemporary South*, asserts that Mary is "torn between the serene seductions of an obsolete lifestyle and the intimidating uncertainties of a variable present and future."

Finally, Mason has been classified as a "minimalist," that is, a writer who creates lean, focused prose, filled with concise details. Because of this identification, her work has been compared and contrasted with that of Raymond Carver, Charles Portis, and Ann Beattie. Barbara Henning undertakes such a study in her essay appearing in *Modern Fiction Studies*. In this piece, Henning carefully reads the details in Mason's work. She contends that both Mason's and Carver's characters "have managed to survive without protesting in a world with reduced economic and emotional possibilities. Their anxieties and disappointments are instead displaced through drug and alcohol use and through an even more deadening activity: a steady focus on the random details of everyday life."

Likewise, Richard Giannone, in an article in *Studies in Short Fiction*, focuses on emotional minimalism, suggesting that "the larger themes in the stories arise from the breakdown of intimacy."

Criticism

Diane Andrews Henningfeld

Henningfeld is an associate professor at Adrian College who writes widely on literary topics for educational publishers. In the following essay, she examines the protagonist's fear of adulthood in "Residents and Transients."

Bobbie Ann Mason's short story, "Residents and Transients," first appeared in the *Boston Review* in 1982, shortly before its inclusion in the collection, *Shiloh and Other Stories*. The volume received high critical praise and several nominations for awards, as well as receiving the Ernest Hemingway Foundation Award in 1983. Readers and critics alike have

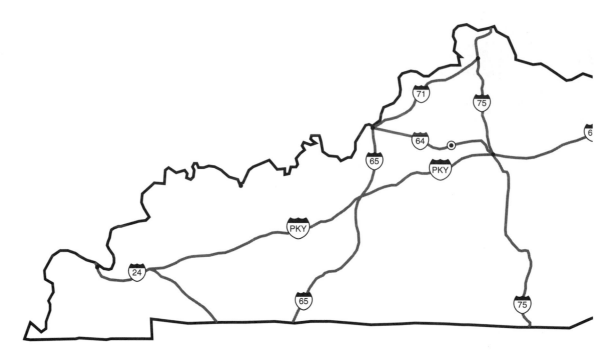

Map of western Kentucky, with the region above the sign for Highway 24 being the general setting for "Residents and Transients."

praised Mason's blunt, straightforward style as well as the way she develops her characters by saying less, rather than more.

"Residents and Transients" has not been anthologized quite so widely as some of Mason's other stories, nor has the story received as much critical attention as her novels. Nevertheless, the story offers a number of interesting features that are worthy of closer examination. Indeed, the story is considerably more complicated than might be thought on first reading.

One of the first features of the story, apparent to anyone who has read Mason's fiction, is that Mary differs from her other female characters in several important ways. In the first place, she left Kentucky for eight years, "pursuing higher learning." Nearly all of Mason's other female characters make their homes in Kentucky and virtually none pursue higher learning. Mason left Kentucky to earn both a master's degree and a doctorate in English, living in the northeast for twenty-eight years before moving back to Kentucky in 1990. The "higher learning" is in all likelihood an advanced degree in English; not only does Mary stay away for eight years, the length of time usually allowed for the completion of a doctorate, she alludes to a Dylan Thomas poem,

"Fern Hill," when she is riding in the plane with Larry.

There are other similarities between the writer and her protagonist. Mason herself grew up on a dairy farm, the same background she gives to Mary. Further, as Mason told Albert Wilhelm in a 1995 interview, "First, you go out into the world in quest of understanding. Then you return to your origins and finally comprehend them. It wasn't until I had pursued my education that I was able to know where the subject of my fiction was. Education has a way of being abstract until you can link it up with experience. I loved the abstractions, but then at some point, I planted a garden, and everything started to come together. Life, art, cats, family, fiction, words, weeds."

Like Mason, Mary wants things to start coming together. She watches the corn grow and she tends to cats. Although it would probably be a mistake to argue too strenuously for an autobiographical link between Bobbie Ann Mason and Mary, certainly Mason has infused Mary with some of her own affection for the land and for cats.

Her story features a series of dichotomies. A dichotomy is a division into two mutually exclusive

What Do I Read Next?

- *In Country* is Bobbie Ann Mason's 1985 novel that chronicles the struggle of Samantha Hughes to understand her dead father in the aftermath of the Vietnam War.

- Bobbie Ann Mason's 1989 collection of short stories, *Love Life*, offers readers another chance to meet the characters that comprise Mason's world.

- *The American Story: Short Stories from the Rea Award* (1993), edited by Michael Rea, presents a superb selection of stories by such authors as Raymond Carver, Joyce Carol Oates, Ann Beattie, Charles Baxter, and Grace Paley.

- *New Women and New Fiction: Short Stories Since the Sixties* is a collection of stories by contemporary women writers such as Cynthia Ozick, Toni Cade Bambara, Anne Tyler, Fay Weldon, and Anne Beattie.

- Raymond Carver's *Where I'm Calling From: New and Selected Stories* (1988) is a collection of stories from one of the important short story writers of the 1980s.

- *The Girl Sleuth: A Feminist Guide to the Bobbsey Twins, Nancy Drew, and Their Sisters* (1975) is Bobbie Ann Mason's intriguing glimpse into the heroines of her childhood.

---

or contradictory groups. By dividing characters, settings, and ideas into two opposite groups, Mason is able to reveal more about each by contrasting it with its opposite. The most obvious dichotomy in the story is the one revealed in its title. Mary explains to Larry the difference between the resident cats and transient cats. This dichotomy also suggests something important about Mary: it is difficult to determine which camp she is in. She is no longer a resident because of her long absence. But she ceased being a transient when she returned to her parents' home. She is caught somewhere in the middle. By establishing oppositions such as this one, Mason reveals this very important feature about Mary: she frequently finds herself caught between two, mutually exclusive oppositions.

Early in the story, Mason contrasts the Kentucky natives with Stephen who is "one of those Yankees who are moving into this region with increasing frequency, a fact which disturbs the native residents." Mary, however, "would not have called Stephen a Yankee," once again revealing her reluctance to classify people or ideas. Mason also divides financial matters and property owners into two groups as well. There are those who prefer "liquid assets," like Stephen, and those who prefer to bury their money in the land, both literally and figuratively. That is, there are those who choose to borrow money to buy property, leaving their cash available for other uses, and those who do not believe in debt, like Mary's parents.

A less obvious contrast in the story is between verbal and non-verbal communication. Stephen is a master of words. Not only does he sell word-processors for a living, he "processes" words when he and Mary talk on the phone or when they visit the financial counselor. His communication is strictly verbal; words are his business and his life. Larry, ironically, who "overhauls" mouths for a living, says very little. He is reticent, quiet and discreet. Again, Mary seems caught in the middle; she is "incoherent" when she speaks to Stephen on the phone, and she falls silent. However, she is also the narrator of the story, the one who relates to the reader what happens. Thus, while she does not "process" words in her conversation with Stephen, she nonetheless is a word processor, someone who links words together to tell a story.

The most important dichotomy in the story, however, is that between childhood and adulthood.

> Her own anxiety over pregnancy is further revealed by her description of her cat, Ellen, who had a vaginal infection, lost a litter of kittens because of an x-ray, and eventually had to be spayed."

There are many clues to suggest that Mary is attempting to return to her childhood. Her allusion to the poem "Fern Hill" by Dylan Thomas underscores this desire. In "Fern Hill," Thomas recalls his own "green" childhood, with longing and nostalgia. Furthermore, Mary is at the moment of transition when she will need to move away from childhood and into adulthood, with all the responsibilities and cares that such a move entails. She is fearful and resistant to making the change. When the story opens, the reader finds that Mary has moved back to Kentucky, to her childhood home, to care for her failing parents. Yet her parents leave Kentucky shortly thereafter to live in Florida, leaving Mary metaphorically orphaned. Their absence, however, signals that it is Mary's turn to take on the responsibility of a household.

Perhaps less obvious, but no less important, is the implication that it is time for Mary to start a family of her own. Certainly, Stephen's search for a home suggests his need to settle down and start a family. Mary's resistance to not only moving to Louisville but also to even visiting Stephen seems to symbolize a deeply rooted fear of sex, pregnancy, and motherhood.

There are many clues pointing in this direction. First, Mary has directed her own maternal instincts toward the cats. She says, "They seem to be my responsibility, like some sins I have committed, like illegitimate children." It would be possible to argue that the sin is her failure to procreate, to carry on her family line. Second, her affair with Larry is essentially immature, as evidenced by Mason's description of them as children. The first time he comes to the house, Larry brings ice cream and drives a truck

with "a chrome streak on it that makes it look like a rocket, and on the doors it has flames painted." While such a truck might be appropriate for a teenager out to see his girlfriend, it seems less appropriate for a divorced dentist pursuing an adulterous affair. Larry does not call her Mary, but Mary Sue, her childhood name. They play Monopoly, and go to eat at a restaurant "where you choose your food from pictures on a wall."

Certainly, nothing in this relationship suggests that two adults are involved. The most obvious absence in the story is any mention of sex. Although Mary and Larry are lovers, the only reference Mary makes to their lovemaking is to note that the "Cats march up and down the bed while we are in it." There are other subtle clues that Mary fears both sex and pregnancy; in some cases, Mason uses phallic symbols to suggest Mary's apprehension about sexual intimacy. For example, when Larry first comes to the house, he frightens Mary by looking in her mouth. Later, she reports that she will not let him get near her mouth. "I clamp my teeth shut and grin widely, fighting off imaginary drills."

While Mary remains in her parents house, away from Stephen, she can avoid pregnancy and motherhood, even though she seems aware of her own biological clock: "I am nearly thirty years old. I have two men, eight cats, no cavities."

Her own anxiety over pregnancy is further revealed by her description of her cat, Ellen, who had a vaginal infection, lost a litter of kittens because of an x-ray, and eventually had to be spayed. Although Mary does not directly relate her worry over the cat to her own body, she nonetheless writes her parents in great detail. She seems unhappy that they do not respond, as if she wants reassurance from them. In the same paragraph, Mary mentions again the house that Stephen wants to buy, indirectly reminding the reader that playing house and keeping house are two different propositions.

The most graphic image appears near the end of the story. Larry suggests that they break up, asserting that he thinks she is bored with him. Mary does not deny this. When Larry says that he wants her to stay with him, Mary responds, "I wish it could be that way. . . . I wish that was right." As soon as Mary implies that staying with him is not right, and that she should go to Louisville, they come upon a rabbit, struggling in the road. "It is hopping in place, the way runners will run in place. Its forelegs are frantically working, but its rear end has been smashed and it cannot get out of the road.'' Mary seems to identify with the rabbit to such an extent that she is incoherent when her husband calls. Moreover, there is little doubt that the rabbit will die, reminding the reader of an old euphemism for pregnancy. Years ago, when people said, ''The rabbit died,'' they meant that a woman's pregnancy test had come back positive.

As the story closes, Mary obliviously shreds the Monopoly money in her hand as she talks to Stephen. Whether or not she will make the next step, from play money to real money, from playing house to keeping house, from illegitimate cats to real babies, is unclear at the end of the story. Like the rabbit, she is caught in the light, neither here nor there, and she waits ''for the light to change.''

Source: Diane Andrews Henningfeld, for *Short Stories for Students*, The Gale Group, 2000.

Thomas E. Barden

Barden is Professor of American Studies and Director of Graduate Studies at the University of Toledo. In the following essay, he discusses thematic and stylistic aspects of the story.

The short story ''Residents and Transients'' is at the center of her 1983 volume *Shiloh and Other Stories* for a reason. Mason confirmed the story's importance in an interview with Wendy Smith in *Publisher's Weekly* shortly after the collection appeared. ''‘Residents and Transients’ is a focal point for the main theme of *Shiloh and Other Stories*, which is the tension between hanging on to the past and racing toward the future'' (*Publisher's Weekly*, 30 August, 1985). The story is significant in its own right—it is a jewel of finely-crafted language and dense symbolic atmosphere and it develops several themes that are fundamental to Mason's work.

This essay will explore the theme of the tension between the past and future in the story in terms of three symbols—the cats that populate the narrator's farmhouse, the *Monopoly* game she plays with her lover, and a half-crushed rabbit they see in the road. It will connect the past/future theme to the one referenced in the story's title, namely the tension between mobility and rootedness. And it will look at some of the methods Mason uses to bring human emotion and complexity to these matters, which in less talented hands could easily have devolved into impersonal socio-economic musings about the new South.

> **Mason's artistic achievement in this story lies in her ability to draw such memorable images and symbols out of the mundane stuff of everyday life--cats, board games, and road-kill."**

As is typical of Mason's economy of language, the first sentence of ''Residents and Transients'' accomplishes a lot in seventeen words. It introduces the three characters: the narrator Mary, her husband, and her lover. In addition, it presents the story's general locale, Kentucky—and, by contrast with Louisville, sets up a rural/urban setting polarity.

Furthermore, it establishes the narrator's oddly passive voice at the outset. She says she is surprised by her own act of having ''taken a lover'' and seems disconnected from it, at least as she reveals herself to her reader. The rest of the paragraph continues in this vein, introducing Mary's dilemma—her husband's involvement in the ''race toward the future'' (he works for a corporation that keeps him constantly moving in an urban world) and her vacillating desire to ''hang on to the past'' by staying in the rural area where she grew up.

The tension between the past and future is quickly presented and personified in the two men in the narrator's life, her husband and her lover. Her husband Stephen is ''one of those Yankees who are moving in;'' her lover, Larry, is a local she has known since high school. As a ''Yankee'' and a native Kentuckian respectively, the two represent the North and the South. This distinction remains significant in Bobbie Ann Mason's contemporary Kentucky because it creates a sense of displacement from 1980s Reagan-era sunbelt America. Mason juxtaposes the local country hicks with people who say ''you guys'' in a Northern brogue, smoke marijuana, and travel to Europe. Even though the old culture of the ''lost cause'' South has been overrun by brand names and subdivisions, these locals feel both cut off from their past and unable to connect with the future that is springing up all around them.

The basic polarity of the story is *past-Southern-rural-simple-resident* versus *future-Northern-urban-sophisticated-transient*, and its dramatic core is Mary's need (but inability) to decide which world to commit to. Her affair with Larry, which she suggests occurred almost without her conscious involvement, is a half- hearted attempt to resist Stephen's orbit of job changes, word processors, and investment counseling. Yet she is unable to hide her boredom with Larry and his provincial life of "smocks and drills" and quiet contentment. She, after all, is a world traveler who has pursued "higher learning" and was one of the first female porters on the National Limited railroad. He is a rural dentist who drives a Ford Ranger and is obviously much more in love with Mary than she is with him.

The cats that live in Mary's parents' old farmhouse constitute the story's major symbol. These eight felines are connected to Mary symbolically, as Mason makes clear when she has her absent-mindedly include herself when she counts them. She reinforces the connection by having Larry unconsciously link Mary and the cats as well. She has the narrator casually point out that "Larry strokes a cat with one hand and my hair with the other." Knowing each cat by name, Mary's character fits nicely with their feline aloofness, their attachment to the farmhouse, and their lack of attachment to anything else.

The cats came with the farm, which places them with the rural past—but they are also cruel to rabbits and homeless cats, which associates them with the "dog eat dog" world of her husband. The cats gang up on transients after initially making them feel at home. After mentioning this cruel feline trait, Mary tells Larry about reading she has done on cat behavior in the wild. The story's title comes from this passage. The issue Mary ponders regarding cats is the same as her own—namely whether it is better to establish a permanent residence or to commit to being a transient, whether she should stay in her parents' country farmhouse with Larry or follow her husband into a rootless future of corporate moves and upward mobility.

Mary explains to Larry, who appears to be interested in everything she has to say, that scientists used to think "resident" cat populations that committed to specific territory were the most successful groups in the wild and that the transients were considered "the bums, the losers." But now this theory has been questioned; the new idea being that maybe the transients are the superior ones, at least the more intelligent. The paradox of all this, of course, is that in Mary's case being a "resident" would mean leaving her marriage, because the marriage is based on the "transient" contemporary lifestyle. To stay (geographically) she has to leave (relationship-wise). She is as confused as the scientists. To be a resident or a transient, that is the question—for cats and for Mary. The story takes place during an interlude of avoiding that inevitable decision.

Like the cats, the board game *Monopoly* symbolically renders the tension between wandering and putting down roots. As a symbol, *Monopoly* aptly combines the idea of aimless meandering with the world of financial investing, mortgage strategies, and getting ahead by "playing the game." Mason reserves her sharpest satire in the story for the idea of money management, having Mary recall a session with a financial counselor who used terminology like "fluid assets" and investment "postures that will maximize your potential." The words remind her of a weird sex therapist's advice.

The *Monopoly* game is the subtext of an evening Larry and Mary spend together, the same one in which they have their cat discussion. It is a curious thing for new lovers to be doing; in a sense the game is taking the place of intimacy for them, just as financial talk substitutes for intimacy between Mary and her husband Stephen. Their long distance calls are mostly about money and/or their new house in Louisville. (It should be noted here that the use of the common brand name game is also a good example of the popular culture many critics have noted as a conspicuous feature of Mason's work.)

While the cats and the *Monopoly* game subtly symbolize the tension Mary feels between following her husband to Louisville and staying with her lover in the country, the wounded rabbit she sees in the road is a blatant and dramatic representation of this conflict. It is an example of what fellow writer Raymond Carver (in the jacket notes to *Shiloh and Other Stories*) called the "aftereffect image" in Mason's fiction—her tendency to create images that, long after one has finished the story, burn in the mind as a vivid and disturbing pictures. Rabbits are mentioned casually earlier in the story—dead ones the cats bring in. Yet in this scene Mary is traumatized by what she sees. As she and Larry are driving back from a restaurant they come across a rabbit that has been hit. "It is hopping in place, the way runners will run in place. Its forelegs are frantically working, but its rear end has been smashed and it cannot get out of the road.''

This image is the closest thing to a climax in this story that, for the most part, carefully avoids the dramatic. The sight of the mangled creature sends Mary into a fit of hysterics. She is inconsolable, and when her husband calls and her lover answers the phone, her whole indecision comes to an abrupt end. Trying to deflect her husband's suspicion about Larry, she hurriedly commits to coming to Louisville, ostensibly ending her affair. In a clever punning reference to the farmhouse felines, Mary says she will have to swear to Stephen ''on a stack of cats'' that nothing sexual is going on. As she and Stephen discuss her ''attachment to place'' and her ''need to be flexible,'' Mary finds herself nervously tearing up the *Monopoly* money she holds in her hands.

Mary has not really resolved her quandary, and her frantic need to do something is both triggered and epitomized by the grisly rabbit image—she sees herself as a helpless creature who is hurt, confused, stuck and immobile, but frantically attempting to move. Mason deftly converges the story's symbols here—the cats, *Monopoly*, and the dying rabbit— and then closes with another striking visual image, the night glow of one of her cats' eyes that appear as one red and one green. Both small animal ''aftereffect images'' combine to make Mary realize the depth of her inner conflict. She thinks of the red and green glow in the cat's eyes as mixed signals from a traffic light, an objective correlative of her indecision.

Mason's artistic achievement in this story lies in her ability to draw such memorable images and symbols out of the mundane stuff of everyday life— cats, board games, and road-kill. But the tone of the story also adds to its success. The flat, emotionless affect of her narrator creates an ambiguity between what is being said and how it is being said. In the mangled rabbit episode, for example, she states that she becomes hysterical. But the reader is never privy to that level of emotion. It is as if the hysteria is happening a long way off. Another example is in the previously mentioned first sentence. Mary says she is cheating on her husband, but she says it as if it were something interesting she read in the newspaper.

Mason has discussed this aspect of her style in an interview in *Contemporary Literature*. ''I try to approximate language that's very blunt and Anglo-Saxon. A lot of this is not just meaning but the sound of the words and the rhythm of the words'' (*Contemporary Literature*, 32, [1991]). Note the phrase

''not just meaning'' here; that indicates that to Mason, meaning is part of the intent of this style. The flat, ''just the facts'' tone of the narrator produces an aura of numbness. One gets the impression Mary is in a kind of shock, like the mangled rabbit, and that she has ironically separated herself from her own existence. Her experience of college is termed ''higher learning.'' When Larry asks if she is bored with him and if he should stop coming to see her, her answer is ''I don't know.''

Many critics have noted Mason's use of rock and roll as a reference in her stories, but in ''Residents and Transients'' she makes one of her rare references to formal literature. The poem the narrator thinks of, but characteristically cannot recall the name of, is Dylan Thomas's ''Fern Hill,'' a beautiful lyric of nostalgia for Thomas's Welsh childhood before he realized the fleeting nature of life and joy. Mary is also nostalgic for her lost past, but she is ironic and arch rather than lyrical about it. Another poetic Dylan, Bob, has penned a line that fits Mary's attitude better than the Welshman's. Dylan's song, ''The Man in the Long Black Coat,'' which coincidentally is also about infidelity, has a line that fits Mary's character to a tee—''people don't live or die, people just float.'' And it is the flat voicing Mason gives her narrator that so effectively conveys this mood.

Source: Thomas E. Barden, ''Symbol and Voice in Bobbie Ann Mason's 'Residents and Transients,''' for *Short Stories for Students*, The Gale Group, 2000.

Liz Brent
Brent has a Ph.D. in American Culture, with a specialization in American cinema, from the University of Michigan. She is a freelance writer/editor and film critic and teaches courses in American cinema. In the following essay, she considers the main character's desire to hang onto her memories of her family farmhouse and small Southern hometown way of life, which is rapidly slipping away from her.

Bobby Ann Mason is a Southern writer known for her stories that express a strong sense of *place*. ''Residents and Transients,'' as the title suggests, is about a woman who is torn between her attachment to her hometown and family farmhouse, where she has been a ''resident'' most of her life, and her attachment to her marriage, which necessitates a ''transient'' lifestyle, as her husband's job requires that they move every few years.

"In some ways, Mary's story is like the mournful 'yowling of a homeless cat,' an expression of her own mourning over the impending loss of her childhood home, and the sense of homelessness it will bring."

On one level, Mary, the narrator, is torn between the two men in her life, her husband and her lover. At a deeper level, however, each man is associated with Mary's two choices: her lover, Larry, is associated with remaining a "resident" in her home town, while her husband, Stephen, is associated with the "transient" life that comes with his job. At the story's opening, Stephen has gone to Louisville, Kentucky, where he has recently been transferred, to look for a new house.

Mary's attachment to Larry is based on his associations with her hometown, family farmhouse, and childhood memories. The two grew up together, he has never moved out of town (and never will), and he even calls her by her childhood name, "Mary Sue." Larry appeals to Mary's sense of home because he wants her to stay there with him. "'You shouldn't go to Louisville,' he pleads. 'This part of Kentucky is the prettiest. I wouldn't change it for anything.'" This deep-rooted attachment to place is also characteristic of the town's residents: "Most people around here would rather die than leave town."

Mary's attachment to her husband, Stephen, on the other hand, necessitates a more "mobile," "flexible" and modern lifestyle in which one doesn't develop any great attachment to a particular location, but is willing to pick up and move anywhere in pursuit of better professional and financial opportunities. His job requires "frequent transfers," from one location to another. Mary even describes him as one of the Yankee outsiders, from the North, who have begun to "invade" her community. This "invasion" of the town represents an element of change which threatens to outmode its rustic, "provincial"

Southern character. Mary explains that this change "disturbs the native residents," herself included.

In the opening paragraph, Mary expresses her strong desire to be a "resident," to stay where she is, in her family farmhouse, in her hometown. "I do not want to go to Louisville. I do not want to go anywhere." A considerable amount of the story is taken up with Mary's loving descriptions of the land and the house. There is a strong sense of *nostalgia* —a longing for, or clinging to, fond memories of a past that is quickly slipping way—in these descriptions. For instance, Mary's description of the farmhouse is rich with majesty and affection: "I love its stateliness, the way it rises up from the fields like a patch of mutant jimsonweeds." The evidence of decay in Mary's description further expresses a strong sense of nostalgia: "I'm fond of the old white wood siding, the sagging outbuildings."

Mary's attachment to her family home even focuses on particular rooms of the house which evoke images of a simpler, more traditional lifestyle. Her description of the "canning kitchen" ties her nostalgia for the house to associations with childhood memories of her mother's old-fashioned home cooking: "The canning kitchen was my mother's pride. There, she processed her green beans twenty minutes in a pressure canner, and her tomato juice fifteen minutes in a water bath."

Even the *view* from the canning kitchen is described in panoramic beauty.

> From the canning kitchen, Larry and I have a good view of the cornfields. A cross-breeze makes this the coolest and most pleasant place to be. The house is in the center of the cornfields, and a dirt lane leads out to the road, about half a mile away.

The great sense of loss Mary feels in seeing even her parents let go of this traditional, rural lifestyle is particularly poignant. Mary's rich associations with her mother's practice of canning her own food is exchanged for the empty, modern practice of grocery shopping: "Now my mother lives in a mobile home. In her letters she tells me all the prices of the foods she buys."

Yet Mary's husband expects her to leave this countryside, rich with association, in order to live in a neighborhood that she disdainfully describes as having other "houses within view." Stephen's description of the new house he has picked out for them in Louisville only intensifies her distaste for modern homes. He describes it as "a three-bedroom brick with a two-car garage, finished basement, dining alcove, patio-"

"Does it have a canning kitchen?" I want to know. Stephen laughs. "No, but it has a rec room." I quake at the thought of a rec room.

Mary clings nostalgically not just to the land and the house, but to many of the *objects* associated with farm life.

"This place is full of junk that no one could throw away," I say distractedly, I'm thinking of the boxes in the attic, the rusted tools in the barn. In a cabinet in the canning kitchen I found some Bag Balm, antiseptic salve to soften cows' udders.

When she and Larry are eating at a cheap diner one night, Mary notices a "framed arrangement of farm tools" hanging on the restaurant wall for decoration. "Other objects—saw handles, scythes pulleys—were mounted on wood like fish trophies." The fact that these farm tools have been framed and hung up on a wall for decoration indicates that they no longer function as *tools*, but have become *artifacts*—remnants of a past way of life no longer useful in the modern world. It's as if they've become museum pieces. Mary is immediately reminded of the tools left in the barn of her family farmhouse, and wonders what they "would look like on the wall of a restaurant." By making this connection between the framed tools on the wall and her father's old tools at home, Mary is faced with acknowledging that the way of life she is clinging to is outdated, a historical relic, no longer a viable option for her in the modern world.

Mary's husband, Stephen, looks down on Mary's attachment to her hometown, telling her it is outdated. "Those attachments to place are so provincial," he tells her. The word "provincial" suggests a small-town, ignorant, behind-the-times outlook on the world. He chides Mary for not having a more modern, up-to-date attitude: "Listen, Mary, you've got to be more open to the way things are," he tells her. Rather than a traditional, old-fashioned, small-town attitude, Stephen tells her she needs to develop a modern, detached attitude toward where and how she wants to live: "You've got to be more flexible," he says.

Even Mary's parents seem to have let go of their home town and family farmhouse in pursuit of a more modern, less rustic, lifestyle. The mobile home in which they are living suggests both a temporary residence and the idea of mobility, which suggests a lack of attachment to any particular location. Furthermore, "their minds are on the condominium they are planning to buy when this farm is sold." Yet Mary's sentiments are the opposite of her parents. "Now they have moved to Florida, but I have stayed here, wondering why I ever went away."

The title of this story, "Residents and Transients," refers literally to Mary's explanation of the "two kinds of cats" that live in the wild, "residents and transients." As the central metaphor of the story, Mary's discussion of these "two kinds of cats" provides a key to understanding her fundamental struggles. Interpreting the cats as metaphors allows for an interpretation of the distinction between "residents" and "transients" as applying to two kinds of *people*: "Some stay put, in their fixed home ranges, and others are on the move. They don't have real homes."

Mary's dilemma is whether or not to "stay put" in her childhood home, her "fixed home range," or follow her husband, who is always "on the move," and has no "real" home. As Mary goes on to discuss these distinctions, she expresses her ambivalence as to whether "staying put" is or isn't really a better option than being "on the move."

"Everybody always thought that the ones who establish the territories are the most successful. They are the strongest, while the transients are the bums and losers."

Mary's description of the "resident" cats characterizes what people *used to* think was the better, more "successful" way to live—to spend one's whole life in one's home town, maintaining a strong attachment to the land. Likewise, a more traditional attitude maintains the perspective that "transients" are "bums and losers." But, again, applying Mary's description to human beings, one can see that the uncertainty of today's "scientists" as to which type of cat is superior is again an expression of Mary's confusion as to which type of lifestyle is better for *her*.

"The thing is—this is what the scientists are wondering about now—it may be that the transients are the superior ones after all, with the greatest curiosity and most intelligence."

Mary ends this explanation with the conclusion that the scientists "can't decide" which type of cat is superior. Again, it is Mary herself who "can't decide" whether to stay where she is or to move on with her husband. In response, Larry inadvertently adds to this metaphor by responding that, "none of this is true of domestic cats." As it is clear that Mary is, by nature, a "domestic cat," Larry's comment that they are "all screwed up" is again indicative of Mary's feelings of being "all screwed up" by her out-dated attachment to the small town farm life of her childhood.

Mary's connection to the cats is indicated in other ways, as well. She even inadvertently categorizes herself as a cat: "One day I was counting the cats and I absentmindedly counted myself." One night she hears a cat, not one of hers, yowling outside her house. "There's nothing so mournful as the yowling of a homeless cat," she says. Mary herself fears becoming like a "homeless cat" if she loses her family home. In some ways, Mary's story is like the mournful "yowling of a homeless cat," an expression of her own mourning over the impending loss of her childhood home, and the sense of homelessness it will bring.

A disturbing image toward the end of the story serves as a metaphor by which Mary comes closer to an understanding of the nature of her dilemma. Driving home one night with Larry, Mary notices a rabbit at the side of the road.

> It is hopping in place, the way runners will run in place. Its forelegs are frantically working, but its rear end has been smashed and it cannot get out of the road.

Like Mary, the rabbit is stuck in one place, its "forelegs are frantically working," an image which resonates with Mary's "frantic" efforts at moving forward into her future. Yet, despite this effort, the rabbit remains where it is, "running in place." In other words, it is as if Mary were *going through the motions* of preparing to move to a new house in Louisville with her husband, yet, for all her efforts, remains stuck in the old house, as if "running in place." Furthermore, the rabbit's back legs have been smashed, so that it is stuck in the road, and cannot move at all. Again, as a metaphor, this correlates with Mary's situation, as her "back legs," or her childhood memories of her home town, have been permanently damaged, in terms of being a part of a past she will never be able to recover. Yet, the sense of emotional loss she feels in clinging to this past leaves Mary, like the rabbit, in a state of agony and unable to move forward.

Source: Liz Brent, for *Short Stories for Students*, The Gale Group, 2000.

G. O. Morphew

In the following excerpt, Morphew examines the qualities of Mason's heroines: their socio-economic status among the rural poor of Kentucky and their feminist struggle to achieve "breathing space in their relationships with their men."

Much has been written about the loss of identity experienced by the characters of Bobbie Ann Mason's short stories; the people of *Shiloh and Other Stories* in particular seem to be confused by the onslaught of pop culture, the media, and other forces of social change. The males, perhaps, seem the more affected, and more ineffectual in their attempts to seize or to create some new center for their lives. The women, at least most of them, react to their frustration and discontent more forcefully; they are or become downhome feminists, and the degree of their feminist responses within their culture is largely determined by education, by economic empowerment, and by age, or by some combination of the three.

Almost all of Mason's characters come *from* the rural poor. This is not to say they *are* poor, either in a strict financial or cultural sense. The older characters, survivors of the deprivations of the Great Depression, have jobs that afford them a comfortable if not luxurious lifestyle; some, like Bill, the retired farmer of "The Ocean," can even afford a "big camper cruiser," which he proudly captains around the backwaters of America even if it is a far cry from the destroyer he served on as a youth during World War II.

The culture of Western Kentucky, although unsophisticated in comparison to the big cities of the East, where so many of the more ambitious characters go, has a solidity, a sophistication even, of its own. In "Nancy Culpepper," the main character, a woman who had fled the unpromising life of her Kentucky youth only to return years later, hears her mother say, "We'll never go anywhere. We've got our dress tail on a bedpost." Puzzled, Nancy asks her mother the meaning of the expression. Her mother gives it, adding, "I guess you think we're just ignorant . . . The way we talk." Nancy responds, "No, I don't." And she doesn't, because this folksy saying is exactly one of the little things that richly differentiate her culture, a culture she once dismissed as backward but now the source of an irresistible longing. (She has used the impending move of her grandmother into a nursing home to justify her visiting her relatives, but she is aware this is really an excuse to test her vague desire to move back to Kentucky.)

It is important to see that the downhome feminists of these stories do not want what their city cousins want: equal legal and political rights, equal access to careers, equal pay, government support of child care, and so on. Mason's women simply want breathing space in their relationships with their men. Sometimes only divorce, always initiated by the women, will provide the degree of change these women seek but sometimes their assertiveness merely aims for a change of pace—casual adultery, for example.

The culture of Mason's Western Kentucky is focused on the lower class, defined by a general lack of higher education, by consumer taste, and, increasingly, by choice of leisure activity. Mason's characters have enough discretionary income to buy such big-ticket items as campers and organs, and enough time to take continuing education classes, or, in the case of Shelby, the preacher in "The Retreat," even the flexibility to follow an avocation which does not support him and his family (he is an electrician during the week). . . .

The most educated women in the book follow a decidely different path in their relationship with their men. Their problems are not as dramatic as their lesser-educated counterparts and their solutions are more ambivalent. Nancy Culpepper was married in 1967 in Massachusetts, where she had gone for graduate school. Her husband, Jack, a Yankee, set up his photography business near Philadelphia after the wedding. Nancy's marriage has produced both a son and relative happiness yet she can't shake a longing for her Kentucky roots, which, to her consternation, were on her mind even during her wedding night. After the ceremony Jack takes Nancy outside to look for the northern lights. She searches the sky diligently but she "kept thinking of her parents at home, probably watching *Gunsmoke*." The *Joy of Cooking*, a wedding gift, makes her wonder what her parents are eating at that very moment. Clumsily, she dances with Jack to a Beatles album. There are no stopping places in the songs and this upsets her: "She was crying. 'Songs used to have stopping places in between.'"

When Nancy learns that she had an ancestor also named Nancy Culpepper, she begins to go by her maiden name. A few years later she insists on visiting Kentucky to help her parents with her invalid grandmother and to look for some lost pictures belonging to her grandmother. Nancy hopes some of the pictures will be of her namesake. This is the catalyst Nancy has been waiting for because lately she had "been vaguely wanting to move to Kentucky." Thus her feminist search for identity is curiously, even atavistically linked to a search for

> **"** Bobbie Ann Mason has an uncanny ability to capture the state of mind of the women of rural Western Kentucky in the 1970s. As that culture becomes more homogenized, more integrated with the general American culture, these women will lose their special identity and their special problems."

roots. She is willing to put a strain on her immediate family in conducting this search: both her husband and her son resent her staying away so long. During a telephone conversation Jack says, "We're your family too." And her son hangs up without saying goodbye, much to Nancy's distress; moreover, neither husband nor son wants to move to Kentucky.

At the end of the story, the grandmother's photo album is found but the grandmother and Nancy's mother disagree on which person in a group picture is the original Nancy Culpepper. The confusion surrounding the identity of the original Nancy perfectly reflects the confusion of identity of the contemporary Nancy. The ending, with Nancy staring both at the woman her grandmother had thought was Nancy's ancestor and at the woman's husband, emphasizes the ambivalence of Nancy's situation:

> This young woman would be glad to dance to "Lucy in the Sky with Diamonds" on her wedding day, Nancy thinks. The man seems bewildered, as if he did not know what to expect, marrying a woman who has her eyes fixed on something so far away.

At that moment Nancy's own husband is far away and he is as uncertain as the reader about Nancy's next move.

The main character of "Residents and Transients," the first-person narrator, has many things in common with Nancy Culpepper. She, too, left Kentucky for "higher learning," which in her case took eight years. She also came back to Kentucky on a family matter, specifically because her parents were in poor health. Even after her parents are recovered and moved to Florida and even though she admits she feels like an outsider, the narrator has stayed on because, like Nancy, she felt the tug of her roots. Or, as she puts it, . . . I have stayed here, wondering why I ever went away.'' And she has a Yankee husband, whom she met when he was transferred by his company into the area.

This woman's story is that she is bored in the absence of her husband, who has been transferred again, to Louisville. He is looking for a house there, while she remains on the farm to oversee the auction of household goods for her parents when the farm is sold. She has taken a lover, her dentist, Larry. That she has been unfaithful to her husband sets her apart from Norma Jean and the others. Although she is somewhat surprised at her behavior, she has the air of a big-city sophisticate, a woman who does what she wants, including what some men have done all along: have a satisfying affair and a satisfying marriage at the same time. The key to her attitude is revealed in a lecture she delivers to Larry about cats:

> "In the wild, there are two kinds of cat populations," I tell him when he finishes his move. "Residents and transients. Some stay put, in their fixed home ranges, and others are on the move. They don't have real homes. Everybody always thought that the ones who establish the territories are the most successful—like the capitalists who get ahold of Park Place."... "They are the strongest, while the transients are the bums, the losers." "The thing is—this is what the scientists are wondering about now—it may be that the transients are the superior ones after all, with the greatest curiosity and most intelligence. They can't decide."

The narrator decides that she misses her husband and that she is going to join him in Louisville. However, one gathers, she would be just as happy without him. The risks she takes while having her fling—going out to dinner with Larry where she may be recognized, even allowing Larry to answer her phone—illustrate confidence, a sense of her *own* superiority. Her identifying with the transient cats is made explicit in the last five lines of the story:

> I see a cat's flaming eyes coming up the lane to the house. One eye is green and one is red, like a traffic light. It is Brenda, my odd-eyed cat. Her blue eye shines red and her yellow eye shines green. In a moment I realize that I am waiting for the light to change.

She is a transient and transients are just as likely to leave mates as they are to leave territories.

Bobbie Ann Mason has an uncanny ability to capture the state of mind of the women of rural Western Kentucky in the 1970s. As that culture becomes more homogenized, more integrated with the general American culture, these women will lose their special identity and their special problems. They will become more like Nancy Culpepper and the narrator of "Residents and Transients" as they become better educated and more economically independent. They will have more complex relationships with their men and families; their lives will be more refined, more introspective—and the trade-off in vigor and earthiness may leave them far less interesting.

Source: G. O. Morphew, "Downhome Feminists in 'Shiloh' and Other Stories," in *Southern Literary Journal*, Vol. XXI, No. 2, Spring, 1989, pp. 41–49.

Maureen Ryan

In the following excerpt, Ryan emphasizes the struggles of Mason's heroines in facing change and their impulses either to cling to the security of the past or to look for something better in a new life.

"Old Things" demonstrates most poignantly the authority of the past in Mason's world. Cleo Watkins is perplexed by the modern predilection for antiques, for she "has spent years trying to get rid of things she has collected. . . . She doesn't want to live in the past." Cleo does not perceive that her avoidance of life, her discontent with contemporary society, anchor her in a past that no longer exists. "Kids never seem to care about anything anymore," she reflects bitterly when her grandchildren act oblivious to their cluttered surroundings, and "she has put a chain on the door, because young people are going wild, breaking in on defenseless older women." Cleo envies a friend who has just taken a trip out West but maintains that she could not "take off like that" because "now there are too many maniacs on the road."

Although she declares that "there's no use trying to hang on to anything. You just lose it all in the end. You might as well not care," the story's denouement teaches Cleo that some of the past cannot—and should not—be forgotten. At a flea market, amidst the Depression glass and rusty farm tools, she spots a familiar object, a miniature whatnot in which her husband used to keep his stamps and receipts. At the sight of the small box, with its drawers that form a scene of a train running through the meadow, Cleo's ''blood is rushing to her head and her stomach is churning.'' As the story ends, she pays three dollars (too much) for the piece and, looking at the train, imagines that her happy family is aboard, crossing the valley, heading West: ''Cleo is following unafraid in the caboose, as the train passes through the golden meadow and they all wave at the future and smile perfect smiles.'' Although the past offers quiet solace from the hectic pace of modern life, Mason is aware of the dangers of ignoring the inexorable changes of society. Cleo, with her refusal to adapt to contemporary culture, personifies another Mason theme—the inordinate fear of life in this strange new world. At fifty-two Cleo feels and acts like an old woman; ''everything seems to distress her, she notices.'' Mack Skaggs is also relatively young (in his late forties), but his agoraphobia and his ineffectual attempts to keep up with his college-student daughter (he struggles with *The Encyclopedia of Philosophy* only to discover that she is studying physics) are the pathetic actions and attitudes of a man completely overwhelmed by the world around him. In ''Still Life with Watermelon,'' Louise's husband goes off to Texas without her because, he claims, she is ''afraid to try new things.'' She is initially angry at his accusations and his wanderlust, but at his return her feelings change. ''Something about the conflicting impulses of men and women has gotten twisted around, she feels. She had preached the idea of staying home, but it occurs to her now that perhaps the meaning of home grows out of the fear of open spaces. In some people that fear is so intense that it is a disease, Louise has read.''

Mary, in ''Residents and Transients,'' has, unlike most of these characters, experimented with various lifestyles, but she has returned to her roots in Kentucky. Now, although her husband has been transferred and has moved to the city to work and find them a home, she stays behind because, she says, ''I do not want to go anywhere.'' Mary loves her parents' old farmhouse and worries about a world that sends her mother off to live in a mobile home in Florida. She knows that her mother, who loved her canning kitchen, would be appalled to find that her daughter has taken a lover and spends her afternoons with him drinking Bloody Marys made with the old woman's canned tomato juice. An obviously more educated and sophisticated woman than many of her neighbors in these stories, Mary too is torn between the serene seductions of an obsolete lifestyle and the intimidating uncertainties of a variable present and future. Eventually she

> ''An obviously more educated and sophisticated woman than many of her neighbors in these stories, Mary too is torn between the serene seductions of an obsolete lifestyle and the intimidating uncertainties of a variable present and future.''

recognizes the dangers of stasis: ''I am nearly thirty years old,'' she proclaims. ''I have two men, eight cats, no cavities. One day I was counting the cats and I absent-mindedly counted myself.'' Near the end of the story Mary relates to her lover the perception that will ultimately send her—however reluctantly—to Louisville and a new life with her husband:

> ''In the wild, there are two kinds of cat populations . . . Residents and transients. Some stay put, in their fixed home ranges, and others are on the move. They don't have real homes. Everybody always thought that the ones who establish the territories are the most successful. . . . They are the strongest, while the transients are the bums, the losers . . . The thing is—this is what the scientists are wondering about now—it may be that the transients are the superior ones after all, with the greatest curiosity and most intelligence. They can't decide. . . . When certain Indians got tired of living in a place—when they used up the soil, or the garbage pile got too high—they moved on to the next place.''

Bobbie Ann Mason's Kentucky is paradigmatic of the contemporary South, and to an extent of modern America. Overwhelmed by rapid and frightening changes in their lives, her characters and her readers must confront contradictory impulses, the temptation to withdraw into the security of home and the past, and the alternative prospect of taking to the road in search of something better. There are no easy answers, Mason tells us, a fact that makes her stories all the more satisfying. They are small stopping places, brief, refreshing respites from a complex world.

Source: Maureen Ryan, "Stopping Places: Bobbie Ann Mason's Short Stories," in *Women Writers of the Contemporary South*, edited by Peggy Whitman Prenshaw, University Press of Mississippi, 1984, pp. 283–94.

Sources

Aldridge, John W. *Talents and Technicians: Literary Chic and the New Assembly-Line Fiction*, Charles Scribner's Sons, 1992.

Brinkmeyer, Robert H., Jr. "Finding One's History: Bobbie Ann Mason and Contemporary Southern Literature," in *The Southern Literary Journal*, Vol. 29, No. 2, Spring, 1987, pp. 20-33.

Giannone, Richard. "Bobbie Ann Mason and the Recovery of Mystery," in *Studies in Short Fiction*, Vol. 27, No. 4, Fall, 1990, pp. 553–66.

Henning, Barbara. "Minimalism and the American Dream: 'Shiloh' by Bobbie Ann Mason and 'Preservation' by Raymond Carver," in *Modern Fiction Studies*, Vol. 35, No. 4, Winter, 1989, pp. 689-98.

Lyons, Gene. Review, in *Newsweek*, Nov. 15, 1982, p. 107.

Mason, Bobbie Ann. "Bobbie Ann Mason: A Conversation with Lila Havens," in *The Story and Its Writer: An Introduction to Short Fiction*, 2nd ed., edited by Ann Charters, St. Martin's, 1987, pp. 1345-349.

Mason, Bobbie Ann, Bonnie Lyons, and Bill Oliver. Interview, in *Contemporary Literature*, Vol. 32, No. 4, Winter, 1991, pp. 449-70.

Morphew, G. O. "Downhome Feminists in *Shiloh and Other Stories*," in *The Southern Literary Review*, Vol. 21, No. 2, Spring, 1989, pp. 41-9.

Ryan, Maureen. "Stopping Places: Bobbie Ann Mason's Short Stories," in *Women Writers of the Contemporary South*, edited by Peggy Whitman Prenshaw, University Press of Mississippi, 1984, pp. 283-94.

Towers, Robert. Review, in *The New York Review of Books*, December 16, 1982, p. 38.

Tyler, Anne. Review, in *The New Republic*, November 1, 1982, p. 36.

Vigderman, Patricia. Review, in *The Nation*, March 19, 1983, p. 345.

Wilhelm, Albert. "An Interview with Bobbie Ann Mason," in his *Bobbie Ann Mason: A Study of the Short Fiction*, Twayne, 1998, pp. 128–34.

———. "Private Rituals: Coping with Change in the Fiction of Bobbie Ann Mason," in *The Midwest Quarterly*, Vol. 28, No. 2, Winter, 1987, pp. 271-82.

———. "Making Over or Making Off: The Problem of Identity in Bobbie Ann Mason's Fiction," in *The Southern Literary Journal*, Vol. 18, No. 2, Spring, 1986, pp. 76-82.

Further Reading

Folks, Jeffrey J., and James A. Perkins, eds. *Southern Writers at Century's End*, Lexington: University of Kentucky Press, 1997.

> Offers essays on twenty-one Southern writers, including Mason, Anne Tyler, Alice Walker, and Lee Smith. The lucid introduction speaks to the fresh and new in Southern literature, as well as to "a continuing tradition of narrative that draws on the South's cultural and human complexity."

Reisman, Rosemary M. and Christopher J. Canfield. *Contemporary Southern Women Fiction Writers: An Annotated Bibliography*, Metuchen, N.J.: Scarecrow Press, 1994.

> A valuable resource for any student who wants to find additional critical sources on not only Bobbie Ann Mason, but on a host of other writers as well. The annotations are both thorough and helpful.

Wilhelm, Albert. *Bobbie Ann Mason: A Study of the Short Fiction*, New York: Twayne, 1998.

> Written by the leading scholar of Mason's work, the book offers students a comprehensive introduction to her fiction.

Silent Snow, Secret Snow

Conrad Aiken

1934

"Silent Snow, Secret Snow" (1934) is not only Conrad Aiken's most anthologized work, but also one of the most widely read twentieth-century American short stories. The story concerns the degeneration of its protagonist, a young boy named Paul Hasleman, into madness. Critics often view this story in light of Aiken's childhood, and search for autobiographical aspects to the work. Some interpret the story using a psychoanalytic framework; but it has been noted that the problem of the psychoanalytic interpretation is that it treats the events of the tale too clinically, diminishing the story's emotional power.

It seems that a valid interpretation of "Silent Snow, Secret Snow" can neither avoid purely psychological issues—the theme of child-parent conflict, for example—nor justifiably ignore the realistic tragedy of a twelve-year-old boy's world demolished by madness.

Author Biography

In 1889 Conrad Aiken was born to parents of Scottish descent in Savannah, Georgia. In 1901, when he was eleven years old, Aiken's father, killed his wife and then committed suicide. Aiken lived with an aunt in New Bedford, Massachusetts, until

he entered Harvard University in 1907. There, he studied with George Santayana, a renowned philosopher and poet. Santayana's philosophy emphasized the utility of human sensory perception and reason. This aesthetic reaction to the world also emerges in Aiken's own poetry and fiction.

Aiken wrote steadily in many genres, but preferred writing poetry and short stories. He also wrote several novels, including *The Blue Voyage* (1927), *Great Circle* (1933), *King Coffin* (1935), and *A Heart of the Gods for Mexico* (1939).

Aiken's poetry ranges from short lyrics to extended "symphonies," as he called them, to more straightforward verse narratives. He received the Pulitzer Prize for his *Selected Poems* (1929) and a National Book Award for his *Collected Poems* (1953). As a poet, Aiken belonged to the modernist school, yet his verse was different from the work of Ezra Pound or Wallace Stevens. As a prose writer, Aiken tended to be more conventional, though such modernistic devices as stream-of-consciousness can be found in his work.

Plot Summary

Aiken divides "Silent Snow, Secret Snow" into four distinct sections. In section I, the story introduces Paul Hasleman, age twelve, a student in Mrs. Buell's sixth-grade classroom. Paul is distracted, however, by his intense memory of an event that occurred several days before. He thinks about the globe that figures in the day's geography lesson and hears Deirdre, the girl who sits in front of him, awkwardly answer a question about the definition of the term "equator." A few days earlier, Paul had the impression that snow had fallen; the sound of the postman's feet on the cobblestones outside his house suddenly sounded muffled. When he got up and looked out, however, the cobblestones were bare and there was no snow. Yet in his own mind, Paul is mysteriously aware of a "secret snow" that signals his growing sense of detachment from the real world.

Paul recalls that the sound of the postman's footsteps grow less and less distinct each day, and are audible only as the postman draws closer and closer to the Hasleman's house. Paul speculates about the necessity of keeping this strange knowledge from others and rehearses a family conversation over dinner as if he were practicing a play. Meanwhile, in the classroom, Mrs. Buell talks about the seventeenth- and eighteenth-century search to discover the Northwest Passage. When Paul rouses himself sufficiently to successfully answer a question about Henry Hudson, Deirdre turns in her chair to smile at him with "approval and admiration." At last the bell rings for dismissal.

In Part II, Paul is on his way home from school. He thinks about the secret snow and how difficult it is to drag himself out of bed each morning when all he wants to do is stay in bed. For Paul, the world grows increasingly more alien, incomprehensible, and repulsive. For example, he takes inventory of the items in a dirty gutter, and stares at tracks left by a dog in the sidewalk when the cement was freshly poured. He then arrives at his own house and is troubled by the thought that it is the sixth house from the corner, when he had all along supposed it to be the seventh. The house seems strange as he comes inside from the street.

In Part III, after supper, Paul's parents grow concerned about their son and call in a doctor to examine him. Paul regards the examination as an inquisition, and becomes emphatically defensive. During the exam, Paul hears the secret snow. The pressure of the doctor's questions forces Paul to admit that his recent state of distraction stems from constantly thinking about the snow. His parents react negatively, and Paul fails to understand the full impact of his revelation.

In Part IV, Paul rushes to his bedroom. The whiteness of the snow has become overwhelming. He now views his mother as a "cruel disturbance," a hostile intruder as she tries to help him. He rejects her defiantly as he finally slips away:

"Mother! Mother! Go away! I hate you!"

And with that effort, everything was solved, everything became all right: the seamless hiss advanced once more, the long white wavering lines rose and fell like enormous whispering sea-waves, the whisper becoming louder, the laughter more numerous.

"Listen!" it said. "We'll tell you the last, most beautiful and secret story—shut your eyes—it is a very small story—a story that gets smaller and smaller—it comes inward instead of opening like a flower—it is a flower becoming a seed—a little cold seed—do you hear? we are leaning closer to you—"

The hiss was now becoming a roar—the whole world was a vast moving screen of snow—but even now it said peace, it said remoteness, it said cold, it said sleep. (Excerpt from "Silent Snow, Secret Snow")

Characters

Deirdre

Deirdre is Paul's classmate. She sits at the desk in front of his. She is not a fully developed character, but her gesture of turning around to smile admiringly at Paul when he answers a question correctly is girlish. Deirdre has freckles on her neck and delicate hands; she is a stereotypical "first love" for a young boy verging on his teens.

Doctor

The doctor is the first to suggest that Paul is suffering from some sort of mental illness. Initially he gives the boy a physical examination. Then, announcing that the problem might be "something else," begins a psychological examination.

Mrs. Hasleman

Mrs. Hasleman obviously cares for and is worried about her son. In the first part of the story, she worries about Paul's condition and speculates that he suffered from "eyestrain." To remedy this, she buys him a new lamp. She tells him one evening that "if this goes on, my lad, we'll have to see a doctor," and she continues reading a magazine, laughing a little, "but with an expression which wasn't mirthful." When she finally understands the seriousness of Paul's mental illness, she falls silent and her mouth "opens in an expression of horror." After he has vanished upstairs to his room, Paul views his mother as a monster chasing after him, though she is merely a terrified parent seeking to save her son from his illness—a task in which, as far as the reader can tell, she fails.

Norman Hasleman

Paul's father, Norman Hasleman, is as concerned as his wife about Paul's welfare, but he is more reticent about expressing his emotions. He also exhibits some impatience with the boy. During his examination by the doctor, for example, Paul recognizes what he calls his father's "punishment voice," which the reader may interpret as a sign that

Conrad Aiken

the father is the disciplinarian of the family. Paul's description of the voice as "resonant and cruel," however, may be attributed to his increasing dementia rather than to reality.

Paul Hasleman

Paul Hasleman, age twelve and presumably in the sixth grade, lives in an American town, probably in New England. Prior to the onset of his madness, Paul was an ordinary boy, good at geometry, and excited about geography. At first he is considered introspective, but it is soon clear that he is detached from reality; this alienation is metaphorically represented in this story as the secret snow.

As the disturbance takes over, Paul feels terribly lonely. As his sickness triumphs, Paul becomes distinctly paranoid regarding the "gross intelligences" that surround him. He only vaguely understands the pain that he is causing others.

Paul's Father
See Norman Hasleman

Paul's Mother
See Mrs. Hasleman

Postman

The first indication of Paul's mental disturbance comes when the usual sound of the postman's footfalls on his early morning rounds are deadened as if by a fresh snowfall. The sound of the muffled footsteps and the fatality of his knock suggest a classic personification of death—if not clinical death, then the death-to-the-world that constitutes psychosis.

Themes

Sanity and Insanity

In "Silent Snow, Secret Snow," sanity is defined as the ability to function in the everyday world and interact with people. Conversely, insanity is measured by the degree to which one is unfamiliar with everyday occurrences and the inability to communicate with others. Deirdre's eagerness to answer Mrs. Buell's geography question is evidence of her sanity. The globe that figures in Mrs. Buell's geography lesson is a symbol for the real and everyday world in which people, as they mature, become increasingly interactive. In contrast, Paul's desire to avoid reality and seek refuge in the sheltering snow is indicative of his increasing behavioral abnormality.

Truth and Falsehood

Saneness may be defined in "Silent Snow, Secret Snow" as a person's ability to distinguish between the truth and lies. Paul's parents are concerned that he is no longer his true self. The doctor investigates the truth of Paul's altered condition; Mrs. Buell teaches the accumulated significant truths about the world to her students; Deirdre admires Paul and flashes her smile to indicate, truthfully, that she is fond of him. Falsehood, on the other hand, is linked to insanity in the story. Paul labors to conceal his knowledge of the snow.

Love and Hatred

Love involves valuing, cherishing, and voluntarily assuming responsibility for another person. Love can also be directed toward institutions or things, like a job, a house, or a dog. Paul loved his parents, but his madness erases his feelings and eventually causes him to reject his mother. Hatred inverts love, for it closes rather than opens personal relationships, and thrives on suspicion and self-involvement. Hatred dissolves the bonds that unite people and in its very intensity constitutes a disturbance of the mind.

Community and Alienation

Community consists of a conscious sharing of values and things. In "Silent Snow, Secret Snow," the schoolroom and the family home symbolize community; Deirdre attempts to establish a more intimate community with Paul by indicating that she admires him for correctly answering a question. Alienation is a disconnection from those shared bonds of community. For Paul, this happens when the snow alters his view of the world and at last obliterates it.

Style

Lyricism

Aiken brought the poet's sensibility and craft to his fiction. He narrates "Silent Snow, Secret Snow" from Paul's point-of-view; this perspective guarantees that the author's stream-of-consciousness prose style will affect readers directly. Not surprisingly, one finds a large number of lyric poems in Aiken's verse. Aiken also utilizes the material properties of words. For example, the pervasive alliteration, with its repeated "s" sounds, already appears in the story's title. In addition, Aiken manages to endow his prose with the naturalness of colloquial speech. Although couched in the third person, Aiken's narration remains faithful to the linguistic style of a twelve-year-old boy.

Grammar

In "Silent Snow, Secret Snow," Aiken's depiction of insanity begins at the grammatical level. In the opening paragraph, for example, Paul thinks of the snow—the initial stages of his madness—and refers to it with the pronoun "it": "Just why *it* should have happened, or why *it* should have happened just when it did, he could not, of course, possibly have said" (emphasis added). The personified "it," then, becomes a thing.

Point of View

Aiken provides Paul's perceptions, as when he stares at the debris in a muddy gutter: "In the gutter, beside a drain, was a scrap of torn and dirty newspaper, caught in a little delta of filth; the word ECZE-

MA appeared in large capitals, and below it was a letter from Mrs. Amelia D. Cravath, 2100 Pine Street, Fort Worth, Texas, to the effect that after being a sufferer for years she had been cured by Haley's Ointment. In the little delta, beside the fan-shaped and deeply funneled continent of brown mud, were lost twigs ... dead matches, a rusty horse-chestnut burr, a small concentration of egg-shell, a streak of yellow sawdust ... a brown pebble, and a broken feather." Aiken does not need to add commentary, since the very randomness of the objects correlates to the randomness of Paul's inner disturbance.

On the other hand, every item described in the gutter metaphorically describes Paul's worsening condition; eczema is an irritating skin condition; a broken feather indicates a bird's inability to fly; and a broken eggshell may suggest the fractured whole-ness of a personality.

The reader should note, finally, that Aiken's consummate usage of the whiteness of the snow may indicate the annihilation of Paul's conscious-ness. This whiteness joins with the cascade of sibilating S's at the end of the story to convey Paul's descent into madness.

Historical Context

The Great Depression

"Silent Snow, Secret Snow" appeared in 1934, the second year of President Franklin Delano Roo-sevelt's first term in office. America was also in the midst of the Great Depression, which disrupted American life, put many people out of work, and left many impoverished. Other nations were affected: Britain, France, Italy, and Germany also suffered from high inflation and unemployment. A fascist government, put in power because of its promise to restore national order and stabilize the economy, had achieved power in Italy in 1922. Another fascist government was established in 1934 in Germany as the Nazis gained control. England, too, had its totalitarian movement around this time, when Oswald Mosley formed the Union of Fascists, the so-called "Black Shirts."

National Mood

In the United States, on the other hand, there was continuing progress in industry and technolo-gy. Although not everyone in 1934 could afford them, a variety of new household conveniences—

Topics for Further Study

- Research the fundamentals of Freud's psycho-logical theory, especially his concepts of the Oedipal complex and the "Primal Scene." How are these concepts related to the clinical concept of madness? To what degree do they explain what happens to Paul Hasleman?

- What human connections will Paul be unable to develop since he has become ill? Explore the implications of his illness.

- As a poet and to a certain extent as a fiction writer, Aiken was identified with the modernist school. What aspects or elements of "Silent Snow, Secret Snow" make it modernistic? Al-ternatively, does anything suggest that the story does not belong to modernism but to some more traditional school of fiction writing?

- Discuss the theme of alienation as it relates to "Silent Snow, Secret Snow." Is alienation in-separable from insanity, or is it possible to imag-ine a perfectly sane individual who is just as alienated from reality?

such as refrigerators and electric ovens—appeared. Air travel increasingly competed with train travel, and radio, the first great mass medium, had come into its own. President Roosevelt's "Fireside Chats," broadcast nationally, brought the country closer together.

Literary and Artistic Trends

Around 1934, there were two important trends in American literature. There was the social con-sciousness movement of writers like John Stein-beck, who portrayed the lives of ordinary people during hard financial times. There was also the modernist movement, as exemplified by the poetry of Ezra Pound and Wallace Stevens, or the novels of John Dos Passos.

Rejecting the literary conventions of the nine-teenth century, the modernist movement concerned

Compare & Contrast

- **1930s:** The American economy is staggering from the impact of the Great Depression. The Wall Street crash of 1929 precipitated a world-wide economic crisis that resulted in devastating circumstances: record unemployment; high inflation; and financial institutions such as banks failing. Many families lose all of their savings and assets, and are forced to rely on charity. In response, the American government implements a number of social programs to relieve suffering, jump-start the economy, and get people back on their feet.

  1990s: The economy is experiencing a record period of affluence and growth. Unemployment is very low, as is the inflation rate. The U.S. budget, at a record deficit in the 1980s, is at a surplus for the first time in many years.

- **1930s:** Fascism is on the rise in Europe as financial and social instability allow leaders such as Benito Mussolini in Italy to gain power.

  1990s: The same powers that embraced fascism in the 1930s now function as republics. For example, Germany has recovered from the effects of two World Wars to once again become a world power, economically and politically. Europe is united to become the European Community, with one currency and concentrated economic resources.

itself with formal experimentation and deliberate disorientation of the reader, often by fragmenting narration into dislodged and discontinuous sections. Modernism also appeared in the non-representational schools of painting and sculpture, as well as in atonal music. Advocates of modernism claimed that the ''alienation'' aspect of the movement accurately reflected the world—human consciousness was becoming progressively detached from its origins.

Critical Overview

Given the interest in the psychoanalytic theory of Sigmund Freud in the 1930s, it is not surprising that early interpretations of ''Silent Snow, Secret Snow'' examined the story from that perspective. Leo Hamalaian provided an early example of psychoanalytic analysis in his ''Aiken's ''Silent Snow, Secret Snow''' of 1948. Frederick Hoffman's 1957 study of *Freudianism and the Literary Mind*, which devotes considerable space to Aiken's fiction, is another case in point, although it should be added

that Hoffman later de-emphasized the Freudian aspect of his reading of Aiken.

Psychoanalysis still influences readings of the tale. As late as 1980, Laura Slap invoked the Oedipus complex as the unconscious theme of Aiken's story: ''My thesis is that Paul Hasleman's illness is a reaction to his realization of his parents' sexual activity.'' When the doctor asks Paul to read a passage from a book taken from the shelves, the passage happens to be from Sophocles' play *Oedipus at Colonus*. This permits Slap to work the Oedipus theme into her discussion.

Some critics have avoided the psychoanalytic approach in favor of a purely aesthetic approach, inspired by the fact that Aiken considered himself a poet first and a prose-writer second. An example of the aesthetic, or formalist, approach is to be found in Elizabeth Tebeux's '''Silent Snow, Secret Snow': Style as Art'' (1983). In the essay, Tebeaux discusses Aiken's careful usage of such poetic devices as ambiguity and polysemy (the endowing of one simple word with many meanings, each of which depends on a particular context); she also looks closely at the use of rhythm and alliteration as a means of reproducing the feelings that accompany

Paul's descent into madness. According to Tebeaux, "focusing only on Paul is to miss the most remarkable literary aspects of the story. Combining sense and symbol and rhythm and tone and sound, Aiken uses his poetic skills to draw the reader into Paul's world."

A more recent tendency is to deconstruct the story by making a deliberately counter-intuitive interpretation. Such interpretations turn insanity into a positive; Paul's behavior is viewed as a symbolic breaking away from an oppressive society and the restrictive bonds of community and family. As such, Paul's growing individuality and independence is seen as insanity. Ann Gossman and Jesse Swan both exemplify this critical trend. Gossman's thesis is that "Paul's withdrawal is not psychopathic, but rather the alienation of the artist from society." Gossman argues that what we mistake for Paul's madness is his flowering "as an artist" or seer who "must die" rather than "'mature' into perhaps another Mr. Hasleman." While admitting that the "reasonable modern reader naturally seems to recoil from accepting" what she calls "Paul's choice" to embrace madness, Jesse Swan nevertheless contends that this same "modern reader" might actually resent "Paul for having the courage" to turn his back on the world and enter the secret, artistic world of the snow.

Criticism

Thomas Bertonneau

Bertonneau is a Temporary Assistant Professor of English and the Humanities at Central Michigan University, and Senior Policy Analyst at the Mackinac Center for Public Policy. In the following essay, he surveys the various critical interpretations of Paul's mental disturbance in Aiken's "Silent Snow, Secret Snow."

Critics do not interpret Conrad Aiken's short story "Silent Snow, Secret Snow" (1934) in a literal way. Upon initial examination, they consistently regard the story as something other than what it is. Thomas L. Erskine, for example, in his 1972 psychoanalytical interpretation of the story, claims that "Silent Snow, Secret Snow" is about the "balance" between "two worlds" and the "discovery" that results by leaving one to enter the other. For

Snow covered spruce tree.

Erskine, each of young Paul Hasleman's deformed or defamiliarized perceptions of the world amount to an "epiphany," an intense vision with deep symbolic meaning.

Appreciating the story on purely aesthetic grounds, Elizabeth Tebeaux calls attention to Aiken's work, stating that he "enables us to feel some of the magic and terrifying wonder that the snow world, whatever it is, offers Paul." Tebeaux concludes by noting that the story "will more than likely continue to be enjoyed long after the nature of Paul's problem has ceased to be of any psychological interest."

What Do I Read Next?

- Edgar Allen Poe's "Ligeia" (1838) and "The Tell-Tale Heart" (1843) both deal with insanity and serve as interesting contrasts to Aiken's "Silent Snow, Secret Snow."

- Ray Bradbury's story, "The Earth Men" (1948), later published in *The Martian Chronicles* (1952), is a story about madness. It is a fascinating inversion of the usual insanity narrative and makes a useful contrast with Aiken's tale.

- Chapter Two of Freud's *Civilization and its*

Discontents (1930) explores the roots of alienation and offers background information for a discussion of Paul Hasleman's detachment from the reality.

- Arthur Rimbaud's "A Season in Hell" (1870) is a long poem that explores the alienation of a young poet.

- "Senlin: A Biography" is a story by Conrad Aiken. It is often discussed in connection with "Silent Snow, Secret Snow."

Moreover, Jesse Swan maintains that we are not to believe that Paul is insane, because madness is a label applied in an arbitrary and oppressive manner. Similarly, Ann Gossman referred to Paul's parents, and to the whole adult world in the story, as "philistine"—an extreme judgment.

Paul Hasleman, the protagonist of "Silent Snow, Secret Snow," suffers the terrible fate of having his life annihilated by a "fixed idea," or an overwhelming obsession. What should one say about those critics who attempt to convert the tragedy into something other than what it is by claiming that Paul's condition corresponds to something other than what the evidence dictates?

Starting from the fact, however, that Aiken understood the effects of insanity—his father killed his mother and then himself in a psychotic fit, and Aiken himself later attempted suicide—I believe that readers need to understand that Paul's disturbance may never qualify as an experience through which he might live and personally or artistically profit, but that his collapse is simply the end of all of his conscious experiences.

Aiken has something in common with Edgar Allan Poe, an earlier American short story writer, who also struggled with madness and wrote about it in such stories as "The Tell-Tale Heart" and

"Ligeia." In the former, insanity is rooted in guilt, while in the latter, it assumes the form of an evil entity.

The term "possession" appears in the first paragraph of "Silent Snow, Secret Snow." The setting is Mrs. Buell's sixth-grade classroom during a geography lesson. Paul ignores her, and instead concentrates on his growing obsession with the snow: "It was like a peculiarly beautiful trinket to be carried unmentioned in one's trouser pocket—a rare stamp, an old coin, a few tiny gold links found trodden out of shape on a path in the park, a pebble of carnelian, a seashell distinguishable from all others by an unusual spot or stripe—and, as if it were any of these, he carried around with him everywhere a warm and persistent and increasingly beautiful sense of possession."

All aspects of Paul's state of mind in regard to his "possession" may strike the reader as sinister foreshadowings of the story's climax. Even at the grammatical level, Aiken's use of the nonspecific pronoun "it" to designate the encroaching psychosis carries a frightening connotation, for a thing that cannot be named cannot be fully understood. Thinking of "it" as a seashell with "an unusual spot or stripe" admits to the oddness of the condition but does nothing to pinpoint or solve it. Thinking of "it" as a broken chain of gold links "trodden out of shape" also anticipates the subsequent breakup and deformation of Paul's mind, not to mention the sundering of his family.

At this early point in the story, Aiken deliberately confounds the idea of possession. Does the word designate an item which one owns, or does it designate an involuntary state to which one submits? Paul mistakenly thinks that he possesses "it," when "it" really possesses him. Moreover, "it" has already drawn Paul out of his world, out of the world in which healthy people live and love. When Deirdre gives an unwittingly silly answer to one of Mrs. Buell's questions, Paul does not join in the laughter—not because he disapproves of it, but because the madness has already abstracted him from the generality of the classroom community.

The scene with Deirdre in part one of "Silent Snow, Secret Snow" tends to slip past in the parade of Paul's confusion, although it offers one key to understanding the story. What Paul notices about Deirdre is not that she is an eager student, willing to rise to answer questions, but that her neck sports a "funny little constellation of freckles . . . exactly like the Big Dipper." Paul has failed to see the full, human Deirdre, and instead reduces her to an anomalous blemish. Aiken skillfully interweaves Paul's autistic inner monologue with brief intrusions from Mrs. Buell's lesson (sometimes reported parenthetically). At one point during the story Mrs. Buell gently admonishes Paul that if he stopped daydreaming he might answer a question about Henry Hudson's success or failure in finding the Northwest Passage. Paul rouses himself momentarily to correctly respond that Hudson "was disappointed." As he sits down, "Deirdre half turned in her chair and gave him a shy smile, of approval and admiration."

Setting all theories aside, consider what Deirdre's smile means in the context of a sixth-grade classroom. All of the children have begun to take an interest in the opposite sex, and all are quite shy about admitting to it. Admitting to such an interest before the eyes of one's classmates is usually dreadful, but Deirdre does just that, spontaneously turning to smile shyly and approvingly at Paul. We cannot discount the episode, for it constitutes a moment of healthy adolescence in that the girl probably wants to establish intimacy with the boy. It is an opportunity for Paul to experience the world of adolescence. The "exploration" theme implied by the geography lesson about Henry Hudson, I would argue, refers to the potential romance offered by Deirdre. Paul's madness prohibits any such explo-

> **Paul's declining interest in and growing aversion to the world is very much a sickness, with physical as well as psychological symptoms."**

ration and any such issue from childhood from taking place. Paul's madness, then, robs him of the possibility of love.

It is suggested that Paul's mental distraction has multiple consequences, for he has become slovenly and neglectful. He has not, for example, recently polished his shoes because (as he rationalizes) "they were one of the many parts of the increasing difficulty of the daily return to daily life, the morning struggle." Paul's declining interest in and growing aversion to the world is very much a sickness, with physical as well as psychological symptoms.

The attraction that Paul ought to feel toward Deirdre is directed toward the hallucinatory snowstorm: "He loved it—he stood still and loved it. Its beauty was paralyzing—beyond all words, all experience, all dream. No fairy story he had ever read could be compared with it." The reader needs to remember, however, that "it" does not exist. At the same time, the snowstorm strikes him as "faintly and deliciously terrifying," a reaction that belongs to that vanishing part of him that is still sane. The psychosis will soon rob Paul of his memory—a terrifying prospect, although Paul will not be able to recognize it as such. When he arrives at the gate of the family home, for example, and sees the stenciled H (for Hasleman), he fails to understand its import.

The final terror comes after Paul is examined by the doctor. Paul feels compelled to divulge the secret of the snow and then, in a panic, he runs upstairs to his bedroom and throws himself into bed. The snow begins to speak to Paul, telling him: "Lie down. Shut your eyes—you will no longer see much—in this white darkness who could see, or want to see? We will take the place of everything."

In conclusion, readers of "Silent Snow, Secret Snow" need to be wary of the numerous interpretations of Paul's affliction. Psychoanalytic approaches tend to reduce the full humanity of the event. More recent approaches which rely on making insanity into something other than what it is, also deserve to be regarded with skepticism. Aiken did not regard insanity either as a purely theoretical or desirable phenomenon. His understanding of insanity might be described as existential, although that, too, is an oversimplification. Perhaps one should simply say that Aiken is a profound observer of the human condition, a lover of life, and a writer who can lead us to appreciate life by giving us the example of someone who loses life by losing his mind.

Source: Thomas Bertonneau, Overview of "Silent Snow, Secret Snow," for *Short Stories for Students*, The Gale Group, 2000.

Jesse G. Swan

In the following excerpt, Swan discusses the major themes of Aiken's "Silent Snow, Secret Snow."

In "Senlin: A Biography" and "Silent Snow, Secret Snow," Conrad Aiken explores the psyches of two people, one an old man, the other a child, who seem to be confronting something much larger than they are. In both pieces, the central figures experience something to which no one else seems to be sensitive. As this experience is uncommon, the depiction of it demands uncommon material. Aiken succeeds in presenting these nebulous experiences by carefully casting silences in his work. Aiken's silences surround man, embody man, and are embodied by man. They also resemble the Christian God in their ubiquity as well as their comprehensiveness. In both pieces, Aiken tries to communicate the import of these silences, and he does this by stretching our consciousness to include the edges of our minds. Although "Senlin" is an early poem of Aiken's and "Silent Snow, Secret Snow" is a later short story, both rely on silence to convey their intendment. Realizing that Aiken employs silence in "Senlin" and develops that employment in "Silent Snow, Secret Snow," we not only develop a greater understanding of Aiken's *Weltanschauung*, we also perceive new possibilities for reading Paul Hasleman's confrontation with the silent snow. . . .

Silence motivates the events of Aiken's greatest work, his short story, "Silent Snow, Secret Snow." Like "Senlin," "Silent Snow, Secret Snow" is an investigation of a psyche that involves much more than only the psyche. Indeed in an even more developed fashion, "Silent Snow, Secret Snow" reveals a struggle that, it appears, Aiken believes we all experience. Some dismiss the confrontation with silence in the story as puberty or madness. However, since the silence in the story develops the silence of "Senlin," it appears that this story, like the poem, depicts a serious confrontation with eternity, with truth, with silence.

A common temptation is to view the silent snow negatively. Paul, we may be tempted to say, is going mad. This conclusion, however, is one that Mr. and Mrs. Hasleman would form. Paul knows that he cannot tell his parents about his silent snow, "No—" he thinks, "it was only too plain that if anything were said about it, the merest hint given, they would be incredulous—they would laugh—they would say 'Absurd!'—think things about him which weren't true. . . ." And clearly the parents would think him insane, but we are not to do so. The parents are "gross intelligences . . . humdrum minds so bound to the usual, the ordinary" that they cannot experience something "irrational." This description from Paul's point of view, if not wholly accurate because of its extremity, does represent the parents' general character. Perhaps it is inappropriate to be so harsh on the parents for being "normal," but they clearly are normal. The parents notice a change in their son's usual, acceptable character and think that something must be wrong with him. If they knew that he was listening to silent snow, they *would* think him mad. They do not see it, so, for them, it is not there. Like any good parent, they decide to call in an authority—the family physician.

The physician epitomizes the typical adult. We believe that there must be a "rational" explanation for everything and that the world is a rationally understandable environment. Anything supernatural cannot be accounted for and is therefore relegated to the realm of "irrationality," "madness," and the like. The parents believe this as does the physician. The physician asks Paul, "Now, young man, tell me,—do you feel all right?" When Paul tells him that he feels fine—indeed Paul feels exceptionally well because of his silent, secret snow—the doctor performs a physical survey of Paul which includes Paul's reading from a passage of a book. When this reveals nothing out of the ordinary, "silence thronged the room", and the doctor asks Paul, moving to a psychological survey assuming that if nothing is physically wrong, something psychologically *must* be wrong with Paul, whether there is "anything that worries you?" Since Paul's answer remains "No," the doctor becomes exasperated and exclaims: "Well, Paul! . . . I'm afraid you don't take this quite seriously enough". The doctor has given Paul numerous chances to declare himself mad, but since he does not, the doctor concludes that Paul is not only mentally troubled but unacceptably obstinate. Thinking about the doctor's and the parents' actions and portraits, it seems that Paul is not so unreasonable. Concluding that the story is about a boy "whose mind finally breaks down" [Edward Stone, *Voices of Despair: Four Motifs in American Literature*, 1996] ignores the possibility, if not fact, that the parents and physician are blind, insensitive and thereby negative agents in the story and that the silent snow and Paul's embrace of it are the positive agents. Such a narrow reading reveals that the readers, like the parents, are "so bound to the usual, the ordinary . . . [that it is] impossible to tell them about" the positive beauty and peacefulness of the silent snow. These readers, like the parents and the doctor, have pushed away the silence which surrounds them and have chosen to embrace the rational, language-centered world. Paul, many try to conclude, is mad, and the parents and doctor, they silently assume, are the standard by which to judge sanity and madness.

That the silent snow is positive not only provides additional support for reading the story as a representation of one of Aiken's favorite points in human development, it also seems rather obvious to the unprejudiced reader. From the very beginning the silent snow is a pleasant experience. In the opening scene where Paul is in class, we find out that

> he was already, with a pleasant sense of half-effort, putting his secret between himself and the [Miss Buell's] words. Was it really an effort at all? For effort implied something voluntary, and perhaps even something one did not especially want; whereas this was distinctly pleasant, and came almost of its own accord.

Although this can be read negatively, as a sign of Paul's ensuing madness, a more positive reading suggests itself as well. The silent secret comes on to Paul, perhaps as "madness" does "a schizoid personality" [William M. Jones, *Explicator*, 18, March 1960], but also as nature's breezes and soothing sounds do. A breeze is not an effort, but we often feel a half-effort to experience it fully. Like the silent secret, a breeze is not voluntary and it is often pleasant. Hence, the silent secret snow is not ipso facto madness and therefore negative. In fact, it seems really quite a positive experience for Paul, much like a mystical experience must be for a devout Christian or a cognitive insight for a critical theorist.

> **The silent snow, after imposing itself on the world, reveals the essential silent entity that embodies everything."**

The development of the silent, secret snow seems to provide further evidence that the snow is a positive force. As in "Senlin," the silence is first a quality that characterizes as well as surrounds, and second it is an entity itself. The silence in the story characterizes the snow which comes to surround Paul's world and then becomes "the most beautiful and secret story" in the end. In class, Paul contemplates the fact that

> All he now knew was, that at some point or other— perhaps the second day, perhaps the sixth—he had noticed that the presence of the snow was a little more insistent. . . . There, outside, were the bare cobbles; and here, inside, was the Snow growing heavier each day, muffling the world, hiding the ugly, and deadening increasingly—above all—the steps of the postman.

The snow is "hiding the ugly" of the world much like Percy Bysshe Shelley claims poetry does in his *A Defence of Poetry* [Roger Ingpen and Walter E. Peck, eds., *A Defence of Poetry: the Complete Works of Percy Bysshe Shelley*, 1965]. Shelley claims that "Poetry turns all things to loveliness; it exalts the beauty of that which is most beautiful, and it adds beauty to that which is most deformed. . . . It subdues to union under its light yoke, all irreconcilable things. It transmutes all that it touches. . . ." The snow, then, may resemble poetry. If the snow resembles poetry, is Paul a poet? Perhaps, but since Aiken concerns himself with Everyman and not just artists, it seems more likely that Paul is an Everyman. The snow may be poetic without Paul being a poet if the silent snow is universal truth that poets, children, and old people are sensitive to.

If the snow is universal truth that includes both the rational and the irrational, as it is in "Senlin," the significance of its "deadening increasingly— above all—the steps of the postman" may be ambiguous. The postman has been seen as representing death as well as, more modestly, "the plain ordinary world in which small boys have to get up, eat breakfast, go to school, listen attentively, and do all the other things expected of small boys'' [Ballew Graham, *English Journal*, 57, May 1968]. The more modest view seems more appropriate especially if we see the silent snow as positive. If the snow hides what is ugly, as poetry does, it would muffle the sound of the postman since the postman is ''the bringer of information from the outside world'' (Jones). The postman, with the parents and the doctor, becomes associated with the adult and loud world that has chosen to ignore the silent truth Paul decides to embrace. By incessantly assaulting the beauty of Paul's newly discovered world with news from the adult's mundane world, the postman must be silenced by the purifying silent snow.

The silent snow, after imposing itself on the world, reveals the essential silent entity that embodies everything. Toward the end of the story, when Paul is being interviewed by the physician, the silent snow becomes an entity that ''Even here, even amongst these hostile presences, and in this arranged light, he could see the snow, he could hear it—it was in the corners of the room, where the shadow was deepest''. The snow occupies the corners—the fringes—of the room much like silence encompasses the edges of sound. Moreover, this silent snow tells Paul to resist his parents and the doctor so that it can provide him with ''something new! Something white! Something cold! something sleepy! something of cease, and peace, and the long bright curve of space!'' This is a rather tempting promise to make, especially when contrasted with what the parents and the world they represent offers him.

The end of the story presents Paul's realization of the silent secret of the universe. The silent snow exclaims:

> Listen! . . . We'll tell you the last, the most beautiful and secret story—shut your eyes—it is a very small story—a story that gets smaller and smaller—it comes inward instead of opening like a flower—it is a flower becoming a seed—a little cold seed—do you hear? We are leaning closer to you.

This statement, compounded by the closing line that describes the snow becoming a fierce ''moving screen of snow—but even now it said peace, it said remoteness, it said cold, it said sleep'', leads many readers to conclude that Paul dies, that his death wish is fulfilled. But the scene has other possibilities, as Jay Martin notes that ''we seem always about to break through to the truths contained in the 'secret' snow. But we never, in the story, transcend

the snow itself, whose meanings remain secret'' [*Conrad Aiken: A Life of his Art*, 1962]. Secret they remain to those who, as ''reasonable'' adults, embrace only what can be understood with mere human language. The snow's depiction of the secret as a flower growing inward back to the beginning of life seems more positive than what is normal—i.e., a flower growing outward and dying! If the secret grows inward it can grow outward again, and repeat this cycle infinitely. The secret that grows inward is related to the silence that developed before Paul dashed up to bed. That ''silence seemed to deepen, to spread out . . . to become timeless and shapeless, and to center inevitably . . . on the beginning of a new sound.'' Hence, we have the most beautiful and secret story; namely, we have the story of the dynamics of eternal life. Life grows out to grow in, indefinitely.

There is certainly more to it than this. However, as the meaning is obviously ultimately silent, all that any of us can do is approximate the truth. Approaching the truth is what Aiken does best. He takes us to the edge of our minds momentarily innumerable times in his poetry and fiction. Senlin has been recognized as a character who probes the problem of understanding who we are. However, Paul, because he is a child, has received incomplete recognition. Like Senlin, Paul is encountering silent truth. Like Senlin, Paul embraces this beauty which ''was simply beyond anything—beyond speech as beyond thought—utterly incommunicable''. But unlike Senlin, Paul is twelve years old and the ''reasonable'' modern adult reader naturally seems to recoil from accepting Paul's choice as courageous and insightful. Perhaps the modern reader recognizes the situation and resents Paul for having the courage that only old men, such as Senlin, usually have. In both cases, Aiken clearly presents a person at a critical point in a human's life—that is, at the edge of sound and silence—and both choose the one which encompasses the other.

Source: Jesse G. Swan, ''At the Edge of Sound and Silence: Conrad Aiken's 'Senlin: A Biography' and 'Silent Snow, Secret Snow,''' in *The Southern Literary Journal*, Vol. XXII, No. 1, Fall, 1989, pp. 41–9.

Elizabeth Tebeaux

In the following excerpt, Tebeaux explores Aiken's development of the narrative and the use of poetical devices in ''Silent Snow, Secret Snow.''

'' Silent Snow, Secret Snow,'' one of Aiken's most famous, most anthologized short stories, has received sparse critical discussion. Most likely because of Aiken's admitted indebtedness to Freud, the core of existing criticism attempts to define Paul's problem in terms of Freudian psychology. Recent criticism gives a general overview of Aiken's short fiction and attempts to place Paul among Aiken's other protagonists, his "lost people" who fail to accept the real world. I would like to suggest, however, that the powerful, intriguing effect of the story emanates less from the enigmatic nature of Paul's problem and more from Aiken's careful manipulation of style to develop the narrative. Aiken is less concerned with our interpreting Paul's problem than in making Paul's journey from reality into the world of snow as credible, sensual, and tangible as possible.

At best, however, Aiken's technique has received passing commentary. Aiken's effective use of symbol has been recognized, but no analysis has been directed to his style or its importance to the development or the effectiveness of the narrative. Close analysis of the story reveals that Aiken carefully implements a number of poetic devices that mesh sound and sense and content to convey the stages, development, and intensity of Paul's experience.

The narrative develops about the constant juxtaposition of the real world and the snow world. These juxtapositions occur within four main settings. The narrative begins during Paul's geography class, shifts to his walk home from school, then focuses on his confrontation with his parents, and finally ends with the description of Paul's final withdrawal after he escapes to the darkness of his bed room. Paul's fate—his rejection of the living world and his acceptance of the snow—the theme of the story, develops through the contrasting descriptions of each world. Shifts within each description, accentuated by Aiken's use of poetic devices and prosody, allow us to follow vividly Paul's changing perception.

The opening paragraph defines this technique. As the narrator brings us into Paul's perception, we become aware that Paul does not understand what is happening to him. He refers to this new dimension of his perception as "it," "the thing." Aiken's choice of words to control the tone of the passage makes clear that Paul's attitude toward "the thing" is, at this point, not only positive but also secretive, defensive, and possessive:

> Just why it should have happened, or why it should
> have happened just the way it did, he could not, of

Sigmund Freud, founder of psychoanalysis, which deals with the treatment of abnormal mental states such as autism and paranoia.

course, possibly have said; nor perhaps would it even have occurred to him to ask. The thing was above all a *secret*, something to be *preciously concealed* from Mother and Father; and to that very fact it owed an enormous part of its *deliciousness*. It was like a peculiarly *beautiful* trinket to be carried unmentioned in one's trouser pocket . . . he carried around with him everywhere a *warm* and *persistent* and increasingly *beautiful* sense of *possession*. Nor was it only a sense of *possession* —it was also a sense of *protection*. It was as if, in some *delightful* way, his *secret* gave him a *fortress*, a wall behind which he could retreat into *heavenly seclusion* . [Italics mine]

Note that even in the opening passage "it" is used polysemically, as a grammatical expletive and as a pronominal substitution for an unknown. In the first and last sentence, the polysemic "it" suggests how entrenched "it" has already become in Paul's mind. In addition, the order of the descriptive adjectives foreshadows the development of the story: possession, protection, fortress, seclusion. "It" begins as a secret possession but leads to total seclusion.

Immediately after this description of Paul's attitude toward "it," the narrative shifts to a description of what Paul sees transpiring during his geography class. The reverie ends abruptly; and

> In nearly every paragraph of the story, Aiken has plied the tools of the poet--rhythm, meter, and common figures--to congeal meaning, sound, and sense."

in contrast to the preceding passage, the descriptive language here is objective, neutral, extremely precise to suggest Paul's boredom and lack of involvement:

> it was the half-hour for geography. Miss Buell was revolving with one finger, slowly, a huge terrestrial globe which had been placed on her desk. The green and yellow continents passed and repassed, questions were asked and answered, and now the little girl in front of him, Deirdre, who had a funny little constellation of freckles on the back of her neck, exactly like the Big Dipper, was standing up and telling Miss Buell that the equator was the line that ran around the middle.

In addition to establishing contrasting styles, the opening passage is stylistically significant for two additional reasons: (1) it serves as a benchmark by which we can compare Paul's shifting view of reality as the narrative develops; and (2) the passage foreshadows the end of the story. The simile—"it was as if, in some delightful way, his secret gave him a fortress, a wall behind which he could retreat into heavenly seclusion"—changes from a comparative device here to reality for Paul. This kind of simile, which Aiken uses repeatedly, becomes, as it occurs, an indicator of Paul's vision as it becomes increasingly snow laden.

In the following paragraphs Aiken introduces us to the story's two central symbols, the postman and the snow. The fading, muffled footsteps of the postman, who represents the real world, mark the stages of Paul's withdrawal. The snow, the idealized world toward which Paul is moving, possesses the transitory magic that covers, transforms, muffles, and harmonizes a temporal reality which Paul rejects. Also operating as a metaphor for the beckoning new world, the snow becomes the comparative intermediary between us and Paul's vision which Aiken wants us to grasp as vividly as possi-

ble. To embody each intrusion of the snow, Aiken develops these descriptions about poetic figures. The repetition of the "s" captures the onomatopoeic, hissing sound of the snow and suggests the transforming effect it has over Paul:

> They [postman's footsteps] were softer, they had a new secrecy about them, they were muffled and indistinct; and while the rhythm of them was the same, it now said a new thing—it said peace, it said remoteness, it said cold, it said sleep.

Note again, as in paragraph one of the story, the use of the polysemic "it" to introduce the final five clauses. Use of anaphora, parallelism, and cadence add a sense of incantation and foreboding. As in paragraph one, the order of the descriptive nouns—peace, cold, remoteness, sleep—suggests the increasing distance that "it" will move from reality. In all the snow passages, the onomatopoeic effect is subtle and enters as softly as the snow:

> All he now knew was, that at some point or other—perhaps the second day, perhaps the sixth—he had noticed that the presence of the snow was a little more insistent, the sound of it clearer; and conversely, the sound of the postman's footsteps more indistinct.

In other snow passages, Aiken combines the onomatopoeic effect with either rhythm or definite meter to capture the movement and momentum of falling snow. In the final clause in the passage below, predominant dactyls created by polysendeton slow the line to develop a sense of inevitable, increasingly ominous depth:

> the long white ragged lines were drifting and sifting across the street, across the faces of the old houses, whispering and hushing, making little triangles of white in the corners between cobblestones, seething a little when the wind blew them over the ground to a drifted corner; and so it would be all day, getting deeper and deeper and silenter and silenter.

Abruptly, as Paul's conscience once again reverts to the classroom, the reality he perceives is described in decidedly non-rhythmic, non-emotive active voice clauses and sentences. These sentences with their pristine clarity contrast sharply with the complex sentence structure of the preceding passage with its twisting, unpredictable structure which moves as steadily, but unpredictably, as the snow:

> (Miss Buell was now asking if anyone knew the difference between the North Pole and the Magnetic Pole. Deirdre was holding up her flickering brown hand, and he could see the four white dimples that marked the knuckles.)

In redirecting Paul's thoughts from the snow vision to the stark reality of the classroom, Aiken uses parenthesis five separate times in Part I. Aiken's choice of parenthesis suggests that Paul's attitude toward reality is indeed ''parenthetical'': it is cut off from his main thought sequence and even now occurs only as interpolated data within the expanding, beckoning snow vision.

Therefore, throughout Part I and Part II, Aiken steadily intensifies the contrast between the snow world and the real world. The tone emerging from the descriptions of his daily, routine activities becomes increasingly less objective, less neutral, more shrill, disjointed, and irritated: ''A new lamp? A new lamp. Yes, Mother, No, Mother, Yes, Mother. School is going very well. The geometry is very easy, The history is very dull.'' As he walks home from school, Paul's view of a living world not covered with snow is composed of black, desiccated lilac stems, dirty sparrows, a gutter, holding ''a scrap of torn and dirty newspaper, caught in a little delta of filth.'' In contrast, the snow passages become steadily and increasingly richer, more ardent, more intense. The addition of assonance to the ''s'' passages slows the pace of the lines, the repetition of the ''o'' throughout the passage producing a visual euphony:

> nevertheless he did in a sense cease to see, or to see the obvious external world, and substituted for this vision the vision of snow, the sound of snow, and the slow, almost soundless, approach of the postman . . . the sound of its seething was more distinct, more soothing, more persistent.

By the end of Part I, the content of the similes has clearly demarcated the advance of Paul's withdrawal: ''as if it was . . . a fortress,'' to ''as if everything in the world had been insulated by snow,'' to ''as if he were trying to live a double life.'' The similes themselves, as they occur periodically, become a kind of motif of transformation by which we can trace Paul's progress toward complete withdrawal. In addition, they also indicate Paul's continuing inability to apprehend his deteriorating condition, in that he can describe his condition only by comparative statements.

By the end of Part II, Paul's shifting, intensifying, sharply contrasting attitudes toward the real world and the snow world are caught in a definite tension as Paul experiences both worlds concomitantly. At one point in Part II, Aiken uses sharp changes in diction and prosody to focus the tension as Paul wrestles with the claims of the two ontologies. The increasing abstraction of the terms used to describe the snow—words, experience, dream, fairy story, ethereal loveliness—and lengthening sentences enforce the sense of ebullition. These sentenc-

es end with an oxymoron and contrast sharply with the monosyllabic cadence, the final sentence, composed of words that are totally neutral, flat, depersonalized:

> He loved it—he stood still and loved it. Its beauty was paralyzing—beyond all words, all experience, all dream. No fairy story he had ever read could be compared with it—none had ever given him this extraordinary combination of ethereal loveliness with a something else unnameable, which was just faintly and deliciously terrifying. *What was this thing*? [Italics mine]

Aiken will use oxymoron and paradox throughout Part II to sustain the conflict of fear and ecstasy that Paul feels as he finds himself steadily drawn to a vision of thickening snow. In the last passage, ''it'' combines ''ethereal loveliness'' with something ''deliciously terrifying.'' The snow ''soothingly and beautifully encroaches with its subtle gradations of menace, in which he could luxuriate.'' ''Every minute was more beautiful than the last, more menacing.''

Part III describes Paul's final alienation from the real world. He sees the doctor as a ''fat fist,'' a ''fixed false smile,'' grinning with ''false amiability.'' His parents are only ''slippers,'' ''voices,'' and ''hostile presences.'' His paranoia comes to a climax appropriately expressed in a series of similes that show Paul's inability to respond to human concern: ''it was as if one had been stood up on a brilliantly lighted stage, under a great round blaze of spotlight; as if one were merely a trained seal, or a performing dog, or a fish, dipped out of an aquarium and held up by the tail'': ''nevertheless he was aware that all three of them were watching him with an intensity—staring hard at him—as if he had done something monstrous, or was himself some kind of monster.'' Those of the living world most concerned about him are totally depersonified in description, while the snow becomes personified and speaks with the onomatopoeic ''s'' controlling the length and slow, steady rhythm of the line. Again, as in earlier snow passages, the order of descriptive words—new white, cold, sleepy, cease, peace, space—forebodes the outcome:

> Ah, but just wait! Wait till we are alone together! Then I will begin to tell you something new! Something white! something cold! something sleepy! something of cease, and peace, and the long bright curve of space!

The conclusion of Part II, which occurs after Paul's hostile, paranoid confrontation with his parents, shifts his apprehension abruptly to the room and to the activities in the house. The imagery is impersonal, Hopkinsesque in its disjoint, acute precision:

> He could hear the soft irregular flutter of the flames; the cluck-click-cluck-click of the clock; far and faint, two sudden spurts of laughter from the kitchen, as quickly cut off as begun, a murmur of water in the pipes; . . .

Then, equally abruptly, in mid-sentence, Paul's thoughts shift to the impending world of snow. Aiken uses anaphora to build a 46-word clause which demarcates the beginning of Paul's irrevocable plunge into the beckoning world of snow. Each segment of the clause lengthens, becoming more heavily accented. The clauses, linked with verbals and prepositions, produce a sense of momentum that ends with two heavily stressed words and a finality of a "new sound."

> and then, the silence seemed to deepen, to spread out, to become world-long and world-wide, to become timeless and shapeless, and to center inevitably and rightly, with a low and sleepy but enormous concentration of all power, on the beginning of a new sound.

While Aiken has used meter as well as major schemes and tropes in Parts I–III, the main effect of Part IV relies on prosody. Part III concludes with a sentence whose prose rhythm captures both the speed and direction conveyed by the meaning:

> Without / another word / he turned / and ran up / the stairs.

Note the use of iambic feet on either side of four stressed feet to suggest Paul's rapid, decisive movement up the stairs. The iambic feet create a rhythm of forcefulness and decision. Note, in contrast, how the speed of this line has changed from the slow, deliberate pace of the preceding 46-word clause.

Part IV then begins with paradox: "The darkness was coming in long white waves," which introduces the paradoxical reversal that has taken place. Before, the snow had been the "thing," but now the real world has become the unknown, the intruder. As Paul's mother suddenly enters his room, the rhythm and sound of intrusion into his relinquishment (sentence 1) are marked by discord and cacophony, which punctuate his loathing toward his mother:

> But then a gash of horrible light fell brutally across the room from the opening door—the snow drew back hissing—something alien had come into the room— something hostile. This thing rushed at him, clutched at him, shook him—and he was not merely horrified, he was filled with such a loathing as he had never known. What was this? This cruel disturbance? this act of anger and hate? It was as if he had to reach up a hand toward another world for any understanding of

it—an effort of which he was only barely capable. But of that other world he still remembered just enough to know the exorcising words. They tore themselves from his other life suddenly—Mother! Mother! Go away! I hate you!

The description utilizes heavily stressed phrases which emphasize the negative words describing Paul's view of reality. Repetition of "something" . . . enforces the point that reality, not the snow, has become the alien thing. While the opening clause, "But then a gash of horrible light fell brutally across the room from the opening door," is perhaps the most cacophonous, jarring line in the entire story, Aiken will use metrical patterns to accentuate the meaning of lines. For example, "This thing / rushed at him / clutched at him / shook him," uses a spondee and light endings on the remaining three feet to accentuate the monosyllabic verbs. Aiken will also use heavy stresses to slow the line— "What was this?"—and anaphora combined with parallel stress pattern—"this cruel / disturbance? / this act / of anger / and hate?"—to embody the intensity of Paul's loathing. The simile—"as if he had to reach up a hand toward another world for any understanding of it"—the final one in the story, serves as the climatic element in the motif of transformation. Aiken will use molossus (to reach up) followed by the anti-bacchic (a hand toward)— five stressed feet—to suggest the momentum of reaching up.

The final sentence of the passage begins decisively with three spondees —"they tore / themselves / from his"—moves to a softer cretic pattern—"other life"—which suggests the lesser importance of reality—and ends with a molossus— "suddenly"—which prepares us for the heavily accented crucial line—"Mother! Mother! Go away! I hate you!"—which appropriately ends with another molossus.

The reversal of worlds and values now complete, everything "was solved"; the final "exorcising words" make everything "all right." The snow advances "once more." Each clause appropriately ends with a spondee to enforce the finality of the resolution. The rhythm of the description again captures the movement of the snow: "the long / white / wavering lines / rose and fell / like enormous / sea waves."

In the closing passage of the narrative, Aiken chooses an image which maintains the paradox of Paul's story. Instead of developing by an organic process, his story has become "smaller and smaller"; it has come inward instead of opening like a flower—"it is a flower becoming a seed." By inversion Paul's problem is solved. Because the tension has been resolved, the passage lacks noticeable, stressed endings, except for two—"shut your eyes" and "do you hear?"—which accentuate the firm hold the snow now has on him. Much of the lulling quality emanates from the parallel soft endings and the parallel trochees. The words used by the snow to describe the "story" are, like the earlier snow passages, regressive: small, smaller, inward, seed, cold seed. Each ending becomes more accented and builds to the molossus "do you hear?" which introduces the incantatory final line of the passage, the four trochees:

> We'll tell you / the last, / the most / beautiful / and secret / story— / shut your eyes / it is / a very / small story—/ a story—/ that gets smaller / and smaller—/ it comes inward / instead of / opening / like a / flower—/ it is / a flower / becoming a seed— / a little cold seed— / do you hear? / we are / leaning / closer / to you—.

In nearly every paragraph of the story, Aiken has plied the tools of the poet—rhythm, meter, and common figures—to congeal meaning, sound, and sense. For example, when Paul first looks out his window and expects to see snow, he sees only bright sunshine enameling the familiar street. This surprising sight is described in words that are crisply objective; the syntax is regular; the rhythm, as sharp and bumpy as the cobbled street Paul sees:

> What he saw instead, was brilliant sunlight on a roof; and when, astonished, he jumped out of bed and stared down into the street, expecting to see the cobbles obliterated by the snow, he saw nothing but the bare bright cobbles themselves.

Yet, Aiken can rapidly shift his rhythm by incorporating alliteration, simile, onomatopoeia, and loose, irregularly patterned sentences composed of words with light endings to preserve the dual vision that Paul carries. In the passage below, which is typical, in part 1 of the sentence, we feel the gentle rhythm of the snow mixed with the accented actuality of the real cobbles in part 2. The repetitive "ing" words also serve as connectives among the phrases in part 1:

> [A ghost of snow falling in the bright sunlight, softly and steadily floating and turning and pausing, soundlessly meeting the snow that covered, as with a transparent mirage,] [the bare bright cobbles.]

Analysis of Aiken's style thus reveals that there is much more to "Silent Snow, Secret Snow" than

defining the nature of Paul's problem. While the story can be called a case history narrative, Aiken's sustained, crafted style suggests that the narrative has more artistic aims. Even the alliterative title suggests such a purpose. Focusing only on Paul is to miss the most remarkable literary aspects of the story. Combining sense and symbol and rhythm and tone and sound, Aiken uses his poetic skills to draw the reader into Paul's world. Through the art of style, then, Aiken enables us to feel some of the magic and terrifying wonder that the snow world, whatever it is, offers Paul. Because of Aiken's skill in shaping the tools of poetry and rhetoric to fit the goal of the narrative—the vivid and sensual illumination of this particular aspect of human experience—"Silent Snow" will more than likely continue to be enjoyed long after the nature of Paul's problem has ceased to be of any psychological interest.

Source: Elizabeth Tebeaux, "'Silent Snow, Secret Snow': Style as Art," in *Studies in Short Fiction*, Vol. 20, No. 2–3, Spring-Summer, 1983, pp. 105–14.

Sources

Erskine, Thomas L. "The Two Worlds of 'Silent Snow, Secret Snow,'" in *From Fiction to Film: Conrad Aiken's "Silent Snow, Secret Snow,"* edited by Gerald R. Barrett and Thomas L. Erskine, Encino, Calif.: Dickenson Publishing Co., 1972, pp. 86–91.

Gossman, Ann. "'Silent Snow, Secret Snow': The Child as Artist," in *Studies in Short Fiction*, Vol. 1, No. 2, Winter, 1964, pp. 123–28.

Hamalian, Leo. "Aiken's 'Silent Snow, Secret Snow,'" in *Explicator*, Vol. 7, 1948, Item 17.

Hoffman, Frederick J. *Conrad Aiken*, New York: Twayne Publishers, 1962.

———. *Freudianism and the Literary Mind*, 2nd ed., Baton Rouge: Louisiana State University Press, 1957.

Slap, Laura. "Conrad Aiken's 'Silent Snow, Secret Snow': Defenses against the Primal Scene," in *American Imago*, Vol. 37, 1980, pp. 1–11.

Swan, Jesse. "At the Edge of Sound and Silence: Conrad Aiken's 'Senlin: A Biography' and 'Silent Snow, Secret Snow,'" in *The Southern Literary Journal*, Vol. XXII, No. 1, Fall, 1989, pp. 41–9.

Tebeaux, Elizabeth. "'Silent Snow, Secret Snow': Style as Art." *Studies in Short Fiction*, Vol. 20, No. 2-3 , Spring-Summer, 1983, pp. 105–14.

Further Reading

Butscher, Edward. *Conrad Aiken: Poet of White Horse Vale*, Athens: University of Georgia Press, 1988.
    Butscher provides biographical context for Aiken's work.

Erskine, Thomas L. "The Two Worlds of 'Silent Snow, Secret Snow,'" in *From Fiction to Film: Conrad Aiken's "Silent Snow, Secret Snow,"* edited by Gerald R. Barrett and Thomas L. Erskine, Encino, Calif.: Dickenson Publishing Co., 1972, pp. 86–91.
    Erskine offers his interpretation of "Silent Snow, Secret Snow," particularly the theme of discovery.

Hoffman, Frederick J. *Conrad Aiken,* New York: Twayne Publishers, 1962.
    Hoffmann evaluates Aiken's achievement. For Hoffman, the snow is a symbol of death, an interpretation which assigns the story firmly to the realm of the tragic.

Glossary of Literary Terms

A

Aestheticism: A literary and artistic movement of the nineteenth century. Followers of the movement believed that art should not be mixed with social, political, or moral teaching. The statement ''art for art's sake'' is a good summary of aestheticism. The movement had its roots in France, but it gained widespread importance in England in the last half of the nineteenth century, where it helped change the Victorian practice of including moral lessons in literature. Edgar Allan Poe is one of the best-known American ''aesthetes.''

Allegory: A narrative technique in which characters representing things or abstract ideas are used to convey a message or teach a lesson. Allegory is typically used to teach moral, ethical, or religious lessons but is sometimes used for satiric or political purposes. Many fairy tales are allegories.

Allusion: A reference to a familiar literary or historical person or event, used to make an idea more easily understood. Joyce Carol Oates's story ''Where Are You Going, Where Have You Been?'' exhibits several allusions to popular music.

Analogy: A comparison of two things made to explain something unfamiliar through its similarities to something familiar, or to prove one point based on the acceptance of another. Similes and metaphors are types of analogies.

Antagonist: The major character in a narrative or drama who works against the hero or protagonist. The Misfit in Flannery O'Connor's story ''A Good Man Is Hard to Find'' serves as the antagonist for the Grandmother.

Anthology: A collection of similar works of literature, art, or music. Zora Neale Hurston's ''The Eatonville Anthology'' is a collection of stories that take place in the same town.

Anthropomorphism: The presentation of animals or objects in human shape or with human characteristics. The term is derived from the Greek word for ''human form.'' The fur necklet in Katherine Mansfield's story ''Miss Brill'' has anthropomorphic characteristics.

Anti-hero: A central character in a work of literature who lacks traditional heroic qualities such as courage, physical prowess, and fortitude. Anti-heroes typically distrust conventional values and are unable to commit themselves to any ideals. They generally feel helpless in a world over which they have no control. Anti-heroes usually accept, and often celebrate, their positions as social outcasts. A well-known anti-hero is Walter Mitty in James Thurber's story ''The Secret Life of Walter Mitty.''

Archetype: The word archetype is commonly used to describe an original pattern or model from which all other things of the same kind are made. Archetypes are the literary images that grow out of the ''collective unconscious,'' a theory proposed by psychologist Carl Jung. They appear in literature as incidents and plots that repeat basic patterns of life. They may also appear as stereotyped characters. The ''schlemiel'' of Yiddish literature is an archetype.

Autobiography: A narrative in which an individual tells his or her life story. Examples include Benjamin Franklin's *Autobiography* and Amy Hempel's story ''In the Cemetery Where Al Jolson Is Buried,'' which has autobiographical characteristics even though it is a work of fiction.

Avant-garde: A literary term that describes new writing that rejects traditional approaches to literature in favor of innovations in style or content. Twentieth-century examples of the literary *avant-garde* include the modernists and the minimalists.

B

Belles-lettres: A French term meaning ''fine letters'' or ''beautiful writing.'' It is often used as a synonym for literature, typically referring to imaginative and artistic rather than scientific or expository writing. Current usage sometimes restricts the meaning to light or humorous writing and appreciative essays about literature. Lewis Carroll's *Alice in Wonderland* epitomizes the realm of belles-lettres.

Bildungsroman: A German word meaning ''novel of development.'' The *bildungsroman* is a study of the maturation of a youthful character, typically brought about through a series of social or sexual encounters that lead to self-awareness. J. D. Salinger's *Catcher in the Rye* is a *bildungsroman*, and Doris Lessing's story ''Through the Tunnel'' exhibits characteristics of a *bildungsroman* as well.

Black Aesthetic Movement: A period of artistic and literary development among African Americans in the 1960s and early 1970s. This was the first major African-American artistic movement since the Harlem Renaissance and was closely paralleled by the civil rights and black power movements. The black aesthetic writers attempted to produce works of art that would be meaningful to the black masses. Key figures in black aesthetics included one of its founders, poet and playwright Amiri Baraka, formerly known as LeRoi Jones; poet and essayist Haki R. Madhubuti, formerly Don L. Lee; poet and playwright Sonia Sanchez; and dramatist Ed Bullins. Works representative of the Black Aesthetic Movement include Amiri Baraka's play *Dutchman,* a 1964 Obie award-winner.

Black Humor: Writing that places grotesque elements side by side with humorous ones in an attempt to shock the reader, forcing him or her to laugh at the horrifying reality of a disordered world. ''Lamb to the Slaughter,'' by Roald Dahl, in which a placid housewife murders her husband and serves the murder weapon to the investigating policemen, is an example of black humor.

C

Catharsis: The release or purging of unwanted emotions—specifically fear and pity—brought about by exposure to art. The term was first used by the Greek philosopher Aristotle in his *Poetics* to refer to the desired effect of tragedy on spectators.

Character: Broadly speaking, a person in a literary work. The actions of characters are what constitute the plot of a story, novel, or poem. There are numerous types of characters, ranging from simple, stereotypical figures to intricate, multifaceted ones. ''Characterization'' is the process by which an author creates vivid, believable characters in a work of art. This may be done in a variety of ways, including (1) direct description of the character by the narrator; (2) the direct presentation of the speech, thoughts, or actions of the character; and (3) the responses of other characters to the character. The term ''character'' also refers to a form originated by the ancient Greek writer Theophrastus that later became popular in the seventeenth and eighteenth centuries. It is a short essay or sketch of a person who prominently displays a specific attribute or quality, such as miserliness or ambition. ''Miss Brill,'' a story by Katherine Mansfield, is an example of a character sketch.

Classical: In its strictest definition in literary criticism, classicism refers to works of ancient Greek or Roman literature. The term may also be used to describe a literary work of recognized importance (a ''classic'') from any time period or literature that exhibits the traits of classicism. Examples of later works and authors now described as classical include French literature of the seventeenth century, Western novels of the nineteenth century, and American fiction of the mid-nineteenth century such as that written by James Fenimore Cooper and Mark Twain.

Climax: The turning point in a narrative, the moment when the conflict is at its most intense. Typically, the structure of stories, novels, and plays is one of rising action, in which tension builds to the climax, followed by falling action, in which tension lessens as the story moves to its conclusion.

Comedy: One of two major types of drama, the other being tragedy. Its aim is to amuse, and it typically ends happily. Comedy assumes many forms, such as farce and burlesque, and uses a variety of techniques, from parody to satire. In a restricted sense the term comedy refers only to dramatic presentations, but in general usage it is commonly applied to nondramatic works as well.

Comic Relief: The use of humor to lighten the mood of a serious or tragic story, especially in plays. The technique is very common in Elizabethan works, and can be an integral part of the plot or simply a brief event designed to break the tension of the scene.

Conflict: The conflict in a work of fiction is the issue to be resolved in the story. It usually occurs between two characters, the protagonist and the antagonist, or between the protagonist and society or the protagonist and himself or herself. The conflict in Washington Irving's story "The Devil and Tom Walker" is that the Devil wants Tom Walker's soul but Tom does not want to go to hell.

Criticism: The systematic study and evaluation of literary works, usually based on a specific method or set of principles. An important part of literary studies since ancient times, the practice of criticism has given rise to numerous theories, methods, and "schools," sometimes producing conflicting, even contradictory, interpretations of literature in general as well as of individual works. Even such basic issues as what constitutes a poem or a novel have been the subject of much criticism over the centuries. Seminal texts of literary criticism include Plato's *Republic,* Aristotle's *Poetics,* Sir Philip Sidney's *The Defence of Poesie,* and John Dryden's *Of Dramatic Poesie.* Contemporary schools of criticism include deconstruction, feminist, psychoanalytic, poststructuralist, new historicist, postcolonialist, and reader-response.

D

Deconstruction: A method of literary criticism characterized by multiple conflicting interpretations of a given work. Deconstructionists consider the impact of the language of a work and suggest that the true meaning of the work is not necessarily the meaning that the author intended.

Deduction: The process of reaching a conclusion through reasoning from general premises to a specific premise. Arthur Conan Doyle's character Sherlock Holmes often used deductive reasoning to solve mysteries.

Denotation: The definition of a word, apart from the impressions or feelings it creates in the reader. The word "apartheid" denotes a political and economic policy of segregation by race, but its connotations—oppression, slavery, inequality—are numerous.

Denouement: A French word meaning "the unknotting." In literature, it denotes the resolution of conflict in fiction or drama. The *denouement* follows the climax and provides an outcome to the primary plot situation as well as an explanation of secondary plot complications. A well-known example of *denouement* is the last scene of the play *As You Like It* by William Shakespeare, in which couples are married, an evildoer repents, the identities of two disguised characters are revealed, and a ruler is restored to power. Also known as "falling action."

Detective Story: A narrative about the solution of a mystery or the identification of a criminal. The conventions of the detective story include the detective's scrupulous use of logic in solving the mystery; incompetent or ineffectual police; a suspect who appears guilty at first but is later proved innocent; and the detective's friend or confidant—often the narrator—whose slowness in interpreting clues emphasizes by contrast the detective's brilliance. Edgar Allan Poe's "Murders in the Rue Morgue" is commonly regarded as the earliest example of this type of story. Other practitioners are Arthur Conan Doyle, Dashiell Hammett, and Agatha Christie.

Dialogue: Dialogue is conversation between people in a literary work. In its most restricted sense, it refers specifically to the speech of characters in a drama. As a specific literary genre, a "dialogue" is a composition in which characters debate an issue or idea.

Didactic: A term used to describe works of literature that aim to teach a moral, religious, political, or practical lesson. Although didactic elements are often found in artistically pleasing works, the term "didactic" usually refers to literature in which the message is more important than the form. The term may also be used to criticize a work that the critic finds "overly didactic," that is, heavy-handed in its delivery of a lesson. An example of didactic literature is John Bunyan's *Pilgrim's Progress.*

Dramatic Irony: Occurs when the reader of a work of literature knows something that a character in the work itself does not know. The irony is in the contrast between the intended meaning of the statements or actions of a character and the additional information understood by the audience.

Dystopia: An imaginary place in a work of fiction where the characters lead dehumanized, fearful lives. **George Orwell's** *Nineteen Eighty-four,* and Margaret Atwood's *Handmaid's Tale* portray versions of dystopia.

E

Edwardian: Describes cultural conventions identified with the period of the reign of Edward VII of England (1901-1910). Writers of the Edwardian Age typically displayed a strong reaction against the propriety and conservatism of the Victorian Age. Their work often exhibits distrust of authority in religion, politics, and art and expresses strong doubts about the soundness of conventional values. Writers of this era include E. M. Forster, H. G. Wells, and Joseph Conrad.

Empathy: A sense of shared experience, including emotional and physical feelings, with someone or something other than oneself. Empathy is often used to describe the response of a reader to a literary character.

Epilogue: A concluding statement or section of a literary work. In dramas, particularly those of the seventeenth and eighteenth centuries, the epilogue is a closing speech, often in verse, delivered by an actor at the end of a play and spoken directly to the audience.

Epiphany: A sudden revelation of truth inspired by a seemingly trivial incident. The term was widely used by James Joyce in his critical writings, and the stories in Joyce's *Dubliners* are commonly called ''epiphanies.''

Epistolary Novel: A novel in the form of letters. The form was particularly popular in the eighteenth century. The form can also be applied to short stories, as in Edwidge Danticat's ''Children of the Sea.''

Epithet: A word or phrase, often disparaging or abusive, that expresses a character trait of someone or something. ''The Napoleon of crime'' is an epithet applied to Professor Moriarty, arch-rival of Sherlock Holmes in Arthur Conan Doyle's series of detective stories.

Existentialism: A predominantly twentieth-century philosophy concerned with the nature and perception of human existence. There are two major strains of existentialist thought: atheistic and Christian. Followers of atheistic existentialism believe that the individual is alone in a godless universe and that the basic human condition is one of suffering and loneliness. Nevertheless, because there are no fixed values, individuals can create their own characters—indeed, they can shape themselves—through the exercise of free will. The atheistic strain culminates in and is popularly associated with the works of Jean-Paul Sartre. The Christian existentialists, on the other hand, believe that only in God may people find freedom from life's anguish. The two strains hold certain beliefs in common: that existence cannot be fully understood or described through empirical effort; that anguish is a universal element of life; that individuals must bear responsibility for their actions; and that there is no common standard of behavior or perception for religious and ethical matters. Existentialist thought figures prominently in the works of such authors as Franz Kafka, Fyodor Dostoyevsky, and Albert Camus.

Expatriatism: The practice of leaving one's country to live for an extended period in another country. Literary expatriates include Irish author James Joyce who moved to Italy and France, American writers James Baldwin, Ernest Hemingway, Gertrude Stein, and F. Scott Fitzgerald who lived and wrote in Paris, and Polish novelist Joseph Conrad in England.

Exposition: Writing intended to explain the nature of an idea, thing, or theme. Expository writing is often combined with description, narration, or argument.

Expressionism: An indistinct literary term, originally used to describe an early twentieth-century school of German painting. The term applies to almost any mode of unconventional, highly subjective writing that distorts reality in some way. Advocates of Expressionism include Federico Garcia Lorca, Eugene O'Neill, Franz Kafka, and James Joyce.

F

Fable: A prose or verse narrative intended to convey a moral. Animals or inanimate objects with human characteristics often serve as characters in fables. A famous fable is Aesop's "The Tortoise and the Hare."

Fantasy: A literary form related to mythology and folklore. Fantasy literature is typically set in nonexistent realms and features supernatural beings. Notable examples of literature with elements of fantasy are Gabriel Garcia Marquez's story "The Handsomest Drowned Man in the World" and Ursula K. LeGuin's "The Ones Who Walk Away from Omelas."

Farce: A type of comedy characterized by broad humor, outlandish incidents, and often vulgar subject matter. Much of the comedy in film and television could more accurately be described as farce.

Fiction: Any story that is the product of imagination rather than a documentation of fact. Characters and events in such narratives may be based in real life but their ultimate form and configuration is a creation of the author.

Figurative Language: A technique in which an author uses figures of speech such as hyperbole, irony, metaphor, or simile for a particular effect. Figurative language is the opposite of literal language, in which every word is truthful, accurate, and free of exaggeration or embellishment.

Flashback: A device used in literature to present action that occurred before the beginning of the story. Flashbacks are often introduced as the dreams or recollections of one or more characters.

Foil: A character in a work of literature whose physical or psychological qualities contrast strongly with, and therefore highlight, the corresponding qualities of another character. In his Sherlock Holmes stories, Arthur Conan Doyle portrayed Dr. Watson as a man of normal habits and intelligence, making him a foil for the eccentric and unusually perceptive Sherlock Holmes.

Folklore: Traditions and myths preserved in a culture or group of people. Typically, these are passed on by word of mouth in various forms—such as legends, songs, and proverbs—or preserved in customs and ceremonies. Washington Irving, in "The Devil and Tom Walker" and many of his other stories, incorporates many elements of the folklore of New England and Germany.

Folktale: A story originating in oral tradition. Folktales fall into a variety of categories, including legends, ghost stories, fairy tales, fables, and anecdotes based on historical figures and events.

Foreshadowing: A device used in literature to create expectation or to set up an explanation of later developments. Edgar Allan Poe uses foreshadowing to create suspense in "The Fall of the House of Usher" when the narrator comments on the crumbling state of disrepair in which he finds the house.

G

Genre: A category of literary work. Genre may refer to both the content of a given work—tragedy, comedy, horror, science fiction—and to its form, such as poetry, novel, or drama.

Gilded Age: A period in American history during the 1870s and after characterized by political corruption and materialism. A number of important novels of social and political criticism were written during this time. Henry James and Kate Chopin are two writers who were prominent during the Gilded Age.

Gothicism: In literature, works characterized by a taste for medieval or morbid characters and situations. A gothic novel prominently features elements of horror, the supernatural, gloom, and violence: clanking chains, terror, ghosts, medieval castles, and unexplained phenomena. The term "gothic novel" is also applied to novels that lack elements of the traditional Gothic setting but that create a similar atmosphere of terror or dread. The term can also be applied to stories, plays, and poems. Mary Shelley's *Frankenstein* and Joyce Carol Oates's *Bellefleur* are both gothic novels.

Grotesque: In literature, a work that is characterized by exaggeration, deformity, freakishness, and disorder. The grotesque often includes an element of comic absurdity. Examples of the grotesque can be found in the works of Edgar Allan Poe, Flannery O'Connor, Joseph Heller, and Shirley Jackson.

H

Harlem Renaissance: The Harlem Renaissance of the 1920s is generally considered the first significant movement of black writers and artists in the United States. During this period, new and established black writers, many of whom lived in the region of New York City known as Harlem, published more fiction and poetry than ever before, the first influential black literary journals were established, and black authors and artists received their first widespread recognition and serious critical appraisal. Among the major writers associated with this period are Countee Cullen, Langston Hughes, Arna Bontemps, and Zora Neale Hurston.

Hero/Heroine: The principal sympathetic character in a literary work. Heroes and heroines typically exhibit admirable traits: idealism, courage, and integrity, for example. Famous heroes and heroines of literature include Charles Dickens's Oliver Twist, Margaret Mitchell's Scarlett O'Hara, and the anonymous narrator in Ralph Ellison's *Invisible Man*.

Hyperbole: Deliberate exaggeration used to achieve an effect. In William Shakespeare's *Macbeth,* Lady Macbeth hyperbolizes when she says, ''All the perfumes of Arabia could not sweeten this little hand.''

I

Image: A concrete representation of an object or sensory experience. Typically, such a representation helps evoke the feelings associated with the object or experience itself. Images are either ''literal'' or ''figurative.'' Literal images are especially concrete and involve little or no extension of the obvious meaning of the words used to express them. Figurative images do not follow the literal meaning of the words exactly. Images in literature are usually visual, but the term ''image'' can also refer to the representation of any sensory experience.

Imagery: The array of images in a literary work. Also used to convey the author's overall use of figurative language in a work.

In medias res: A Latin term meaning ''in the middle of things.'' It refers to the technique of beginning a story at its midpoint and then using various flashback devices to reveal previous action. This technique originated in such epics as Virgil's *Aeneid*.

Interior Monologue: A narrative technique in which characters' thoughts are revealed in a way that appears to be uncontrolled by the author. The interior monologue typically aims to reveal the inner self of a character. It portrays emotional experiences as they occur at both a conscious and unconscious level. One of the best-known interior monologues in English is the Molly Bloom section at the close of James Joyce's *Ulysses*. Katherine Anne Porter's ''The Jilting of Granny Weatherall'' is also told in the form of an interior monologue.

Irony: In literary criticism, the effect of language in which the intended meaning is the opposite of what

is stated. The title of Jonathan Swift's ''A Modest Proposal'' is ironic because what Swift proposes in this essay is cannibalism—hardly ''modest.''

J

Jargon: Language that is used or understood only by a select group of people. Jargon may refer to terminology used in a certain profession, such as computer jargon, or it may refer to any nonsensical language that is not understood by most people. Anthony Burgess's *A Clockwork Orange* and James Thurber's ''The Secret Life of Walter Mitty'' both use jargon.

K

Knickerbocker Group: An indistinct group of New York writers of the first half of the nineteenth century. Members of the group were linked only by location and a common theme: New York life. Two famous members of the Knickerbocker Group were Washington Irving and William Cullen Bryant. The group's name derives from Irving's *Knickerbocker's History of New York*.

L

Literal Language: An author uses literal language when he or she writes without exaggerating or embellishing the subject matter and without any tools of figurative language. To say ''He ran very quickly down the street'' is to use literal language, whereas to say ''He ran like a hare down the street'' would be using figurative language.

Literature: Literature is broadly defined as any written or spoken material, but the term most often refers to creative works. Literature includes poetry, drama, fiction, and many kinds of nonfiction writing, as well as oral, dramatic, and broadcast compositions not necessarily preserved in a written format, such as films and television programs.

Lost Generation: A term first used by Gertrude Stein to describe the post-World War I generation of American writers: men and women haunted by a sense of betrayal and emptiness brought about by the destructiveness of the war. The term is commonly applied to Hart Crane, Ernest Hemingway, F. Scott Fitzgerald, and others.

M

Magic Realism: A form of literature that incorporates fantasy elements or supernatural occurrences into the narrative and accepts them as truth. Gabriel Garcia Marquez and Laura Esquivel are two writers known for their works of magic realism.

Metaphor: A figure of speech that expresses an idea through the image of another object. Metaphors suggest the essence of the first object by identifying it with certain qualities of the second object. An example is "But soft, what light through yonder window breaks?/ It is the east, and Juliet is the sun" in William Shakespeare's *Romeo and Juliet*. Here, Juliet, the first object, is identified with qualities of the second object, the sun.

Minimalism: A literary style characterized by spare, simple prose with few elaborations. In minimalism, the main theme of the work is often never discussed directly. Amy Hempel and Ernest Hemingway are two writers known for their works of minimalism.

Modernism: Modern literary practices. Also, the principles of a literary school that lasted from roughly the beginning of the twentieth century until the end of World War II. Modernism is defined by its rejection of the literary conventions of the nineteenth century and by its opposition to conventional morality, taste, traditions, and economic values. Many writers are associated with the concepts of modernism, including Albert Camus, D. H. Lawrence, Ernest Hemingway, William Faulkner, Eugene O'Neill, and James Joyce.

Monologue: A composition, written or oral, by a single individual. More specifically, a speech given by a single individual in a drama or other public entertainment. It has no set length, although it is usually several or more lines long. "I Stand Here Ironing" by Tillie Olsen is an example of a story written in the form of a monologue.

Mood: The prevailing emotions of a work or of the author in his or her creation of the work. The mood of a work is not always what might be expected based on its subject matter.

Motif: A theme, character type, image, metaphor, or other verbal element that recurs throughout a single work of literature or occurs in a number of different works over a period of time. For example, the color white in Herman Melville's *Moby Dick* is a "specific" *motif,* while the trials of star-crossed lovers is a "conventional" *motif* from the literature of all periods.

N

Narration: The telling of a series of events, real or invented. A narration may be either a simple narrative, in which the events are recounted chronologically, or a narrative with a plot, in which the account is given in a style reflecting the author's artistic concept of the story. Narration is sometimes used as a synonym for "storyline."

Narrative: A verse or prose accounting of an event or sequence of events, real or invented. The term is also used as an adjective in the sense "method of narration." For example, in literary criticism, the expression "narrative technique" usually refers to the way the author structures and presents his or her story. Different narrative forms include diaries, travelogues, novels, ballads, epics, short stories, and other fictional forms.

Narrator: The teller of a story. The narrator may be the author or a character in the story through whom the author speaks. Huckleberry Finn is the narrator of Mark Twain's *The Adventures of Huckleberry Finn.*

Novella: An Italian term meaning "story." This term has been especially used to describe fourteenth-century Italian tales, but it also refers to modern short novels. Modern novellas include Leo Tolstoy's *The Death of Ivan Ilich,* Fyodor Dostoyevsky's *Notes from the Underground,* and Joseph Conrad's *Heart of Darkness.*

O

Oedipus Complex: A son's romantic obsession with his mother. The phrase is derived from the story of the ancient Theban hero Oedipus, who unknowingly killed his father and married his mother, and was popularized by Sigmund Freud's theory of psychoanalysis. Literary occurrences of the Oedipus complex include Sophocles' *Oedipus Rex* and D. H. Lawrence's "The Rocking-Horse Winner."

Onomatopoeia: The use of words whose sounds express or suggest their meaning. In its simplest sense, onomatopoeia may be represented by words that mimic the sounds they denote such as "hiss" or "meow." At a more subtle level, the pattern and rhythm of sounds and rhymes of a line or poem may be onomatopoeic.

Oral Tradition: A process by which songs, ballads, folklore, and other material are transmitted by word of mouth. The tradition of oral transmission predates the written record systems of literate society.

Oral transmission preserves material sometimes over generations, although often with variations. Memory plays a large part in the recitation and preservation of orally transmitted material. Native American myths and legends, and African folktales told by plantation slaves are examples of orally transmitted literature.

P

Parable: A story intended to teach a moral lesson or answer an ethical question. Examples of parables are the stories told by Jesus Christ in the New Testament, notably ''The Prodigal Son,'' but parables also are used in Sufism, rabbinic literature, Hasidism, and Zen Buddhism. Isaac Bashevis Singer's story ''Gimpel the Fool'' exhibits characteristics of a parable.

Paradox: A statement that appears illogical or contradictory at first, but may actually point to an underlying truth. A literary example of a paradox is George Orwell's statement ''All animals are equal, but some animals are more equal than others'' in *Animal Farm*.

Parody: In literature, this term refers to an imitation of a serious literary work or the signature style of a particular author in a ridiculous manner. A typical parody adopts the style of the original and applies it to an inappropriate subject for humorous effect. Parody is a form of satire and could be considered the literary equivalent of a caricature or cartoon. Henry Fielding's *Shamela* is a parody of Samuel Richardson's *Pamela*.

Persona: A Latin term meaning ''mask.'' Personae are the characters in a fictional work of literature. The persona generally functions as a mask through which the author tells a story in a voice other than his or her own. A persona is usually either a character in a story who acts as a narrator or an ''implied author,'' a voice created by the author to act as the narrator for himself or herself. The persona in Charlotte Perkins Gilman's story ''The Yellow Wallpaper'' is the unnamed young mother experiencing a mental breakdown.

Personification: A figure of speech that gives human qualities to abstract ideas, animals, and inanimate objects. To say that ''the sun is smiling'' is to personify the sun.

Plot: The pattern of events in a narrative or drama. In its simplest sense, the plot guides the author in composing the work and helps the reader follow the work. Typically, plots exhibit causality and unity and have a beginning, a middle, and an end. Sometimes, however, a plot may consist of a series of disconnected events, in which case it is known as an ''episodic plot.''

Poetic Justice: An outcome in a literary work, not necessarily a poem, in which the good are rewarded and the evil are punished, especially in ways that particularly fit their virtues or crimes. For example, a murderer may himself be murdered, or a thief will find himself penniless.

Poetic License: Distortions of fact and literary convention made by a writer—not always a poet—for the sake of the effect gained. Poetic license is closely related to the concept of ''artistic freedom.'' An author exercises poetic license by saying that a pile of money ''reaches as high as a mountain'' when the pile is actually only a foot or two high.

Point of View: The narrative perspective from which a literary work is presented to the reader. There are four traditional points of view. The ''third person omniscient'' gives the reader a ''godlike'' perspective, unrestricted by time or place, from which to see actions and look into the minds of characters. This allows the author to comment openly on characters and events in the work. The ''third person'' point of view presents the events of the story from outside of any single character's perception, much like the omniscient point of view, but the reader must understand the action as it takes place and without any special insight into characters' minds or motivations. The ''first person'' or ''personal'' point of view relates events as they are perceived by a single character. The main character ''tells'' the story and may offer opinions about the action and characters which differ from those of the author. Much less common than omniscient, third person, and first person is the ''second person'' point of view, wherein the author tells the story as if it is happening to the reader. James Thurber employs the omniscient point of view in his short story ''The Secret Life of Walter Mitty.'' Ernest Hemingway's ''A Clean, Well-Lighted Place'' is a short story told from the third person point of view. Mark Twain's novel *Huckleberry Finn* is presented from the first person viewpoint. Jay McInerney's *Bright Lights, Big City* is an example of a novel which uses the second person point of view.

Pornography: Writing intended to provoke feelings of lust in the reader. Such works are often condemned by critics and teachers, but those which can be shown to have literary value are viewed less harshly. Literary works that have been described as pornographic include D. H. Lawrence's *Lady Chatterley's Lover* and James Joyce's *Ulysses*.

Post-Aesthetic Movement: An artistic response made by African Americans to the black aesthetic movement of the 1960s and early 1970s. Writers since that time have adopted a somewhat different tone in their work, with less emphasis placed on the disparity between black and white in the United States. In the words of post-aesthetic authors such as Toni Morrison, John Edgar Wideman, and Kristin Hunter, African Americans are portrayed as looking inward for answers to their own questions, rather than always looking to the outside world. Two well-known examples of works produced as part of the post-aesthetic movement are the Pulitzer Prize-winning novels *The Color Purple* by Alice Walker and *Beloved* by Toni Morrison.

Postmodernism: Writing from the 1960s forward characterized by experimentation and application of modernist elements, which include existentialism and alienation. Postmodernists have gone a step further in the rejection of tradition begun with the modernists by also rejecting traditional forms, preferring the anti-novel over the novel and the anti-hero over the hero. Postmodern writers include Thomas Pynchon, Margaret Drabble, and Gabriel Garcia Marquez.

Prologue: An introductory section of a literary work. It often contains information establishing the situation of the characters or presents information about the setting, time period, or action. In drama, the prologue is spoken by a chorus or by one of the principal characters.

Prose: A literary medium that attempts to mirror the language of everyday speech. It is distinguished from poetry by its use of unmetered, unrhymed language consisting of logically related sentences. Prose is usually grouped into paragraphs that form a cohesive whole such as an essay or a novel. The term is sometimes used to mean an author's general writing.

Protagonist: The central character of a story who serves as a focus for its themes and incidents and as the principal rationale for its development. The protagonist is sometimes referred to in discussions of modern literature as the hero or anti-hero. Well-known protagonists are Hamlet in William Shakespeare's *Hamlet* and Jay Gatsby in F. Scott Fitzgerald's *The Great Gatsby*.

R

Realism: A nineteenth-century European literary movement that sought to portray familiar characters, situations, and settings in a realistic manner. This was done primarily by using an objective narrative point of view and through the buildup of accurate detail. The standard for success of any realistic work depends on how faithfully it transfers common experience into fictional forms. The realistic method may be altered or extended, as in stream of consciousness writing, to record highly subjective experience. Contemporary authors who often write in a realistic way include Nadine Gordimer and Grace Paley.

Resolution: The portion of a story following the climax, in which the conflict is resolved. The resolution of Jane Austen's *Northanger Abbey* is neatly summed up in the following sentence: "Henry and Catherine were married, the bells rang and every body smiled."

Rising Action: The part of a drama where the plot becomes increasingly complicated. Rising action leads up to the climax, or turning point, of a drama. The final "chase scene" of an action film is generally the rising action which culminates in the film's climax.

Roman a clef: A French phrase meaning "novel with a key." It refers to a narrative in which real persons are portrayed under fictitious names. Jack Kerouac, for example, portrayed various his friends under fictitious names in the novel *On the Road*. D. H. Lawrence based "The Rocking-Horse Winner" on a family he knew.

Romanticism: This term has two widely accepted meanings. In historical criticism, it refers to a European intellectual and artistic movement of the late eighteenth and early nineteenth centuries that sought greater freedom of personal expression than that allowed by the strict rules of literary form and logic of the eighteenth-century neoclassicists. The Romantics preferred emotional and imaginative expression to rational analysis. They considered the individual to be at the center of all experience and so placed him or her at the center of their art. The Romantics believed that the creative imagination reveals nobler truths—unique feelings and attitudes—than those that could be discovered by logic or by scientific examination. "Romanticism" is also used as a general term to refer to a type of sensibility found in all periods of literary history and usually considered to be in opposition to the principles of classicism. In this sense, Romanticism signifies any work or philosophy in which the exotic or dreamlike figure strongly, or that is devoted to individualistic expression, self-analysis, or a pursuit of a higher realm of knowledge than can be discovered by human reason. Prominent Romantics include Jean-Jacques Rousseau, William Wordsworth, John Keats, Lord Byron, and Johann Wolfgang von Goethe.

S

Satire: A work that uses ridicule, humor, and wit to criticize and provoke change in human nature and institutions. Voltaire's novella *Candide* and Jonathan Swift's essay ''A Modest Proposal'' are both satires. Flannery O'Connor's portrayal of the family in ''A Good Man Is Hard to Find'' is a satire of a modern, Southern, American family.

Science Fiction: A type of narrative based upon real or imagined scientific theories and technology. Science fiction is often peopled with alien creatures and set on other planets or in different dimensions. Popular writers of science fiction are Isaac Asimov, Karel Capek, Ray Bradbury, and Ursula K. Le Guin.

Setting: The time, place, and culture in which the action of a narrative takes place. The elements of setting may include geographic location, characters's physical and mental environments, prevailing cultural attitudes, or the historical time in which the action takes place.

Short Story: A fictional prose narrative shorter and more focused than a novella. The short story usually deals with a single episode and often a single character. The ''tone,'' the author's attitude toward his or her subject and audience, is uniform throughout. The short story frequently also lacks *denouement*, ending instead at its climax.

Signifying Monkey: A popular trickster figure in black folklore, with hundreds of tales about this character documented since the 19th century. Henry Louis Gates Jr. examines the history of the signifying monkey in *The Signifying Monkey: Towards a Theory of Afro-American Literary Criticism,* published in 1988.

Simile: A comparison, usually using ''like'' or ''as,''of two essentially dissimilar things, as in ''coffee as cold as ice'' or ''He sounded like a broken record.'' The title of Ernest Hemingway's ''Hills Like White Elephants'' contains a simile.

Social Realism: The Socialist Realism school of literary theory was proposed by Maxim Gorky and established as a dogma by the first Soviet Congress of Writers. It demanded adherence to a communist worldview in works of literature. Its doctrines required an objective viewpoint comprehensible to the working classes and themes of social struggle featuring strong proletarian heroes. Gabriel Garcia Marquez's stories exhibit some characteristics of Socialist Realism.

Stereotype: A stereotype was originally the name for a duplication made during the printing process; this led to its modern definition as a person or thing that is (or is assumed to be) the same as all others of its type. Common stereotypical characters include the absent-minded professor, the nagging wife, the troublemaking teenager, and the kindhearted grandmother.

Stream of Consciousness: A narrative technique for rendering the inward experience of a character. This technique is designed to give the impression of an ever-changing series of thoughts, emotions, images, and memories in the spontaneous and seemingly illogical order that they occur in life. The textbook example of stream of consciousness is the last section of James Joyce's *Ulysses.*

Structure: The form taken by a piece of literature. The structure may be made obvious for ease of understanding, as in nonfiction works, or may be obscured for artistic purposes, as in some poetry or seemingly ''unstructured'' prose.

Style: A writer's distinctive manner of arranging words to suit his or her ideas and purpose in writing. The unique imprint of the author's personality upon his or her writing, style is the product of an author's way of arranging ideas and his or her use of diction, different sentence structures, rhythm, figures of speech, rhetorical principles, and other elements of composition.

Suspense: A literary device in which the author maintains the audience's attention through the build-up of events, the outcome of which will soon be revealed. Suspense in William Shakespeare's *Hamlet* is sustained throughout by the question of whether or not the Prince will achieve what he has been instructed to do and of what he intends to do.

Symbol: Something that suggests or stands for something else without losing its original identity. In literature, symbols combine their literal meaning with the suggestion of an abstract concept. Literary symbols are of two types: those that carry complex associations of meaning no matter what their contexts, and those that derive their suggestive meaning from their functions in specific literary works. Examples of symbols are sunshine suggesting happiness, rain suggesting sorrow, and storm clouds suggesting despair.

T

Tale: A story told by a narrator with a simple plot and little character development. Tales are usually relatively short and often carry a simple message. Examples of tales can be found in the works of Saki, Anton Chekhov, Guy de Maupassant, and O. Henry.

Tall Tale: A humorous tale told in a straightforward, credible tone but relating absolutely impossible events or feats of the characters. Such tales were commonly told of frontier adventures during the settlement of the west in the United States. Literary use of tall tales can be found in Washington Irving's *History of New York,* Mark Twain's *Life on the Mississippi,* and in the German R. F. Raspe's *Baron Munchausen's Narratives of His Marvellous Travels and Campaigns in Russia.*

Theme: The main point of a work of literature. The term is used interchangeably with thesis. Many works have multiple themes. One of the themes of Nathaniel Hawthorne's ''Young Goodman Brown'' is loss of faith.

Tone: The author's attitude toward his or her audience may be deduced from the tone of the work. A formal tone may create distance or convey politeness, while an informal tone may encourage a friendly, intimate, or intrusive feeling in the reader. The author's attitude toward his or her subject matter may also be deduced from the tone of the words he or she uses in discussing it. The tone of John F. Kennedy's speech which included the appeal to ''ask not what your country can do for you'' was intended to instill feelings of camaraderie and national pride in listeners.

Tragedy: A drama in prose or poetry about a noble, courageous hero of excellent character who, be-cause of some tragic character flaw, brings ruin upon him- or herself. Tragedy treats its subjects in a dignified and serious manner, using poetic language to help evoke pity and fear and bring about catharsis, a purging of these emotions. The tragic form was practiced extensively by the ancient Greeks. The classical form of tragedy was revived in the sixteenth century; it flourished especially on the Elizabethan stage. In modern times, dramatists have attempted to adapt the form to the needs of modern society by drawing their heroes from the ranks of ordinary men and women and defining the nobility of these heroes in terms of spirit rather than exalted social standing. Some contemporary works that are thought of as tragedies include *The Great Gatsby* by F. Scott Fitzgerald, and *The Sound and the Fury* by William Faulkner.

Tragic Flaw: In a tragedy, the quality within the hero or heroine which leads to his or her downfall. Examples of the tragic flaw include Othello's jealousy and Hamlet's indecisiveness, although most great tragedies defy such simple interpretation.

U

Utopia: A fictional perfect place, such as ''paradise'' or ''heaven.'' An early literary utopia was described in Plato's *Republic,* and in modern literature, Ursula K. Le Guin depicts a utopia in ''The Ones Who Walk Away from Omelas.''

V

Victorian: Refers broadly to the reign of Queen Victoria of England (1837-1901) and to anything with qualities typical of that era. For example, the qualities of smug narrow-mindedness, bourgeois materialism, faith in social progress, and priggish morality are often considered Victorian. In literature, the Victorian Period was the great age of the English novel, and the latter part of the era saw the rise of movements such as decadence and symbolism.

Cumulative
Author/Title Index

Nationality/Ethnicity Index

Subject/Theme Index